FOREWORD TO THE SECOND EDITION

"The team making the fewest mistakes wins." Many years ago, I made my way through college on a football scholarship. Before each game our coach would go over "game axioms," of which this was always the first and the most important. Since that time I have learned that it is equally applicable to the conduct of a lawsuit.

Lawsuits, like battles, are won by avoiding mistakes and by capitalizing on the mistakes of one's opponents. As all experienced trial lawyers know, thorough trial preparation, that is, a complete knowledge of the entire body of evidence as well as the identification of the legal issues likely to surface during trial, is the first step toward avoiding mistakes. But thorough preparation is not enough. Throughout the course of a lawsuit, a trial lawyer also must continually evaluate the opposing lawyer and anticipate that lawyer's tactics and strategy. It is only by doing so that a trial lawyer can be adequately prepared to respond to those tactics and to turn those tactics to his or her advantage.

Today relatively few lawsuits go to trial, and many trial lawyers actually have little trial experience. It is often difficult, therefore, for a lawyer to anticipate the tactics of the opposing lawyer. Justice Frankfurter once observed, "Litigation is the pursuit of practical ends, not a game of chess;" in reality trial practice is often a series of moves and countermoves. It is for this reason that Mark Dombroff's book, *Dombroff on Unfair Tactics,* is so useful. For the neophyte lawyer, this book is invaluable as a source that details the tactics that may be employed by the opposing lawyer and the various responses that can be used to neutralize those tactics. It also demonstrates how litigation can be conducted, aggressively but ethically, when it is in the client's best interest to "play hardball." Mr. Dombroff addresses all the stages of litigation, from the investigatory phase through the appeal, with practical suggestions of how to proceed.

Dombroff on Unfair Tactics is no less valuable for the experienced trial lawyer. It identifies situations commonly encountered by trial lawyers during the course of litigation and analyzes the strategic possibilities. And, it serves not only to remind the experienced trial lawyer of tactics that can be successfully employed, but also suggests innovative applications of those tactics. Insight into the mind of opposing counsel provides a tremendous advantage to the trial attorney. As Job, bemoaning his fate, said, "[W]ould

. . . that mine adversary had written a book." Mr. Dombroff's book comes as close as possible to answering that call, and it should be read and reread in preparation for aggressive litigation.

Furthermore, this second edition of Mr. Dombroff's book contains several new chapters on sanctions. The issue of sanctions, including the circumstances under which attorneys' fees can be recovered, is becoming more and more important as our society becomes more litigious and as more unfounded lawsuits are filed. This book is an excellent resource in this rapidly developing area of the law. In a comprehensive fashion, it describes the circumstances under which sanctions are available, with a discussion of the applicable rules of civil procedure and the relevant case law. Mr. Dombroff discusses not only how to prevail on a motion for sanctions, but also how to protect oneself from such a motion.

Whether it is in the area of sanctions, of discovery, or of the actual trial of a lawsuit, this book can aid the trial lawyer in minimizing his mistakes and in maximizing the effect of his opponents' mistakes. I recommend it to all trial lawyers, and suggest that it is an essential component of a complete law library.

Nashville, Tennessee JAMES F. NEAL
January, 1988

FOREWORD TO THE FIRST EDITION

Ever since I tried my first lawsuit 30 years ago at the tender age of 21, I have been a consistent critic of the meager legal training afforded our prospective trial lawyers. The efforts of various law schools vary widely in attacking this problem, but none has succeeded, in my opinion, in a meaningful way.

The handling of a lawsuit demands considerable talent from those in charge. They are warriors, compromisors, conciliators, and mediators, possessing, hopefully, a combination of fearlessness and good judgment. Entrusted to them are enormous stakes, ranging from huge sums of money to human life itself. In an adversarial system of regulating disputes in human affairs, trial lawyers are critically important to society, for the published results of their advocacy exert a pervasive influence on the judgment of the many who do not go to the mat, but are interested in telling their clients where the point of wise compromise may lie.

As in every undertaking, there is a limit to what can be taught short of actual field experience. In the case of early airmen, the perimeters of safe flight had to be learned by each pilot in an airplane with a crash the price of a mistake. As aviation has progressed, we have used simulators to "teach out" those mistakes most frequently made without paying twisted aluminum and injury or death as the price of a slip.

In legal practice, as Chief Justice Burger has been saying for some years now, we need better training of this type. A trained person is by definition one who avoids those mistakes which an untrained person does not perceive, or perceives too late to make timely corrections. And while we use simulators of a sort in legal training, called "moot courts," the bulk of what lawyers learn about mistake avoidance is done at the expense of real clients in real cases. This unfortunate circumstance is tantamount to training young surgeons on actual triple by-pass cases, or student pilots in the cockpits of commercial airliners. The pressure is and should remain upon the profession to make greater use of simulators and less use of live clients in the training process.

This book is an answer to that challenge. An office lawyer is a force who does work with whatever time may be required to reflect and revise, to consult with colleagues, and to redraft as often as the need for a good product may require. A trial lawyer is a power—force with a time factor—

who often gets only one chance to make a quick decision on a particular issue, and thus has a much greater chance of making a mistake. The avoidance of mistakes in a fast-changing environment requires the ability to anticipate what is next to come, judge the availability of numerous options, and rapidly select the best option available. No lawyer can ever confront every possible dilemma in trial practice under circumstances where he or she can calmly sort out the options and carefully reason the way to the best decision. To accomplish this end, the advocate must draw on personal experience and the experiences of others. This book is chock-full of such experience, setting forth the options commonly available, and the pros and cons which flow from the selection of each option.

Strategy is an armchair or a conference game, where long-range plans are worked out, organized, and committed to the war. Tactics involve the skirmishes of battle under ever-changing conditions, where experience and knowledge must be swiftly applied to the circumstances at hand. This book is about that more difficult area—tactics. While the partners in the boardroom may map out the strategy, the advocate on the front lines is responsible for tactical decisions. This book is in my judgment of immense value to trial lawyers at all levels, from those new at the game to seasoned professionals. It offers a wealth of pointers on mistake avoidance by example after example, by discussing the options likely to accompany each decision-confrontation and by giving the advice of an experienced field general as to how those options should be evaluated. I have tried many cases of many sorts in many jurisdictions, and yet I found myself constantly learning new twists and nuances as I read through this book.

I strongly recommend it to my colleagues at the Bar. For lawyers over whom I have the power of direction in my own practice, it will be required reading. And if I succeed in helping to establish—as I have promised for many years to do—a specialized course for the training of advocates leading to a Master's Degree in Advocacy, this book will be a standard text. In a profession which badly needs more simulators, I view Mr. Dombroff's effort as a quantum leap forward.

Nassau, Bahamas
July 30, 1984

F. LEE BAILEY

PREFACE TO THE SECOND EDITION

In the four years which have transpired since this book first appeared, I have received an enormous amount of comment from colleagues representing all segments of the bar. The sentiments expressed run the gamut from "great book" to "I wouldn't turn my back on you." In the latter category are those who would rather not acknowledge the existence of a distinction between improper tactics which are designed to thwart the litigation process and those which are entirely proper and are nothing more than good lawyering. Properly used and effectively implemented, the tactics described in this book fall into the latter category.

Perhaps the most significant activity in the legal profession in the last four years has been in the area of sanctions. The 1983 amendments to Federal Rule of Civil Procedure 11 make it clear that good faith is no longer a defense and that an attorney's signature is, in many respects, a warranty of what he signs. The fact of the matter is that, in such an environment, a trial lawyer cannot afford to be anything but "fair." The failure to do so will most assuredly result in the imposition of sanctions.

Don't let the title of this book fool you, however. The tactics contained in this book are tried and tested, all the result of the effective application and interpretation of the rules, and designed to give you a substantial advantage over your opponent. Perhaps an appropriate way to leave the reader of this book is with the words of The Client's Twenty-third Psalm:

> The attorney is my Shepard,
>   I shall not worry.
> He maketh me to sign on the
>   dotted line.
> He leadeth me down courthouse corridors.
> He restoreth my goal.
> He guideth me in legal paths for
>   my claim's sake.
> Yea, though I walk through the valley
>   of the shadow of the courthouse,
> I shall fear no evil, for my
>   Attorney is with me.

His subpoenas and his depositions,
  they comfort me.
He prepares a fable beforehand,
  In the presence of mine enemies.
He hath anointed my story with oil.
His final statement runneth over.
Surely He shall appeal my case
  to the Supreme Court.
And I shall dwell in his Reception Room
  forever.

Reprinted with the permission
of the LPBA Journal, Fall 1987

Washington, D.C.
March, 1988

MARK A. DOMBROFF

PREFACE TO THE FIRST EDITION

In law school, all prospective lawyers learn that the practice of law frequently is and should be an adversarial profession. While all lawyers are to a certain extent combatants, litigators personify the adversary process. The courtroom is the ultimate battleground and the trial lawyer the ultimate warrior.

Trial strategy and tactics are not dissimilar to battle plans, and the frame of mind which a lawyer brings to planning his or her case parallels the organization and structure of an infantry commander seeking to destroy his opponent. However, while "all is fair in love and war," the same is not true in law, for as lawyers we are bound by rules of evidence and rules of procedure.

Any lawyer who has spent considerable time in the adversarial atmosphere of litigation knows that passions run high and the zealous pursuit of a cause on behalf of a client can often cloud good judgment. On occasion this is inadvertent. However, in all too many circumstances, such "clouded judgments" are deliberate, well-planned, and quite successful in their execution. When judgments are made or actions occur, either deliberately or inadvertently, which contravene the rules of procedure or rules of evidence, the result is often an unfair advantage or the utilization of evidence that would otherwise be improper.

The rules of evidence and the rules of procedure, state or federal, provide the guidelines and the parameters for "fair" litigation. However, the philosophy of "win at all costs" does not necessarily contravene the rules and it is only when this philosophy is applied and the end result is weighed against the bounds of fair play that one can make judgments as to whether an opponent has been unfair.

Use of unfair tactics should be guarded against. The protection of the record against inadmissible evidence is a goal for which a litigator must be ever vigilant. Recognizing the importance of this fact, the question then presented is how to recognize the onset of unfair tactics and, in the event that they are employed against you, how to protect yourself, your record, and your client, and, in the final analysis, turn that unfair tactic against your opponent. Similarly, when an opponent has taken a piece of evidence which would otherwise be inadmissible and packaged it in a form in which it is likely to be received into the record, how do you anticipate that tactic, meet it, and turn it on its proponent?

These are questions which focus themselves not on the rules of procedure but rather on the tactics and strategies for effective litigating techniques. Accepting the conventional wisdom that the most effective witness against an opponent is that opponent's own witness, whether an individual or a document, it follows that the most effective tactic against an opponent is to turn the opponent's tactic around and use it as a weapon.

The chapters which follow address themselves to the area of unfair tactics, inadmissible evidence, and: (1) how the rules of procedure and the discretion of the judge can be used to shift the burden of proof at trial; (2) how the use of opinion questions can effectively overcome foundation problems; and (3) the use of summaries as a device to cure defects in documents, depositions, and other proofs.

When confronted with an attorney who has breached a rule of evidence or procedure in the courtroom, the typical reaction by the judge to cure the defect is to instruct the jury to disregard what they have heard. Obviously, the "unringing of the bell" is not something that can be accomplished. No matter how completely a jury is instructed or how hard a judge attempts to disregard matters which should not have been presented in the first instance, human nature makes it impossible to erase from one's memory banks information of which a person has become aware.

The most effective means for preventing this sort of difficulty in the courtroom is to be able to spot one of these situations as it develops, anticipate what is happening, and either prevent it from occurring at all or, preferably, turn it into your own weapon. The techniques and tactics discussed in this book will provide you with the means for accomplishing this end.

As used in this book, the terms *prejudice* or *unfair* are not necessarily bad. From your perspective everything which you offer into evidence should be perceived as unfair and prejudicial in favor of your case by your opponent. By the same token, everything which your adversary introduces in support of his or her case should be considered as unfair and prejudicial by you. The difficulty which you confront is discerning where the fine line of propriety and/or admissibility is within the context of the Federal Rules of Civil Procedure, the Federal Rules of Evidence, or the Code of Professional Responsibility, and when you step over it. Until you or your opponent do so, the techniques and tactics discussed in the following chapters are fair game. The key to success is making it *your* game.

Washington, D.C.
May, 1984

MARK A. DOMBROFF

SUMMARY CONTENTS

DETAILED CONTENTS

CHAPTER 1

PRETRIAL DISCOVERY

§ 1.1 Introduction

It is not uncommon for the discovery phase of litigation to commence almost simultaneously with the filing of the complaint or answer. Indeed, one of the most offensive or aggressive litigation tactics is the filing of interrogatories or requests for admissions with the complaint or answer.

In any event, discovery typically commences within a very short time of the initial pleadings having been filed. Because a significant amount of the civil litigation process is discovery-oriented, it is in this pretrial discovery phase of the process when you often encounter the first indications of the tone or tenor which the litigation will have.

In large part, the response which you present to an aggressive discovery program on the part of your opponent will dictate the atmosphere of the litigation and send a signal to your opponent as to what he or she may expect as the litigation progresses toward trial. Indeed, in some instances, your reaction to an aggressive opponent may determine whether the case ever reaches trial or is sidetracked by way of settlement at some earlier stage.

§ 1.2 Playing Hardball

Trial lawyers are often accused of pursuing a "scorched earth" approach to litigation. Most typically this is associated with lawyers representing large corporate defendants, such as insurance companies, the idea being to beat the smaller or less resource-rich opponent into submission.

As a practical matter, playing hardball is what litigation is all about, and you should not become incensed because your opponent chooses to pursue a hard line in the conduct of the case. Rather, you should take an approach which is, if possible, even more aggressive than that taken by your opponent. Furthermore, unlimited resources are not needed to succeed in such an approach.

The question which is raised by all observers of litigation, as well as by those who have been on the receiving end of aggressive litigation tactics, usually centers on the subject of ethics. As a practical matter, the only ethical limitations which we as litigators operate under are those associated with the formal canons of ethics and the broader considerations of propriety and fair play. Simply stated, there is no restriction against being an aggressive or hardball litigator. As long as you do not run afoul of the rules of procedure or the rules of evidence, an aggressive approach to litigation often is a winning one.

Because the tone of litigation is typically established during the discovery and, to some extent, the initial pleadings stage of the case, it is imperative that, when confronted with an aggressive opponent, you immediately establish yourself as an equally and, if possible, more aggressive litigator. The desired effect of such an approach is to shut down your opponent and establish firm control over the litigation. However, it is not enough to do this on a "hit and run" basis. Rather, once this tone is established, it is important to maintain it on a continuing basis and manifest it throughout the litigation in all of your activities as well as your responses to the activities of your opponent.

§ 1.3 When to Start

As any experienced litigator knows, litigation commences well before the filing of a complaint or answer. However, it is not until a formal filing that the adversaries, as distinguished from the issues, are joined. Despite this fact, with ever-increasing frequency we are finding that fact gathering, investigation, and discovery are commencing before the filing or service of a complaint.

When representing a plaintiff, it is important that the factual underpinnings of a case be established and prepared *prior* to the filing of that case. Accordingly, factual investigation, document collection, and evolution of theories of liability all must predate the filing of any complaint.

Similarly, when representing a defendant, you must begin prior to the filing of the complaint against your client. The obvious question is: "How do I know that my client is going to be a defendant?" The answer to this question is not easy, except to state that the likelihood of a lawsuit being filed against an individual or group usually is well known by the potential defendant. In such circumstances it is imperative that the client be advised of the type of tactics to which it may be subjected prior to the filing of the lawsuit. Failure to do so may result in discovery being taken against your client that is later admissible in the litigation but which was "discovered" outside the context of litigation, and the rules of procedure applicable in discovery may be unavailable to protect the interests of the client.

On the question of timing of discovery for maximum benefit, the following guidelines should be observed:

1. Setting the tone of your case at an early stage through an aggressive discovery program will yield substantial benefits down the road.
2. It's never too early to start. Plaintiffs should file their first wave of discovery with the complaint. Defendants should file it with the answer.
3. Plaintiffs must do all preliminary factual investigation and the initial formulations of theories of liability before formal discovery starts. Failure to do so typically results in a lot of wheel spinning and the waste of time and money.

4. Clients and prospective defendants must be aware that litigation starts against them *before* the filing of a complaint. They should be sensitized to public inquiries in potential areas of litigation, e.g., product failures, and attuned to contacting counsel immediately.
5. You must be familiar with techniques for perpetuating evidence or testimony, both formal and informal, not only for the purpose of using them, but also to guard against their abuse. Subsequent sections of this chapter discuss several such techniques.

§ 1.4 Discovery Before Service or Filing: Motions to Perpetuate

One of the most significant concerns of many lawyers and a primary cause of legal malpractice actions is failure to observe statutes of limitations in the filing of complaints. Because of the potential problems surrounding this area, many complaints are filed simply in order to toll the statute of limitations, even though counsel is either not convinced or essentially unaware of whether a cause of action truly exists. However, consistent with state rules of procedure, such complaints may not and need not be served on the defendant at the same time the complaint is filed with the court. Although filing of the complaint tolls the statute of limitations, it does not create an adversarial relationship until proper service has been effected.

This procedure has been incorporated into the Federal Rules of Civil Procedure in Rule 4(j).

> Summons: Time limit for service. If the service of the summons and complaint is not made on a defendant within one hundred twenty (120) days after the filing of the complaint and the party on whose behalf such service was required cannot show good cause why such service was not made within that period, the action shall be dismissed as to that defendant without prejudice upon the court's own initiative with notice to such party or upon motion. The subdivision shall not apply to service in a foreign country pursuant to subdivision (i) of this rule.

The question then arises as to the kinds of discovery attempts which may be made on a defendant against whom a complaint has been filed but not yet served, so that the defendant has not had notice of the fact that a complaint has been filed. Because the adversary process has not yet begun, the types of discovery which will take place typically fall outside applicable state or federal rules.

The likelihood is that if a potential defendant is confronted with discovery requests in the form of either motions to perpetuate or informal requests from a potential adversary, the fact of a complaint's being on file but unserved will become known. Under such circumstances, opposing the discovery requests by way of either a response to a motion to perpetuate or simply declining an informal inquiry will usually suffice. Remember, the purpose of a motion to perpetuate is not to provide evidence for the framing of a complaint but rather to preserve the existence of evidence which is in danger. This purpose remains valid whether the complaint has been served and filed or simply filed.

For example, as established by the Federal Rules of Civil Procedure and uniform state rules, a motion to perpetuate is provided for by Rule 27. Specifically, it states:

RULE 27. Depositions Before Action or Pending Appeal

(a) Before Action.

(1) Petition. A person who desires to perpetuate his own testimony or that of another person regarding any matter that may be cognizable in any court of the United States may file a verified petition in the United States district court in the district of the residence of any expected adverse party. The petition shall be entitled in the name of the petitioner and shall show: 1, that the petitioner expects to be a party to an action cognizable in a court of the United States but is presently unable to bring it or cause it to be brought, 2, the subject matter of the expected action and his interest therein, 3, the facts which he desires to establish by the proposed testimony and his reasons for desiring to perpetuate it, 4, the names or a description of the persons he expects will be adverse parties and their addresses so far as known, and 5, the names and addresses of the persons to be examined and the substance of the testimony which he expects to elicit from each, and shall ask for an order authorizing the petitioner to take the depositions of the persons to be examined named in the petition, for the purpose of perpetuating their testimony.

(2) Notice and Service. The petitioner shall thereafter serve a notice upon each person named in the petition as an expected adverse party, together with a copy of the petition, stating that the petitioner will apply to the court, at a time and place named therein, for the order described in the petition. At least 20 days before the date of hearing the notice shall be served either within or without the district or state in the manner provided in Rule 4(d) for service of summons; but if such service cannot with due diligence be made upon any expected adverse party named in the petition, the court may make such order as is just for service by publication or otherwise, and shall appoint, for persons not served in the manner provided in Rule 4(d), an attorney who shall represent them, and, in case they are not otherwise represented, shall cross-examine the deponent. If any expected adverse party is a minor or incompetent the provisions of Rule 17(c) apply.

(3) Order and Examination. If the court is satisfied that the perpetuation of the testimony may prevent a failure or delay of justice, it shall make an order designating or describing the persons whose depositions may be taken and specifying the subject matter of the examination and whether the depositions shall be taken upon oral examination or written interrogatories.

The depositions may then be taken in accordance with these rules; and the court may make orders of the character provided for by Rules 34 and 35. For the purpose of applying these rules to depositions for perpetuating testimony, each reference therein to the court in which the action is pending shall be deemed to refer to the court in which the petition for such deposition was filed.

(4) Use of Deposition. If a deposition to perpetuate testimony is taken, it would be admissible in evidence in the courts of the state in which it is taken, it may be used in any action involving the same subject matter subsequently brought in a United States district court, in accordance with the provisions of Rule 32(a).

Thus, a motion to perpetuate may be used as a discovery device for the purpose of preserving evidence when a complaint, under either state or federal rules, has been filed but not yet served. It is not in and of itself improper. You must examine the justifications presented for the motion to perpetuate in order to determine whether it is being properly used. If there is a question in your mind as to the propriety of the motion to perpetuate, filing such a motion, while at the same time filing but not yet serving a complaint, can be made to appear as if opposing counsel is attempting to subvert the appropriate discovery process. This fact should be reflected in any opposing papers or motions to strike.

§ 1.5 In-House or Insurance Investigations

The taking of discovery prior to the commencement of litigation is a tactic which itself is not necessarily bad but can be unfair if motivated by and used for the wrong reason. Virtually all insurance companies and more and more law firms undertake some sort of investigation prior to commencement of litigation. This is true whether the insurance company or law firm is representing a potential plaintiff or a potential defendant.

Characteristic of this type of investigation can be sworn statements from witnesses or, on some occasions, from potential plaintiffs or defendants themselves. On occasion, such sworn statements may take the form of transcripts where a court reporter or stenotypist is present and the witness is thereafter asked to sign the statement.

The only manner to defend effectively against such a tactic is, in the first instance, to have been involved as a lawyer at an early enough stage of the potential litigation to have been able to advise the client not to talk with anyone without having contacted you first. Frequently this is not the case, and you are unable to control what transpires at such early stages of a potential lawsuit. The best approach to take to combat what could be damaging admissions or evidence already adduced by your opponent is to file immediately either requests for production or interrogatories designed to obtain disclosure of the existence of insurance investigations, sworn statements, interviews, or transcripts.

Since such information is typically collected for use in connection with litigation, the authorities are clear that they are discoverable under the appropriate rules of procedure if they have not been gathered in anticipation of litigation. For example, Rule 26(b)(3) of the Federal Rules of Civil Procedure provides:

> (3) *Trial Preparation: Materials.* Subject to the provisions of subdivision (b)(4) of this rule, a party may obtain discovery of documents and tangible things otherwise discoverable under subdivision (b)(1) of this rule and prepared in anticipation of litigation or for trial by or for another party or by or for that other party's representative (including his attorney, consultant, surety, indemnitor, insurer, or agent) only upon a showing that the party seeking discovery has substantial need of the materials in the preparation of his case and that he is unable without undue hardship to obtain the substantial equivalent of the materials by other means. In ordering discovery of such materials when the required showing has been made, the court shall protect against disclosure of the mental impressions, conclusions, opinions, or legal theories of an attorney or other representative of a party concerning the litigation.

If material is provided to you in response to your request for production which is damaging to your case but which was gathered prior to the initiation of litigation, a tactic to be considered is the filing of a motion *in limine* or *threshold* motion to preclude the use of such information during the litigation because your client was not represented at the proceedings.

The most which can usually be expected from such an approach is a requirement that the discovery be retaken within the formal context of the applicable rules of procedure. Frequently, this is enough to balance the scales and bring about a more equitable situation. However, if, for example, the witness whose statement is at issue and has been discovered changes his story at the subsequent discovery session, the previously existing statement can, in all likelihood, be used against him for impeachment purposes. Thus, if the prior statement was given in the form of a deposition, Federal Rule of Civil Procedure 32(a)(1) and similar state rules of procedure would permit the deposition to be used by any party for the purpose of contradicting or impeaching the deponent as a witness or for any other purpose.

Similarly, Federal Rule of Evidence 803(5) would permit a memorandum or record concerning a matter about which a witness once had knowledge, but now has an insufficient recollection to be able to testify fully, to be introduced into evidence. This latter circumstance is one of the exceptions to the hearsay rule and is generally known as the *doctrine of recorded recollection.* In addition, Federal Rule of Evidence 804 and its state counterparts permit earlier testimony given by a witness into evidence, as well as statements made against interest by a witness or declarant. Each of these provides some basis for the introduction of the prior statement for the purpose of impeaching or otherwise attacking the present testimony of an individual who gave a previous statement or testimony prior to your involvement in the case.

A troubling area when representing insurance companies relates to the question of protecting your reports prepared for the insurance company but done so outside the context of litigation. A recent case from Missouri, *May Department Stores Co. v. Ryan,* 699 S.W.2d 134 (Mo. Ct. App. 1985), addresses this issue and comes down on the side of the defendant.

In *Ryan,* the Missouri Court determined that a report made by an employee to an employer regarding an incident alleged by a customer to constitute false imprisonment and transmitted to the employer's insurer was protected by the insurer-insured privilege and could not be discovered. While certainly there are a number of cases addressing the question of the work product privilege, there are few cases dealing with the so-called insurer-insured privilege. Accordingly, *Ryan* is an important case from defense counsel's perspective whenever seeking to protect such reports within the context of litigation.

The following two sections contain, respectively, an example of a motion to compel production of insurance company investigative reports and a sample order granting that motion.

§ 1.6 —Motion to Compel Production of Insurance Company Investigative Reports

MEMORANDUM IN SUPPORT OF DEFENDANT'S MOTION FOR AN ORDER COMPELLING PRODUCTION OF DOCUMENTS

Pursuant to Rule 26 of the Federal Rules of Civil Procedure, parties may obtain discovery regarding any matter "not privileged," which is relevant to the subject matter involved in the pending action. In the present case, the documents sought by Defendant relate to the aircraft that is the subject of this lawsuit. Plaintiff is suing the United States of America for the amount that it paid to the aircraft's owner as a result of the accident. Among the documents sought are the evaluation of the adjuster as to the value of the aircraft; the amounts recovered in salvage; and statements, reports and documents relating to Plaintiff's investigation of the accident. Since the cause or causes of the accident are directly at issue in this litigation, the documents are certainly relevant or may lead to the discovery of relevant evidence.

The production request for documents which is at issue herein is as follows:

3. Entire claims file relating to the subject aircraft including but not limited to all claim forms, reports, and other writings procured by the insurance carrier

in its investigation and handling of the claim but not limited to the evaluation of the adjusters and claims manager regarding this accident.

Plaintiff responded as follows:

Response: Plaintiff objects to the production of its claim file relating to the subject aircraft as the said claim file contains only materials prepared in anticipation of litigation by this party and its representatives pursuant to Rule 28(b)(3) of the Federal Rules of Civil Procedure.

Plaintiff's objection that the requested documents "contain only materials prepared in anticipation of litigation" is not supported by either the Federal Rules of Civil Procedure or case law.

Litigation is a truthseeking procedure. "Justice is truth in action," Disraeli. In *Monier v. Chamberlain,* 35 Ill. 2d 351, 221 N.E.2d 410 (1966), the Illinois Supreme Court stated as follows:

> . . . attention must be focused upon the words "made in preparation for trial." Although it may feasibly be said that all memoranda, reports or documents made by or for a party prior to the actual trial are "made in preparation for trial," present day concepts of discovery . . . *look to the ultimate ascertainment of the truth.* (emphasis added) [by movant]

Plaintiff's employees and agents conducted a complete investigation regarding the cause or causes of the subject accident. The United States of America has requested Plaintiff's reports concerning the accident. Courts have emphasized the importance of making available to the litigants in civil actions all information about the cause of an accident in the "interest of discovering the truth and insuring a just result in civil litigation." *Kline v. Martin,* 345 F. Supp. 31 (E.D. Va. 1972).

A motion for the production of documents is entitled to broad and liberal treatment. *In re Folding Carton Antitrust Litigation,* 76 F.R.D. 420 (D.C. Ill. 1979).

The United States of America states that inspection of the requested documents is necessary to prepare its case adequately for trial and that a failure to order production would prejudice the United States and result in hardship to the United States. Plaintiff has in its possession statements of witnesses, regarding the accident, made immediately after the accident. The United States of America has substantial need for these statements which were made when the witnesses had complete recall of the facts and circumstances of the accident. In *Southern Railway Co. v. Lanham,* 403 F.2d 119 (5th Cir. 1968), the Court held that statements of witnesses taken by a claims agent of an insurance company, as well as facts personally observed by him, were proper objects of discovery.

CONCLUSION

For all of the foregoing reasons, the United States of America submits that its motion for an order compelling the Plaintiff to produce the requested claims file should be granted.

It is urged that the Plaintiff should not be permitted to cause the Defendant to incur an inordinate expenditure and time-consuming process in order to obtain full and complete disclosure to which it is entitled. Rule 37(a)(4) provides:

Award of Expenses of Motion

If the motion is granted, the Court shall, after opportunity for hearing, require the party or deponent whose conduct necessitated the motion or the party or attorney advising such conduct or both of them to pay to the moving party the reasonable expenses incurred in obtaining the order, including attorney's fees, unless the Court finds that the opposition to the motion was substantially justified or that other circumstances make an award of expenses unjust.

§ 1.7 —Order Granting Motion to Compel Production of Insurance Company Investigative Reports

MEMORANDUM OPINION AND ORDER

Plaintiff, as subrogee of John Doe, brings this suit against defendant United States of America for money that Plaintiff paid in settlement to a passenger of an aircraft that crashed on March 2, 1977. Plaintiff is also seeking compensation for money it paid to the aircraft's owner for damage to the aircraft. Currently pending is Defendant's motion for an order compelling Plaintiff to further answer interrogatories and Defendant's motion to compel production of documents. Each motion will be discussed below.

MOTION FOR AN ORDER COMPELLING PLAINTIFF TO FURTHER ANSWER INTERROGATORIES

On January 23, 1980, Defendant submitted a set of interrogatories to Plaintiff pursuant to F[ed]. R. Civ. P. 33. Plaintiff did not answer any of the interrogatories until June 23, 1980, six months later. Even after the answers to the interrogatories were finally submitted, Plaintiff failed to answer, objected to, or answered incompletely over half of them. As a result, the United States filed this motion to compel Plaintiff to further answer the interrogatories. The government also points out that plaintiff has not answered the interrogatories under oath as required by the Federal Rules of Civil Procedure. Plaintiff is ordered to comply with its representation that it will correct this inadvertence by amending the answers to indicate that they are under oath. After the filing of this motion, the Plaintiff voluntarily answered several of the disputed interrogatories, and the government withdrew its motion to compel with respect to those interrogatories.

Plaintiff opposes Defendant's motion on the ground that the government's request is premature since discovery is just commencing. Consequently, Plaintiff argues that the interrogatories are burdensome and oppressive and need not be answered until discovery has been completed.

Plaintiff's argument, however, overlooks the fact that the accident which is the subject of this litigation took place over three years ago. Plaintiff has had this set of interrogatories for close to a year. Plaintiff clearly has under its control the means to answer the interrogatories. As such, it cannot lawfully avoid answering. *Hickman v. Taylor,* 329 U.S. 495, 504 (1947); *Olmert v. Nelson,* 60 F.R.D. 369, 370 (D.D.C. 1973).

If Plaintiff lacks the necessary information to answer the interrogatories adequately, then it should so state under oath and set forth in detail the efforts it has made to obtain the necessary information. *Miller v. Doctor's General Hospital,* 76 F.R.D. 136 (W.D. Okla. 1977). Moreover, this court orders Plaintiff to supplement its incomplete answers as information becomes available. F[ed]. R. Civ. P. 26(e)(3).

Plaintiff's reliance on *Krantz v. United States,* 56 F.R.D. 555 (W.D. Va. 1972), for the proposition that Defendant's request is premature and therefore burdensome and oppressive, is misplaced. In *Krantz* the government propounded over 1,500 questions in regard to a tax refund case. Additionally, in *Krantz* the government had within its control most of the information it sought to discover. In the present case, the government has submitted a manageable number of relevant questions and does not have the information under its control. Consequently, Plaintiff must answer the government's interrogatories.

Two interrogatories, Nos. 2(b) and 14(h), must be considered separately since Plaintiff specifically objects to answering them on the grounds that the information sought was developed in anticipation of litigation. Interrogatory 2(b) requests the names and addresses of persons having information about the accident and a description of any statement such a person may have made. Such information is obviously necessary in order to prepare for depositions in the case. Plaintiff's claim that the material was prepared in anticipation of litigation is without merit. F[ed]. R. Civ. P. 26(b)(3) only protects from discovery "documents and tangible things" prepared in anticipation of litigation, unless the party making the discovery request makes a showing of substantial need for the materials. First, defendant does not seek discovery of "documents or tangible things." Second, the government has a substantial need for this information in order to prepare for depositions. Finally, names of witnesses obtained by an attorney through investigation must be given in response to interrogatories. *Roberson v. Ryder Truck Lines, Inc.,* 41 F.R.D. 166 (N.D. Miss. 1966).

Interrogatory 14(h) seeks to discover each and every fact, document, item, photograph or tangible object supplied to the expert witnesses Plaintiff intends to call at trial. To the extent this interrogatory seeks to discover the information supplied to an expert retained by plaintiff in anticipation of litigation and who is not expected to be called as a witness, the interrogatory need not be answered. F[ed]. R. Civ. P. 26(b)(3)(B). Moreover, if plaintiff has not yet decided what experts it intends to call at trial, it may state so in its answer and such answer will be an adequate response to the interrogatory. The Federal Rules do not permit such detailed discovery of an expert's basis for testimony. The Federal Rules allow a party to discover "the facts and opinions to which the expert is expected to testify and a *summary* of the grounds for each opinion." (Emphasis supplied) [by court] F[ed]. R. Civ. P. 26(b)(3)(A). Thus, Plaintiff need submit only a summary of the information upon which the expert will base his opinion. Such summary should be detailed enough to allow the government to conduct effective and thorough cross-examination. Additionally, Plaintiff must supply Defendant with any facts or opinions to which such expert is expected to testify.

MOTION TO COMPEL PRODUCTION OF DOCUMENTS

The Defendant submitted the following request for production of documents:

> Entire claims file relating to the subject aircraft including but not limited to all claim forms, reports and other writings procured by the insurance carrier in its investigation and handling of the claim but not limited to the evaluation of the adjusters and claims manager regarding this accident.

Plaintiff objects to producing the claims file because it was allegedly prepared in anticipation of litigation. See F[ed]. R. Civ. P. 26(b)(3). Plaintiff particularly objects to producing statements of witnesses which were interviewed by Plaintiff between four and eighteen days after the accident. The government argues that the claims file was not prepared in anticipation of litigation and that it has substantial need for the documents because: they contain factual information necessary to its defense; it cannot obtain the information from other sources; and interviewing the witnesses some three years after the accident would not give them the same information as the statements of witnesses that were made when the accident was fresh in their minds.

Plaintiff's contention that the government can easily interview the witnesses itself and consequently Plaintiff should not have to produce the witnesses' statements is untenable. Where statements were made by witnesses soon after an accident, the courts have ordered their production even where the witnesses are still available for deposition. *See, e.g., Tiernan v. Westext Transport, Inc.*, 46 F.R.D. 3 (D.R.I. 1969).

Plaintiff's second argument—that all information contained in its claims file was "prepared in anticipation of litigation"—is also without merit. An insurance company's investigation of an accident is made in order to settle and pursue claims. Such an investigation is made in the ordinary course of the insurance company's business. To hold that this claims file was prepared in anticipation of litigation would mean that any time an insurance company investigates an accident, the results of that investigation would not be discoverable. A long line of cases, however, has held that most accident reports, made soon after the accident, are made in the ordinary course of business and therefore discoverable. *O'Boyle v. Life Insurance Co. of America*, 299 F. Supp. 704 (W.D. Mo. 1969); *Atlanta Coca-Cola Bottling Co. v. Transamerica Insurance Co.*, 61 F.R.D. 115 (N.D. Ga. 1972); *Westhemeco Ltd. v. New Hampshire Insurance Co.*, 82 F.R.D. 702 (S.D.N.Y. 1979).

Defendant, in its request for Plaintiff's claims file, also seeks discovery of material relating to damages and Plaintiff's claims adjuster's evaluation of the value of the aircraft as well as the amounts recovered in salvage. Plaintiff again objects to discovery on the grounds that this material was prepared in anticipation of litigation. Clearly, under Rule 26, an insurer's evaluation of a claim from a policyholder is prepared in the ordinary course of business and not in anticipation of litigation. *Atlanta Coca-Cola Bottling Co. v. Transamerica Insurance Co., supra.* Consequently, Plaintiff must produce the claims report requested by the defendant.

For the reasons stated above, Defendant's motion for production of documents is granted; Plaintiff is ordered to answer Defendant's interrogatories in accordance with the views expressed in this memorandum. The request for reasonable expenses incurred in obtaining this order, including attorney's fees, is continued until Plaintiff complies with this order.

Enter:

____

United States District Judge

Dated: ____________________

§ 1.8 Contention Interrogatories

As a general rule, interrogatories have questionable value as a discovery device. While they have the advantage of being inexpensive and easy to prepare, they suffer from several rather substantial disadvantages. Included among these is the fact that, as a practical matter, answers to interrogatories are typically drafted by counsel as opposed to the client. In addition, the fact that you are unable to immediately follow up answers to interrogatories except by filing supplemental interrogatories makes effective use of interrogatories problematical. One area which can provide an exception to the rather substantial drawbacks of interrogatories involves *contention interrogatories.*

Since the advent of notice pleading, a skillfully drafted complaint frequently reveals virtually nothing about the cause of action being presented against your client. Similarly, a skillfully drafted answer will be vague in its response and in the joining of the issues. One technique for sharpening the issues is the use of contention interrogatories, wherein either a plaintiff or a defendant attempts to focus on the allegations of the complaint or the answer using the interrogatory format. Although such interrogatories, even when used for these purposes, can suffer from the usual drawbacks, e.g., the inability to follow up answers with additional questions or answers provided by counsel, if skillfully drafted, a contention interrogatory can be an effective tool for pinning down your opponent.

In its simplest form, the contention interrogatory focuses on a particular allegation or paragraph of the complaint or answer and requests all facts and information on which that specific statement is premised, for example, "In paragraph seven of the complaint you have stated that the defendant was negligent; please set forth all facts and other information upon which you base this statement." The inherent weakness in this approach is that it encourages generalized and conclusionary answers, often provided by counsel.

A far more effective tack to be taken in the use of contention interrogatories is to seek objective information and not to permit an opponent to be creative in responding. Thus, for example, a contention interrogatory which seeks all documents or witnesses which support a particular paragraph of a complaint or answer is far more difficult to evade than one which seeks a statement of "all facts and other information."

Whatever the type of contention interrogatory used, one of the most effective tactics in using them is to file them with the complaint. Pursuant to Rule 33 of the Federal Rules of Civil Procedure, as well as many state court rules, interrogatories "may, without leave of court, be served upon the plaintiff after commencement of the action and upon any other party with or after summons and complaint upon that party." Thus, an effective tactic would be to file contention interrogatories with either the complaint or the answer. The primary benefit of doing so is that your opponent has not yet had an opportunity to shape his or her position to the point of being able to answer the interrogatories in a manner which may prove advantageous to the opponent's case at a later point. Thus, answers given after discovery has proceeded to some degree may be entirely different.

There are several approaches to dealing with such a tactic. It is imperative, however, that under no circumstances should misleading or evasive answers be filed, even at such an early stage. The problem with doing this, notwithstanding the fact there may be no substantive information available to answer an interrogatory, is that such answers bolster a court's tendency to view with suspicion the contentions of parties which answer in an evasive fashion. *Ruiz v. Hamburg-American Line,* 478 F.2d 29 (9th Cir. 1973). Generally, an evasive statement made to avoid answering an interrogatory is no answer at all. *Bollard v. Volkswagen of America, Inc.,* 56 F.R.D. 569 (W.D. Mo. 1971).

The question then becomes how to respond to such a tactic, i.e., the filing of contention interrogatories at the very outset of the lawsuit, when you have no real substantive information available and do not wish to limit yourself in your later contentions at trial. There are several responses, any of which will blunt the effectiveness of this tactic when used against you.

A party upon whom interrogatories have been served shall, pursuant to most rules of procedure, *see, e.g.,* Fed. R. Civ. P. 33(a), serve a copy of the answers or objections within 30 days of the service of interrogatories except that a defendant may serve answers or objections within 45 days of the service of the summons and complaint on the defendant. This latter provision takes into account the situation when a plaintiff has served interrogatories at approximately the same time when the complaint was served, so that the defendant is given 15 additional days, for a total of 45 days, in which to file an answer. However, virtually all rules permit the court to allow a longer time within which to answer. *Id.* Initially, then, you should be aware that a defendant has longer than 30 days to answer interrogatories filed by the plaintiff with the complaint.

In addition to ascertaining the precise amount of time you have to answer threshold discovery, there are a number of matters to consider:

1. The first issue is whether to obtain an extension of time to keep your options open regarding liability theories or defenses.
2. A possible answer which straddles the line between an extension and an answer is: "Until there has been discovery on the liability issues associated with this case, the [plaintiff/defendant] is unable to provide a response. A further answer will be provided when additional discovery has taken place."
3. Do not forget to follow up on interrogatories or answers to interrogatories for which supplementation is required. The failure of an opponent to provide supplemental answers to interrogatories may result in a motion in limine to prevent any such evidence from being offered.
4. An approach to safely handling threshold discovery to avoid having your proofs subject to a motion in limine is to object to the interrogatories. By doing so, unless a motion to compel is filed or the court orders otherwise, you will probably free yourself of the need to supplement your answers.

Notwithstanding the fact that the rules provide the time frame in which answers are to be filed, they further give the trial judge discretion to permit longer times. There is authority that answers need not be provided where interrogatories call for mixed responses of law and fact until discovery has been completed. *Mid-America Facilities, Inc. v. Argonaut Insurance Co.,* 78 F.R.D. 497 (E.D. Wis. 1978). Furthermore, a district court has authority to grant an ex parte extension of time for the defendant to answer or otherwise respond to the plaintiff's interrogatories. *Equal Employment Opportunity Commission v. New Enterprises Stone and Lime Co.,* 74 F.R.D. 628 (E.D. Pa. 1977). A party seeking an extension of time for answering interrogatories will often find that the fact that discovery is not completed may provide grounds for objecting to interrogatories on the basis that the interrogatories are premature.

In *In re Folding Carton Antitrust Litigation,* 83 F.R.D. 260 (N.D. Ill. 1979), the court held that the defendant's interrogatory seeking identification of co-conspirators was relevant and not objectionable on the ground that answering an interrogatory prior to completion of discovery was premature. However, in that case, discovery had been completed except for supplemental depositions, and plaintiffs were to supplement their interrogatory answers if additional information identifying co-conspirators was obtained through the remaining depositions. This would clearly suggest that when discovery has been neither substantially nor totally completed, a valid ground for objecting to interrogatories is the fact that the interrogatories are premature at the time they are filed. This is particularly true with contention interrogatories, which are meant to limit the issues and define the contours of the case.

Accordingly, while contention interrogatories, if skillfully drafted and used, can be an effective tool for putting an adversary at a disadvantage if they have been filed at the right stage of the case, this tactic can be deflected when used against you. The key is not to attempt to evade the interrogatories but rather to meet them head-on, with responses indicating inability to answer them at that stage of the case or with objections. However, assuming that your own contention interrogatories are successfully deferred, you should remember to re-ask them at a more appropriate time of the litigation and, when they have been posed to you and successfully defended against, you should insure that you are not setting yourself up for sanctions under either Federal Rule of Civil Procedure 37 or one of its state counterparts.

Furthermore, whenever you are considering the filing of early contention interrogatories, note that their use was limited in *In re Convergent Technologies Securities Litigation,* No. C-84-20749-RPA (N.D. Cal., decided Oct. 28, 1985). In this decision, United States Magistrate Wayne D. Brazil held that the burden of justification for using contention interrogatories should be placed on the party who seeks answers to those kinds of questions before substantial documentary or testimonial discovery has been completed.

If you plan to file contention interrogatories, perhaps as early as with the complaint if you are acting as a plaintiff, and certainly when you are filing your answer when defending a client, bear in mind that Rule 11 and the sanctions provided in that rule are becoming more and more preeminent in the conduct and management of litigation. This decision, albeit from a federal magistrate, is interesting in that context, since it focuses on contention interrogatories which are frequently not capable of being answered at such an early stage of the litigation.

§ 1.9 Damage Interrogatories and Statements

An area of discovery which is perhaps better suited to the use of interrogatories than any other single area is the collection of damage data. As a general rule, the value of interrogatories as a discovery device is limited in direct proportion to the amount of subjective information being sought.

When contention-type information is being sought and there is room for subjective responses, a skilled opponent will provide answers to the interrogatories which are of virtually no value. On the other hand, damage interrogatories which seek damage-type information such as employment history, income, claimed losses, etc., and leave little room for subjective manipulation of the information can provide valuable discovery data for the case.

Notwithstanding the fact that damage interrogatories are themselves effective, some counsel use a tactic which, though it can be both effective and attractive to the court under some circumstances, can place your client at a substantial disadvantage in the proofs relative to damage. Damage statements, or interrogatories which incorporate a damage statement and go beyond the normal collection of damage data by requiring counsel to do economic calculations, step over the line of factual discovery tools and enter the realm of expert opinion evidence. This technique is one which originated in mass disaster litigation and has typically been used in the multiple-plaintiff situation.

Sometimes found in the form of a court order requiring plaintiffs to provide certain damage information without the requirement that the defendant file damage interrogatories, this technique is typified in **§ 1.10**, which contains an order requiring a statement in the nature of a pretrial outline of proof on the issue of damages and contentions of plaintiffs as to method, items, and amount of total damages, as suggested in Appendix 1.51 of the *Manual for Complex Litigation.*

§ 1.10 —Order Requiring Pretrial Outline of Proof

Good Cause appearing therefore,

IT IS HEREBY ORDERED that counsel for Plaintiffs prepare and file in the above-numbered case, with a copy mailed to opposing counsel and the undersigned, on or before ____________________ a statement in the nature of pretrial contentions and offer of proof, using the following outline as near as possible:

PRETRIAL STATEMENT IN THE NATURE OF OUTLINE OF OFFER OF PROOF ON THE ISSUE OF DAMAGES, AND CONTENTIONS OF PLAINTIFFS AS TO METHOD, ITEMS, AND AMOUNT OF TOTAL DAMAGES

I

a. Name of decedent and birth date:
b. Life expectancy in years:
c. Name of spouse and birth date:
d. Life expectancy in years:
e. Same information as to other survivors, and relationship of each to decedent:

II
Employment

a. Position and title of decedent at time of accident:
b. Period or periods of employment in years, and by whom:
c. Past rate of compensation: State periods to which compensation was applicable and whether hourly, weekly, or monthly:
d. Monthly, weekly, or hourly compensation at date of death:
e. Prospective future monthly or weekly earnings from date of death to retirement:
f. Payroll record for five years prior to death, giving gross annual earnings, income tax deductions, and take-home net, if available: If not available, so state:
g. If decedent was self employed, set forth data corresponding to above "a" to "f":

III

Retirement benefit and age of retirement, if compulsory: If not compulsory, state general terms:

IV

Additional income (dividends, interest, etc.):

V
State of Health

a. Of decedent at and for five years prior to his death:
b. Of each survivor:
c. State any illnesses requiring doctor's treatment or hospital care as to any of the above during the five years prior to death of decedent:

VI

Monthly expenses which were purely personal to decedent:

VII

Brief statement of medical testimony, if any:

VIII
Special Damages

a. Funeral expenses itemized:
b. Loss of personal effects, if any, itemized:

IX

Facts relating to damages other than above:

X

Set forth a computation of your contentions as to damages with a breakdown thereof as near as possible as follows:
Name:
Age: Life expectancy of decedent in years:
Earning expectancy in years:

Annual Earning Rate:
At date of death: $
At date of trial: $
Maximum in future: $

Earnings:
Yearly average earnings over work expectancy: $
Less estimated income tax: $
Net per year: $

Monthly Average Take-home Pay:
Less decedent's personal expenses: $
Net for family: $

Decedent's contribution in dollar value per month in care, comfort, society, protection, etc.:

Total family monthly benefit:

19_____ [insert current date] value of sum required:

To produce $ __________ per month for earning capacity $
To produce $ __________ per year to pay income tax on income from investments $

TOTAL
Discount percentage used:
Inflation factor:

Special Damages:
Funeral Expenses: $
Personal Property Loss: $

Add to the above total any benefits claimed to accrue to the family from things which are peculiar to this case such as:
1. Income derived by decedents on investments: $
2. Retirement pensions and benefits: $

Dated this _____ day of __________, 19_____.

____
Judge

In the more typical single plaintiff versus single defendant case, as opposed to the mass disaster case in which the damage calculation may be ordered by the court along the lines of the order above, the substance of the order can be embodied in a set of damage interrogatories. If this particular tactic is followed, it is not necessary to file a motion seeking an order, but rather the interrogatories may be filed pursuant to Rule 33 of the Federal Rules of Civil Procedure or any of its state counterparts.

Section 1.11 contains the format of a set of interrogatories which embody the substance of a court order requiring damage calculations over and above the typical damage information to be collected through a more traditional set of damage interrogatories.

§ 1.11 —Interrogatories Incorporating Court Order on Damage Calculations

Please take notice that pursuant to the Rules of Procedure, the Defendant propounds the following interrogatories to the Plaintiff—

Note: Items I through IX in the extracted appendix in **§ 1.10** are changed from the statement form to the question form.

— Set forth the annual earning rate of the decedent at date of death.

— Set forth the annual earning rate of the decedent projected by you at date of trial had he lived.

— Set forth the maximum annual earning rate of the decedent projected by you in the future had he lived.

What is the yearly average earnings projected by you over the decedent's work expectancy had he lived?

Note: Each of the additional elements in the order is simply changed to interrogatory form.

Pursuant to the rule of discovery, specifically Rule 26 of the Federal Rules of Civil Procedure, your opponent would probably be entitled to this type of information, i.e., the inflation rate applied by your experts, the manner in which your experts calculated the economic loss, etc. However, the question is not so much whether they are entitled to the information but rather *when* they are entitled to it.

Rule 33 of the Federal Rules of Civil Procedure and any of its state counterparts dealing with interrogatories clearly permit the gathering of information which is not otherwise objectionable or privileged. Such damage information typically does not fall into the objectionable or privileged category. However, there is no provision in the Federal Rules of Civil Procedure or state counterparts which, as a matter of course, requires you to "process" that information in any way by doing calculations or reaching conclusions before providing it to your opponent. Although this is generally true, there are means by which you or your opponent can obtain processed information. For example, requests for admissions, which are discussed in **§ 1.13**, are not designed as a discovery tool but rather as a means of limiting the issues and proofs at trial. They can be used to obtain processed information in the form of admissions or denials.

Rule 26 of the Federal Rules of Civil Procedure and its state counterparts dealing with the discovery of opinion evidence require, in effect, the providing of evidence processed in the form of opinions to your opponent. It is in this latter area that damage calculations more properly fit. Since you as an attorney are usually not qualified to perform calculations for purposes of litigation, though you can do them on scratch paper for your own purposes, it is necessary to obtain the services of an economist not only to do the calculations but also to testify to their significance within the context of the case.

Thus, the seeking of damage information in whatever form, including interrogatories, is in the nature of seeking expert witness testimony. The objection to be filed when such interrogatories are filed against you, or when a motion seeking a court order of the same nature is filed, is that this is more properly to be considered expert witness discovery and should be deferred until a later point in the discovery process. In addition, you can indicate that you have not as yet obtained an expert on the subject of damages and, as a result, have not formulated opinions associated with the area of inquiry.

There is an argument to be made that such discovery is more properly treatable as expert discovery within the realm of expert opinion evidence and is thereby more properly reserved for that phase of the discovery process. Accordingly, when faced with an opponent seeking your answers or those of your client relative to this damage information and damage calculations, your response should be in the nature of an objection or opposition papers laying out the improprieties associated with using that form of discovery at that particular time.

§ 1.12 —All-Purpose Damage Interrogatories

The interrogatories which follow represent a good all-purpose set of damage interrogatories from the defendant to the plaintiff which are capable of being modified for special cases you confront. They should include, as appropriate, a definition and instruction section.

INTERROGATORIES

1. Since the date of the accident set forth in the complaint, has plaintiff engaged in one or more gainful occupations? If so, state:

(a) The names and addresses of his employers and the dates between which he worked for each such employer; and

(b) The nature of the work in each such occupation and the wage or salary received by him in each such occupation.

2. (a) State the total amounts earned by plaintiff in each full year for the preceding five years and the total amounts earned by plaintiff in the present calendar year up until the date of the answer to this interrogatory.

(b) State the sources (by names and addresses) and amounts of all income received by plaintiff from gainful employment during these periods from each employer.

3. Has plaintiff been absent from work at any time or times since the date of the accident set forth in the complaint? If so, state:

(a) The dates of all absences from work and the reasons therefor; and

(b) Plaintiff's rates of pay on the dates of such absences, and, if so, for what reason.

4. State whether plaintiff has been unable to perform satisfactorily any of the duties required of him in any of his employments since the date of the accident set forth in the complaint, indicating with particularity what duties he was unable to perform and the names and addresses of all persons having knowledge of such facts, including plaintiff's supervisors and employer at the time of such incapacities.

5. Has plaintiff, or has anyone acting in plaintiff's behalf, obtained from any person or persons any report, statement, memorandum, or testimony concerning the accident involved in this cause of action?

6. If so, what is the name and last known address and present whereabouts, if known, of each such person?

7. If so, when, where and by whom was each such report, statement, memorandum, or testimony obtained or made?

8. If so, where is each located?

9. What is the name and last known address and present whereabouts, if known, of each person whom plaintiff or anyone acting in plaintiff's behalf knows or believes to have witnessed said accident?

10. What is the name, last known address, and present whereabouts, if known, of each person whom plaintiff or anyone acting in plaintiff's behalf knows or believes to have any relevant knowledge of the conditions at the scene of the accident existing prior to, at, or immediately after the same?

11. Exactly where did the accident occur, stated in feet from specific landmarks?

12. Is plaintiff or any representative of plaintiff in possession of any photographs of ________________ involved in this accident, the locale or surrounding area of the site of the accident, or any other matters or things involved in this accident?

13. If plaintiff's answer to the preceding interrogatory is in the affirmative, state:

(a) The date(s) when such photographs were taken;

(b) The name and address of the party taking them;

(c) Where they were taken;

(d) The object(s) or subject(s) or the particular site or view each photograph represents; and

(e) The present whereabouts of the photographs and the name and address of whomsoever is in possession or custody thereof.

14. Was the plaintiff's work governed by any rule(s) promulgated by his employer and in effect at the time of the accident?

15. If your answer to the preceding interrogatory is in the affirmative, specify the number(s) of employer's operating or safety rules which is (are) claimed by plaintiff to apply to plaintiff's activities at the time of the accident.

16. State the names, addresses, and job classifications of plaintiff's supervisors, if any, at the time of the accident.

17. State the names, addresses, and job classifications of plaintiff's fellow crew or gang workers, if any, who were working with the plaintiff at the time of the accident. State where each was and what each was doing at the time of the accident.

18. State the rate of pay which plaintiff was earning at the time of the injury and indicate whether the rate of pay for the work which the plaintiff did at the time of the injury has been since increased. If so, state the amount of increase and when it occurred.

19. Has the plaintiff worked since the accident? If so, indicate whether such work is the same as that done before the accident. If not, specify the type of work done since the date of the accident and the rate of pay therefor.

20. How much time from work has plaintiff lost since this accident, computed up to the date of your answer?

21. How many days was plaintiff absent from work:

(a) In the year of his accident and prior to said accident;

(b) In the two full years prior to the year of the accident (except absences for holidays, vacations, layoffs, furloughs, and Sundays or relief days); and

(c) State the explanation for any of such absences, other than those excepted.

22. State how much plaintiff's gross earnings were for each of the two full years preceding the year of his accident.

23. State the total of plaintiff's gross earnings for the year in which he was hurt, indicating the amount earned before and the amount earned after the injury.

24. State how much plaintiff's gross earnings were for each of the years subsequent to the year in which he was hurt, computed up to the date of your answer.

25. State whether and how often periodic inspections or examinations were made of the (machinery, equipment) (condition) involved in this case.

26. State when inspections were made last preceding and first following this accident of (machinery, equipment) (condition) involved herein, giving the

names, addresses, and job classifications of the persons making each inspection.

27. State whether:

(a) Written or typed reports were made of the inspections referred to in the preceding interrogatory, and, if so, indicate the present location of copies of said reports; and

(b) Any such oral reports were made of the inspection referred to in the preceding interrogatory, and, if so, from whom and to whom.

28. State what physical facts, if any, were disclosed by the inspection.

29. State:

(a) The dates of any repairs, alterations, or modifications made last preceding and first following this accident;

(b) The names, addresses, and job classifications of the persons making such repairs, alterations, or modifications;

(c) The nature and extent of such repairs, alterations, or modifications; and

(d) If written records were made of the repairs, alterations, or modifications referred to above, state the present location of such records and the names and addresses of the persons having custody thereof.

30. State the present location of the object (machinery, equipment) (condition) involved in the alleged occurrence and the name, residential address, and job classification of the person having custody of same.

31. State whether any alterations, repairs, or replacements were made to the said object (machinery, equipment) (condition) subsequent to the alleged accident and, if yes, state:

(a) The nature thereof;

(b) The date and time of day the same was done;

(c) The name, address, and job classification of the person making same and, if not in your employ, the name and address of his employer; and

(d) If any report, record, or memorandum was made concerning the repairs, state the nature thereof, the date thereof, and the name, address, and job classification of the person having possession and custody thereof.

32. State whether any photographs were taken of the object (machinery, equipment) (condition) or site of the alleged occurrence. If yes, state:

(a) The subject matter of said photographs;

(b) The date and time of day said photographs were taken;

(c) The name, address, and job classification of the person taking same, and the name and address of his employer if not in your employ; and

(d) The name, address, and job classification of the person having custody of the photographs.

33. State whether any plans, drawings, blueprints, sketches, or diagrams exist or were made, other than by counsel, of the object (machinery, equipment) (condition) or site of the alleged accident, and, if so, state:

(a) The identity of each said plan, drawing, blueprint, sketch, or diagram by subject matter;

(b) The date and times of day when each of the same was made if subsequent to the occurrence.

(c) The name, address, and job classification of the person making same, if made subsequent to the occurrence; and

(d) The name, address, and job classification of the person having custody of the plans, drawings, blueprints, sketches or diagrams.

34. State whether or not any notice was given or complaints were made relating to the said object (machinery, equipment) (condition) prior to the alleged occurrence. If yes, state:

(a) Name, address, and job classification of the person making same, and the name and address of his employer;

(b) The nature of said notice or complaint;

(c) The date and time of day thereof;

(d) The name, address, and job classification of the person to whom made; and

(e) Whether any report, record, or memorandum was made thereof. If so, the date, place and name and address of the person having custody of same.

35. State whether the plaintiff submitted to any physical examinations in connection with employment either prior to or subsequent to the commencement of his employment, and, if yes, state as to each examination:

(a) The date or dates thereof;

(b) The name and address of any hospital facility where made;

(c) Describe the nature of any written report, record, or memorandum thereof;

(d) The name and address and job classification of the person at whose instance said examination was made;

(e) Identify the person or company who paid for the examination;

(f) State the doctor's employer; and

(g) Give the name, address, and job classification of the person having custody of such medical records.

36. State whether any first aid or medical attention was given to the plaintiff subsequent to the alleged occurrence and, if yes, state as to each:

(a) The name, address, and job classification of all individuals, and the name and address of all physicians, medical facilities and/or hospitals;

(b) The date or dates thereof;

(c) Whether any reports, records, or memoranda were made thereof;

(d) The dates of said reports, records, or memoranda; and

(e) The name and address of the person having custody of such reports, records, or memoranda.

37. State whether any disciplinary action was taken against the plaintiff within three years prior to the alleged occurrence and up to the present time and, if so, specify the nature of said action, the dates thereof, and if any report, record, or memorandum exists relating thereto, describe the same and state the name, address, and job classification of the person having custody of same.

38. State whether any safety or operating rules exist relating to the activity in which plaintiff was engaged at the time of the alleged occurrence and, if yes, identify the same by:

(a) Subject matter;

(b) Source of authority therefor;

(c) Date the same went into effect;

(d) If published, the identity and title, publisher, date of publications, and place of publication; and

(e) Give the name, address, and job classification of the person having custody of such publication.

39. Did plaintiff ever suffer any injuries, sickness, disease, or abnormality of any kind prior to the accident alleged in this action involving any part or function of the body claimed in this suit to have been injured?

40. If so, when? What was the said injury, sickness, disease, or abnormality?

41. Was plaintiff ever examined or treated for any injuries, sickness, disease, or abnormality prior to the accident alleged in this action involving any part or function of the body claimed in this suit to have been injured?

42. If so, when, where, and by whom?

43. Does the plaintiff have photographs, drawings, or plans which are relevant to this action other than as prepared by counsel?

44. When, where, by whom, and of what subject were they taken or made?

45. Exactly what total wage loss did plaintiff sustain as a result of this accident?

46. Exactly how does the plaintiff compute this sum?

47. Has plaintiff been known by any name other than that in which action is brought at any time since the date of the accident involved in this action?

48. To the support or maintenance of what person or persons did decedent contribute during the five years preceding his death, and when and in what amounts or in what form was each such contribution made?

49. From whom, on what dates, and in what amounts did decedent receive any pay, wages, earnings, or other compensation from one year prior to the accident involved in this action to the date of his death?

50. Upon what days from one year prior to the accident involved in this action was decedent employed, by whom, and in exactly what kind of work?

51. What specific expenses were incurred by decedent or his estate as a result of this accident?

§ 1.13 Requests for Admissions

Requests for admissions are the most dangerous discovery tool available to any litigator. Used properly against you they can be devastatingly effective, and used properly by you they can be your most powerful tool in litigation. The purpose of a request for admission is generally not to discover new evidence; rather, it is to narrow the issues at trial, expedite the proceedings, and eliminate the need for proofs at trial and discovery.

Requests for admissions are unique in the context of available litigative and discovery techniques in being in effect self-executing. As provided by Federal Rule of Civil Procedure 36, requests for admissions are admitted "unless within thirty (30) days of the service of the request or within such shorter or longer time as the court may allow, the party to whom the request is directed serves upon the party requesting the admission a written answer or objection addressed to the matter . . . ." Thus, failure to do anything at all, e.g., admit, deny, object, etc., with respect to a request for admissions, unlike the situation of interrogatories where a motion to compel answers to interrogatories or a motion for sanctions must be filed, has a result. The requests are deemed admitted if they are not responded to within the time provided for in the rules or by the court. This fact makes requests for admissions, when properly used, extremely dangerous.

If a matter is deemed to be admitted under Rule 36, that matter is conclusively established unless the judge permits a withdrawal or amendment of the admission based upon the motion against whom the admission is operating. In the face of a showing of prejudice by the party seeking to enforce the admission, the relief being sought by way of withdrawal or amendment will, at least theoretically, not be permitted. Specifically, Rule 36(b) provides that relief from an admission will be permitted "when the presentation of the merits of the action will be subserved thereby and the party who obtained the admission fails to satisfy the court that withdrawal or amendment will prejudice him in maintaining his action or defense on the merits." The question then becomes one of prejudice.

In many respects, however, Rule 36 regarding the effect of admissions and the relief to be given to nonresponding parties must be read in concert with Rule 16 of the Federal Rules of Civil Procedure. Rule 16 governs amendments of the pretrial order and, in pertinent part, provides for the court to make an order "which recites the action taken at the conference, the amendments allowed to the pleadings, and the agreements made by the parties as to any of the matters considered, and which limits the issues for trial to those not disposed of by admissions or agreements of counsel."

Once there is a pretrial order in effect entered by the court, it dictates the further contours of the trial and the evidence. Matters which have been stipulated to and which are contained in the pretrial order need not be the subject of proof any longer and are thus already determined. Although the order can be modified at trial, it may only be done so—in the terms of Rule 16—to "prevent manifest injustice."

Reading Rule 36 together with Rule 16 is important when you find yourself in a situation where an opponent is seeking relief from admissions which have not been responded to but which, by virtue of Rule 16, have been incorporated into the pretrial order. The showing which must be made by an opponent to avoid an admission which has been made under Rule 36 is significantly greater after a trial has begun and its course is being dictated by a Rule 16 pretrial order than it would have been before the trial began.

On occasion, you may encounter a situation in which your opponent has overlooked responding to requests for admissions filed by you. From a into evidence the admitted facts. Those admitted facts may or may not, depending upon the practice in the court where you are trying the case, already be the subject of the pretrial order. In any event the trial will have begun.

As a result, when you find yourself confronted with an opponent who is seeking to use the prejudice standard to obtain relief from an admission during trial, be sure to turn to Rule 16. A recent case on this point is *Brook Village North Associates v. General Electric Co.,* 687 F.2d 66 (1st Cir. 1982). *Brook Village* involved a situation in which the district court held that, because the plaintiff elected to go forward with the presentation of certain evidence that touched on matters deemed to have been admitted by the defendant, the plaintiff was no longer in a position to rely upon those admissions. In addition, the court held that it would no longer be bound by the admissions because their withdrawal would not prejudice the plaintiffs. On appeal, the First Circuit found that the district court's application of Rule 36 was in error.

Essentially, the First Circuit in *Brook Village* held that requiring a party to elect between (1) relying on admissions which had been admitted through default and introducing no evidence at all on those points and (2) introducing evidence but foregoing the binding force of the admissions would unfairly place the party who makes the decision to use admissions by default as a means to limit the proof at trial to the scope of the admissions. In so ruling, the court of appeals determined that a party who obtains admission through default by an opponent does not waive the right to rely on those admissions and may introduce additional evidence at trial which overlaps the matters controlled by the admission.

The reasoning in *Brook Village* is applicable whether or not you are dealing with an admission-by-default situation. If you have an opponent who has made admissions either by choice or by default, you are still able under the rationale of *Brook Village* to introduce additional evidence which overlaps the matters controlled by the admission. Any other reading or application of the rule would be overly technical. Thus, when confronted by an opponent who seeks to undo an admission by virtue of the fact that you introduce evidence at trial bearing on the subject matter of the admission, be sure to raise the reasoning in *Brook Village* to the court.

In summary, requests for admissions enjoy several advantages as well as disadvantages. The most obvious advantage is that they limit the issues at trial and thus reduce the amount of discovery time needed and resulting time at trial. To the extent they have a disadvantage, it usually arises when you are on the receiving end of a comprehensive set of requests. Since they require responses, you find yourself confronting the issues of a case sooner than you otherwise might want to do so. On balance, however, there is no question that requests for admissions are highly effective in virtually all respects.

§ 1.14 —Use with Interrogatories

A technique sometimes used by the propounder of a comprehensive set of requests for admissions in order to discourage an opponent from either denying a request or filing a qualified answer is to include a formatted interrogatory at the beginning of the requests for admissions which covers the entire set of requests or an interrogatory with respect to each request. In general, this interrogatory requests each and every fact on which a full or partial denial is based if the request is to any extent denied. The idea of including such an interrogatory is to discourage the party to whom requests are addressed from denying the requests in light of the fact that responding to the interrogatory can be burdensome.

A type of formatted interrogatory which is frequently used in this manner follows:

If your response to any requests for admissions contained herein is other than an unqualified admission, please answer the following interrogatory for each such response:

1. All facts which you contend support your refusal to unqualifiedly admit the request.
2. For each such fact listed in response to subsection one (1) above, identify all documents, notes, reports, memoranda, electronic and/or tape recordings, photographs, or oral statements or any other tangible or intangible thing which supports your refusal to unqualifiedly admit the request. The said identification should be sufficient to identify the items listed in a request for production.
3. The name, address, and telephone number of the custodian of records of all tangible or intangible things identified in response to interrogatory two (2) above.
4. The name, address, and telephone number of all persons, including consultants and/or experts, purporting to have any knowledge or factual data upon which you base your refusal to make an unqualified admission to the request. The purpose of this interrogatory is to have you reveal everything presently known by you that bears on your refusal to respond to the request with an unqualified admission.

The [plaintiff] [defendant] will, at the time of trial, move the court for an order excluding from evidence all tangible or intangible things known to you at the time of your responses to these requests and interrogatories not disclosed in your responses thereto.

There is little doubt that, when faced with the alternative of responding with an unqualified admission to a request for admission as opposed to providing the extensive type of information requested in the interrogatory, most litigants will opt for the former. However, this use of an interrogatory by your opponent as a bludgeon to obtain admissions must not simply be accepted.

An appropriate response to this sort of tactic is to file a motion to strike the interrogatory as an improper use of both interrogatories and requests for admissions. Remember, a request for admission is not a discovery tool but is rather to be used to limit the proofs at trial. An interrogatory coupled with a request for admission can be argued to be counterproductive to the underlying rationale for requests for admissions.

§ 1.15 —Partial Admissions and Denials

Another unfair tactic in connection with requests for admissions has to do with qualified admissions or denials and their phrasing. As a general matter, the possible responses to a request are an admission, a denial, a statement of inability to either admit or deny, an objection, or a request for an extension of time in which to respond. Thus, the rules themselves make no provision for qualified or partial admissions or denials. However, it is clear that any responses made by you must be unambiguous, because it is likely that any ambiguity will be interpreted against your client.

Although not provided for explicitly within the rules, partial admissions or denials nevertheless are frequent. Thus, an admission that reads "admitted but deny . . ." is common. A tactic that is sometimes used against such qualified responses is that your opponent may seek to strike everything following the word *admitted* or *denied* as an improper response under the rules. Sometimes you may find yourself with an admission or denial that may be inaccurate as well as prejudicial to your cause.

A technique for avoiding entrapment by an opponent who moves to strike qualified admissions or denials is to follow the *reversal rule.* Although under normal circumstances you might state "admitted, but denied . . . ," in order to protect yourself against that rare opponent who may take the tack of moving to strike everything after the *admitted,* you should respond to such requests by denying everything but admitting only specific portions. Thus, when following this approach, the response would be "denied, but admit. . . ."

If you follow this latter format, it is not likely that your opponent will seek to strike that part of the response following the first word. If he or she does so, however, you are in no worse position for having made a total denial. Further, you are in a better position to resist the imposition of sanctions or costs in the event your opponent must introduce evidence proving what he or she asserts should have been admitted.

The best response to a motion to strike is simply to point out to the court that, by making the type of response you did, you were attempting to avoid a partially correct response in favor of a completely correct response and that to grant the motion to strike would be counterproductive, despite the fact that the rules themselves do not provide for qualified admissions or denials.

In the event that you do not prevail and the motion is granted, you are no worse off than before by virtue of having protected yourself through a reversal of the response.

§ 1.16 —Creating Prejudice

Rule 36 of the Federal Rules of Civil Procedure and its state counterparts provide in subsection (b):

> [T]he court may permit withdrawal or amendment [of responses to requests] when the presentation of the merits of the action will be subserved thereby and the party who obtained the admission fails to satisfy the court that withdrawal or amendment will prejudice him in maintaining his action or defense on the merits.

As a general matter, it is quite clear that unless a party securing an admission has the right to rely on that admission, he or she cannot safely avoid the expense of preparing to prove the matter on which the party secured the admission. However, the rules do not go so far as to totally bar the granting of relief but provide that such relief may be afforded in the absence of a showing of prejudice.

Typical of the circumstances in which relief must be sought is when requests are not responded to within the time limits allowed and are thereby deemed admitted, or when requests are responded to but, because of either inadvertence or late discovery, the responses are found to be incorrect. In such circumstances, the party to whom the requests were directed would be obliged to seek relief from the court, and the party who propounded the requests would be obliged to show that prejudice has occurred or would occur if relief were granted to the responding party.

You may encounter circumstances in which your opponent attempts to take advantage of the fact that you are seeking relief from a failure to respond to a request or, alternatively, attempts to change a response to a request by asserting prejudice. The first point to consider is whether your opponent reasonably knew or should have known at the time the response was filed or the request was deemed admitted that the requests had not been responded to and were thus deemed admitted, or whether it was obvious that the responses as filed were incorrect. If you conclude that your opponent actually possesses or should have possessed such knowledge, the odds are your opponent is attempting to "create" prejudice to defeat your request for relief.

Such a tactic amounts to a set-up, and if this is properly pointed out in your papers to the court, there may be a dual benefit. First, your request for relief will probably be granted; second, the tactic of your opponent will be recognized for what it is. A good approach to turning this situation around, to the extent you are able to do so, is not to attack your opponent in the moving papers in which you seek relief in the first instance. Rather, when you either failed to respond to requests for admissions at all and this should have been apparent to your opponent or when your responses were patently in error, your original moving papers should simply set forth the request for relief and the general basis for that relief, including the appropriate rules and citations.

If your opponent has filed opposition papers setting forth prejudice, you should respond by asserting that the prejudice was purposely and voluntarily created by your opponent despite the fact that it should have been apparent either that the answers to the requests were wrong or that no responses had been filed. Remember, courts today do not favor trial by ambush. If it becomes apparent to the judge that you are being set up, despite the fact that you may not have done something which you should have done, i.e., respond to requests for admissions, it is not unlikely that the judge will view your opponent as attempting to take unfair advantage of a situation.

Although you will not emerge from such a situation unscathed in terms of either credibility or the perception of the court, this approach can minimize and contain the damage which might otherwise occur in such unfortunate circumstances. Obviously, the best way to avoid such a tactic is to pay careful attention to requests for admissions and ensure that they are properly responded to in a timely fashion.

§ 1.17 —Timing

One tactic you should carefully watch out for, no matter which side of the case you are on, is the filing of requests for admissions with the complaint or with the answer. Since this discovery tactic is typically not anticipated at such an early stage of the case, it is easy to overlook their filing and thus not respond to them at that time. In such a circumstance, you set yourself up for a prejudice claim, because there is a great deal of discovery yet to come and an opponent may, in reliance on your failure to respond, purposely fail to take certain types of discovery, if this failure, though prejudicial, would not be fatal to his or her case.

The argument then to be anticipated in opposition to your request for relief is that certain discovery was deliberately omitted from the discovery plan in reliance on the responses or failure to respond to the requests for admissions filed at an early date. Further, you may expect that your opponent will assert that the reason for filing the requests at such an early date was to limit the issues and thereby the areas of discovery which would be required. Only a careful and measured approach toward the management of discovery and control of case files can keep this from happening in the case of early-filed, self-executing requests for admission.

§ 1.18 Document Production

One aspect of the discovery process which is susceptible to abuse by both plaintiffs and defendants is document production. Rule 34 of the Federal Rules of Civil Procedure and its state counterparts provide for the production of documents and other things as well as for entry on land for inspection and other purposes. In light of the ever-increasing complexity of litigation, documentary evidence is becoming increasingly important, and, as a result, the pretrial discovery of that material has become a key information-gathering device in the litigation process. This has led to unfair use of this procedure by both plaintiffs and defendants.

Ideally, the production of documents should be an organized and cooperative effort between and among counsel with the common goal of minimizing costs associated with a potentially costly process and, ultimately, expediting the litigation. As a practical matter, however, reality indicates this is more often the exception than the rule. Document production is used as a bludgeon on occasion and is the frequent cause of the often-criticized expense of the litigative process, due primarily to the use of certain tactics directed at impeding discovery and the ultimate resolution of the litigation. However, each of these tactics can be effectively countered and turned against an opponent who attempts to improperly use production discovery devices.

As a general matter, tactics used by counsel to pervert Rule 34 document production fall into three broad categories. These are the "boxcar" request, the "shuffled deck" response, and the "smoking gun" response. The first of these three is used by the party requesting document production, while the latter two are used in responding to requests for production. Each is an unfair tactic, and each has a number of responses which can turn it against the user as a very effective weapon.

§ 1.19 —"Boxcar" Requests

The "boxcar" request typically is used as an intimidation tactic. It amounts to a request for production of documents that, if responded to, would require a boxcar to deliver the responsive documents. When exposed for what it is—an intimidation tactic to discourage the other side from pursuing the litigation and perhaps to take advantage of superior resources of the requesting party—the boxcar approach typically will boomerang.

The appropriate response to this request usually is a motion to strike the request or for a protective order, setting out the nature of the tactic and, perhaps, including affidavits which delineate the volume of documentation needed to respond to the request for production of documents.

A usual response in such a circumstance, from a judge who is focusing on judicial and litigative economies, will be either to put the requesting party on the spot to narrow the request for production of documents voluntarily or to order that the requests be limited. This requires first that the party of whom the request is made make an informal or voluntary effort along with the requesting party to narrow the request and be in a position to attest to the court that the requesting party has refused to cooperate in the limiting of requests for production of documents.

The boxcar response is also used as an intimidation tactic by the responding party's side. Assuming that producing the boxcar or van load full of documents will discourage the requesting party from reading the documents, responding parties who have the capability will frequently produce documents of questionable relevance or materiality for the purpose of overwhelming the party for whom the documents are being produced. This approach is similar to the technique for dealing with either the "shuffled deck" or the "smoking gun" responses.

§ 1.20 —"Shuffled Deck" and "Smoking Gun" Responses

A "shuffled deck" response to a request for production occurs when the party producing documents produces them in a format or manner which approximates what occurs after a deck of cards has been shuffled. The documents have been "reorganized," and all original structure or format has been removed.

In a "smoking gun" response, a responding party attempts to hide an incriminating or particularly damaging document in a "boxcar" load of documents and makes the gratuitous offer to permit the requesting party to review all the documents in the load, hoping to intimidate the opponent into submission.

The response to each of these tactics is a motion filed pursuant to Rule 34(b) of the Federal Rules of Civil Procedure or its state counterpart requiring the party producing the documents to produce them as they are "kept in the usual course of business" or organized and labeled to correspond to the various categories of the request for production itself.

The Section of Litigation of the American Bar Association has recognized that "it is apparently not rare for parties deliberately to mix critical documents with others in the hope of obscuring significance." Report of the Special Committee for the Study of Discovery Abuse 22 (1977).

Coupled with a motion for sanctions or costs against offending counsel, a Rule 34 compliance motion is an effective response to an unfair tactic designed to abuse the production process.

§ 1.21 Discovery of Experts' Reports

Although all the discovery tools of the Federal Rules of Civil Procedure and state counterparts are available in the nonexpert area as a matter of right, with the exception of physical examinations or inspections of property, the same is not true with respect to discovery against expert witnesses. Indeed, the only device provided for under the Federal Rules for discovery as a matter of right as against expert witnesses is interrogatories. Even with interrogatories, the scope of discovery is limited to the identity of the expert, the opinion, and the basis for the opinion.

The different results in two recent cases illustrate the distinctions between discovery from expert witnesses and from nonexperts.

Delcastor, Inc. v. Vail Associates, Inc., 108 F.R.D. 405 (D. Colo., 1985), dealt with the question of discoverability of experts' reports. In *Delcastor*, the court granted the plaintiff's motion to compel discovery of an expert's report containing opinions as to the cause of a mud slide. The defendant had been planning to call the expert as a witness, but only with respect to his observations of the mud slide as to rain and the proximity of drainage ditches following the mud slide. In order to make effective cross-examination of the expert's testimony regarding the facts surrounding the mud slide, the court felt that discovery of the opinion as to the cause of the slide would be appropriate. In addition, the report would also be necessary for effective cross-examination and possible impeachment of another expert.

Another case dealing with the question of expert testimony was *Puerto Rico Aqueduct & Sewer Authority v. Clow Corp.*, No. 82-2421 (HL) (D.P.R., decided Nov. 12, 1985). The *Clow* case involved an action against 12 defendants for alleged defects discovered by the plaintiff in approximately 20,000 cold-water service connections. The court determined that the defendants were not entitled to compel the plaintiff to disclose information, including facts, opinions, and identities of its experts. The defendants did not show that they did not have other means to obtain facts or opinions on the same subject.

When representing defense interests and seeking discovery from the plaintiff's expert, two approaches can be taken. The first is to seek to obtain such discovery by stipulation or agreement from plaintiff's counsel. Usually the best approach to accomplishing this is to offer your experts for discovery in exchange for taking discovery from the plaintiff's experts. Failing such an agreement, it will be necessary to seek an order from the court to take discovery beyond interrogatories. In order to get such discovery, it will further be necessary for you to make a showing that the information is not reasonably obtainable from other sources. In effect, a showing of need must be made in order to avail yourself of discovery from plaintiff's experts in a manner other than through the interrogatories provided for in the rules.

§ 1.22 Sources of Document Discovery

One of the greatest problems which you will encounter when representing a corporate-type defendant has to do with document production. Oftentimes, as has been exhibited in recent years, obtaining documents which have been requested through the discovery process is a significant undertaking. This is true for a number of reasons, including the fact that many corporate-type defendants, particularly those in the product manufacturing area, do not have document retention procedures or, if they do, their document retention procedures are not geared toward litigation. For example, the defendant may have document destruction policies which are carried out despite the fact that litigation is pending; for example, perhaps the individuals charged with this responsibility never "got the word" regarding the litigation or the need to retain documents. As a result, adverse inferences are sought and, on occasion, obtained.

Another problem frequently encountered with respect to corporate defendants is the "private" file. This is nothing more than the employee who, usually contrary to company regulations or procedures, has a personal file on a particular project, problem, or other matter kept at work or, perhaps, at home. Into this same category falls the retired employee who has brought with him into retirement a large number of documents. They usually reside in his garage or attic and come to light only after you have inevitably made representations regarding the nonexistence of the very documents in his possession.

Keeping in mind the fact that you can be in the position of being taken advantage of by virtue of certain procedures followed by your client, you should be aware of the following discovery considerations which touch upon document discovery matters, as well as others, whenever you represent corporate defendants.

1. Determine whether the manufacturer or other corporate defendant has a library, either formal or informal. Check that library for any documents which may be relevant to the litigation. In addition, determine whether the library or some other place in the corporation has copies of patent applications which may be relevant. Oftentimes, representations may be made in such patent applications that

are inconsistent with the position being taken in litigation. The time to learn about this fact is not in the courtroom.

2. Check all patent application files and documents, wherever they are maintained, including the United States Patent Office. Don't rely on the fact that what is reflected in the corporate files regarding patent applications is the same as what is on file with the Patent Office. Once again, the way to learn about this is not from your opponent in court.
3. Check all indexes to articles, including masters theses and doctoral dissertations, that may involve the particular product or products in issue in the case. Also, be sure to check any indexes to periodicals such as newspapers, magazine reports, or other materials that may be relevant to the product. Be on the lookout for any interviews with corporate officials that may touch on the product.
4. Talk to any reporters who may be knowledgeable about the particular industry or product involved. Oftentimes, national or local news organizations, including newspapers and televisions, assign particular reporters to cover specific types of beats, by industry, company, or otherwise. It can be helpful to talk to these reporters and possibly exchange information in order to determine the types of leads which you might need to follow up and which your opponent might be following up.
5. Review all past company reports to see the types of representations that were made regarding the product.
6. Review all in-house publications, including newsletters, to find the names of retired employees.
7. Have the company check the list of stockholders to determine whether any of the attorneys or clients on the other side are stockholders in the corporation. It is not unheard of for an attorney or client to purchase one share of stock simply to receive publications from the company and have access to certain company-related information. If you determine that either the attorneys or clients on the other side are in fact shareholders, be sure to review any information that may have been supplied to them as shareholders.
8. Review all trade association or trade organization types of publications; they may contain information relevant to either the industry in general or the specific company and product.
9. Be wary when inquiries are made of the company either directly or through company representatives regarding the nature of the product, warranties, and related matters. On occasion you may run into situations in which an opponent specifically sends someone to a product retailer authorized by the manufacturer to sell the product for the purpose of determining what types of representations regarding

the product are being made by the retailer. Although it may not be possible to stop your opponent from doing this, it is important that you not have unfair advantage taken of you. As a result, be sure to determine yourself the types of representations which the sales and marketing department is making regarding the product and how those representations are being carried out by retailers who are suppliers of the product.

§ 1.23 Protecting Internal Company Reports

Protecting internal company reports from discovery in litigation is a problem being addressed more frequently by the courts. In *Hardy v. New York News, Inc.*, No. Civ. 1147 (MGC) (S.D.N.Y., Jan. 28, 1987), the court found that the self-evaluative privilege is based on a concern that documents which reflect the candid self-evaluation of a company if disclosed will likely deter useful evaluations or compliance with either professional or legal standards. In *Urseth v. City of Dayton, Ohio,* No. C-3-84-103 (S.D. Ohio, May 5, 1986), the court held that self-evaluative materials generally are subject to protection. Exceptional circumstances, however, can bring about their disclosure.

Section 1.24 contains a sample document management agreement and protective order which can be adapted according to the facts of your case.

§ 1.24 —Sample Document Agreement and Protective Order

PROPERTY MANAGEMENT AND RETURN AGREEMENT AND PROTECTIVE ORDER

Pursuant to Rules of the Court, the defendant, ________________, respectfully requests that the Court order the protection of confidential and proprietary information and documents requested of the defendant, pursuant to the standards and guidelines outlined below, for the purpose of limiting the use of confidential and proprietary information or documents given or produced by defendant in this action.

The subject matter of plaintiffs' action involves the design, manufacture, and testing of a sophisticated product and plaintiffs' discovery does, and in the future may, seek information involving trade secrets, confidential research, development, and commercial information which must be protected from disclosure and dissemination outside of the scope of this action. Protection from disclosure of such confidential and proprietary information is necessary in order for the defendant to avoid the undue burden, expense, and oppression that would be placed upon defendant thereby in order to protect and maintain its competitive position in the development and marketing of such sophisticated products and components in the commercial and military marketplace.

Defendant would more specifically ask the Court to enter an order as follows:

1. This order shall apply to all documents, drawings, reports, data, information, and other materials provided by defendant to plaintiffs throughout the course of this action, unless otherwise agreed to by all counsel to this action in writing and all materials subject to this order shall be identified with a proprietary stamp as being the property of defendant.

2. That plaintiff's attorneys shall acknowledge receipt of all such confidential and proprietary information.

3. That plaintiffs, plaintiffs' attorneys, plaintiffs' experts, and others who have been or will be provided any such confidential and proprietary information (whether in the form of a document or simply the information itself) will not disclose any such information other than to disclose it to persons who require such information for preparation for trial and for use at depositions and trial in this case only. More specifically, that plaintiffs, plaintiffs' attorneys, plaintiffs' experts, and others who have access to any such proprietary information will not disclose it to the public in general, to the news media, to other manufacturers, subcontractors or suppliers, designers, experts, or consultants of any type or nature, whatsoever, or to other attorneys and any other organizations not specifically and solely related to preparation and use at the trial of this case.

4. Prior to any such disclosures or exhibition, plaintiff's counsel shall first present a copy of the Property Management and Return Agreement Protective Order to any such person, and such person shall sign an acknowledgment, the form of which is attached hereto as Exhibit "A," stating that such person has read this Order and agrees to be bound by its terms. All such persons shall be bound by the terms of this Order, and shall not permit disclosure of the documents or the information contained therein other than pursuant to the terms of the Order.

5. If at any time, when confidential and proprietary information or documents are in the possession of any party, such information or documents are subpoenaed by any court, administrative or legislative body, or any other persons purporting to have authority to subpoena such documents, the party to whom the subpoena is directed will not produce such documents without first giving written notice of the subpoena (including the delivery of a copy thereof) to defendant within twenty-four hours after receipt of the subpoena. In the event that a subpoena purports to require production of such materials on less than twenty-four hours' notice, the party to whom the subpoena is directed shall give immediate telephonic notice of the receipt of such subpoena and forthwith hand-deliver a copy thereof to counsel for the defendant.

6. The parties to this Order shall be entitled to designate additional documents which may become subject to this Order during the remainder of this litigation. Such additional documents may include, but are not limited to, answers to interrogatories, responses to requests for admissions, deposition exhibits, and responses to requests for production of documents.

7. All pleadings, motion papers, memoranda, affidavits, exhibits, transcripts, and other papers filed with the Clerk of the Court that contain any confidential and proprietary information, including any quotations or summaries from any documents designated by UTC as containing confidential and proprietary business information, or any information or material derived from any documents or other discovery material designated by defendant as containing confidential and proprietary business information, shall be marked: "CONFIDENTIAL PURSUANT TO COURT ORDER" and shall be filed with the Clerk of the Court under seal and kept under seal until further order of the Court. The party filing the pleading, motion paper, memorandum, affidavit, exhibit transcript, or other paper shall also ensure that the service photocopies are marked: "CONFIDENTIAL PURSUANT TO COURT ORDER" and that precautions are taken to prevent disclosure to anyone other than the parties being served. Where possible, only those portions of filings with the Clerk of the Court which contain confidential and proprietary information shall be held under seal.

8. Notwithstanding the foregoing provisions, this Order shall not be construed as a waiver by defendants or plaintiffs of any objections which might be raised as to the admissibility at trial of any evidentiary material.

9. The provisions of this Order shall not terminate at the conclusion of these actions. Within ninety days after the completion of this cause of action either by settlement, trial with a verdict and judgment or appellate decision, and prior to any payment, if any, of the settlement or judgment, plaintiffs will return to defendant's attorney all such confidential and proprietary information covered by this court order and will provide the defendant and the court a certificate attesting to the return of any and all such proprietary information and will further certify that no such proprietary information has remained in the hands of any experts or others working on the case or has been disseminated in violation of said court order.

Approved and Agreed to by:

Dated: ________________ Plaintiff

By: ____________________________

Dated: ________________ Defendant

By: ____________________________

ORDER

It is so ordered this _____ day of __________, 1987.

____

Judge

EXHIBIT "A"

ACKNOWLEDGMENT

STATE OF ____________________)
)
COUNTY OF __________________)

I have reviewed and studied the Property Management and Return Agreement Protective Order attached hereto as Exhibit "A" and do hereby acknowledge that I understand the terms and conditions of the Protective Order and agree to be bound by its terms.

____

____
(Printed Name)

SUBSCRIBED AND SWORN TO before me, by the said ________________ to certify which, witness my hand and seal of office on this _____ day of ___________, 19_____.

____
NOTARY PUBLIC IN AND FOR
THE STATE OF ___________

§ 1.25 Combating Unfair Tactics

One tactic which you may occasionally run into is the situation in which a document production request has been filed and, shortly after that filing, settlement discussions are commenced by your opponent. Superficially, there seems to be very little relationship between the discovery process or, more particularly, the production of documents and the resolution of the whole litigation through settlement. However, it is not at all uncommon for a party receiving a discovery request for the production of documents to be confronted with having to turn over to an opponent a document or documents which can be likened to the proverbial "smoking gun."

For all practical purposes under such circumstances, the production of those documents will end the case insofar as they put the party producing them at a substantial disadvantage if the case goes forward to trial or, alternatively, in any settlement negotiations. As a result, the party faced with such a dilemma immediately undertakes steps to attempt the settlement of the case without the need for disclosing, in response to the document production request or other types of discovery requests, the information which is so damaging to the litigation. Sometimes that information is simply embarrassing to the party. On other occasions the information is so crucial to the success of the case that its disclosure will effectively end the case.

Confronted with this situation, the party immediately initiates settlement negotiations in either a relatively offhand fashion, or in a more formalized fashion—"Rather than getting bogged down in further discovery, let's simply shelve it for the time being and discuss settlement. By doing this we can focus our entire attention on the settlement prospects and not be confronted with splitting our attention and thus possibly failing in settlement."

Oftentimes, you will find yourself in the situation of not really being able to discern the motive for an opponent raising settlement questions. However, you should be particularly suspicious how you react to settlement overtures which to that point in time have not been made and come shortly after the filing of a round of discovery by you. This is particularly true if your opponent at that point suggests that discovery either be formally or informally stayed while the settlement negotiations are ongoing. The best approach to take for expediting the settlement as well as for determining the motive behind the settlement discussions is to press ahead with the discovery and advise your opponent that you certainly have no objection to discussing settlement but you don't want to do so at the cost of moving the case forward. As a result, you should tell your opponent that you are certainly prepared to sit down whenever and wherever it is convenient to both sides to discuss the settlement, but you would request that the discovery and responses to your discovery requests proceed in the normal schedule of things.

The response you receive can tell you a great deal about the motives of your opponent. If your opponent intensifies his or her efforts to settle the case, you can be relatively sure that your discovery is striking close to home. If, on the other hand, your opponent simply accedes to your request, you are not in a position to read as much into the settlement overtures as before. However, even under such circumstances, you may be able to use the leverage of the discovery process to move the settlement along.

Turning the tables for a moment, the question arises how to react when you are confronted with the discovery request from an opponent and having in your hand the so-called smoking gun. Obviously, you cannot simply destroy or hide the document, because to do so would be, at a minimum, illegal and unethical. The best approach under such circumstances is to proceed with the discovery process while at the same time pursuing the settlement process. This is not to say that you shouldn't seek to get an agreement that the discovery process will either stop or slow down while settlement is being discussed; but, by the same token, you do not want to take any steps which would lead your opponent to believe that he or she has struck pay dirt and should forge ahead at all costs.

On December 5, 1985, the United States District Court for the Western District of Michigan held that a plaintiff, acting through his attorney, was to immediately cease all ex parte contact with the defendant corporation's managerial employees.

In *Massa v. Eaton Corp.,* 109 F.R.D. 312 (W.D. Mich. 1985), the court determined that informal discovery without the prior knowledge or consent of the defendant's counsel conducted by interviewing several managerial-level employees of the defendant corporation regarding the subject matter of the litigation was improper. In so deciding, the district court reversed a decision of the magistrate and determined that the employees who were contacted in the *Massa* case were precisely the types of corporate employees that would be covered by an ex parte prohibition regarding communications under Disciplinary Rule 7-104(A)(1) of the Michigan Code of Professional Responsibility, which prohibits a lawyer from communicating with a party he or she knows to be represented by counsel on the subject of the controversy without the consent of that counsel.

Whenever representing large corporate defendants, defense counsel always runs the risk of having those employees contacted. One suggestion which can help prevent such problems is to have defense counsel seek either agreement from plaintiff's counsel at an early stage of the litigation, or an order from the court at an early stage of the litigation. In either event, this is an eventuality which must be kept in mind and guarded against in order to ensure that employees of the company do not speak to plaintiff's counsel. Certainly the best way to approach this is by getting either a stipulated agreement or a court order prohibiting plaintiff's counsel from undertaking any such efforts.

§ 1.26 Depositions—In General

There is little doubt that the most widely used and abused discovery device available to litigators is the deposition. There is neither a surer nor a quicker way to increase the cost of litigation than to go on a deposition binge. Opponents who do this to you in a particular case or who, in a more moderate approach, abuse the deposition process must be dealt with quickly.

As a general rule, most courts will permit depositions to be taken. Indeed, depositions can be the most effective and, when properly used, expeditious way of taking discovery and readying a case for trial. However, when an opponent is insistent on pursuing tactics which increase the cost, lengthen the process, and, from an overall perspective, abuse the rules, all the advantages of the deposition process are lost.

For a discussion of the relative merits and demerits of depositions generally, *see* Dallas, *Effective Use of Interrogatories and Depositions: Some Practical Pointers,* 45 Brooklyn L. Rev. 297 (1979).

§ 1.27 How Depositions Should Be Taken

Many depositions need not be taken face to face. Just because your opponent has noticed an in-person deposition, you should not assume that a deposition in that form is necessary. Such a notice may have been filed for any number of reasons, including increasing the cost of the litigation and perhaps attempting to intimidate you. Other ways of accomplishing this same intimidation include ordering expedited copies of the deposition, thereby requiring you to consider ordering such expedited copies, noticing depositions in distant cities, or refusing to bring witnesses under the control of an opponent to a more convenient city and thus necessitating extended and costly travel.

In addition, you may meet opponents who insist on lengthy depositions, all directed at attempting to intimidate your witnesses, your client, and you into either not pursuing or not defending the case.

In the first analysis, a deposition ought to be considered in the context of whether it is necessary. You should not take it for granted that when an opponent notices a live deposition, the deposition is required. Accordingly, you should consider whether a telephone deposition may be appropriate. Although this technique has not been used on a wide-scale basis, it can save a considerable amount of costs and is much quicker in terms of both attorney time and witness time than an in-person deposition. Telephone depositions are especially useful when you are confronted with an opponent who notices a large number of depositions of peripheral witnesses which would require an extensive amount of travel. If those peripheral witnesses, often eyewitnesses with a limited amount of factual information, are not within the control of your opponent, you are not in a position to go to the court seeking an order that they be produced in a particular city. Under such circumstances, the approach you should take is to go to the court to seek an order requiring that the depositions of your opponent's witnesses be taken by telephone. See §§ **1.31** through **1.42** for detailed discussion of telephone deposition procedures.

§ 1.28 Controlling Depositions—In General

On far too many occasions, depositions are interminable and, as compared to what is actually used from those depositions at the trial, seem to bear little relationship to the discovery process, at least in terms of relevance.

The pleading and practice order is certainly one means for controlling the overall discovery process and setting the ground rules for the litigation at an early stage. However, oftentimes you will find yourself dealing with an opponent who is able to use the deposition process as a means of not only gathering discovery but also harassing both your client and you. Oftentimes, this is a function of an opponent's personality as distinct from a tactic. Frequently, it is a function of the litigation. In either event, you are usually able to tell early on whether the discovery process is likely to be abused in a particular litigation. If so, there are a number of steps which you can take either within the context of inclusion in the pleading and practice order or, alternatively, by way of seeking a protective order under Rule 37 of the Federal Rules of Civil Procedure or state counterparts from the trial judge.

Underlying the control of the deposition process are limitations on (1) the number of depositions to be taken, (2) the amount of time to be permitted in the deposition process in terms of hours, as distinguished from a discovery cut-off date, or (3) a limitation on the number of deposition pages which a particular side may generate.

The first and second of these suggestions, namely the limitations on the number of depositions and the amount of time to be expended on them, may be combined. For example, if you anticipate an opponent's taking an inordinate amount of time in the deposition process or using it in an abusive fashion, you can suggest to the judge that no more than, for example, 10 depositions per side be taken and that the depositions last no more than three hours each. The form which this suggestion can take is a protective order.

§ 1.29 —Protective Order Regarding Depositions

The following form is an example of a protective order regarding depositions.

(Plaintiff) (defendant) moves this court for a protective order pursuant to ________ the Federal Rules of Civil Procedure for the purpose of defining and setting limits on the scope of deposition discovery which may be taken in this litigation.

As grounds for this motion, (plaintiff) (defendant) asserts that the deposition process in this litigation is likely to be a costly and time-consuming process. Counsel have attempted to voluntarily agree upon limits relative to the number of depositions which may be taken as well as the length of those depositions. To date, the parties have been unsuccessful in reaching any agreement on this matter.

Attached hereto is a proposed order defining limits to the deposition process.

Respectfully submitted,

____

PROPOSED ORDER

It is hereby ordered the ______ day of ___________, 19______ that the following limitations, pursuant to Federal Rules of Civil Procedure 16 and 26(f) are set on the process of taking depositions in the above-captioned litigation.

(1) All depositions in this litigation must be completed no later than ________ (days) (months) (years) from the date of entry of this Order.
(2) Notwithstanding the cut-off date for the taking of depositions established in Paragraph 1 of this Order, each party to this litigation may notice no more than (insert number) depositions.
(3) No deposition to be taken in this litigation may, including all direct and cross-examination, exceed (insert length in hours or pages).
(4) This Order will be subject to modification only upon a showing of good cause by the party seeking said modification.
(5) Any party violating this order will be subject to the imposition of sanctions, including, but not limited to, attorney's fees, costs, a reduction in the amount of discovery to be afforded that party and/or the enlargement of the amount of discovery to be afforded other parties.
(6) Notwithstanding motions for modification to be made by any party, this Order and the limitations established hereunder will be subject to a periodic review of the court *sua sponte*.

SO ORDERED.

§ 1.30 —Advantages of Deposition Limitations

There are several advantages to being the party suggesting that limitations be imposed on depositions consistent with a protective order of the type described in § **1.29**.

Perhaps the single greatest advantage of this type of protective order is the fact that you are the party proposing the limitation on discovery. Unfortunately, even in today's environment of litigation in which much is made of over-discovering the case and the costs associated with that process, attorneys typically do not come forward themselves and suggest discovery limitations. By doing so, you will immediately get the court's attention in a favorable fashion.

In addition, the use of this sort of discovery order is, in large measure, self-executing. Since the judge no longer has to visit the question of limiting depositions, the necessity for bringing discovery-type motions is lessened. Remember, each party is limited not only with respect to the number of depositions it may take, but also the length of time that those depositions may continue. As a result, since time is at a premium, a party who wastes time will simply be doing so at his or her own peril. Repetitive questioning is less likely, as are lengthy discovery discussions or disputes on the record. Thus, the entry of this sort of discovery order can have the effect of "taming" an unruly opponent who uses the deposition process to harass you or your client.

The use of this type of order has the additional benefit of holding out the prospect that, if abused, the discovery process taking place under such an order will be substantially altered, giving you more discovery and your opponent less. This is certainly not something which your opponent desires. As a result, if you encounter an opponent who you anticipate by his or her past performance in litigation is likely to abuse the deposition process, this type of discovery order can have quite a sobering effect.

The overall benefits of these types of limitations on the deposition process relate not only to the number of depositions but to their quality as well. Little need be said as to the reality of asking only relevant and essential questions of important witnesses when the deposition process has been curtailed in terms of time.

§ 1.31 Telephone Depositions

The discovery techniques available under the Federal Rules of Civil Procedure were designed to meet, among other things, the fact-finding needs of the parties and narrow the issues brought to trial. Misuse and overuse of those techniques as a competitive strategy rather than a fact-finding tool has created problems for counsel attempting to use the rules as designed. These difficulties led to a 1970 amendment to the rules authorizing stiffer sanctions for failure to properly participate in discovery. Fed. R. Civ. P. 37; *see* Lundquist, *In Search of Discovery Reform,* 66 A.B.A.J. 1071 (1980). But this amendment did not end all complaints arising out of the discovery process. In his opening remarks to the Pound Conference in 1976, Chief Justice Burger expressed concern over expensive, unthoughtful, and massive discovery. The follow-up task force of that conference gave major attention to discovery abuse and asked the Section of Litigation of the American Bar Association to select a special committee to study discovery abuse and suggest streamlined discovery procedures. The Special Committee for the Study of Discovery Abuse was established in 1977. Lundquist, *In Search of Discovery Reform,* 66 A.B.A.J. 1071 (1980).

That committee's first report suggested a comprehensive series of amendments, based on a three-pronged approach of deterring misuse of discovery, avoiding overuse of discovery, and reducing unnecessary costs. That third aspect, reducing unnecessary costs, discussed use of telephone depositions. *Id.* at 1072. The Judicial Conference's Advisory Committee on Civil Rules issued a second draft of this report with proposed amendments that dealt less drastically with the scope of discovery and abuse of interrogatories, and with encouraging cost-cutting devices by stipulation of the parties. This diluted proposal package evoked dissent by Justices Powell, Stewart, and Rehnquist when presented to the Supreme Court for consideration. *Id.*

The proposals finally adopted by the Supreme Court, and approved by Congress as amendments to the rules effective August 1, 1980, did, however, retain many of the reforms first suggested by the special committee of the American Bar Association, one of which is the increased availability of flexible means of taking depositions.

Rule 30(b)(7), which governs the taking of depositions upon oral examination, having been amended, now reads:

> The parties may stipulate in writing or the court may upon motion order that a deposition be taken by telephone. For the purposes of this rule and Rules 28(a), 37(a)(1), 37(b)(1) and 45(d), a deposition taken by telephone is taken in the district and at the place where the deponent is to answer questions propounded to him.

The other rules referred to in this subsection deal with procedures for taking depositions within the United States, its territories or its insular possessions, the location of the appropriate courts with which motions relating to the taking of a deposition may be filed, which court may hold a recalcitrant deponent in contempt, and the reach of a subpoena issued to require a deponent to attend. They are specifically mentioned to answer obvious questions about the location of the deposition when the deponent is in one district and the telephone examiner is in another.

The language of the rule is simple and actually does not create a new discovery device. Depositions by telephone had previously been available upon stipulation of the parties. *See* Fed. R. Civ. P. 29, allowing parties by written stipulation to have depositions taken before anyone, at any time or place, upon any notice, in any manner, and used like any other deposition. The 1980 amendment authorized the method by order of the court. Notes of Advisory Committee on Rules, 1980 Amendment to Fed. R. Civ. P. 30(b)(7), 28 U.S.C.A. (West Supp. 1981). The advantage of this amendment, therefore, is that prior to it, a telephone deposition was not available if the parties could not agree on that procedure. Also, if the only stipulation that the parties could arrive at was that the deponent was to testify before someone who was not authorized to administer the oath, that deponent could not be held in contempt or convicted of perjury for lying. Acomb, *Foreign Depositions: The Problems, Pitfalls and Procedures,* 14 FORUM 440, 452 (1979).

When a telephone deposition is taken pursuant to a written stipulation, that stipulation should clearly set forth all the particulars of the proceeding to avoid any future questions of validity. When the proceeding is governed by court order, of course, all the specifics of the order should be followed to the letter. But some aspects of the deposition may not be expressly mentioned in the order, so the requirements for taking depositions found elsewhere in the rules should be used to fill in these gaps. The following sections examine specific problems inherent in telephone depositions, with suggestions on how to safely solve these under the rules. The suggestions may also be helpful in preparing stipulations when a telephone deposition is taken pursuant to written stipulation of the parties. A sample set of stipulations is included in § **1.42**. The problems dealt with here are peculiar to the taking of depositions by telephone. The elements of this discovery device common to all other types of depositions, e.g., notice of deposition or preparation of examination and deponent, are not considered.

§ 1.32 —Procedure for Taking

Before the attorney picks up the telephone receiver, two essential questions must be answered: (1) how the testimony will be recorded, and (2) if a court reporter is used, from what point that reporter will record the testimony. These questions are rarely a problem when resources for an in-person deposition are available. Even in the telephone deposition setting, the questions can be answered easily but should never be ignored.

§ 1.33 —Manner of Recordation

The problem of recording a telephone deposition has two possible solutions: (1) stenographic recording by a court reporter or (2) recording by any other means which is accurate and trustworthy and performed pursuant to court order or stipulation under Rule 30(b)(4). The more traditional manner of stenographic recordation presents some special problems, which are dealt with in § **1.32**. The most obvious alternative means in the telephone deposition setting is to tape record the proceeding.

Tape recording is not unique to telephone depositions and has long been an available means of reducing discovery costs by court order. *See* Notes of Advisory Committee on Rules, 1980 Amendment to Fed. R. Civ. P. 30(b)(4), 28 U.S.C.A. (West Supp. 1981). Precedent concerning when a court order for recordation by other than stenographic means will issue should guide this determination, whether the deposition is taken in person or by telephone. Such precedent supports the granting of a motion to record by other than stenographic means when requested as long as the party opposing the motion does not specify why the proposed manner would be insufficient, *Colonial Times, Inc. v. Gasch,* 509 F.2d 517, 521 (D.C. Cir. 1975), or at least when the proposed method satisfies the individual court, in its discretion, as to reliability, accuracy, and necessity, *Barham v. IDM Corp.,* 78 F.R.D. 340, 341–42 (N.D. Ohio 1978). The United States District Court for the Eastern District of Pennsylvania approved a comprehensive plan or recordation that should insure accuracy and trustworthiness and would bolster any motion for a court order to allow tape recording of a deposition. The plan was:

(1) Two original recordings of the proceeding
(2) Good quality equipment provided
(3) An operator not involved in the actual examination
(4) Oath or affirmation administered by one authorized to do so by law
(5) Identification of speakers whenever necessary for clarity
(6) At the end of the deposition, one original tape would be appropriately labelled in a sealed envelope and deposited with the court
(7) The movant would have all needed testimony transcribed, filed with the court, and supplied to opposing counsel
(8) All objections as to accuracy would be made within ten days of receipt of the transcript
(9) The court could review those objections by reference to the tape in its custody or other appropriate means
(10) The transcript finally agreed upon could constitute the official record
(11) The opposing party could provide a stenographer or independent recorder at its own expense
(12) The above procedures would be in lieu of other proceedings for transcription, filing, signing, and certifying under the rules.

Lucas v. Curran, 62 F.R.D. 336, 339 (E.D. Pa. 1974).

When such an alternative method of recording is used, Rule 30(b)(4) requires that the stipulation or court order so providing is to designate the person before whom the deposition will be taken. This requirement is "to encourage the naming of the recording technician as that person, eliminating the necessity of the presence of one whose only function is to administer the oath." Notes of Advisory Committee on Rules, 1980 Amendment to Fed. R. Civ. P. 30(b)(4), 28 U.S.C.A. (West Supp. 1981). The nuance here is that, strictly under the rules, the deponent should first be put under oath by one authorized to do so. Fed. R. Civ. P. 30(c). When the court orders recording by tape recorder and appoints the technician as the person before whom the deposition is to be taken, then that person is automatically authorized to administer the oath. Fed. R. Civ. P. 28(a). Within the United States, territories, and insular possessions, the person appointed by the court to take the deposition "has the power to administer oaths and take testimony," and that person is the "officer" referred to in later rules dealing with certification, filing, etc. *Id.*

When the parties stipulate to a nonstenographic recording, care should be taken to have someone authorized to administer the oath and fulfill the officer's duties of certifying and filing, since the language of the rules does not explicitly give the technician by stipulation the authority to administer oaths. An argument can be made that the rules implicitly authorize the recording technician by stipulation to administer the oath, since Rule 28(a) states, "The term officer as used in Rules 30, 31, and 32 includes a person appointed by the court or designated by the parties under Rule 29." Rule 30(c) states, "The officer before whom the deposition is to be taken shall put the witness on oath . . . ." This, along with liberal language of the Advisory Committee Notes, could be read to allow a recording technician by stipulation to administer the oath. Rule 28(a), however, does explicitly provide that the technician by court order is authorized to give the oath, with no reference at that point to authorization of the technician by stipulation. This could raise a negative implication that the technician by stipulation must be independently authorized to administer oaths. With such uncertainty, and to impress on the deponent the seriousness of the proceeding and to preserve the sanctions of contempt or perjury conviction, see **§ 1.31**, the safest course is to employ someone who is, in the deponent's presence, expressly authorized to administer the oath in the particular stipulation situation. The recording by stipulation would be usable even without the oath, but if an oath is desirable, this safest course might be the best.

§ 1.34 —Location of Court Reporters

When a court reporter is used in a telephone deposition, all normal precautions should be taken to insure that the reporter, at a minimum, *hears,* all questions and responses, even if the reporter does not physically observe all participants. When depositions are taken pursuant to stipulation, the parties can agree that the reporter is to listen to and record the testimony from a telephone station separate from that of the deponent. *See, e.g.,* Lempert, *Judges, Lawyers See Phones as Effective Cost Cutter,* Legal Times, May 4, 1981 (testimony of deponent in Korea taken with court reporter in California and consular officer in Korea administering the oath).

The problem of how to get the deponent on oath, discussed in the preceding section in the context of tape recording a deposition, also arises in this situation; the parties may agree to proceed without an oath or arrange for someone to appear where the deponent testifies to administer it. It is unlikely that a distant court reporter would administer an oath over the phone by stipulation of the parties, since local state rules may prohibit this and the reporter would probably be unable to identify the voice of the deponent to certify that the voice heard and recorded was that of the deponent. Indeed, the Code of Professional Responsibility of the National Shorthand Reporters Association requires that the reporter "shall avoid any appearance of conflict of interest by conducting himself with impartiality toward all participants in every case," and the impartiality of administering an oath over the phone, when the reporter has never met or heard the purported deponent, might be questionable. *National Directory of Shorthand Reporters: Deposition Directory* 2 (1980). Thus, the attorney arranging a stipulated telephone deposition during which the court reporter will only hear the deponent over the conference line might do well to arrange that someone authorized to administer the oath be present with the deponent.

If the telephone deposition is taken by court order rather than stipulation under Rules 29 and 30(b)(7), the order might not specify from where the court reporter is to record the testimony. If this is the case, the language of Rule 30(c) can be referred to: "The officer before whom the deposition is to be taken shall put the witness [deponent] on oath and shall personally, or by someone acting under this direction and in his presence, record the testimony of the witness [deponent]." This language seems to indicate that the court reporter, if that person does not administer the oath, must still be in the presence of the person giving the oath to the deponent. This problem can be effectively avoided simply by petitioning the court to specify in its order the logistics of how the oath is to be administered and before whom the deposition is to be taken.

These subtleties of recording a telephone deposition and getting the deponent under oath require forethought by the attorney preparing such a deposition. Any problems that might subsequently arise should be dealt with expressly in the stipulations or court order governing the deposition. This is when the creativity of the attorneys and the exigencies of the particular case come into play. *See Marlboro Products Corp. v. North American Philips Corp.,* 55 F.R.D. 487, 490 (S.D.N.Y. 1972) ("[a]s to the need of an independent 'officer' to administer oaths, certify, seal and file, the court relies complacently upon our illustrious bar to cope by creative stipulation with these aspects of the enterprise"). After these particulars have been considered and dealt with in some written form, the stage is set for the actual deposition.

§ 1.35 —Making Contact

The attorney wishing to set up or participate in a telephone deposition should become familiar with available communications facilities. If all participants are congregated in one or the other of two locations, no peculiar problems are presented as long as extensions or speakerphones are available. When compared to travel expenses for attorneys, speakerphone procurement requests should be favorably received. Particular care should be taken to assure that the court reporter, if used, is physically able both to listen to the deposition and to record it accurately. The reporter should not be expected to record conversation accurately while balancing the receiver of an extension phone on his or her shoulder. A functioning speakerphone at the reporter's location should be adequate in most situations. (For an interesting article on the importance of establishing good rapport with court reporters, *see* Van Patten, *The Lawyer and the Deposition*

Reporter, 53 Cal. St. B.J. 40 (1978)). But even if the parties, the deponent, and the attorneys are in several locations, all may participate in the deposition through conference calls.

Even with the capacity to include many participants, it is a good idea to have a representative of the noticing party in the same room as the deponent. This is to protect the noticing party's interest in preventing unfair coaching or note passing to the deponent during the course of the deposition.

Once a telephone connection has been made with all participants necessary to the deposition, there should be careful identification of everyone on the line. All persons listening in should be asked to acknowledge their presence orally so that similarities in voices can be noted. The attorneys should also be prepared to require identification of the speaker at any time for clarity. Difficulties with telephone connections at any station should be dealt with at this early stage, and everyone should be reminded to speak slowly and clearly. When the physical aspects of the proceeding are to everyone's satisfaction, the formal deposition may begin.

§ 1.36 —Recording Terms of Court Orders or Stipulations

Besides the normal caveats which relate to stipulations at the beginning of any deposition, see **§ 1.31**, all stipulations as to the conduct of a telephone deposition should be read into the record initially to remind all participants of the ground rules of the proceeding and prevent any confusion at a later date about mutual understandings. It might not be a bad idea, when the deposition is pursuant to court order, to read the order so that the record will clearly reflect what was expected by the court of all participants.

§ 1.37 —Conduct of Examination

The actual testimony of the deponent in a telephone deposition is taken following the same format used for an in-person examination. The deponent is normally sworn first. For a discussion of how to put the deponent under oath in a telephone deposition, see **§§ 1.33–1.35**. Direct and cross-examination proceed in regular fashion. The only difference in the telephone deposition is the communications medium, a factor that should never be forgotten. If a court reporter is used, he or she may at times ask for repetition or identification of a speaker, but the reporter usually makes "all reasonable efforts to avoid the unnecessary interruption of proceedings." Code of Professional Responsibility of National Shorthand

Reporters Association, *National Directory of Shorthand Reporters: Deposition Directory* 2 (1980). Gestures and nods cannot be used to clarify over the telephone, so statements such as "Um-hum" or "Un-huh" may need more clarification in telephone depositions. The attorneys should assume full responsibility for clarity and understanding without relying on the competence of the court reporter or others. Common sense is the best guide for conduct at this stage of the proceeding.

§ 1.38 —Handling of Documents

The effective use of documents at a face-to-face deposition can be difficult enough without the additional complication of a telephone. In addition to the basic considerations to be observed in using documents, several special techniques should be followed:

1. Documents to be used at the deposition should be in the hands of all counsel no less than 24 hours prior to commencement of the deposition.
2. Counsel should agree on a system for the marking of documents prior to the deposition and insure that the reporter fully understands the system.
3. If practicable, the reporter should retain custody of the exhibits actually marked at the deposition and bind them either into the deposition transcript or in a separate volume.
4. The witness should not be asked to mark on documents.
5. In referring to documents, indefinite words like "this," "that," etc., should be avoided at all costs.

§ 1.39 —Wrapping Up the Deposition

When examination of the deponent is complete, the technicalities of the deponent's reading and signing the transcript, or waiver of reading and signing, should be dealt with as in any deposition. Care should be taken that all parties, particularly in the instance of a telephone deposition, know the specific timetable and methods by which the reporter, the appointed recording technician, or other officer who will transport, certify, and file the deposition performs those functions. This is especially necessary when the procedure is to be expedited for a proximate trial date.

One technicality that may merit special attention at the end of a telephone deposition is the wording of the certification to be filed with the court along with the deposition. Many reporters and notaries simply attach a form certification to all depositions, and the form may not reflect the actual facts of the proceeding. In a telephone deposition of a deponent in Korea, for instance, the certification of the California court reporter referred to the reporter as having put the deponent under oath, when that had actually been done in Korea by the United States consular officer. Lempert, *Judges, Lawyers See Phones as Effective Cost Cutter,* Legal Times, May 4, 1981. A suggestion might be made if some unusual event occurred that the certification reflect the actual state of the facts. This should be done only when the event was out of the ordinary, as when the oath was given in a peculiar manner, and should always be requested in the friendliest manner so as not to insult the officer certifying the record. This should not be overemphasized, for it is just a technicality, but technicalities sometimes have a way of coming back to haunt the unprepared.

§ 1.40 —Sample Instructions to Witness

The following excerpt from a deposition conducted by the author illustrates the opening instructions to a witness. All names (except that of the author) have been changed.

Q. Mrs. Brown, my name is Mark Dombroff and I am an attorney representing one of the defendants in the lawsuit that you are presently here testifying in connection with. I represent Big Resort. Now I am going to ask you some questions regarding materials that you may have reviewed or opinions which you may have formulated. Do you understand that?

A. Yes.

Q. And do you understand that my client Big Resort is in a position adverse to the party in connection with whom you are testifying, Lisa Moore.

MR. PRICE [Plaintiff's attorney]: Well—

MR. DOMBROFF: Let me withdraw that.

BY MR. DOMBROFF:

Q. Do you understand that Lisa Moore is suing my clients?

A. Yes, I do.

Q. Now if for some reason you don't understand one of my questions, will you tell me that?

A. Yes, I will.

Q. And I will rephrase or try to clarify that question. Is that agreeable?

A. Okay.

Q. And if for some reason you don't hear one of my questions, will you tell me that?

A. Yes, I will.

Q. We have some traffic noise out here and my voice might fade into the background, as unlikely as that is. If a train does go by, it may fade in, and I will restate the question or repeat the question, is that agreeable?

A. Fine.

Q. Is it also fair on my part to assume that if you don't indicate any lack of understanding of my question or any failure to hear my question that you heard and understood my question?

MR. PRICE: Well, she thought she did.

THE WITNESS: To the best of my ability, yes.

MR. DOMBROFF: Okay.

BY MR. DOMBROFF:

Q. And that your answers are truthful to the very best of your ability?

A. Yes, sir.

* * * *

MR. DOMBROFF: You know you have the right to read and sign this deposition.

MR. PRICE: She waives.

MR. DOMBROFF: Signature and signing is waived, is that correct, Mrs. Brown?

THE WITNESS: If David says so, that is all right.

§ 1.41 —Checklist of Procedures

In making the decision to conduct a deposition by telephone, the time-saving, money-saving, and tactical advantages of this technique should always be weighed against the disadvantages of inability to see the deponent and the physical difficulties with telephonic communication. Once you decide that a telephone deposition is the proper mode of discovery from a particular deponent, a deposition plan to deal with problems peculiar to telephone discovery should be devised. A good plan to follow might include the following points, with other considerations for extraordinary situations to be dealt with on an ad hoc basis:

____ **1.** Decide on a method of recordation. The simplest would be to arrange for a court reporter authorized to administer the oath to be present at the place where the deponent will testify.

____ **2.** Arrange for all equipment necessary to complete the deposition. Basically, the most important aspect of this would be to insure that the reporter will hear all parties and the deponent over a speakerphone, rather than an extension.

____ **3.** Draft stipulations or seek a court order delineating the specifics of the proceeding. This should be done in writing, and include, inter alia, the location of all parties, the manner of recordation, the manner of giving the oath, any prohibitions as to making gestures or passing notes to the deponent, stipulations on documents to be referred to during the examination, and arrangements for payment of expenses. See sample stipulation in § **1.42**.

____ **4.** If possible, arrange for a representative of the noticing party to be where the deponent will actually testify. This is an extra safeguard to protect against improper coaching of the deponent out of the sight of examining counsel.

____ **5.** Make contact and clearly identify all participants and listeners (including the reporter or recording technician).

____ **6.** Read all stipulations and court orders pertaining to conduct of the telephone deposition into the record.

____ **7.** Put the deponent under oath. This is most easily done with a court reporter authorized to do so in the deponent's presence.

____ **8.** Conduct the examination. Always remember problems of communication and multiple speakers.

____ **9.** Arrange for reading and signing, or waiver of reading and signing.

____ **10.** Arrange with the officer taking the deposition (probably the court reporter) the details of transcription, certification, filing, and transport of the deposition and copies.

____ **11.** Remind the officer taking the deposition of any peculiarities of the proceeding that may need to be reflected in his or her certification. This probably need only be done in unusual situations, as when the oath is given by one other than the person who records and certifies the testimony.

These points are by no means exhaustive, and some may not be relevant in particular instances. Planning, however, should never be overlooked, especially when the telephone deposition is new to any attorney participating.

As the telephone deposition technique is employed by a larger segment of the bar, the procedure will become commonplace, and the trial attorney can spend less time worrying over minute technicalities and focus on the "qualitative character" of his or her discovery, with the increased potential that telephone discovery can afford. Lundquist, *In Search of Discovery Reform,* 66 A.B.A.J. 1071, 1073 (1980).

§ 1.42 —Form: Stipulation

It is hereby stipulated that the telephone depositions which will be taken in the above-captioned case, pursuant to the Federal Rules of Civil Procedure, and in particular Rules 29 and 30(b)(7), shall be recorded in the following manner:

1. The deposition shall be taken by a certified court reporter who shall take the necessary precautions to assure that the recorded testimony will be accurate and trustworthy.
2. The court reporter will be with the deponent and shall utilize a speakerphone to record the comments of counsel communicating by telephone.

3. Unless otherwise agreed, counsel noticing the deposition shall have the responsibility of obtaining the court reporter and the responsibility of providing the speakerphone for the deposition.
4. If documents are to be used, all counsel of record shall be provided with a copy of these documents at least twenty-four hours in advance of the deposition.
5. All expenses and arrangements of the conference call with the telephone company will be borne by the party noticing the deposition.
6. Counsel desiring to attend the deposition in the presence of the deponent are not precluded from doing so.
7. Each individual attending the deposition in the presence of the deponent and/or listening to the deposition by conference line shall be properly identified in his or her own voice and restricted pursuant to the Federal Rules of Civil Procedure and local rules of practice governing the attendance of such individuals.
8. There will be no notes passed, gestures made, or assistance given to the deponent in any form. Any such notes passed, gestures made, or assistance given will be noted on the record by the reporter and all notes will be attached to the deposition.

§ 1.43 Instructions Not to Answer

When dealing with an aggressive opponent in a deposition setting, you will frequently encounter a situation in which your opponent instructs a witness noticed by you for deposition not to answer a particular question. As a general matter, absent the existence or invocation of a privilege, e.g., attorney-client or work product, there are no grounds for an attorney's instructing a witness not to answer a question.

Both state and federal rules of procedure typically provide that all objections except as to form are reserved until time of trial. Accordingly, if an attorney has an objection to a deposition question, the proper procedure is to state the objection if it goes to form or, in the event it does not go to form, to simply remain silent and assert the objection at trial.

On occasion you may run into a circumstance where your opponent not only instructs a witness to refrain from answering a particular question without invoking a privilege but also makes repeated objections other than to form. The purpose of such objections is often to hint to the witness how to answer particular questions.

There is little question but that these instructions not to answer questions and inappropriate objections are improper and unfair tactics in a deposition setting. The proper response to such tactics is not to react too quickly but rather to build a record in order to go to the judge on the firmest possible footing.

When opposing counsel instructs a witness not to answer a question, you should inquire into the basis for the instruction. If your opponent refuses to give any basis or gives a basis other than assertion of a privilege, you should proceed to build the record as solidly as you can.

Where objections to matters other than form are concerned, you should not immediately jump on your opponent and thus tip your hand as to what you are doing. Rather, you should permit him or her to make such objections as fully and completely as desired at the outset, thus having the other side build your record as to how he or she is coaching the witness. When you have done so and the record is complete, you should indicate on the record at the next objection that you take exception to counsel's repeatedly violating the rules regarding the making of objections solely for the purpose of coaching the witness at the deposition and, in effect, testifying personally.

The question which then presents itself in the situation of either an instruction not to answer or an improper objection is whether to terminate the deposition and immediately see the judge or, alternatively, allow the deposition to proceed and present it to the judge later. This question has no single answer; it must be determined within the context of a particular case.

The cardinal rule is that you should not threaten to go to the judge unless you are prepared to do so. If you make a threat and then back down for whatever reason, you will have played a very important card and run a bluff to which your opponent will be wise in the future. Accordingly, when you are ready to go to the judge you should insure that your record is not only complete but is favorably weighted toward your position and, after indicating that you are terminating the deposition and immediately seeking a hearing or calling the judge on the telephone, you should do so. Failure to do so will impair your credibility with your opponent and make it that much more difficult to take an aggressive stance during further discovery in the case.

§ 1.44 Deposing Attorneys

A tactic which usually can be described only as harassment is the noticing of counsel of record for a deposition by the opposing party. Although there may be circumstances justifying such a deposition, the usual reason for the noticing of the deposition is to harass the attorney and the party he or she is representing.

Your likely response when served with a notice of a deposition for you or one of your co-counsel will be the emotional one of "they can't do that." However, what is called for is a more measured response which takes into account the facts and circumstances of a given situation.

The first thing to be done is to examine the notice in light of the factual information which the noticed attorney, be it yourself or a co-counsel, could provide. Such information usually falls into one of several categories. The most difficult to deal with is when the attorney noticed for the deposition actually possesses factual information which may bear on some aspect of the litigation. This situation sometimes arises in connection with a good faith settlement wherein one defendant enters into a settlement agreement which may call for the performance or accomplishment of certain other conditions. If that settlement is found by the court to have been in good faith, that defendant will be protected in certain jurisdictions from any indemnity actions by a co-defendant. The co-defendant may have the right to take the deposition of the attorneys who entered into the agreement for the purpose of ascertaining the facts and circumstances surrounding the agreement, all directed toward the good faith question.

The second situation in which an attorney might be subject to deposition relates to privileged categories such as attorney-client communications or work product information. Existence of a privilege and whether the deposition is being noticed for harassment purposes can usually be ascertained if an honest assessment is made of what is really being sought. The obvious response in such a circumstance is to seek a protective order. However, a protective order or motion to quash should not necessarily be the first response in the situation of an attorney noticed for either factual or protected information. Rather, it may sometimes be better and more productive to file a motion or request through the court that the noticing party be required to make a written, detailed, and extensive offer of proof as to what that party would expect to be able to elicit or prove through your deposition.

Most judges are not receptive to having the attorneys themselves deposed in litigation. At a minimum, the judge will want to hear what is being sought in order to decide whether the deposition should go forward. By filing a motion for a protective order or motion to quash, you are in effect taking the burden of going forward and, as a result, the burden of proof to support the relief you are seeking.

On the other hand, by requesting, through the court, that your opponent make an offer of proof as to what he or she expects to obtain through the deposition, you are placing that burden of going forward where it should be under such circumstances.

If your opponent files an offer of proof regarding the noticing of your deposition, the appropriate response is dictated by the type of information being sought. Assuming that the information being sought is protected by the work product or attorney-client privilege, the response in opposition to the offer of proof should take the form of a motion for a protective order or a motion to quash. The strength of following this approach is that you are able to *respond* by having the position of your opponent revealed first.

In the event that the information being sought is not protected by a privilege but rather is factual in nature and bears some relationship to the issues in the case, you should not automatically proceed to the deposition but rather should oppose it and alternatively suggest that discovery be taken by way of interrogatories or requests for admissions.

Since judges are not necessarily sympathetic toward attempts to depose counsel, if there is a feasible alternative to a deposition, most courts will probably be inclined to require the party noticing the deposition to pursue discovery through another means. The obvious advantage of this is that you will have a greater degree of control over the nature of the responsive information provided because of lack of timeliness of other types of discovery in contrast to depositions.

If you find yourself in a situation in which either you conclude independently or the court orders that the deposition should go forward, you should insure that counsel representing you is knowledgeable in all the ramifications of the subject matter which will be addressed by the scope of examination of the deposition.

A word of caution—if you have resisted the attempt to have a deposition taken and the judge has ordered that it be taken, you are not in the best position to go back before the judge during the course of the deposition and object to the area of questioning. As a result, if you are going to permit the deposition to be taken or if you are to have it taken through court order, you should have a specific court order or stipulation in advance that lays out the procedure to be followed and the parameters of inquiry at the deposition. Although this may have the form of a protective order in terms of those areas which may be explored at the deposition, it should not be characterized as such when sought, inasmuch as a protective order may have certain other connotations relating to preventing the deposition from going forward. An order regarding the taking of the deposition seems more positive and yet accomplishes the same purpose.

Overall, you should notice attorney depositions only when there is a genuine factual basis for taking them within the context of the case. To do otherwise is to set yourself up for a significant fall before the court.

Similarly, when your own deposition has been noticed, you should examine the underlying reason why the deposition is being requested and proceed accordingly. Such depositions have the potential to turn into name-calling contests and frequently have ramifications far beyond the deposition, with the ultimate problem being a motion to disqualify the attorney being deposed because of the nature of the attorney's involvement in the factual transactions giving rise to the litigation. Obviously, this is to be avoided; it is not in the best interest of the client or of expediting the litigation.

§ 1.45 Deposing Experts

More often than not, the deposition of expert witnesses is mutually agreed to between plaintiff and defense counsel. In effect, it's a "you can depose my experts and I'll depose your experts" sort of thing. Remember, there is no right to take the deposition of expert witnesses absent a showing of exceptional circumstances, particularly with respect to nontestifying experts.

The scope of expert discovery is illustrated by *Grindell v. American Motors Corp.,* 108 F.R.D. 94 (D.N.Y. 1985). The court found that the plaintiffs in this action were not entitled to depose a nontestifying expert regarding tests he had performed as a consultant for the defendants. Without a showing of exceptional circumstances, the plaintiffs could not depose the expert regarding factual matters surrounding his relationship with the defendant.

See also § **1.21**.

§ 1.46 Deposing Nonmanagement Employees of a Corporate Defendant

One of the most difficult problems oftentimes encountered in representing corporations is the flow of information out of the corporation from individuals who may not be directly involved in the litigation. Moreover, when the word has been spread about the litigation, employees will be aware that they should not be speaking to attorneys who seek to talk to them about the litigation. Given the greatly increased number of products liability cases in court during the last several years and the fact that more and more aspects of corporate involvement are being subject to the discovery process, particularly when punitive damages are at stake, it is important that all employees of the corporation who may have any contact with the subject matter of the litigation be made aware of what is occurring.

Wright v. Group Health Hospital, 103 Wash. 2d 192, 691 P.2d 564 (1984) presents a particularly interesting example of what occurs when you do not take steps to ensure that employees are properly attuned to litigative considerations. In *Wright,* a medical malpractice action was brought against the Group Health Hospital. The hospital administration issued orders prohibiting the nursing staff who were involved in caring for the plaintiff from discussing the case with anybody other than the attorneys representing the hospital. Defense counsel's position was that the nurses were essentially clients of the firm and that no contacts could be made with them by plaintiff's counsel without going through defense counsel. Based upon this position, the defendant sought a protective order covering the nurses and, after that protective order was denied, took an appeal.

On appeal, the Washington Supreme Court determined that a corporate defendant such as the hospital could not prohibit counsel for the plaintiffs from communicating with employees of the corporation. Obviously, the implications of this sort of decision and its reasoning when applied in any litigation involving corporations acting through its employees is particularly significant to counsel.

In upholding the denial of the protective order, the Washington Supreme Court determined that the knowledge of the nurses with respect to underlying facts would not fall within any attorney-client privilege and thus would not preclude contacts by the plaintiff's counsel with the nonmanagement-level employees.

The hospital also argued that the canons of professional ethics would preclude ex parte communications, absent prior consent, with employees of the defendant. The Washington Supreme Court determined that the purpose of such a rule was to prevent an adverse party from having improper advantage taken of it. However, the court did acknowledge that, under one interpretation of the disciplinary rules, such ex parte contacts would not be permitted, while under another, they would be permitted. Focusing on the American Bar Association's guidelines, the Washington Supreme Court determined that ex parte contacts with employees would be permitted unless the employees had the power to bind the corporation. If they did have that power, they would be considered as parties to the litigation, as opposed to witnesses.

Obviously, this ruling would not extend to former employees or nonmanagement-type employees, neither of whom would have the power to bind a corporate defendant. Finding that the reasoning in *Upjohn Co. v. United States,* 449 U.S. 383 (1981), which allowed certain lower-level employees to enjoy the attorney-client privilege not applicable in the *Wright* situation, the Washington Supreme Court determined that the policy underlying the Supreme Court's reasoning in *Upjohn* was designed to afford the attorney-client privilege to a greater number of individuals, as distinguished from a disciplinary rule which was enacted to protect a corporate defendant from having agents with the power to affect the corporate position in litigation from being unduly or improperly influenced. Finding that the plaintiff could talk to lower-level employees who are not management agents, the Washington Supreme Court further found that the hospital could not tell its employees not to speak to the plaintiff's attorney.

From a defendant's perspective, the reasoning in *Wright* is particularly troublesome and requires that counsel take all steps necessary to ensure that all employees of the defendant corporation are apprised of the rights and responsibilities which they have and which they owe to the defendant. In this regard, when you find yourself in the position of representing a corporate defendant and have a situation involving nonmanagement or nonbinding-type employees involved in your case, consider taking the following steps:

1. Ensure that you review *Upjohn Co. v. United States,* 449 U.S. 383 (1981), regarding the question of attorney-client privilege and its application to lower-level employees.
2. Consider meeting with all employees who are or may be involved in the litigation for the purpose of conveying to them the corporate

position on the litigation. In this regard, you may well give some thought to communicating certain work product type information and engaging in work product type discussions for the purpose of asserting the work product privilege regarding any contacts over the litigation.

3. Determine at an early stage of the litigation, preferably before the discovery process is under way with your opponent, if former employees of the company are involved in the case. If so, they should be contacted and included in whatever briefings may be held. It is important that all employees, both present and former, understand the position of the corporation in the litigation. Oftentimes, this helps shape the recollection of the employees as well as the position which they may take at any depositions or in any interviews with opposing counsel.
4. No matter what, take a hard line with respect to the representation of nonmanaging agent employees. As a general rule, when representing the corporate defendant, you should always assume that all employees, high level or low level, are off limits. This should be a position which you take at the outset of the case and establish as a hard line throughout the case. Oftentimes, the mere taking of this position will be enough to dissuade an opponent, even the most enthusiastic opponent, from pursuing employees of the corporate defendant.
5. At any time your opponent seeks to interview a nonmanaging employee of the corporate defendant, take the position that you have a right to be present. If the employee says that he or she doesn't want you present, you probably will be facing a situation in which the employee may not be particularly friendly to the corporate defendant's position. However, as a practical matter, the employment relationship is a strong one and is likely to temper what the employee is willing to say. In the overwhelming majority of circumstances, your presence at any such interview will more likely than not be a given fact.
6. Make sure that all employees who may be contacted in connection with the litigation, including former employees, have been instructed immediately to get in touch with either you or corporate in-house counsel. This requires that the employees be given some insight into not only the nature of the litigation but also the attorneys who may be contacting them.

An approach which many attorneys may take in this regard is to contact employees before litigation is actually filed. See the discussion regarding discovery before litigation in §§ **1.3** through **1.5**. Typically, you will be aware of the fact that litigation is going to be filed against the defendant even before it is filed. After all, the occurrence giving rise to litigation normally takes place before the litigation. In light of this fact, make sure that proper steps are taken within the corporate structure to notify present and former employees as to what may occur. Failure to do so may result in information being provided by the corporation in either documentary or other form which will ultimately come back to haunt the corporation in litigation.

§ 1.47 Deposing Managing Agents and Principals

In litigation where either party is a corporation, one of the favorite tactics of some lawyers is to file a notice of deposition listing senior management officials from the chief executive officer down through middle management executive ranks. One purpose of doing this may be to harass the corporation by requiring its executives and management to expend inordinate amounts of time in the litigation.

Some plaintiff's counsel notice such depositions of the defendant's executives for the professed purpose of attempting to intimidate them into settling the case by pointing out to them at the deposition how grievous the conduct of their corporation was in the factual transactions involved in the lawsuit.

More often than not, corporate officials noticed for the deposition have no substantive or factual knowledge to offer in the context of the litigation that is either relevant or material itself or reasonably calculated to lead to relevant or material evidence. However, although this may at first seem like a justifiable reason for filing an immediate motion for a protective order, such motions frequently fail by virtue of the fact that the court is reluctant to in effect pre-decide whether an individual has relevant factual material, notwithstanding the fact that the individual may be a high corporate officer not directly involved in the factual transactions.

An effective tactic for countering such deposition notices is frequently to permit one or two of the depositions to go forward. During the briefing of those executives prior to deposition, you should see to it that they are prepared to provide answers either directly or indirectly, whether or not the questions are asked, that establish the frame of reference regarding not only their involvement but also that of other peripherally involved corporate officers.

Once that has been accomplished, you are in a position to file a motion for a protective order supported with selections from the deposition. The strength of this approach over the early filing of a motion for a protective order, even attaching affidavits from the corporate officers involved, is that it gets around the judge's initial reaction of not wanting to limit discovery without giving the attorney some chance. More important, an immediate protective order provides for no cross-examination of your assertions as to the noninvolvement of corporate officers. By permitting one, possibly two, of the corporate officers to be examined and "priming" them to set forth the nature of involvement or noninvolvement of the other individuals noticed, you are in a far better position to file the motion for a protective order and obtain the desired relief.

An alternative response when you are faced with a deposition noticing corporate executives by name or title and you believe the deposition is being taken for harassment purposes is to contact your opponent and seek some sense of the type of information he or she wants. This may also be done in the form of a motion for a protective order, not to preclude the deposition from being taken, but rather to require a more definite statement as to why it is being taken.

In either event, you may then be in a position to offer for deposition a corporate employee who is more factually involved and knowledgeable and thus more responsive to your opponent's lines of inquiry. If your opponent refuses to respond at all, you are then in a far better position to expose the tack being taken for what it is, and your client will not be characterized as the litigant seeking to impede discovery.

Another tactic frequently encountered when, with good intentions, you file a notice for corporate executives by title or category, i.e., "John Doe or other corporate executives who are knowledgeable in . . . ," is that you receive a long list of corporate executives and employees who will be made available for deposition. These executives or employees are "served up" to you on a scheduled basis that makes it appear as if your opponent is attempting to do everything possible to accommodate your desires and expedite the case.

As a practical matter, when you look beyond the actual response, you will often learn that the cooperation of your opponent is not what it seems to be. Typically, the attorney representing the party you have noticed provides you with a list of witnesses scheduled in an order which serves up for deposition those who know the least first, thereby subjecting you to the additional expense of working your way through the list of witnesses.

Obviously, the witness who knows the most essential facts which are central to the deposition and whom you are really after is always placed last on the list in the hopes that you will never get to that witness because you will give up or simply forget. Throughout the depositions, such attorneys use every tactic known to the street fighter to slow progress of the case and increase the cost of the litigation without incurring sanctions.

When faced with this tactic, you often have no one to blame but yourself, because you should be thoroughly versed in what each witness has to say about the issues of the case prior to the deposition. This can be accomplished through judicious use of interrogatories which ask about the identity of the individuals, their roles in the case, and the facts and information which they can provide.

Obviously, you should assume that answers to interrogatories are provided by counsel. As a result, you should also assume that the answers are calculated to give you the least amount of information possible while at the same time being responsive enough to avoid a motion to compel further answers. You should not accept the answers and, if the purpose of the interrogatories is to seek information regarding persons to be deposed, you should go back and get further answers until you have an adequate factual basis to make a decision.

The same is true of a request for production in that you should use a request for production only to determine whether an individual should be deposed. Often, after having compared the list of witnesses provided by your opponent in response to a "John Doe" notice to a corporation to answer to interrogatories and requests for document production previously made, you are in a position to judge whether the list of witnesses is responsive.

In the event you find the list of witnesses not to be responsive, it is often a good idea to go back to the court with a motion to compel or, in today's atmosphere of sensitivity to discovery abuse, for sanctions, setting forth what your opponent is attempting to do in terms of abusing the discovery, and attaching to that motion copies of whatever interrogatories or documents support your position.

Even though you may not obtain the sanctions you are seeking, you will still have brought to the court's attention the manner in which your opponent is handling the case, and you will have accomplished the dual purpose of educating the judge and telling your opponent that such tactics are not going unnoticed.

Weaver v. Gross, 605 F. Supp. 210 (D.D.C. 1985), held that an officer of an employer could not take a purposefully restricted approach to discovery by furnishing only that information within his immediate knowledge or profession.

The court found that the information sought to be elicited was relevant to the officer's motive and intent in an employee termination action and that an artificial distinction between the officer and his activities as chief executive officer of the corporation and the activities of the corporation as a separate legal entity were totally unwarranted. Thus, the employee was entitled to recover sanctions against the defendant employer.

Defense counsel will oftentimes find themselves dealing with corporations which, of necessity, must be represented by individuals at depositions. Care should be taken to ensure that the individual witness is not artificially compartmentalizing the information being presented and thus walking themselves into the situation set forth by the court in *Weaver.*

§ 1.48 Deposing Chief Executive Officers—In General

Sections 1.48–1.54 are adapted from an article by Alan N. Salpeter and Richard A. Salomon, both of Mayer, Brown & Platt, Chicago, Illinois. The article, entitled *Discovery Rule Changes End Open Season On CEOs,* originally appeared in the May 13, 1987, issue of *The National Law Journal.* Reprinted with permission.

CEO does not and should not stand for "cross-examined often." Indeed, chief executive officers should rarely, if ever, be subjected to depositions in litigation. Certainly, all CEOs subscribe to that view, and now courts are moving in that direction.

Granted, CEOs should not be excused from a deposition simply because they are busy people. They should be excused because 99 times out of 100 they lack firsthand knowledge of the facts of the case. The sad truth is that the typical party seeking the CEO's deposition is not trying to acquire probative evidence and narrow the issues for trial but is trying to harass the CEO at the outset of a case to coerce a settlement.

The CEO's task is to manage the business; in doing so, he derives his knowledge of the business from others. It follows that the information being sought from the CEO in a deposition in a typical commercial case can almost always be obtained elsewhere more easily and less expensively. Under the recently amended federal discovery rules, litigants are required to go elsewhere first.

Armed with the recent amendments to the Federal Rules of Civil Procedure, other calls for discovery reform, and some useful court decisions, lawyers for CEOs now can argue more effectively than ever that the CEO belongs in the boardroom managing the corporation, not in the conference room answering questions at a deposition.

In a commercial case, a plaintiff's lawyer often will start the discovery program by noticing the deposition of the corporate defendant's CEO. Upon learning that his deposition has been noticed, the CEO's initial response is that he does not know anything about the issues in the case or the facts giving rise to it. That is usually true. In a products liability case, the CEO typically will know nothing about the design, manufacture, or sale of the product that allegedly injured the plaintiff. In a breach of contract case, the CEO usually will know nothing about the negotiation, execution, or performance of the contract which his company allegedly breached. In an antitrust price-fixing case, the CEO ordinarily will know nothing about any of the meetings where the competitors allegedly met and fixed prices.

The party seeking to depose the CEO responds to the "I don't know anything" rebuff with contempt and moves to compel the CEO's deposition under Rule 37 of the Federal Rules of Civil Procedure. Opposing counsel points to some article or book written by or about the CEO that tangentially relates to the subject matter of the case and argues that the CEO's testimony "appears reasonably calculated to lead to the discovery of admissible evidence." In other words, even if he doesn't know anything, he might give opposing counsel a lead. The CEO's lawyer cries harassment, and the battle is on.

Section 1.49 examines the pre-1983 authority for quashing the deposition of CEOs. **Sections 1.50** through **1.53** focus on the emerging law concerning the deposing of the CEO and the significant changes that were made to the federal discovery rules in 1983. Finally, a checklist of defensive strategies to try to protect CEOs from unnecessary depositions is provided in § **1.54**.

§ 1.49 —Pre-1983 Authority for Protecting CEOs

Generally, little attention has been paid to the early cases in which courts quashed depositions of high-ranking government officials and senior corporate officers. The common threads running through those cases were that the individual to be deposed possessed little, if any, firsthand knowledge about the facts of the case and that the party seeking discovery could have obtained the information by other means or from more knowledgeable individuals.

For example, depositions of governmental officials frequently have been quashed when they were unable to testify from personal knowledge about the material facts of the case. *See, e.g., Community Federal Savings & Loan Association v. Federal Home Loan Bank Board,* 96 F.R.D. 619, 621–22 (D.D.C. 1983) (no unique personal knowledge by these board members with respect to the underlying issues); *Cornejo v. Landon,* 524 F. Supp. 118, 122 (N.D. Ill. 1981) (deposition of acting commissioner of the Immigration and Naturalization Service quashed as unnecessary because the information sought could be obtained through other means, including the "depositions of other defendants or persons"); *Wirtz v. Local 30, International Union of Operating Engineers,* 34 F.R.D. 13 (S.D.N.Y. 1963) (no need or basis shown for taking the deposition of the secretary of labor). *See also Capitol Vending Co. v. Baker,* 36 F.R.D. 45, 46 (D.D.C. 1964). Professor Moore in his treatise, 4 *Moore's Federal Practice* ¶ 26.69 (2d ed. 1985), recognizes that the taking of the deposition of "the busiest member of the corporate hierarchy or a government agency, when the information sought could be obtained by deposing subordinate officials," is a common but abusive litigation tactic frequently intended to coerce a favorable settlement unrelated to the merits of the underlying claim.

There also are numerous cases, predating the 1983 discovery rule amendments, in which courts quashed depositions of senior corporate officers. By way of illustration, in *M.A. Porazzi Co. v. Mormaclark,* 16 F.R.D. 383 (S.D.N.Y. 1951), the district court vacated a notice to take the deposition of a party's vice president when it appeared to the court that he could "contribute nothing beyond that which would be gleaned from an examination" of a lower ranking official. *Id.* at 383. Other courts have reached the same conclusion. In *Skookum Co. v. Sutherlin Machine Works Inc.,* 33 F.R.D. 19, 21 (D. Or. 1963), the district court refused to grant a motion requiring the plaintiff to produce its president, the inventor of the patent in dispute, because his only knowledge of matters in litigation resulted from his capacity as an inventor and not as an officer of the corporation. In *Campbell v. General Motors Corp.,* 13 F.R.D. 331, 332–33 (S.D.N.Y. 1952), the District Court quashed the deposition of a corporate director who had no day-to-day corporate responsibilities and did not acquire any knowledge through his role as director that was germane to the litigation.

Colonial Capital Co. v. General Motors Corp., 29 F.R.D. 514, 518 (D. Conn. 1961) is a significant case. There, the court quashed the deposition of the chairman of the board and CEO of General Motors. The depositions of other employees of General Motors already had been taken, and the CEO had no personal knowledge of matters involved in the suit. *Accord Mitchell v. American Tobacco Co.,* 33 F.R.D. 262, 263 (M.D. Pa. 1963).

Thus, even before the discovery rules were amended, a number of courts recognized that, in many instances in which a party was insisting on taking the CEO's deposition, that party really was trying to extort a settlement. These courts did not hesitate to quash the attempted deposition. *Amherst Leasing Corp. v. Emhart Corp.,* 65 F.R.D. 121, 123 (D. Conn. 1974). *See also Armstrong Cork Co. v. Niagara Mohawk Power Corp.,* 16 F.R.D. 389, 390–91 (S.D.N.Y. 1954), in which the district court held that

> "[i]n the absence of any reasonable relief that the persons have some knowledge of the *facts* concerning which their testimony is to be taken, there is no reason why they should be compelled to appear. . . . The Court should be alert to see that the liberal deposition procedure provided in the Federal Rules . . . is not used as a litigation tactic to harass the other side or cause it wasteful expense" (emphasis added).

To the same effect is *Hughes v. General Motors Corp.,* 18 Fed. R. Serv. 2d 1249, 1250 (S.D.N.Y. 1974), in which the district court refused to allow the deposition of the president of the company when "it [was] clear that the information plaintiff wants [was] available through other employees of defendant, and such employees have been questioned or on plaintiff's request can be questioned. The request borders on harassment and would at best result in a duplication of testimony."

§ 1.50 —Alternative Approaches to Depositions

Rule 26(c) of the Federal Rules of Civil Procedure empowers a court to "make any order which justice requires to protect a party or person from annoyance, embarrassment, oppression, or undue burden or expense," including an order that "the discovery may be had only by a method of discovery other than that selected by the party seeking discovery." Rule 26(d) authorizes a court, "for the convenience of parties and witnesses and in the interests of justice," to control the sequence and timing of discovery. Rule 26(b)(1), as amended in 1983, states that discovery "shall" not be "unreasonably cumulative or duplicative." These rules, taken together, provide a court with a variety of options that on the one hand will allow a plaintiff to pursue discovery fully and fairly, while on the other hand will protect a defendant company and its CEO against unnecessarily burdensome and wasteful discovery.

One option open to the court when a CEO's deposition is sought is to require that other discovery proceed first. *Marrese v. American Academy of Orthopedic Surgeons,* 726 F.2d 1150, 1161 (7th Cir. 1984) (en banc) (Rule 26(d) should be used to "schedule the sensitive [and highly questionable] discovery last"), *rev'd on other grounds,* 470 U.S. 37 (1985); *Salter v. Upjohn Co.,* 593 F.2d 649, 651 (5th Cir. 1979) (emphasizing the importance of controlling the timing of discovery when the witness was "extremely busy" and denied "direct knowledge of the facts").

A second option for the court is to order that written interrogatories be directed to officers of the company. *Mitchell v. American Tobacco Co.,* 33 F.R.D. 262, 263 (M.D. Pa. 1963); *Community Federal Savings & Loan Association v. Federal Home Loan Bank Board,* 96 F.R.D. 619, 621–22 (D.D.C. 1983). *See also Capitol Vending Co. v. Baker,* 36 F.R.D. 45, 46 (D.D.C. 1964). After written interrogatories are answered and after other discovery is taken, the court can reexamine the propriety of allowing the chief executive officer's deposition to proceed and can evaluate whether the CEO has relevant evidence (or information that will lead to relevant evidence) that cannot be obtained elsewhere in a less intrusive and less cumbersome manner. At this juncture, the party seeking the CEO's deposition must demonstrate two things: (1) that there is an independent justification for proceeding with it, and (2) that the deposition will not be redundant or duplicative. *Cf. Colonial Capital Co. v. General Motors Corp.,* 29 F.R.D. 514, 518 (D. Conn. 1961) (deposition of CEO allowed to proceed only if "answers to the interrogatories with regard to his participation in or knowledge of the matters forming the subject matter of this suit appear to the court to warrant it").

In determining whether to quash or defer the CEO's deposition, a court must "compare the hardship" if the CEO is subjected to deposition with any adverse impact on the discovering party's ability to obtain information elsewhere relating to its claims. *See Marrese v. American Academy of Orthopedic Surgeons,* 726 F.2d at 1159 (7th Cir. 1984). In most cases in which the CEO or other high-ranking corporate officer has little or no firsthand knowledge of the material facts in a case, a balancing of hardships should favor the responding company.

The balancing-of-hardships approach and the other-discovery-first approach flow directly from the language of Rules 26(b) and (c). If a CEO (or other senior corporate official) is required to give a deposition in every commercial case in which he may have some generalized opinion (based on years of experience in a given industry), he literally would be unable to perform the duties of his office. If such a requirement were extended to key executives throughout the country, the disruption to corporate America would be immeasurable.

In contrast, a protective order precluding the deposition of such an official would typically impose no burden whatsoever on the discovering party. The responding party can make available for deposition individuals possessing firsthand knowledge of the material facts involved in the lawsuit. In addition, the responding company may agree to answer written interrogatories directed to the company or even directed to the person sought to be deposed. Until these or other avenues are pursued or at least considered, the testimony of the CEO would be, at best, cumulative and, at worst, irrelevant and wasteful.

§ 1.51 —1983 Amendments to Rule 26(b)(1)

If there were ever any doubt about the appropriateness of a protective order quashing or at least deferring the CEO's deposition, that doubt was dispelled by the 1983 amendment to Rule 26(b)(1) of the Federal Rules of Civil Procedure. Specifically, the amendment provides that "the frequency or extent of use of the discovery methods . . . shall be limited by the court if it determines that . . . the discovery sought is unreasonably cumulative or duplicative, or is obtainable from some other source that is more convenient, less burdensome or less expensive." The drafters of the amendment correctly perceived an undue reluctance by district judges "to limit the use of discovery devices" if the information sought by the discovering party appeared to be "relevant" under the broad test of relevance in the federal discovery rules. The amended rule therefore was "intended to encourage judges to be more aggressive in identifying and discouraging discovery overuse." 1983 Advisory Committee Note to Amended Rule 26(b)(1).

This reluctance of judges to enter into the discovery fray and to control discovery abuses is also borne out by empirical research. A 1978 nationwide survey of federal judges, responding to a questionnaire prepared under the auspices of the Office of Improvements of the Unites States Department of Justice, indicated a general unwillingness by the members of the judiciary to take the time needed to "enmesh" or involve themselves in discovery disputes. *See* Ellington, *A Study of Sanctions for Discovery Abuse* 96–101 (Office of Improvements in the Administration of Justice of the U.S. Department of Justice, Nov. 27, 1976). In particular, the new rule was designed to "remind federal district judges of their broad powers—and . . . correlative responsibilities—under rule 26" to limit unnecessary discovery of even relevant information. *See Marrese v. American Academy of Orthopedic Surgeons,* 726 F.2d 1150, 1162 (7th Cir. 1984) *rev'd,* 470 U.S. 373 (1985).

One of the principal drafters of the 1983 rules revisions has explained that district courts now have a *duty* to enter a protective order if the party seeking discovery can obtain that discovery "from some other source" or at a lesser cost to the party against whom the discovery is sought. A. Miller, *The August 1983 Amendments to the Federal Rules of Civil Procedure: Promoting Effective Case Management and Lawyer Responsibility* 32–33 (Federal Judicial Center Workshop 1984):

> Until last August, the last sentence in rule 26(a) said: 'Unless . . . the court orders otherwise, the frequency and use of discovery is not limited.' Unless the court says otherwise, go ye forth and discover. That had been the message of the last sentence of rule 26(a). In 1984, we decided it was a lousy message. That sentence has been stricken and replaced, quite literally, by the reverse message, which you now find in rule 26(b). Rule 26(b) now says that the frequency and extent of use of discovery shall be limited by the court if certain conditions become manifest. Just realize the 180-degree shift between the last sentence of the old rule 26(a) and the new sentence. Judges now have the obligation to limit discovery if certain things become manifest. The things that are then listed in that paragraph are basically the evils of redundancy and disproportionality. Because one says that if discovery is unreasonably cumulative, or duplicative, or obtainable from some other source, that is redundancy. If you can get it more cheaply, or if you already have got it—stop asking the same questions.

Although this section focuses on protecting CEOs from unnecessary depositions, "the evils of redundancy and disproportionality," to use Professor Miller's words, also are present in situations when a party serves blunderbuss document requests or hundreds of interrogatories or imposes otherwise abusive discovery.

When a party attempts to depose a CEO with little or no knowledge of the facts of the case, the evils of redundancy and disproportionality are present. Often there is no serious question that relevant information sought by the discovering party from a high-ranking corporate officer can be obtained from "some other source [and] . . . more cheaply." The taking of the deposition of a CEO, when more detailed and specific information is available from other personnel within the company, is precisely the evil at which the discovery amendments are directed.

The Advisory Committee Note to Rule 26(b)(1) cites several protective order cases as illustrative of the use to which the new amendment should be put. One of these cases provides general support for the entry of a protective order when a CEO's deposition is sought. In *Mitchell v. American Tobacco Co.,* 33 F.R.D. 262, 263 (M.D. Pa. 1963), in which the defendant corporation successfully moved for an order excusing its president from a deposition, the district court stated: "[P]laintiff's purpose would be adequately served at this time by means of written interrogatories. If on the return of the interrogatories and answers they are shown to be insufficient, an application may then be made for taking his testimony by oral depositions."

If inconvenience, burden, and expense are to be minimized substantially by new Rule 26(b)(1), a corporation that cannot quash its CEO's deposition outright should be able to persuade a court to proceed first with written interrogatories or some other alternate form of discovery.

§ 1.52 —Is a CEO an "Expert" Witness?

In resisting a CEO's deposition, a valid argument also can be made that the CEO may not be compelled to become an involuntary "opinion" expert for his adversary.

In *Kaufman v. Edelstein,* 539 F.2d 811, 822 (2d Cir. 1976), Judge Henry J. Friendly articulated the factors that should be considered in determining whether opinion testimony may be compelled from such an involuntary "expert":

1. Whether the expert is called to testify because of his knowledge of *facts* relevant to the case at bar or to give opinion testimony
2. Whether the expert is testifying about *previously* formed or expressed opinions or is being forced to prepare and formulate "new" opinions
3. Whether the witness has unique expertise
4. Whether the party seeking discovery is unable to obtain a comparable witness willing to testify voluntarily, and
5. Whether the witness will be "oppressed by having continually to testify." (Emphasis added.)

Each of the factors identified by Judge Friendly favors protection of the CEO whose opinions are being compelled. First, the CEO typically has no firsthand knowledge of facts relevant to the underlying case. Second, if called upon to give opinion testimony, the CEO would have to prepare in order to formulate opinions germane to the case. Third, the CEO frequently is not an expert or specialist and does not hold himself out as such; therefore, he has no unique qualifications to testify about the matters in litigation. Fourth, plaintiffs easily can find an expert of their own to use at trial.

Finally, if the CEO is forced to testify in the initial case, he may be forced to testify in numerous subsequent cases. Just as the hypothetical world-renowned surgeon described in the *Kaufman* opinion would be "forced to spend a considerable share of his time in the courtroom rather than in the operating room," the CEO would be compelled to spend many of his working hours in the deposition room rather than the boardroom. This would, of course, substantially interfere with the performance of his duties to the company and its stockholders.

§ 1.53 —Discovery Conferences

When the party seeking discovery is adamant about taking the deposition of the CEO, it probably is time to request a Rule 26(f) conference under the Federal Rules of Civil Procedure, first with the party seeking the discovery and then, if that is not fruitful, with the court. Requesting a discovery plan from the party seeking discovery forces that party to define the principal issues in the case and to demonstrate the necessity of the depositions that counsel is seeking. Should opposing counsel fail to provide a "proposed plan and schedule of discovery," counsel for the responding party can file a motion with the court for a discovery conference.

A Rule 26(f) motion for a discovery conference must provide the court with:

1. A statement of the issues as they then appear
2. A proposed plan and schedule of discovery
3. Any limitations proposed to be placed on discovery (including requested protective orders)
4. Any other proposed orders with respect to discovery
5. A statement showing that the attorney making the motion has made a reasonable effort to reach agreement with opposing attorneys on the matters set forth in the motion. All parties and their attorneys are under a duty to participate in good faith in the framing of a discovery plan if a plan is proposed by the attorney for any party.

Rule 26(f) states that upon the filing of such a motion, the court "shall" conduct such a conference and "enter an order tentatively identifying the issues for discovery purposes, establishing a plan and schedule for discovery, setting limitations on discovery, if any; and determining such other matters, including the allocation of expenses as are necessary for the proper management of discovery in the action."

The Advisory Note to Rule 26(f) states that requests for discovery conferences should not be "made routinely" and that narrow discovery disputes can be resolved by resort to Rules 26(c) or 37(a). Nonetheless, Rule 26(f) remains an option to consider when abusive discovery occurs, such as noticing the CEO's deposition.

A discovery conference under Rule 26(f) also can be combined by a court with a pretrial conference under Rule 16. Such a conference also may be used to simplify the issues for trial and avoid unnecessary and cumulative discovery.

§ 1.54 —Checklist for Protecting CEOs

In addition to the limitations on discovery contained in Rule 26(b)(1) of the Federal Rules of Civil Procedure, the local rules of selected district courts contain proscriptions against discovery abuse. For example, Standing Rule 10 of the United States District Court for the Eastern District of New York recognizes that "[o]ften the chief executive officer of the company may know nothing regarding the subject matter but is noticed or subpoenaed [for deposition] for harassment purposes." Under Standing Rule 10, a corporate executive served with a notice of deposition who has no personal knowledge of the relevant facts may submit an affidavit to that effect, naming witnesses who do have knowledge. The intent of the rule is to discourage the opposing party from proceeding further and to provide a factual basis for a protective order if the party brings one.

The proposed *Manual for Complex Litigation 2d* also contains proscriptions against discovery abuse and excess. The drafters of the proposed *Manual* (February 1985 draft) have recognized the need for district judges to play a more active role in the discovery process, including curtailing excessive discovery. The manual states:

> Unless appropriate limitations and procedures are established in advance, the deposition process may unduly prolong pretrial procedures and result in an enormous cost to the litigants, far outweighing the actual value of the discovery. Under Fed. R. Civ. P. 26 the attorneys and judges have an affirmative duty to curtail excessive discovery of all types, including depositions.

The manual recommends that, in appropriate cases, limits be placed on the scope, number, and length of depositions. In addition, the manual outlines certain cost-saving measures with respect to depositions, including written interrogatories in lieu of oral testimony. *Manual for Complex Litigation 2d* 21-16, 21-17, 21-30, 29-40, 29-41, 29-42 (February 1985 draft).

When and if the CEO of your client is noticed for a deposition, there are a variety of steps you can take:

1. Try to persuade opposing counsel through an informal conference to proceed with other discovery first. Suggest that opposing counsel go forward with document requests, interrogatories, requests to admit, and depositions of other individuals.
2. If a voluntary plan of discovery fails, consider filing a motion to quash the deposition outright or to alter the sequence or method of discovery. Highlight in the motion the deponent's lack of knowledge of the facts (accomplished by an affidavit) and the availability of other discovery methods.
3. In lieu of step 2, request a formal Rule 26(f) conference with your adversary. As a part of this conference, propose a discovery plan that has two-way obligations and focuses the discovery on the real issues in the case. (The proposed plan obviously will not call for the depositions of CEOs.)
4. If your opponent refuses to convene a Rule 26(f) conference and persists in seeking to depose your client's CEO, file with the court a formal Rule 26(f) motion for a discovery conference. In filing the motion, follow the requirements of Rule 26(f) literally. Remember that the court—and not a magistrate—should hear the motion and "shall" enter an order. Although it is preferable to have the Rule 26(f) conference with the court near the beginning of a case, that is not required.
5. If the district court has ordered the CEO to appear for deposition either as part of an overall discovery plan or otherwise, appellate review may be available. In fact, the recent amendments to the discovery rules increase the likelihood of obtaining that review. Although interlocutory appellate review of a discovery order may be difficult (*but see Belcher v. Bassett Furniture Industries, Inc.*, 588 F.2d 904, 906 n.4 (4th Cir. 1978)), particularly when a district court made no findings and failed to consider or apply the factors set forth in revised Rule 26(b)(1), a writ of mandamus may be possible. *Compare Schlagenhauf v. Holder,* 379 U.S. 104 (1964) ("advisory" mandamus granted to review a new and recurring question of interpretation under a federal discovery rule) *with La Buy v. Howes Leather Co.,* 352 U.S. 249 (1957) ("supervisory" mandamus exercised because of a deliberate regard of the provisions of a rule). *See also* 16 C. Wright & A. Miller, *Federal Practice and Procedure* § 3935 (1977) (discussing

discovery orders and mandamus relief); Note, *Supervisory and Advisory Mandamus Under the All Writs Act,* 86 Harv. L. Rev. 595 (1973).

6. Whichever strategy you follow, avoid at all costs making the argument that the CEO is too busy and too important for a deposition. Instead, emphasize that the new rules adopt a least expensive-least intrusive test to curb abusive discovery. It is not enough that the discovery might lead to relevant evidence.

§ 1.55 Deposing Insurance Companies

One of the risks that is always present in representing a corporate defendant in litigation, especially an insurance company whose executives may possess little or no factual information regarding the incident giving rise to coverage questions, is that the plaintiff will notice the deposition of management. This is typically done for harassment purposes, although the plaintiff does not admit to such tactics.

The approach usually taken by the noticing party is framed in the context of the insurance company's being the real party in interest, since the defendant is not itself exposed financially because there is full insurance coverage. The defendant, so the plaintiff's argument goes, is a defendant only in name, and the real party in interest is the insurance company, which is fair game for discovery.

You must turn to state law to explore the question of who the real party in interest is when a plaintiff has been fully compensated for a loss and the insurance company which has compensated the plaintiff is suing in the plaintiff's name. The same question must be answered when the defendant has no financial risk personally or through the corporation, but rather has full and complete insurance coverage.

State law generally holds that an insurance company may sue in the name of its insured and that this does not necessarily make the insurance company itself a real party in interest so that the other side would have direct access to insurance company management for purposes of deposition and other discovery. Of course, should those individuals have some information relevant or material to the issues in the lawsuit, that information would be discoverable, like any other factual material, under appropriate rules of procedure.

§ 1.56 Summaries

Summaries can be used to present cases in a relevant fashion which is understandable, persuasive, and comprehensible. *See* M. Dombroff,

Dombroff on Demonstrative Evidence (1983). The obvious benefits of a summary, whether of records or of a deposition, are that it shortens and simplifies what would otherwise be a complex and bulky set of records or a large volume of facts; it "processes" the records into a new form that removes extraneous material and focuses the jury's attention on the details which are important to your case; and, finally, it permits each juror to have a summary at the appropriate time during the trial. Although two of these three benefits of summaries, the first and the third, do not have built into them any sort of unfair advantage for either side, the second, the processing of records, has the capabilities for abuse.

Assume for a moment that your opponent intends to use deposition testimony in proving a case against your client or establishing a defense to a case you are attempting to prove. The deposition testimony may require several hours of reading to the jury which, notwithstanding the best efforts of even the most talented attorneys, frequently is an excruciating process.

Rule 1006 of the Federal Rules of Evidence permits the use of a summary in lieu of the underlying document when certain conditions are met:

1. The direct evidence in a suit must involve "voluminous writings, recordings, or photographs."
2. The writings, recordings, or photographs at issue cannot be such that they may be conveniently examined in court.
3. The originals or duplicate originals from which the summaries have been prepared must be made available to your opponent for examination at a reasonable time and place prior to use of the summaries in court.
4. There should be a reasonable guarantee that the summary, be it in tabular, narrative, or chart form, is accurate.
5. The individual who prepared the summary, whether an expert or other witness, should be available to testify at trial relative to the method of preparation and the underlying documentation or to give an explanation of the summary.

Providing that these guidelines are met, Rule 1006 makes it clear that the summaries are received into evidence and may be considered as direct evidence and that the underlying documents, i.e., the voluminous records themselves, need not be offered into evidence nor need they be directly considered by the jury. *See Weinstein's Evidence* § 1006 [01] (1978); *United States v. Skalicky,* 615 F.2d 1117 (5th Cir. 1980).

Using Rule 1006, your opponent has taken the several hundred pages of deposition testimony that would otherwise be offered into evidence and summarized it pursuant to the rule. Then, instead of offering the deposition itself, your opponent offers to read the narrative summary into the record. The summary as prepared is not unlike an offer of proof, except that it does not contain the qualifying language which might accompany such an offer, e.g., "if permitted to testify, Mr. Jones would say, . . ." Thus, a narrative deposition of an eyewitness to an automobile accident might read: "On December 12th, George Jones was walking across Elm Street when he saw a red truck driven by a woman . . . ."

Section 1.57 contains excerpts from two narrative summaries.

§ 1.57 —Sample Narrative Deposition Summaries

Deposition of J. F.

J. F. resides at 140 Street Address, Anytown, Anystate. Prior to retirement he worked with the international organization which is the plaintiff in this action. Mr. F. is an attorney, a 1953 graduate of Harvard Law School, and a pilot with a private pilot's rating and 250 total hours of flight time.

In 1957, Mr. F. began working for Air Lines, Inc. and Air Transportation Company in Taiwan as assistant legal counsel, responsible for doing everything there was to do.

Air Lines was a maintenance organization wholly owned by Air Limited with its base in Taiwan. Air Lines did maintenance work for its own aircraft fleet and the U.S. government. It had more than 25 different types of aircraft, including four-engine jet types (Convair 880), three-engine jet types (727s), C-47s, C-46s, BB4s, Dornier, Pilatus Porters, C-54s, DC-6s, C-45s, and helicopters. The company did maintenance for the Air Force on F-86s, F-100s, F-4-Zs, and a variety of aircraft. Generally, Air Lines serviced aircraft for anyone who could pay for it.

Mr. F. served as Air Lines' assistant legal counsel until 1966 and was primarily responsible for negotiating the company's contracts. Air Lines was also a certified FAA repair station, which meant that it could do minor to major repairs on a variety of aircraft instruments as well as on American registered aircraft.

For eight years, Mr. F. worked as an attorney advisor for the Agency for International Development (A.I.D.) in Washington, D.C. He was primarily responsible for government contracting under two international programs and was involved with air transportation contracts during 1980 and 1981.

He developed some standard phraseology or standard clauses that ended up in the aviation contracts. He also worked on Requests for Proposals (FRP's) which are solicitations, to the general public, requesting contract proposals. . . . In doing aviation contracting, one should know about technical aspects of aviation as well. In addition, as Air Lines' chief representative, he had to know a good deal about maintenance and contract pricing.

In 1981 he joined the organization and served as its Deputy General Counsel. He was principally responsible for the organization's aviation-related contracts, but was assisted by a contracting officer, L. P., who was responsible for getting the requirements, negotiating price, etc. by technical people who established requirements for the lift—i.e., who was to be carried and when, by commercial airline or charter. Mr. F. was involved in formulating and developing the organization's standard charter contract and was instrumental in negotiating the Defendant's Exhibit 30 contract.

L. P. was responsible for deciding the capability of an air carrier to perform the contract. Mr. F. does not know what L. P. did to reach his decision, but generally he knows that a contracting officer must satisfy himself that the contractor has the capability and capacity to perform the services specified in whatever writing is used to establish the requirement. The contracting officer is free to do anything that he wants to do, including looking at the contractor's facilities.

Through the time he left the organization none of the contracting officers told him that they were dissatisfied with Z Air's service. No one told him that the organization was dissatisfied with Z Air's service, or that Z Air was unsafe.

During Mr. F.'s tenure with the organization, there were no indications that the organization had been fraudulently induced into entering into the charter contracts. The language in paragraph 9, page 10 of Defendant's Exhibit 11, the inspection services clause, was probably authored by the contracting officer. Mr. F. would have reviewed this clause, because he normally reviewed all general clauses. The clause gives the organization the right to inspect services, including services, such as maintenance, being performed in conjunction with the service that was primary the requirement of the contract, air transportation.

Deposition of D. E.

Mr. E. lives at a certain address in Arlington, Virginia, and is employed by the Department of Justice as a contracting officer. He is 39 years old. Immediately prior to being employed by the Justice Department, he was self employed as a management consultant.

Mr. E.'s job responsibilities at the Justice Department include distribution of incoming contract actions for staff, negotiating complex contracts, negotiating contract terminations, issuing contracting officer final decisions, and cradle-to-grave contracting (from the inception of the contract to the conclusion of the contract). He also administers the contract.

He works with technical people who might be technically involved in the day-to-day workings of the contract or the subject matter of the contract in order to perform his responsibilities. Invoices from contractors are first sent to the accounting department for their review. Then they are sent to Mr. E. who checks the contracts to make sure the Justice Department is paying for what is in the contract. If these contracts are out in the field, Mr. E. checks with someone to see whether the services have been delivered properly. If they are in-house, he has first-hand knowledge and would not have to check with anyone to make sure.

The contracting officer's technical representative signs off on the same sheet. A technical representative is an individual assigned to assist the contracting officer in the administration of the contract. Normally, the contracting officer's technical representative would be a specialist in the area. His signature indicates that the quality of the technical services performed are satisfactory under the contract. That is a general government procedure.

[Mr. E.'s education and employment background prior to his joining the Justice Department are summarized in detail. He went to work for the international organization as a contracting officer, reporting to L. P.]

Mr. E. was the contracting officer on the contract for the organization's air transportation services involving Z Air. Mr. E. saw that contract about an hour or two before the deposition. He made a basic review of the contract and he was told the nature of the case. He was also told that the organization filed a lawsuit against Z Air. He was told that the organization asserts in that lawsuit that Z Air fraudulently induced the organization to enter into the charter contracts. He had never heard of such an assertion or a position being taken by the organization prior to an hour before the deposition. He was not told by the organization's lawyers that it had asserted in its lawsuit that Z Air was an unsafe airline, nor did he hear during his tenure at the organization that Z Air was an unsafe airline.

In the process of negotiating technical contracts, Mr. E. tended to rely upon his staff and the technical representative to let him know if a firm was capable of performing in a technical fashion. If there were problems, problem areas, or perceived problem areas, then he would negotiate those based on his technical advice. He would rely upon his technical representatives. In this case, it was Mr. W. If it was a nontechnical area, he could rely upon his own experience.

Unless the contract was a fixed price type of contract where the only worry is about price, through some means or device he, as a contracting officer, had to satisfy himself that the contractors were able to perform. In the case of certain kinds of services such as air transportation services, he had to be satisfied that the contractor could perform safely, and, at least in the area of air transportation services, that was something where he would rely upon his technical representative. He would make a certification to Mr. E. of his areas of technical expertise. Mr. E. would look to him and would also look on past performance if the organization had had a contractor with whom they had dealt with before.

> Question: Would you tell me what you did, either by yourself or in conference with Mr. W., to satisfy yourself on the fact that Z Air was capable of performing this contract, defendants' Exhibit 11?
>
> Answer: Well, there was two areas: one, the reputation that Z Air had in the industry.
>
> Question: What was it?
>
> Answer: An excellent safety record. Good management performance, as related to me by Mr. W. and also on past performance with us.
>
> Question: What was that? What did he tell you about that?
>
> Answer: That they had a very high reputation. That they had very good pilots, good maintenance, and they just did not have any trouble.
>
> And the second part of that was that I reviewed their past performance myself on a contract and found them to be very satisfactory.

Mr. E. would characterize his experience with Z Air as a contractor who was responsive, without problems, and he found them to be concerned about doing a good job.

The contractor's technical representative, Mr. W., would bring problem areas to the attention of Mr. E. If there was a problem with performance he would expect to hear from Mr. W. If there was a safety problem, he would expect to hear from him. If there was a failure to comply with the contract, he would expect to hear from him. If there was a conclusion on his part that Z Air was incapable of performing this contract, he would expect to hear from Mr. W. If he had heard any of these things, he would call the contractor himself and schedule a meeting to find out what was going on. It would depend on the severity of the problem. He would assemble all the facts first, then get hold of the contractor and see what the situation was.

During the period of time that he was at the organization, he had no meetings with Mr. W. or anybody regarding the performance of Z Air other than technical discussions when they were evaluating proposals prior to the award of the contract. Mr. W. confirmed to Mr. E. that Z Air was performing satisfactorily and they were technically able to continue to fulfill the contract terms.

Mr. E. does not believe that the organization was fraudulently induced into entering into the contract which he signed with Z Air. It was his job as a contracting officer to see that this did not happen. He felt satisfied before he signed the contract that they were technically capable of performing.

§ 1.58 —Dealing with Summaries

Perhaps the most effective tactic for dealing with a summary is to use it first. Given the fact that litigation is becoming a battle of paper and judges look kindly on litigants who offer alternatives to this approach, it is often difficult to have to oppose the use of a summary proffered by your opponent when the summary is more effective than the actual records or deposition.

If you oppose the summary, you can find yourself in the role of an obstreperous litigant who wants the court to expend time and effort unnecessarily while your opponent is attempting to innovate and offer alternate approaches. This is not a desirable perception to have attached to you or your client.

In the event that you find yourself at the receiving end of the summary, the most important thing you can do is to insure that your input is included and that the summary as proposed by your opponent is accurate. In addition, you should examine your case with an eye toward preparing summaries of your evidence that are effective in terms of presentation and innovation.

One approach to blunting an opponent's summary is to point out to the court that the summary is not as innocuous as your opponent would lead the court to believe. Rather, through the process of capsulizing, the evidence which remains takes on an even greater significance and is emphasized out of proportion in the overall patchwork of the evidence. The response of the court may be that, even assuming there is some truth to this position, the effect is minimal at worst. However, you may be able to use the records in their entirety while your opponent simply uses a summary.

Obviously, if all this is done before a jury, there are additional risks in that the jury may resent your tactic as an attempt to confuse the record while your opponent is attempting to streamline it.

§ 1.59 Authentication of Other Evidence

One of the most troubling aspects of preparing for trial often comes when deciding what foundation materials are needed or what actions must be taken in connection with authenticating other types of evidence. This typically arises when you have a large number of documents which you must use at trial and you must establish an appropriate foundation for their use. Under the Federal Rules of Civil Procedure, in particular Rule 36 dealing with admissions, the genuineness of documents can be established through requests for admissions. This is perhaps one of the most effective uses of requests for admissions and one which serves the purpose of narrowing the proofs at trial and eliminating the need for other types of evidence, particularly in the foundation area.

On occasion, you may find an opponent who uses requests for admissions to go beyond what is contemplated and to have you validate matters beyond the scope of what the rule was contemplated to cover. For example, an opponent may ask you to admit that an expert is qualified to testify in a given area. Obviously, this is not a proper use of a request for admission, and such a request should be denied as an improper use of the request for admission as a discovery device with a reservation of all rights regarding proofs and cross-examination until time of trial; you should answer that, without having heard either the direct examination or the context in which the evidence is being offered, you are unable to admit the request within the context of the case.

Another way in which opponents often attempt to take unfair advantage of your witnesses is by confronting them during depositions with particular pieces of documentary or factual evidence that are not directly related to their depositions. You will not have prepared your witness for such an examination, and your witness, seeing nothing particularly evil about the line of questioning being pursued, may be asked to agree repeatedly with your opponent regarding the authentication, validity, or factual accuracy of the evidence with which the questioning is concerned.

The underlying motive for this technique is typically your opponent's attempt to verify factual or evidentiary data for use by one of his or her own experts in formulating opinions adverse to your case. Unfortunately, all too often the response of counsel confronted with such a tactic is, "this doesn't hurt, so I won't object."

Although within the limited context of the questioning of the witness, the response is probably correct, within the broader scheme of things, the evidence that is being addressed through this witness can be devastating.

The approach you should take to such a line of questioning during a deposition is to consider the questioning within the broader context of the case and, most important, the burden of proof which your opponent must meet. If you conclude that your opponent is attempting to use your witness to validate, authenticate, or otherwise lend credence to factual information which is either outside or peripheral to the witness's scope of knowledge, you should note your objection and indicate that it goes beyond the scope of the deposition and the knowledge of the witness.

Such an objection might be characterized as a "prompt" to the witness who, assuming that he or she has been properly briefed, will thereafter indicate an inability to answer questions about the matter outside the scope of his or her knowledge. Certainly, the record should not appear as if you are coaching the witness, but there is also no question that you should get your objections on the record in as full and complete a form as possible. Failure to do so can only result in a witness who, if left unguided, can do significant damage in a matter totally unrelated to his or her expertise or scope of knowledge.

The ideal way to forestall such occurrences is careful preparation and briefing of the witness. Thus, in addition to briefing the witness on his or her area of involvement both as to overall parameters of the deposition and substantive questions which may be expected, you are well advised to give the witness a greater overall perspective as to those particular evidentiary or foundational problems which your opponent may have and may seek to cure through the upcoming deposition. By doing so, you will minimize or eliminate the necessity for prompting the witness through the use of objections and the possibility of being accused of coaching the witness.

§ 1.60 Simultaneous Depositions

With ever-increasing frequency, courts are setting discovery cutoffs. As a practical matter, the establishment of a discovery cutoff, be it 30 days, 60 days, six months, or one year from the date on which it is set, acts as a powerful impetus to get the parties on track toward bringing the litigation into the courtroom for trial. Obviously, the shorter the discovery period, the greater the pressure on the litigants.

Often at the beginning of the discovery process, parties to litigation do not appreciate the amount of discovery which they contemplate as measured against the time frame in which discovery may take place. Rarely do attorneys have the luxury of spending all their time on a single case. The exceptions are those major cases in which a number of attorneys spend all or significant portions of their time on the litigation. The typical circumstance is that a single case is only one of many in a larger caseload.

What this means in terms of time available for discovery is that, as the parties approach the discovery cutoff, they often find that there is more discovery to be taken than there is time available. You and your opponent may realize that the remaining depositions cannot be taken unless they are taken simultaneously. In effect, this means that more than one deposition is taken at the same time with teams of attorneys taking the depositions in different locations at the same time or within overlapping time frames. This discovery tactic or procedure must be carefully planned early in the case in order to insure proper representation.

On occasion, an opponent may have been carefully planning for such multiple-track depositions throughout preceding discovery. As the end of discovery approaches, the opponent suggests multiple-track depositions. All too frequently in such circumstances, you are not prepared for multiple-track depositions because you are inadequately staffed in terms of number and knowledgeability of lawyers.

In order to protect yourself against what could be an extremely effective tactic for bringing pressure on you and thrusting your opponent into a commanding position in the eyes of the court, you should take several steps early in the litigation to assess the question of multiple depositions and prepare for them in the event it appears they will become necessary:

1. Given the scheduled discovery, at what point is it likely that multiple-track depositions will commence? Under some circumstances witnesses for more than one party may be deposed simultaneously, although this is not a desirable circumstance from your perspective. Rather, more than one witness from your opponent should be deposed, thereby making it more difficult to prepare the witnesses and properly cover the depositions.
2. Because more than one deposition will be going on at a time at some stage, it is necessary that the depositions be properly covered by attorneys. It is virtually impossible for attorneys to "catch up" to get a picture of the litigation and the discovery which has taken place to the date of commencing the simultaneous depositions. Although it may not be absolutely necessary to have more than one attorney involved in a day-to-day role in the litigation up to the point of commencing the simultaneous depositions, it will be necessary for one or more attorneys to maintain a continuing awareness of the factual issues and discovery in order that they may step in at the appropriate time and participate in the discovery without being disadvantaged when your opponent has anticipated the simultaneous depositions and you have failed to do so.
3. The court reporter should be advised far enough in advance of the commencement of simultaneous depositions so that arrangements can be made for multiple reporters.
4. Duplicate copies of exhibits should be available in the event that witnesses use the same exhibits.
5. Logistical arrangements should be such that the depositions take place in the same physical location, e.g., two conference rooms in the same law firm offices. This makes for easier coordination and avoids unnecessary scheduling and practical problems.
6. A paralegal should be available to coordinate between the attorneys taking the two or more separate depositions. Often what is being discovered in one deposition may be tremendously relevant to an ongoing deposition in another room. When this is the case, there should be a means of communications between the two attorneys without the need for either deposition to adjourn. This is typically a role which a paralegal or law clerk can play extremely effectively, insuring that there is maximum coordination between the two depositions.

The tactic of simultaneous depositions, if planned for by one party at an early stage of a case and implemented when the discovery period becomes short and the pressure from the trial judge becomes great, can put an unsuspecting litigant in a highly disadvantageous position. Unfortunately, the response to a judge either that your firm is not structured to do it or that you do not have enough attorneys seems to indicate failure to plan properly and thus is usually not acceptable. Careful preplanning and "brainstorming" early in the case as to what might occur and adequate contingency planning are absolute necessities when there is any possibility that depositions may take place on multiple tracks.

§ 1.61 Privileges—In General

One of the most abused objections to discovery relates to whether a privilege protects the sought-after material. Within the context of litigation, the privilege may focus on doctor-patient or attorney-client relationships or, most likely, work product.

The doctrine of work product privilege is frequently abused by counsel both deliberately and because of lack of understanding of the work product privilege. The mere assertion by an opponent that something is protected by this privilege should not under any circumstances be accepted. Sometimes such an assertion is merely an attempt to throw a blanket over documents or other discoverable material when there is no other specific privilege or objection available to your opponent.

§ 1.62 —Attorney Work Product

The attorney work product privilege is embodied in Federal Rule of Civil Procedure 26(b)(3):

> (3) Trial Preparation: Materials. Subject to the provisions of subdivision (b)(4) of this rule, a party may obtain discovery of documents and tangible things otherwise discoverable under subdivision (b)(1) of this rule and prepared in anticipation of litigation or for trial by or for another party or by or for that other party's representative (including his attorney, consultant, surety, indemnitor, insurer, or agent) only upon a showing that the party seeking discovery has substantial need of the materials in the preparation of his case and that he is unable without undue hardship to obtain the substantial equivalent of the materials by other means. In ordering discovery of such materials when the required showing has been made, the court shall protect against disclosure of mental impressions, conclusions, opinions, or legal theories of an attorney or other representative of a party concerning the litigation.

One of the most extensive and definitive discussions of the attorney work product privilege is found in *Hickman v. Taylor,* 329 U.S. 495 (1947). Discussing the relative equities, the Supreme Court found, in effect, that Rules 26, 33, and 34 of the Federal Rules of Civil Procedure do not require production as a matter of right of written or oral statements of witnesses obtained by counsel in anticipation of litigation.

Since *Hickman v. Taylor* was decided in 1947, the doctrine of attorney work product has been applied to a wide variety of cases. At one time or another, this rule has been used to protect statements obtained in anticipation of litigation by an investigator who was working with an attorney, *Sersted v. American Can Co.,* 535 F. Supp. 1072 (E.D. Wis. 1982), documents that reveal the identity of outside consultants, disclosure of which would reveal the theories of a litigant, *Exxon v. FTC,* 476 F. Supp. 713 (D.D.C. 1979), a manual prepared by a computer company detailing proposed litigation strategy and plans for discovery, *Id.* and notes taken by counsel during pretrial discovery interviews of expert witnesses, *Bristol-Myers Co. v. FTC,* 598 F.2d 18 (D.D.C. 1978).

However, it is well accepted that the work product privilege is not absolute. In order to pierce the privilege, the party seeking disclosure of attorney work product items must establish that the sought-after document or information is essential to preparation of the case. Such necessity may arise when the information is the sought-after documents is unavailable through other means or can be reached only with great difficulty. *See, e.g., United States v. Lipshy,* 492 F. Supp. 35 (N.D. Tex. 1979).

Today, when many cases involve huge numbers of documents, the question of what constitutes "great difficulty" often poses an interesting question. This is particularly true when documents are culled or selected from a larger group of documents and then used, for example, to assist in the briefing of a witness. This question was confronted by the courts in *In re International Systems and Controls Corp. Securities Litigation,* 91 F.R.D. 552 (S.D. Tex. 1981), in which it was held that documents in the hands of the client were not protected by the attorney work product doctrine. However, the court stated that in cases in which materials were selected from a large group of documents and assembled meaningfully, they were protected as attorney work product.

From this case, one can readily see how the principles enunciated by the court in *In re International Systems* would be applied to the deposition preparation situation. If counsel, mindful of the theories and strategies of a case, assembles a briefing package of documents from a larger collection of documents that itself is discoverable, the package assembled for briefing purposes would be privileged. The privilege would attach, not because of the nature of the documents themselves, but rather due to the thought process that would be revealed and evidenced by the selection made by counsel. Certainly, although the concept is not directly embraced in the more usual application of the attorney work product doctrine, the mental impressions of counsel as to which documents are important to a particular theory or witness by logical extension would fall within the doctrine.

Recent developments and experience with the Federal Rules of Evidence indicate that the conventional approach to attorney work product has undergone a thorough reexamination by the courts. Federal Rule of Evidence 612 provides that if your witness uses a document to refresh his or her memory while testifying, your opponent is entitled to have it produced. In addition, the rule provides that, at the court's discretion, your opponent may even be able to have produced the writings used to refresh your witness's memory before testimony. The relationship of this rule to the attorney work product doctrine can produce some difficult problems for a lawyer who does not fully appreciate the interplay between the Federal Rules of Civil Procedure and the Federal Rules of Evidence.

In *James Julian Inc. v. Raytheon Co.,* 93 F.R.D. 138 (D. Del. 1982), plaintiff's counsel learned the hard way that the Federal Rules must be read together, particularly Fed. R. Civ. P. 26(b)(3) with Fed. R. Evid. 612. During the course of preparing a witness for a deposition, plaintiff's counsel selected a few key documents from among thousands of pages of documents, which then were placed in binders and shown to the witness prior to the deposition.

In resisting a discovery request under Rule 612, counsel argued that the selection process constituted attorney work product in that the selection of a few documents from a larger collection reflected the mental processes of counsel and evidenced his theories of the case. Thus the plaintiff in *Julian* asserted the very same argument upheld by the court in *In re International Systems.*

Although acknowledging that, in the first instance, the binders prepared by counsel were entitled to protection as work product, citing *Berkey Photo, Inc. v. Eastman Kodak Co.,* 74 F.R.D. 613 (S.D.N.Y. 1977), the court in *Julian* went on to order their production after discussing Rule 612 and its legislative history. Citing and discussing a number of cases, including District Judge Marvin E. Frankel's opinion in *Berkey Photo, Inc.,* District Judge Murray M. Schwartz found:

> The binder at issue contains various documents selected and arranged by plaintiffs' counsel and given to various witnesses prior to their depositions. Without reviewing those binders defendants' counsel cannot know or inquire into the extent to which the witnesses' testimony has been shaded by counsel's presentation of the factual background. The instant request constitutes neither a fishing expedition into the plaintiff's files nor an invasion of counsel's "zone of privacy." Plaintiff's counsel made a decision to educate their witnesses by supplying them with the binders and the Raytheon defendants are entitled to know the content of that education.

93 F.R.D. at 146. The lesson to be learned from *Julian* is that prudent trial counsel must think well in advance about ramifications of what is disclosed to witnesses as part of the preparatory process. There is little doubt

that the attorney work product privilege is pierced if counsel permits witnesses to enter the "zone of privacy."

The risk-benefit analysis accompanying such judgments must take into account the fact that "counsel cannot have it both ways." *Ramsey v. County of Fresno,* 7 Fed. R. Evid. Serv. (Callaghan) 950 (E.D. Cal. 1980).

§ 1.63 Discovery Memoranda

Recent amendments to Rule 26 of the Federal Rules of Civil Procedure provide for the holding of a discovery conference at any time after commencement of an action as directed by the court. In addition, if requested by one of the litigants, the court may order a discovery conference.

As provided in Rule 26(f) of the Federal Rules of Civil Procedure, the motion must include the following items:

1. A statement of the issues as they appear
2. A proposed plan and discovery schedule
3. Any limitations proposed to be placed on discovery
4. Any other proposed orders with respect to discovery
5. A statement that the moving attorney has made a reasonable effort to reach agreement with the opponent on the matters set forth in the motion.

The rule also provides that "objections or additions to matters set forth in the motion shall be served not later than 10 days after service of the motion."

Following the discovery conference, a judge is directed under the rule to enter an order identifying the issues with discovery purposes, establishing a plan and schedule of discovery, setting any limitations on discovery, and determining a number of other matters, possibly including the assessment of expenses.

It is clear that this rule may be used as an unfair device, positioning one litigant more favorably than another. If you are on the receiving end of such a motion for a discovery conference and order, you should review it from several perspectives with an eye toward framing your response:

1. Is the statement of issues fair and accurate?
2. Is the proposed plan or schedule of discovery realistic, and does it take into account the needs of all the litigants? Furthermore, is the timing of the proposed discovery plan consistent with the logical and natural progression and order of proof in the case?
3. Are the limitations proposed for discovery fair and reasonable? Do they benefit or favor one side over the other?

4. Has your opponent made a genuine effort to work out agreements with you regarding discovery? If so, has that effort been reflected in the motion, and do you, as a result, come across to the court as unreasonable and unwilling to expedite the handling of the case?

It is quite clear that a litigant who is able to get a discovery plan adopted and frame the issues in a manner consistent with clients' interests has seized control of the case and is in a better position to direct its further progress than one who is on the defensive. Accordingly, you should be especially cautious about refusing to agree with opponents on an otherwise reasonable discovery plan simply because of natural adversary instincts.

Gestetner Corp. v. Case Equipment Co., 108 F.R.D. 138 (D. Me. 1985), is an interesting case focusing on the question of the logistical management of discovery. United States District Judge Gene Carter determined that there was no showing of good cause why a magistrate's scheduling order setting a deadline for completion of discovery in the filing of all pretrial motions should be extended. The district court found that counsel had failed to express disagreement with the schedules set by the magistrate and did not request a conference to review any aspect of it. The motion made by counsel made no showing that the complete lack of attention paid to the case over a period of some four months was due to any mistake, excusable neglect, or any other factor which might have understandably accounted for the failure of counsel to undertake to comply with the order.

In any sort of situation when there is a standard scheduling order propounded by the court or a magistrate, you should immediately review that order and the dates contained therein. If there is any disagreement noted with it or difficulty in complying with it, you should immediately bring it to the attention of the court. By the same token, the failure to do so on the part of opposing counsel should be treated in the context of this case, and an argument should be propounded that opposing counsel is estopped from taking issue with the discovery schedule.

§ 1.64 Pleading and Practice Memoranda

Another approach to the discovery conference or plan is the use of pleading and practice memoranda or motions. The discovery, pleading, and practice memorandum is a pleading, filed either in the form of a "Motion Seeking a Discovery, Pleading and Practice Order" or as a "Memorandum In Re: Discovery, Pleading and Practice," with several complementary purposes, all aimed at maximizing the effective preparation and presentation of your case:

1. It sets out several suggested pretrial procedures that the judge can adopt to expedite the pretrial and trial proceedings in your case.
2. It distinguishes you as the party seeking to move the case along using a series of innovative procedures.
3. It provides a vehicle for your pretrial and trial procedures to be adopted over those proposed by your opponent.
4. It places a burden on your opponent to accept or reject or to come up with alternative procedures.

Too often, inexperienced trial lawyers tend to litigate on an ad hoc basis without giving thought to long-term phases of the litigation until it is too late to do anything but react. If you use long-term planning in making judgments as to the course the case should take, you are in a decidedly better position to control what happens. The pleading and practice memorandum can be used to better achieve that end.

The memorandum should be filed as a memorandum or a motion. Some or all of the following provisions may be included as desirable in the context of your specific case.

**MEMORANDUM OF [PLAINTIFF OR DEFENDANT, AS APPROPRIATE]
IN RE: DISCOVERY, PLEADING AND PRACTICE**

INTRODUCTION

The [plaintiff or defendant, as appropriate] for the purpose of expediting the pretrial preparation and trial of this action, suggests the adoption of the following procedures for the discovery, pretrial and trial aspects of this litigation.

The introductory language is purely a matter of style. One of the advantages of a motion seeking a discovery, pleading, and practice order is that your opponent and the judge are required to act. If a motion is filed, the introductory language would be different. One form it might take follows:

Please take notice that the [plaintiff, defendant] moves this Honorable Court to enter an order on discovery, pleading and practice in this matter. Attached hereto and filed in support hereof is a memorandum and a proposed order.

1. Discovery in the liability and damages aspects of the case should be bifurcated with separate discovery being permitted, pursuant to local rules, for each aspect of the case.

You should also consider other types of bifurcations or severances, e.g., parties or issues. Obviously, if you suggest them at all, you should include requests for separate discovery with respect to each party or issue.

Most rules of procedure, state and federal, give the court a broad range of discretion in allowing separate trials of any claim, cross-claim, counterclaim, or third-party claim or any separate issue or any number of claims, cross-claims, counterclaims, third-party claims, or issues. Furthermore, if a local rule limits the number of depositions, interrogatories, or admissions, severance or bifurcation may also allow for expanded discovery if separate discovery is provided in each separate part of the case.

2. Whenever a party has an objection to responding to either an interrogatory, a request for production or a request for admission, all answers or documents that are not objectionable will be filed and/or served as appropriate. Simultaneously, the objection(s) will be filed and served with all legal and factual arguments in support of the objection. Also filed at this time, but *in camera* only, will be the objectionable response or document.

   If the objection goes to the voluminous nature of the information sought, no *in camera* submission need be made initially. However, counsel should submit affidavits attesting to the voluminous nature of material being sought.

   Within five days of receipt of the objection and supporting authorities, opposing counsel will file a response. The court, with or without argument or further briefing as it may deem appropriate, may then rule upon the objections without further delay and if it overrules them, make the responsive information immediately available to counsel. Following this procedure should substantially expedite the process and aid in making counsel more responsive to discovery requests.

This procedure was developed for complex tort litigation. Although it imposes a burden on you as well as your opponent, it does have the effect of substantially expediting that phase of discovery surrounding objections.

When an objection is based on the voluminous nature of the information sought, the very act of providing it to the court in camera defeats the objection. Under such circumstances, an in camera inspection would not be carried out.

3. Pursuant to an order of this court, a Special Master should be appointed to preside over all discovery with full power to exercise all powers granted by the rules of procedure, and such additional powers as are usually exercised by Special Masters. The expenses of the Master should be borne equally by the parties with the accumulated costs to be assessed against the losing party at the conclusion of the proceedings.

You should reserve the use of a master for those unusual cases in which the discovery process will be either so broad or, due to personalities of counsel, so difficult as to require some continued judicial presence and control. Such cases are, luckily, the exception.

4. In order to minimize the repetitive use of damage interrogatories, plaintiff(s) should be required to provide damage information within 10 days of filing their complaint.

This procedure is most effectively utilized in a multiparty case.

5. For the purpose of expediting discovery and minimizing cost—unless the court manifests a contrary desire—all status conferences, motions hearings, and preliminary pretrials should be handled via telephone.

This procedure does nothing other than track a trend that is becoming more and more predominant.

6. In order to simplify the handling of documents and exhibits during both discovery and trial, the use of a consecutive numbering system, without regard to which party produces or offers a document, should be observed. By doing so, reference to documents will be simplified inasmuch as that document marked, for example, as exhibit 3 in the Jones deposition will always be Exhibit 3, be it in subsequent depositions or trial.

The benefit of this procedure is self-evident. If adopted, no longer are there multiple exhibits bearing the same number which, assuming renumbering is required by local rule for trial, is inconsistent with the references to the exhibit in the deposition. Such a procedure, in order to be maximally effective, should be followed from the outset of the litigation and, for that reason, should be suggested early.

In order to accommodate exhibits marked at trial (e.g., exhibits used on cross-examination and not premarked, demonstrative exhibits, court-marked exhibits, etc.), blocks of numbers can be reserved for each party (e.g., 1–1000 would be for premarked exhibits, 1001–2000 for plaintiff's trial exhibits, 2001–3000 for defendant's trial exhibits, and so forth).

If your local rules require renumbering for trial (e.g., numbers for plaintiff, letters for defendant), you may require leave of court for a single sequential numbering system.

7. To the maximum extent practicable and in lieu of the verbatim reading of depositions at trial, either straight narratives of proffered deposition testimony, or a combination of narrative and verbatim extracts, should be utilized. The party intending to offer deposition testimony will have the obligation of preparing the narrative which will then be submitted to opposing counsel for additions and/or objections. Those objections, to either form or substance, which cannot be resolved by counsel will be referred to the court for resolution.

   A similar procedure will be utilized in the event either party intends to rely upon voluminous documentary evidence for the preparation of summaries.

There is no question but that the pleading and practice memorandum is an extremely effective technique. It is most effective when a motion seeking its imposition is filed early in the litigation. Accordingly, if representing the plaintiff, you should request a pleading and practice order at the same time you file your complaint. Alternatively, if you are representing a defendant, you should seek a pleading and practice order when you file your answer. This immediately establishes you as the party seeking to take control of the case and the one with innovative ideas for managing the case in an expeditious and economic fashion. Recognizing that this is a primary concern of judges today, you are well positioned to gain the favor of the court at an early stage.

The advantage of filing a motion seeking a pleading and practice order, as opposed to simply filing a memorandum, is that the motion demands action not only by your opponent in the form of a response but also by the court in the form of an order. Alternatively, by simply filing a memorandum suggesting the procedures, you or your opponent will, in effect, be filing an informational pleading as opposed to an action pleading.

On the receiving end of pleading and practice memoranda one must react in a calculated and careful fashion. If you oppose the motion too strongly, you will be cast in the role of the "bad guy," because you can be characterized as not wishing to expedite or innovate in the case. As a practical matter, opposing the use of the procedures which might be contained in the vehicle of a pleading and practice order simply for the sake of litigative purposes or adversarial gains is something less than good faith.

The approach to be taken when responding to such a motion must be contemplated looking to the rules. A suggested response to the pleading and practice motion is to characterize it as nothing more than a request for a discovery conference or a discovery order as a result of that conference. By doing this, you can validly characterize your opponent as seeking to circumvent the requirement of joint attempts to resolve discovery concerns and problems under Rule 26(f) of the Federal Rules of Civil Procedure. If you indicate in your response that you are willing to sit down with your opponent and work out reasonable areas of agreement or of agreement to disagree, it is highly unlikely that the court will respond affirmatively to the motions seeking a pleading and practice order, because most judges will opt for the litigants' working out their difficulties as opposed to imposition of judicially mandated decisions.

Accordingly, your response to a motion seeking a pleading and practice order should be calculated not to cause the judge to deny the motion on its merits, because many of the ideas contained in such orders are sound. Rather, it should be calculated to cause the judge to defer to the litigants in resolving the question. By characterizing your opponent as one who is in effect seeking a discovery conference and order and yet has failed to attempt to jointly work out all matters, you will appear cooperative to the court, assist the court in placing such motions (which are not provided for in the rules of procedure) in their proper perspective, and implement some very effective techniques and tactics for the litigation.

Section 1.65 contains two sample memoranda regarding pleading and practice procedures and a sample stipulation and protective order regarding privileged information.

§ 1.65 —Sample Pleading and Practice Orders

DEFENDANT'S MEMORANDUM CONCERNING PROPOSED PLEADING AND PRACTICE PROCEDURES

_______________ (Defendant), for the purpose of expediting the pretrial preparation and trial of this action, suggests the adoption of the following procedures for the discovery, pretrial, and trial aspects of this litigation.

I. Discovery

A. Written discovery

Defendant proposes that the first phase of discovery be limited to written discovery consisting of interrogatories, requests for production of documents, and requests for admission. All requests for such discovery shall be filed so that the responses to such discovery will be due on or before ___________, 19__, as calculated under the Federal Rules of Civil Procedure.

Whenever a party has an objection to responding to such written discovery, that party, on the date that the responses to such discovery are due pursuant to the Federal Rules of Civil Procedure, will:

(1) Serve and file with the Court all objections to the requested discovery, with all legal and factual arguments in support of such objections;

(2) Serve all answers or documents that are responsive to discovery to which an objection has not been asserted;

(3) Submit to the Court, *in camera,* all answers or documents that are responsive to the discovery to which an objection has been asserted where such objection is not based on the voluminous nature of the information sought; and

(4) Serve and file supporting affidavits for any objection based on the voluminous nature of the information sought.

Within five days of receipt of such an objection, opposing counsel may file a response. The Court, with or without argument or further briefing as it may deem appropriate, may then rule upon the objections without further delay. If the Court overrules an objection, it will release the responsive information immediately, or, in the case of objections based on the voluminous nature of the material sought, order the objecting party to produce the response as early as possible.

B. Depositions

Defendant proposes that all depositions of fact witnesses be conducted between ___________, 19__, and ___________, 19__. Defendant also proposes: (1) that plaintiffs name their experts and file their Federal Rule of Civil Procedure 26(b)(4) statements on or before __________, 19__, and (2) that defendants name their experts and file their Federal Rule of Civil Procedure 26(b)(4) statements on or before __________, 19__. Expert depositions shall be conducted between __________, 19__, and __________, 19, with all parties bearing the costs of their own experts. All depositions and discovery will be completed on or before __________, 19__.

C. Location of Depositions.

In order to coordinate and expedite the deposition process, Defendant proposes that depositions be conducted at the following locations:

1. Depositions of fact witnesses pertaining to __________ or __________ shall be conducted at __________.

2. Depositions of fact witnesses pertaining to Defendant shall be conducted in __________.

3. Depositions of plaintiffs and all expert witnesses shall be conducted in New York City.

II. Bifurcation of Damages and Liability

Defendant strongly urges that the trial be bifurcated with respect to damages and liability.

III. Pretrial Motions

Defendant proposes that: (1) all motions relating to joinder of parties, claims, or remedies, and amendment of pleadings be filed on or before __________, 19__; (2) all motions to dismiss based on the pleadings be filed on or before __________, 19__; and (3) all motions for summary judgment be filed on or before __________, 19__.

IV. Documents

A. Identification

In order to simplify the handling of documents and exhibits during both discovery and trial, Defendant proposes that each party that produces documents number such documents consecutively with the following letter prefixes to designate the party producing the documents:

Party	*Prefix*
Defendant A	"S"
Defendant B	"A"
Plaintiff A	"D"
Plaintiff B	"W"
Plaintiff C	"T"
Plaintiff D	"H"

In addition, documents used or referred to at depositions shall be marked consecutively, without regard to the deposition or to which party produces or offers such a document. By doing so, reference to a document marked, for example, as Exhibit 3 in the "Jones" deposition will always be Exhibit 3, even in subsequent depositions or at trial.

B. Depository

Defendant proposes that a document depository for all documents produced be established at Hughes Hubbard & Reed, One Wall Street, New York, New York, with costs for maintaining such to be borne equally between plaintiffs and defendants.

V. Appointment of a Special Master

Defendant proposes that a special master be appointed to preside over all discovery and settlement matters, with full power to exercise all powers granted by the rules of procedure and such additional powers as are usually exercised by special masters. The expenses of the master should be borne equally by plaintiffs and defendants.

DEFENDANT ABC'S MEMORANDUM CONCERNING PROPOSED PLEADING AND PRACTICE PROCEDURES TO BE ADOPTED IN THIS ACTION

Defendant ABC, for the purpose of expediting the pretrial preparation and trial of this action, suggests the adoption of the following procedures for the discovery, pretrial, and trial aspects of this litigation.

I. Discovery

A. Class Certification

Although ABC does not believe this case is appropriate for certifying as a class action, should this court determine that plaintiffs' demand merits further investigation, ABC requests that sixty (60) days be allocated for discovery relating to individual members of the proposed class. This discovery should be limited as follows:

(1) The identity of members of the class;

(2) The bases of claims of the individual plaintiffs;

(3) The uses and maintenance history for each allegedly defective aircraft owned by the class member; and

(4) The issue of whether the plaintiffs will fairly and adequately protect the interests of the class.

B. Liability

ABC proposes that plaintiffs be required to name their experts on or before ___________, 19__, with plaintiffs' Federal Rule of Civil Procedure 26(b)(4) statements being filed at that time, and that defendants be required to name their experts on or before ___________, 19__, with defendants' Federal Rule of Civil Procedure 26(b)(4) statements being filed at that time.

ABC proposes that depositions of plaintiffs' experts occur between ___________, 19__ and ___________, 19__, that deposition of defendants' experts occur between ___________, 19__ and ___________, 19__, and that all parties bear the costs of their own experts.

C. Damages

ABC strongly urges that the trial be bifurcated with respect to damages and liability.

ABC proposes that plaintiffs be required to file, within thirty (30) days of the signing of this Order, a comprehensive list of all damages claimed, detailing the date of loss and a description of the loss incurred. ABC also proposes that plaintiffs be required to provide, at the time of such filing, all documentation (if any) substantiating the loss.

ABC suggests that damage discovery as to the named plaintiffs be limited to thirty (30) days.

D. Location of Depositions

To coordinate and expedite the deposition process, GM proposes that the following locations be established for depositions:

(1) Depositions of fact witnesses pertaining to CDE shall occur in __________.

(2) Depositions of fact witnesses pertaining to ABC shall occur in __________.

(3) Depositions of plaintiffs and all experts shall occur in __________.

E. Written Discovery

ABC proposes that the following procedure be followed with respect to written discovery.

Whenever a party has an objection to responding to an interrogatory, a request for production, or a request for admission, all answers or documents that are not objectionable will be filed and/or served as appropriate. Simultaneously, the objection(s) will be filed and served with all legal and factual arguments in support of the objection. Also filed at this time, but *in camera* only, will be the objectionable response or document.

If the objection goes to the voluminous nature of the information sought, no *in camera* submission need be made initially. However, counsel must submit affidavits attesting to the voluminous nature of material being sought.

Within five days of receipt of the objection and supporting authorities, opposing counsel will file a response. The court, with or without argument or further briefing as it may deem appropriate, may then rule upon the objections without further delay and if it overrules them, make the responsive information immediately available to counsel.

II. Document Identification

In order to simplify the handling of documents and exhibits both during discovery and trial, ABC proposes that the use of a consecutive numbering system, without regard to which party produces or offers a document, should be adopted. By doing so, reference to documents will be simplified inasmuch as that a document marked, for example, as Exhibit 3 in the "Jones" deposition will always be Exhibit 3, be it in subsequent depositions or at trial.

III. Document Depository

ABC proposes that a document depository for all documents produced be established at ________________, with the costs for maintaining such to be borne equally between plaintiffs and defendants.

IV. Previous Deadlines Established By The Court

A. All motions relating to joinder of parties claims or remedies, class certification, and amendment of pleadings must be filed on or before ____________, 19__.

B. All motions to dismiss based on the pleadings must be filed on or before ____________, 19__.

C. Discovery is to be completed on or before ____________, 19__.

D. All motions for summary judgment are to be filed on or before ____________, 19__.

STIPULATION AND PROTECTIVE ORDER

IT IS HEREBY STIPULATED and agreed between the parties to this action, through their respective counsel, as follows:

Defendants ABC and CDE contend that the documents, data, information, and other materials provided by defendants in the defense of this action and/or pursuant to plaintiffs' pretrial discovery requests are privileged because they afford other entities and corporations the opportunity to take competitive advantage. This material shall be deemed confidential and proprietary information which shall be used by plaintiffs solely for the purposes of this action. Such information will not be revealed or disclosed or made available for inspection and copying to any competitors of ABC or CDE or to any third parties.

It is contemplated by the parties to this stipulation that the use of confidential and proprietary information encompassed within this stipulation may be permitted in preparation of the trial of this action, but not so as to be potentially injurious to defendants' business interests, such as by disclosure of information sensitive to the national defense or competitively sensitive to defendants. If defendants ABC and CDE deem that such information is being used by plaintiffs or others in such a manner as to violate the intent and spirit of this stipulation, defendants, individually or jointly, may give plaintiffs or their agents notice that such materials could be subject to this stipulation and bring the issue to the attention of the Court for further order.

This Stipulation and Protective Order shall apply to all documents, data, information, and other materials provided by the defendants to the plaintiffs throughout the course of this action, unless otherwise agreed by all counsel to this action in writing.

Notwithstanding the foregoing provisions, this Stipulation and Protective Order shall not be construed as a waiver by defendants or plaintiffs of any objections which might be raised as to the admissibility at trial of any evidentiary material.

Upon final termination of this action, plaintiffs shall immediately return to defendants ABC and CDE all information, documents, data, and other materials produced by defendants and all copies thereof. Plaintiffs, their attorneys, expert consultants, and any agents of any of them, shall also destroy any extracts, summaries or copies of the same of any such documents which have been prepared during the course of the litigation. Finally, plaintiffs' counsel shall prepare a sworn affidavit, certifying that plaintiffs have complied with the requirements of this final paragraph of the Stipulation and Protective Order.

____

[signatures]

____

SO ORDERED:

____

United States District Judge

§ 1.66 Trial Preparation Checklist

In the final analysis, litigation of all types is strikingly similar. Not only does the trial lawyer have to know about the tactics and techniques of trying a lawsuit, but he or she may have to possess the knowledge of a doctor, the information of a banker, the technical acumen of an engineer, the ability of an accountant, or, depending on the nature of the case, the skills of several other specialists. Simply stated, trial lawyers must possess a large number of diverse skills and expertise. What then sets apart litigators who are actually trying lawsuits from the general legal population?

Most trial lawyers acknowledge that lawsuits are usually won or lost before the lawyers ever set foot in the courtroom. Skillfully taken depositions, extensive document discovery, and the ability to put everything together into a scenario that either proves or disproves the case, depending on whether one is a plaintiff or a defendant, typically marks the successful litigator.

If you had to sum up the secret of winning cases into one word, it would be all-inclusive and yet neither surprising nor very innovative. That word is *preparation.* As obvious as it may seem, the key to winning lawsuits is preparation, not only preparation to insure the successful outcome of the pretrial process, but preparation needed to insure the successful outcome of the trial.

This section presents a checklist for procedures commencing approximately 100 days before trial. The purpose of this checklist is not to focus on, for example, settlement or the discovery process, but rather to establish a series of guidelines by which a litigator can compare the steps taken to prepare his or her case to those needed in order to insure that preparation is complete and the case is postured for victory. Although certainly no one can guarantee that the outcome will be a successful verdict, the one thing that can be guaranteed is that a less-than-successful verdict is attributable to less-than-successful preparation.

You should feel free and indeed are encouraged to take this checklist and duplicate it, placing one copy in each case file and using it as a guideline as the case approaches the trial date. By using this "tickler" system, important steps can be highlighted and details remembered. After all, in litigation, as in many other things in life, the small things really are the ones which count.

100 Days Before Trial

1. Complete discovery.

____ Review all depositions, interrogatories, requests for admissions, and document production requests.

____ Finish those which haven't been completed.

____ Follow up on those that require responses.

____ Insure that those which should be filed have been filed with the court.

____ Review all answers to which your opponent may have deferred responding until more discovery had been taken in the case.

2. Prepare for expert depositions.

____ Unless you have already done so, notice the depositions of all expert witnesses being offered by your opponent.

____ If you do not know their identity as yet, file a set of interrogatories to ascertain their identity.

____ Unless you have the right to take their depositions, seek to do so by stipulation with your opponent. The best way to do this is to offer your experts for deposition while taking those of your opponent, with each party bearing its own costs.

3. File cleanup interrogatories.

____ Draw up and file a set of "cleanup" interrogatories which, in some measure, overlap prior interrogatories but are designed to get all that last-minute information. Among other things, they could include the following:

- Inquiry into the names of all witnesses
- The subject matter of the testimony of all witnesses
- The names of expert witnesses
- The subject matter and opinions of the expert witnesses
- Any factual basis for the denial of assertions of negligence or for the allegation or affirmative defenses

- Inquiry into any demonstrative evidence which will be utilized at trial and which previously may not have been disclosed (including such things as charts, graphs, diagrams, experiments, demonstrations, recreations, videotapes, computer-generated evidence, motion picture films, and photographs).

____ Based upon the responses you receive to these interrogatories, you are in a position to draft and file a motion in limine to preclude certain issues from the case, define the nature of other issues, or obtain preliminary rulings on certain evidence.

4. Complete investigation.

____ To the extent you have not already done so, finish up all interviews with nonexpert witnesses, including eyewitnesses. In the event certain witnesses have not yet been located, make a final attempt to do so.

____ Statements from the witnesses should already be in your possession; to the extent necessary, they should be verified. Double check that any wreckage or product type exhibits will be available to the extent necessary for trial; if appropriate, take custody of those portions of the wreckage or product which are important to your case.

____ Double check that any witnesses being requested from government agencies will, to the extent allowed by the agency, be available for trial. If they will not be available for trial, insure that their depositions are obtained.

____ Make a list of all witnesses for whom subpoenas must be issued.

____ Make a list of all documents and other materials for which subpoenas must be issued.

____ Be sure that you know who the document custodian is with respect to the production of any documents for trial.

60 to 45 Days Before Trial

1. Prepare for settlement, if appropriate.

____ Consider whether a final settlement conference should be requested.

____ If so, or if a settlement conference is ordered by the judge, consult with the client and prepare a damages brochure or day-in-the-life type settlement videotape. See **Chapter 9**.

____ From the defense perspective, confer with the principals to determine the latest position on settlement and make a settlement offer if it is deemed appropriate.

2. Prepare for pretrial conference and order.

____ The pretrial conference should be prepared for by preparing the pretrial order.

____ Check local rules for the precise format of the pretrial order for a particular court.

____ Consider the following elements for the pretrial order:

- Agreed-upon facts
- Disputed issues of fact
- Legal issues
- Defenses
- Claimed damages
- Exhibits expected to be introduced at trial
- Witnesses expected to be called at trial
- Pending motions
- Estimates of time for trial.

____ Following the pretrial conference, finalize the pretrial order based upon whatever rulings the judge may have made and enter the order.

45 Days Before Trial

1. Prepare your files.

____ Review all files in connection with the case to determine whether they have been organized in a way which facilitates maximum access of information. More important, determine whether they are logically organized.

____ Suggested file folders may be as follows:

- Correspondence
- Complaint, answer, and related motions
- Motions for summary judgment
- Motion to dismiss
- Deposition notices
- Expenses
- Folders for individual witnesses, including experts
- Folders for each exhibit
- Jury instructions.

____ For a complete explanation of an extensive case organization system which may be accomplished without the use of a computer, see M. Dombroff, *Litigation Organization and Management: Effective Tactics and Techniques* ch. 5, *The LITIDEX System: A Computer Compatible Means of Effectively Organizing and Managing Litigation* (Law and Business, Inc., Harcourt Brace Jovanovich 1984).

2. **Prepare your trial notebook.**

    ____ The trial notebook should be prepared as soon as the case becomes a case and should be updated and rearranged as needed throughout the preparation process. See § **1.67**.

45 to 30 Days Before Trial

1. **Outline all elements of proof.**

    ____ Draft out in detail all allegations which you must prove to support your position.

    ____ Along with each allegation, list the witnesses and exhibits necessary to sustain it.

2. **Prepare depositions for trial.**

    ____ Determine which witnesses will be presented through the use of depositions.

    ____ Obviously, if a witness is going to testify live or is within the subpoena power, a deposition will not be used. However, all depositions, even those of witnesses who will be testifying live, should be indexed in detail to permit you to have rapid access to the information.

    ____ With respect to those witnesses who will testify via deposition, determine which portions of the deposition will be offered.

    ____ Determine the manner in which the deposition testimony will be offered. For example, will it be read verbatim in open court? Will it be submitted in an underlined form? Will you use narrative deposition summaries? On the last technique, see M. Dombroff, *Dombroff on Demonstrative Evidence* ch. 4 (John Wiley & Sons 1984, 1985 Supp.).

    ____ Make sure that videotape depositions have been edited and prepared for use in the courtroom.

3. **Prepare the client.**

    ____ Whether you represent the plaintiff or the defendant, begin preparation of your client at an early date. Generally, this involves a meeting about what is going to occur up until the point of trial. In addition, you might want to brief your client on the general aspects of being a witness.

____ Provide the client with a copy of any interrogatory answers prepared by him or her, as well as any deposition that he or she has given. This gives the client ample opportunity to review potential grounds of impeachment that may be used by opposing counsel.

4. Update medical examination.

____ If you represent the plaintiff in a personal injury case, you are well advised at this point to have a current medical examination of your client.

____ When representing the defendant, you should seek to have all the medical information updated and, if possible, to have a current medical examination.

5. Prepare nonexpert witnesses.

____ Contact all nonexpert witnesses and interview them by telephone or in person, depending upon the particular witness. Witnesses' statements or depositions should be reviewed, and, when appropriate, witnesses should be supplied with copies of their statements or depositions.

____ Review with each witness all exhibits that will be used with his or her testimony to ensure that he or she fully understands the exhibits.

____ To the extent possible, advise nonexpert, nonparty witnesses of scheduling and seek to clear any conflicts.

30 Days Before Trial

____ Be sure that all relevant government records have been certified.

____ Check to make sure that all weather records have been obtained and that both certified and uncertified copies, as necessary, are available.

____ Make sure that sufficient copies of all documents and other records are available. You should plan on having available at least six copies of any record which you intend to offer into evidence. This includes the original, one for the witness, one for the judge, one for you, one for the court reporter, and one for your opponent. In addition, consider whether additional copies should be available for inclusion in the jury book. See M. Dombroff, *Dombroff on Demonstrative Evidence* § 1.18.

____ Ensure that foundation is available for all records and other documents. In the event that you cannot obtain stipulations with respect to admissibility, make sure that you have a witness available, be it a custodian of records or someone else, who is in a position to testify as to the particular documents.

____ Review all records to determine what material, if any, may require the preparation of motions in limine, particularly with regard to items of evidence which you may want to keep out of the record.

____ Review the investigative report of any government agency to determine what segments of the report are admissible and to determine if there are hearsay problems or statutory bars.

____ Highlight exhibits to flag key portions in order to ensure that the information is readily available to you during the examination of witnesses.

____ File your exhibits in your case organization system in a manner that is case specific. For example, you may wish to set up your exhibit files along the lines of the witnesses who will testify to the particular exhibits. Alternatively, you may wish to set them up by issue or some other means. In any event, make a determination as to how you wish to have the exhibits structured in your file system so that you are able to access them rapidly during trial.

____ Get stipulations from opposing counsel regarding as many exhibits as possible.

____ Prepare short "pocket" briefs on exhibits which you expect will be at issue. Such briefs should be no more than two or three pages long and should be ready to be handed up to the judge during the trial when an evidentiary question is raised as to a particular exhibit.

____ Review all demonstrative evidence for foundation requirements. With respect to each piece of demonstrative evidence, whether it is a chart, graph, diagram, model, or videotape, be sure that you have a foundation package to support its admissibility. Included with this foundation package should be the following:

- A "pocket" brief which addresses the legal discretion of the judge with respect to the particular evidence
- Copies of all information used to prepare the exhibit (for example, in the case of a photograph, the time it was taken, the date, the camera, lens, and film used, and so forth)
- Copies of any deposition testimony which might be needed to support the admissibility of the evidence if a live witness will not testify to foundation. See M. Dombroff, *Dombroff on Demonstrative Evidence.*

____ Prepare medical records for ready access. One of the greatest problems in accessing medical records is that they often are not arranged in any particular form. Consider indexing medical records and tabbing them in several categories such as the following:

- Medical history
- Initial physical examination
- Laboratory reports
- Surgical notes
- Doctors' orders
- Nursing notes
- Progress notes
- Anesthesia notes and records
- Discharge summaries.

15 Days Before Trial

1. Prepare trial objections.

____ Consider the trial objections which may be made and whether an in limine motion or pocket brief may be appropriate.

____ Do some background preparation for the handling and response of those objections. In this regard, see M. Dombroff, *Trial Objections* (Ford Publishing 1985); M. Dombroff, *Trial Hearsay* (Ford Publishing 1985).

2. Prepare your trial brief.

____ In order to be effective, a trial brief must be simple, concise, and well organized. It should contain the following.

a. Facts (Section I). The factual discussion should be as complete as possible with citations to the source of the facts (e.g., depositions, admissions, documents, etc.). The slant of the factual statement should be adversarial and put as favorable an interpretation on them as fairness permits. Remember, you want the judge to utilize your brief as a yardstick against which he or she measures what is unfolding in the courtroom.

Too many lawyers do not recognize the persuasive potential of a clearly written factual statement. Do not fall into the trap of giving short shrift to the facts in favor of the law. By far, most tort actions are factual disputes the successful resolution of which depends on an interpretation of the facts that is favorable to your client.

b. Applicable Law (Section II). In this section you should attempt to parallel, relative to the law, what you have done in Section I relative to the facts. The court should have presented to it, in a persuasive format, the law as you would have it applied to your case. Included within this section should be citations and, where appropriate, excerpts from cases. If there is a case, or a number of cases, which are especially favorable to your position, they should be appended to the trial brief for easy reference by the court.

c. Factual Issues (Section III). Careful attention should be given to framing the factual issues in a manner which gives your position the best chance of prevailing.

For example, assume you represent a merchant in a slip-and-fall action which has, as a central issue, the existence or nonexistence of a pool of water in the vicinity of the fall. Representing the plaintiff in this action, an effective framing of this issue might be, "Was the defendant negligent in permitting a pool of water to accumulate on the floor in the area where the plaintiff slipped and fell?"

If the issue is framed in this fashion and accepted by the court, the defendant is effectively faced with overcoming the presumption that water was on the floor and that the only remaining issue is one of negligence.

Your task in framing the factual issues is to cause the judge to accept your version of what occurred. By doing so, you are in a position to be able to subtly influence evidentiary rulings, instructions to the jury, and, it is to be hoped, the outcome of the case.

d. Legal Issues (Section IV). Legal issues should be presented in much the same way as you present the factual issues in the preceding section: in a fashion calculated to maximize their likely resolution in your favor.

e. Witnesses (Section V). Accompanying each witness's name and identity should be a brief summary of the element(s) of the case to which that witness will testify.

f. Exhibits (Section VI). Exhibits are frequently the central evidence in any case. Since the philosophy of civil litigation has done away with the concept of trial by ambush, all exhibits must usually be made available to opposing counsel prior to trial. The only exception which you will typically find to this broad rule relates to exhibits used for cross-examination, including impeachment, or rebuttal. Similarly, many rules require the completion and submission to the court of exhibit lists prior to trial. This section of the trial brief should contain a listing of all exhibits required to be disclosed. It would also be a good idea, notwithstanding local rules, to include as an attachment to the trial brief an exhibit list for the use of the court during trial.

Sufficient copies should also be available for the court reporter, court clerk, law clerk, and opposing counsel.

The format you should utilize in an exhibit list for the judge is as follows:

COURT NAME
(e.g., In the __________ Court for the
(State) (District) of __________)

Caption } Civil Number

(PLAINTIFF'S) (DEFENDANT'S) EXHIBIT LIST

Exhibit Number	Description	Date Marked For Identification	Date Received Evidence
__________	__________	__________	__________
__________	__________	__________	__________
__________	__________	__________	__________

3. Consider motions in limine.

____ A motion in limine is a "threshold" motion and a vehicle which can be used to obtain evidentiary and other types of rulings from the judge. Focus on various issues which you believe will come up during the trial and are susceptible of resolution prior to the trial.

____ Beyond the ability to obtain a pretrial ruling, one of the advantages to a motion in limine is that you are able, in effect, to educate the judge about the case. Consider which issues might be presented in this manner. See M. Dombroff, *Dombroff on Unfair Tactics* § 2.2 (John Wiley & Sons 1984).

4. Consider motion for summary judgment.

____ You may find it advisable to file a motion for summary judgment as to certain matters that are susceptible of resolution prior to commencement of trial. Often an objection made to a motion for summary judgment filed at an earlier stage is that certain discovery has not yet been taken. However, a motion for summary judgment filed 15 days prior to trial is not really susceptible to such a response. In addition, if it appears to the judge that the case is likely to go to trial, he or she may be more disposed to grant summary judgment on certain issues for the purpose of limiting those issues which are actually tried.

5. **Finalize jury instructions.**

____ You probably should have done your initial draft of jury instructions when you outlined the elements of proof. They should now be finalized in order to ensure that you introduce all required elements supporting a particular instruction.

____ It is always a good idea to file your jury instructions with the judge before the trial begins, even if the judge does not require such a filing. Having such jury instructions permits the judge to better understand the context of the evidence as it is received into the record and to follow your proofs in a logical sequence.

6. **Prepare for selecting the jury.**

____ Begin to think about the kind of jury which you would like to have decide your case. For example, would you prefer men or women, older or younger jurors? What level of education is desirable? Although you may change every element of this preliminary evaluation during the actual jury selection process, at least some forethought in this area will permit you to work from a logical starting place when actually selecting the jury.

____ Begin drafting the voir dire questions which you will use during the jury selection process. If you are trying the case in federal court, it is unlikely that the judge will permit you to ask questions directly of the jury. However, it is not unlikely that the judge will permit you to submit questions to him or her to be asked of the jury. It is surprising how few lawyers participate in the jury selection process in federal court through the device of submitting questions directly to the judge. Accordingly, give thought to the kinds of questions which you would ask if you were in a position to question the jury directly. It is not at all unlikely that the judge will in fact ask the questions.

7. **Prepare subpoenas for all witnesses.**

____ Do this whether or not the witness has already expressed an agreement to testify. In the case of a cooperative witness, simply explain to the witness that the subpoena is a formality and is not to imply that he or she is uncooperative.

____ Be sure that the subpoenas are issued in sufficient time to allow their being served.

____ With respect to nonparty witnesses who are required to take time off from work, consider whether you should offer to reimburse them for their time lost. This is particularly important with respect to eyewitnesses, who normally are third party in nature and have no direct interest in the outcome of the case.

Five Days Before Trial

1. **Know your judge.**

    ____ Whether the case is jury or nonjury, learn everything you possibly can about the judge. Obviously, in the federal system, you may already know a great deal about the judge, because you probably will have appeared before him or her on status conferences, pretrials, and the like.

    ____ Check any of the numerous publications which can give you biographical background and information about the judge, including the *Federal Judiciary Almanac* (John Wiley & Sons) and the *Almanac of the Federal Judiciary* (Law Letters Press, Chicago, IL).

    ____ Consider running a LEXIS or Westlaw search of the judge's prior decisions in order to determine whether he or she has ruled on any similar matters, motions, or related areas on prior occasions.

2. **Know your opposition.**

    ____ Just as you learn about the judge, you should also learn as much as you possibly can about your opponent. Check Martindale-Hubbell to determine whether he or she is listed. Chat with colleagues to determine whether they have had any experience with him or her.

3. **Review the file.**

    ____ At this stage, you should review your *entire* case file at least once. This review is not so much for the purpose of learning anything new, but rather to refresh you as to those items which are in the case file. You would be surprised as to how many things you will pick up in this final review and which will return to you as the evidence unfolds at trial.

4. **Determine your final settlement position.**

    ____ It is not at all unlikely that the judge will focus on settlement one final time prior to commencement of the trial. Review your settlement position and be prepared to take a final settlement position at the trial.

5. **Review order of proof.**

    ____ Review your order of proof one final time to see if it is the most logical and persuasive order which can be achieved.

One Day Before Trial

1. Double check your personal and professional schedules.

____ Ensure that all other professional obligations have been accounted for or otherwise resolved. Make sure that someone is covering your other cases in the office.

____ Make sure your personal obligations are accounted for and that your family understands the nature of the trial process.

2. Double check hotel reservations.

____ If you are trying a case out of town, make sure that all your hotel reservations have been confirmed at an earlier date.

____ Ensure that hotel reservations and other arrangements for witnesses have been taken care of and are double checked.

3. Consider your personal appearance.

____ Think about your clothing for the trial so that you don't have to think about it on a day-to-day basis. This is particularly important if you are going to be out of town.

The foregoing checklist will provide you with a working outline of matters to be considered before commencing a trial. It is not meant to be all inclusive. Rather, it is structured in such a way so as to permit you to add additional elements and time frames as appropriate.

Virtually all litigation is won or lost before the case in the courtroom ever begins. As a result, the well-organized trial lawyer starts off with an advantage that his opponent may never be able to overcome. The key to successful preparation is to insure that none of the details are overlooked. Using this checklist as adapted to your own particular case can help give you the added assurance of knowing that all details have been accounted for prior to trial.

§ 1.67 Trial Notebook

The key to a successful trial notebook is organization and access. As described in Chapter 9 of M. Dombroff, *Litigation Organization and Management: Effective Tactics and Techniques* (Law and Business Inc., Harcourt Brace Jovanovich 1984), the following trial notebook system will give you both speed of access and ready availability of information.

A trial notebook should be everything a yellow pad is not. It should be indexed and organized, easily maintained, built as the case develops, capable of reorganization as the case develops, and, most important, should provide a permanent and easily accessible means for preserving information. Although much has been written about trial notebooks, the ultimate trial notebook has yet to be developed. However, there is an approach to case organization and trial preparation through the use of trial notebooks which possesses a number of advantages. Such a system actually consists of two separate notebooks—one organized by litigation segment (*litigation book*) and the other organized chronologically (*chronological book*).

The day a case becomes a case, when the complaint is either filed or received, the litigation book is established. It is not a substitute for case files, but rather is a working manual or "battle plan." The sections it contains may vary but typically would consist of at least the following:

Discovery
Pretrial motions
Jury selection
Opening statement
Direct case
Expert witnesses
Demonstrative evidence
Exhibits (other than demonstrative exhibits)
Cross examination
Rebuttal case
Closing argument
Jury instructions
Posttrial motions
Costs.

Obviously each section can be further subdivided. Thus, the sections on the direct case of expert witnesses would likely be subdivided by individual witnesses, issues, or proofs.

Within each section of the notebook, a particular portion of the case should be developed. For example, notes on the opening statement, including its outline, should be in that section. As the opening statement is further developed, updated notes and/or drafts can be included until it exists in final outline or whatever form is going to be used at trial.

Cross-references to other sections of the notebook would also be indicated, as would references to exhibits, documents, or depositions in the case. In some instances, copies of transcript or exhibit excerpts might actually be placed in the litigation book. Often the use of plastic page protectors can be used to accomplish this, thereby obviating the need to punch holes in the documents in the event the originals are used.

The great strength of this approach is that the litigation notebook provides a structured means of developing pretrial, trial, and posttrial strategy. It is built as the case progresses and avoids the loss of an idea or thought which may have been recorded but cannot be found. This approach to a trial or litigation notebook is simple enough, but it is all too infrequently utilized. However, an effective trial notebook system does not stop at this point.

The chronological notebook is a second and separate notebook which becomes the permanent repository of all notes from hearings, depositions, and trial. It is established the first time there is some adversarial activity in the case other than the filing of pleadings or discovery. Each activity is entered on an index sheet in the front and each daily section is tabbed with the date. An example of an index sheet might reveal:

Jan 16	Hearing—Motion to Dismiss	2.00
Jan 17	Deposition—John Smith	6.00
Jan 18	Deposition—John Smith	6.00
Jan 19	Pretrial	1.00
Jan 23	Trial—Jury selection openings	5.00
Jan 24	Trial—Direct case Johnson	5.00
Jan 25	Trial—Direct case Johnson Wilson	6.00

The numbers in the right hand column are times and provide a convenient place for collecting billing or timekeeping data. The notes within each section are kept only on the fronts of the pages, with the backs reserved for annotations and trial notes. In this area, the real strength of the dual notebook system manifests itself—the annotation and combining of the litigation and chronological notebooks.

As the litigative process proceeds, those sections of the litigation notebook appropriate to what is occurring are transferred to the chronological notebook. For example, on the day of the opening statements, the opening statement section of the litigation or battle-plan notebook is transferred to the appropriate date section of the chronological notebook. The advantage of this approach is that everything having to do with your opening statement is then located in a single place. The added strength of this technique is that once the case is completed, you have a single comprehensive and chronological record of the case which is highly indexed and of inestimable value for not only the appellate process of this case but also for future cases. If the same witnesses are encountered in other cases, your thoughts and plans regarding those witnesses as well as your notes on their examination are readily retrievable.

In addition to any other benefit, the practical value of this approach at the trial itself is substantial. Because events often unfold with some rapidity in the trial environment, the desirability of shifting from file folder to file folder to yellow pad to notebook is questionable. Although the dual notebook approach is not guaranteed to eliminate the need to shift your focus of attention, it is guaranteed to minimize it, because the pertinent portions of the litigation notebook have already been placed in the chronological notebook prior to the commencement of the trial day.

CHAPTER 2

MOTIONS PRACTICE

§ 2.1 Introduction

There is little question that the bulk of time and money spent in litigation is associated with pretrial discovery. The elimination of "trial by ambush" in civil matters has brought about discovery which is not only long but also expensive. A direct outgrowth of this is the fact that lawyers on all sides often spend an enormous amount of time and effort on the discovery process with an eye toward winning the case on motion during that phase of the litigation. Sometimes this is possible; typically it is not.

In connection with the discovery process, as well as independent of it, motions practice is one of the most crucial and result-producing aspects of a case. If not carefully controlled by you, the motions practice conducted by your opponent can bring some extremely adverse results to your case.

Motions practice conducted by you can have equally disastrous results, inasmuch as you may obtain rulings which, in the process of denying your motions, also destroy the underpinnings of your theory or position. As a result, you must be especially careful not only to guard against motions which are calculated to achieve results for your opponent which, although not dispositive, will substantially weaken your case, but also to guard against bringing motions yourself which will give your opponent an unfair advantage, either in responding to them or in obtaining a ruling.

In general, motions practice by anyone is a risk-benefit proposition. In each case you should measure the result you hope to achieve, if you are fully successful, against the most negative results which can occur if you are totally unsuccessful. For example, as is discussed in **§ 2.6**, summary judgment motions used by your opponent to educate the judge regarding a theory of the case can have a potentially disastrous backfire effect either on their own or with a little help from you. Under the best circumstances for your case, in denying your opponent's motion the judge will, in effect, rule for you or against your opponent's theories. You must be especially careful when dealing with certain types of motions filed by your opponent or when filing those motions yourself that you have not set yourself up.

§ 2.2 In Limine Motions

Generally stated, an *in limine* or *threshold* motion is a device for obtaining preliminary rulings from the court. At least one court has indicated that motions in limine as a procedural device for obtaining evidentiary rulings are not favored. In *Scarboro v. Travelers Ins. Co.,* 91 F.R.D. 21 (E.D. Tenn. 1980), the court felt that the better practice was to deal with evidentiary questions and the admissibility of evidence as they arose during trial. The more enlightened view is that pretrial evidentiary rulings help expedite litigation. As stated by the United States Court of Appeals for the Ninth Circuit in *United States v. Cook,* "prior planning helps both parties and the court." 608 F.2d 1175, 1186 (1979); *see also* Dombroff, *Innovation Needed to Narrow Issues for Litigation,* Legal Times, Mar. 15, 1982, at 15.

Despite the fact that evidentiary matters are the most frequent subject of in limine motions, virtually any aspect of the case can be their subject. In any event, the granting of such motions is in the sound discretion of the court. See *United States v. Certain Land,* 547 F. Supp. 680 (E.D. Mich. 1982). For example, a plaintiff may file an in limine motion to preclude the introduction of a particular kind of evidence at trial on a particular issue, e.g., evidence of a settlement. Alternatively, a motion in limine may be used to preclude the introduction of any evidence on a particular issue. *Vergott v. Deseret Pharmaceutical Co.,* 463 F.2d 12 (5th Cir. 1972). A good example of this situation is an instance in which a party either has failed to respond to discovery requests or has responded in an unsatisfactory manner, and the moving party seeks to preclude the introduction of any evidence on the subject matter of the requests. *United States v. Mucci,* 630 F.2d 737 (10th Cir. 1980). No matter when a motion in limine is used, if granted it has the effect of limiting the issues and evidence at trial and shortening the trial.

One area in which motions in limine are frequently used is to obtain pretrial rulings on the admissibility of trial evidence. The importance of strict compliance with pretrial orders in this regard that require objections to the admissibility of proposed exhibits to be made pretrial is demonstrated by the Eleventh Circuit's decision in *Woods v. Burlington Northern Railroad,* 768 F.2d 1287 (11th Cir. 1985) (per curiam). In this personal injury case, the district court's pretrial order required the parties to exchange exhibit lists prior to trial. The order further provided that, unless written objections were filed with the court within five days after receiving an opposing party's exhibit list, the parties would be deemed to have agreed that each of the items on the exhibit list was admissible at trial.

Despite the pretrial order, no exhibit lists were exchanged in this case. Nevertheless, prior to trial the parties did exchange the actual exhibits they planned to introduce. No objections were filed to the exhibits that were exchanged. At trial, defense counsel objected to one of plaintiffs' exhibits. When asked by the court why no objection to the exhibit had been filed before trial, defense counsel argued that, although the parties had exchanged exhibits, he had not been provided with the exhibit list called for by the pretrial order, and that, therefore, the pretrial order did not require him to file written objections to plaintiffs' exhibits. The district court overruled the objection, noting simply that the pretrial order required objections to exhibits to be made before trial.

On appeal, defense counsel argued that, by enforcing the pretrial order's requirement of written objections prior to trial while waiving the requirement of exchanging exhibit lists, the district court unfairly allowed into evidence inadmissible exhibits. The Eleventh Circuit affirmed enforcement of the order, noting the district court's broad discretion in controlling pretrial procedures. The district court's treatment of the parties' exchange of the exhibits themselves as substantial compliance with the pretrial order's requirement of exchanging exhibit lists was approved as being a reasonable application of the pretrial order. The exhibits in question were held to be properly admissible. Nevertheless, the Eleventh Circuit noted that, even if the exhibits were not otherwise admissible, it would not have considered the district court's actions to be erroneous. Thus, the *Woods* case demonstrates that, by failing to raise objections to exhibits in the manner required by a pretrial order, one may be forever waiving one's right to object to their admission, even if on appeal the exhibits are found to have been otherwise inadmissible.

A motion in limine has been held to be the appropriate vehicle for adjudicating the trustworthiness of findings of fact made in an investigation pursuant to authority created by law. *Zenith Radio Corp. v. Matsushita Electric Industrial Co.,* 505 F. Supp. 1125 (E.D. Pa. 1980). This suggests that admissibility of government investigative reports and similar documents would be a proper subject of an in limine proceeding.

Keeping evidence of subsequent remedial measures from the jury is frequently the subject of in limine motions and was recently the focus of decisions in a number of recent cases.

In *Koonce v. Quaker Safety Products,* 789 F.2d 700 (5th Cir. 1986), the court held that Federal Rule of Evidence 407 barring subsequent remedial measures does not bar evidence of such measures when those measures are undertaken by persons other than the party against whom the evidence is offered. However, it is within the discretion of the trial judge to exclude such evidence under Rule 403 to avoid confusing or misleading the jury.

In *Rocky Mountain Helicopters, Inc. v. Bell Helicopters Textron,* 805 F.2d 907 (10th Cir. 1986), evidence of safety improvements made after an accident were held to be inadmissible. However, the court also held that if certain parts were redesigned as a result of the accident, those redesigns would not be a subsequent remedial measure, and the evidence would be inadmissible.

Finally, in *Albrecht v. Baltimore & Ohio Railroad,* No. 85-1789 (4th Cir. Jan. 5, 1987) the court held that a plaintiff may not include feasibility as an issue and thereafter place evidence of subsequent remedial measures before the jury. Feasibility is not an issue in the case unless and until it is contraverted by the defendant.

Although no rules limit use of in limine motions, several approaches can enhance their effectiveness. For example, coupling motions in limine with requests for admissions or interrogatories provides a foundation for obtaining a favorable order precluding introduction of evidence. Requests for admissions would in fact be framed relative to specific issues in the case. For example, if the answer to the interrogatory "Do you contend that the defendant was negligent in failing to provide further warnings?" is "No," an in limine order precluding the introduction of any evidence on this issue would be appropriate.

Although it may seem that a negative answer to the interrogatory would be sufficient, you run the risk of an argument that additional evidence is now known that justifies a change of position. If, however, an in limine order is granted immediately after either the interrogatories are answered or there has been an admission of no negligence, a change of position is unlikely to be allowed.

In limine motions also are effective when used by a defendant immediately after a complaint is filed to narrow the scope of issues on which discovery must be taken. This can be coupled with requests for admissions or interrogatories; in certain circumstances, it can be filed by itself. In this latter circumstance, however, it is not as likely that the motion will be granted early in the litigation without the taking of any discovery at all.

The reciprocal to filing an in limine motion during the early pleading stage of a case is to file it either at the close of discovery or just prior to trial. The advantage of filing it at either of these times is twofold. First, opposing counsel cannot assert that resolution of the motion is premature, because discovery will have been completed, and second, if opposing counsel argues against the motion in limine, this will probably give you the details of all the trial evidence that will be relied on relative to the issue(s) in question. It is clear that the motion must be made in a timely fashion. See *United States v. Neal,* 692 F.2d 1296 (10th Cir. 1982). However, denial of the motion is not reversible error. In order to preserve all rights on appeal, appropriate and timely objections should be made at trial to those matters which were the subject of the motion in limine. See *Collins v. Wayne Corp.,* 621 F.2d 777 (5th Cir. 1980).Although it has been held that an in limine ruling is not reviewable before a trial on the merits, *United States v. Mack,* 604 F.2d 336 (5th Cir. 1979), it also has been held, in *United States v. Santiago,* 582 F.2d 1128 (7th Cir. 1978), that a matter that has been handled on a motion in limine need not be reconsidered at trial.

Although *Santiago* seems to suggest that appeal rights are preserved without necessity for further objection at trial, prudence dictates that a trial record include the subject matter of the in limine motion or an offer of proof along with appropriate objections.

As with any litigative tactics, there is a risk associated with the filing of a motion in limine. In many respects, this risk is similar to that associated with motions for summary judgment (see **§ 2.6**). There is always the possibility that, after considering the merits of an argument, the court will judge the substance in the context of the motion and, in effect, deal a serious blow to the moving party's case.

The risk analysis that accompanies consideration of a motion in limine must take into account what possible damage can occur to the case if the motion is denied. Although you cannot guard against all eventualities, you can and should recognize them in advance so that you are aware of the worst possible outcome.

Checklist for Filing Motions in Limine

____ **1.** Should the motions be filed?

____ **2.** What are the downside risks?

____ **3.** If denied, will the order result in a damaging decision on the merits of the movant's case or a central issue thereof?

____ **4.** When should the motion be filed?

____ **5.** Can the motion be filed during the early pleading stages of the case in order to effectively limit the scope of discovery?
____ **6.** Would the filing of a motion in limine be more effective at the conclusion of discovery?
____ **7.** What support is there in the record for a motion in limine?
____ **8.** Have interrogatories and/or requests for admission been filed? Have depositions been taken which support the motion?

The form that a motion in limine should take is not significantly different from the form of any other motion. One very important aspect of a motion in limine, whether or not required by rules of procedure, is a proposed order to insure that the preclusion order clearly sets forth those areas of the evidence or those issues that are proscribed. Even if the court does not sign the proposed order, it still provides a guide or format for the court in framing its own order.

In addition to a proposed order, a detailed memorandum with appropriate attachments, including affidavits, should be filed. The later in the discovery process a motion in limine is filed, the more attachments there are likely to be.

Section 2.3 contains a sample motion in limine, supporting memorandum of points and authorities, and order.

§ 2.3 —Sample Motion in Limine

MOTION IN LIMINE

COMES NOW Defendant, Open Air Company, by and through counsel, and hereby moves this Court to limit the testimony of Plaintiff's proposed expert, Mr. C. M. Defendant requests that this Court not permit Mr. M. to testify as to any Federal and/or State regulations allegedly violated by this Defendant. The Plaintiff and Mr. M. have not identified the particular regulations that were allegedly violated by Defendants in the operation of Open Airport. Therefore, this Defendant is unable to prepare for Mr. M.'s testimony at trial and would be prejudiced severely if Mr. M. is allowed to testify at trial on these matters. The Court is respectfully referred to the attached Memorandum of Points and Authorities in support of this Motion.

MEMORANDUM OF POINTS AND AUTHORITIES

This is a suit for personal injuries suffered by the Plaintiff on December 11, 1984 when a Piper Lance in which she was a passenger crashed shortly after take-off from Open Airport in Roanoke, Virginia. Plaintiff alleges that Defendants Open Air Company and J. Open, the operator of the airport, negligently operated and maintained the airport.

The Plaintiff has named Mr. C. M. as an expert on airport safety. Plaintiff, in her Answer to Interrogatories, stated that Mr. M. would "testify that Open Airport was held open for operations while it was in violation of the relevant obstruction criteria and federal and state rules for clear zones . . . ." Plaintiff, however, failed to cite any specific regulations which the Defendants allegedly violated.

Defendant thereafter deposed Mr. M. On examination Mr. M. was unable to identify any specific regulations he was relying on in rendering his opinion. Mr. M., a lawyer, was unable to establish that any federal or state regulations applied to this airport. We submit that Mr. M. should not be permitted to testify as to violations of the unidentified regulations or to testify as an expert on regulations.

It is well settled law in Virginia that the facts must show that an expert possesses sufficient knowledge, skill, or experience to make him competent to testify as an expert on the subject matter of the inquiry. *Noll v. Rahal,* 219 Va. 795, 250 S.E.2d 741, 744 (1979), *citing Commonwealth v. Larkin,* 88 Va. 422, 13 S.E. 901, 902 (1891). *See also* Va. Code § 8.01-401.1(1983). It is within this Court's discretion to determine whether an expert is qualified to express an opinion. *Id.*

Part of the knowledge required of an expert is familiarity with the legal relationship of his opinion to applicable laws and regulations. "[I]t should always be required of an expert that he should at least be sufficiently acquainted with the subject matter of his testimony to know what its laws are, and not merely to conjecture or have an idea about it." 7B *Michie's Jurisprudence* Evidence § 168. In this case, Mr. M., by his own admission, is not competent to testify concerning the applicability of federal and state regulations. Therefore, any testimony in this area which Plaintiff intends to proffer through Mr. M.'s testimony should be inadmissible.

Mr. M. testified in response to questioning by counsel for Defendants that he had not concluded whether Part 77 of the Federal Aviation Regulations applied to Open Airport. *See* M. Deposition Transcript 56, 59. Rather, Mr. M. stated that people from the Federal Aviation Administration or the National Transportation Safety Board would be properly qualified to determine whether the federal regulations applied to Open Airport. *Id.* at 18.

When asked to identify any particular federal regulations which formed the basis for his opinion Mr. M. declined to venture an opinion. He stated that he does not "keep those numbers in the back of [his] head, . . . [and] it's been a long time since I looked at them." *Id.* at 62. Clearly, Mr. M. is not sufficiently acquainted with the federal regulations to be qualified to testify as to their applicability in this case. Therefore, Mr. M.'s testimony must be limited to other areas where the Plaintiff can establish his qualifications and knowledge.

Mr. M.'s testimony concerning the Virginia regulations also showed a complete lack of knowledge concerning the regulations and clearly was inadequate to allow him to testify concerning the regulations at trial. When Mr. M. was asked if he had reviewed the Commonwealth of Virginia's Aeronautical Regulations, he responded that he had seen a pamphlet dealing with the Virginia regulations but he did not pay much attention to the Commonwealth of Virginia material. *Id.* at 60. As a result, Mr. M. was unable to answer counsel's questions as to his opinions on applicability of the Virginia regulations to Open Airport and this accident.

Mr. M.'s inability to testify at deposition concerning the federal and state regulations has frustrated Defendants' efforts to prepare for trial and to cross examine Mr. M. Defendant therefore requests that the Court disallow Mr. M. to testify at trial on the applicability and violations of any federal and state regulations.

ORDER

Upon consideration of Defendant Open Air Company's Motion In Limine and Opposition thereto:

It is this _____ day of __________, 1987,

ORDERED that the aforesaid Motion be and the same is, granted; and it is further

ORDERED that C. M., identified by the Plaintiff as an expert, is precluded from testifying at trial in this case on any matter relating to the applicability or violation of federal or Commonwealth of Virginia regulations in this action.

____

Judge

§ 2.4 Summary Judgment Motions

Rule 56 of the Federal Rules of Civil Procedure and its state counterparts provide for the filing of summary judgment motions. In essence, such motions seek entire or partial dispositions of the case as a matter of law.

Two particular points should be considered. The first is that summary judgment motions may be directed at a disposition of the entire case or at a partial disposition of the case. The second point to be remembered is that summary judgment motions may rely on matters outside the record. In particular, they may rely on affidavits made on personal knowledge setting forth facts which would otherwise be admissible into evidence and establishing that the person making the affidavit is competent to testify to the matter stated in the affidavit. Obviously, the potential for misuse is substantial.

Also to be considered in any discussion of summary judgment motions as a tactic are Rule 12(c) of the Federal Rules of Civil Procedure and its state counterparts which provide for judgment on the pleadings. The significant difference between a motion for judgment on the pleadings and a motion for summary judgment is that a motion for a judgment on the pleadings is confined to the pleadings and may not rely on matters outside the pleadings, such as affidavits. If such a motion does in fact go beyond the pleadings, the rules instruct the court to treat the motion as one for summary judgment.

In many situations, the pleadings that have been filed in a case do not represent the actual state of the litigation. The best example of this is when pleadings have been framed in such adversarial terms as to make it appear that a true controversy exists when in fact there is no such controversy. Alternatively, the pleadings may be drafted to make it appear that no controversy exists. In the latter case, your opponent may take advantage of this situation by filing a motion for judgment on the pleadings which, at least pursuant to the rules, will be decided based on the pleadings. This is an approach which is meant to put you at a disadvantage and get a resolution from the court with less than full disclosure of the facts.

Your response should be to turn your opponent's motion into one for summary judgment by responding to it and including materials outside the pleadings which clearly indicate the existence of a controversy. Such materials may include affidavits, depositions, and other types of discovery.

When the situation is reversed and you find yourself filing a motion for judgment on the pleadings and your opponent attempts to turn it into a summary judgment proceeding by filing affidavits and responses, the appropriate reaction is to point out to the court that your opponent is attempting to turn the instant controversy into a war of affidavits and to divert the court's attention from the true fact that the motion is one for judgment on the pleadings. The downside risk of such a development is that the court may find the factual issue to be truly present and may deny the motion, allowing the litigation to proceed. There is very little that can be done, except to bring your opponent's tactic to the attention of the court and hope for a long-term benefit.

Defense counsel will be particularly interested in a recent case decided by the United States Court of Appeals for the Ninth Circuit. In *Bulthuis v. Rexall Corp.,* 789 F.2d 1315 (1986), the court discussed the interrelationship between Federal Rule of Civil Procedure 56(e), dealing with summary judgment motions, and Rule 705 of the Federal Rules of Evidence.

This action was a products liability action against the manufacturer of diethylstilbestrol (DES) in which the defendants moved for summary judgment. The district court granted summary judgment, declining to consider the affidavits presented by the plaintiff's experts in opposition to the motion. The court determined that the affidavits were insufficient to defeat the summary judgment finding that "a declaration which simply presents an expert opinion without factual support is inadequate to defeat summary judgment." *Id.* at 1317.

Federal Rule of Evidence 705 provides that "the expert may testify in terms of opinion or inference and give his reasons therefor without prior disclosure of the underlying facts or data unless the court requires otherwise." The district court rejected the plaintiff's expert's declaration on the ground that the affidavit did not include facts on which the opinion was based. However, it would appear on its face that the district court's reason for rejecting the expert's affidavit was inconsistent with Rule 705. At a minimum, if the court felt that the affidavit were inadequate, the court should have permitted the plaintiff to supplement the affidavit.

In reversing the district court's finding, the Ninth Circuit found that expert opinion not accompanied by underlying facts or data is admissible and may be used to defeat a summary judgment motion if it appears that the person giving the affidavit is competent to give an expert opinion as to the matters addressed. However, if the trial court requires further facts or determines that such further facts are desirable, the moving party may request and the district court may require their disclosure.

Defense counsel should carefully consider this decision within the context of summary judgment motions, whether they are made by the defendant or against the defendant. In either event, there must be a reconciliation between the requirements of Federal Rule of Civil Procedure 56(e) and Federal Rule of Evidence 705. A failure to recognize the interrelationship between the two can result in a problem.

On June 25, 1986, the Supreme Court decided a case which should prove to be of significant assistance to trial counsel in all types of civil litigations. *Celotex Corp. v. Catrett,* 477 U.S. ——, 91 L. Ed. 2d 265, arose out of the 1979 death of the plaintiff's husband allegedly due to his exposure to certain asbestos products which were, according to the complaint, manufactured or distributed by the defendants including Celotex Corp.

Suit was filed September 1980, and one year later the defendant filed a motion for summary judgment pursuant to Rule 56 of the Federal Rules of Civil Procedure. The motion asserted that, during the discovery process, the plaintiff had failed to develop any evidence to support the allegation that her husband had been exposed to any products manufactured or distributed by Celotex.

In opposing the motion made by Celotex, the plaintiff produced some documents which tended to show such exposure, but the defendant asserted that the documents were inadmissible as hearsay and thus could not be considered by the district court in deciding the motion.

The district court granted the summary judgment motion in July 1982, holding that there was an absence of any evidence demonstrating exposure by the decedent to the defendant's products.

On appeal, the United States Court of Appeals for the District of Columbia reversed and held that the grant of summary judgment was improper due to the defendant's failure to support its motion with affirmative evidence tending to negate such exposure. In reversing, the Court of Appeals relied, at least in part, on Rule 56(e).

The Supreme Court, in its decision of June 25, 1986, squarely rejected the decision of the Court of Appeals and handed a major victory to the defendant in *Celotex.* The Court found the decision of the Court of Appeals to be inconsistent with the standard for summary judgment prescribed in Rule 56(c) which provides that summary judgment is proper "if the pleadings, depositions, answers to interrogatories, and admissions on file, together with the affidavits, if any, show that there is no genuine issue as to any material fact and that the moving party is entitled to judgment as a matter of law." In doing so, the Court found that the plain language of Rule 56(c) mandates the entry of summary judgment after the plaintiff has had adequate time for discovery and the plaintiff fails to make a showing sufficient to establish the existence of an element essential to the plaintiff's case and on which the plaintiff will bear the burden of proof at trial. The Court rejected the Court of Appeals' position that Rule 56 imposes a requirement upon the moving party to support its motion with affidavits or other materials negating the plaintiff's claim. As the Court found:

> Rule 56 must be construed with due regard not only for the rights of persons asserting claims and defenses that are adequately based in fact to have those claims and defenses tried to a jury, but also for the rights of persons opposing such claims and defenses to demonstrate in the manner provided by the Rule, prior to trial, that the claims and defenses have no factual basis.

91 L. Ed. 2d at 269.

The Supreme Court reversed and remanded the decision of the Court of Appeals with instructions that it determine whether an adequate showing of exposure by the decedent to the defendant's product had been made in opposition to the motion for summary judgment and whether such a showing, if admissible, would be sufficient to carry the burden of proof for the plaintiff at trial.

Celotex represents a recent pronouncement of the Supreme Court on the use of summary judgment motions as a device to resolve cases. The usual situation in which a summary judgment is made is, as in *Celotex,* a defendant seeking a preliminary resolution of a case without trial but after the plaintiff has had an opportunity to take discovery. In such situations, especially in cases which revolve around factual disputes, it has appeared in the past that many courts have been reluctant to grant summary judgment. In most cases, that reluctance has centered on the party against whom the summary judgment motion is made when that party opposes the motion by asserting that either there is additional discovery yet to be taken or the defendant has not offered or developed evidence which contradicts the plaintiff's theory or simply that the issue is not appropriate for a summary disposition.

In large measure, *Celotex* goes a long way forward in making it less likely that such situations will occur and that a summary judgment motion will be denied. As Justice Brennan pointed out, the burden upon the moving party in a summary judgment situation is to demonstrate to the court that "the nonmoving party's evidence is insufficient to establish an essential element of the nonmoving party's claim. . . . If the nonmoving party cannot muster sufficient evidence to make out its claim, a trial would be useless and the moving party is entitled to summary judgment as a matter of law." *Id.* 279.

Given the decision in *Celotex,* parties moving for summary judgment would be well advised not only to recognize the risks and benefits of summary judgment motions but also to keep in mind a number of tactical aspects associated with such motions.

§ 2.5 —Timing

Timing of the filing of a motion for summary judgment can be particularly important. The plaintiff may file such a motion after 20 days following the filing of the complaint; a defendant can file at any time. In either case, a party against whom a summary judgment motion has been filed can be at a disadvantage, because the time of the battle is chosen by the moving party within the provisions of the rules.

Recognizing the predisposition of many judges to resolve a case early without expending large amounts of judicial time, your response to a summary judgment motion which has been filed at a preliminary state of the case should be not only substantive but also directed at the timing question.

The obvious advantage to filing a summary judgment motion early is the chance to get a resolution of the case before the facts have developed. Your response should point out that, even though the rules permit summary judgment motions to be filed early in litigation, it would not be appropriate for the court to resolve the particular case on a summary judgment proceeding. In support of this response, you should be prepared not only to point out the tactic pursued by your opponent, i.e., an early resolution without a full airing of the facts, but also to file an affidavit from either a potential witness or yourself which sets forth factual issues justifying denial of your opponent's motion.

§ 2.6 —As an Educational Tool

One factor to consider in the filing of any summary judgment motion is that such motions can often educate your opponent about the merits of your case when you are the moving party. Because you will be relying on materials that are both within the record and outside the record to support your motion and will be asking for a judgment as a matter of law, you will frequently find yourself exposing far more about your case than you would otherwise wish to expose.

A tactic which you may encounter is that your opponent may file a summary judgment motion which, although complete on its face, reveals very little about your opponent's case, because the purpose of filing a summary judgment motion is not so much to get a favorable disposition as to require you in your response to lay out your case and show your hand to your opponent.

Unfortunately, there are many, many occasions when you will be unable to definitively ascertain from the face of the moving papers your opponent's motive in filing. However, in responding to summary judgment motions, you should pay particular care to the manner in which you are exposing your case, keeping in mind that the summary judgment motion itself may be used to obtain disclosure rather than as a tactic for disposition.

Remember, if the motion really has no chance of being granted and yet you have been successful in drawing out your opponent in terms of fact, opinions, and other materials in support of the case, you may have accomplished much of your trial preparation.

§ 2.7 Inadmissible Supporting Materials

A favorite tactic of many litigants in motions practice, particularly summary judgment motions, is to include materials in support of the motion that would otherwise be inadmissible under the rules of evidence. This is an important "back door" into the record.

Virtually all rules covering the filing of summary judgment motions, including Federal Rule of Civil Procedure 56, provide that, for example, supporting affidavits must be made on personal knowledge and demonstrate that the person making the affidavit is competent to testify to the matters stated in the affidavit. Accordingly, there would seem to be a number of categories of items which are not proper supporting material for summary judgment motions either independently or by inclusion in an affidavit, for example, hearsay evidence, conclusions of law, or, depending on the competence of the individual making the affidavit, opinions. However, you should not construe the fact that these are improper bases for a summary judgment motion as indicating that they are not in fact used as the bases of a summary judgment motion.

You should be especially leery of summary judgment motions supported by attorney affidavits premised on information and belief as opposed to personal knowledge. Clearly, at least according to Federal Rule of Civil Procedure 56, this is an improper supporting basis for a summary judgment motion. Again, however, the fact that this may be an improper basis for a summary judgment motion does not mean that your opponent will not use it, and, indeed, the use of attorney affidavits is relatively common.

The approach to take when your opponent attempts to use evidence in support of a summary judgment motion which is inadmissible in its substantive form or inadmissible in the form in which it is being filed, e.g., an attorney's affidavit, is to point out to the judge the attempts which your opponent is making to cure what are obvious defects in the case through use of inadmissible evidence. Furthermore, you should not permit such inadmissible assertions to remain in the record. If there are aspects of the summary judgment motion which are well supported, you might consider moving to strike those portions which are improper.

Your aim is to eliminate the inadmissible evidence from the record, because such evidence has a way of surfacing again when referred to by your opponent in the context of another proceeding. You want to guard against giving any improperly introduced evidence validity which it does not otherwise have.

§ 2.8 Order of Proof: Changing the Rules of the Game

Trial judges in both the state and federal systems have a tremendous amount of discretion. An important area of discretion to expedite proceedings involves the question of consolidation of cases for trial or separate trials. This point is addressed within the federal system in Rule 42 of the Federal Rules of Civil Procedure, which gives trial judges the power to have joint trials when there are common questions of law or fact or to "make such orders concerning proceedings therein as may tend to avoid unnecessary costs or delay." In addition, trial judges within the federal system and most state systems are empowered to allow for separate trials when this would be conducive to the expeditious and economic disposition of justice. Finally, trial judges may order separate trials of any claim, cross-claim, counterclaim, or third-party claim, or of any separate issue or any number of claims, cross-claims, counterclaims, third-party claims, or issues if to do so would be consistent with the expeditious and economic disposition of justice.

Applying Rule 42 of the Federal Rules of Civil Procedure or any of its state counterparts is usually no problem for trial judges. However, it can pose a substantial problem for *you* if your opponent seeks to use the discretion of the judge to move a case along in a manner which substantially prejudices your position. For example, by motion to invoke the discretion of the court, your opponent may seek to either reorder the trial, e.g., to deal with damages before liability, or change the order of proof, thereby in effect shifting the burden of proof. The latter tactic often can be effectively pursued by plaintiffs who have sued multiple defendants who, in turn, have filed cross-claims among themselves.

The motion filed by the plaintiff under such circumstances would be to change the order of proof and essentially have a separate and first trial on the issue of cross-claims. The justification for such a motion is that by litigating the cross-claims in the first instance and establishing liability among defendants, there is a possibility that no trial of the plaintiff versus the defendants will be necessary. As characterized by the plaintiff in such circumstances, the litigation is essentially a dispute among the defendants as to how much of the loss, if any, each should bear and not whether any or all of them are liable to the plaintiff.

The obvious effect of such a motion is to shift the burden of proof to the defendants, allowing the plaintiff to become simply a spectator to the litigation. It is imperative that you be aware of this tactic when representing a defendant. The proper response is to redirect the court's attention to the basic question at issue—namely, whether one or more of the defendants is liable to the plaintiff and whether the plaintiff can meet its burden of proof as to one or more of the defendants. By granting the plaintiff's motion, the court will eliminate this latter and preliminary requirement and turn the litigation into a matter of contribution rather than that of the plaintiff's proving liability and damages in the first instance.

To combat such motions effectively, it may be necessary for the defendants to temporarily lay aside their differences and join in a common opposition. This is frequently the best and most effective approach, because it highlights the fact that the litigation is basically plaintiff versus defendant and not defendant versus defendant.

§ 2.9 Sanctions Motions

Motions practice is one aspect of pretrial proceedings which can take an inordinate amount of time and attention, depending on your opponent. Although the device of motions, whatever their character, is generally used to get interim rulings from a judge on matters smaller than the entire case, there is an aspect of motions and a segment to motions practice which have greater implications.

Several kinds of motions are used to seek relief from the court in the nature of characterizing an opponent as violating the procedures of discovery or orders of court. Thus, when a party files a sanctions motion or certain type of discovery motion, such as a motion to compel, the implication is that the party against whom it is filed is guilty of some wrongdoing. Such a motion immediately requires that the latter party come forward and prove to the court that the relief being sought is not warranted.

From the movant's point of view, the strength of such a motion is that it puts an opponent on the defensive and, in addition, clearly casts suspicion on opposing counsel. In many circumstances, such motions are filed simply for tactical reasons and do not have any necessary relationship to what is actually transpiring at a given time.

It is important when confronting motions of this type, filed without a complete foundation and for the purpose of establishing a broad picture, to deal with the specific allegations on a point-by-point basis and thereby avoid meeting your adversary on a battleground chosen by him or her for prejudicial purposes.

One of the most effective preventive techniques for accomplishing this goal, while at the same time responding in a manner calculated to do you the most good, is to maintain a log during the discovery process of all the efforts which you have made to respond to discovery or to work out discovery differences with your opponents. Such a log could include copies of all correspondence between you and your opponent attempting to resolve discovery disputes. Sanctions and other types of discovery motions filed for the purpose of prejudicing your cause frequently deal in generalities. Your ability to respond with detailed statements of what really happened will often turn the tables on your opponent.

Another technique for protecting yourself against motions of this type is to maintain a telephone log of all conversations which may relate to a particular case. This puts you in an excellent position to reconstruct events. Finally, your conduct of discovery sessions, especially production sessions, on the record (along with the written responses to all such discovery requests addressed to you) is always a substantial benefit in attempting to reconstruct the record later.

One tactic sometimes attempted in responding to discovery motions of this type is to file a countermotion. Frequently, this is not a good tactic to pursue, because it can prejudice you and make it appear as if your taking the offensive through the countermotion is nothing more than an attempt to cloud the issues.

Denial of a discovery motion filed against you can frequently be a far greater benefit than the granting of your countermotion, because your opponent will lose credibility with the court, and, in the event that a true discovery dispute arises in which your position is not sound, your opponent may not be in a position to make a second trip to court.

There are several tactical and practical considerations to remember in dealing with sanctions motions, motions to compel, and similar types of discovery motions:

1. Deal with each allegation on a specific and detailed basis.
2. Do not make general responses painted with a broad brush.
3. Attach as many supporting documents to your response as possible, including copies of correspondence, copies of discovery pleadings, transcript excerpts, or, when appropriate, affidavits.

4. Clearly consider whether you should file a countermotion or responsive motions. The downside risk of this is that it may be characterized as a tactic to unjustifiably shift the attention of the court. Often it is better simply to meet your opponent's allegations head-on and point out to the court how frivolous they really are.
5. Always attach a proposed order to your responsive pleadings specifically detailing precisely what action you wish the court to take in dealing with your opponent's motion.
6. If possible, without being too obvious about how you accomplish it, characterize your opponent's motions as a personal attack on you as distinguished from a justified attempt to seek the aid of the court in a valid discovery dispute.
7. Always step back from the dispute in question and judge its merits as they will be perceived by a third person, i.e., the judge. Remember, in the thick of the battle you are sometimes not the best person to determine the merits of allegations directed at you or your position. If your opponent loses the motion, his or her credibility will be severely impaired before the court, especially if you are able to shape the judge's response. By the same token, however, if you lose the motion, your credibility will be similarly impaired.

For detailed discussion of sanctions motions, see **Chapter 4**.

§ 2.10 Aggressive Litigation Tactics and Disqualification of Counsel

One of the most aggressive tactics that can be pursued in litigation is to seek the disqualification of opposing counsel. A situation which may give rise to a motion seeking disqualification is when opposing counsel is or is likely to be a witness in the case. Under such circumstances not only is the individual attorney subject to disqualification, but the attorney's firm is as well.

The new American Bar Association Model Rules of Professional Conduct (Mode 1 Rules) on the attorney-witness situation provide in (a)(1)–(3), Rule 3.7, 52 U.S.L.W. 19 (Aug. 16, 1983) that:

> . . . [a] lawyer shall not act as an advocate at a trial in which the lawyer is likely to be a necessary witness except where: (1) the testimony relates to an uncontested issue; (2) the testimony relates to the nature and value of legal services rendered in the case; or (3) disqualification of the lawyer would work substantial hardship on the client.

However, the new Model Rules do permit an attorney to appear in a trial in which another lawyer from his or her firm is likely to be called as a witness. The exception to this is when there is a conflict of interest with the attorney's client or another client of the firm. Model Rules of Professional Conduct Rule 3.7(b), 52 U.S.L.W. 19 (Aug. 16, 1983).

These new rules issued by the ABA, which are subject to adoption by individual jurisdictions, replace former DR 5-102(A) of the Code of Professional Responsibility (Code) which provided for the disqualification of not only the individual attorney but the firm as well. DR 5-101(B)(4) however, provided for the same type of "substantial hardship" exception as is provided for in the Model Rules.

Because both the new and the old rules contemplate disqualification at trial, as distinguished from pretrial, the timing associated with making and resolving a disqualification motion is important. This is easily understood because disqualification must be premised upon the issues of the particular case. Because the issues and related facts are frequently not fully disclosed or known until after discovery, any attempt to disqualify counsel prior to the trial stage would be premature. *See, e.g., Beaver Falls Thrift Corp. v. Commercial Credit Business Loans, Inc.,* 563 F. Supp. 68 (W.D. Pa. 1983); *Miller Electric Construction, Inc. v. Devine Lighting Co.,* 421 F. Supp. 1023 (W.D. Pa. 1976).

The irony of courts recognizing that disqualification is such a drastic step that they will refuse to rule on motions seeking it until after discovery is completed is that the potentially disqualified attorney is put in a better position to seek a substantial hardship exception. Assuming that disqualification would be proper, it is evident that counsel would be more easily replaced prior to the completion of what can prove to be long and complex discovery and pretrial proceedings. If the issue is not confronted by the court until after discovery is completed, a substantial hardship which may not have existed before discovery will virtually always be argued to exist after discovery.

The ABA itself has, in some sense, sanctioned this created hardship exception. In Formal Opinion 339 (1975), the ABA Committee on Ethics and Professional Responsibility recognized the unfairness to a client if it is compelled to obtain new trial counsel, incur additional expense, and possibly seek a later trial date, all because counsel has been disqualified after discovery is completed. In *Kenosha Automobile Transport Corp. v. United States,* 206 Ct. Cl. 888 (1975), the court held that a substantial hardship would exist if counsel were disqualified after two years of extensive pretrial investigations. A similar result was reached in *Ross v. Great Atlantic & Pacific Tea Co.,* 447 F. Supp. 406 (S.D.N.Y. 1978), which recognized that disqualification should be avoided if possible, because a party has an interest in retaining counsel of choice, particularly when counsel's service to the client has been long and faithful.

In light of the fact that the disqualification of trial counsel is such a serious step, there are a number of considerations to keep in mind when dealing with such situations. These are particularly important because moves to disqualify opposing counsel, rightly or wrongly, have become a regular weapon in the litigator's arsenal.

1. Distinct from the plain words of the applicable rule, the standard to be argued for is one which will most insure fairness to all in the litigation. *See, e.g., Freschi v. Grand Coal Venture,* 564 F. Supp. 414 (S.D.N.Y. 1983); *Greenbaum-Mountain Mortgage Co. v. Pioneer National Title Insurance Co.,* 421 F. Supp. 1348 (D. Colo. 1976).
2. Can disqualification be avoided by fashioning an alternative means of relief? For example, in *Schaible v. Michigan Mutual Insurance Co.,* 321 N.W.2d 860 (Mich. 1982), counsel who was called as a witness was disqualified, but his firm was not, and he was allowed to sit at counsel table.
3. From the perspective of an attorney whose disqualification is being sought, can an argument be made that resolution of the motion ought to be delayed until the completion of discovery?
4. From a movant's perspective, will a substantial hardship exception be created if resolution of the motion is delayed until after discovery? If so, can an offer of proof or some other means be devised to put the issue before the judge at an early stage, thus preventing a bootstrap defense to disqualification?
5. What are the downside risks versus the benefits of attempting to get an opposing law firm and/or attorney disqualified? For example, does it really do you any good, especially when there are multiple firms on the other side? Will you have to coexist with that attorney and/or firm, and, through your motion, are you irrevocably poisoning that relationship? Do you really have grounds for a disqualification, or are you simply making it as a tactical move? If the latter, are you running the risk of making an enemy of the judge?
6. Is there a procedural means for defining a disqualification situation or, at a minimum, containing it? For example, can the parties or issues be severed or bifurcated for trial pursuant to Federal Rule of Civil Procedure 42, thus minimizing those areas of the case which will be impacted by a disqualification?

There is little doubt but that aggressive litigators will continue to use disqualification of opposing counsel as a trial weapon. However, the ramifications of this tactic to the bar at large are so significant that one must be fully knowledgeable about it before using it as an offensive weapon designed not so much to carry the day with your case as to remove the other side's warrior from the field of battle.

The comment to Model Rule 37(a)(3), 52 U.S.L.W. 20 (Aug. 16, 1983) provides:

> A balancing is required between the interests of the client and those of the opposing party. Whether the opposing party is likely to suffer prejudice depends on the nature of the case, the importance and probable tenor of the lawyer's testimony, and the probability that the lawyer's testimony will conflict with that of other witnesses. Even if there is a risk of such prejudice, in determining whether the lawyer should be disqualified due regard must be given to the effect of disqualification on the lawyer's client.

The ABA's new attorney-witness Model Rule provides that

> [a] lawyer shall not act as advocate at a trial in which the lawyer is likely to be a necessary witness except where: (1) the testimony relates to an uncontested issue; (2) the testimony relates to the nature and value of legal services rendered in the case; or (3) disqualification of the lawyer would work substantial hardship on the client.

Model Rules of Professional Conduct Rule 3.7(a)(1-3), 52 U.S.L.W. 19 (Aug. 16, 1983). The ABA's new rule expressly permits "[a] lawyer [to] act as advocate in a trial in which another lawyer in the lawyer's firm is likely to be called as a witness unless precluded from doing so by [a conflict of interest with his client or another client]." Model Rules of Professional Conduct Rule 3.7(b), 52 U.S.L.W. 19 (Aug. 16, 1983).

The former ABA rule on the attorney-witness issue in the code provides that

> [i]f after undertaking employment in contemplated or pending litigation, a lawyer learns or it is obvious that he or a lawyer in his firm ought to be called as a witness on behalf of his client, he shall withdraw from the conduct of the trial and his firm, if any, shall not continue representation in the trial.

Code of Professional Responsibility DR 5-102(A)(1974). The Code also contains essentially the same exceptions to disqualification as in the Model Rules. *See* Code of Professional Responsibility DR 5-101(B)(1-4)(1979). The substantial hardship exception in the Code provided that disqualification of an attorney and his or her firm was not appropriate if such disqualification "would work a substantial hardship on the client because of the distinctive value of the lawyer or his firm as counsel in the particular case." Code of Professional Responsibility DR 5-101(B)(4)(1979).

It should also be noted that courts do not mechanically apply the rules of professional conduct as adopted by any jurisdiction, and that is true when the federal court's rules adopt the rules of professional conduct of the local jurisdiction. *E.g., International Electronics Corp. v. Flanser,* 527

F.2d 1288, 1293 (2d Cir. 1975) (indicating that the court did not consider itself bound by a modification of the ABA attorney-witness rule even though that modification had been adopted by the local jurisdiction and by the district court); *Freschi v. Grand Coal Venture,* 564 F. Supp. at 417 n.2 (in refusing to disqualify plaintiff's law firm on the ground that a member of a branch office was likely to be a plaintiff, the court relied on Rule 3.7 of the Proposed Final Draft of the ABA's Model Rules of Professional Conduct, which has now been adopted as the ABA's present attorney-witness rule); *see Greenbaum-Mountain Mortgage Co. v. Pioneer National Title Insurance Co.,* 421 F. Supp. at 1351.

Rather, the critical question in deciding an attorney-witness issue is what procedure will most likely result in the litigation being "conducted in fairness to all." *E.g., Freschi v. Grand Coal Venture; Greenbaum-Mountain Mortgage Co. v. Pioneer National Title Insurance Co.,* 421 F. Supp. at 1353. To resolve that question, the court should "examine afresh" the considerations bearing upon possible disqualification and consequences of any disqualification. *E.g., International Electronics Corp. v. Flanser,* 527 F.2d at 1293; *Greenbaum-Mountain Mortgage Co. v. Pioneer National Title Insurance Co.,* 421 F. Supp. at 1351. Because the ABA itself has newly examined the attorney-witness issue and adopted a new rule on the subject, that new rule should be given great weight by courts deciding attorney disqualification issues.

Courts generally refrain from deciding attorney disqualification issues at an early stage of a case. Both the new Model Rules and the former Code are concerned only with disqualification of counsel *at trial,* when counsel may be a witness. Model Rules of Professional Conduct Rule 3.7(a), 52 U.S.L.W. 19 (Aug. 16, 1983); Code of Professional Responsibility (DR 5-102(A)(1979). *E.g., Beaver Falls Thrift Corp. v. Commercial Credit Business Loans, Inc.,* 563 F. Supp. at 70–71 (refusing to rule on a motion to disqualify an attorney prior to discovery); *Smith v. New Orleans Federal Savings & Loan Association,* 474 F. Supp. 742, 750–51 (E.D. La. 1979) (refusing to rule on such a motion prior to deposition of lawyer whose disqualification was at issue); *Miller Electric Construction, Inc. v. Devine Lighting Co.,* 421 F. Supp. at 1023–24 (refusing to rule on such a motion prior to discovery on substantive issues).

No decision to disqualify an attorney for purposes of trial should be made on the strength of barebones pleadings. *Cf. Bottaro v. Hatton Associates,* 680 F.2d 895, 896 (2d Cir. 1982); *Ross v. Great Atlantic & Pacific Tea Co.,* 447 F. Supp. at 409 (both stating that disqualification is a drastic step which should be avoided if possible). Dispositive motions filed after the pleadings may end the prospect of trial altogether. A partial summary judgment could limit the nature of the issues to be tried, and thereby either eliminate any need for attorney testimony or limit the range of the testimony in a way that makes it abundantly plain that disqualification is unduly burdensome. Furthermore, the nature and scope of the issues to be tried—and the identity of facts in dispute or not in dispute—cannot be determined until discovery has been taken. *See, e.g., Beaver Falls Thrift Corp. v. Commercial Credit Business Loans, Inc.,* 563 F. Supp. at 70–71; *Smith v. New Orleans Federal Savings & Loan Association,* 474 F. Supp. at 750–51; *Miller Electric Construction, Inc. v. Devine Lighting Co.,* 421 F. Supp. at 1023.

In sum, courts generally refrain from disqualifying counsel without knowing what issues may be tried, what subjects may be testified to by attorneys, what the nature of or need for that testimony will be, and, most important, what hardship will be imposed on a client if the attorney were disqualified as trial counsel. All of these issues are relevant to the issue of disqualification. *See, e.g.,* Model Code of Professional Conduct Rule 3.7(a)(3) comment, 52 U.S.L.W. 20 (Aug. 16, 1983):

> [A] balancing is required between the interests of the client and those of the opposing party. Whether the opposing party is likely to suffer prejudice depends on the nature of the case, the importance and probable tenor of the lawyer's testimony, and the probability that the lawyer's testimony will conflict with that of other witnesses. Even if there is risk of such prejudice, in determining whether the lawyer should be disqualified due regard must be given to the effect of disqualification on the lawyer's client.

A court, at a minimum, should delay ruling on attorney disqualification until discovery has concluded and any dispositive motions have been decided, because only then will it be in a sound position to decide the critical disqualification issue—whether the hardship imposed on the parties outweighs the need for disqualification. In considering such hardship, the court must weigh the impact of disqualification on both the attorney's client and the opposing party. Model Rules of Professional Conduct Rule 3.7(a)(3), 52 U.S.L.W. 19 (Aug. 16, 1983). To decide that issue properly, a court needs to know which issues are to be tried and the type of evidence needed to try those issues. The former consideration requires pretrial rulings on motions; the latter requires discovery.

Both the new Model Rules and the former Code recognize a substantial hardship exception to the general requirement that an attorney who will be a witness at a trial should not act as trial counsel. The substantial hardship exception may be somewhat broader under the Model Rules than under the Code. The Model Rules provide simply that disqualification of a lawyer is not appropriate when the disqualification "would work substantial hardship on the client," while the Code indicates that the hardship to the client must result from "the distinctive value of the lawyer or his firm as counsel in the particular case." Model Rules of Professional Conduct Rule 3.7(b), 52 U.S.L.W. 19 (Aug. 16, 1983); Code of Professional Responsibility DR 5-101(b)(94) (1979).

In ABA Formal Opinion 339 (1975), the ABA Committee on Ethics and Professional Responsibility set forth the underlying purposes of the attorney-witness rule and explained the substantial hardship exception. That opinion notes that the exception should be involved "where a complex suit has been in preparation over a long period of time and a development which could not be anticipated makes the lawyer's testimony essential." *Id.* at 3. According to ABA Formal Opinion 339, it would be "manifestly unfair to the client" in such circumstances if he were "compelled to seek new trial counsel at substantial additional expense and perhaps to have to seek a delay of the trial." *Id. Accord, Chuck v. St. Paul Fire & Marine Insurance Co.,* 606 F.2d 1320 (Haw. 1980). In *Chuck,* the defense required the trier of fact to revisit litigation which "involved numerous individual claims and a factual background spanning the course of over ten years." The court held that "loss of [the attorney] and his peculiar knowledge of the facts underlying the charges made [in the earlier litigation] will undoubtedly work a substantial hardship [on the plaintiff's] ability to present this case." *Id.* at 1325. *See also Kenosha Automobile Transport Corp. v. United States,* 206 Ct. Cl. 888, 891 (1975) (disqualification of counsel after two years of "extensive pretrial investigations" would work a substantial hardship); *Ross v. Great Atlantic & Pacific Tea Co.,* 447 F. Supp. at 409 (fashioning a remedy other than disqualification because "the plaintiffs have an interest in retaining the services of the counsel of their choice" and "this interest is particularly compelling, in light of the long and faithful services [counsel] has rendered to the [client]"). The *Ross* case is an example of the well-established principle that attorney disqualification is a drastic step which should be avoided whenever possible. *See also, Bottaro v. Hatton Associates,* 680 F.2d at 896. In light of that principle, courts should attempt to shape an alternative remedy to disqualification which will assure fairness to the parties and integrity to the judicial process. E.g., *Ross; Greenbaum-Mountain Mortgage Co. v. Pioneer National Title Insurance Co.,* 421 F. Supp. at 1351.

In addition to the foregoing considerations, the new ABA attorney-witness Model Rule expressly provides that "[a] lawyer may act as advocate in a trial in which another lawyer in the lawyer's firm is likely to be called as a witness." Rule 3.7(b), 52 U.S.L.W. 19. This new rule, which prevents disqualification of a firm, is based on the ABA's conclusion that "[t]he interests protected by the rule are not endangered where one lawyer appears as a witness and another [in his firm] as advocate." ABA Commission on Evaluation of Professional Standards, Model Rules of Professional Conduct 152 (Proposed Final Draft May 30, 1981); *see* Wydick, *Trial Counsel as Witness: The Code and the Model Rules,* 15 U.C. Davis L. Rev. 651, 659–65, 675–80 (1982). Thus, if a court applies the new rule, it will not be confronted with the question of whether entire law firms are disqualified.

The former ABA attorney-witness rule, by its terms, authorized disqualification of a lawyer's firm if a lawyer in the firm was disqualified. If a court were to apply the old rule, it should generally read the substantial hardship exception of that rule in light of the fact that the ABA itself has now flatly rejected disqualification of the firm as overbroad and unnecessary to carry out the policies of the rule. *See Freschi v. Grand Coal Venture,* 564 F. Supp. at 417 n.2 (in refusing to disqualify plaintiff's law firm on the ground that a member of a branch office was likely to be a plaintiff, the court relied on Rule 3.7 of the Proposed Final Draft of the ABA's Rules of Professional Conduct, which has now been adopted as the ABA's new attorney-witness rule); *International Electronics Corp. v. Flanser,* 527 F.2d at 1293 (indicating that the court was not bound by a modification to the ABA attorney-witness rule even though that modification had been adopted by the local jurisdiction and by the local rules of the district court). *See also In re A.,* 554 F.2d 479 (Or. 1976) court analyzed a case involving withdrawal of counsel in light of the ABA's 1974 amendment to its applicable disciplinary rule although that disciplinary rule had not been adopted by the state bar association).

Even before the ABA rejected disqualification of an attorney's firm, courts refrained from disqualifying the firm when that would impose substantial hardship on the client. *Greenbaum-Mountain Mortgage Co. v. Pioneer National Title Insurance Co.,* 421 F. Supp. at 1353–54; *Freschi v. Grand Coal Venture,* 564 F. Supp. at 417–18; *see International Electronics Corp. v. Flanser,* 527 F.2d at 1293 (firm not disqualified from representing former partner who was a defendant because, among other things, disqualification was not necessary to carry out the purposes of the rule); *Schaible v. Michigan Mutual Insurance Co.,* 321 N.W.2d 860 (Mich. 1982) (although counsel called as a witness was disqualified, he was allowed to sit at counsel table and his firm was allowed to continue representation of the client).

The answer to what can be a difficult predicament for counsel is to guard against the situation in which you find yourself having to form part of the foundation for a particular evidence. Keep in mind at the formative stages of litigation what evidence is going to be needed and, more important, what foundation considerations will be encountered in getting that evidence received into the record. If you are in a situation in which, due to time or other constraints, it is necessary for an attorney to be directly involved in the evidence-gathering process, turn the task over to a colleague who will be in a position, if necessary, to testify to foundation considerations. Do not put yourself in a situation in which, even if you prevail, you are leaving it up to the judge to determine the question of disqualification.

§ 2.11 Motions for Costs

Perhaps no single issue in the legal profession today generates as much peripheral litigation as discovery and its attendant costs. Litigation by its very nature is an expensive process and, in far too many instances, the expense associated with the process bears little relationship to the substantive matters at issue.

In recent years, a number of amendments to the Federal Rules of Civil Procedure have been directed at minimizing discovery proceedings and their attendant costs. At best, these recent amendments are of problematical effectiveness. Although they do a great deal to encourage litigants to be more economical and to resolve litigation in a shorter time, they tend to rely on recommendations and judicial discretion to accomplish their purposes. Even when there has been a clear abuse of the rules, courts have been reluctant to impose costs on an offending party. As a result, you must not only be prepared to combat the imposition of costs but also should be aware of how to build a record in order to obtain costs when appropriate or arguable. The area which is most susceptible to abuse and in connection with which expenses most often run high is depositions.

Typically, your opponent attempts to conduct a "scorched earth" discovery program, directed at either depleting your resources or delivering the message to you that this case will be very expensive to litigate. In today's litigative environment, such tactics are not well received and may be dealt with swiftly by the courts.

You must be aware of the approach taken by courts to awarding deposition costs which, in most instances, are viewed as discretionary. Several states take the position that deposition expenses may be taxed to a losing litigant as a cost item only when the deposition was necessary for use and, in fact, was actually used at trial. *Barrett v. Singer Co.,* 60 Ohio St. 2d 7, 396 N.E.2d 218 (1979); *Casey v. Williams,* 87 Nev. 137, 482 P.2d 824 (1971); *Kendall v. Curl,* 22 Or. 329, 353 P.2d 227 (1960); *Platts v. Arney,* 46 Wash. 122, 278 P.2d 657 (1955). *Morrison-Maierle, Inc. v. Selsco,* 606 P.2d 1085, 186 Mont. 180 (1980); *Morris v. Redak,* 124 Colo. 27, 234 P.2d 908 (1951); *Wood v. Gautier,* 201 Kan. 74, 439 P.2d 73 (1968).

A minority of states will admit deposition costs to be taxed as litigation expenses even though the deposition is not used at trial. Parties seeking to recover costs must demonstrate that the deposition was taken in good faith and is either actually or reasonably necessary for preparation of the case or protection of the rights of the prevailing party. *Stocker v. Wells,* 155 Neb. 472, 52 N.W.2d 284 (1952); *Lawson Supply Co. v. General Plumbing & Heating, Inc.,* 27 Utah 2d 84, 493 P.2d 607 (1972); *Lomita Land & Water Co. v. Robinson,* 154 Cal. 36, 97 P. 10 (1908); *Kaps Transportation, Inc. v. Henry,* 572 P.2d 72 (Alaska 1977).

There is little question that, if your opponent notices a large number of depositions, you must do one of two things—either obtain a protective order striking the depositions or attend the depositions. Unfortunately, the latter approach is the one most frequently required, inasmuch as open discovery makes it unlikely that deposition notices will be stricken, particularly as cases become more complex. Perhaps the only redeeming feature of this whole situation is that your opponent must attend depositions if you notice them.

Prior to deciding whether to expend enormous amounts of time and money in a discovery process which has degenerated into a discovery battle, a number of factors must be considered:

1. Your likelihood of obtaining a protective order or order limiting discovery
2. Your likelihood of recovering costs as part of the litigation expenses
3. From an objective point of view, the necessity of your attending the depositions. Although litigants are always reluctant not to attend some sort of discovery, there are situations in which nonattendance may not in fact be prejudicial. For example, assume that the only controversy in the litigation is among the defendants in terms of apportionment of liability. In such a situation, a plaintiff may not be required to attend a deposition.

In the federal court system, costs have typically been allowed for depositions or parts of depositions read into evidence, used for cross-examination, used in connection with a motion for summary judgment, or used to preserve testimony of a witness. *See, e.g.,* 6 J. Moore, W. Taggert & J. Wicker, *Moore's Federal Practice* ¶ 54.77[4] (2d ed. 1981). However, the general rule in the federal court system is to disallow the costs of depositions which are used only for discovery and not in connection with the trial or a related proceeding. *See, e.g.,* 4 *Moore's Federal Practice* ¶ 26.82, at 26–581 to –582.

The question of deposition expenses can be difficult if not dealt with early in the case. Although you may not be able to resolve the overall question, you will at least have a better understanding of the ground rules with which you must live and a better capability for dealing with the opponent who tries to overwhelm you with depositions.

§ 2.12 Case Study in Motions Practice

Motions practice can be one of the most effective tools for pressuring an opponent into doing any number of things, from discovery-related actions to outright dismissal. Separate and distinct from any benefits which motions practice may have in the context of legal questions is the fact that an active motions practice in the discovery phase of the case can often send a message that will give your opponent second thoughts about not only certain types of discovery tactics to pursue but whether to pursue the case at all. This can best be illustrated by an example from my own experience.

On January 13, 1982, an Air Florida Boeing 737 aircraft crashed shortly after takeoff from Washington National Airport. The litigation brought on behalf of the deceased and injured passengers and the litigation on behalf of the deceased cockpit crew members were consolidated pursuant to order of the judicial panel on multidistrict litigation. This consolidation took place in the United States District Court for the District of Columbia and was done for the purpose of consolidating liability proceedings. Discovery on liability questions went at a very rapid and intensive pace for several months. Following completion of the greatest portion of that discovery, the United States was dismissed with prejudice by all passenger plaintiffs. This left the United States as a defendant only in the cases brought on behalf of the deceased cockpit crew members.

On December 3, 1982, after the United States had been dismissed out of the passenger plaintiffs' cases, the district court ordered that the United States would have leave to file a set of contention interrogatories with the crew plaintiffs no later than December 8, 1982. These contention interrogatories were filed as ordered by the court. Their form was essentially to take the allegations of the plaintiffs' complaints and request the specific details of the factual bases on which the allegations were premised.

The crew plaintiffs waited until the day the interrogatories were due, January 10, 1983, to request an extension of time within which to answer. The United States responded by pointing out that it would be prejudiced by any extension, particularly in light of a January 31, 1983 discovery cutoff date, a fact which had previously been pointed out to counsel for the crew on December 23, 1982.

On January 12, 1983, the court, based on the objection of the United States to any extension, order the crew to respond to the United States' interrogatories by January 17, 1983.

At the close of the business day on January 17, 1983, the United States received the responses. Of 24 interrogatories filed by the United States, the plaintiffs responded to 17 of them by stating, "the crew plaintiffs do not intend to pursue this claim at trial." As to the remaining seven interrogatories, the crew plaintiffs' answers were incomplete and/or evasive.

Section 2.13 contains an example of the interrogatory and the response made by the crew plaintiffs along with the position taken by the United States on that response in a motion in limine to exclude evidence at trial pertaining to the United States' interrogatories and/or to exclude expert testimony offered by the crew plaintiffs.

§ 2.13 —Memorandum in Support of Motion

UNITED STATES OF AMERICA'S MEMORANDUM IN SUPPORT OF ITS MOTION IN LIMINE TO EXCLUDE EVIDENCE AT TRIAL PERTAINING TO DEFENDANTS' INTERROGATORIES NOS. XV, XVI, XVII, XVIII, XXII, AND/OR TO EXCLUDE CREW PLAINTIFF'S EXPERT TESTIMONY AT TRIAL AND TO EXCLUDE EXPERT TESTIMONY AT TRIAL CONCERNING INTERROGATORIES NOS. XV, XVI, XVII, XVIII, XXII

On December 3, 1982, this Court ordered that the United States of America's First Set of Contention Interrogatories to Crew Plaintiffs be propounded no later than December 8, 1982. Defendant served the interrogatories as required by this order. Crew Plaintiffs waited until the day the interrogatories were due, January 10, 1983, to request an extension of time in which to answer these interrogatories. Defendant United States responded by arguing they would be prejudiced by any extension, particularly in light of the January 31, 1983 discovery cutoff date, a fact previously expressed to ________________, Crew Plaintiffs' liaison counsel, on December 23, 1982.

On January 12, 1983, this Court ordered Crew Plaintiffs to respond to Defendants' First Set of Contention Interrogatories by January 17, 1983. (A copy of the order is attached as Exhibit A.) At the close of the business day on January 17, 1983, Defendants received Crew Plaintiffs' filed responses (attached as Exhibit B). Of 24 Interrogatories, Crew Plaintiffs responded to 17 of them by stating "The crew plaintiffs do not intend to pursue this claim at trial." As to the remaining 7 interrogatories, Crew Plaintiffs' answers were incomplete and/or evasive.

Set forth below are the 7 United States Interrogatories, Crew Plaintiffs' response and the United States position as to each interrogatory.

XV. State and describe in full and complete detail every fact known to you that supports your contention that the United States of America breached the nondelegable duty "to investigate aircraft incidents and accidents involving the safety of flight" as alleged in Paragraph 113, page 22, of Plaintiffs' Complaint, including but not limited to: a list of any and all depositions, setting forth the deponent's name, date of said deposition, volume number of said deposition where applicable, and any and all page numbers which you believe support your contention as set forth above; a list of all exhibits which have been produced by X, Inc., Y, Inc., the Z Company, or the United States of America which you believe support your contention as set forth above; and any documents you have in your possession or control which you believe support your contention as set forth above.

A. The person and/or persons failing to perform the act or acts set forth in your response to Interrogatory No. XV.

B. The exact date on which you contend the act or acts set forth in your response to Interrogatory No. XV were performed or not performed.

C. The circumstances under which you contend the act or acts set forth in your response to Interrogatory No. XV were or were not performed.

D. The specific manner in which you contend the act or acts set forth in your response to Interrogatory No. XV were performed or not performed.

E. What you contend should or should not have been done instead.

F. The specific manner in which you contend such altered performance would have been non-negligent.

G. Whether you contend the performance or non-performance of the act(s) and/or omission(s) alleged in Paragraph 113 of the Complaint, as set forth in Interrogatory No. XV, violated any applicable standard of care or performance and, if so, as to each contended violation, state the following:

1. The standard of care and/or performance involved.
2. The specific manner in which you contend the performance or non-performance of the act and/or omission violated the standard of care and/or performance.
3. The specific manner in which you contend the violation led to or resulted in the injury alleged in your complaint.
4. What you contend should have been done or not been done instead so as to comport with the standard of care and/or performance.
5. The specific manner in which you contend such altered performance or non-performance would have avoided the injury alleged in your complaint.

CREW PLAINTIFFS' RESPONSE XV

Defendant United States, since its certification of the aircraft, negligently failed to perform adequately its non-delegable duty to investigate and evaluate aircraft incidents and accidents involving the safety of flight which indicated that the aircraft exhibited characteristics indicating that the accumulation of even imperceptible quantities of snow or ice on certain parts of the aircraft posed an extraordinary potential hazard. The United States negligently failed to carry out these responsibilities in a manner that would alert airline pilots and air carriers which operate the aircraft about the aforementioned safety deficiency of the aircraft. Specifically, the United States and the Z Company have since 1970 received numerous warnings and reports from aircraft operators, the British Civil Aviation Authority and others alerting them to the unexpected hazards of abrupt pitch-up or roll-off immediately after lift-off when there were accumulations of even imperceptible quantities of snow or ice on certain parts of the aircraft.

The persons who negligently failed to adequately perform these non-delegable duties include all United States personnel involved in or responsible for the performance of these duties, including persons deposed or described in depositions or other documents produced during the current, ongoing discovery processes.

Adequate performance of these duties should have alerted the United States about this characteristic and caused the United States to take the actions described in the answers to Interrogatories Nos. XVI-XVIII below.

UNITED STATES POSITION XV

That Crew Plaintiffs' answer is incomplete is patent. To list only a few of those questions intrinsic within Defendant's interrogatory and not addressed by Crew plaintiffs:

1. What specific "aircraft incidents," that the FAA was aware of, are Crew Plaintiffs referring to;
2. What documents and/or exhibits produced to date support Crew Plaintiffs' contention that this Defendant had a "non-delegable duty to investigate incidents and accidents," . . .
3. What standard of care was violated and what should have been done instead.

Further, as to Defendant's request to the person or persons failing to perform the act, Crew Plaintiffs response, "*include* all United States personnel involved in or responsible for the performance of these duties." (emphasis added); that this answer is evasive is obvious. Crew Plaintiffs must know 14 days before discovery cutoff who performed or failed to perform the acts they complain of.

§ 2.14 —Action on Motion

The United States filed its motion in limine to exclude the evidence based on Rule 37(a)(3) of the Federal Rules of Civil Procedure which provides that an incomplete or evasive answer is to be treated as a failure to answer. Asserting that the answers were both incomplete and evasive, the United States sought exclusion of evidence pertaining to unanswered interrogatories and exclusion of any expert testimony on issues related to the matters under inquiry.

The court did not grant the defendant's motion outright but gave the plaintiff until noon on a Saturday, a day or two after the hearing on the defendant's motion, to provide full and complete answers to the defendant's interrogatories. At approximately 11:00 A.M. on that Saturday, the plaintiffs telephoned defense counsel at home and indicated that they would be dismissing the case with prejudice in exchange for which the defense would not seek any costs. Obviously, this "offer" was accepted, and the case was terminated in its entirety.

A motions practice which is well thought out and planned in advance will not always result in a dismissal of the action. However, there are few circumstances in which it will not yield some long-term benefit as long as all the risks are taken into account and minimized within the context of the relief being sought.

§ 2.15 Mandamus Motions

During the lifetime of every litigator, he or she frequently is confronted with situations posed by trial judges which ring of manifest injustice. By far the greatest numbers of these result from being on the losing side. The avenue of relief in such circumstances is the appellate process. Sometimes there is a reversal on the merits, and justice is done.

Far less frequent are situations in which a litigator is confronted with a judge who refuses to do something such as, for example, follow the mandate of the Court of Appeals or enter an order. In these circumstances, there typically is little likelihood that the "offending" judge will certify his actions or order for an interlocutory appeal pursuant to 28 U.S.C. § 1292(b).

The aggrieved lawyer in such a situation is usually left with only one viable option—a writ of mandamus. 28 U.S.C. § 1651(a) provides: "The Supreme Court and all courts established by Act of Congress may issue all writs necessary or appropriate in aid of their respective jurisdictions and agreeable to the usage and principles of law . . . ."

The jurisdiction of the federal court system to issue writs of mandamus is thus clear. In *Green v. Occidental Petroleum Corp.,* 541 F.2d 1335 (9th Cir. 1976), the court set forth the principle that the issuance of a writ of mandamus is within the power of the Court of Appeals under the All Writs Statute [28 U.S.C. § 1651(a)], particularly if the Court of Appeals could later entertain an appeal on the issues presented. And, in *In re Virginia Electric & Power Co.,* 539 F.2d 357 (4th Cir. 1974) the court stated: "The All Writs Statute authorizes [a Circuit Court] to issue writs of mandamus to district courts in the circuit." *Id.* at 365.

The Tenth Circuit made a similar finding in *Estate of Whitlock v. Commissioner of Internal Revenue*, 547 F.2d 506 (10th Cir. 1976). "Mandamus may be used to compel a court to exercise authority when it has the duty to do so." *Id.* at 510 (citing *Kerr v. United States District Court for the Northern District of California,* 426 U.S. 394, 402 (1976)). *See also Prater v. Boyd,* 263 F.2d 788 (6th Cir. 1959); *Bartsch v. Clarke,* 293 F.2d 283 (4th Cir. 1961).

There is little doubt that a mandamus directed to a United States District Judge is an extraordinary measure. *Bancohio Corp. v. Fox,* 516 F.2d 29 (6th Cir. 1975); *Dow Chemical Co. v. Taylor,* 519 F.2d 352 (6th Cir. 1975); *National Farmers' Organization, Inc. v. Oliver,* 530 F.2d 815 (8th Cir. 1976). However, when it is sought, counsel inevitably believes that the set of circumstances manifests the necessity for such exceptional relief.

In *Kerr v. United States District Court for the Northern District of California,* 426 U.S. 394 (1976), the court set forth the situation in which a writ of mandamus is most frequently utilized:

> The writ "has traditionally been used in the federal courts only 'to confine an inferior court to a lawful exercise of its prescribed jurisdiction or to compel it to exercise its authority when it is its duty to do so.'"

Id. at 402. *See also Bankers Life & Casualty Co. v. Holland,* 346 U.S. 379 (1953); *Estate of Whitlock v. Commissioner of Internal Revenue,* 547 F.2d 506 (10th Cir. 1976); *Guerra v. Board of Trustees of California State Universities,* 572 F.2d 700 (9th Cir. 1978).

Further, mandamus will lie only in the exceptional case in which there is a clear abuse of discretion or usurption of judicial power. *Bankers Life & Casualty Co., supra.*

Mandamus is especially proper when all that remains to be done is the execution of a purely ministerial act. *Kirby v. Thomas,* 336 F.2d 462 (6th Cir. 1964); *Whittier v. Emmett,* 281 F.2d 24 (D.C. Cir. 1960). In *Higginson v. Schoeneman,* 190 F.2d 32 (D.C. Cir. 1950), the court stated: "Mandamus is employed to compel the performance, when refused, of a ministerial duty, this being its chief use." *Id.* at 34 (quoting *Wilbur v. United States,* 281 U.S. 206 (1930)).

Many other cases have set forth the idea that the doing of a ministerial act is foremost within the realm of mandamus. In *United States ex rel. Roughton v. Ickes,* 101 F.2d 248 (D.C. Cir. 1938), the court reiterated that idea. A definition of a *ministerial act* for the purposes of the writ is given in *United States ex rel. McQueen v. Wangelin,* 527 F.2d 579 (8th Cir. 1979):

> The writ of mandamus . . . is an extraordinary remedy reserved for a few exceptions such as . . . failure to complete a ministerial act whose performance is "positively commanded and so plainly prescribed as to be free from doubt. *Richardson v. United States,* 465 F.2d 844, 849 (3d Cir. 1972), *cert. denied,* 410 U.S. 955 (1973).

Id. at 582. *See also Central South Carolina Chapter, Society of Professional Journalists, Sigma Delta Chi v. United States District Court,* 551 F.2d 559, 561–562 (4th Cir. 1977).

Because of the extraordinary nature of mandamus, the courts have been firm in the requirement that no other adequate remedy be available to the petitioner seeking such a writ. *Ex parte Newman,* 81 U.S. 152 (1872); *In re Press Printers & Publishers,* 12 F.2d 660 (3d Cir. 1926); *Albert v. United States District Court for the Western District of Michigan, Northern Division,* 283 F.2d 61 (6th Cir. 1960); *United States v. Richardson,* 204 F.2d 552 (5th Cir. 1953); *Clarke v. Memolo,* 174 F.2d 978 (D.C. Cir. 1949); *Ex parte Fahey,* 332 U.S. 258 (1947).

In *Albert v. United States District Court,* the court set forth the requirements which must be fulfilled by the petitioner before a writ may be granted:

> Before petitioner may resort to the extraordinary writ of mandamus, he must establish that he has a clear and certain right and that the duties of

> the respondent are ministerial, plainly defined and preemptory. . . . The writ may be granted only where it is clear and undisputable that there is no other legal remedy.

Id. at 62. *See also Redpath v. Kissinger,* 415 F. Supp. 566 (W.D. Tex. 1976); *Carter v. Seamans,* 411 F.2d 767 (5th Cir. 1969); *In re B & B Properties, Ltd.,* 423 F. Supp. 23 (W.D. Ga. 1976).

Further, in *Kay Ferer, Inc. v. Hulen,* 160 F.2d 146 (8th Cir. 1947), the court stated that the petitioner must show that: "it has no other plain, adequate and complete method of redressing the wrong or obtaining the relief to which it is entitled so that without the issuance of the writ there would be a failure of justice." *Id.* at 149. *See also Clark v. Memolo,* 174 F.2d 978 (D.C. Cir. 1949); *United States v. Richardson,* 204 F.2d 552 (5th Cir. 1953); *Ex parte Newman,* 81 U.S. 152 (1872); *In re Press Printers & Publishers,* 12 F.2d 660 (3d Cir. 1926); *Rayburn v. Jones,* 282 F.2d 410 (6th Cir. 1960).

Finally, in *Rees v. United States District Court for the Central District of California,* 572 F.2d 700 (9th Cir. 1978), in addition to the requirement that no other means of obtaining relief be available, the court set forth the criterion that: "The petitioner will be damaged or prejudiced in a way not correctable on appeal . . . . *Id.* at 702 (citing *Bauman v. United States District Court,* 557 F.2d 650 (9th Cir. 1977)).

It is established that a writ of mandamus is not awarded to control or review an exercise of authority or discretion with respect to actions by the court which are not within the discharge of a ministerial duty. *Ex parte Roe,* 23 U.S. 70 (1914). It is also established and understood that mandamus does not lie to direct the lower court with respect to *how* to proceed. In *Schendel v. McGee,* 300 F.273 (8th Cir. 1924), the court stated: "Of course, an appellate court cannot by mandamus control a subordinate judicial officer to reach any particular conclusion or decide a case in any particular way. It can, however, compel such court to render a final judgment, so that appellate jurisdiction can be exercised." *Id.* at 276. *See also Kendall v. United States,* 37 U.S. 522 (1838).

The courts have also addressed the question of the propriety of mandamus prior to the time an appeal is perfected. In *American Fidelity Fire Insurance v. United States District Court for the Northern District of California,* 538 F.2d 1371 (9th Cir. 1976), the court directed its attention to that part of 28 U.S.C. 1651(a) which states that writs may be granted by the courts as long as such writs are "in aid of their respective jurisdictions" and stated

> As the jurisdiction of the circuit court of appeals is exclusively appellate, its authority to issue writs of mandamus is restricted by statute to those cases in which the writ is in aid of that jurisdiction. Its authority is not confined to the issuance of writs in aid of a jurisdiction already acquired

> by appeal but extends to those cases which are within its appellate jurisdiction although no appeal has been perfected. . . . *Roche v. Evaporated Milk Association,* 319 U.S. 21, 25 (1943).

538 F.2d at 1373.

See also Application of President and Directors of Georgetown College, Inc., 331 F.2d 1000 (D.C. Cir. 1964); *National Farmers' Organization, Inc. v. Oliver,* 530 F.2d 815 (8th Cir. 1976).

Quite distinct from the legal questions and difficulties associated with successfully obtaining an order in the nature of a writ of mandamus are the tactical risks associated with it. Whether counsel wins or loses before a court of appeal is in some measure irrelevant to what may be expected from the trial judge against whom the order has been sought. This is especially true if the district court proceedings are still at some pretrial stage and counsel must continue to litigate in the district court.

If the Court of Appeals denies the petition, the district court judge has received what is in effect an appellate imprimatur on the action being complained of. If mandamus is granted, successful counsel can potentially face an even more difficult problem in the form of a district judge over whose head counsel has successfully gone. Although certainly the system provides for such procedures, human nature being what it is, the potential for a "whiplash" effect is very real.

Despite the fact that our legal system provides for writs of mandamus, the key question which all litigators must face is whether they and their clients can afford the risk of mandamus.

CHAPTER 3

SANCTIONS: DISCOVERY ABUSE

§ 3.1 Introduction

This chapter and the several which follow address one of the most dangerous areas which a lawyer can confront, whether representing plaintiffs or defendants—sanctions. Since the amendments to Federal Rule of Civil Procedure 11 were made in 1983, the courts have undertaken with vigor the imposition of sanctions and evaluation of attorneys' actions relative to sanctions.

In the next several chapters the full range of sanctions which a court can impose are addressed, including attorneys' fees, costs, Rule 11 sanctions, and discovery expenses.

The thrust of these chapters is to focus your attention on the standards underlying the various types of sanctions so you can both avoid them as well as, when appropriate, seek them. The practical checklists such as the one in **§ 3.11** are keyed toward immediate application and are aimed at maximizing your position in litigation while minimizing that of your opponent.

At present, the public has a fairly low regard for lawyers and the civil litigation system. Plaintiffs have been accused of bringing meritless actions, which defendants settle for nuisance value rather than subject themselves to extensive, costly, and possibly embarrassing discovery. *See, e.g., Blue Chip Stamps v. Manor Drug Stores,* 421 U.S. 723, 740 (1975); *Amendments to the Federal Rules of Civil Procedure,* 85 F.R.D. 521 (1979) (Powell, Stewart and Rehnquist, JJ., dissenting). Defendants with greater economic resources are viewed as drowning less affluent plaintiffs in a sea of paper. *Amendments to the Federal Rules of Civil Procedure,* 85 F.R.D. 521. Courts are sensitive to complaints that the public has lost respect for the judicial system because those with limited means cannot afford to litigate just claims or fight unjust actions. *Id.* As the Seventh Circuit recently noted, "[m]ounting federal caseloads and growing public dissatisfaction with the costs and delays of litigation have made it imperative that the federal courts impose sanctions on persons and firms that abuse their right of access to these courts." *Dreis & Krump Manufacturing v. International Association of Machinists,* 802 F.2d 247, 255 (7th Cir. 1986). Therefore, judges now are receptive to imposing sanctions for a variety of practices, some of which previously were considered within the range of zealous advocacy. In fact, if the number of cases being decided on sanctions issues is any indication, judges are being flooded with requests to impose sanctions.

Although the actual extent of discovery abuse is disputed, *compare* Renfrew, *Discovery Sanctions: A Judicial Perspective,* 67 Cal. L. Rev. 263 (1979) (widespread) *with* Federal Judicial Center, *Controls and the Civil Litigative Process: Discovery* 24 (P. Connally, E. Holleman, & M. Kuhlman eds. 1978) (sanctions requested for less than 1 percent of discovery requests studied), it is not surprising that the tension between a self-executing discovery policy and the adversary system has resulted in attorneys testing the limits of zealous advocacy within the bounds of law. *See, e.g.,* Ebersole, *Discovery Problems: Is Help on the Way,* 66 A.B.A. J. 50 (1980); Brazil, *The Adversary Character of Civil Discovery: A Critique and Proposals for Change,* 31 Vand. L. Rev. 1295 (1978). Optimistically establishing a policy that litigants willingly exchange relevant information conflicts with the role of the attorney as an advocate who resolves all disputes in the client's favor. *See* Cohn, *Federal Discovery: A Survey of Local Rules and Practices in View of Proposed Changes to the Federal Rules,* 63 Minn. L. Rev. 253, 256 n.25 (1979).

Moreover, some of the reasons why counsel engage in extensive discovery or employ dilatory practices are endemic to our system of litigation. *See generally* Sofaer, *Sanctioning Attorneys for Discovery Abuse Under the New Federal Rules: On the Limited Utility of Punishment,* 57 St. John's L. Rev. 684, 720–29 (1983); *see also* Edelstein, *The Ethics of Dilatory Motion Practice: Time for Change,* 44 Fordham L. Rev. 1069, 1076 (1976). For example, the nominal costs of bringing an action and the general ban on requiring the loser to pay the winner's attorneys' fees fosters litigation and expensive discovery requests. The inability to obtain prejudgment interest in many cases and low pre- and postjudgment interest rates encourages defendants to use extensive discovery as a means of delaying the proceedings. In addition, courts are now being used as forums for complex political and social issues which by their nature generate vast amounts of discovery, often on sensitive issues.

The willingness of courts to expand theories of liability also provides plaintiffs with an incentive to test the bounds of relevance. Moreover, the difficulty of obtaining summary judgment results in weak cases going to trial unless a defendant is willing to settle for nuisance value. In general, because most civil cases settle, pretrial practice has become big business for lawyers, who generate much of their billings from discovery and motions and who are also concerned that limiting discovery or acquiescing without a fight to discovery requests may result in a malpractice action if the case is lost. *See* Rosenberg & King, *Curbing Discovery Abuse in Civil Litigation: Enough is Enough,* 1981 B.Y.U. L. Rev. 570, 582.

Until recently these systemic pressures went unchecked by judges, who were reluctant to become involved in discovery because they felt that taking sides in discovery disputes is unseemly, interferes with their role as impartial factfinders, exacerbates personal conflict between the attorneys, discourages the loser from later litigating legitimate discovery disputes, and wastes the court's time because the case is likely to settle regardless of the outcome of the dispute. *See, e.g.,* Cavanagh, *The August 1, 1983 Amendments to the Federal Rules of Civil Procedure: A Critical Evaluation and a Proposal for More Effective Discovery Through Local Rules,* 30 Villanova L. Rev. 767, 795–97 (1985); Berger, *Sanctions Under Rule 37: The Growing Irritation with Discovery Abuses,* N.Y.S.B.J. 106, 108 (Feb. 1979). Many attorneys as well as the public became disappointed with the failure of judges to impose sanctions for discovery abuse, *e.g.,* Brazil, *Views from the Front Lines: Observations by Chicago Lawyers About the System of Civil Discovery,* 1980 A.B.F. Res. J. 217, 245, because there appeared no other way to set the adversarial limits of discovery practice. Without appropriate checks, discovery abuse had become simply another tactical weapon of the adversary system. Some even felt that the negative side of discovery, which is manifested by both overdiscovery and resistance to discovery, outweighed its positive values.

§ 3.2 Revisions of the Federal Rules of Civil Procedure

The 1983 revisions of the Federal Rules of Civil Procedure focused on the judge's power and responsibility to control litigation and for the first time explicitly provided relief for the problems associated with overdiscovery. *See* Schwarze, *Sanctions Under the New Federal Rule 11—A Closer Look,* 104 F.R.D. 181, 183 (1985). Changes to Rules 11, 16, and 26 were adopted to force litigators and judges to reassess previous practices. Rule 26(g) requires the person signing a discovery request, response, or objection to certify its reasonableness. Rule 11 applies this standard to every pleading, motion, and other legal paper filed in an action. A violation of Rule 11 or 26(g) can result in the striking of an unsigned document and the imposition of appropriate sanctions, including attorneys' fees, for improper certifications. Violations of Rule 26(g) reach overdiscovery as well as resistance to proper discovery.

Ethical responsibilities in discovery were also clarified by prohibiting lawyers from making a frivolous discovery request and requiring them to make a reasonably diligent effort to comply with legally proper discovery requests of the opposing party. Model Rules of Professional Responsibility Rule 3.4(d).

In addition, federal judges were explicitly encouraged to become case managers by the revisions to Rule 16. *See generally* Resnik, *Managerial Judges,* 96 Harv. L. Rev. 374 (1982). Paragraphs 16.1–16.3 of the rule list among the objectives of pretrial conferences (1) establishing early and continuing control so that the case will not be protracted because of lack of management and (2) discouraging wasteful pretrial activities. Rule 16(b) mandates that the court must enter a scheduling order which limits the time to file and hear motions and complete discovery. Rule 26(f) permits the court or a party to enter a formal discovery plan setting limitations on discovery if the attorneys have not been able to reach agreement after reasonable effort. Failure to participate in good faith in framing the plan subjects the party or its attorney to pay the reasonable expenses, including attorneys' fees, caused by the failure. Parties and their attorneys can also be sanctioned under Rule 16(f) for failure to obey a scheduling or pretrial order, not appearing at such conferences, or being substantially unprepared to participate in the conference or to participate in good faith. Sanctions for such Rule 16 violations include preclusion orders, striking pleadings, staying the proceedings, entering a dismissal or default, and contempt, as well as paying the reasonable expenses, including attorneys' fees, incurred because of the noncompliance.

Rule 26(b) was adopted specifically to correct problems associated with overdiscovery. It provides that the court shall limit the frequency or extent of use of discovery if:

1. The discovery sought is unreasonably cumulative or duplicative or is obtainable from some other source that is more convenient, less burdensome, or less expensive

2. The party seeking discovery has had ample opportunity by discovery in the action to obtain the information sought, or
3. The discovery is unduly burdensome or expensive, taking into account the needs of the case, the amount of controversy, limitations on the parties' resources, and the importance of the issues at stake in the litigation.

§ 3.3 —Courts' Applications of the Rule Revisions

The number of sanctions motions in federal courts has clearly increased in the last few years, adding to the costs of litigation, *see, e.g.*, Cavanagh, *The August 1, 1983 Amendments to the Federal Rules of Civil Procedure: A Critical Evaluation and a Proposal for More Effective Discovery Through Local Rules,* 30 Villanova L. Rev. 767, 794 (1985), and potentially delaying the resolution of the underlying actions. Similarly, the changes to Rule 16 have resulted in what many litigators believe to be overly expensive and complex requirements aptly described as "pretrial by ordeal." Comment, *Recent Changes in the Federal Rules of Civil Procedure: Prescription to Ease the Pain?,* 15 Texas Tech. L. Rev. 887, 904–08 (1984).

Significant numbers of cases have been terminated for discovery and pretrial abuses. Furthermore, as the Seventh Circuit has noted, a dismissal caused by an attorney's misconduct may result in a successful malpractice action against the plaintiff's attorney. *Tolliver v. Northrop Corp.,* 786 F.2d 316, 318 (7th Cir. 1986). Costs and attorneys' fees are now routinely levied against practitioners as well as their clients. *See, e.g.,* Burger, *Abuses of Discovery: Judges Are Correcting the Problem,* 30 Trial 18, 19–20 (Sept. 1984). In fact, many judges are more comfortable sanctioning attorneys than imposing sanctions which will affect the merits of the action. Therefore, the certification requirements mandated by Rules 7, 11, and 26(g), as well as the trial court's explicit power to curtail discovery under Rule 26(b)(1) and to manage the litigation process under Rule 16 must be considered when you evaluate discovery strategy.

Because not all judges have wholeheartedly embraced the role of case manager and not all attorneys are willing to request sanctions, the likelihood of obtaining relief for abusive pretrial tactics varies significantly. There are also real differences in how the circuits approach discovery sanctions on appeal. *See, e.g.,* Epstein, Corcoran, Krieger, & Carr, *An Up-Date on Rule 37 Sanctions After National Hockey League v. Metropolitan Hockey Clubs, Inc.,* 84 F.R.D. 145 (1979). For example, the Third Circuit appears to be the most hostile to the imposition of severe sanctions, while the First and Second Circuits consistently affirm sanctions which terminate cases.

§ 3.4 —Tactical Considerations for Attorneys

Although you should not tolerate unethical or sharp practices, you should not be deterred from aggressive lawyering on your client's behalf because of the modification of the rules. However, some uncertainty exists whether requiring attorneys to certify their reasonableness has fundamentally changed counsel's role as an advocate. For example, requiring aggressive litigators to certify unconditionally that a motion or discovery request or response is not interposed solely for improper reasons should not result in hindering discovery. But excessive use of interrogatories, boilerplate interrogatories, overly long depositions, numerous inconsequential depositions, and excessive requests for production of documents should be regarded as suspect.

On the other hand, if tactical considerations are not considered proper reasons, who can truly certify that requests and motions are not interposed for any improper purpose, as Rules 11 and 26(g) require? Lawyers handling large cases who responded to a survey said that tactical considerations affected how they conducted or responded to discovery in 99 percent of their cases. Brazil, *Civil Discovery: Lawyers' View of Its Effectiveness, Its Principal Problems and Abuses,* 1980 A.B.F. Res. J. 787, 871; Brazil, *Civil Discovery: How Bad Are the Problems?,* 67 A.B.A. J. 450, 451 (1981). Unless these attorneys have changed their behavior, certifications signify only that some proper purpose supports the position taken, not that no improper purpose exists.

You should be aware that the modifications to the rules may also result in the de-emphasis of previously important goals such as ease of access to courts, procedural simplicity, and self-executing discovery, because of the shift to more complex rules overseen by the judge as case manager. *See* Roberts, *The Myth of Uniformity in Federal Civil Procedure: Federal Civil Rule 83 and District Court Local Rulemaking Powers,* 8 U. Puget Sound L. Rev. 537, 538 (1985). Uniformity of practice in federal courts also appears to be disappearing with the enactment by district courts and individual judges of some 3,000 local rules which if violated may result in the imposition of sanctions.

§ 3.5 Authority for and Standards of Review of Sanctions

Rules, statutes, and the inherent power of courts to manage their dockets provide the basic authority which judges rely upon for imposing sanctions. The requirements for any particular sanction vary with the authority cited.

On appeal, sanctions usually are reviewed under the following standards: factual inquiries are reviewed under the clearly erroneous standard; legal conclusions are reviewed de novo; and the appropriateness of the sanction is reviewed for abuse of discretion. *See, e.g., United States v. National Medical Enterprises, Inc.,* 792 F.2d 906, 910–11 (9th Cir. 1986) (Rule 37); *In re Itel Securities Litigation,* 791 F.2d 672, 674 (9th Cir. 1986) (28 U.S.C. § 1927 and Rule 11), *cert. denied,* _____ U.S. _____, 107 S.Ct. 880 (1987); *Eastway Construction Corp. v. City of New York,* 762 F.2d 243, 254 n.7 (2d Cir. 1985) (Rule 11); *Eastway General Hospital Ltd. v. Eastway Women's Clinic, Inc.,* 737 F.2d 503, 505 (5th Cir. 1984), *cert. denied,* 470 U.S. 1052 (1985) (Rule 37).

§ 3.6 —Awards of Attorneys' Fees

Attorneys' fees can be awarded pursuant to a number of rules and statutes as well as by reference to the court's inherent powers. The following authorities are most frequently cited for imposition of attorneys' fees.

1. **Rules 11 and 26(g)** permit an appropriate sanction to be invoked for improperly certifying that an attorney or party has made a reasonable inquiry into the factual and legal basis of any pleading, motion, or paper submitted to the court and any discovery request, response, or objection. Monetary sanctions can be awarded against the attorney or party without any showing of bad faith.
2. **28 U.S.C. § 1927** provides that any attorney who multiplies the proceedings in any case unreasonably and vexatiously may be required personally to satisfy the excess costs, expenses, and attorneys' fees reasonably incurred because of such conduct. Bad faith is a prerequisite, *Kamen v. AT&T Co.,* 791 F.2d 1006, 1010 (2d Cir. 1986); *Dreiling v. Peugeot Motors of America, Inc.,* 768 F.2d 1159, 1164–65 (10th Cir. 1985); *Baker Industries, Inc. v. Cerberus Ltd.,* 764 F.2d 204, 209 (3d Cir. 1985), although a few circuits appear to permit such sanctions for reckless behavior.
3. **Various rules**, including **Rule 37(a) (4)**, provide for attorneys' fees for bringing motions or defending against them when the opposition is not justified.

§ 3.7 —Sanctions Affecting the Merits of the Action

Some of the same rules discussed in **§ 3.6** can be used to obtain sanctions affecting the merits of the action, but there is not a complete overlap.

The following authorities support imposition of outcome-determinative sanctions:

1. **Rule 37** remains the main weapon in your arsenal against abuse caused by total or partial resistance to valid discovery requests. It applies to all parties and their attorneys as well as nonparty deponents. Unlike the modifications to the rules which focus on imposing monetary sanctions on lawyers and parties to discourage abuse, Rule 37 is directed primarily at sanctions which affect the merits of the action. Judges appear to apply Rule 37 more frequently, because the rules have been changed to encourage sanctions and case management. Sanctions for a party who disobeys a court order concerning discovery or for total discovery failure under Rule 37(d) range from issue preclusion, establishment or designated facts, and contempt to dismissal and default.

   Rule 37 explicitly permits the imposition of any order which is just in regard to the failure. Willfulness is usually thought necessary for a court to terminate an action under this rule, although some circuits permit dismissals for gross negligence. Lesser sanctions may be applied for all types of conduct which results in failure to comply with court orders. Monetary sanctions can be imposed against the attorney and the party under this rule as well as an award of expenses, including reasonable attorneys' fees, for successfully bringing or defeating a discovery motion.
2. **Rule 41(b)** permits a defendant to obtain the dismissal of an action for the plaintiff's failure to prosecute or obey the rules or any court order. Although courts vary as to the length of time a case must be inactive before dismissal, federal courts are generally much stricter than state courts in meting out such dismissals. This rule mentions only dismissals, but less severe sanctions can be imposed. Sanctions under Rules 41(b) and 37 often overlap when aimed at abusive tactics of a plaintiff.
3. Courts have **inherent power** to manage their own affairs to achieve the orderly and expeditious disposition of cases. *See Link v. Wabash Railroad,* 370 U.S. 626, 630–31 (1962). Judges can terminate cases or impose other sanctions, including assessments of attorneys' fees, to control their own dockets. The court can sua sponte initiate sanctions similar to Rule 41(b) sanctions to ensure that cases are prosecuted and court orders obeyed. Courts' inherent powers also include the ability to hold an individual in criminal or civil contempt. In addition, some courts fine litigants and attorneys for behavior not reaching contempt. Inherent powers are strictly construed and require bad faith of the individual being sanctioned.

4. **Rule 16(f)** provides that most of the sanctions available under Rule 37 can be imposed for failure to obey a scheduling or pretrial order, failure to appear at a scheduling or pretrial conference, or failure to prepare or participate in good faith at the conference. This rule is rarely cited as the sole justification for severe sanctions and is treated as codifying some of the court's inherent powers for failure to prosecute and obey court orders.

§ 3.8 —Sanctions for Other Pretrial Abuses

Sanctions such as fines and contempt can also be imposed for other civil pretrial abuses. The authority for such sanctions is as follows:

1. **Local rules** may expand the obligations of counsel and provide sanctions for their violation.
2. **Criminal contempt** is authorized by statute, 18 U.S.C. § 401 (1982); Fed. R. Crim. P. 42, as well as under Rule 37 and the court's inherent powers.
3. **Civil contempt** is also available as a sanction, although its use is strictly construed.

§ 3.9 —Citing Appropriate Authority for Specific Sanctions

A quick review of the alternatives indicates that the same behavior of counsel and/or a party may justify imposition of a sanction under one rule which is prohibited under another. For example, conduct which is not in bad faith cannot result in attorneys' fees under 28 U.S.C. § 1927 or the court's inherent powers, but such relief may be available under Rules 11 and 37.

The basis for any sanctions motion must be carefully set forth to ensure that the conduct falls within the rule you have cited for support. If you cite the wrong rule, the judge can deny the sanction.

Conversely, when defending against a sanctions motion, you should be careful to ascertain whether the cited authority supports the particular sanction requested. If any sanction is awarded incorrectly, the appellate court may remand the case of findings under the appropriate rule rather than affirming the award under the correct standard. *See, e.g., Roadway Express, Inc. v. Piper,* 447 U.S. 752, 767–68 (1980); *see also In re Yaman,* 796 F.2d 1165, 1184–87, *modified on other grounds,* 803 F.2d 1085 (9th Cir. 1986).

§ 3.10 Review of Sanction Orders

Most orders compelling discovery or imposing sanctions are not immediately appealable. *See, e.g., Robinson v. Tanner,* 798 F.2d 1378, 1380–81 (11th Cir. 1986) (extensive citations). For example, the majority of circuits do not permit interlocutory appeals of an order requiring a party to pay monetary sanctions for a routine discovery failure, *Coleman v. Sherwood Medical Industries,* 746 F.2d 445, 447 (8th Cir. 1984); *see D&H Marketers, Inc. v. Freedom Oil & Gas, Inc.,* 744 F.2d 1443, 1444–46 (10th Cir. 1984); *Mulay Plastics, Inc. v. Grand Trunk Western Railroad,* 742 F.2d 369, 370–71 (7th Cir. 1984), *cert. denied,* 470 U.S. 1037 (1985); *Meche v. Dan-Tex International, Inc.,* 681 F.2d 264, 265 (5th Cir. 1982); *Johnny Pflocks, Inc. v. Firestone Tire & Rubber Co.,* 634 F.2d 1215, 1217 (9th Cir. 1980). Such orders are not usually a proper subject for mandamus. Even important discovery issues raised by the sanctions order may not result in immediate appeal. *Compare Boreri v. Fiat S.P.A.,* 763 F.2d 17, 21–22 (1st Cir. 1985) (denying review of order rejecting primacy of Hague Convention in discovery of foreign parties) *with Ohio v. Arthur Andersen & Co.,* 570 F.2d 1370, 1372 (10th Cir. 1978), *cert. denied,* 439 U.S. 833 (1979) (permitting review when compliance with discovery order could have resulted in violation of foreign law). Similarly, the judge's certification of a monetary award for immediate appeal under Rule 54(b) was ineffective to permit appeal because the order did not affect a substantial claim. *Mulay Plastics, Inc. v. Grand Trunk Western Railroad,* 742 F.2d 369, 371 (7th Cir. 1984), *cert. denied,* 470 U.S. 1037 (1985). In some circuits, if the award of attorneys' fees is part of a sanction, the amount of the award must be determined before preview is appropriate, even if the action has been dismissed with prejudice. *See Jaffe v. Sundowner Properties, Inc.,* 808 F.2d 1425, 1427 (11th Cir. 1987); *cf. Phelps v. Washburn University,* 807 F.2d 152, 154–55 (10th Cir. 1986) (1988 action surveying general case law).

If a party is held in contempt, *United States v. Ryan,* 402 U.S. 530, 532–33 (1971), or the sanction results in dismissal, an immediate appeal is appropriate. *See, e.g., Robinson v. Tanner,* 798 F.2d 1378, 1380–81 (11th Cir. 1986) (extensive citations). A sanction which affects the granting or denial of an injunction can also be appealed when imposed. *Aurora Bancshares Corp. v. Weston,* 777 F.2d 385, 386 (7th Cir. 1985). An order imposing a sanction upon counsel or other nonparties in the underlying action is often considered final and appealable as a collateral order when the sanction is imposed. *See Estate of Blas through Chargualaf v. Winkler,* 792 F.2d 858, 860 n.2 (9th Cir. 1986); *Knorr Brake Corp. v. Harbil, Inc.,* 738 F.2d 223, 226 (7th Cir. 1984); *Cheng v. GAF Corp.,* 713 F.2d 886, 888–889 (2d Cir. 1983). Even here, however, not all circuits agree. *See In re Light v. Semonoff,* 796 F.2d 569 (1st Cir. 1986) (surveying case law).

§ 3.11 Sanctions Checklist

General Considerations

____ **1.** Was there a total failure of discovery warranting an immediate motion for sanctions?

____ **2.** Is a motion to compel necessary before sanctions other than recovery of the costs of obtaining the order can be requested?

____ **3.** Has the plaintiff failed to prosecute the action?

____ **4.** Has the party failed to obey a court order?

____ **5.** Has any party violated a local rule?

____ **6.** Is the pleading, motion, or other paper

- ____ **a.** Well grounded in fact?
- ____ **b.** Warranted by existing law or by a good faith argument for its modification?
- ____ **c.** Not interposed for any improper purpose, such as to harass or to cause unnecessary delay or needless increase in the cost of litigation?

____ **7.** Is the discovery request, response or objection

- ____ **a.** Warranted by existing law or a good faith argument for its modification?
- ____ **b.** Not interposed for any improper purpose, such as to harass or to cause unnecessary delay or needless increase in the cost of litigation?
- ____ **c.** Not unreasonable or unduly burdensome or expensive, given the needs of the case, the discovery already had in the case, the amount in controversy, and the importance of the issues at stake in the litigation?

____ **8.** Does the adversary's misconduct warrant recovery of attorneys' fees?

____ **9.** Does the adversary's misconduct warrant sanctions regarding the merits of action?

____ **10.** Does the adversary's misconduct warrant dismissal or default of the action?

- ____ **a.** Does the conduct involve bad faith, willfulness, or fault?
- ____ **b.** What is the extent of the party's personal responsibility?
- ____ **c.** What prejudice has been caused by the misconduct?
- ____ **d.** Is there a history of dilatoriness?
- ____ **e.** Will sanctions other than dismissal be effective?

Procedural Requirements for Motions to Compel and Sanctions Motions

____ **1.** Is there a requirement to meet and confer before the motion can be brought?

____ **2.** Is a joint statement required

  ____ **a.** Concerning factual matters?

  ____ **b.** Concerning legal questions?

____ **3.** Is a supporting memorandum of law required?

____ **4.** Have affidavits, declarations, or any other evidentiary support concerning factual disputes been submitted with the motion?

____ **5.** Has a request been included for the expenses associated with the motion, including attorneys' fees?

____ **6.** Have the appropriate sanctions been specified in detail?

____ **7.** Is any reply to the adversary's opposition permitted?

Oppositions to Motions to Compel and Sanctions Motions

____ **1.** Is a written opposition required

  ____ **a.** Concerning factual matters?

  ____ **b.** Concerning legal questions?

  ____ **c.** As part of a joint statement?

    ____ (1) Is any reply to the joint statement permitted by either party?

____ **2.** Is a request for a protective order appropriate?

  ____ **a.** Was a timely objection made to the discovery in dispute?

____ **3.** Should a Rule 26(f) discovery conference be requested?

____ **4.** Have affidavits, declarations, or any other evidentiary support concerning factual disputes been submitted with the motion?

____ **5.** Has a request been included for the expenses associated with successfully defending the motion, including attorneys' fees?

Authority for Granting Sanctions

____ **1.** **Rule 11**: Can any appropriate sanction, including attorneys' fees, be assessed for improperly certifying that a paper is

  ____ **a.** Well grounded in fact?

  ____ **b.** Warranted by existing law or by a good faith argument for its modification?

____ c. Not interposed for any improper purpose, such as to harass or to cause unnecessary delay or needless increase in the cost of litigation?

____ 2. **Rule 16(f)**: Can Rule 37(b) (2) (B), (C), and (D) sanctions (including case terminating and evidentiary sanctions), as well as expenses (including attorneys' fees caused by the noncompliance) be assessed because a party or attorney

____ a. Failed to obey a scheduling or pretrial order?

____ b. Was absent from a pretrial conference?

____ c. Was unprepared or failed to participate in good faith in a pretrial conference?

____ 3. **Rule 26(g)**: Can any appropriate sanction, including attorneys' fees, be assessed for improperly certifying that a discovery request, response, or objection is:

____ a. Warranted by existing law or a good faith argument for its modification?

____ b. Not interposed for any improper purpose, such as to harass or to cause unnecessary delay or needless increase in the cost of litigation?

____ c. Not unreasonable or unduly burdensome or expensive, given the needs of the case, the discovery already had in the case, the amount in controversy, and the importance of the issues at stake in the litigation?

____ 4. **Rule 37**: Can any of a full range of sanctions be assessed against parties for discovery abuse and an award of expenses be imposed against any offending party or attorney as well as reasonable expenses including attorneys' fees be assessed for successfully bringing or defending against a motion? (See Rule 37 checklist in § **6.11**.)

____ 5. **Rule 41(b)**: Could the case be dismissed or lesser sanctions assessed for failure of the plaintiff to

____ a. Prosecute the action?

____ b. Comply with the rules?

____ c. Comply with any order of court?

____ 6. **28 U.S.C. § 1927**: Can an attorney be assessed any excess costs, expenses, and attorneys' fees caused by conduct which unreasonably and vexatiously multiplied the proceedings?

____ 7. **Local rules**: Can sanctions be imposed for violations of any of their requirements?

____ 8. **Statute, rules, and the court's inherent powers**: Is civil or criminal contempt available

____ **a.** For failure to obey court orders?

____ **b.** For other contemptuous misbehavior by attorneys or parties?

____ **9. Local rules, the court's inherent powers, Rule 11, and sanctions for contempt by attorneys or parties**: Are fines authorized?

____ **10. Inherent powers of the court**: Can any of a full range of sanctions be assessed for misconduct by attorneys or parties?

CHAPTER 4

SANCTIONS: RULE 11

§ 4.1 Introduction

Rule 11 of the Federal Rules of Civil Procedure, as amended in 1983, provides a relatively broad standard for the imposition of sanctions, including attorneys' fees:

> The signature of an attorney or party constitutes a certificate by him that he has read the pleading, motion or other paper; that to the best of his knowledge, information, and belief formed after reasonable inquiry it is well grounded in fact and is warranted by existing law or a good faith argument for the extension, modification, or reversal of existing law, and that it is not interposed for any improper purpose, such as to harass or to cause unnecessary delay or needless increase in the cost of litigation.

Perhaps one of the most striking things about Rule 11 as amended is not so much the language of the rule itself but rather the manner in which it contrasts with its predecessor. The previous wording of Rule 11 indicated that a lawyer's certification of a pleading amounted to an assertion that "to the best of his knowledge, information, and belief, there [was] good ground to support it." As a result, the inquiry on a sanctions proceeding was premised upon the *subjective knowledge* of the attorney who certified the pleading at the time it was signed. In effect, this amounted to an inquiry into the subject of bad faith.

With the amendments in 1983, the drafters of the new rule clearly indicated that bad faith was no longer going to be the only requirement, because the standard was no longer subjectivity. Rule 11 now focuses on a far broader range of requirements, including the following:

1. The attorney must have read the pleading.
2. The attorney must have made reasonable inquiry regarding the contents of the pleading.
3. The pleading must be well grounded in fact.
4. The pleading must be warranted by
   - **a.** Existing law, or
   - **b.** A good faith argument for an extension of existing law, or
   - **c.** A modification of existing law, or
   - **d.** A reversal of existing law.
5. The pleading must not be interposed for a purpose such as harassment, delay, or increase in the cost of the litigation.

Clearly, the wording of Rule 11 permits a far greater degree of scrutiny of the particular pleading in question. In some measure, attorneys sign pleadings of any kind at their own risk. Although this has always been the case, the subjective standard previously applicable under the original Rule 11 has given way to a standard which now exposes lawyers to second guessing and the broad range of judicial discretion.

The Notes of the Advisory Committee on the 1983 amendment to Rule 11 indicate that the purpose of the rule was not to "chill an attorney's enthusiasm or creativity in pursuing factual or legal theories." Rather, "the court is expected to avoid using the wisdom of hindsight and should test the signer's conduct by inquiring what was reasonable to believe at the time of the pleading, motion, or other paper was submitted." Although in some respects one could read "good faith" into this note, the application of Rule 11 to date makes it clear that good faith is not the test.

A reading of the advance sheets clearly indicates that the imposition of Rule 11 sanctions is being taken on a serious note by most federal court judges. On occasion, as with any exercise of discretion, there may be an abuse. However, there is little doubt but that the ability of the court to sanction attorneys under Rule 11, when properly utilized, can have the effect of resolving litigation more expeditiously and at lower cost. The task confronting lawyers is to be aware of Rule 11 whenever affixing a signature to any document in order to ensure that the broad power given to trial judges by Rule 11 to sanction attorneys is not exercised against them.

§ 4.2 Judicial Application of Rule 11—Viability of Pleadings

On May 21, 1985, the United States Court of Appeals for the Second Circuit decided one of the first appellate level cases focusing on Rule 11 as amended, *Eastway Construction Corp. v. City of New York,* 762 F.2d 243 (2d Cir. 1985).

The case involved an antitrust action brought after a bribery scandal involving New York City's program for rehabilitating public housing. The outgrowth of that scandal was a decision that contracts would no longer be entered into with firms which had defaulted or were in arrears with respect to any loans. The policy was also extended to prevent firms that had contracts with the city or were under city supervision from contracting with such defaulting firms. The principals of the plaintiff firm controlled entities which had default on city loans and, as a result, found themselves precluded from contracting with companies that were engaged in city finance reconstruction projects. The resulting antitrust action was subsequently dismissed.

On appeal, the City of New York asserted that under Rule 11, it should have been entitled to its attorney's fees. After reviewing Rule 11, both historically as well as subsequent to the 1983 amendments, Judge Kaufman of the Second Circuit, writing for the court, stated:

> [W]e cannot say for a certainty that Eastway or its counsel acted in subjective bad faith in bringing or maintaining this lawsuit, or that its actual motive was to harass the City. It might just as well have been acting out of frustration or desperation. We can say, however, that its claim of an antitrust violation by non-competitors, without any allegation of antitrust injury, was destined to fail. Moreover, a competent attorney, after reasonable inquiry, would have had to reach the same conclusion.
>
> Accordingly, we hold that it was error for the district court to deny the municipal defendant's motion for attorney's fees incurred in defending against the antitrust claim.

Id. at 254.

Thus, for perhaps the first time, a United States court of appeals focused on Rule 11 and stated quite explicitly that attorneys may no longer find comfort in the fact that they acted with what they believed to be subjective good faith. Rather, attorneys must now make an affirmative inquiry into the viability of the pleading and be prepared to justify that pleading and their signature thereon in an after-the-fact inquiry. The Second Circuit stated:

> No longer is it enough for an attorney to claim that he acted in good faith, or that he personally was unaware of the groundless nature of an argument or claim. For the language of the new Rule 11 explicitly and unambiguously imposes an affirmative duty on each attorney to conduct a reasonable inquiry into the viability of a pleading before it is signed. Simply put, subjective good faith no longer provides the safe harbor it once did.

Id. at 253.

There is little doubt that, in response to a Rule 11 sanctions motion, attorneys frequently will assert that their actions were undertaken in good faith and motivated by the good faith belief that what was contained in the pleading they signed was reasonable.

However, the *Eastway* court pointed out that good faith is no defense to the imposition of sanctions under Rule 11, and the rule does not require that an attorney act in bad faith for sanctions to be imposed.

Furthermore, the purpose of the amendments to Rule 11 was to make judges less reluctant to impose sanctions. The standard which an attorney was expected to meet in affixing his signature to a pleading was meant to be more stringent than the good faith requirements that had traditionally been utilized as a measure of whether or not sanctions would be imposed. The decision of the Second Circuit clearly reflects the intent of the drafters of the amended Rule 11 that subjective bad faith is not necessary as a trigger to sanctions under Rule 11. Rather, sanctions should be awarded against an attorney or the client whenever a pleading has been interposed for any improper purpose or when a competent attorney would conclude that the pleading had no merit.

A recent decision from the United States District Court for the Southern District of New York also focused on the amendments to Rule 11. In *Burlington Coat Factory Warehouse v. Belk Brothers Co.,* 621 F. Supp. 224 (S.D.N.Y. 1985), the court held that an attorney has an affirmative duty to reasonably inquire into the viability of pleadings, motions, or other papers before they are signed.

Rule 11 sanctions are mandatory against an attorney and/or client when it appears the pleading has been interposed for any improper purpose or if, after reasonable inquiry, a competent attorney could not form a reasonable belief that the pleading is well grounded in fact and is warranted by existing law or good faith extension, modification, or reversal of existing law. However, the standard of this new rule is not meant to "stifle the enthusiasm or chill the creativity that is the very lifeblood of the law," *Eastway,* 762 F.2d at 254, but rather, to punish those who manipulate the federal court systems for ends inimical to those for whom it was created.

§ 4.3 —Inadequate Factual Basis for Complaint

A recent case arising in a products liability context focused on the filing of the complaint. In *Albright v. Upjohn Co.*, 780 F.2d 1217 (6th Cir. 1986), the United States Court of Appeals for the Sixth Circuit held that the failure of the plaintiff's attorney to investigate properly the medical records of the client prior to the filing of the action was ground for the imposition of Rule 11 sanctions because the complaint was not well grounded in fact at the time it was filed.

It appears that the plaintiff provided for her attorney copies of all the medical records in her possession, but she was apparently unable to locate records from two other treating physicians. Thereafter, the defendant and other codefendants sought summary judgment on the ground that they had not been identified as the manufacturers of the drugs which were taken by the plaintiff. As a result of the filing of that motion, an amended complaint was filed which excluded Upjohn and the other defendants who had filed a summary judgment motion. The district court granted Upjohn's motion for summary judgment but denied a Rule 11 motion seeking the imposition of sanctions against the plaintiff.

On appeal, the United States Court of Appeals reversed and remanded to the district court for the imposition of sanctions. In doing so, the court of appeals pointed out that Rule 11 requires a prefiling inquiry of not only the facts but the law as well to determine whether the complaint is well grounded in fact and is warranted by existing law. In making this inquiry, the standard for evaluating the conduct of any attorney in the context of Rule 11 is reasonableness under the circumstances.

Plaintiff's attorneys asserted in their defense that they had made an adequate inquiry prior to the filing of the complaint as to the identity of the manufacturers involved in the drug. They further asserted that the medical records of the plaintiff were old and often illegible, that the records of one doctor apparently were lost, and that the efforts to obtain the records from the other doctors were continuing. Furthermore, they asserted that Upjohn was known to be a lead defendant in other similar actions involving drugs.

In reversing, the court of appeals determined that plaintiff's attorneys had brought the claim against Upjohn with the knowledge that there was no factual basis for a claim and that they continued to assert that claim long after it would have been reasonable to enter a dismissal against Upjohn. In addition, the court of appeals found that the plaintiff had not shown any likelihood that additional medical records would be located that could not have been found through reasonable inquiry prior to filing.

It is clear that counsel should never take the complaint for granted insofar as Rule 11 sanctions are concerned. In this regard, as a plaintiff, you should always examine the complaint against the Rule 11 standards. See

§ **4.10**. As a defendant, this tactic is best utilized when you file a set of requests for admissions immediately after the complaint is filed. If the responses you receive from the plaintiff all assert that, without discovery being taken, the plaintiff is not in a position to respond substantively to the requests, you should seriously consider whether a Rule 11 motion should be filed. By its very terms, Rule 11 requires this inquiry to predate the filing of the complaint.

§ 4.4 —Motion to Disqualify

In today's more aggressive litigation atmosphere, Rule 11 clearly acts to temper not only the filing of frivolous complaints but, in the final analysis, the filing of any pleading or document which is being interposed for reasons other than those found by the judge to be justified within the context of the litigation.

For example, motions attempting to disqualify opposing counsel are being filed with increasing frequency. It seems that, in many instances, motions for such disqualification are premised more on technical than on substantive grounds. Rule 11 provides a substantial deterrent for the bringing of such motions.

In *Wold v. Minerals Engineering Corp.,* 575 F. Supp. 166 (D. Colo. 1983), the plaintiff corporation's motion to disqualify a law firm from representing the defendant was found not to have been based on a reasonable inquiry into relevant facts, but rather to have been interposed for improper purposes. The district court found that the motion was filed to harass opposing counsel, cause unnecessary delay in the lawsuit, and needlessly increase the cost of the litigation. As a result, counsel for the plaintiff was required to pay reasonable expenses of the defendant incurred as a result of the filing of the motion to disqualify, including attorneys' fees.

§ 4.5 —Discovery Abuse

There is always a major risk of a litigant's failing to comply with discovery orders. The ultimate sanction is dismissal. In *Jaffe v. Grant,* 793 F.2d 1182 (11th Cir. 1986), the United States Court of Appeals for the Eleventh Circuit determined that sanctions were appropriate and that the trial court had not abused its discretion in striking both the answer filed by the plaintiff and defenses to counterclaims made by the defendant. The order was entered as a sanction for the plaintiff's refusal to comply with discovery orders in the case.

On appeal, the court of appeals affirmed the sanction which had been opposed by the district court and found that the award of attorneys' fees had twice been imposed for an unjustified failure to attend scheduled depositions. As a result, the court of appeals determined that the district court was warranted in finding that any lesser sanctions which may have been contemplated under Federal Rule of Civil Procedure 37 would not have been effective in compelling the plaintiff to respond to the discovery requests in a timely manner.

Aruba Bonaire Curacao Trust Co. v. Commissioner of Internal Revenue, 777 F.2d 38 (D.C. Cir. 1985) presents, in the court's own words, an example "of how attorneys should not operate." In that case, the United States Court of Appeals for the District of Columbia upheld the very serious sanction of dismissal, which had been imposed by the Tax Court against the appellants for failure to present evidence at a discovery hearing.

As the court pointed out, the sanction of dismissal is severe and should be employed only when absolutely necessary. After reviewing the facts of this case, the court upheld the dismissal, finding that it was the proper sanction for failure to produce documents after numerous extensions and four years of litigation.

Obviously, defense counsel never wants to be in the position of having to explain to a client why a case was dismissed or why pleadings have been stricken. Given the attitude of the courts toward the more aggressive enforcement of discovery sanctions, especially insofar as discovery proceedings may impact upon the progress of the litigation, defense counsel would be well advised to review this case as an object lesson.

Parkinson v. Houlihan's/D.C., Inc., No. 84-02038 (D.D.C., decided Dec. 9, 1985), is a decision by United States District Judge Lewis F. Oberdorfer which, as a result of discovery abuses, required the defendant and defense counsel to pay the plaintiff the amount of her costs, including attorneys' fees, for proceedings necessitated by the defendant's obstructive, uncooperative behavior.

The court found that, despite the large number and severity of the discovery abuses, neither the postverdict entry of default against the defendant nor a grant of a third trial was warranted. The record demonstrated that the jury was able to reach a fair determination in favor of the defendant on the merits on the second trial of the personal injury case.

Much of the final resolution of whether such fees and costs are in fact paid depends upon the judge's personality. In this regard, defense counsel must carefully weigh and evaluate the kind of judge with which he or she is dealing and determine whether it is likely that the judge will impose sanctions under Rule 11 or other rules.

§ 4.6 —Withholding Information

Itel Containers International Corp. v. Puerto Rico Marine Management, Inc., No. 83-2673L (D.N.J., decided Oct. 29, 1985), involved the imposition of a $5,000 sanction upon a defendant and his attorney. United

States District Judge Frederick B. Lacey, who has since stepped down from the bench, found that a $5,000 sanction was appropriate for an abuse of the judicial process. He determined that the defendant and his counsel had been aware from the time they received the complaint that the plaintiff had mistakenly invoked diversity jurisdiction. Notwithstanding this knowledge, the defendant and his counsel willfully elected to pursue a litigation strategy of actively concealing from the plaintiff and the court as long as possible the fact that the court was without power to hear the matter. Sanctions ensued.

There is a real balancing of interests which all defense counsel must consider when "sitting on information." Oftentimes, perhaps not as frequently as we might like as defense counsel, we become aware of the fact that something the plaintiff has pleaded is inaccurate either from a factual or legal perspective; the task then is to decide what is the way most advantageous to our clients to bring this to the attention of the court. Frequently the decision is made not to reveal the information at the outset but retain it for some later time when defense counsel can get a greater tactical advantage.

The risk associated with such a course of action is highlighted in the *Itel Containers* case. The court felt that, quite separate and distinct from any advantage or disadvantage to which the plaintiff may have been put, the judicial system had been taken advantage of in a way that justified the imposition of Rule 11 sanctions. Given the wide discretion with which the court is vested in the imposition of such sanctions, it seems clear that defense counsel must carefully consider the ramifications associated with not revealing to the court defective positions taken by the plaintiff.

§ 4.7 —Violation of Local Rule

It is not at all infrequent that plaintiff's counsel plays fast and loose with the rules. This is particularly true when defense counsel is from out of town and the plaintiff's attorney is a member of the local bar. Under such circumstances, it is not unusual to have pleadings filed at the last minute, thereby depriving defense counsel of any opportunity for meaningful reply. *Toombs v. Leone,* 777 F.2d 465 (9th Cir. 1985) stands for the proposition that such tactics are not to be condoned and justify the imposition of sanctions against plaintiff's counsel for attempting to use them.

The Ninth Circuit determined in the *Toombs* case that it was not an abuse of discretion for the district court to impose monetary sanctions on plaintiff's counsel when granting a continuance to the defendants for the plaintiff's failure to comply with a local rule requiring that brief and exhibits be filed seven days before trial. In *Toombs,* plaintiff's counsel filed a 148-page brief and 282 exhibits on the morning of trial. Counsel acknowledged that they were aware of the seven-day rule and admitted that they had deliberately flouted it in order to produce a thorough and complete brief and set of exhibits.

§ 4.8 Practical Considerations

From a trial lawyer's perspective, a number of steps should be taken in order to protect against the possibility of the imposition of sanctions under Rule 11. Among others to be kept in mind and considered are the following:

1. Prior to signing any pleading which you have reason to believe, whether realistically or unrealistically, may subject you to a motion for sanctions, specifically and consciously take Rule 11 into account and review it. This is important not so much for the exercise of going through the rule prior to signing the pleading, but rather for the ability later to file an affidavit, when resisting Rule 11 sanctions, that you specifically did consider the rule and its individual provisions.

   In this regard you should go through the mental process of determining what steps you took to make the reasonable inquiry required by the rule:

   a. That the facts of the case justify the filing of the particular pleading
   b. Whether you are filing the pleading in question based upon existing law or whether you are seeking an extension, modification, or reversal of existing law
   c. That your intent with filing the pleading was not to harass, delay, or increase the cost of the litigation.

   Although each of these simply is an element of the rule itself, the ability to execute an affidavit in opposition to Rule 11 sanctions which may be sought by your opponent that you in fact went through this mental process in some detail prior to filing the actual pleading can provide a substantial tool for combating such sanctions. The checklist in § **4.10** can assist you in proving that such an inquiry was made.

2. When resisting the imposition of sanctions, consider the amount of time which you had available to you for investigation prior to signing the pleading. For example, if the pleading in question is one arising in a temporary restraining order (TRO) setting, the amount of time involved which you may have available to investigate or make your "reasonable inquiry" would be far less than that involved in other kinds of litigation. As a result, there is no purely objective standard

to be utilized in determining what is a reasonable inquiry. Rather, the question of what is a reasonable inquiry must be determined on the circumstances of the litigation, and this should be referred to in opposition papers.

3. Consider the source of the information upon which you are relying in filing a certain pleading. For example, in many instances the information must come by way of the client. What additional inquiry, if any, can be made beyond the client? As a practical matter, is any additional inquiry necessary or fruitful? Be sure to aver that "reasonable inquiry" or the reason that the reasonable inquiry was limited to the sources which it was under the circumstances.
4. Consider whether the pleading in question was based on, as the Advisory Committee's notes indicate, a "plausible view of the law."
5. Consider whether forwarding counsel or some other member of the bar was relied upon in connection with representations, knowledge, or other aspects of the pleading. This may in fact provide some sort of mitigation with respect to whether sanctions are appropriate under Rule 11.

Keep in mind that Rule 11 does not require an attorney to disclose either privileged communications or work product for the purpose of demonstrating that the signing of pleadings was justified. The Advisory Committee Notes to the 1983 amendments make it quite clear that Fed. R. Civ. P. 26(c) is still available for the purpose of protecting work product or attorney-client communications when either one of those sources of information has been utilized as the basis for the signing of a pleading.

§ 4.9 —Timing

Generally, as noted in the Advisory Committee Notes to the 1983 amendments, a party to litigation who seeks sanctions should give notice to the court and the party against whom the sanctions are being sought promptly upon a basis for such sanctions becoming known. However, the question of when the sanctions are imposed quite obviously rests within the broad discretion of the trial judge. More often than not, as in many sanction-related matters, this will be determined at the conclusion of the litigation in its entirety. Indeed, sanctions may be imposed even against the prevailing party if the basis for the sanctions is independently viable and separate from a resolution of the case.

When an opponent does not promptly bring to the attention of the court conduct which may in fact justify the imposition of Rule 11 sanctions, an argument may be made that sanctions are waived. Certainly, an equitable estoppel argument should be made. However, whether such a defense to otherwise sanctionable conduct will prevail rests within the broad discretion of the trial judge.

§ 4.10 Rule 11 Checklist

Given the increasing propensity of lawyers to file Rule 11 motions, there is an excellent technique available which can help protect you against the successful imposition of sanctions in a case. Let's call this technique the "Rule 11 Checklist."

Assume that you are involved in a case in which you think it is likely that sanctions motions will be filed. Furthermore, assume that you are about to sign a pleading which, due to either the substance of the pleading or the nature of your relationship with opposing counsel, may well draw a Rule 11 motion. Frequently, Rule 11 controversies come down to questions of credibility—that is, what an attorney did prior to signing a pleading.

Rule 11 no longer depends upon good faith inquiries on the part of an attorney, but rather upon whether he has read the pleading, and to the best of his knowledge, information, or belief formed after reasonable inquiries, it is well grounded in fact and warranted by existing law or an extension of existing law. The Rule 11 checklist can provide an excellent piece of contemporaneous evidence from which you can argue that Rule 11 sanctions should not be imposed.

The procedure which you will follow in connection with utilizing the Rule 11 checklist is to complete a single page form similar to the one which follows. You should do this at the time when you affix your signature to the pleading. As you can see, this form is nothing more than Rule 11 put into checklist form with other appropriate entries which will permit you later to argue quite persuasively to the court that Rule 11 was very much on your mind at the time you signed the pleading.

An additional benefit of this form is that it requires you to make an item-by-item examination of Rule 11 for the purpose of insuring that such sanctions cannot be imposed. The mere fact of doing this frequently is enough to persuade you not to file something or to satisfy you that sanctions are not justified.

Rule 11 Checklist

Case: ____________

Rule 11. Signing of Pleadings, Motions, and Other Papers; Sanctions

Every pleading, motion, and other paper of a party represented by an attorney shall be signed by at least one attorney of record in his individual name, whose address shall be stated. A party who is not represented by an attorney shall sign his pleading, motion, or other paper and state his address. Except when otherwise specifically provided by the rule or statute, pleadings need not be verified or accompanied by affidavit. The rule in equity that the averments of an answer under oath must be overcome by the testimony of two witnesses or of one witness sustained by corroborating circumstances is abolished. The signature of an attorney or party constitutes a certificate by him:

____ That he has read the pleading, motion, or other paper

____ That to the best of his knowledge, information, and belief formed after reasonable inquiry it is well grounded in fact and is warranted by existing law or a good faith argument for the extension, modification, or reversal of existing law, and

____ That it is not interposed for any proper purpose, such as to harass or to cause unnecessary delay or needless increase in the cost of litigation.

If a pleading, motion, or other paper is not signed, it shall be stricken unless it is signed promptly after the omission is called to the attention of the pleader or movant. If a pleading, motion, or other paper is signed in violation of this rule, the court, upon motion or upon its own initiative, shall impose upon the person who signed it, a represented party, or both, an appropriate sanction, which may include an order to pay to the other party or parties the amount of the reasonable expenses incurred because of the filing of the pleading, motion, or other paper, including a reasonable attorney's fee.

In connection with the filing of [*insert name of pleading to be signed*], I have reviewed Rule 11 and the requirements of that rule prior to signing the pleading.

Date: ________________ ____________________________

Signature

____

Typed Name

§ 4.11 Responding to Rule 11 Motions

Motions practice is one aspect of pretrial proceedings which can take an inordinate amount of time and attention. The device of motions, whatever their character, is generally used to get interim rulings from a judge on matters smaller than the entire case. However, there is an aspect of motions practice which has larger implications.

Several kinds of motions are used to seek relief from the court in the nature of characterizing an opponent as violating the procedures of discovery or orders of court. Thus, when a party files a sanctions motion or a certain type of discovery motion, such as a motion to compel, the implication is that the party against whom it is filed is guilty of some wrongdoing.

Such a motion immediately puts the latter party on the defensive, requiring that it come forward and prove to the court that the relief being sought is not warranted.

From the movant's point of view, the strength of such a motion is that it puts an opponent on the defensive and clearly casts suspicion on opposing counsel. In many circumstances, such motions are filed simply for tactical reasons and do not have any necessary relationship to what is actually transpiring at a given time.

When confronting motions of this type, filed without a complete foundation and for the purpose of establishing a broad picture, it is important to deal with the specific allegations on a point-by-point basis and thereby avoid meeting your adversary on a battleground chosen by him or her for prejudicial purposes.

One of the most effective preventive techniques for accomplishing this goal, while at the same time responding in a manner calculated to do you the most good, is to maintain a log during the discovery process of all the efforts which you have made to respond to discovery or to work out discovery differences with your opponents. Such a log could include copies of all correspondence between you and your opponent attempting to resolve discovery disputes. Sanctions and other types of discovery motions filed for the purpose of prejudicing your cause frequently deal in generalities. Your ability to respond with detailed statements of what really happened will often turn the tables on your opponent.

Another technique for protecting yourself against motions of this type is to maintain a telephone log of all conversations which may relate to a particular case. This will put you in an excellent position to reconstruct events. Finally, your conduct of discovery sessions, especially production sessions, on the record (along with the written responses to all such discovery requests addressed to you) is always a substantial benefit in attempting to reconstruct the record later.

One tactic sometimes attempted in responding to discovery motions of this type is to file a countermotion. Frequently, this is not a good tactic, because it can prejudice you and make it appear as if your taking the offensive through the countermotion is nothing more than an attempt to cloud the issues.

Denial of a discovery motion filed against you can frequently be a far greater benefit than the granting of your countermotion; your opponent will lose credibility with the court, and, in the event that a true discovery dispute arises in which your position is not sound, your opponent may not be in a position to make a second trip to court.

There are several tactical and practical considerations to remember in dealing with sanctions motions, motions to compel, and similar types of discovery motions:

1. Deal with each allegation on a specific and detailed basis.
2. Do not make general responses which paint with a broad brush.

3. Attach as many supporting documents to your response as possible, including copies of correspondence, copies of discovery pleadings, transcript excerpts, and, when appropriate, affidavits.
4. Consider whether you should file a countermotion or responsive motion. The downside risk is that such a motion may be characterized as a tactic to shift unjustifiably the attention of the court. Often it is better simply to meet your opponent's allegations head-on and point out to the court how frivolous they really are.
5. Always attach a proposed order to your responsive pleadings specifically detailing precisely what action you wish the court to take in dealing with your opponent's motion.
6. If possible, without being too obvious about how you accomplish it, characterize your opponent's motions as a personal attack on you as distinguished from a justified attempt to seek the aid of the court in a valid discovery dispute.
7. Always step back from the dispute in question and judge its merits as they will be perceived by a third person—the judge. Remember, in the thick of the battle you may not be the best person to determine the merits of allegations directed at you or your position. If your opponent loses the motion, his or her credibility will be severely impaired before the court, especially if you are able to shape the judge's response. By the same token, however, if you lose the motion, your credibility will be impaired.

CHAPTER 5

SANCTIONS: FAILURE TO PROSECUTE OR OBEY COURT ORDERS

§ 5.1 Introduction

Because Federal Rule of Civil Procedure 37 applies only to discovery abuses, courts have used their inherent powers as well as Rules 41 and 16 to impose sanctions for failure to prosecute and otherwise obey court orders. Rule 41 is directed primarily at plaintiffs; inherent powers and Rule 16 permit sanctions against all litigants.

§ 5.2 Rule 41(b)—Overview

Rule 41(b) provides that a defendant can move for dismissal of an action or claim for failure by the plaintiff to prosecute or to comply with the federal rules or any order of the court. Unless otherwise specified, such dismissals operate as an adjudication upon the merits. Fed. R. Civ. P. 41 (b). *But see Combined Network v. Equitable Life Assurance Society,* 805 F.2d

1292, 1298 (7th Cir. 1986). Unlike Rule 37, which can be invoked by either party, Rule 41 provides sanctions solely against claimants. Therefore, a defendant's conduct can be reached through Rule 41(b) only as to any counterclaim, cross-claim or third party action which it has brought.

A dismissal under Rule 41(b) or the court's inherent power is reviewed for abuse of discretion. *Link v. Wabash Railroad,* 370 U.S. 626, 633 (1962). Dismissals without prejudice are reviewed under the same standard as dismissals with prejudice when they result in time barring of a claim. *McGowan v. Faulkner Concrete Pipe Co.,* 659 F.2d 554, 556 (5th Cir. 1981).

Most circuits have adopted basically identical standards for evaluating sanctions imposed under Rules 41(b) and 37. *See, e.g., Scarborough v. Eubanks,* 747 F.2d 871, 874–78 (3d Cir. 1984). Often it is difficult to tell which of these rules is being invoked to authorize a given sanction. *See, e.g., Fletcher v. Southern Farm Bureau Life Insurance Co.,* 757 F.2d 953, 956 (8th Cir. 1985); *Corchado v. Puerto Rico Marine Management, Inc.,* 665 F.2d 410, 413 (1st Cir. 1981), *cert. denied,* 459 U.S. 826 (1982). Although the Supreme Court has distinguished them on the basis that Rule 37 applies to discovery failures, whereas Rule 41 is concerned with trials, *Societe Internationale v. Rogers,* 357 U.S. 197, 206–07 (1958), it is often appropriate to cite both rules when the plaintiff is guilty of both dilatory discovery conduct and violating court orders. Courts appear to treat failures to prosecute interchangeably with failures to comply with court orders. *See* 5 J. Moore *et al., Moore's Federal Practice* ¶ 41.12, at 41–152 (2d ed. 1986) [hereinafter *Moore's Federal Practice*].

Although Rule 41(b) provides only for dismissal, courts can and do invoke lesser sanctions, including fines, costs, damages, attorney disciplinary measures, formal reprimands, placing the case at the bottom of the calendar, the temporary suspension of culpable counsel from practice before the court, preclusion of claims or defenses, dismissal unless new counsel is secured, and dismissal without prejudice. *See, e.g., Sturgeon v. Airborne Freight Corp.,* 778 F.2d 1154, 1159 (5th Cir. 1985); *Titus v. Mercedes Benz of North America,* 695 F.2d 746, 749 n.6 (3d Cir. 1982); *Zavala Santiago v. Gonzalez Rivera,* 553 F.2d 710, 712 n.1 (1st Cir. 1977). In fact, most circuits require the judge to consider or make express findings that less drastic sanctions would not be effective before permitting a Rule 41(b) dismissal. *See Shea v. Donohoe Construction Co.,* 795 F.2d 1071, 1072 (D.C. Cir. 1986); *Webber v. Eye Corp.,* 721 F.2d 1067, 1070 (7th Cir. 1983); *Harding v. Federal Reserve Bank of New York,* 707 F.2d 46, 50 (2d Cir. 1983); *Titus v. Mercedes Benz,* 695 F.2d at 747; *Raiford v. Pounds,* 640 F.2d 944, 945 (9th Cir. 1981) (per curiam). Rule 41(b) dismissals usually are reserved for those cases in which there is a clear record of delay or contumacious conduct. *See, e.g., Jackson v. Schoemehl,* 788 F.2d 1296, 1299 (8th Cir. 1986); *Webber v. Eye Corp.,*

721 F.2d at 1069, 1070; *Madesky v. Campbell,* 705 F.2d 703, 704 (3d Cir. 1983); *Gonzalez v. Firestone Tire & Rubber Co.,* 610 F.2d 241, 247 (5th Cir. 1980). Simple negligence is not thought to warrant dismissal. *McKelvey v. AT&T Technologies, Inc.,* 789 F.2d 1518, 1520 (11th Cir. 1986).

In general, when deciding Rule 41(b) motions, the district court weighs the court's need to manage its docket, the public interest in expeditious resolution of litigation, and the risk of prejudice to the defendants against the policy favoring disposition of cases on their merits. *Mir v. Fosburg,* 706 F.2d 916, 918 (9th Cir. 1983); *see Lyell Theatre Corp. v. Loew's Corp.,* 682 F.2d 37, 43 (2d Cir. 1982).

Several circuits view the following specific factors as relevant to determining whether a dismissal with prejudice is appropriate:

1. The degree of the plaintiff's personal responsibility for the delay
2. Prejudice to the defendant occasioned by the delay
3. Any history that the plaintiff proceeded in a dilatory manner, and
4. The effectiveness of sanctions other than dismissal.

Donnelly v. Johns-Mansville Sales Corp., 677 F.2d 339, 342 (3d Cir. 1982); *Morris v. Ocean Systems, Inc.,* 730 F.2d 248, 252 (5th Cir. 1984); *Davis v. Williams,* 588 F.2d 309, 312 (2d Cir. 1986); *Ash v. Cvetkow,* 739 F.2d 493, 496 (9th Cir. 1984), *cert. denied,* 470 U.S. 1007 (1985).

Irreparable harm to the adverse party is probably the most important factor considered. *See, e.g., Raiford v. Pounds,* 640 F.2d at 945. A court may also consider whether the plaintiff had received notice that further delays would result in dismissal. *See Hamilton v. Neptune Orient Lines, Ltd.,* 811 F.2d 498, 500 (9th Cir. 1987); *Cohen v. Carnival Cruise Lines, Inc.,* 782 F.2d 923, 925–26 (11th Cir. 1986); *Harding v. Federal Reserve Bank of New York,* 707 F.2d at 50.

These criteria should be kept in mind when structuring motions and responses even in those circuits not requiring their mandatory consideration. Counsel should also be aware that Rule 41(b) motions which are brought well after the offending conduct are not likely to be granted. *See, e.g., Stock Pot Restaurant, Inc. v. Stockpot, Inc.,* 737 F.2d 1576, 1581 (Fed. Cir. 1984). It is also rare that the court's refusal to dismiss an action for failure to prosecute will be an abuse of discretion. *See, e.g., United States v. Berney,* 713 F.2d 568, 571 (10th Cir. 1983).

§ 5.3 —Failure to Prosecute and Delays

Lawyers who are used to state systems in which it is usual for cases to drag on for several years with no activity are often unprepared for the swiftness with which federal judges dismiss actions for failure to prosecute. Because federal rules rather than state procedures govern such dismissals in diversity actions, *see Olympic Sports Products, Inc. v. Universal Athletic Sales Co.,* 760 F.2d 910, 916 (9th Cir. 1985), cert. denied, _____ U.S. _____, 106 S. Ct. 804 (1986) (California five-year rule does not apply in federal court), you must be prepared to proceed quickly, although a plaintiff will not be penalized for any dilatory conduct in state court prior to removal. *Nealey v. Transportacion Maritima Mexicana, S.A.,* 662 F.2d 1275, 1279 (9th Cir. 1980). In some district courts, the goal is to try cases within 12 to 18 months of filing, and the local rules are written accordingly to prod lawyers into action at the risk of sanctions ranging from fines to dismissals. *See, e.g.,* Cal. C.D. Rules 6 and 9. A significant number of such dismissals are ordered sua sponte by the court without any notice of hearing; therefore, you can rely on the defendant's acquiescence to dilatory conduct. If a plaintiff's counsel is experiencing difficulty in obtaining discovery or witnesses, the court should be notified of any reasons causing the delay to avoid a sua sponte dismissal. *See Sturgeon v. Airborne Freight Corp.,* 778 F.2d 1154, 1160–61 (5th Cir. 1985).

A single failure to attend a pretrial hearing or otherwise prosecute or comply with the court's order is usually not considered sufficient to warrant a dismissal. *Link v. Wabash Railroad.,* 370 U.S. 626, 634–35 (1962); *Jones v. Graham,* 709 F.2d 1457, 1462 (11th Cir. 1983); *Harding v. Federal Reserve Bank of New York,* 707 F.2d 46, 50, (2d Cir. 1983); *see Stevens v. Greyhound Lines, Inc.,* 710 F.2d 1224, 1230 (7th Cir. 1983). However, a court can rely on all circumstances in the case, including earlier delays, in justifying its dismissal. *Garrison v. International Paper Co.,* 714 F.2d 757, 760 (8th Cir. 1983); *see Link v. Wabash Railroad,* 370 U.S. at 633; *Lyell Theatre Corp. v. Loew's Corp.,* 682 F.2d 37, 43 (2d Cir. 1982).

Although there is no magic time beyond which dismissal is justified, the newer the case, the more likely an appellate court will reverse a dismissal. *See Shea v. Donohoe Construction Co.,* 795 F.2d 1071, 1072 (D.C. Cir. 1986); *Batson v. Neal Spelce Associates, Inc.,* 765 F.2d 511, 516 n.2 (5th Cir. 1985); *Webber v. Eye Corp.,* 721 F.2d 1067, 1070 (7th Cir. 1983); *Harding v. Federal Reserve Bank of New York,* 707 F.2d at 50; *Titus v. Mercedes Benz of North America,* 695 F.2d 746, 749 (3d Cir. 1982); *Raiford v. Pounds,* 640 F.2d 944, 945 (9th Cir. 1981) (per curiam). However, even an action which is pending only for one year can warrant dismissal when it has been neglected by counsel and court orders are ignored. *See Chira v. Lockheed Aircraft Corp.,* 634 F.2d 664, 665–66 (2d Cir. 1980).

The length of delay may be an indication that prejudice has occurred, but it is not clear whether delay alone justifies dismissal. *See Mir v. Fosburg,* 706 F.2d 916, 919 n.2 (9th Cir. 1983). In a few circuits, prejudice cannot be presumed or established by conclusory allegations. *E.g., Tamini v. M/V Jewon,* 808 F.2d 978, 981 (2d Cir. 1987); 9 C. Wright & A. Miller,

Federal Practice and Procedure § 2370, at 216 (1971) [hereinafter *Federal Practice and Procedure*]; *see Washington v. Walker,* 734 F.2d 1237, 1240 (7th Cir. 1984); *Garrison v. International Paper Co.,* 714 F.2d at 760. In other circuits, unreasonable delay spanning several years appears to entitle a court to presume prejudice. *Shea v. Donohoe Construction Co.,* 795 F.2d. If a plaintiff comes forth with a nonfrivolous excuse for the delay, the burden of production shifts to the defendant to show at least some actual prejudice. *Nealey v. Transportacion Maritima Mexicana, S.A.,* 662 F.2d at 1281. The plaintiff must then persuade the court that such prejudice is either illusory or relatively insignificant when compared to the reason for the delay. *Id.*

§ 5.4 —Local Rules

Local rules should always be consulted, because it is common for such rules to obligate plaintiffs to take affirmative action to bring the case to trial and authorize dismissal for inactivity. Often such rules can reverse the normal presumption that a dismissal is with prejudice and authorize dismissals without prejudice in the absence of a court directive to the contrary.

In the absence of local rules, a plaintiff is not obligated to notify the court of its readiness or procure a trial date after the completion of discovery. *See Ace Novelty Co. v. Gooding Amusement Co.,* 664 F.2d 761, 763 (9th Cir. 1981). When faced with delay in the absence of a local rule, defense counsel can request or the judge can sua sponte impose a discovery and trial schedule, the violation of which can result in dismissal. *See* Rules 16(b) and 26(f); *see also Mir v. Fosburg,* 706 F.2d 916, 919 (9th Cir. 1983).

§ 5.5 —Misconduct of Counsel

Many dismissals for failure to prosecute turn on the conduct of counsel. In *Link v. Wabash Railroad,* 370 U.S. 626, 633-34 (1962), the Supreme Court made clear that a plaintiff cannot avoid dismissal by disclaiming counsel's unexcused conduct, because the party voluntarily chose counsel and cannot avoid the consequences of counsel's acts or omissions. Most circuits temper this language with the requirement that the client knew of or participated in the attorney's failure to prosecute as a prerequisite to dismissal, *see, e.g., Carter v. Albert Einstein Medical Center,* 804 F.2d 805, 807 (3d Cir. 1986); *Shea v. Donohoe Construction Co.,* 795 F.2d 1071, 1077–78 (D.C. Cir. 1986); *Taylor v. Combustion Engineering, Inc.,* 782 F.2d 525 (5th Cir. 1986); *but see Corchado v. Puerto Rico Marine Management, Inc.,* 665 F.2d 410, 413 (1st Cir. 1981), *cert. denied,* 459 U.S. 826

(1982), unless no other sanction would cure the harm caused to the defendant, *Goforth v. Owens,* 766 F.2d 1533, 1535 (11th Cir. 1985); *see Shea v. Donohoe Construction Co.,* 795 F.2d at 1071. For example, the D.C. Circuit has held that an attorney's failure to attend three separate status calls was not sufficient to justify dismissal, but only a sanction directed against the attorney, unless the plaintiff had been previously notified that any recurrence of the attorney's misconduct would result in dismissal. *Id.* at 1078–79.

Similarly, when the plaintiff was blameless, dismissals have been reversed, even though counsel's efforts were wholly insufficient. *See Haley v. Kansas City Star,* 761 F.2d 489, 491 (8th Cir. 1985); *Carter v. City of Memphis,* 636 F.2d 159, 161 (6th Cir. 1980). Courts have suggested that the offending attorney be required to pay costs and expenses or face attorney disciplinary proceedings in lieu of dismissing a plaintiff who lacked culpability. *See Shea v. Donohoe Construction Co.,* 795 F.2d at 1077–78; *Hollis v. United States,* 744 F.2d 1430, 1433 (10th Cir. 1984); *Webber v. Eye Corp.,* 721 F.2d 1067, 1069 n.2 (7th Cir. 1983). On the other hand, it was not an abuse of discretion to refuse to reinstate the action of an initially blameless plaintiff who waited several months after learning of the dismissal to request reconsideration. *Kagan v. Caterpillar Tractor Co.,* 795 F.2d 601, 611–12 (7th Cir. 1986).

§ 5.6 —Pro Se Litigants

The complaints of pro se litigants can be dismissed for failure to prosecute. *See, e.g., Bomate v. Ford Motor Co.,* 761 F.2d 713, 714 (D.C. Cir. 1985) (with prejudice); *Stevens v. Greyhound Lines, Inc.,* 710 F.2d 1224, 1230 (7th Cir. 1983) (with prejudice); *Schooley v. Kennedy,* 712 F.2d 372, 373–74 (11th Cir. 1983) (without prejudice). However, dismissals of pro se litigants who are incarcerated for failure to appear have been reversed. *Reynolds v. Foree,* 771 F.2d 1179, 1181 (8th Cir. 1985); *Sisk v. United States,* 756 F.2d 497, 499–500 (7th Cir. 1985); *Holt v. Pitts,* 619 F.2d 558, 562 (6th Cir. 1980); *cf. Romandette v. Weetabix Co.,* 807 F.2d 309, 312 (2d Cir. 1986) (41(b) dismissal reversed when failure of incarcerated plaintiff to serve complaint was because of delay by marshal).

A delay in paying a filing fee after being denied in forma pauperis status did not justify dismissal. *Rodgers v. Bowen,* 790 F.2d 1550, 1553 (11th Cir. 1986). However, the Sixth Circuit has permitted dismissal of an indigent plaintiff's complaint when the failure to produce witnesses resulted from lack of funds to pay attendance fees. *Johnson v. Hubbard,* 698 F.2d 286, 291 (6th Cir.), *cert. denied,* 464 U.S. 917 (1983). In some circuits the failure of the district judge to warn a pro se litigant of the consequences of neglect may result in a reversal of a dismissal for failure to prosecute. *See, e.g., Schilling v. Walworth County Parks & Planning Commission,* 805 F.2d 272, 277–78 (7th Cir. 1986).

§ 5.7 —Failure to Comply with Court Orders and Other Rules

Unlike Rule 37, which does not permit a dismissal for failure to pay monetary sanctions unrelated to the merits, a Rule 41(b) dismissal for failure to prosecute or comply with court orders may be upheld when a plaintiff who was able to pay court-ordered sanctions failed to do so. *See Hornbuckle v. Arco Oil & Gas Co.,* 770 F.2d 1321, 1322 (5th Cir. 1985), *cert. denied,* _____ U.S. _____, 106 S. Ct. 1198 (1986); *Gibbs v. Maxwell House,* 738 F.2d 1153, 1154–55 (11th Cir. 1984).

Similarly, a dismissal without prejudice may be turned into a dismissal with prejudice if a party fails to follow a court's directive. For example, a dismissal is granted without prejudice under Rule 41(b) if no amendment is served. *See Toyota Landscape Co. v. Building Material & Dump Truck Drivers Local 420,* 726 F.2d 525, 528 (9th Cir.), *cert. denied,* 469 U.S. 825 (1984).

The Ninth Circuit has cautioned that a plaintiff who takes dismissal with prejudice under Rule 41(b) to challenge the denial of a dismissal without prejudice under Rule 41(a)(2) proceeds at its peril. *Kern Oil & Refining Co. v. Tenneco Oil Co.,* 792 F.2d 1380, 1389 (9th Cir. 1986).

Failure to comply with Federal Rule of Civil Procedure 8 to set forth a short, clear, concise statement of a claim can also support a Rule 41(b) dismissal. *Nevijel v. North Coast Life Insurance Co.,* 651 F.2d 1380, 1389 (9th Cir. 1986).

§ 5.8 —Opportunity to Respond to a Rule 41(b) Dismissal

The Supreme Court has specifically held that the absence of notice and an adversary hearing did not render a Rule 41(b) dismissal void, *Link v. Wabash Railroad,* 370 U.S. 626, 632 (1962), because a party's knowledge of the circumstances surrounding the dilatory conduct may be taken to show notice of the consequences of the party's misconduct. Therefore, counsel cannot be assured of obtaining notice and a hearing prior to dismissal. *See, e.g., Price v. McGlathery,* 792 F.2d 472, 475 (5th Cir. 1986) (per curiam); *Colokathis v. Wentworth-Douglass Hospital,* 693 F.2d 7, 10 (1st Cir. 1982), *cert. denied,* 461 U.S. 915 (1983).

If it is unclear whether the dismissal was with prejudice, a motion for clarification or, alternatively, to vacate judgment should be brought. *See, e.g., In re Jee,* 799 F.2d 532, 534 (9th Cir. 1986). If the action is dismissed with prejudice or after the statute of limitations has run, the plaintiff should always bring a Rule 60(b) motion to reopen the case in order to establish whatever justification exists for the dilatory or contumacious conduct. Failure to do so is often considered as a factor weighing against reversal, because the court can assume that the offending behavior was deliberate rather than negligent in the absence of adequate explanations given in a Rule 60(b) motion. *See, e.g., Link v. Wabash Railroad,* 370 U.S. at 632, 635–36; *Price v. McGlathery,* 792 F.2d at 476.

Because the Rule 60(b) motion does not extend the time to appeal, you must be careful to appeal from the underlying dismissal as well as the denial to reopen, because a Rule 60(b) motion does not permit the review of the underlying judgment, even if it was erroneous. *Carter by Carter v. United States,* 780 F.2d 925, 927–28 (11th Cir. 1986); *see Kagan v. Caterpillar Tractor Co.,* 795 F.2d 601, 606–07 (7th Cir. 1986). If a timely appeal was not filed, counsel should request the appellate court to treat a Rule 60(b) motion made within 10 days of judgment as a Rule 59(e) motion to alter judgment, because the denial of that motion would permit an otherwise untimely appeal of the underlying dismissal. *See, e.g., Jackson v. Schoemehl,* 788 F.2d 1296, 1297–99 (8th Cir. 1986); *Lyell Theatre Corp. v. Loew's Corp.,* 682 F.2d 37, 41 (2d Cir. 1982).

§ 5.9 Sanctions Pursuant to the Court's Inherent Powers

Inherent powers are those which are necessary to the exercise of all others. *Roadway Express, Inc. v. Piper,* 447 U.S. 752, 764 (1980). Because they are shielded from direct democratic controls, inherent powers are required to be exercised with restraint and discretion. *Id.* Although the court has inherent power to enter appropriate orders to facilitate the deposition of court business, *Holcomb v. Allis-Chalmers Corp.,* 774 F.2d 398, 401–02 (10th Cir. 1985), the entry of such orders must comport with due process. *Id.* at 402. The court has inherent power to sanction attorneys as well as parties.

Attorneys' fees can be awarded under the court's inherent power on a finding of bad faith, *see Roadway Express, Inc. v. Piper,* 447 U.S. 752, 766–67 (1980), even if the litigation had a factual and legal basis, because bad faith may be found not only in bringing the litigation but in its conduct. *Id.; Hall v. Cole,* 412 U.S. 1, 15 (1973); *Lipsig v. National Student Marketing Corp.,* 663 F.2d 178, 182 (D.C. Cir. 1980). An attorney's failure to file answers by the date ordered by the court can also result in monetary sanctions under the court's inherent power.

Courts can terminate cases under their inherent powers. Although Rule 41(b) provides for dismissal only upon motion of a defendant, the courts have inherent power to dismiss an action sua sponte for plaintiffs' failure to prosecute or obey court orders, *Goforth v. Owens,* 766 F.2d 1533, 1535 (11th Cir. 1985); *see Shea v. Donohoe Construction Co.,* 795 F.2d 1071 (D.C. Cir. 1986), and frequently use this power. This authority is vested in courts so that judges can manage their own affairs to achieve the orderly and expeditious disposition of cases. *Id.* Such power is considered necessary in order to prevent undue delays in the disposition of pending cases and to avoid congestion in the court's caseload under the inherent authority in Rule 16(f).

The court also has inherent power to dismiss an action if a party has willfully deceived the court and engaged in conduct utterly inconsistent with the orderly administration of justice. *Fjelstad v. American Honda Motor Co.,* 762 F.2d 1334, 1338 (9th Cir. 1985). Such dismissals are imposed only in extreme circumstances in which the deceptive conduct is willful or in bad faith or relates to the matters in controversy in such a way as to interfere with the rightful decision of the case. *United States v. National Medical Enterprises, Inc.,* 792 F.2d 906 (9th Cir. 1986). Similarly, a default was proper to vindicate the integrity of court proceedings when the defendants purposely misled the judge, even though the conduct leading to the default was technically within Rule 37. *Brockton Savings Bank v. Peat Marwick, Mitchell & Co.,* 771 F.2d 5, 11–12 (1st Cir. 1985), *cert. denied,* _____ U.S. _____, 106 S. Ct. 1204 (1986). On the other hand, a partial default imposed pursuant to the court's inherent powers was reversed when the party's failure to provide information occurred before it was joined as a defendant. *Fjelstad v. American Honda Motor Co.,* 762 F.2d at 1338. When the deceit related to a peripheral matter, a default was also improper. *Phoceene Sous-Marine, S.A. v. U.S. Phosmarine, Inc.,* 682 F.2d 802, 806 (9th Cir. 1982).

§ 5.10 Rule 16(f) Sanctions

Rule 16(f) provides that if a party or party's attorney fails to obey a scheduling or pretrial order, fails to appear at a conference, or is unprepared for or does not participate in good faith at a pretrial conference, the judge can apply sanctions as provided in Rule 37(b)(2)(B), (C), and (D) as well as imposc attorney's fees incurred by the noncompliance. Therefore, a full range of discovery sanctions, including dismissal, default, preclusion orders, contempt, and awards of expenses are available for breaches of pretrial practice. *Rabb v. Amatex Corp.,* 769 F.2d 996, 999 (4th Cir. 1985); *see generally* 3 *Moore's Federal Practice* ¶ 16.22 (2d ed. 1985).

Although this rule has not been frequently cited, it has been considered as an alternative reason to justify a dismissal for failure to prosecute or obey a court order. *Sherman v. United States,* 801 F.2d 1133, 1134–35 (9th

Cir. 1986); *Goforth v. Owens,* 766 F.2d 1533, 1535 (11th Cir. 1985). The rule is intended to encourage forceful judicial management, but the Second Circuit has noted that it "did not loose a strange and capricious new beast." *Salahuddin v. Harris,* 782 F.2d 1127, 1133 (2d Cir. 1986).

Rule 16(f) is designed to punish lawyers and parties for conduct which unreasonably delays or otherwise interferes with the expeditious management of trial preparation. *In re Baker,* 744 F.2d 1438, 1441 (10th Cir. 1984) (en banc), *cert. denied,* 471 U.S. 1014 (1985). Therefore, when the misconduct is caused by counsel, sanctions should be directed against that individual rather than the party. *Seismic International Research Corp. v. South Ranch Oil Co.,* 793 F.2d 227, 230 (10th Cir. 1986).

Common pretrial failings which are subject to sanctions under either Rule 41(b) or Rule 16(f) include ignoring discovery deadlines or requirements for disclosure of expert witnesses, not filing or failing to amend pretrial statements, and unexcused absences from pretrial conferences. Rule 16(f) has also been cited as authority to assess a fine on attorneys who have not been held in contempt. *Smith v. Rowe,* 761 F.2d 360, 366 (7th Cir. 1985); *In re Baker,* 744 F.2d at 1440. The Fifth Circuit has noted that the same criteria developed for evaluating Rule 41(b) dismissals apply to Rule 16(f), *Price v. McGlathery,* 792 F.2d 472, 474 (5th Cir. 1986) (per curiam), while the Second and Fourth Circuits have considered such sanctions as more appropriately falling with Rule 37, *see Salahuddin v. Harris,* 782 F.2d at 1133; *Rabb v. Amatex Corp.,* 769 F.2d at 999. As a practical matter, most circuits apply virtually identical criteria to Rules 37 and 41 sanctions. The Ninth Circuit has required notice and an opportunity to be heard before the imposition of Rule 16(f) sanctions, *Ford v. Alfara,* 785 F.2d 835, 840 (9th Cir. 1986), but not all circuits can be expected to follow this procedure.

There appears to be some disagreement whether Rule 16(f) sanctions are appropriate if there has been no violation of an explicit order. *Compare Salahuddin v. Harris,* 782 F.2d at 1133 (no sanctions if order implicit) *with In re Baker,* 744 F.2d at 1440 (not necessary to violate court order). Rule 16(f) sanctions were not considered appropriate as a means for clubbing the parties into an involuntary settlement by assessing attorneys' fees against a defendant who failed to settle a case prior to trial. *Kothe v. Smith,* 771 F.2d 667, 669 (2d Cir. 1985). The validity of a Rule 16(f) dismissal for failure to file a timely pretrial order depends upon the circumstances of the case and whether the failure is willful as opposed to merely negligent. *See Woodmore v. Git-N-Go,* 790 F.2d 1497, 1498–99 (10th Cir. 1986); *Ford v. Fogarty Van Lines, Inc.,* 780 F.2d 1582, 1583 (11th Cir. 1986) (dismissals reversed). As with other dismissals, a Rule 60(b) motion should be made to proffer the reasons for the specific pretrial retrial violation. *Price v. McGlathery,* 792 F.2d at 476.

Often Rule 16(f) is not mentioned at all when dealing with pretrial violations. For example, whether to exclude testimony or exhibits proffered in violation of the pretrial order is a frequently litigated issue. Courts established standards to resolve this problem well before the advent of Rule 16(f) and continue to refer to previous case law rather than to Rule 16(f). The test enunciated in *Meyers v. Pennypack Woods Home Ownership Association,* 559 F.2d 894, 904 (3d Cir. 1977), which considers (1) the prejudice or surprise in fact of the party against whom the excluded witnesses would have testified, (2) the ability of that party to cure the prejudice, (3) the extent to which waiver of the rule against calling unlisted witnesses would disrupt the orderly and efficient trial of the case or of other cases in the court, and (4) bad faith or willfulness in failing to comply with the court's order, is the most commonly cited.

See, e.g., Kickapoo Oil Co. v. Clark Oil & Refining Corp., 788 F.2d 11, 17–18 (Temp. Emer. Ct. App. 1985); *United States v. Koziy,* 728 F.2d 1314, 1320–21 (11th Cir.), *cert. denied,* 469 U.S. 835 (1984); *Smith v. Ford Motor Co.,* 626 F.2d 784, 797 (10th Cir. 1980), *cert. denied,* 450 U.S. 918 (1981).

The Meyers criteria have also been applied in determining whether documents were properly excluded. *Smith v. Rowe,* 761 F.2d at 365. Other courts weigh essentially the same factors and consider the reasons why the witness was not named, the importance of the witness's testimony, the time needed to prepare for the testimony, and whether a continuance would be useful. *See Patterson v. F.W. Woolworth Co.,* 786 F.2d 874, 879 (8th Cir. 1986); *Murphy v. Magnolia Electric Power Association,* 639 F.2d 232, 235 (5th Cir. 1981); 8 *Federal Practice and Procedure* § 2050, at 327. The Ninth Circuit presumes that failure to give notice of an expert's testimony until immediately before trial was clearly prejudicial when earlier disclosure was required by the local rules and no justification for noncompliance was offered. *Sealy, Inc. v. Easy Living, Inc.,* 743 F.2d 1378, 1382–83 (9th Cir. 1984). As with other discovery rulings, such orders are reviewed for abuse of discretion. *See, e.g., Perry v. Winspur,* 782 F.2d 893, 895 (10th Cir. 1986); *Young v. City of New Orleans,* 751 F.2d 794, 797 (5th Cir. 1985).

CHAPTER 6

SANCTIONS: RULE 37 DISCOVERY ABUSES

§ 6.1 Sanctions Affecting the Merits of an Action

Rule 37 of the Federal Rules of Civil Procedure is the primary weapon in the war against abusive discovery. Because it applies only to the discovery process, *see, e.g., Loctite Corp. v. Fel-Pro, Inc.,* 667 F.2d 577, 585 (7th Cir. 1981), you may decide to cite Rule 37 in conjunction with Rule 11 or Rule 41(b), 28 U.S.C. § 1927, or the court's inherent power to obtain sanctions in cases when other conduct is also implicated. However, unlike Rule 11's mandatory approach, the award of sanctions under Rule 37 is more permissive. *See, e.g., Westmoreland v. CBS, Inc.,* 770 F.2d 1168, 1174 n.8 (D.C. Cir. 1985).

Sanctions against nonparty deponents are limited to contempt of court, Fed. R. Civ. P. 37(b)(1), and an award of expenses, including attorneys' fees, incurred in obtaining an order to compel the deponent to answer a question, Fed. R. Civ. P. 37(a)(4). Because Rule 37 provides for recovery of costs only for obtaining or opposing orders compelling discovery from nonparties, it cannot be used to obtain relief from other orders such as a frivolous petition to hold the deponent in contempt. *Westmoreland v. CBS, Inc.*, 770 F.2d at 1173 (applying Rule 11 when petition was groundless).

Rule 37 sanctions which affect the merits of the action apply to parties and persons who are officers, directors, or managing agents of a party or designated by the party to testify on its behalf. Fed. R. Civ. P. 37(b)(2); *see, e.g., Founding Church of Scientology v. Webster,* 802 F.2d 1448, 1451–59 (D.C. Cir. 1986) (affirming termination for repeated failure of managing agent to attend deposition). It can be used to sanction the United States as well as private litigants. *See* 28 U.S.C. § 2412(b)(Supp. III 1985); *Potlatch Corp. v. United States,* 679 F.2d 153, 159 n.1 (9th Cir. 1982). The rule provides for whatever sanctions are just in the circumstances and specifically mentions:

1. An order which designated matters or facts for the purposes of the action, Fed. R. Civ. P. 37(b)(2)(A)
2. An order refusing to allow the disobedient party to support or oppose designated claims or defenses or prohibiting the introduction of designated matters in evidence, Fed. R. Civ. P. 37(b)(2)(B)
3. An order striking out pleadings or parts thereof, staying further proceedings until the order is obeyed, dismissing the action in whole or part, or rendering a default against the disobedient party, Fed. R. Civ. P. 37(b)(2)(C)
4. An order treating the failure to obey an order as a contempt of court, except for an order to submit to a physical or mental examination
5. Payment of reasonable expenses, including attorneys' fees, for any failure which was not substantially justified, unless other circumstances make an award of expenses unjust, Fed. R. Civ. P. 37(b)(2).

Rule 37 also provides that all sanctions other than contempt are available if a party fails to comply with an order under Rule 35(a) which requires the production of another individual for examination, unless the party is unable to produce the individual. Fed. R. Civ. P. 37(b)(2)(E). Expenses for wrongfully failing to admit the genuineness of any document or the truth of any matter as requested under Rule 36 are also provided in Rule 37(c).

§ 6.2 Procedures for Obtaining Rule 37 Sanctions

There are two methods by which you can obtain relief under Rule 37, depending upon whether there is a partial or complete failure of discovery. First, if there has been a complete failure of discovery, such as failure of a party to attend a deposition, answer interrogatories, or provide a written response to a Rule 34 request, you can move immediately for sanctions under Rule 37(d) without any previous order to compel discovery. *Charter House Insurance Brokers, Ltd. v. New Hampshire Insurance Co.,* 667 F.2d 600, 604 (7th Cir. 1981); *Guidry v. Continental Oil Co.,* 640 F.2d 523, 533 (5th Cir.), *cert. denied,* 454 U.S. 818 (1981); 8 C. Wright & A. Miller, *Federal Practice and Procedure* § 229 (1970) [hereinafter *Federal Practice and Procedure*]. Second, if there is a partial discovery failure, you must invoke two steps before sanctions can be awarded: (1) you may move to compel the requested discovery under Rule 37(a) and may be awarded expenses for obtaining the court order; (2) only if the order compelling discovery is violated can you move for sanctions affecting the outcome of the case to be assessed pursuant to Rule 37(b). **Section 6.11** contains a checklist for consideration of a Rule 37 motion when there has been a total or partial discovery failure.

The two-step process is mandated whenever (1) a party or deponent fails to answer a deposition question, (2) a corporation fails to designate a person to speak on its behalf, (3) a party fails to answer an interrogatory, or (4) a party fails to permit Rule 34 productions or responds that it will not permit production as requested. A party need not formally move to compel if the court has issued an oral or written order. *See Tamari v. Bache & Co. (Lebanon) S.A.L.,* 729 F.2d 469, 473 (7th Cir. 1984); *Professional Seminar Consultants, Inc. v. Sino American Technical Exchange Council, Inc.,* 727 F.2d 1470, 1474 (9th Cir. 1984); *Properties International Ltd. v. Turner,* 706 F.2d 308, 310 (11th Cir. 1983). The order need not refer to the specific discovery in dispute as long as it is clear. Therefore, an order to provide complete answers to interrogatories is sufficient, without reference to individual interrogatories. *See Fjelstad v. American Honda Motor Co.,* 762 F.2d 1334, 1339 (9th Cir. 1985). A party's failure to object to the production of the disputed material, *Penthouse International, Ltd. v. Playboy Enterprises, Inc.,* 663 F.2d 371, 389–90 (2d Cir. 1981), and an attorney's promise in open court to produce documents, *Charter House Insurance Brokers, Ltd. v. New Hampshire Insurance Co.,* 667 F.2d 600, 604 (7th Cir. 1981), have been treated as the equivalent of an order for Rule 37(b) purposes. However, if no order is violated, the court must rely on its inherent power to impose sanctions. *Penthouse International, Ltd. v. Playboy Enterprises, Inc.,* 663 F.2d at 389–90.

Although the rule itself does not specify any timing requirements, local rules may mandate that discovery motions be brought within a given time after the noncompliance to avoid waiver. The Second Circuit has indicated that a motion will be deemed waived if it is not made prior to judgment, unless the issue is expressly reserved in the judgment, and that generally a motion should be brought prior to trial to avoid waiver, unless a later motion is made within a reasonable time after the noncompliance. *Mercy v. County of Suffolk,* 748 F.2d 52, 55–56 (2d Cir. 1984); *see Airtex Corp. v. Shelley Radiant Ceiling Co.,* 536 F.2d 145, 155 (7th Cir. 1976).

Many local rules also provide that before a motion can be made, counsel must meet and confer regarding the disputed discovery and certify that they are unable after reasonable effort to resolve the dispute, *see Crown Cork & Seal Co. v. Chemed Corp.,* 101 F.R.D. 105, 106 n.1 (E.D. Pa. 1984) (listing all courts with such rules), although such conferences may be limited to partial rather than total discovery failures. Delegation of this obligation to someone other than an attorney has been considered insufficient compliance. *Id.* at 107. In some courts, a joint motion is required, which often has the practical effect of deterring parties from requesting sanctions based on minor differences due to the increased cost of such motions to both parties as well as the inevitable delay in bringing them. Parties who cannot agree on discovery matters often cannot even agree about whose word processor will be used to create the final document.

§ 6.3 The *National Hockey League* Standard

In *National Hockey League v. Metropolitan Hockey Club,* 427 U.S. 639, 643 (1976), the Supreme Court approved a standard for terminating an action for discovery abuse which requires a minimum of willfulness, bad faith, or fault. A dismissal cannot be granted when the failure to comply is solely due to inability. *Societe Internationale v. Rogers,* 357 U.S. 197, 212 (1958). Therefore, a pro se plaintiff who informs the court he is unable to pay a monetary sanction cannot be dismissed without a showing that he had the ability to pay. *Thomas v. Gerber Products,* 703 F.2d 353, 356–57 (9th Cir. 1983). Inability is often an issue when the discovery materials are located in a country which has a statute blocking its production. *See Societe Internationale v. Rogers,* 357 U.S. at 212; *General Atomic Co. v. Exxon Nuclear Co.,* 90 F.R.D. 290, 291 (S.D. Cal. 1981). Some circuits hold that fault can justify a dismissal or default in the absence of willfulness or bad faith, *United Artists Corp. v. La Cage Aux Folles, Inc.,* 771 F.2d 1265, 1270 (9th Cir. 1985), permitting terminations for gross negligence, *see, e.g., Rabb v. Amatex Corp.,* 769 F.2d 996, 1000 (4th Cir. 1985); *Weisberg v. Webster,* 749 F.2d 864, 871 (D.C. Cir. 1984); *Penthouse International, Ltd. v. Playboy Enterprises, Inc.,* 663 F.2d 371, 388 (2d Cir. 1981); *Affanato v. Merrill Brothers,* 547 F.2d 138, 141 (1st Cir. 1977), or recklessness, *Hritz v. Woma Corp.,* 732 F.2d 1178, 1183 (3d Cir. 1984).

National Hockey League also adopted deterrence as a legitimate goal in meting out sanctions in order to prevent other parties from engaging in discovery abuses. 427 U.S. at 643; *see generally* Note, *The Emerging Deterrence Orientation in the Imposition of Discovery Sanctions,* 91 Harv. L. Rev. 1033 (1978). Therefore, even if the noncomplaining party appears repentant and tenders the disputed materials after the dismissal motion is filed, the trial judge can still dismiss the action. *See, e.g., Wyle v. R.J.*

Reynolds Industries, Inc., 709 F.2d 585, 591 (9th Cir. 1983); *G-K Properties v. Redevelopment Agency*, 577 F.2d 645, 647–48 (9th Cir. 1978). The deterrence rationale has even been used to affirm dismissal of an entire case, although the discovery dispute focused on a single claim. *See Weisberg v. Webster*, 749 F.2d 864, 872 (D.C. Cir. 1984).

When applying sanctions, courts are guided by the Supreme Court's decision in *Insurance Corp. of Ireland v. Compagnie Des Bauxites de Guinee*, 456 U.S. 694, 707 (1982), which limited the district court's discretion in assigning sanctions to Rule 37(b)(2)'s by requiring that (1) sanctions must be just and (2) the sanction must be specifically related to the particular claim which was at issue in the order to provide discovery. Due process is satisfied as long as the conduct supports an inference that the refusal to provide the requested information is an admission of the lack of merit of the claim or defense. *Id.* at 705–06; *see Hammond Packing Co. v. Arkansas*, 212 U.S. 322, 350–51 (1909). If the behavior does not support this presumption, due process is violated. *Insurance Corp. of Ireland v. Compagnie Des Bauxites de Guinee*, 456 U.S. at 706. Therefore, a case cannot be terminated merely to punish a litigant who fails to comply with an order to deposit money in the court's registry. *Hovey v. Elliott*, 167 U.S. 409, 413–14 (1897). Similarly, refusal to pay a monetary sanction is not sufficient, by itself, to support a default. *SEC v. Seaboard Corp.*, 666 F.2d 414, 416–17 (9th Cir. 1982). A partial default has also been reversed because the failure to supplement a response concerning potential witnesses did not give rise to a presumption that the denials in its answer to the complaint were untrue or that its defenses were meritless. *Fjelstad v. American Honda Motor Co.*, 762 F.2d 1334, 1342 (9th Cir. 1985).

§ 6.4 Review of Discovery Sanctions

National Hockey League limited the appellate court's review of discovery sanctions to whether the district court abused its discretion. *National Hockey League v. Metropolitan Hockey Club*, 427 U.S. 639, 642 (1976) (per curiam). This reduces the possibility of a reversal on appeal because the appellate court believes the sanction is too harsh in the circumstances, as long as the behavior supports a dismissal or default. *Id.* at 642–43; *Aruba Bonaire Curacao Trust Co. v. Commissioner*, 777 F.2d 38, 44 (D.C. Cir. 1985), *cert. denied*, ______ U.S. ______, 106 S. Ct. 1469 (1986). Similarly, it is rare that an appellate court will reverse a trial court's decision not to impose a Rule 37 sanction, because Rule 37, unlike Rule 11, is permissive as to the imposition of any sanction as well as the nature of any sanction imposed. *Compare Dellums v. Powell*, 566 F.2d 231, 236 (D.C. Cir. 1977)(sanction required) *with Augustine v. United States*, 810 F.2d 991, 996 (10th Cir. 1987) *and Hazen v. Pasley*,

768 F.2d 226, 229 (8th Cir. 1985) *and Forro Precision Inc. v. IBM Corp.,* 673 F.2d 1045, 1053 (9th Cir. 1982)(sanction not required).

Although the appropriateness of the sanction is reviewed under an abuse of discretion standard, factual inquiries under Rule 37 are reviewed under the clearly erroneous standard, and any legal conclusions are reviewed de novo. *United States v. National Medical Enterprise, Inc.,* 792 F.2d 906, 910–11 (9th Cir. 1986); *Eastway General Hospital, Ltd. v. Eastway Women's Clinic, Inc.,* 737 F.2d 503, 505 (5th Cir. 1984), *cert. denied,* 470 U.S. 1052 (1985).

When reviewing the propriety of sanctions for failure to cooperate in discovery, the court also reviews the propriety of the underlying discovery order. *Patton v. Aerojet Ordnance Co.,* 765 F.2d 604, 608 (6th Cir. 1985); *Hastings v. North East Independent School District,* 615 F.2d 628, 631 (5th Cir. 1980). If the order disobeyed was invalid, any sanctions must necessarily fail. *Donovan v. Mosher Steel Co.,* 791 F.2d 1535, 1537 (11th Cir. 1986), *cert. denied,* _____ U.S. _____, 107 S. Ct. 874 (1987); *Holcomb v. Allis-Chalmers Corp.,* 774 F.2d 398, 400–01 (10th Cir. 1985); *Hastings v. North East Independent School District,* 615 F.2d 628, 631 (5th Cir. 1980). Therefore, if no reasonable notice of the order was given, *Holcomb v. Allis-Chalmers Corp.,* 774 F.2d at 400–01, or the disputed discovery was not relevant to the action or was privileged, a dismissal cannot be sustained. *See, e.g., Fonseca v. Regan,* 734 F.2d 944, 948 (2d Cir.), *cert. denied,* 469 U.S. 882 (1984); *Savola v. Webster,* 644 F.2d 743, 747 (8th Cir. 1981); *Dunbar v. United States,* 502 F.2d 506, 509–10 (5th Cir. 1974). However, the reason for the invalid order must be raised before the trial judge, or it will not be heard on appeal. *See United States v. Rylander,* 460 U.S. 752, 755–57 (1983); *Rainbow Pioneer v. Hawaii-Nevada Investment Corp.,* 711 F.2d 902, 905 (9th Cir. 1983).

§ 6.5 —Review of Sanctions Which Terminate the Action

The circuits vary in their approaches to Rule 37 sanctions. At one end of the spectrum, some circuits affirm dismissals and defaults even if the judge did not consider lesser sanctions, because Rule 37 does not state or suggest this requirement. *Damiani v. Rhode Island Hospital,* 704 F.2d 12, 15 (1st Cir. 1983). Similarly, the First Circuit noted that the claim of abuse of discretion does not receive its sympathetic ear, as shown by its affirmance of all dismissals but one from 1964 to 1983. *Id.* at 17. On the other hand, most of the circuits view dismissals and defaults as a draconian remedy or a sanction of last resort. *Patton v. Aerojet Ordnance Co.,* 765 F.2d 604, 607 (6th Cir. 1985); *Batson v. Neal Spelce Associates, Inc.,* 765 F.2d 511, 515 (5th Cir. 1985); *Searock v. Stripling,* 736 F.2d 650, 653 (11th Cir.

1984). These circuits require that the judge consider less drastic sanctions which would be equally effective before terminating the action, *e.g., Batson v. Neal Spelce Associates, Inc.,* 765 F.2d at 516; *United Artists Corp. v. La Cage Aux Folles, Inc.,* 771 F.2d at 1270 (9th Cir. 1985); *Searock v. Stripling,* 736 F.2d at 653; *Hritz v. Woma Corp.,* 732 F.2d 1178, 1182 (3d Cir. 1984), and explicitly articulate the resolution of the factual, legal, and discretionary issues presented, *Patton v. Aerojet Ordnance Co.,* 765 F.2d 604, 608 (6th Cir. 1985); *Quality Prefabrication, Inc. v. Daniel J. Keating Co.,* 675 F.2d 77, 81 (3d Cir. 1982).

The use of an ultimate sanction is upheld without explicit balancing only if the conduct clearly justifies dismissal. *See Batson v. Neal Spelce Associates, Inc.,* 765 F.2d at 516 n.2. Even if the transgression is willful, some circuits require the punishment to fit the crime rather than generally approving sanctions which terminate the action. *See Givens v. A.H. Robins Co.,* 751 F.2d 261, 263 (8th Cir. 1984) (dismissal for willful failure to comply with discovery deadline reversed). Although a showing of prejudice or irreparable harm may not be required, it is a relevant factor that courts consider before terminating an action. *United States v. National Medical Enterprises, Inc.,* 792 F.2d 906, 913 (9th Cir. 1986); *Searock v. Stripling,* 736 F.2d at 653; *Marshall v. Segona,* 621 F.2d 763, 768 (5th Cir. 1980).

Probably the most stringent review of severe sanctions occurs in the Third Circuit, which has established a strong presumption against sanctions that decide the issues of a case. *Ali v. Sims,* 788 F.2d 954, 958 (3d Cir. 1986). The trial judge must consider the following factors before terminating an action as sanction: (1) the extent of the party's personal responsibility; (2) the prejudice to the adversary caused by the failure to meet scheduling orders and respond to discovery; (3) a history of dilatoriness; (4) whether the conduct of the party or the attorney was willful or in bad faith; (5) the effectiveness of sanctions other than dismissal, which entails an analysis of alternative sanctions; and (6) the meritoriousness of the claim or defense. *Poulis v. State Farm Fire & Casualty Co.,* 747 F.2d 863, 868–70 (3d Cir. 1984), *followed in Ennis v. New Jersey Bell Telephone Co.,* 782 F.2d 396, 397 (3d Cir. 1985), cert. denied, ____ U.S. ____, 106 S. Ct. 1461 (1986). Most of these criteria also are required by the Fourth Circuit. *Chandler Leasing Corp. v. Lopez,* 669 F.2d 919, 920 (4th Cir. 1982). The Ninth Circuit also applies several of these factors as well as evaluating whether notice and warning have been given to the recalcitrant party before dismissal. *See In re Rubin,* 769 F.2d 611, 616 (9th Cir. 1985). These criteria are useful as guidelines in bringing or defending against sanctions motions even in circuits not requiring that the entire standard be applied.

It is a common practice for trial courts to issue warnings or make dismissal or default orders conditional on a party's continued noncompliance with an outstanding order to compel. *See id.* The district court can also order discovery to determine whether the original discovery violation was willful and assess the costs of such discovery against the noncomplying party. *See, e.g., Tamari v. Bache & Co. (Lebanon) S.A.L.,* 729 F.2d 469, 471–72 (7th Cir. 1984). As a practical matter, the district court usually looks to a pattern of discovery abuse before terminating a case. *See, e.g., United States Freight Co. v. Penn Central Transportation Co.,* 716 F.2d 954, 954–55 (2d Cir. 1983). Therefore, although the violation which brings the motion to the court's attention may be minor, dismissal can be ordered if it is part of a continuing saga of dilatory or obstructive conduct. *See id.* at 955; *Penthouse International, Ltd. v. Playboy Enterprises, Inc.,* 663 F.2d 371, 388–90 (2d Cir. 1981).

§ 6.6 —Terminations for Attorney Misconduct

If the fault lies with the attorney rather than the party, some circuits consider dismissal too severe a sanction. *See, e.g., D.G. Shelter Products Co. v. Forest Products Co.,* 769 F.2d 644, 645 (10th Cir. 1985); *In re MacMeekin,* 722 F.2d 32, 35 (3d Cir. 1983). Others cite the Supreme Court's admonition in *Link v. Wabash Railroad,* 370 U.S. 626, 633–34 (1962), that the party "voluntarily chose this attorney as his representative in the action, and he cannot now avoid the consequences of the acts or omissions of this freely selected agent." *See United Artists Corp. v. La Cage Aux Folles, Inc.,* 771 F.2d 1265, 1271 (9th Cir. 1985); *Damiani v. Rhode Island Hospital,* 704 F.2d 12, 16 (1st Cir. 1983). Usually the deciding factor is whether counsel was guilty of repeated abuse of the judicial process and indifference to court orders. *See, e.g., Vela v. Western Electric Co.,* 709 F.2d 375, 376–77 (5th Cir. 1983).

§ 6.7 Lesser Sanctions Affecting the Merits

Lesser sanctions than those terminating the action are employed for mere failures to respond to discovery, *Weisberg v. Webster,* 749 F.2d 864, 871 (D.C. Cir. 1984); *see Societe Internationale v. Rogers,* 357 U.S. 197, 212–13 (1958), or other negligent behavior, *Fjelstad v. American Honda Motor Co.,* 762 F.2d 1334, 1343 (9th Cir. 1985); *Tamari v. Bache & Co. (Lebanon) S.A.L.,* 729 F.2d 469, 474 (7th Cir. 1984). Therefore, a preclusion order which does not result in a dismissal need not be based on willfulness. *See Cope v. McPherson,* 781 F.2d 207, 209 (D.C. Cir. 1985). Lesser sanctions such as striking a defense or a preclusion order which is tantamount to dismissal are usually treated under the *National Hockey League* standard, discussed in §§ **6.3** and **6.4**. *See Rabb v. Amatex Corp.,* 769 F.2d 996, 1000 (4th Cir. 1985)(applying gross negligence standard); *Parrott v. Wilson,* 707 F.2d 1262, 1273 n.26 (11th Cir.), *cert. denied,* 464 U.S. 936 (1983).

In *Insurance Corp. of Ireland v. Compagnie Des Bauxites de Guinee,* 456 U.S. 694 (1982), the Supreme Court permitted personal jurisdiction to be presumed as a discovery sanction. The Court noted that the sanction was just because the defendants had been warned that the judge would presume personal jurisdiction unless the requested materials were produced, they had repeatedly promised compliance and then defaulted, the claim that personal jurisdiction existed was not frivolous, and they were allowed to present evidence contradicting the presumption. *Id.* at 707–08. Subject matter jurisdiction cannot be presumed as a sanction, *see id.* at 701–02, although sanctions can be invoked against parties whose misfeasance involves procedures connected with the court's determination of whether it has subject matter jurisdiction. *Davis v. Cluet, Peabody & Co.,* 667 F.2d 1371, 1374 n.8 (11th Cir. 1982).

Rule 37 sanctions can be invoked even if the disputed information is not admitted at trial. For example, the Second Circuit has affirmed a Rule 37 sanction denying a victorious antitrust plaintiff attorneys' fees amounting to $10 million for its intentional concealment of evidence which was ultimately ruled inadmissible. *Litton Systems, Inc. v. AT&T Co.,* 700 F.2d 785, 827 (2d Cir. 1983), *cert. denied,* 464 U.S. 1073 (1984). Other sanctions not specifically mentioned in Rule 37 which have been applied include presuming exhibits admissible when authentication and hearsay problems were caused by the adverse party's misconduct, *General Atomic Co. v. Exxon Nuclear Co.,* 90 F.R.D. 290, 309 (S.D. Cal. 1981), and assessing attorneys' fees and office expenses for a second deposition required because of an expert's lack of preparation, *Admiral Theatre Corp. v. Douglas Theatre Co.,* 585 F.2d 877, 899 (8th Cir. 1978).

A compensatory award under Rule 37 is limited to the actual losses sustained as a result of contumacy. *See United States v. National Medical Enterprises, Inc.,* 792 F.2d 906, 910 (9th Cir. 1986). Sanctions cannot be assessed against one party because of the failure of another party to comply with discovery, absent a showing that the sanctioned party controlled the actions of the noncomplying party. *Letelier v. Republic of Chile,* 748 F.2d 790, 795 n.2 (2d Cir. 1984), *cert. denied,* 471 U.S. 1125 (1985); 4A J. Moore *et al., Moore's Federal Practice* ¶ 37.05 (2d ed. 1984) [hereinafter *Moore's Federal Practice*]. A pattern of dilatory conduct may also be used to support a judge's refusal to grant a continuance for trial. *See, e.g., Watson v. Miears,* 772 F.2d 433, 437–38 (8th Cir. 1985).

§ 6.8 Expenses for Rule 37 Violations

The plain language of Rule 37(b)(2)(E) provides that only those expenses, including attorneys' fees, caused by the failure to comply may be assessed against the noncomplying party. Therefore, attorneys' fees for discovery matters not related to failure to comply with discovery orders are not recoverable under Rule 37, *Batson v. Neal Spelce Associates, Inc.,* 765 F.2d 511, 516 (5th Cir. 1985), although in a given case another rule or statute or the court's inherent power may justify such awards.

A reviewing court may view an extraordinarily large award of Rule 37 attorneys' fees as unreasonable on its face if not supported by documentation. *Id.; In re Yagman,* 796 F.2d 1165, 1180–81, *modified on other grounds,* 803 F.2d 1085 (9th Cir. 1986). Because an appellate court can remand an action for the trial judge to articulate reasons for its assessment of fees, *Batson v. Neal Spelce Associates, Inc.,* 765 F.2d at 517, counsel obtaining a fee award should always ensure that the record is sufficient on this issue. Specific findings may also be required to determine the allocation of expenses between the noncomplying party and attorney. *See Weisberg v. Webster,* 749 F.2d 864, 873–74 (D.C. Cir. 1984).

Some circuits are strict about the type of documentation necessary to recover attorneys' fees, *see, e.g., Day v. Allstate Insurance Co.,* 788 F.2d 1110, 1113 (5th Cir. 1986)(following *Johnson v. Georgia Highway Express, Inc.,* 488 F.2d 714, 717–19 (5th Cir. 1974)), requiring contemporaneous, complete, standardized time records which accurately reflect the work done by each attorney. *See Weisberg v. Webster,* 749 F.2d 864, 872–73 (D.C. Cir. 1984)(following *National Association of Concerned Veterans v. Secretary of Defense,* 675 F.2d 1319, 1327 (D.C. Cir. 1982)(per curiam)). Attorney's fees on appeal have also been awarded based on the rationale that such costs were caused by the discovery failure. *Mickwee v. Hsu,* 753 F.2d 770, 770 (9th Cir. 1985)(per curiam); *Tamari v. Bache & Co. (Lebanon) S.A.L.,* 729 F.2d 469, 475 (7th Cir. 1984).

§ 6.9 Hearings

There is no right to a jury trial in Rule 37 proceedings, *Wyle v. R.J. Reynolds Industries, Inc.,* 709 F.2d 585, 592 (9th Cir. 1983), even though termination of the action is equivalent to an adjudication of the merits, *id.; see Woods v. Tsuchiya,* 754 F.2d 1571, 1582 (Fed. Cir.), *cert. denied,* _____ U.S. _____, 106 S. Ct. 81 (1985). *Roadway Express Inc. v. Piper,* 447 U.S. 752, 767 (1980), specifically states that "[l]ike other sanctions, attorney's fees certainly should not be assessed lightly or without fair notice and an opportunity for a hearing on the record." However, a hearing, though desirable, is not considered necessary in all circumstances, even if the sanction terminates the action. *See id.; Professional Seminar Consultants, Inc. v. Simo American Technical Exchange Council, Inc.,* 727 F.2d 1470, 1473 (9th Cir. 1984); *Vela v. Western Electric Co.,* 709 F.2d 375, 377 (5th Cir. 1983).

Factors considered in determining the necessity of holding a hearing include the judge's familiarity with the disruptive behavior, the type of notice given the noncomplying party that sanctions would be imposed, the vagueness or specificity of the discovery order, and the opportunity of the noncomplying party to respond. Similarly, Rule 55(b)(2) concerning defaults, which provides that the court can conduct a hearing if necessary to determine the amount of damages, does not mandate hearings in all cases, see *Brockton Savings Bank v. Peat, Marwick, Mitchell & Co.*, 771 F.2d 5, 12–13 (1st Cir. 1985), *cert. denied,* ____ U.S. ____, 106 S. Ct. 1204 (1986); *United States v. DeFrantz,* 708 F.2d 310, 312–13 (7th Cir. 1983), although a few circuits require a hearing unless the amount of damages claimed is a liquidated sum or can be mathematically calculated, *see Adolph Coors Co. v. Movement Against Racism,* 777 F.2d 1538, 1543–44 (11th Cir. 1985); *United Artists Corp. v. Freeman,* 605 F.2d 854, 857 (5th Cir. 1979)(per curiam). However, if a hearing is mandated, the rule provides that the court must afford a right to a jury trial when and as required by a statute of the United States. *See* Fed. R. Civ. P. 55(b); 6 *Moore's Federal Practice* ¶ 55.09. Because such a statute would have to require a jury for damages, it is extremely rare for a case to indicate that a jury trial on damages has been granted for a default entered as a discovery sanction. *See, e.g., Griffin v. Swim-Tech Corp.*, 722 F.2d 677, 679 (11th Cir. 1984).

If the defaulting party appeared in the action, Rule 55(b)(2) requires that three days' notice of the default hearing be given, although it is unclear whether this is engrafted onto Rule 37 procedures. *See Au Bon Pain Corp. v. Artect, Inc.*, 653 F.2d 61, 65 (2d Cir. 1981) (default entered for discovery failure required Rule 55 procedures). At the damage inquest, the court accepts as true all of the factual allegations of the complaint except those relating to damages. *Id.*

Rule 37(a)(4) specifically mentions opportunity for a hearing, but the judge's perusal of transcripts of disputed deposition testimony and memoranda justifying counsel's position has been held sufficient. *Hayden Stone, Inc. v. Brode,* 508 F.2d 895, 897 (7th Cir. 1974). Counsel should request a hearing after the imposition of sanctions, if one has not previously been afforded.

§ 6.10 Setting Aside Defaults and Dismissals

A Rule 55(c) motion is appropriate to set aside an entry of default before judgment has been entered, while a Rule 60(b) motion requesting relief from judgment based on mistake, inadvertence, surprise, or excusable neglect should be addressed to the trial court if sanctions result in termination of the action. *See* 7 *Moore's Federal Practice* ¶ 60.09–.30. Even if the judge does not grant the motion, its presence may be a factor considered by the appellate court. At a minimum, it enables the noncomplying party to proffer whatever reasons it has for excusable neglect, because an appellate court will not consider any affidavits concerning justification which were not presented below. *Rainbow Pioneer v. Hawaii-Nevada Investment Corp.,* 711 F.2d 902, 906 (9th Cir. 1983).

You must be careful to appeal both the judgment of dismissal and the denial of the Rule 60(b) motion, because Rule 60(b) denials are reviewed more narrowly in scope than dismissals so as not to vitiate the requirements of a timely appeal. *Vela v. Western Electric Co.,* 709 F.2d 375, 376 (5th Cir. 1983). Filing a Rule 60(b) motion does not toll the time in which an appeal can be taken from judgment. *Barta v. Long,* 670 F.2d 907, 909 (10th Cir. 1982); 11 *Federal Practice and Procedure* § 2871. Denials of Rule 60(b) motions are reviewed for abuse of discretion. *Id.*

Motions to set aside the default under either Rule 55(c) or Rule 60(b) must be filed within a reasonable time and require an acceptable reason for the default as well as the existence of a meritorious defense. *Barta v. Long,* 670 F.2d at 909. The culpability of the defendant's conduct and the prejudice to the plaintiff should also be considered. *Hritz v. Woma Corp.,* 732 F.2d 1178, 1181 (3d Cir. 1984). A court can order conditions on reopening a default, such as waiver of the statute of limitations, to avoid hurting the adverse party. *Id.* at 1182 & n.3. It is also common to require that the defaulting party cure all previous discovery violations. *See Tolliver v. Northrop Corp.,* 786 F.2d 316, 319 (7th Cir. 1986). A Rule 60 movant should always tender any outstanding discovery with the motion to ensure that the reviewing court does not consider its absence as justifying a denial of relief. *See id.*

§ 6.11 Rule 37 Checklist

Total Failure of Discovery

No motion to compel is necessary before Rule 37(d) sanctions can be assessed for failure of a party or officer, director, or managing agent of a party or a person designated as a deponent under Rule 30(b)(6) or 31(a) to

____ **1.** Appear for deposition after proper notice
____ **2.** Serve answers or objections to properly served interrogatories
____ **3.** Serve a written response to a properly served Rule 34 request.

Partial Failure of Discovery

____ **1.** Failure to answer an oral or written deposition question
____ **2.** Failure to make a Rule 30(b)(6) or 31(a) deponent designation

____ **3.** Failure to answer or making an evasive or incomplete answer to a Rule 33 interrogatory

____ **4.** Failure to respond that a Rule 34 inspection will be permitted as requested

____ **5.** Failure to permit a Rule 34 inspection as requested.

Obtaining Expenses

____ **1.** Expenses are available for any motion granted under Rule 37(a), (b), (d), or (g).

____ **2.** A party or deponent and/or an attorney is liable for the reasonable expenses incurred in successfully bringing or defending against a motion

  ____ **a.** To obtain a Rule 37(a) order

  ____ **b.** Caused by the failure to comply with a Rule 37(a) order

  ____ **c.** Caused by a Rule 37(d) failure

  ____ **d.** Caused by a failure to participate in good faith in framing a Rule 26(f) discovery plan

  ____ **e.** Deponents and/or their attorneys are liable for expenses under **2a** or **2b**.

____ **3.** Reasonable expenses include attorneys' fees.

____ **4.** The court must make the expense award unless the motion or opposition was substantially justified, unless other circumstances make an award of expenses unjust.

Other Sanctions

____ **1.** Sanctions are available for a Rule 37(d) failure or a Rule 37(b) failure by a party or an officer, director, or managing agent of a party or a person designated as a deponent under Rule 30(b)(6) or 31(a) to obey an order issued under Rule 37(a), 35(a) or 26(f).

____ **2.** Any order which is just in regard to the aforementioned discovery failures can be assessed, including

  ____ **a.** Designating facts as established for the purpose of the action

  ____ **b.** Refusing to allow the disobedient party to support or oppose designated claims or defenses

  ____ **c.** Prohibiting the disobedient party from introducing designated matters in evidence

  ____ **d.** Striking pleadings or parts thereof

  ____ **e.** Staying proceedings until the order is obeyed

  ____ **f.** Dismissing the action, or any part thereof

____ **g.** Rendering a default judgment against the disobedient party

____ **h.** Citing the disobedient party for contempt of court.

____ **3.** A party's failure to produce another for examination under Rule 35(a) can result in the imposition of any sanction except contempt, unless the party shows inability to produce the required person for examination.

____ **4.** A deponent who fails to be sworn or to answer a question after being ordered can be held in contempt.

Failure to Admit a Rule 36 Request

____ **1.** Failure to admit the genuineness of any document or the truth of any matter requested which is proved at trial permits the following sanctions to be assessed pursuant to Rule 37(c).

____ **a.** Reasonable expenses incurred in making the proof

____ **b.** Reasonable attorneys' fees incurred in making the proof.

____ **2.** The court must make the expense award unless

____ **a.** The request was objectionable under Rule 36(a)

____ **b.** The admission was of no substantial importance

____ **c.** The party failing to admit had reasonable ground to believe that it might prevail on the matter

____ **d.** Other good reason existed for the failure to admit.

Where to Bring the Motion

____ **1.** If the motion concerns a deposition

____ **a.** Of a party, it may be brought in the district where the action is pending or in the district where the deposition is being taken

____ **b.** Of a nonparty, it may be brought in the district where the deposition is being taken.

____ **2.** Other matters must be brought in the district in which the action is pending.

CHAPTER 7

SANCTIONS: ATTORNEYS' FEES

§ 7.1 Introduction

The American rule concerning attorneys' fees is that parties to litigation must bear their own fees. *See Alyeska Pipeline Service Co. v. Wilderness Society,* 421 U.S. 240, 247, 257–59 (1975). This avoids unjustly discouraging the poor from instituting actions to vindicate their rights or penalizing litigants for merely defending or prosecuting lawsuits. *F.D. Rich Co. v. United States,* 417 U.S. 116, 129 (1974). However, federal courts invoke their inherent powers as well as 28 U.S.C. § 1927 to permit awards of attorneys' fees in limited circumstances.

§ 7.2 Inherent Powers of the Court and 28 U.S.C. § 1927

Federal courts have created an exception to the American rule in order to assess attorneys' fees against parties and counsel who willfully abuse judicial process or otherwise conduct litigation in bad faith. The Supreme Court expressly upheld this use of inherent powers in *Roadway Express, Inc. v. Piper,* 447 U.S. 752, 764–66 (1980). Bad faith can justify the withholding of statutory attorneys' fees as well as the award of attorneys' fees.

See Litton Systems, Inc. v. AT&T Co., 700 F.2d 785, 827 (2d Cir. 1983), *cert. denied,* 464 U.S. 1073 (1984).

The bad faith exception for attorney conduct, *see generally* 6 J. Moore *et al., Moore's Federal Practice* ¶ 54.77[2] (2d ed. 1986); Mallor, *Punitive Attorneys' Fees for Abuses of the Judicial System,* 61 N.C.L. Rev. 613 (1983); Note, *Attorneys' Fees—Nemeroff v. Abelson and the Bad Faith Exception to the American Rule,* 58 Tulane L. Rev. 1519 (1984); *see also* Axelberg, *Sanctions Available for Attorney Misconduct: A Glimpse at the "Other" Remedies,* 47 Mont. L. Rev. 87 (1986), has been codified in 28 U.S.C. § 1927. Because of its penal nature, § 1927 is strictly construed. *Indianapolis Colts v. Mayor of Baltimore,* 775 F.2d 177, 182 (7th Cir. 1985). Similarly, because inherent powers are shielded from direct democratic controls, they must be exercised with restraint and discretion. *Roadway Express, Inc. v. Piper,* 447 U.S. at 764 (1980).

Although a party will not be penalized for maintaining an aggressive litigation posture, advocacy simply for the sake of burdening an opponent can result in an award of attorneys' fees. *See Batson v. Neal Spelce Associates, Inc.,* 805 F.2d 546, 550–51 (5th Cir. 1986); *Lipsig v. National Student Marketing Corp.,* 663 F.2d 178, 181 (D.C. Cir. 1980). Such fees are not limited by Rule 37(d)'s requirement that they must be caused by the failure to comply with the discovery order but can encompass all fees caused by an attorney's misconduct. *Batson v. Neal Spelce Associates, Inc.,* 805 F.2d at 551. However, because § 1927 applies to excess fees, a blanket award of all fees is not justified. *In re Yagman,* 796 F.2d 1165, 1184, *modified on other grounds,* 803 F.2d 1085 (9th Cir. 1986). Often § 1927 and inherent powers are jointly invoked to ensure that fees can be assessed against the adverse party as well as the attorney. Such sanctions apply to diversity cases as well as other actions. *Sterling Energy, Ltd. v. Friendly National Bank,* 744 F.2d 1433, 1435 n.2 (10th Cir. 1984).

Most circuits appear to refer to the bad faith exception and § 1927 interchangeably when dealing with attorney misconduct, *see, e.g., Ford v. Temple Hospital,* 790 F.2d 342, 346–47 (3d Cir. 1986), applying identical standards and procedures. The only variation that has emerged is whether bad faith is a prerequisite to § 1927 actions, *Kamen v. AT&T Co.,* 791 F.2d 1006, 1010 (2d Cir. 1986); *Dreiling v. Peugeot Motors of America, Inc.,* 768 F.2d 1159, 1164–65 (10th Cir. 1985); *Baker Industries, Inc. v. Cerberus Ltd.,* 764 F.2d 204, 209 (3d Cir. 1985), or whether some different and lower standard applies, because the statute refers solely to conduct which unreasonably and vexatiously multiplies the proceedings. Some circuits find that reckless behavior as well as bad faith satisfies § 1927. *United States v. Associated Convalescent Enterprises, Inc.,* 766 F.2d 1342, 1346 (9th Cir. 1985); *United States v. Ross,* 535 F.2d 346, 349 (6th Cir. 1976). A few apply a less stringent standard which mirrors Rule 11, assessing sanctions when an attorney who is not guilty of conscious impropriety intentionally pursues a claim that lacks a plausible legal or factual basis or uses tactics which needlessly obstruct the litigation of a nonfrivolous claim. *Jones v. Continental Corp.*, 789 F.2d 1225, 1230 (6th Cir. 1986); *Knorr Brake Corp. v. Harbil, Inc.*, 738 F.2d 223, 226–27 (7th Cir. 1984).

Except in those circuits permitting an award of attorneys' fees for conduct not reaching bad faith, it is usually easier to recover attorneys' fees under Rules 11 or 37 than § 1927 or the court's inherent power. *See Zaldivar v. City of Los Angeles,* 780 F.2d 823, 831 (9th Cir. 1986) (Rule 11). Moreover, § 1927 is specifically limited to attorney misconduct and cannot be used against parties. *See F.T.C. v. Alaska Leasing Inc.*, 799 F.2d 507, 510 (9th Cir. 1986). Therefore, counsel should not invoke § 1927 or the court's inherent power unless the offending conduct does not violate any rule which permits recovery on a lesser standard than bad faith.

§ 7.3 Defining Bad Faith

Bad faith generally falls within one of three categories:

1. Bad faith during the course of the litigation
2. Bad faith in bringing or causing an action to be brought, and
3. Bad faith in the acts giving rise to the substantive claim.

The bad faith in filing an action or maintaining a defense must be distinguished from the bad faith in the acts giving rise to the claim, because one circuit has refused to award attorneys' fees based on bad faith in the act underlying the substantive claim. *Shimman v. International Union of Operating Engineers,* 744 F.2d 1226, 1231 (6th Cir. 1984) (en banc), *cert. denied,* 469 U.S. 1215 (1985). *But see Richardson v. Communications Workers,* 530 F.2d 126, 133 (8th Cir.), *cert. denied,* 429 U.S. 824 (1976). Other circuits find § 1927 inapplicable to initial pleadings, because it addresses only the multiplication of proceedings. *See, e.g., In re Yagman,* 796 F.2d 1165, 1187, *modified on other grounds,* 803 F.2d 1085 (9th Cir. 1986). Several circuits have held that a party acts in bad faith in bringing the action only when the claim is entirely without color and has been asserted wantonly for purposes of harassment, delay, or other improper reasons. *Sterling Energy Ltd. v. Friendly National Bank,* 744 F.2d 1433, 1435 (10th Cir. 1984); *Browning Debenture Holders' Committee v. DASA Corp.,* 560 F.2d 1078, 1088 (2d Cir. 1977).

The fact that the litigation had a factual and legal basis is not dispositive, because bad faith may be found not only in bringing the litigation but in its conduct. *Roadway Express, Inc. v. Piper,* 447 U.S. 752, 766 (1980); *Lipsig v. National Student Marketing Corp.,* 663 F.2d 178, 182 (D.C. Cir. 1980). For example, the filing of an untimely complaint did not demonstrate bad faith, because the statute of limitations is an affirmative defense which may be waived or subject to estoppel, but when it became evident that a valid defense was asserted, fees could be assessed for continued litigation. *See Ford v. Temple Hospital,* 790 F.2d 342, 347–50 (3d Cir. 1986). Bad faith in the conduct of the litigation has also been found when counsel brought a meritless disqualification motion for tactical reasons, *Optyl Eyewear Fashion International Corp. v. Style Cos.,* 760 F.2d 1045, 1050–51 (9th Cir. 1985), and when counsel breached their stipulation not to appeal the decision of a referee, *Baker Industries, Inc. v. Cerebus, Ltd.,* 764 F.2d 204, 211 (3d Cir. 1985). Bad faith can even be demonstrated by deliberately misquoting precedent. *See McCandless v. Great Atlantic & Pacific Tea Co.,* 697 F.2d 198, 202 (7th Cir. 1983); *Lipsig v. National Student Marketing Corp.,* 663 F.2d at 181.

Unlike Rule 11, which requires a sanction to be imposed, once a finding of bad faith or its equivalent under § 1927 has been made, the appropriateness of assessing fees is a matter for the court's discretion. Therefore, a district court may refuse to award fees even if it finds bad faith, if in balancing the equities it determines that an award would not serve the interests of justice. *See Ford v. Temple Hospital,* 790 F.2d at 347–50. If neither party litigated in good faith or the guilty party had financial difficulties, an award can be denied or reduced. *Id.* The party or attorney who has acted in bad faith has the burden of proving any mitigating factors. *Id.*

Courts vary as to what, if any, factors must be set forth in determining the amount of an award. For example, the actual attorneys' fees balanced against the possible chilling effect of the award on future representation by counsel has been considered sufficient. *See McCandless v. Great Atlantic & Pacific Tea Co.,* 697 F.2d at 202; *Lipsig v. National Student Marketing Corp.,* 663 F.2d at 181. The Seventh Circuit has even permitted the reasonable fee to be determined without reference to the amount of fees actually incurred by the wronged party when in-house counsel was used, although recognizing that actual fees could serve as a rational starting point for determining the size of the award. *Textor v. Board of Regents of Northern Illinois University,* 711 F.2d 1387, 1396 (7th Cir. 1983). The First Circuit permitted a lodestar fee calculated by multiplying a reasonable hourly rate by the number of hours reasonably expended on the lawsuit, adjusted to reflect factors such as the quality of legal representation. *United States v. Nesglo, Inc.,* 744 F.2d 887, 892 (1st Cir. 1984). The Ninth Circuit is not consistent as to whether the 12-factor test, *Kerr v. Screen Extras Guild, Inc.,* 526 F.2d 67, 70 (9th Cir. 1975), *cert. denied,* 425 U.S. 951 (1976), which it applies to other attorneys' fee awards must be considered. *Compare General Signal Corp. v. Donallco., Inc.,* 787 F.2d 1376, 1380 (9th Cir. 1986) *and Beaudry Motor Co. v. Abko Properties, Inc.,* 780 F.2d 751, 757 (9th Cir.) (citing *Kerr* standard), *cert. denied,* _____ U.S. _____, 107 S. Ct. 100 (1986) *with In re Yagman,* 796 F.2d at 1185 *and Toombs v. Leone,* 777 F.2d 465, 471 (9th Cir. 1985) *and Masalosalo v. Stonewall Insurance Co.,* 718 F.2d 955, 957 (9th Cir. 1983) (detailed review of *Kerr* standard not necessary).

§ 7.4 Hearings

Fair notice and an opportunity for a hearing on the record appear to be mandated before attorneys' fees can be assessed under § 1927 or the court's inherent powers. *See Roadway Express, Inc. v. Piper,* 447 U.S. 752, 767 (1980); *T.W. Electric Service v. Pacific Electric Contractors Association,* 809 F.2d 626, 638 (9th Cir. 1987). Notice can be either actual or constructive. *F.T.C. v. Alaska Land Leasing, Inc.,* 799 F.2d 507, 510 (9th Cir. 1986). However, such hearings prior to awarding attorneys' fees, although desirable, are not invariably required. For example, when the court had no reason to believe the motion was opposed, *United States v. Nesglo, Inc.,* 744 F.2d 887, 891 (1st Cir. 1984), or when the court had extensive familiarity with the case, *id.; cf. Copeland v. Marshall,* 641 F.2d 880, 905 (D.C. Cir. 1980) (civil rights action), hearings were not necessary.

§ 7.5 Review

Factual inquiries, including the finding of bad faith, are reviewed under the clearly erroneous standard; legal conclusions are reviewed de novo, and the appropriateness of the sanction is reviewed under an abuse of discretion standard. *In re Itel Securities Litigation,* 791 F.2d 672, 674 (9th Cir. 1986), *cert. denied,* ______ U.S. ______, 107 S. Ct. 880 (1987); *Dreiling v. Peugeot Motors of America, Inc.,* 768 F.2d 1159, 1165 (10th Cir. 1985). If no express finding of bad faith is made, an appellate court can remand for finding of facts, *see Barnd v. City of Tacoma,* 664 F.2d 1339, 1342–43 (9th Cir. 1982), or reverse the sanction, *see Estate of Blas through Chargualaf v. Winkler,* 792 F.2d 858, 860–61 (9th Cir. 1986), unless bad faith is evident from the record, *see Optyl Eyewear Fashion International v. Style Cos.,* 760 F.2d 1045, 1051 (9th Cir. 1985). For example, there is no basis to assume that counsel acted in bad faith from the fact that a suit was unsuccessful, so a hearing is necessary to impose attorneys' fees under § 1927 when counsel's conduct is as indicative of incompetence as it is of bad faith. *See Textor v. Board of Regents of Northern Illinois University,* 711 F.2d 1387, 1395 (7th Cir. 1983). On the other hand, Rule 11 sanctions may be appropriate without a hearing if the claim which was dismissed was legally or factually frivolous.

§ 7.6 Recovery of Expenses Associated with Discovery Motions

Federal Rule of Civil Procedure 37(a)(4) mandates the court to require the party, deponent, or attorney who unsuccessfully brings or defends a discovery motion to pay the winning party's reasonable expenses, including attorneys' fees, for conduct falling within its ambit and shifts the burden to the losing party to demonstrate that its conduct was substantially justified or other circumstances make an award of expenses unjust. *See Merritt v. International Brotherhood of Boilermakers,* 649 F.2d 1013, 1019 (5th Cir. 1981). Substantial justification exists if reasonable people could differ whether the position taken is appropriate. *Reygo Pacific Corp. v. Johnston Pump Co.,* 680 F.2d 647, 649 (9th Cir. 1982); 8 C. Wright & A. Miller, *Federal Practice and Procedure* § 2288 (Supp. 1985). When the expenses are levied against the parties, an appellate court will not permit them to shift the blame to their attorneys for the failures when nothing in the record indicates that the attorneys were acting outside the scope of their authority. *Merritt v. International Brotherhood of Boilermakers,* 649 F.2d at 1019.

The court may apportion reasonable expenses incurred in a just manner if the motion is partially granted. The provisions of Rule 37(a)(4) also apply to an award of expenses for protective orders. Fed. R. Civ. P. 26(c). Similarly, noncompliance with Rule 16 procedures results in the imposition of reasonable expenses including attorneys' fees, under the Rule 37(a)(4) standard, regardless of other sanctions imposed. Fed. R. Civ. P. 16(f). Rule 37(g) also provides for an award of expenses, including attorneys' fees, for failure to participate in good faith in framing a Rule 26(f) discovery plan. These rules provide that an opportunity for hearing must be afforded before monetary compensation is awarded.

§ 7.7 Other Sources for Awards of Attorneys' Fees as Sanctions

In patent cases, 35 U.S.C. § 285 permits the award of reasonable fees for "exceptional" cases. Such awards are reserved for willful misconduct or bad faith. *See, e.g., Loctite Corp. v. Fel-Pro, Inc.,* 667 F.2d 577, 584–85 (7th Cir. 1981). Fees are recoverable for the entire lawsuit rather than just for expenses arising out of abusive conduct. *Id.* at 585. The Ninth Circuit requires a finding of bad faith or frivolity for an award of attorney fees under 17 U.S.C. § 505 in copyright actions. *Cooling Systems & Flexibles, Inc. v. Stuart Radiator, Inc.,* 777 F.2d 485, 493 (9th Cir. 1985). In civil rights actions, a prevailing defendant may be awarded counsel fees if the plaintiff's claim is frivolous, unreasonable, or without foundation. *Christiansburg Garment Co. v. EEOC,* 434 U.S. 412, 422 (1978). An explicit finding may be required to uphold such a decision. *See Batson v. Neal Spelce Associates, Inc.,* 765 F.2d 511, 517 (5th Cir. 1985).

CHAPTER 8

SANCTIONS: CONTEMPT

§ 8.1 Civil versus Criminal Contempt

There are several sources for applying contempt as a sanction, including the court's inherent power, 18 U.S.C. § 401, Federal Rules of Civil Procedure 37 and 41, and Federal Rule of Criminal Procedure 42. As a practical matter, many courts appear to require that criminal contempts brought as sanctions for abuse of discovery or pretrial orders follow the requirements established under 18 U.S.C. § 401 and Federal Rule of Criminal Procedure 42. For example, the Ninth Circuit has noted that there is nothing to indicate that Rule 37 has changed the law relative to civil and criminal contempt or traditional concepts of the due process limitations on the exercise of contempt power. *Falstaff Brewing Corp. v. Miller Brewing Co.,* 702 F.2d 770, 783 (9th Cir. 1983).

It is important to distinguish civil and criminal contempt, because the procedural requirements and standards vary depending upon the type of contempt involved. However, it is often difficult to determine whether a contempt proceeding is criminal or civil in nature, because the same facts can give rise to both types of contempt. *See United States v. United Mine Workers of America,* 330 U.S. 258, 298–99 (1947). For example, when an attorney was ordered to pay a remedial fine for failing to appear and misrepresenting his whereabouts to the court, the contempt was considered civil rather than criminal. *In re Jacques,* 761 F.2d 302, 304–06 (6th Cir. 1985). The focus in determining the nature of the contempt is not the fact of the punishment but rather its character and purpose. *Shillitani v. United States,* 384 U.S. 364, 369 (1966).

Criminal contempt vindicates the authority of the court and places great reliance upon the discretion of the trial judge. *United States v. United Mine Workers,* 330 U.S. at 302–03. Civil contempt attempts to coerce the defendant into compliance with the court's order and compensates the complainant for its losses. *Id.* at 303–304. Therefore, some courts view the discretion of the trial judge as more limited in civil contempt, because the rights of the complainant, not the authority of the court, are at stake. *See Thompson v. Cleland,* 782 F.2d 719, 721 (7th Cir. 1986).

Imprisonment and monetary fines are available in both types of contempt proceedings. *In re Kave,* 760 F.2d 343, 351 (1st Cir. 1985). However, if a money fine is not compensatory or conditioned on the occurrence of future violation of court orders, it raises a presumption that the fine is punitive in nature. *Id.; see McDonald's Corp. v. Victory Investments,* 727 F.2d 82, 87 (3d Cir. 1984). Usually a criminal fine is paid to the court, while a civil fine is paid to the aggrieved party.

When a judgment contains a mixture of criminal and civil elements, the criminal aspects of the order fix its character for purposes of procedures on review. *Falstaff Brewing Corp. v. Miller Brewing Co.,* 702 F.2d 770, 778 (9th Cir. 1983). The imposition of civil contempt does not preclude later criminal contempt sanctions based on the same conduct under either the double jeopardy clause, *see Yates v. United States,* 355 U.S. 66, 74 (1957); *United States v. Monteleone,* 804 F.2d 1004, 1008–09 (7th Cir. 1986), or the res judicata doctrine, *United States v. Ryan,* 810 F.2d 650, 654 (7th Cir. 1987). Similarly, collateral estoppel does not bar the second action if the defendant did not prevail on the relevant issues in the first prosecution. *Id.* at 654–55.

§ 8.2 Civil Contempt

Civil contempt occurs when a party fails to comply with a court order. *General Signal Corp. v. Donallco, Inc.*, 787 F.2d 1376, 1379 (9th Cir. 1986). Sanctions for civil contempt are considered wholly remedial and are aimed at coercing compliance with a court order or compensating the injured party for the results of the contemptuous behavior or both. *United States v. United Mine Workers of America,* 330 U.S. 258, 303–04 (1947); *see generally* 11 C. Wright & A. Miller, *Federal Practice and Procedure* § 2960 (1973) [hereinafter *Federal Practice and Procedure*].

Civil contempt issues usually concern refusals to testify, disobedience of injunctions, and refusals to produce documents to the grand jury or in IRS enforcement actions. Failure to obey a protective order can also result in a civil contempt citation. In a discovery setting, any refusal to produce existing documents can be treated as civil contempt, but courts usually do not use this procedure, favoring Rule 37 sanctions which affect the merits of the action. Similarly, although the only remedy against nonparties for noncompliance of subpoenas duces tecum is contempt, judges usually resort to criminal rather than civil proceedings.

§ 8.3 —Procedures for Invoking Civil Contempt

Civil contempt is a civil action governed by the Federal Rules of Civil Procedure, *Rogers v. Webster,* 776 F.2d 607, 610 (6th Cir. 1985); 3 *Federal Practice and Procedure* § 705, including the pleading requirements of Rule 8, *Rogers v. Webster,* 776 F.2d at 610; *Shakman v. Democratic Organization of Cook County,* 533 F.2d 344, 352 (7th Cir.), *cert. denied,* 429 U.S. 858 (1976). Therefore, if a defendant in a civil contempt proceeding fails to file a responsive pleading admitting or denying the accusation, a district court could ordinarily deem the opponent's averments as admitted. *Rogers v. Webster,* 776 F.2d at 611. A court can also require that affidavits on file be controverted by counteraffidavits and treat uncontroverted affidavits as containing true facts. *Id.; Hoffman v. Beer Drivers & Salemen's Local Union No. 888,* 536 F.2d 1268, 1277 (9th Cir. 1976). If the defendant responds by invoking the Fifth Amendment privilege, this is considered the equivalent of a specific denial which requires the plaintiff to provide proof of its claims. *Rogers v. Webster,* 776 F.2d at 611; *see National Acceptance Co. of America v. Bathalter,* 705 F.2d 924, 926, 932 (7th Cir. 1983). Privilege should be raised in a formal answer or response to ensure that the court will not find a technical waiver. *See Rogers v. Webster,* 776 F.2d at 611 n.4. If a Fifth Amendment claim is denied, the defendant is given an opportunity to reconsider its response before being penalized for a refusal to answer. *Garner v. United States,* 424 U.S. 648, 663 (1976). Therefore, refusing to accept the defendant's affidavits as untimely and prohibiting him from testifying because of his earlier invocation of the Fifth Amendment privilege was reversible error, even though the defendant admitted the alleged misconduct, *Rogers v. Webster,* 776 F.2d at 612, because the defendant was entitled to offer matter in explanation of his conduct or in mitigation of any coercive punishment. *Id.; cf. Groppi v. Leslie,* 404 U.S. 496, 502–03 (1972).

It is unclear whether willfulness is an element of civil contempt. *Compare SEC v. Ormont Drug & Chemical Co.,* 739 F.2d 654, 656 (D.C. Cir. 1981) *and Shuffler v. Heritage Bank,* 720 F.2d 1141, 1146 (9th Cir. 1983) (willfulness necessary) *with Rogers v. Webster,* 776 F.2d at 612 *and* 3 *Federal Practice and Procedure* § 705 (willfulness not necessary). However, the contemnor's state of mind, such as good faith or reliance on the advice of counsel, is always considered relevant to mitigation of any penalty. Compensatory awards are limited to actual losses sustained as a result of the contumacy. *Shuffler v. Heritage Bank,* 720 F.2d at 1148; *see United States v. United Mine Workers of America,* 330 U.S. 258, 304 (1947). If the fine is coercive, it will be paid to the court rather than the opposing party. *General Signal Corp. v. Donallco, Inc.,* 787 F.2d 1376, 1380 (9th Cir. 1986); *In re Winner Corp.,* 511 F.2d 1010, 1015 (6th Cir. 1975). Coercive sanctions consider the character and magnitude of the harm threatened by the continued contumacy and the probable effectiveness of any suggested sanction. *United States v. United Mine Workers,* 330 U.S. at 304.

In civil contempt proceedings, the plaintiff has the burden of establishing that the defendant disobeyed the orders of the district court. If compensation is sought, similar to tort action, the complainant must prove that the defendant's actions in violation of the court order caused the injury. *Thompson v. Cleland,* 782 F.2d 719, 722 (7th Cir. 1986); *Vuitton et Fils, S.A. v. Carousel Handbags,* 592 F.2d 125, 130 (2d Cir. 1979). Clear and convincing evidence, rather than proof beyond a reasonable doubt, is required for such violations. *Hayden v. Oak Terrace Apartments,* 808 F.2d 1269, 1270 (7th Cir. 1987); *Neely v. City of Grenada,* 799 F.2d 203, 207 (5th Cir. 1976); *In re Kitchen,* 706 F.2d 1266, 1271 (2d Cir. 1983); *see Rogers v. Webster,* 776 F.2d at 612 n.6; 3 *Federal Practice and Procedure* § 705.

No right to a jury exists in civil contempt cases. *In re Kitchen,* 706 F.2d at 1271. However, a trend exists to afford the same or similar procedural safeguards to persons charged with civil contempt as to those charged with criminal contempt. *In re Rosahn,* 671 F.2d 690, 697 (2d Cir. 1982); *see In re Grand Jury Proceedings,* 795 F.2d 226, 234 (1st Cir. 1986), *cert. denied,* ______ U.S. ______, 107 S. Ct. 950 (1987). The extent of any required hearing varies with the nature of the contempt. *See In re Grand Jury Proceedings,* 795 F.2d at 234.

§ 8.4 —Defenses to Civil Contempt

Present inability to comply is a complete defense to civil contempt. *See United States v. Rylander,* 460 U.S. 752, 757 (1983); *Shillitani v. United States,* 384 U.S. 364, 371 (1966); *Maggio v. Zeitz,* 333 U.S. 56, 59, 69 (1948). Substantial compliance is also a defense if the violating party has taken all reasonable steps to comply with the court order. *General Signal Corp. v. Donallco, Inc.,* 787 F.2d 1376, 1379 (9th Cir. 1986). The defendant has the burden to produce evidence supporting such defenses. *United States v. Rylander,* 460 U.S. 752, 757 (1983). For example, if the defendant shows that the documents do not exist or are not in that person's custody or control, contempt is unavailable. Similarly, financial inability to comply with an order is a complete defense to civil contempt. *Badgely v. Santa Croce,* 800 F.2d 33, 37 (3d Cir. 1986); *SEC v. Ormont Drug & Chemical Co.,* 739 F.2d 654, 657 (D.C. Cir. 1984). The mere existence of a foreign law blocking access to documents located in another country usually is not sufficient to excuse noncompliance with a court order. *See, e.g., In re Grand Jury Proceedings Bank of Nova Scotia,* 740 F.2d 817, 832 (11th Cir. 1984), *cert. denied,* 469 U.S. 1106 (1985); *In re Marc Rich & Co.,* 736 F.2d 864, 866 (2d Cir. 1984).

A previous finding of ability to comply is not res judicata, because only present inability is required to avoid civil contempt. *United States v. Rylander,* 460 U.S. at 757. However, if a court finds that a defendant could have previously complied with a court order, it presumes a present ability to comply, which imposes a burden of producing contrary evidence on the defendant. *Id.; United States ex rel. Thom v. Jenkins,* 760 F.2d 736, 739–40 (7th Cir. 1985). Once this burden of production is met, the burden of persuasion shifts back to the party seeking contempt. *United States ex rel. Thom v. Jenkins,* 760 F.2d 736, 740 (7th Cir. 1985). The defendant's invocation of the Fifth Amendment is not a substitute for relevant evidence meeting the defendant's burden of producing evidence in support of a defense. *United States v. Rylander,* 460 U.S. at 761.

When the underlying order is held invalid, such as the imposition of fees on attorneys whose conduct did not fall within Rule 37 or 18 U.S.C. § 1927, the civil contempt adjudication must fail. *In re Air Crash Disaster Near Saigon,* 671 F.2d 564, 568 (D.C. Cir. 1982); *see United States v. United Mine Workers of America,* 330 U.S. 258, 294–95 (1947). However, a party cannot raise defenses to the underlying court order in the contempt proceeding if they were not previously raised to challenge the validity of the original order. *United States v. Rylander,* 460 U.S. at 757.

§ 8.5 —Review of Civil Contempt Orders

Both the determination of contempt and the sanctions imposed are reviewed for abuse of discretion, *Gifford v. Heckler,* 741 F.2d 263, 266 (9th Cir. 1984), although factual decisions are reviewed on a clearly erroneous standard, *Anderson v. City of Bessemer City,* 470 U.S. 564, 573 (1985); *United States v. Seetapun,* 750 F.2d 601, 604 n.4 (7th Cir. 1984). Counsel should always request clarification of the ruling if its basis is not apparent, because several circuits will remand for entry of a statement of the purpose and basis of the sanction to aid appellate review. *See, e.g., Shuffler v. Heritage Bank,* 720 F.2d 1141, 1147 (9th Cir. 1983); *Perfect Fit Industries,*

Inc. v. Acme Quilting Co., 646 F.2d 800, 810 (2d Cir. 1981), *cert. denied,* 459 U.S. 832 (1982).

An order adjudging a party in civil contempt is not an appealable final order. *Fox v. Capital Co.,* 299 U.S. 105, 107 (1936); *but see N.Y. State Urban Development Corp. v. VSL Corp.,* 738 F.2d 61, 64–65 (2d Cir. 1984) (finding limited exception to rule). However, in many cases, appeal is proper, because the civil contempt proceeding is the sole action before the court. *See, e.g., Shuffler v. Heritage Bank,* 720 F.2d 1141, 1145 (9th Cir. 1983). Even if the contempt is appealable, some circuits prohibit review until sanctions have been imposed. *Motorola, Inc. v. Computer Displays International, Inc.,* 739 F.2d 1149, 1154 (7th Cir. 1984); *Donovan v. Mazzola,* 761 F.2d 1141, 1147 (9th Cir. 1985); *see United States Steel Corp. v. Fraternal Association of Steel Haulers,* 601 F.2d 1269, 1273 (3d Cir. 1979). For example, if a party can purge the contempt by complying with the order, it is considered interlocutory, whereas if the fine or penalty cannot be avoided, the order is immediately appealable. *Combs v. Ryan's Coal Co.,* 785 F.2d 970, 976 (11th Cir.), *cert. denied,* ______ U.S. ______, 107 S. Ct. 187 (1986). A judgment of civil contempt entered against a nonparty is appealable as a final judgment. *New York Times Co. v. Jascalevich,* 439 U.S. 1317, 1319 (1978) (White, J., in chambers); *Lamb v. Cramer,* 285 U.S. 217, 221 (1932); *United States v. Johnson,* 736 F.2d 358, 359 n.1 (6th Cir. 1984). Paying an ordered fine ends the civil contempt aspect of a case or controversy for appeal, *McDonald's Corp. v. Victory Investments,* 727 F.2d 82, 85–86 (3d Cir. 1984); *In re Cordova Gonzalez,* 726 F.2d 16, 21 (1st Cir.), *cert. denied,* 466 U.S. 951 (1984); *In re Campbell,* 628 F.2d 1260, 1261 (9th Cir. 1980), unless the court has permitted a motion for refund to be entertained, *see Falstaff Brewing Corp. v. Miller Brewing Co.,* 702 F.2d 770, 777 (9th Cir. 1983).

§ 8.6 Criminal Contempt

Criminal contempt is punitive and is imposed for conduct which affronts the honor and dignity of the court. Criminal contempt citations for discovery and pretrial abuses are uncommon, because of the formalities surrounding their imposition and the reluctance of judges to hold attorneys in contempt. Moreover, some courts will not impose a contempt sanction for conduct not punishable under the judge's inherent powers. *See United States v. Stoneberger,* 805 F.2d 1391, 1394 (9th Cir. 1986).

Criminal contempt can occur in a variety of pretrial situations, because any willful violation of a court order can be considered contemptuous. For example, a lawyer was held in criminal contempt under 18 U.S.C. § 401(3) for failure to comply with an order directing her to submit a written narrative witness statement prior to trial. *Chapman v. Pacific Telephone &*

Telegraph Co., 613 F.2d 193, 194 (9th Cir. 1979). Dilatory tactics by lawyers who have "sold out to the client" have also been treated as contempt. *E.g., Pesaplastic, C.A. v. Cincinnati Milacron Co.,* 799 F.2d 1510 (11th Cir. 1986).

§ 8.7 —Procedures for Invoking Criminal Conduct

Summary disposition of contempt charges is reserved for exceptional circumstances such as acts threatening the judge, disrupting a hearing, or obstructing court proceedings. *Harris v. United States,* 382 U.S. 162, 164 (1965). Conduct outside the actual presence of the court must follow normal procedures established in Federal Rule of Criminal Procedure 42(b). *Id.* at 164–65. Summary contempt usually occurs during jury trials when attorneys are questioning witnesses and become embroiled in disputes with the judge, *see, e.g., United States v. Lowery,* 733 F.2d 441, 442–44 (7th Cir.), *cert. denied,* 469 U.S. 932 (1984), not in pretrial proceedings. Rule 42(a), which provides for summary adjudication, cannot be used to punish an attorney for statements made in a written paper. *See In re Jafree,* 741 F.2d 133, 136 (7th Cir. 1984); *United States v. Lee,* 720 F.2d 1049, 1052 (9th Cir. 1983). Similarly, summary adjudication ordinarily cannot be used when an attorney fails to attend a scheduled court appearance. *United States v. Nunez,* 801 F.2d 1250, 1253 (11th Cir. 1985); *United States v. Onu,* 730 F.2d 253, 255–56 (5th Cir.), *cert. denied,* 469 U.S. 856 (1984); *In re Allis,* 531 F.2d 1391, 1392 (9th Cir.), *cert. denied,* 429 U.S. 900 (1976). *But see In re Niblack,* 476 F.2d 930, 933 (D.C. Cir.), *cert. denied,* 414 U.S. 909 (1973). However, when counsel had previously informed the court of the reasons for an intended absence, summary contempt was upheld. *United States v. Baldwin,* 770 F.2d 1550, 1555–56 (11th Cir. 1985), *cert. denied,* _____ U.S. _____, 106 S. Ct. 1636 (1986). A pro se litigant's refusal to proceed with trial also warranted summary contempt. *United States v. Brown,* 791 F.2d 577, 578 (7th Cir. 1986).

Rule 42(b) provides for notice which allows a reasonable time for the preparation of the defense and states the essential facts constituting the charge as well as the time and place of the hearing. The contemnor is protected by a presumption of innocence, *In re Kave,* 760 F.2d 343, 351 (1st Cir. 1985), and can be convicted only by proof beyond a reasonable doubt, *Gompters v. Bucks Stove & Range Co.,* 221 U.S. 418, 444 (1911); *Falstaff Brewing Corp. v. Miller Brewing Co.,* 702 F.2d 770, 778 (9th Cir. 1983). No right exists for a jury trial in a criminal contempt proceeding unless the judge imposes a prison sentence exceeding six months. *Bloom v. Illinois,* 391 U.S. 194, 210–11 (1968). When the contempt involves disrespect or criticism of a judge so that he becomes personally embroiled in the controversy or when there is likelihood of bias or the appearance of bias, recusal is required. Fed. R. Crim. P. 42 (b); *Taylor v. Hayes,* 418 U.S. 488, 501 (1974); *Mayberry v. Pennsylvania,* 400 U.S. 455, 464–65 (1971). Although a private attorney can be appointed as prosecutor in the contempt action, the Supreme Court recently prohibited counsel for a party that is the beneficiary of a court to prosecute the contempt. *See Yound v. United States ex rel. Vuitton et Fils S.A.,* _____ U.S. _____, 107 S. Ct. 2124, 2128, 2130 (1987).

Willfulness is an essential element of criminal contempt, *United States v. McCargo,* 783 F.2d 507, 510 (5th Cir. 1986); *United States v. Armstrong,* 781 F.2d 700, 706 (9th Cir. 1986), and implies a deliberate or intended violation, as distinguished from an accidental, inadvertent, or negligent violation of an order, *Falstaff Brewing Corp. v. Miller Brewing Co.,* 702 F.2d at 782, *quoted in United States v. Baldwin,* 770 F.2d at 1558; *accord Hubbard v. Fleet Mortgage Co.,* 810 F.2d 778, 781 (8th Cir. 1987). Conduct which is merely disrespectful is not contemptuous. *Tyler v. City of Milwaukee,* 740 F.2d 580, 582 (7th Cir. 1984); *see In re Little,* 404 U.S. 553, 555 (1972) (per curiam). A good faith belief that the party is complying with the order may also prevent a finding of willfulness. *United States v. Armstrong,* 781 F.2d at 706 (9th Cir. 1986). It is unclear whether good faith reliance on the advice of counsel to disobey a court order is a defense to criminal contempt. *Compare id.* (not a defense) *with Williamson v. United States,* 207 U.S. 425, 453 (1908) (court cited instruction approving the defense).

18 U.S.C. § 401 authorizes either a fine or imprisonment for criminal contempt, but not both. *United States v. McCargo,* 783 F.2d at 510. However, 18 U.S.C. § 3013 provides for specific fines in criminal cases which can be imposed in addition to any other punishment. In determining what sentence to impose in a criminal contempt case, the court considers the extent of the willful and deliberate defiance of the court's order, the seriousness of the consequences of the contumacious behavior, the necessity of effectively terminating the defendant's defiance as required by the public interest, and the importance of deterring such acts in the future. *United States v. United Mine Workers of America,* 330 U.S. 258, 303 (1947).

§ 8.8 —Review of Criminal Contempt Orders

A party usually can appeal a criminal contempt ruling, *see United States v. Ryan,* 402 U.S. 530, 532–33 (1971), but an appeal does not necessarily permit review of the validity of the order whose violation led to the contempt. *See, e.g., Walker v. City of Birmingham,* 388 U.S. 307, 317–21 (1967). If the underlying order is not appealable and compliance will bring irreparable harm, the individual disobeying the order can raise its invalidity as a defense in a subsequent contempt proceeding. *Maness v. Meyers,* 419 U.S. 449, 460 (1975); *United States v. Ryan,* 402 U.S. at 532–33

(1971). In such cases, if the underlying order is invalidated, the contempt judgment falls with it. *Id.* at 533. However, if the order is appealable, some circuits do not permit its invalidity to be raised as a defense to a contempt proceeding if review of the order was not sought. *See Marrese v. American Academy of Orthopaedic Surgeons,* 726 F.2d 1150, 1157 (7th Cir. 1984) (en banc), *rev'd on other grounds,* 470 U.S. 373 (1985); *Halderman v. Pennhurst State School & Hospital,* 673 F.2d 628, 636–37 (3d Cir. 1982) (en banc), *cert. denied,* 465 U.S. 1038 (1984). Similarly, when compliance with the disputed order posed no irreparable harm, its invalidity was not permitted to be raised as a defense to a contempt charge. *Pennsylvania v. Local Union 542, International Union of Operating Engineers,* 552 F.2d 498, 505–06 (3d Cir. 1977), *cert. denied,* 434 U.S. 822 (1977).

Usually issues of privilege are considered as resulting in irreparable harm. *See, e.g., Maness v. Meyers,* 419 U.S. at 460; *United States v. Pearce,* 792 F.2d 397, 401 n.5 (3d Cir. 1986); *In re Grand Jury proceedings,* 601 F.2d 162, 169 (5th Cir. 1979). The circuits are split as to when clients can appeal orders for their attorneys to produce documents which are allegedly privileged. The Supreme Court permitted such an appeal in *Perlman v. United States,* 247 U.S. 7, 12–13 (1918). *Perlman* has been interpreted by most circuits as always permitting clients to appeal as soon as their attorneys are required to produce documents, while a minority permit an appeal in advance of a citation for contempt only when contempt is unlikely as a practical matter. *In re Klein,* 776 F.2d 628, 630 (7th Cir. 1985) (extensive citations); *see* Comment, *The Perlman Exception; Limitations Required by the Final Decision Rule,* 49 U. Chi. L. Rev. 798 (1982). Contempt orders against nonparties, such as attorneys, are appealable. *Combs v. Ryan's Coal Co.,* 785 F.2d 970, 977 (11th Cir.), *cert. denied,* ____ U.S. ____, 107 S. Ct. 187 (1986); see 9 J. Moore, et al., *Moore's Federal Practice* ¶ 110.14[1], at 198 (2d ed. 1986). Criminal contempt sanctions are reviewed for abuse of discretion. *United States v. McCargo,* 783 F.2d 507, 510 (5th Cir. 1986).

§ 8.9 Fines

Most circuits permit fines to be imposed against attorneys and litigants absent a finding of contempt. *See, e.g., Eash v. Riggins Trucking Inc.,* 757 F.2d 557, 568 (3d Cir. 1985) (en banc); *Miranda v. Southern Pacific Transportation Co.,* 710 F.2d 516, 521–22 (9th Cir. 1983); *Martinez v. Thrifty Drug & Discount Co.,* 593 F.2d 992, 993–94 (10th Cir. 1979); *In re Sutter,* 543 F.2d 1030, 1036–68 (2d Cir. 1916); *J.M. Cleminshaw Co. v. City of Norwich,* 93 F.R.D. 338, 358–60 (D. Conn. 1981); *see also Cotner v. Hopkins,* 795 F.2d 900, 903 (10th Cir. 1986); *White v. Raymark Industries, Inc.,* 783 F.2d 1175, 1177 (4th Cir. 1986) (litigants as well as attorneys can be fined). Often such fines arise out of violations or failures to prosecute or obey court orders under Rules 16(f) or 41(b) or the court's inherent powers.

Fines have also been imposed for Rule 11 violations. *Cotner v. Hopkins,* 795 F.2d 900, 903 (10th Cir. 1986). However, it appears that notice, an opportunity to respond, and a hearing are required before a fine can be invoked. *See Eash v. Riggins Trucking Inc.,* 757 F.2d 557, 570–71 (3d Cir. 1985) (en banc); *Miranda v. Southern Pacific Transportation Co.,* 710 F.2d at 522–23. As a practical matter, courts resort to such fines as a way of sanctioning attorneys without having to worry about the consequences that a finding of contempt may have upon an attorney's reputation or practice.

§ 8.10 Sanctions for Violations of Local Rules

Often local rules specifically authorize sanctions which can be invoked for noncomplying conduct. A district court's authority to adopt local rules stems from its inherent power, 28 U.S.C. § 2071, and Federal Rule of Civil Procedure 83 *White v. Raymark Industries,* 783 F.2d 1175, 1176–77 (4th Cir. 1986); *Transamerica Corp. v. Transamerica Bancgrowth Corp.,* 627 F.2d 963, 965 (9th Cir. 1986). The only requirement for such rules is that they be consistent with the federal statutes and rules of practice. *White v. Raymark Industries,* 783 F.2d. at 1176–77.

One common rule enables the court to consider a motion unopposed when no opposition or an untimely response is made. Another permits the court to impose monetary sanctions for failure to follow local rules. It is rare that such rules are challenged, *see generally* Cohn, *Federal Discovery: A Survey of Local Rules and Practices in View of Proposed Changes to the Federal Rules,* 63 Minn. L. Rev. 253 (1979); Roberts, *The Myth of Uniformity in Federal Civil Procedure: Federal Civil Rule 83 and District Court Local Rulemaking Powers,* 8 Univ. Puget Sound L. Rev. 537 (1985), in part because such sanctions cannot usually be immediately appealed. However, when local rules conflict with the federal rules, they will be overturned. *Cf. Miner v. Atlass,* 363 U.S. 641, 647 (1960) (Admiralty Rules). Therefore, local rules which provide for sanctions which terminate a case are judged by the same standard as other sanctions resulting in dismissals and defaults. *See Hall v. Commissioner,* 805 F.2d 1511, 1514–15 (11th Cir. 1986). For example, dismissals of actions for failure to file a memorandum of points and authorities have been reversed when there was no other evidence of dilatoriness. *See, e.g., Witt v. United States,* 681 F.2d 1144, 1149 (11th Cir. 1986). Similarly, a dismissal for failure to notify the clerk of the name, address, and telephone number of defendant's counsel was reversed as being too severe. *Farmers Plant Food, Inc. v. Fisher,* 746 F.2d 451, 452 (8th Cir. 1984). Several circuits have held that summary judgment cannot be granted for violation of a local rule when it would not otherwise be appropriate, *Dixie Stevedores, Inc. v. Marinic Maritime, Ltd.*, 778 F.2d 670, 672–73 (11th Cir. 1985); *John v. Louisiana*, 757 F.2d 698, 707–09 (5th Cir. 1985), although a few circuits uphold dismissals for failure to file an opposition. *See, e.g., Lepkowski v. United States Department of Treasury*, 804 F.2d 1310, 1312–13 (D.C. Cir. 1986).

Local rules are narrowly constructed. When suspension from the district court bar was not specifically mentioned as a sanction for an attorney's tardiness, the appellate court refused to interpret a local rule governing conduct unbecoming a member of the bar to include a late appearance. *See United States v. Stoneberger*, 805 F.2d 1391, 1393–94 (9th Cir. 1986). Sanctions for violating a judge's unwritten rules were also overturned when the party was not given fair warning. *In re Richardson*, 793 F.2d 37, 41 (1st Cir. 1986). On the other hand, excluding an expert witness from testifying because the expert's designation was untimely under a local rule, *Sturgeon v. Airborne Freight Corp.*, 778 F.2d 1154, 1159 (5th Cir. 1985), or refusing to permit discovery beyond the period provided by a local rule, *Public Loan Co. v. FDIC*, 803 F.2d 82, 86 (3d Cir. 1986), were not abuses of discretion.

CHAPTER 9

SETTLEMENT TACTICS AND STRATEGIES

§ 9.1 Introduction

Of all aspects of the litigative process that are susceptible to the use of unfair tactics, settlement is one in which lawyers are most prone to play "hardball," with conduct frequently bordering on the unethical. The settlement process is definitely adversarial.

Whether you litigate a case or settle it, the amount of advocacy skill required is enormous. Indeed, more often than not, it takes a more knowledgeable tactician and strategist to resolve a case in a nontrial setting through settlement than to resolve it in the courtroom.

In many respects, the courtroom is the easy way out. By taking a case to trial, the lawyers are turning the decision-making process, in terms of both imposition of liability and measure of damages, over to someone else. By resolving a case through settlement, the lawyers are required to make, justify to their clients, and live with their own evaluations of both liability and damages and, more important, they are required to act on those judgments.

Virtually none of this happens when cases are resolved by the judge or the jury. The losing side can always say "they were wrong and we were right and we'll prove it to them on appeal." Even if the adverse verdict is upheld on appeal, the losing side can simply say, "the standards on appeal are so narrow that we never had a chance." The same thing cannot be said for disputes resolved through settlement. Each side must be prepared to accept and live with the consequences of its decisions and, if those decisions are bad ones, must take responsibility for them.

In recognizing the motivations that are often present in the settlement of litigation by opponents, it is imperative that you gain more understanding not only of the merits of your case and your opponent's case, but of your opponent as well, in order to understand what prompts certain actions and why certain actions are not being taken.

Often settlement tactics are pursued not for the sake of settlement but rather to gain an advantage in the litigation by feeling out the strengths and weaknesses of an opponent. Similarly, certain settlement tactics may be pursued to educate the judge in a biased fashion or to put an opponent in an unfavorable light in the eyes of the judge. All of these tactics and strategies, although unfair, are pursued regularly and, for the most part, yield the results at which they are aimed.

Although evidence of settlement negotiations is, as a general rule, inadmissible under Federal Rule of Evidence 408, there are instances when it may be admitted. Two recent cases illustrate such situations.

In *Bituminous Construction, Inc. v. Rucker Enterprises, Inc.*, 816 F.2d 965 (4th Cir. 1987), evidence of settlement negotiations was determined to be admissible to show the understanding of its obligations by one of the parties.

In Davidson v. Beco Corp., 1986 Opinion No. CA-139 (Idaho Ct. App. Dec. 12, 1986), evidence of settlement negotiations was determined to be admissible for the purpose of showing prior inconsistent statements made during the negotiations when the circumstances suggest that witness at trial is committing perjury and/or the danger of unfair prejudice is insubstantial.

Admissibility of certain aspects of settlement negotiations is further discussed in §§ **9.4** (settlement brochures) and **9.7–9.9** (day-in-the-life videotapes).

§ 9.2 Taking the Measure of Your Opponent

One of the most significant differences between the litigative process as it takes place in the courtroom and the litigative process as it takes place in the settlement arena has to do with the importance of the individual lawyer in the overall outcome. In the instance of settlement, the individual personality, character, and overall tactical sense of a lawyer are far more important than in the courtroom.

Remember, in the courtroom you are a litigator. Although perhaps you may be the master of ceremonies and director of the production, you are not the sole actor. Witnesses, other lawyers, the jury, the judge, and many other persons and matters are outside your control. On the other hand, in settlement negotiations, whether or not they involve the judge, you are typically the only character in the play as well as its director, writer, and producer. Although you certainly have responsibilities to your client, and although there is an opponent on the other side as well as a judge, the outcome of the settlement negotiation is within your control to a far greater extent than the trial process.

Accordingly, it is incumbent on you to be sure you have a good understanding of your opponent in order to better represent your client in settlement negotiations. Similarly, such an understanding permits you to avoid being subject to unfair pressure tactics and the type of hardball negotiation strategy favored by many lawyers.

§ 9.3 Settlement Books or Brochures

It is typical in personal injury or wrongful death cases for an attorney to prepare what is commonly known as a *settlement brochure* or *settlement book.* Generally, the brochure contains a number of sections, including the plaintiff's version of the facts, incorporating items such as accident reports, maps, or diagrams that may be pertinent to the case, along with photographs that may be illustrative of the plaintiff's argument; a statement of the law along with copies of cases which may be of special import to the plaintiff's case; and copies of medical records as well as prognoses. In a death case, the book may include a copy of a death certificate; personal papers or materials relating to the plaintiff, including family photographs, birth certificates, and graduation certificates; and copies of pertinent income tax returns and an economic analysis typically compiled by an expert setting forth further damages along with the assumptions built into those calculations.

Settlement brochures can be as simple or as elaborate as the facts and damages of a particular case may dictate. In some instances they may consist of nothing more than several typewritten pages discussing damages put together and included as an attachment to a letter making a settlement demand. In other cases, where the damages are substantial, the settlement brochure may be relatively elaborate, possibly bound in a leather covered loose-leaf notebook with plastic insert pages for pictures and other documents.

Without regard to the form in which the settlement brochure is assembled, its purpose remains the same—to present the damages claimed by your client in the most effective and persuasive fashion.

The following table of contents represents a sampling of the kind of information which can be included in a settlement brochure dealing with a typical automobile personal injury case. Obviously whatever changes that are necessary, be they additions or deletions, can be made as a particular case may dictate.

1. Letter of transmittal and amount of demand.
2. Factual statement summarizing accident and effects.
3. Copy of police report.
4. Survey of premises involved.
5. Photo of premises involved.
6. List of factual witnesses to be called.
7. List of technical expert witnesses to be called.
8. List of medical expert witnesses to be called.
9. Copy of reports of technical experts.
10. Copy of reports of medical experts.
11. Copy of hospital reports.
12. Copies of all bills for medical, surgical, and hospital fees.
13. Photos of plaintiff showing all scars or other deformities.
14. Copy of life expectancy table with plaintiff's life expectancy circled for easy reference.
15. Summary of injuries and special damages.
16. Factual and legal analysis.
17. Damage analysis, showing how damages claimed were arrived at, followed by a restatement of the demand, "expressly without prejudice."

The damages analysis (item 15 on table of contents) is one of the most important aspects of the settlement brochure. A suggested format follows:

Name of plaintiff ______________________________ Age __________

Date of accident __________ Place of accident ______________________

____

Description of Injuries:

(a) ______________________ (d) ______________________

(b) ______________________ (e) ______________________

(c) ______________________ (f) ______________________

Confined to ____________ Hospital, from __________ to __________

Confined to bed from __________ to __________ Total __________ Weeks

__________ Days

Confined to home from ________ to __________ Total __________ Weeks

__________ Days

Names and addresses of doctors, and bills to date:

__________________ $__________

__________________ $__________

__________________ $__________

__________________ $__________

__________________ $__________

Total doctor bills $__________

Total hospital bills to date __________ 19______ $__________

X-rays taken at __________________________ Hospital $__________

X-rays taken at office of Dr. ______________________ $__________

Total medical bills $__________

Time lost from employment at ___________________________________

____________ Days

from __________ to __________ Weeks @ $________ $__________

Itemize all other losses or expenses:

____ $__________

____ $__________

Total $__________

Settlement brochures, when properly done for maximum effect, usually are assembled in a looseleaf notebook with clear acetate pages, resembling a scrapbook. They are designed to impress an opponent with not only the merits but also the worth of a case and are used to help force a settlement. They are, in many respects, a tactic susceptible of considerable misuse if not clearly understood for what they are and, most important, what they are not.

The ideal situation for the use of a settlement brochure is when both the plaintiff and the defendant have evaluated the issue of liability as favorable for them and damages are relatively substantial. If either one of these situations is not present, you as a defense attorney should view any use of a settlement brochure with a suspicious eye.

Defense attorneys can misuse this technique as a discovery tool by soliciting such settlement brochures or books from plaintiff's counsel as a means of obtaining what is essentially work product and discovery without going through the formalities. The analysis that the plaintiff's attorney makes of the evidence respecting liability or calculations regarding damages may either reveal the attorney's thought processes regarding theories of the case or preliminarily reveal experts' opinions and testimony.

A settlement brochure or book can be of tremendous assistance to you as a defense lawyer in evaluating the plaintiff's case. However, you should also recognize that compilation is an adversarial undertaking slanted toward the best aspects of the plaintiff's case and designed to maximize the plaintiff's damages. In its most basic form, it is a sales brochure aimed at selling you the case for the asking price of the plaintiff. If you fail to recognize this fact when dealing with any kind of settlement brochure, you are responding just as the plaintiff intended when preparing and submitting a brochure to you.

You should approach the settlement brochure with suspicion and cynicism as to its contents and conclusions. Your rule should be, "I don't accept any of it unless, after review, I am persuaded." This is very like the rule of thumb for cross-examination that you should not cross-examine a witness unless you have a good reason to do so.

If you start with the opposite assumption, i.e., accepting everything in the settlement brochure unless you have reason to doubt it, you will be giving unjustified weight to it and playing into the plaintiff's hands. However, if you reject everything subject to accepting it on a proper showing of its worth, you will be better served, and your ability to evaluate the material contained in the settlement brochure will be that much better.

You should also be aware that a settlement brochure or book is effective only in certain kinds of cases. All too often, a plaintiff may attempt to use the technique to make much ado about nothing. For example, if liability is clear but damages are relatively small, a settlement brochure may be used to dress up the damages aspect of the case and try for a free ride on the liability. Alternatively, if damages are exceedingly good but liability is shaky, the plaintiff may attempt to use a settlement brochure as a means of steamrolling the defendant with the damages and thus intimidating a settlement out of the other side.

Plaintiffs' attorneys should be cautious about revealing this information and should weigh the merits of laying it out against the liabilities. On the other hand, a defense lawyer should solicit such settlement brochures, because, notwithstanding the fact that they are biased and adversarial in nature, they do yield a substantial amount of information regarding the other side's case.

§ 9.4 —In Evidence

A technique which you as a defense lawyer should be leery of when dealing with settlement brochures is any attempt on the part of the other side to use the settlement brochure in evidence. Remember, a settlement brochure is adversarial and is quite likely to contain a substantial amount of inadmissible information in the form of opinions, conclusions, speculations and other types of "puff" regarding both the cause of action and the damages.

Much of this "evidence" would undoubtedly not be admissible in any form, so you should guard against any attempt by plaintiff's counsel to use the settlement brochure to get such information into the record. One of the ways a plaintiff is most likely to approach this is to have an expert rely on it in formulating his or her opinions respecting the loss suffered by the plaintiff. For example, if an economist has formulated certain opinions regarding the loss due to the wrongful death of the plaintiff's decedent, as part of the preliminary questioning the plaintiff may elicit the fact that the economist has reviewed certain factual information regarding the occurrence, damage information regarding the plaintiff, and certain other documentary evidence associated with the case. The form in which this information was presented to the expert may have been the settlement brochure, in which case on cross-examination the other side's expert may indicate that he or she reviewed this information bound in a "black book with acetate pages and documents under these pages." When this happens, you, as defense counsel, must resort to traditional rules of evidence regarding what experts may rely on, and the appropriate motions to strike, or, if you have advance notice, in limine should be filed to preclude the possibility of ambush.

§ 9.5 Day-In-The-Life Presentations

Of all the settlement tactics available to a plaintiff in wrongful death and personal injury litigation, perhaps the most effective is a *day-in-the-life presentation. Effective* is probably not a very good word to describe such presentations which, when properly prepared, are prejudicial and unfair and have a tremendous impact on the viewer. However, do not confuse the fact that they are unfair or prejudicial with the issue of whether they are admissible in evidence. With proper attention to foundation and careful preparation, day-in-the-life presentations are relevant and material evidence that can properly be placed before a trier of fact, whether judge or jury, in order to better permit an evaluation of the loss.

The key to proper preparation and ultimate admissibility of a day-in-the-life presentation is foundation. Whether you are a plaintiff preparing such a presentation and using it to prove your case or a defendant attempting to respond to or cross-examine on the basis of a day-in-the-life presentation, there is no substitute for preparation.

§ 9.6 —Use in Personal Injury Cases

In my earlier work, *Dombroff on Demonstrative Evidence* §§ 6.13–6.15 (1983), I discussed day-in-the-life presentations as part of the larger subject of using motion pictures and videotape effectively in a courtroom. I pointed out that the value of a day-in-the-life presentation is multidimensional:

1. It shows the impact of the injuries on the plaintiff's everyday life and on the daily activities which so many of us, including the jurors, take for granted, such as rising in the morning, eating, and bathing.
2. It shows the injured plaintiff's dependence on others, i.e., what family members and others must do to assist the plaintiff. Thus, the day-in-the-life presentation focuses not only on a day in the life of the injured plaintiff but also on a day in the life of the injured plaintiff's family.
3. It illustrates the strain which the plaintiff's injuries have placed on the family by permitting viewers psychologically to put themselves into family members' roles and judge their own responses to such circumstances.
4. It graphically and effectively illustrates the limitations which the injury has caused, and depicts the frustration which can be associated with those limitations, not only on the part of the injured party but also among family members and friends.
5. It graphically and effectively illustrates the care which the plaintiff will require in a manner that is far more demonstrative than any sort of verbal explanation could possibly convey.

Recognizing that a day-in-the-life presentation in a personal injury case has such a significant impact and is so unfair in the way it favors a plaintiff, you must, when preparing to offer such a presentation, be especially careful about your foundation and avoid several pitfalls that can cause such a presentation to cross the line from unfair and prejudicial but admissible into unfair and prejudicial but inadmissible.

A day-in-the-life presentation used in a personal injury case, for example, one involving a quadriplegic or a serious burn case, is so powerful that it speaks for itself. You need not introduce any theatrical elements to make it more effective. Indeed, by doing so you may well be making it inadmissible rather than more effective.

The message you should get across in using the presentation is that the injured person is attempting to be self-sufficient despite the physical handicap and problems associated with it. The message should be a positive one, calculated to get the jury "rooting" for the plaintiff as opposed to feeling sorry for the plaintiff. This latter effect will naturally flow from the substantive presentation and need not be drawn out of the jury.

You should be sure that the finished product is an accurate representation of the normal daily activities of the injured person. Any outtakes from the finished product should be available for viewing by your opponent. Typically such outtakes are harmless as long as the presentation itself has not been staged or contrived. If it has been contrived, this will come across and will provide a fertile ground for your opponent's arguments that you have stepped out of bounds into the area of inadmissibility. Similarly, if the edited-out material is not available, you may find yourself on the defensive and the recipient of a ruling that your day-in-the-life presentation is not admissible.

One technique that can be used with some success for heightening the impression created by a day-in-the-life presentation but which is patently unfair and prejudicial is the combining of day-in-the-life footage with home movies or still photographs. By incorporating and editing such preexisting scenes into a day-in-the-life presentation, a plaintiff will be showing the jury a *before and after* type of comparison.

In its most effective form, you might see a still photograph or segment from a home movie showing the plaintiff playing ball with his son immediately followed by a segment from the day-in-the-life footage showing the plaintiff sitting in a wheelchair watching his son bounce the ball against a wall. In an area as explosive and innately prejudicial as day-in-the-life presentations already are, such a format certainly goes beyond admissibility, and you should vehemently object to it if you are on the receiving end.

§ 9.7 —Preparation

Whether you are offering a day-in-the-life presentation in a personal injury case as a plaintiff or examining such a presentation as a defendant for the purposes of deciding whether you should object, there are a number of points you should be aware of.

First, if offering a day-in-the-life presentation, you should have a "pocket" brief available which lays out the law applicable to such pieces of evidence and the discretion of the judge in admitting them into the record. On the other hand, if you anticipate your opponent's offering such a piece of evidence into the record, you should have a brief that lays out the discretion of the court to refuse admission of this evidence into the record. Given the fact that day-in-the-life presentations fall into the category of demonstrative evidence and are thus within the sole discretion of the court regarding admissibility, the more substance and precedent which you can provide to the judge regarding discretion on the question of admissibility, the greater the likelihood you will prevail on the question.

Second, in order to keep the day-in-the-life presentation from appearing contrived or staged, a working script should be prepared in consultation with your client. This working script should essentially be a chronology of the day; this step should be followed by a walk-through by the people who will do the actual videotaping, to give them a working familiarity with the subject and allow them to set up camera angles and other technical details that will be most effective yet avoid the staged look.

Third, an extremely effective plaintiff's tactic which will put the defendant on the defensive even more than the litigation itself is to advise the defendant that you will be doing a day-in-the-life presentation and invite the defendant to the taping session itself. By doing so you will appear to be an open and forthcoming plaintiff, in no way intent on ambushing your opponent, but rather solely concerned with creating a piece of evidence which can be effectively used to aid the trier of fact in resolving the dispute. Your response as a defendant to such an invitation must be carefully measured. If you accept the invitation, you may well be compromising any objections to a day-in-the-life presentation, because you will have been present at the actual taping and may find yourself unwittingly part of an introductory statement at the beginning of the presentation wherein your opponent indicates what is transpiring and who is present. Certainly the argument will be made that you have waived any objection by being present, and you must be careful, assuming you are to be present, that you preserve any objection and do not permit your presence and perhaps your silence on the scene to be construed as a waiver of any right.

On the other hand, if you arc not present, you may find yourself characterized as uncooperative and unwilling to move the case along on an expeditious and economic basis by requiring your opponent to undertake the considerable expense of this presentation without attempting to join in and make it as informative and admissible a piece of evidence as possible. The response to an invitation to attend a day-in-the-life taping should attempt to walk the middle ground between accepting the invitation and rejecting it. One proper response in this situation would be to file a pleading noting the invitation and declining to accept it, reserving all your objections to it and noting that, by declining the invitation, you are not in any way attempting to cause the plaintiff to incur added expense or lengthy litigation, but pointing out that your presence at the taping could serve no useful purpose except to compromise your objections. As long as you file such a position prior to the taping, you probably cannot be characterized as obstreperous or otherwise attempting to make the litigation process any more expensive than it already is.

Fifth, you should consider superimposing a real clock face on the screen. This will enable viewers to place in temporal perspective what they are observing, and will also indicate where editing has taken place, in order to insure integrity of the finished product.

Placement of a real clock face on the screen is done through a signal generator and in no way interferes with or changes the actual taping. This matter should be discussed with the technicians doing the videotaping.

Sixth, you should ensure that everyone appearing in the day-in-the-life presentation—the injured person, doctors, nurses, and other individuals—is fully aware of what is going to occur and that it is important to act in a natural and relaxed manner. In no way should they "play to" the camera or alter their activities in any way.

Finally, coupled with the videotape itself, you should have a detailed log prepared in final form for introduction into evidence with the videotape. This log should be keyed to particular points on the videotape. In addition, you should maintain a log of any segments which have been edited out to make it easier to deal with objections interposed solely to attempt to defeat receipt into evidence of the day-in-the-life presentation.

§ 9.8 —Objections

As a general matter, objections to day-in-the-life presentations fall into one of three broad categories: hearsay, prejudicial and improper, or lack of foundation. In dealing with such powerful pieces of evidence, you, as a defense lawyer, should realize that day-in-the-life presentations properly prepared for use in personal injury litigation are both unfair and prejudicial to your case. However, the fact that a piece of evidence may be both unfair and prejudicial does not necessarily mean that it is inadmissible or is either too unfair or too prejudicial to merit evidentiary consideration. Rather, you must be prepared to argue that the evidence is prejudicial and unfair within the context of the rules of evidence as distinguished from the context of its impact on the case. Although a day-in-the-life presentation is undoubtedly hearsay, because it is not susceptible to cross-examination, having taken place outside the courtroom, the response to such an objection is typically framed in terms of the catchall exception to the hearsay rule set forth in Federal Rule of Evidence 803(24) and its state counterparts.

According to that rule, any statement which would otherwise be hearsay but which is not covered by any of the specific exceptions to the hearsay rule is admissible if it has the equivalent circumstantial guarantees of trustworthiness and if: (1) the court determines that the statement is offered as evidence of material fact; (2) the statement is more probative on the point for which it is offered than any other evidence which the proponent can procure through reasonable efforts; and (3) the general purposes of the rules and the interests of justice will best be served by admission of the statement into evidence. However, a statement generally may not be admitted under this exception unless its proponent makes known to you as an adverse party, sufficiently in advance of the trial or hearing to provide you with a fair opportunity to prepare to meet it, the intention to offer the statement and the particulars of it, including the name and address of the declarant or, in the case of a day-in-the-life presentation, the plaintiff.

An objection to a day-in-the-life presentation under this catchall exception to the hearsay rule should focus on the question whether a day-in-the-life presentation is more probative than other types of evidence, including doctors' testimony, regarding the physical condition of the injured party. The question of prior notice is also important. Specifically, if you are not offered an opportunity to be present at the preparation of the day-in-the-life presentation and have had no prior notice of it before being advised by your opponent that it is going to be offered, you should vigorously argue that you were not given sufficient advance notice and were deprived of any opportunity to prepare to meet the presentation and that this renders it inadmissible. For this reason, you should be particularly wary about invitations to be present at the taping of a day-in-the-life presentation made by your opponent. Such offers are typically made not out of the goodness of your opponent's heart, but rather as a means of filling foundation gaps that may show up later.

In one case, *Grimes v. Employer's Mutual Liability Insurance Co.*, 73 F.R.D. 607 (D. Alaska 1977), the court held that a day-in-the-life videotape was admissible under the catchall exception to the hearsay rule because it was more probative on the question of the pain and suffering of the plaintiff and loss of enjoyment of the plaintiff's life than any other evidence which could be procured through the exercise of reasonable efforts. The question of trustworthiness was dealt with by the court in that case by subjecting the plaintiff and a verifying witness to cross-examination by the defense. *Id.* at 611.

Perhaps the best objection to be made to day-in-the-life presentations in personal injury cases when hearsay is not a viable approach is the question of prejudice. There is a fine line between admissibility and nonadmissibility when dealing with the question of the prejudicial character of day-in-the-life evidence.

By its very nature, a day-in-the-life presentation in a personal injury case is prejudicial. Accordingly, it is incumbent on plaintiffs as proponents of such evidence to be especially careful that they do not overstep the bounds of admissibility, while at the same time preserving the unfair and prejudicial character of the evidence which favors their case.

As defense counsel, in reviewing such a presentation, you should be especially sensitive to gruesome shots or sound effects, whether real and unrehearsed or contrived for the purpose of playing to the sympathy of the observer. In addition, you should object to any use of a narrated sound track, because use of sound tends to turn what is supposed to be a day-in-the-life presentation into a documentary.

For example, an objection to a day-in-the-life videotape on the ground that it was prejudicial was sustained in a case in which the videotape depicted a burn victim's physical therapy. *Thomas v. C.G. Tate Construction Co.,* 465 F. Supp. 566 (D.S.C. 1979). The videotape in question included several pained facial expressions and grimaces, as well as spoken expressions by the injured person. In sustaining defense objections to this piece of evidence, which was an accurate portrayal of what was being undergone by the burn victim, the court stated that the videotape would "destroy the jury's objectivity because it would inflame the average person." *Id.* at 569.

In *Bolstridge v. Central Maine Power Co.,* No. 84-0128-P (M. Nov. 21, 1985), the court determined that a day-in-the-life videotape was not admissible in a personal injury action brought by the plaintiff. The videotape was intended to depict a typical day in the life of the plaintiff in order to demonstrate to the jury the impact of her injuries on her day-to-day activities. Finding that almost always an edited tape necessarily raises issues as to every sequence portrayed of whether the events shown were fairly representational of the facts after the editing process and whether it was unduly prejudicial because of the manner of presentation, the district court found the tape not to be properly admissible against the defendant. Furthermore, the court found the fact that a plaintiff is aware of being videotaped for such a purpose is likely to cause self-serving behavior, consciously or otherwise. Finally, the court concluded that use of a videotape for such purposes is also troublesome because it dominates evidence more conventionally adduced simply because of the nature of its presentation.

There is little question that a day-in-the-life type presentation is one of the most effective pieces of evidence which a plaintiff can utilize against a defendant in a personal injury case. Properly prepared and carefully edited, the tape will be admissible unless it can be shown that, pursuant to Rule 403 of the Federal Rules of Evidence or its state counterparts, the danger of unfair prejudice from the tape is not outweighed by its probative value.

In objecting to such a presentation in general, you should keep in mind the questions of objectivity, sympathy, and inflaming the jury's passions. Indeed, you need not even go so far as to object to facial expressions or expressions of pain; rather, you should object to the overall presentation as playing to the jury's sympathy and destroying any sense of objectivity which jury members may possess.

Another possible objection, one which is more tenuous depending on the manner of presentation of the day-in-the-life videotape, relates to cumulativeness. The objection, if made, should be premised on the fact that a day-in-the-life presentation in a personal injury case is merely cumulative of the medical testimony from treating and other physicians and any personal testimony offered by the plaintiff. Furthermore, this objection should be coupled with another relating to the prejudicial nature of the presentation.

The problem with this objection is that, if the presentation of the day-in-the-life videotape has been properly structured by its proponent, e.g., if it is supplemental to the medical testimony in demonstrating the operative extent of the plaintiff's injuries as distinguished from simply setting forth the injuries themselves, you may find yourself without a well-founded objection. Accordingly, you should look to whether the day-in-the-life presentation is supplemental to or indeed cumulative of other evidence.

The following considerations should be taken into account when cross-examining the foundation of videotape presentations.

1. Whether a witness who was present at the time the videotape was shot is required to testify that it accurately depicts events as the witness saw them when they occurred
2. Whether a witness is required to testify regarding the competence of the camera operator
3. Whether information regarding the type of camera used and mechanics is required
4. Whether information regarding the type of film is required
5. Whether information regarding the type of lens and its adjustment is required
6. Whether information regarding lighting arrangements and weather conditions is required
7. Whether the videotape has been speeded up or slowed down

8. Whether any editing was done to the videotape. If so, ask for a screening of any outtakes. If the outtakes are not available, an objection should be made on the basis of inability to properly cross-examine the foundation of the evidence.

§ 9.9 —Wrongful Death Cases

You may occasionally encounter an attempt to use a day-in-the-life presentation as evidence in a wrongful death case to aid in proof of damages. By its very nature, a day-in-the-life presentation does not seem to have any place in a wrongful death case, because the injured plaintiff is in fact deceased and, thus, there is no day in a life to portray.

However, a day-in-the-life presentation here becomes, in effect, a day in the life of the survivors. Thus, a day-in-the-life presentation in a wrongful death case would purport to show the impact of the death on the survivors' everyday life, the strain which has been placed on the family, and the change brought about by the death.

Clearly, because a day-in-the-life presentation is, when properly admissible, admissible only because it is more probative on the question of the loss than any other evidence which could be procured through reasonable efforts and is subject to verification by cross-examination, this type of presentation should be strongly objected to as improper and inadmissible. It has none of the safeguards attached to it which arguable are present in a personal injury case, in which there may be a valid purpose served by demonstrating the extent of the injuries and there is no other reasonable means of showing this other than a day-in-the-life presentation.

Thus, as defendant's counsel, you should safeguard against any attempted use of a day-in-the-life presentation which, for example, purports to show how the death of the decedent has affected the plaintiff's life, the decedent's children's lives, or the enjoyment of daily activities by the survivors. Such presentations can only be calculated to inflame passions, are hearsay of the highest order that is incapable of being cross-examined by any means, and lack any probative value whatsoever.

§ 9.10 —Use as Settlement Documentary

A technique which is being used increasingly is the preparation of a day-in-the-life presentation that might be more accurately characterized as a settlement documentary designed to present, in an adversarial fashion, the plaintiff's case to the defendant. This technique can, as a practical matter, encompass personal injury and wrongful death, as well as any other type of case, because the technique is documentary in style and its user need not be concerned with the rules of evidence.

As with a day-in-the-life presentation, the effective use of this technique in presenting the plaintiff's case without interruption depends on a combination of several circumstances. Thus, when damages are significant, such a documentary may be used to illustrate in a concise format the quantum of damages. In addition, when the physical damage is highly graphic, use of a video settlement brochure can be very effective. Finally, as with a day-in-the-life presentation, a plaintiff with a strong liability case can use this technique to maximize the already powerful aspects of that case and perhaps bring about a more rapid disposition through settlement.

In an article discussing the merits of such a technique in the settlement context, one plaintiff's attorney has pointed out several advantages to such a video settlement documentary:

1. Because of its format, it reaches the decision-making claims adjuster without being edited or sanitized by defense counsel. It forces that claims adjuster to review the case in its entirety.
2. It affords plaintiff's counsel an opportunity to tell the story without interruptions or questions.
3. It provides the plaintiff with the opportunity to present family members and witnesses in their best and most effective light as distinguished from exposing them to the defendant for the first time in the courtroom where, as a practical matter, defense counsel is on home ground. In addition, this technique eliminates the possibility of a witness's performing in a fashion which would be adverse to the case and peripheral to its merits.
4. It can answer the question that is always in the minds of adversaries of whether you are indeed ready to go to trial.

Turley, *The Video Documentary—A Powerful Settlement Tool,* Trial, July 1982, at 88.

The strengths of this technique within the settlement context raise several questions which a defense attorney must consider. First, the defense must realize that such video productions are susceptible to manipulation and distortion. Indeed, the whole idea of such a production is to characterize the plaintiff's case in its most desirable, sympathetic light, and it is designed to keep the defense away from the courtroom. Defense counsel must keep this in mind, particularly if an insurance company adjuster or claims person is going to view such a presentation in its entirety.

The great strength of the presentation is that typically it is viewed in its entirety, while its great weakness is that it does not come out and state its adversarial nature. It is incumbent on defense attorneys to make sure that their principals are aware of these facts.

The tactic which must be guarded against when dealing with these sorts of presentations is their transfer into the trial arena. A video documentary prepared for settlement and made in an adversarial fashion calculated for maximum impact will probably be, for the most part, inadmissible. This, however, may not be apparent on the face of the presentation but rather will be inherent in its very nature.

If you as a defense lawyer sense any attempt by the plaintiff's lawyer to use a video presentation which was prepared for settlement purposes in court during the damages phase of the trial, you should take immediate steps to stop that attempt, arguing that the presentation is prejudicial, contains hearsay, and contains opinions, speculation, and other materials that have no place in the courtroom.

§ 9.11 Principals at Settlement Conferences

One of the most aggressive settlement tactics used by plaintiffs' attorneys to leverage defendants into settlement, especially in cases involving insurance companies or corporate clients, is to request of the court that the principal in the person of either a corporate executive or insurance executive be present at the settlement conference. Such a tactic is especially effective when, for example, the case is pending in San Francisco and the insurance company executive is in New York or at some other distant location.

The leverage occasioned by the court's "requesting" or ordering the presence of a principal can work because the judge may then be able to bring pressure on the defendant to settle, especially when the court itself does not care to try the case.

As a practical matter, such requests can actually come about in one of two ways. As mentioned, the plaintiff may make the request of the court or, alternatively, the court itself may initiate the request. Unfortunately, at least from a defendant's point of view, the latter approach is being taken by more and more courts in this country with the judges themselves initiating the request that a principal be present at the settlement conference.

Typically such a request is phrased not in terms of principal, but rather as a request that an individual with settlement authority be present. The defense attorney usually does not wish to represent that he or she personally has settlement authority, because this may detract from the ability to conduct effective negotiations, making it impossible to say, "I have to go back to my clients and check with them." It is precisely for this reason that more and more judges are ordering that an individual with settlement authority be present at the settlement conference.

Obviously, if you are a plaintiff's attorney, you can get considerable mileage out of such pressure. If, however, you are representing a defendant, there are a number of ways to respond to such situations. The first thing a defense attorney must do when evaluating the response to a request or order that a principal be present in person is to look at the source of the request. If the request has been made initially by the plaintiff's attorney through the court, you can characterize that request as merely tactical. Under such circumstances, unless you believe the actual presence of a principal at the settlement conference would be a real benefit, your response should be that the plaintiff's request is merely designed to bring pressure on the defense and that there is no practical purpose to be served by requiring the physical presence of principals, because they will be available instantaneously by telephone and can give all necessary authority through that medium. In many instances, this will effectively respond to the tactic and satisfy any valid concern which the court may have because of the request from the plaintiff.

If the request is initiated by the courts, you must be more careful in characterizing it. Certainly you cannot characterize it as a tactic. As a result, your response, unless you are agreeable to having your principal present, should be simply that the principal will be available by telephone and able to make immediate decisions. Under these circumstances, you must always be prepared with the fallback position of agreeing to having the principal present.

An aggressive approach to such a request, whether it originates with the plaintiff's attorney or with the court, is to in effect make a counterrequest that the plaintiff be present in person or, in the case of a corporation, that a principal of the plaintiff be present as well. Although this may seem like a "tit for tat" response, it is valid given that settlement is going to be discussed and that persons with immediate authority should be present.

If the response is that opposing counsel has authority to accept or reject an offer, your response can be that offers must ethically be communicated to the client and that, without that client's being present, just as they have requested that your client be present, effective settlement negotiations cannot take place. Frequently, when you respond in kind to such a request, you will find your opponent backing off, or, alternatively, you will find the court to be receptive to some intermediate position, such as availability of the principals by telephone.

When representing the defense, you may sometimes find it desirable to initiate the situation just described by offering or suggesting that the principals be present and indicating that your principal will be present at the settlement conference. This has the effect of taking the offensive and putting the plaintiff on the defensive. The benefit of this approach is that it demonstrates to the court your good will and earnestness in this situation, while at the same time grasping control of the situation and requiring your opponent to respond. Often, in litigation, it is better to be the hunter than the hunted.

§ 9.12 Offers in Judgment

One of the most effective settlement devices available to litigators is an offer in judgment. Whether made pursuant to Rule 68 of the Federal Rules of Civil Procedure or to any of the state procedures which may permit similar offers, a party can offer to allow judgment to be taken against him or her for the money or property or to the effect specified in the offer.

Such an offer typically must be made at least 10 days prior to trial and is irrevocable during that period of time. In addition, it must include costs then accrued by the party to whom the offer is made, and, although it is neither a motion nor a pleading, it must be served on the adverse party in accordance with service rules. However, the offer is filed with the court only if it is accepted by the party to whom it is made.

If the offer is not accepted and the ultimate judgment following trial is less favorable than the offer itself, the party to whom the offer was made is liable for costs incurred by the party making the offer after the date of the offer, the idea being that the party to whom the offer is made must seriously consider the offer and face a penalty of having to pay the offering party's costs, even if the party to whom the offer is made wins the case; this rule applies whenever judgment is less favorable than the offer.

One of the great leverage strengths of this technique is that the court has no discretion on whether to impose costs when dealing with an offer in judgment. If the judgment is less favorable than the offer, the court must impose costs. *Mr. Hanger, Inc. v. Cut Weight Plastic Hangers, Inc.,* 63 F.R.D. 607 (E.D.N.Y. 1974); *Dual v. Cleland,* 79 F.R.D. 696 (D.D.C. 1978).

The format of an offer in judgment is illustrated by the following:

OFFER OF JUDGMENT

COMES NOW Defendant ____________, and, pursuant to Rule 68 of the Federal Rules of Civil Procedure, makes the following Offer of Judgment to Plaintiff ____________ as follows:

1. Defendant hereby offers to allow judgment to be taken against it for ____________, with costs presently accrued, for a period of ten (10) days after the service of this offer upon Plaintiff ____________.
2. If within ten (10) days after service of this offer Plaintiff ____________ does not accept it, said offer is withdrawn pursuant to Rule 68.

Respectfully submitted,

____

CERTIFICATE OF SERVICE

I HEREBY CERTIFY that a true and correct copy of the Defendant's Offer of Judgment was mailed this ______ day of ____________, to the following counsel:

____

____

§ 9.13 —Notice

It is important to remember that, although the offer in judgment must be served on the other side, it is not filed with the court unless it is accepted. You should be particularly aware of this when dealing with offers in judgment, because failure to follow this exact procedure may be used by your opponent to gain a tactical advantage.

On occasion you may encounter an opponent who, in addition to serving the offer in judgment on you, also files a copy with the court. This may be done either out of ignorance or deliberately. In either event, it is contrary to the procedure, and, if it is done deliberately, it is probably for the purpose of educating the judge as to the fact than an offer in judgment has been made.

The proper response is to advise the party making the offer in judgment that you do not consider it to be a proper offer in judgment because it was not made consistent with the rules.

The worst that can happen in taking this position is that you will inflame the court against you by causing the judge to perceive you as an unreasonable litigant unwilling to entertain a nontraditional resolution of the case. For this reason, you should also indicate to your opponent that, although you will not consider the offer as an offer in judgment consistent with the rules for the purpose of giving your opponent any right to costs in the event that the ultimate judgment is less favorable than the offer in judgment, you will consider the offer in judgment as a straight settlement offer and deal with it on that basis.

The reciprocal to the offering party's filing a copy of the offer in judgment with the court is the situation in which the receiving party advises the court that an offer in judgment has been made. One way of doing this is by sending the court a copy of a letter of rejection within the 10 days or by filing with the court a pleading which rejects the offer in judgment within the 10-day time frame. Once again, this is done either as a tactic or out of ignorance of procedure.

As a practical matter, without regard to motivation, the response of an offering party, when the court has been advised of the offer in judgment and this fact has the potential to perhaps prejudice the court against the offering party's position, should be either to withdraw the offer in judgment as having been improperly disclosed to the court or to advise your opponent that what was originally an offer in judgment should now be considered a settlement offer. In so advising your opponent, you should serve a copy of any such letter or pleading on the court as well.

§ 9.14 —Nuisance

Another tactic sometimes pursued is to make an offer in judgment in what can only be characterized as a nuisance amount that does not constitute a good faith offer. By doing so, the party making the offer has placed the burden on the receiving party to evaluate its likelihood of success in the case, because, no matter how unrealistic the offer, if the judgment is less favorable, costs will be assessed against the party to whom the offer was made. Thus, by making what would be considered an unrealistically low offer or judgment, the offering party risks little but builds a protection into the record that may yield costs in the long run.

The problem with this tactic is that Rule 68 of the Federal Rules of Civil Procedure does not address the question of what constitutes a good faith offer and whether, in fact, an offer need be in what would otherwise be considered a realistic amount. Although this issue was presented to the Supreme Court of the United States in *August v. Delta Airlines, Inc.*, 450 U.S. 346 (1980), it was not addressed. Although *August* was actually decided on the merits as a civil rights dispute, the United States Court of Appeals for the Seventh Circuit agreed with the district court that an offer must be in a realistic amount and in good faith. *August v. Delta Airlines, Inc.*, 600 F.2d 699, 700 n.3 (7th Cir. 1979).

One more point which must be considered when dealing with offers in judgment is the fact that in *August,* the Supreme Court did decide that an offer in judgment made pursuant to the Federal Rules of Civil Procedure is effective as a means of shifting costs only when the plaintiff prevails in an amount less than the defendant's offer in judgment. Thus, even though a defendant may have made an offer in judgment in a realistic amount, if the defendant prevails in the ultimate judgment, the offer in judgment does not operate to entitle the defendant to costs regardless of the exercise of any discretion by the court. For a defendant to obtain an award of costs, the plaintiff must prevail but in a dollar amount smaller than the offer in judgment. Thus, when representing the plaintiff, you should be aware of the fact that a judgment for the defendant in effect commits the question of costs back to the discretion of the court.

§ 9.15 Structured Settlements—In General

A detailed discussion of the economics of structured settlements is beyond the scope of this chapter. It is enough to say that a structured settlement is simply a settlement device currently seeing heavy use in all types of litigation in which damages can be reduced to monetary terms. This device is most widely used in personal injury and wrongful death litigation involving compensatory and other damages. However, in recent years, it has been employed increasingly in domestic relations litigation in the area of property settlement.

In its simplest form, a structured settlement is nothing more than a settlement in which the defendant buys, for a fixed, one-time premium, an annuity. That annuity makes payments over a specified time schedule to the plaintiff. The annuity may take into account particular events during the life of the plaintiff, including, for example, college years or special financial needs or may call for lump sum payments at specified times. In addition, most such annuities have an increasing payment schedule based on a fixed percentage. Thus, the payout to the plaintiff might, for example, increase at 3 percent per year during life. The question of percentage, as well as the other factors which affect payout, are matters for negotiation between the plaintiff and defendant.

§ 9.16 —Advantages and Disadvantages

The advantages of a structured settlement to a plaintiff include the near-absolute security offered by it and the increased amounts which may be received over the life of the plaintiff. The major advantage to the plaintiff is that the payments received are not taxable, because the manner in which the annuity settlement is set up never vests actual or constructive possession of the principal in the hands of the plaintiff. Thus, the income received is tax free. *See* Rev. Rul. 77-230, 1977-2 C.B. 214; Rev. Rul. 79-220, 1979-2 C.B. 74. *See also* the Periodic Payment Settlement Act of 1982, 26 U.S.C. § 104(a) *et seq.* (1983).

The disadvantages to the plaintiff are, in many regards, reciprocal of the advantages. Thus, there is no flexibility in the investment options available to the plaintiff for maximizing dollars. Furthermore, there is a certain element of risk associated with the payout, because the vitality of the annuity depends on the financial security of the company from which the annuity is purchased.

Totally separate and apart from the tax advantages of a structured settlement, there may be investment advantages for both the plaintiff and the defendant. Because of its great investment power, a large financial institution such as an insurer typically can realize a greater return on its investments than an individual. As a result, defendants may be able to negotiate settlements on a structured basis with payment of a single premium even though they are unwilling to negotiate a lump sum settlement, because the former may cost less than the latter.

This point can present the greatest advantage to the defendant in the structured settlement area. Because the defendant is purchasing an annuity policy at more advantageous rates than might otherwise be available to the individual investor, the premium cost is less than a lump sum settlement. As a result, from the defendant's perspective, selling the settlement concept to the plaintiff means persuading the plaintiff that he or she is getting more. The result when the parties are able to achieve a meeting of the minds will be a settlement when, were the parties still talking about lump sums, no settlement would be possible.

Notwithstanding all the advantages of the structured settlement device, there are a number of tactics and strategies of which you should be aware to be better able to evaluate the merits of a structured settlement in any particular case. Similarly, tactics used to make such settlements seem attractive should not distract you from the basic elements to be considered in evaluating the merits and appropriateness of such an approach to settlement.

§ 9.17 —"Selling" the Settlement

One tactic often used by defendants in attempting to sell a structured settlement is to point out all its advantages. If appropriate, it should be noted, of course, that a structured settlement is the best way of resolving the case. It relieves the plaintiff of financial management and guarantees absolute security in the future. In addition, the tax burden is substantially lessened.

However, notwithstanding these very real advantages, you should not lose sight of the means of evaluating the structure in the rush to resolution. The inherent flexibility of a structure is often used as a selling point and, in many instances, it is just that. For example, a structured settlement can be and typically is set up so as to increase the income by predetermined percentages to offset anticipated inflation. Alternatively, or perhaps in addition to this, the structure can provide for the payment of life insurance premiums or for lump sum payments at predetermined times during the plaintiff's life, for example, during the college years or at predetermined ages of minor children.

Because the whole concept of settling a case is to replace monetary benefits which have been lost as a result of the death or injury, the flexibility of the structured settlement approach allows a settlement to approximate the interrupted cash flow as much as possible as if the deceased or injured person were still capable of earning regular income.

Notwithstanding the apparent flexibility, you should not lose sight of the fact that the bottom line of a structured settlement is how much that settlement costs the defendant. This area should be inquired into and, despite protestations to the contrary by many defendants, is a proper area of inquiry if for no other reason than attorneys' fees. You should not have to resort to an economic consultant who will charge a fixed fee to evaluate the structured settlement and advise you of out-of-pocket costs to the defendant. As a practical matter, such advice may be incorrect, because the cost of a particular settlement package to a particular defendant may vary depending on the defendant's leverage in the marketplace.

Assuming you do get what you consider to be a fair offer, your task is not necessarily completed, because, when representing plaintiffs, particularly individuals as opposed to corporations, you may still have to "sell" the settlement to your client. This is particularly true if your client has formed an expectation, either with or without your help, and the settlement offer doesn't meet that expectation. There are a number of arguments you can present to your client in such circumstances.

1. The case is not the best on liability and, as a result, there is a realistic possibility of a zero jury verdict.
2. The ability to prove pain and suffering, permanence or injury, or any other aspect of the damages is less than an absolute certainty.
3. Even if a verdict is returned, under the best of circumstances, the verdict could be less than the settlement offer.
4. A settlement is probably a certainty if a jury verdict is returned which is substantially higher than the settlement offer.
5. You believe the settlement is fair and adequate.

Obviously, if the client refuses to accept a settlement offer even after your best efforts, you go to trial in the absence of an increased settlement offer.

§ 9.18 —Attorneys' Fees

From the defendant's perspective, the structured settlement concept provides considerably more flexibility in fashioning settlement and, in some cases, costs the defendant less. This latter point has led to less than full acceptance of the structured settlement among the plaintiffs' bar. Although one would think that evaluation of a settlement offer should turn on the benefits it provides to the plaintiff, far too many plaintiffs' lawyers judge a settlement by what it costs the defendant. A far more serious problem to the plaintiffs' bar is the fact that computation of attorneys' fees on a structured settlement has the potential for placing plaintiffs' counsel in a conflict-of-interest situation.

An example illustrates the dilemma of plaintiffs' counsel regarding fee questions and the potential for conflict of interest brought about by defense counsel's tactics. Assume that the injured person in an automobile accident was a 26-year-old woman who suffered brain damage in the accident, leaving her a quadriplegic. In a settlement conference, her attorney stated that he wants $2 million in settlement of her case. The defense offers a structured settlement consisting of:

— $675,000 cash, plus
— $55,000 per year increasing at 6% compounded annually for life or 10 years, whichever is longer, costing the defendant approximately $675,000.

In considering and evaluating the defendant's offer, the plaintiff's attorney goes through a thought process in which he determines that 38 years is a reasonable life expectancy for his client. Accordingly, reason tells him that he does not want to let this money run out before 38 years have passed.

He has considered what his client could safely earn on an after-tax basis over the next 38 years. He has made a detailed analysis of the next 38 years of his client's life, using various interest and tax rate assumptions. For instance, he has assumed that his client would use half the money for tax-exempt bonds and half the money for taxable instruments. He has assumed that his client can make 13 percent on her taxable portfolio this year, 12 percent next year, 11½ percent, on average, over the following five years, and 10½ percent on average thereafter.

He has assumed that 70 percent of everything his client spends will be deductible for medical or other reasons. He has assumed that the tax tables will be adjusted annually for inflation and that inflation will be 9 percent compounded annually for the next five years, and 7½ percent compounded annually thereafter.

Plaintiff's counsel, with the assistance of a consultant, has taken all these life-simulating assumptions and has had generated a quarter-by-quarter computer printout of the next 38 years of his client's life. Of course, this is done with the assistance of a financial analytical computer program that simulates the life of the client per very detailed specifications.

Through this process of analysis, the plaintiff's attorney has come to the realization that, if he were standing 38 years in the future and looking back at how his client's portfolio would have performed, he would see that there is relatively little chance that after-tax yield on the portfolio would exceed 8½ percent compounded annually. In fact, with the plethora of advice available—well-meaning and opportunistic, competent and incompetent—and taking into account unforeseeable volatility in securities markets, worse results might be significantly more likely than better results.

The plaintiff's attorney has further determined that, because of the other great strength of a structured settlement—tax advantages that are not available in either a verdict or a lump sum settlement—a lump sum settlement or verdict of approximately $2 million would be needed, assuming an 8 ½ percent after-tax rate of return, to benefit the plaintiff to the same extent as the cash plus annuity offer. This is true because, as noted in **§ 9.16**, the Internal Revenue Service and the Periodic Payments Act holds that a structured settlement of this type and its income, when the beneficiary never has actual or constructive possession of the principal, is exempt from taxes. On the other hand, all the income of a lump sum settlement or verdict is taxable.

The plaintiff's attorney has prepared his case well. He has taken the position that he will not settle the case for any amount that would do less than a $2 million verdict or settlement would do for his client. Because his contingency agreement calls for a 25 percent fee, his fee for such a settlement would be $500,000. He argues that his case is worth $2 million, and that is what he wants from the defendant. He further recognizes that if he were to recommend acceptance of the defendant's structured settlement offer, while he would be getting better than a $2 million result for his client, he would be setting himself up for a greatly reduced fee for his efforts, because the basis for his fee would be 25 percent of $1.35 million ($675,000 in cash plus $675,00 representing the total cost of the annuity portion of the settlement) and not 25 percent of $2 million.

Defense counsel now increases the pressure and presents his opponent with a serious dilemma. He shows him that five annuity companies were contacted for quotations on this case, and that the lowest quoted a cost of $675,000. One other was in the $700,000—750,000 range. There were two others in the $800,000 to $1 million range. The highest quote was $1.28 million. However, the more expensive quotes assumed a longer life expectancy and provided a lower rate of return than the one selected by the defense which yielded the greatest return to the plaintiff and, overall, was the best available source for the annuity.

Defense counsel tells plaintiff's counsel that if plaintiff's counsel wants the defen e to spend more, the defense could go to the more expensive company, purchase less annuity, and obtain less value for the client. This would, according to the basis of fee computation being used (25 percent of the total *cost* of settlement) entitle the plaintiff's attorney to a higher fee, in return for having obtained less for the client.

This dilemma is not isolated or unusual but to some degree presents itself in every single case in which a structured settlement of the type outlined is considered. Whatever the kind of settlement contemplated, the plaintiff's attorney always wants the defense to spend more. Yet, when faced with a structured settlement offer, plaintiff's counsel realizes that the defense could give him a greater amount in cash, thereby spending more, and quite possibly do less for his client than is possible through the structured annuity. Also, the defense could choose a less competitive quote (perhaps from a company that it deems to be larger and safer), spend more money, and do less for the plaintiff. Yet by spending more money, it would be entitling the plaintiff's attorney to a higher fee.

The defendants face a decision when various annuity companies quote different prices for the same product. They want to pick an annuity that will save them money, but they will be back on the hook if they pick a company that becomes insolvent. How much an annuity costs is a function of, among other things, the company from which it is purchased. Defense counsel and his client have a choice of which company to purchase from and at what cost. The cost of purchasing an annuity and the contingent liability risks so incurred are matters for the business judgment of the defendant. There is simply no reason why plaintiff's counsel should benefit at all from this exercise of judgment.

If plaintiff's counsel does what he believes to be the best thing for his client in the way of a periodic payment settlement, he benefits his client and the defendant but may well decrease his fee entitlement. On occasion, this conflict may prevent acceptance of the more beneficial structured settlement.

In addition to the problems posed by inherent cost factors associated with structured annuity-type settlements, there is a tactic available to defense counsel which in effect forces plaintiff's counsel into a conflict situation. Assume that defense counsel makes an offer in the alternative to the plaintiff—$1 million in cash *or* $800,000 in cash *plus* an annuity that costs the defendant an additional $150,000 for a total out-of-pocket cost of $950,000. Assuming a 25 percent contingent fee agreement, counsel's fee on the lump sum settlement would be $250,000, but on the structured settlement it would be something less than $250,000. Although the attorneys' fees on the structured settlement package are less than on the lump sum settlement, there is a substantial argument to be made that the structured settlement package is of far greater benefit to the client. It is tax free, totally secure, and, over its term, pays out an amount far in excess of the alternative lump sum settlement.

The approach suggested by defense counsel in order to obtain a fair and objective evaluation of *all* structured settlement offers whenever they are made is that they be evaluated on the client's behalf by the judge, a magistrate, or outside counsel acting in an amicus capacity. In the absence of the fee questions, a better and more objective evaluation of whether a structured settlement is in the best interests of the injured party may result.

If defense counsel seeks a third-party evaluation, plaintiff's counsel will most assuredly object to such a procedure. Those objections, however, are no basis for depriving the client of a totally objective evaluation devoid of the self-interest which counsel brings to the process.

§ 9.19 —Checklist for Evaluating a Settlement Proposal

In every settlement situation, a number of factors should be taken into account to determine whether the settlement is appropriate in terms of both its amount and its nature. This is particularly necessary in the case of a structured settlement—a settlement device completely different from a lump sum settlement.

These factors, although generally known, must be applied in every circumstance, not only by plaintiffs but also by defendants, to ensure that the use of a structured settlement in a given situation is proper and does not unfairly prejudice either party in terms of the resolution of the case.

1. Does the nature of the injury justify a structured settlement? Is it a long-term injury which will require constant payout? Are there minors involved?
2. Does the plaintiff have the financial sophistication to manage a lump sum settlement?
3. Does the structured settlement provide for sufficient cash up front, not only to take care of attorneys' fees but also to leave the plaintiff a reasonable amount?
4. Has the structured settlement document itself been prepared so as to maximize the protection against tax?
5. Is the company from which the annuity is being purchased financially sound?
6. Is the defendant willing to guarantee the annuity, and, if not, is a surety bond an appropriate vehicle?
7. If a surety bond is to be used, how much will the surety bond cost, and who will bear that cost?
8. Is the inflation rate an appropriate one to be used in the structured settlement?
9. Has the structured settlement been devised so as to provide lump sum payments at appropriate times throughout the lifetime of the plaintiff, i.e., educational needs, family needs, and so forth?
10. Does the amount of damage justify use of a structured settlement?
11. Have all future activities which might necessitate expenditure of capital amounts been taken into account in structuring the settlement?
12. Is it advisable to get an independent evaluation of the financial solvency of the company from which the annuity is being purchased?
13. What is the out-of-pocket cost of the annuity to the defendant?

14. What is the verdict value of the structured settlement, i.e., what amount of money if awarded by verdict after trial would be required, taking into account the tax consequences on the income generated by that verdict, to equal the tax-free nature of the structured settlement?

§ 9.20 —Sample Settlement Agreement

The following example of a settlement agreement can be considered for use in settling cases using structured devices. It is by no means the only type of agreement which will fulfill this purpose but is simply an example of an approach to this task.

SETTLEMENT AGREEMENT

THIS AGREEMENT is entered into this ______ day of ____________, between (plaintiff/claimant) and the (defendant);

WHEREAS, (plaintiff/claimant) has heretofore made claim against the (defendant) seeking damages arising from injuries sustained by (plaintiff/claimant) on or about the ______ day of ____________, at the (location of alleged negligence or description of negligent act) and alleged to be the result of negligence of the (defendant); and

WHEREAS, the (defendant) has denied any negligence on its part resulting in said injuries and damages to (plaintiff/claimant); and

WHEREAS, the parties hereto have agreed upon a compromise settlement of all claims of (plaintiff/claimant) against the (defendant) arising from or in any way connected with (description of alleged negligence);

NOW, THEREFORE, in consideration of the mutual covenants contained herein, the parties agree to the following terms of settlement in full satisfaction of all claims of (plaintiff/claimant) against (defendant), either known or unknown, resulting from or in any way related to the claim against the defendant arising from (describe incident).

I. WARRANTIES

(a) All parties warrant and represent, each to the other, that they have been fully informed and have full knowledge of the terms, conditions, and effects of this Agreement.

(b) All parties warrant and represent, each to the other, that they have, either personally or through their attorney or attorneys, fully investigated, to such party's full satisfaction, all facts surrounding the various claims, controversies, and disputes and are fully satisfied with the terms and effects of this Agreement.

(c) All parties warrant and represent, each to the other, that no promise or inducement has been offered or made except as herein set forth, nor has there been any representation made by defendant or any person on behalf of defendant as to any tax effects or consequences resulting to the plaintiff arising out of or under the terms of this Agreement, and that this Agreement is executed without reliance upon any statement or representation by any other party or his agent.

II. PAYMENTS TO PLAINTIFF

In consideration for the compromise and full settlement of the various contentions, claims, counterclaims, and disputes between and among the parties related directly or indirectly to the claims of (plaintiff/claimant), the parties hereto agree to be bound by the following distribution provisions.

(a) *Initial Payments.* The (defendant) shall pay to (plaintiff/claimant) the lump sum of (fill in amount).

(b) *Monthly Payments and Deferred Lump Sums.* As soon as practicable after the execution of this Agreement, defendant shall pay to (name of ________________/annuity company) the sum of (insert amount) for the purchase of annuities that will result in the following distributions on behalf of the defendant:

1. ___________ dollars per month increasing at annual compounded rate of _____ percent per annum. Said payment will commence during the first month following the purchase of the annuity and will continue for the life of (plaintiff/claimant), or _____ years certain whichever is longer. In the event of the death of (plaintiff/claimant) prior to expiration of the _____ years following the due date of the first payment, such remaining payments during the balance of the _____ year period shall be made to her estate or designee.

2. On the _____ anniversary of the settlement, a lump sum payment of $___________ shall be paid to (plaintiff/claimant). In the event of the death of (plaintiff/claimant) prior to the date this payment comes due, said sum shall be paid to the estate of (plaintiff/claimant) or such beneficiary or designee as she may designate by her Last Will and Testament.

(c) *Ownership of Annuities.* The annuities to be purchased and owned by ________________ shall be purchased for an insurance company chosen by ________________. (Plaintiff/Claimant) shall have no right to accelerate or increase any of the above referenced payments.

(d) *How Payments Made.* All payments called for herein shall be mailed first class via the United States Postal Service to (plaintiff/claimant) at (address) or such other person or place as may be designated by (plaintiff/claimant) or her legally appointed representative in writing.

(e) *Purchase of Annuity.* The annuity herein referred to shall be purchased from an insurance company or companies having a rating of at least "A" by A.M. Best Company, Oldwich, New Jersey.

(f) *Rights in Annuity.* The ________________ or its designee shall be the sole owner of the annuity contract purchased by ________________ and shall have all rights of ownership including without limitation, the right to change the beneficiary of said annuity contract.

(g) *Reliance on General Credit of Parties for Collection of Monthly and Deferred Payments.* (Plaintiff/Claimant) agrees to rely solely on the general credit of the insurance company from which the annuities are purchased for collection of the payment obligations hereunder, and said party has no obligation to set aside assets to secure its obligations to make any monthly or other deferred payments.

(h) *Monthly Payments Not Income.* The monthly payments required to be paid hereunder are intended solely as compensation for the personal injuries and the pain and suffering sustained by (plaintiff/claimant) as a result of (describe incident) and are not nor are they intended by the parties to be compensation for lost income and the provisions of this instrument shall be construed to give effect to such intent.

III. ATTORNEYS' FEES

In addition to the distributions referenced in Section II of this Agreement attorneys' fees of $__________ shall be paid to plaintiff/claimant's attorneys __________________.

IV. RELEASE OF (DEFENDANT)

In consideration of the purchase of the annuity and payment of the lump sum referred to in Section II of this Settlement Agreement, plaintiff/claimant hereby releases, covenants not to sue, and forever discharges (defendant), its present and former officers, agents and employees from all liability, claims, and demands of whatsoever nature arising from the said incident or circumstances giving rise to these claims. Furthermore, plaintiff/claimant agrees to indemnify and hold harmless (defendant) from any and all claims, causes of action, rights, subrogated interests or proceedings of whatever nature which may hereafter be asserted or brought by or on behalf of plaintiff/claimant, her heirs, executor, administrator, assigns, successors in interest, or other third parties, to recover for personal injuries or death, contribution or indemnification arising out of or, related to (describe incident).

V. GENERAL INDEMNIFICATION TO SECURE PERFORMANCE

In order to induce every party to execute and deliver this Agreement, and to pay the consideration required hereby, each party warrants (the "Warranting Party") to every other party (i) that such Warranting Party or such Warranting Party's heirs, descendants, successors, assigns, or legal representatives, individually and collectively, shall perform all duties and obligations hereunder and shall scrupulously abide by each and every term, condition, provision, covenant, and agreement contained herein, and (ii) that those of a Warranting Party's heirs, descendants, successors, assigns and legal representatives not parties hereto, shall abide by, observe and perform each and every term, condition, agreement, obligation, covenant, and release contained herein the same as if those such heirs, descendants, successors, assigns, and legal representatives were signatory parties hereto.

VI. MISCELLANEOUS PROVISIONS

(a) *Additional Instruments.* Additionally, such party agrees that he or it shall execute and deliver such other and further instruments of assignment and all notices, releases, acquittances and other documents as may be necessary to implement fully the terms and provisions hereof.

(b) *Agreement to Survive.* All warranties, covenants, agreements, and releases contained herein shall survive this Agreement.

(c) *Entire Agreement.* This Agreement constitutes the entire agreement among the parties pertaining to the subject matter contained herein.

(d) *Invalid Provisions.* If, after the date hereof, any provision of this Agreement is held to be illegal, invalid, or unenforceable under present or future laws effective during the term of this Agreement, such provisions shall be fully severable. In lieu thereof, there shall be added a provision as similar in terms to such illegal, invalid, or unenforceable provision as may be possible and be legal, valid and enforceable.

(e) *Amendment.* This Agreement shall not be modified or amended except by an instrument in writing signed by all the parties.

(f) *Law Governing.* The validity, construction, interpretation and administration of this Agreement shall be governed by the substantive laws of the State of ___________.

(g) *Titles, Headings, and Captions.* All titles, headings, and captions used in this Agreement have been intended for administrative convenience only and do not constitute matters to be construed in interpreting this Agreement.

IN TESTIMONY WHEREOF, this Settlement Agreement has been signed and sealed by (plaintiff/claimant) and (defendant).

____
Plaintiff/Claimant

____
Plaintiff's Attorney

____
Defendant

____
Defendant's Attorney

§ 9.21 —Sample Settlement Agreement and Release

The following example of a settlement agreement and release can be considered for use in settling cases using structured devices. It is by no means the only type of agreement and release which will fulfill this purpose but is simply an example of an approach to this task.

SETTLEMENT AGREEMENT AND RELEASE

THIS SETTLEMENT AGREEMENT AND RELEASE ("Settlement Agreement") is made and entered into this ______ day of __________, 19_____ by and among __________________ and __________________ (the "Plaintiffs"), and _______________, a California corporation (the "Insurer").

RECITALS

A. On or about __________, 19_____, the Plaintiffs filed a complaint (the "Complaint") against _______________ et al. (the "Defendants") in the __________ Court of the State of __________, __________ County (Court Action No. _____) which Complaint arose out of certain alleged negligent acts or omissions by the Defendants.

B. The Insurer is the liability insurer of the Defendants and as such would be obligated to pay any judgment obtained against the Defendants which is covered by its policy.

C. The parties desire to enter into this Settlement Agreement in order to provide for certain payments in full settlement and discharge of all claims which are the subject of the Complaint, upon the terms and conditions set forth herein.

AGREEMENT

The parties hereto hereby agree as follows:

1. *Release and Discharge.* In consideration of the payments called for herein, the Plaintiffs and each of them hereby completely release and forever discharge the Defendants and each of them, the Insurer, and said parties' past, present and future officers, directors, stockholders, attorneys, agents, servants, representatives, employees, subsidiaries, affiliates, partners, predecessors and successors in interest, and assigns and all other persons, firms, or corporations with whom any of the former have been, are now or may hereafter be affiliated, of and from any and all past, present or future claims, demands, obligations, actions, causes of action, wrongful death claims, rights, damages, costs, losses of services, expenses and compensation of any nature whatsoever, whether based on a tort, contract or other theory of recovery, and whether for compensatory or punitive damages, which the Plaintiffs or any of them now have, or which may hereafter accrue or otherwise be acquired, on account of, or in any way growing out of, or which are the subject of, the Complaint (and all related pleadings) including, without limitation, any and all known or unknown claims for bodily and personal injuries to Plaintiff (_______________) and the consequences thereof, which have resulted or may result from the alleged negligent acts or omissions of the Defendants or any of them. This release, on the part of the Plaintiffs, shall be a fully binding and complete settlement between the Plaintiffs, the Defendants and the Insurer and all parties represented by or claiming through the Plaintiffs, save only the executory provisions of this Settlement Agreement. The Plaintiffs agree to defend,

indemnify and hold the Defendants and the Insurer harmless from and against all such claims, demands, obligations, actions, causes of action, damages, costs and expenses.

2. *Payments.* In consideration of the release set forth above, the Insurer on behalf of the Defendants hereby agrees to pay the following sums in the following manner:

a. Initial Payment

Concurrently with execution of this Agreement, the Insurer agrees to pay to the Plaintiff the sum of ____________ ($____________). Said Plaintiff agrees to pay from said sum all of the Plaintiffs' attorneys' fees, and all other costs and expenses resulting to the Plaintiffs or incurred by or on behalf of the Plaintiffs in connection with the Complaint and the settlement set forth herein.

b. Monthly Payments

Subject to the other terms and conditions of this Settlement Agreement, the Insurer further agrees to pay to the Plaintiff the sum of ____________ ($____________) per month increasing at ______% compounded annually for life or ______ payments, whichever is longer. Should the Plaintiff die prior to the ______ payment, pursuant to this paragraph 2b, such monthly payments shall continue to be made from the date of said Plaintiff's death until ______ payments have been made to such person or entity as may be designated in accordance with Section 4 hereof. Payments in this section shall commence on the starting date, which if an annuity is purchased, shall be one month from the date that the annuity company receives a valid premium check. In no event shall the starting date be later than ______________, 19______.

3. *Attorneys' Fees.* Each party hereto shall bear all attorneys' fees and costs arising from the actions of its own counsel in connection with the Complaint, this Settlement Agreement and the matters and documents referred to herein, the filing of a dismissal of the Complaint, and all related matters.

4. *Designation of Contingent Beneficiary and Revocation of Designation.* Any payments to be made after the death of the Plaintiff (________________) pursuant to Section 2 hereof shall be made to such persons or entity as shall be designated in writing by said Plaintiff to the Insurer. If no person or entity is so designated by said Plaintiff, such payments shall be made in equal shares to ________________ and ________________ (or the survivor of them), and if neither shall be alive at the time of payment, then to the estate of the Plaintiff (________________). No such designation nor any revocation thereof shall be effective unless it is in writing and delivered to the Insurer.

5. *Right to Purchase an Annuity.* For its own convenience, the Insurer reserves the right to fund its obligation(s) under paragraph 2b above through the purchase of any financial vehicle it chooses, including, but not limited to an annuity policy from the ____________ Life Insurance Company. For its own convenience, the Insurer shall have the annuity carrier mail payments directly to the Plaintiff. The Plaintiff shall be responsible for maintaining proper mailing address and mortality information with the Insurer.

6. *Discharge of Obligation.* The obligations of the Insurer to make each monthly installment of the annual payments and the lump sum payment shall

be discharged upon the mailing of a valid check in the amount of such payment to the address designated by the party to whom the payment is required to be made under this Settlement Agreement, and the Insurer shall not be liable for failure of the appropriate persons to receive any such check if said check is so mailed.

7. *General Release.* The Plaintiffs hereby acknowledge and agree that the release set forth in Section 1 hereof is a general release and they further expressly waive and assume the risk of any and all claims for damages which exist as of this date but which the Plaintiffs do not know of or suspect to exist, whether through ignorance, oversight, error, negligence, or otherwise, and which, if known, would materially affect their decision to enter into this Settlement Agreement. The Plaintiffs further acknowledge that they have read the provisions of California Civil Code Section 1542 [substitute applicable statute] and they waive all rights thereunder, which Section provides:

> A general release does not extend to claims which the creditor does not know or suspect to exist in his favor at the time of executing the release, which if known by him must have materially affected his settlement with the debtor.

The Plaintiffs further agree that they have accepted payment of the sums specified herein as a complete compromise of matters involving disputed issues of law and fact and they fully assume the risk that the facts or the law may be otherwise than they believe.

8. *Delivery of Dismissal with Prejudice.* Concurrently with the execution of this Settlement Agreement, counsel for the Plaintiffs has delivered to counsel for the Insurer an executed Dismissal with Prejudice of the civil action described in Recital A above. The Plaintiffs have authorized their attorneys to execute this Dismissal on their behalf and hereby authorize counsel for the Insurer to file said Dismissal with the Superior Court of the State of California, County of Sacramento [modify as appropriate] and enter it as a matter of record.

9. *Warranty of Capacity to Execute Agreement.* The Plaintiffs represent and warrant that no other person or entity has or has had any interest in the claims, demands, obligations, or causes of action referred to in this Settlement Agreement; that they have the sole right and exclusive authority to execute this Settlement Agreement and receive the sums specified in it; and that they have not sold, assigned, transferred, conveyed, or otherwise disposed of any of the claims, demands, obligations, or causes of action referred to in this Settlement Agreement.

10. *Disclaimer of Liability.* The Plaintiffs agree and acknowledge that they accept payment of the sums specified in this Settlement Agreement as a full and complete compromise of matters involving disputed issues; that neither payment of the sums by the Insurer nor the negotiations for this settlement (including all statements, admissions, or communications) by the Insurer, the Defendants, or their attorneys or representatives shall be considered admissions by any of said parties; and that no past or present wrongdoing on the part of the Defendants shall be implied by such payment or negotiations.

11. *Entire Agreement and Successors in Interest.* This Settlement Agreement contains the entire agreement between the Plaintiffs, the Defendants and

the Insurer with regard to the matters set forth in it and shall be binding upon and inure to the benefit of the executors, administrators, personal representatives, heirs, successors and assigns of each.

12. *Construction by (State) Law.* This Settlement Agreement is entered into in the State of __________ and shall be construed and interpreted in accordance with its laws.

13. *Representation of Comprehension of Document.* In entering into this Settlement Agreement the Plaintiffs represent that they have relied upon the legal advice of their attorneys, who are the attorneys of their own choice, and that the terms of this Settlement Agreement have been completely read and explained to them by their attorneys, and that those terms are fully understood and voluntarily accepted by them.

14. *Additional Documents.* All parties agree to cooperate fully and execute any and all supplementary documents and to take all additional actions which may be necessary or appropriate to give full force and effect to the basic terms and intent of this Settlement Agreement.

15. *Effectiveness.* This Settlement Agreement shall become effective immediately following execution by all of the parties.

Executed at ______________, ______________, this _____ day of __________, 19_____.

By: ____________________

____

____

§ 9.22 Nonjury Cases and Settlement Judges

A tactic often used by both plaintiffs and defendants in cases which are to be tried without a jury, although it is used in jury cases as well, is to seek settlement conferences or discussions with the judge present, because the trier of fact will be the judge.

The only purpose for having settlement discussions under the auspices of the trier of fact is to educate the trier of fact. As a result, if you find yourself in a nonjury case in which your opponent requests that the court oversee settlement discussions or if the court suggests that it oversee settlement discussions, you should pursue one of the following courses of action.

Your immediate response to such a situation should be respectfully to suggest to the ourt that you have no objection whatsoever to judicial involvement in settlement discussions, but that because the court will be the trier of fact in the nonjury situation, another judge should oversee the settlement discussions in a *settlement judge* capacity. This is not at all an unusual circumstance and, if suggested in this form, should not offend or anger the court.

When the suggestion that the court act in a settlement capacity originates with the court itself, the same approach can be taken, namely, that your client welcomes the involvement of the court in the settlement aspects of the case, but you respectfully suggest that this be done by another judge who will act in a settlement capacity and will not be the trier of fact.

Notwithstanding the significant differences between the nonjury and the jury situations when dealing with a judge in a settlement capacity, there are also certain tactical advantages, even in a jury situation, to having the trial judge preside over the settlement discussions. Remember, the judge will do a number of things during the case which will manifest his or her attitude toward the case and will undoubtedly influence the jury. The judge will rule on objections, displaying an attitude toward you and your client, and will question witnesses and through that questioning, despite the statement to the jury not to give it any greater weight than any other questioning, is quite likely to display a bias or attitude toward the testimony. Thus, it is incumbent on you as an advocate for your client to get the judge on your side to stay. The device of using the judge as a settlement judge prior to trial is an excellent way of informally educating him or her to your case.

It is more difficult to handle such a situation in a jury case, because the judge will not be the trier of fact. Thus, whether the suggestion originates with your opponent or with the court, you should take as much advantage of it as your opponent. The most effective way of doing this is by undertaking your own campaign to educate the judge, with a carefully prepared and adversarially written settlement brochure or brief.

This brief should be similar to a settlement brochure or book. The significant difference is that the audience is not your opponent but rather the court, and, as a result, the brief should focus on the particular role which the judge will play in the trial. It should include case citations, copies of cases if appropriate, discussions of key evidentiary points, discussions of witness testimony, and other matters on which the judge will have to focus in the case. The settlement brief should be heavily indexed and organized to permit the judge rapid access to any part of it and to show your case in its most favorable light.

The great advantage of this tactic is that, notwithstanding whether the case settles, you have another opportunity to preeducate or prebrief the judge regarding the merits of your case. Coupling this with a trial brief or an opening statement, as well as with any motions for summary judgment which may have been filed as an educational device, you are constantly conditioning the judge to your case and the particular aspects which are crucial to its successful outcome.

§ 9.23 Nonbinding Arbitration

An approach to settlement which has gained widespread use as an alternative means of dispute resolution is arbitration. When litigants are truly interested in resolving the case outside the judicial process, such arbitration may be binding. However, when the litigants need a shove to encourage them to settle, either within the context of liability or more typically within the context of damages, nonbinding arbitration is frequently resorted to as an alternative.

Generally, such a procedure works through use of a panel of three arbitrators. Often these individuals may be retired judges. They hear a case in a highly abbreviated form with strict time limits imposed. However, the rules of evidence typically are not strictly adhered to, and the presentations often are made solely by the attorneys. On occasion, depending on the agreements of the parties, witnesses may be presented briefly and only if they are important to a determination of the case. Usually, no experts are presented. Once the presentations have been completed, the arbitrators retire and render what becomes an advisory result which the parties are free to either accept or ignore. On occasion, this result may be submitted to the trial judge for his or her information, although frequently the parties may agree that the result will not be brought to the attention of the court, but that they will only advise of the fact of whether the parties have been able to settle following the arbitration.

As with many other aspects of the litigative process which have strengths, nonbinding arbitration can easily become a tactic to leverage either party into settling. This can be done either by the party suggesting the arbitration or, by appropriate response, by the party to whom request is addressed. The whole key to successfully controlling an arbitration and, if things work out as planned, prevailing in its outcome is seizing the initiative and properly presenting your case to the panel or arbitrator.

Assume you are representing the plaintiff and intend to suggest a nonbinding arbitration because of the reluctance of the defendant to settle because of belief that liability is doubtful and excessive damages are being sought by your client. With respect to the reluctance of the defendant, assuming the accuracy or partial accuracy of the grounds given, either one of those beliefs is a valid basis for not settling. However, in suggesting the arbitration to defendant's counsel and the court, you request that the arbitration be limited to the question of damages so that both parties may benefit from the guidance of a third party on the question of the monetary loss.

By skipping over the question of liability, you are able to guarantee a dollar result on the damages question and, depending on the strength of your case, the dollar result may be substantial. However, if in fact the defendant is right and you are overreaching on the question of damages, the nonbinding arbitration tactic and limiting it to the damages question will certainly boomerang on you.

If you are going to seek a damages arbitration and if you do so for the purpose of getting a dollar figure down in black and white which you can then use as a club against the defendant on the issue of liability, you must not overvalue your case.

Looking at the other side of this scenario, assume you are representing the defendant. Again assuming that your reluctance to settle has some basis in the case and is not simply a "take them to the courthouse steps" tactic, it is incumbent on you not to permit your opponent to isolate the issues involving sympathy, injury, and loss and those which deal with emotion. Rather, you must do all you can to insure that the arbitration focuses on the merits of the case in their entirety and not on the emotion of the case in isolation. Accordingly, you should resist any attempt to break up an arbitration and suggest that if there is to be such an arbitration on a nonbinding basis, it must focus not only on damages but on liability as well.

Whichever side you are representing in an arbitration proceeding, recognizing that brevity and compactness are the ends to be achieved, it is incumbent on you to prepare a brief, not unlike the settlement brief, calculated to sway the arbitrator in your direction and provide a readymade basis on which to rule. What this means is that any such brief or pleading should include a proposed order which lays out precisely what you want and the basis on which you feel entitled to it. Failure to do so opens you to the risk of the arbitrator's signing an order proposed by your opponent or, alternatively, issuing an order which, while ruling in your favor, does not give you what you want or what you are entitled to under the evidence.

§ 9.24 Sharing Agreements

A tactic which has been pursued by defendants with considerable success for purposes of minimizing damages recoverable against them while at the same time preserving their rights as against one another is the device of a *sharing agreement*. Historically, in many tort lawsuits, the issue has not been whether the plaintiff recovers but rather the amount of money which the plaintiff recovers and by which of several defendants the money will be paid. This is typically the situation in mass disaster-type tort litigation.

In such situations, the plaintiffs may institute suit against several defendants and then, in effect, sit back and let the defendants fight it out among themselves. The net result of this tends to be that the defendants end up paying in whatever proportions were probably appropriate all along, yet the damages are substantially greater because of the passage of time. In addition, legal fees are that much higher, and litigation costs become astronomical. The burden on the judicial system is immense, and the entire piece of litigation takes on a life of its own while the plaintiff sits back and watches his or her case inflate in value.

Recognizing this fact, defendants have begun entering into sharing agreements for the purpose of undercutting this tactic of the plaintiff and bringing a rapid conclusion to the plaintiff versus defendant dispute while preserving the defendant versus defendant dispute. In its simplest form, a sharing agreement provides for multiple defendants to settle jointly with the plaintiff or plaintiffs in equal shares and either negotiate the ultimate percentages or, if such a voluntary negotiation is not possible, litigate the ultimate percentages.

This device has several advantages, including the fact that it undercuts and eliminates the plaintiff from the case. From the plaintiff's perspective, this is not entirely bad, because the plaintiff gets paid at an early date when the money may yield more through prudent investment. Most important, by a rapid disposition of the plaintiff's cases, the defendants are able to avoid paying the premium on those cases as a result of their own disputes.

The sharing agreement has its greatest effect when it is entered into early in the litigation, preferably shortly after complaints are filed and before the parties have solidified their positions. When confronted with the prospect of such a sharing agreement, both plaintiffs and defendants must consider several matters.

From a defendant's perspective, the concept of a sharing agreement presents the question of degree of exposure as opposed to its fact. If some exposure is acknowledged, the best device for keeping the plaintiff's damages down while at the same time preserving the rights of the defendant as against others is the sharing agreement.

The downside risk of such a sharing agreement is that it often removes a potential ally in the form of a plaintiff proving a case against other defendants. Thus, you must determine when representing defense interests whether your client is a "target" defendant. If so, it may be in your best interest to suggest that a funding or sharing agreement be entered into with co-defendants, thus eliminating you as the focus of the plaintiff's case. Of course, in such a circumstance, your co-defendants may also be making the same assessment, thus making it more difficult to bring about a funding agreement.

On occasion, when a funding agreement is difficult to work out among defendants for whatever reason, the aid of the court can be solicited. Because the court has a vested interest in moving its calendar along, bringing the funding agreement to the attention of the court and noting that the parties are having some difficulty in reaching such an agreement can frequently aid in leveraging reluctant co-defendants while at the same time making it extremely difficult for them to raise tactical objections to such an agreement.

From a plaintiff's perspective, a funding agreement has both advantages and disadvantages. The obvious advantage from the plaintiff's perspective is that without expenditure of large amounts of money on the litigation, the plaintiff receives its damages early, notwithstanding the fact that the defendants may not have agreed among themselves as to who bears what portion of the loss.

In most cases, the fact of the matter is that the plaintiff does not care who pays but only that they pay promptly the full amount of damages. A plaintiff is often willing to discount damages in order to get paid early without getting into the expensive and time-consuming process of litigation.

The only possible downside risk in a sharing agreement from the plaintiff's perspective is that the damages are not going to be inflated by virtue of the defendants' fighting among themselves. Experience demonstrates that the greater the passage of time between a loss and payment for it, the greater the likelihood that the damages will take into account the passage of time as well as the actual value of the loss.

Although it might be argued that damages are not inflated by virtue of the squabbling but rather by the passage of time, there is little question that infighting among defendants makes cases worth more than they might be otherwise. Thus, some plaintiffs might take the position that when defendants shortcut the process and pay up front, the plaintiffs are not getting their full measure of damages. This is not a position which can be put before the court, but it must be kept in mind by both plaintiffs and defendants.

One tactic which is sometimes considered as a possible means of defeating use of a sharing agreement is to claim punitive damages against the defendants. If, for example, a plaintiff claims punitive damages against one or all of the defendants, the defendants may find themselves unable to agree on a sharing arrangement because of the very nature of damages aimed at punishing a defendant.

Because an award of punitive damages is often many times greater than the amount of compensatory damages in a particular case, the division of punitive damages (assuming any division at all is possible) under a sharing arrangement is a virtually impossible task. Thus, a count seeking punitive damages can have the effect of frustrating the parties from entering into a sharing arrangement.

Use of such a technique by a plaintiff can also be a bargaining chip in bringing about an ultimate settlement. By bargaining away the punitive damages aspect of a case, the defendants may agree not to contest liability as against the plaintiff and to either litigate damages or fund damages, reserving to themselves the later litigation of their respective percentages.

If defendants suspect that inclusion of a punitive damages count in a complaint is simply a tactical device, an appropriate response would be to file a joint motion to strike the punitive damages aspect of the complaint and attempt to get a complete resolution of that claim, bringing to the attention of the court the long-term effect that such a demand has on the settlement prospects of the litigation.

It goes without saying that, if there is any substance to the allegations regarding punitive damages, it is likely that such a motion will fail, thereby giving greater leverage to the plaintiff in the pursuit of this aspect of the case. A risk-benefit decision must be made by defense counsel before undertaking this particular method of containing damages.

§ 9.25 —Sample Sharing Agreement

The sample sharing agreement contained in this section has terms which are in no way fixed and must be adjusted to the particular case at issue and the concerns of the defendants. However, you should note that the plaintiff is not a party to this agreement; it is an agreement among the defendants to settle the plaintiff's case. As a result, a separate compromise document will be necessary between the plaintiff and the defendants for the purpose of removing the plaintiff from the case.

SHARING AGREEMENT

WHEREAS, (defendants) wish to resolve by settlement and without any admission of liability the claims brought against them by plaintiff, in order to limit their potential exposure to liability in the civil actions pending in the United States District Court for the District of__________, (hereinafter referred to as "the actions") arising from injuries caused to (plaintiff and/or plaintiff's decedent) as the result of (incident description); and,

WHEREAS, settlement of the actions has been reached with and accepted by plaintiff for the amount of (amount); and

WHEREAS, there remain cross-claims and a third-party complaint for indemnity and/or contribution which have not been resolved; and

WHEREAS, all defendants to the actions (including the defendant not party to this Agreement) have been fully informed of the pendency of settlement negotiations with plaintiff and have had opportunity to participate therein, but one defendant does not agree to join in such settlement;

IT IS HEREBY STIPULATED AND AGREED by and between defendants and by their respective attorneys:

1. That (defendants)(hereinafter referred to as "the fund contributors") shall each contribute one-third of the total settlement amount of__________to a settlement fund from which plaintiff's claims may be settled with respect to all defendants to the actions;

2. That the claims of plaintiff against all defendants shall be settled for the amount of__________, and that a dismissal of all claims of plaintiff shall be entered in the actions;

3. That a release shall be given by plaintiff releasing all defendants in the actions from further liability to plaintiff, but that such release shall not operate to release cross-claims for indemnity and/or contribution;

4. That the settlement with plaintiff is reasonable and made in good faith;

5. That all defendants in the actions have been given opportunity to participate in the settlement negotiations with plaintiff;

6. That the litigation shall proceed to trial on the merits of the cross-claims for indemnity and/or contribution, for apportionment of relative fault, if any, among defendants;

7. That the percentage or amounts paid into the fund by the fund contributors, or the existence of such a fund or contributions thereto, shall in no way be relevant to or affect the determination of the relative fault, if any, of those parties, and the fact-finder at trial shall not be informed of the fact, percentage, or amount of each fund contributor's share of the settlement fund;

8. That, after trial and appeal, if any, of the cross-claims for indemnity and/or contribution, the obligations of the defendants to one another with respect to amounts paid by the fund contributors in settlement of the claims of the plaintiff shall be determined in accordance with the relative fault of the defendants and the applicable principles of indemnity, contribution and comparative negligence among joint or concurrent tortfeasors;

9. That upon the conclusion of trial and satisfaction of judgments in accordance with this Agreement, the defendants shall execute the appropriate releases of claims brought in cross-claims.

§ 9.26 Good Faith Settlements

Over the last several years a number of states have enacted statutes designed to encourage settlements among plaintiffs and defendants. Such settlements are typically characterized as *good faith settlements* and, when entered into in the proper circumstances, protect a settling defendant from any cause of action premised on contribution or indemnity from a nonsettling co-defendant.

One factor which often discourages one or several defendants from settling a case with the plaintiff is the risk of being held liable for contribution or indemnity to a co-defendant. Thus, a number of states, recognizing this problem and wishing to encourage settlements, have enacted statutes which protect co-defendants who have settled with a plaintiff from actions for contribution or indemnity brought by nonsettling defendants.

Typical of these statutes is California Civil Procedure Code § 877:

> Where a release, dismissal with or without prejudice, or a covenant not to sue or not to enforce judgment is given in good faith before verdict or judgment to one or more of a number of tortfeasors claimed to be liable for the same tort . . .

(b) It shall discharge the tortfeasor to whom it is given from all liability for any contribution to another tortfeasor.

Such a statute, designed to encourage settlements and protect settling defendants, has been construed by the California Supreme Court in *American Motorcycle Association v. Superior Court,* 20 Cal. 3d 578, 604, 578 P.2d 899, 149 Cal. Rptr. 182 (1978), to apply not only to actions for contribution, but also to actions for partial or comparative indemnity.

When the settlement is properly entered into pursuant to the terms of the statute, a settling defendant is completely protected.

When settlements are reached between a plaintiff and a defendant following a verdict against a co-defendant but before a verdict or judgment is entered as to a nonsettling defendant, the settling defendant has a tremendous advantage. Assuming a plaintiff is amenable to settlement and has prevailed against a nonsettling defendant, the settling defendant is able to view the case and make much better informed judgments whether to settle and, if so, for how much.

A tactic which can thus be pursued, when there is a good faith settlement statute or equivalent judge-made law in place in a given jurisdiction, is for a culpable defendant to settle for a minimal amount of money and protect itself against a contribution/indemnity action by a less culpable defendant. The question under these circumstances revolves around what *good faith* means and whether the settlement was merely a subterfuge as opposed to being in good faith.

From a settling defendant's perspective, there are a number of matters to be considered before entering into what is intended to be a good faith settlement:

1. Has the judgment or verdict been entered?
2. Does the amount contemplated to be paid under the settlement agreement allow an argument to be made that the settlement is in good faith?
3. Is the settlement merely a subterfuge to escape greater liability to a co-defendant or is its purpose truly to settle the rights of the plaintiff versus the settling defendant?

From the perspective of a co-defendant wishing to attack a settlement as not cutting off indemnity or contribution rights, the following factors should be considered.

1. A cross-claim should be filed against any co-defendants when you feel your client is entitled to indemnity/contribution. Despite the fact that you do not lose the right to indemnity, you may find your client in a less advantageous position to argue against a settlement

agreement by a co-defendant with a plaintiff when no contribution or indemnity action in the form of a cross-claim has been filed.

2. Has a verdict or judgment been entered against the settling co-defendants? If so, the settlement typically will not qualify as one cutting off your client's rights to contribution or indemnity.
3. Look to the amount of the settlement and whether it genuinely qualifies as good faith or whether it is so small as to be patently a device for limiting the settling defendants' liability and perhaps financing the litigation against your client.
4. When you have prior notice that a co-defendant intends to enter into a settlement with the plaintiff which would have the effect of qualifying as good faith for the purpose of cutting off your indemnity rights, consider whether your client's interests would be better served by attempting to bring about a joint or total settlement of the case.
5. It should be noted that settlement by a co-defendant may actually benefit your client in that the sympathy factor of the plaintiff will be removed from the case, and it will become a question of defendants fighting between or among themselves.

In terms of format, an ordinary stipulation of settlement can be used for the purpose of entering into a settlement in a multidefendant case when the settlement is consummated between the plaintiff and one of the defendants. Thereafter, a good faith determination should be sought in order to protect the settling defendant from an action for contribution or indemnity by a co-defendant. No special language is required; however, the stipulation should embody all the terms of the settlement so you cannot be accused of having side arrangements about which the question of good faith can be raised.

CHAPTER 10

TACTICAL NEGOTIATIONS

§ 10.1 Introduction

The negotiating process is one aspect of litigation capable of being turned into a weapon against the unwary or inexperienced litigator. The art of negotiation is one of which all successful trial lawyers must, at a minimum, have a high degree of knowledge. Whether or not you consider yourself a master negotiator, the ability to know when you are being taken advantage of in order to avoid that happening is a skill which all trial lawyers must possess.

There are any number of self-help or self-improvement type books on the market today which address the question of negotiations. This is a process which, at least in some measure, should be distinguished from the settlement process. As used within the context of this chapter, *negotiation* is the process by which a settlement may be achieved and is only one technique for achieving that settlement. However, it is far and away the most important technique for achieving successful settlements in that the negotiation process provides the framework for the resolution of disputes outside the courtroom. Indeed, it is the primary factor in the settlement process that brings about successful settlements.

Lawyers involved in all aspects of practice engage in the negotiating process. This is true whether the lawyer is handling a civil case involving contract questions or monetary damage questions or a criminal case involving the plea bargaining process. Likewise, negotiations are an integral part of the regulatory or administrative sector of the practice. Notwithstanding the aspect of litigation in which one may be involved, the principles and techniques of negotiations remain essentially the same and have the same effect in whatever setting they are applied.

Generally speaking, the *process of negotiation* can be defined as the exchange of information between or among parties achieved for the purpose of influencing the behavior of one or more of those parties. In light of this fact, the negotiating process actually takes place on several levels simultaneously. First, there is a person-to-person or individual level of negotiating. In the context of litigation, it may be one lawyer sitting down face-to-face with another lawyer and negotiating between themselves, for example, on procedural matters.

The second level of negotiation occurs on an organization-to-organization basis and can be equated with the individual lawyer negotiating on behalf of a client on substantive matters. Absent a lawyer having final authority to reach a result, the lawyer is actually doing nothing more than negotiating on behalf of client who, in the final analysis, has the ultimate say as to whether negotiations will be successful. In this instance, although the level of negotiations is between the individual lawyers and may take place on an individual basis, the lawyers are acting not on their own behalves but rather on behalf of clients.

The final level of negotiation involves international transactions. In this instance, the negotiating process may involve not only lawyers, their clients, or law firms but the interests of nations as well. In such circumstances, the interests of the lawyer are usually only incidental, while the interests of the nation or the client are certainly paramount. This level of negotiation typically is not encountered by most lawyers. By far the most typical negotiating situation encountered by most lawyers involves a lawyer's representing the interests of a client.

When a criminal prosecutor sits down with defense counsel, the prosecutor is representing not only the interests of the community but also, in some respect, no matter how small, the interests of the accused, because the accused is a member of the community. As a result, the interests represented by the prosecutor do in some measure conflict. This conflict can be characterized in the following ways:

1. Removing the defendant from the street versus the presumption of innocence
2. Saving the community the cost of full trial versus giving the defendant his day in court
3. Obtaining the maximum penalty available under law versus the certainty of obtaining a conviction through a plea bargain arrangement.

In performing these functions, it is incumbent upon the prosecutor to be aware of the effect that these conflicting needs present and the fact that there is not a total degree of consistency in the position the prosecutor represents. The prosecutor must also recognize the policies which he or she represents, the effectiveness of the prosecuting organization as an arm of the judiciary, and the absolute requirement of arriving at a resolution of the case that is fair not only to the defendant but also to the community.

Recognizing the multilevel considerations which a prosecutor has to keep in mind when representing a client, the task of a defense attorney is simplicity itself. The defense has one and only one goal in mind in representing a client in negotiations: to obtain the best possible deal under the circumstances which he or she is capable of obtaining for the defendant.

The extent to which a defense lawyer succeeds in accomplishing the goal of getting a client the best possible deal in large measure depends almost entirely upon the ability for free exchange of information with his or her opponent. Knowledge is truly power in this circumstance, be it in the criminal or the civil context. Exchanging information will hopefully result in a bargain which both the prosecutor and the defense lawyer can later sell to their clients.

The essential features which form the foundation of any bargain in a criminal case are the following:

1. The strength of the prosecutor's case
2. The absence or presence of a valid defense for the defendant
3. Whether there are any witness problems
4. The length of the trial
5. The likelihood of winning at trial

6. The likelihood of there being an error committed at trial which would cause a reversal on appeal.

Whether you are dealing with a criminal case or a civil case, the process of negotiations is strikingly similar. The same elements which have just been listed in the context of a criminal case are equally applicable to negotiations in a civil case and will impact upon the negotiations process.

Be it civil or criminal litigation, the tool of negotiation is available to achieve settlements in all types of cases. Through the use of information, you are in a better position to persuade your opponent that the best result would be achieved outside the courtroom and, presumably, at least in your opinion, would better serve your client's interests.

Although you will find that settlements will not always occur even if both you and your opponent are in favor of a settlement, they will generally occur when the parties are of a like mind to resolve the dispute through negotiations in order to avoid either a trial or a deadlock in negotiations.

§ 10.2 Style of Negotiation

As with most other aspects of the trial process, there are any number of approaches to negotiating that are designed to yield long-term benefits. The question of style is one of the foremost considerations which you should always keep in mind when approaching the negotiating process.

Generally speaking, you will find that the most effective approach to negotiations attempts to set an atmosphere in which all parties to the negotiation see themselves as benefiting from a successful result. This approach can be characterized as the *cooperative style* of negotiating. For example, in the criminal situation, the prosecutor negotiates for an assured conviction based on a guilty plea that is protected on appeal, because no such appeal will take place; at the same time, the defense is negotiating for the lightest sentence which can be achieved, perhaps the possibility of probation without any prison at all, or an early probation and a shorter prison sentence.

The alternative to this sort of resolution is an *all-or-nothing* gamble on everybody's part. The prosecutor goes for a conviction and risks a finding of not guilty or reversal on appeal. The defense seeks an acquittal and risks a conviction or a reversal on appeal. In either case, the prosecutor or the defense is risking a loss, and expensive trial, and the possibility of an outcome far less favorable to what might have been achieved with a negotiated settlement.

In the civil context, the plaintiff who settles a case for $100,000 rather than holding out for the $1 million ad damnun requested in the complaint is guaranteed a sure thing. The alternative is a defense verdict or, assuming a victory at trial, reversal on appeal. The defendant in the civil case has the same benefit with a settlement, because the risk of a runaway verdict is eliminated, the fixed damages of the settlement are known, the expense and time of a lengthy trial are eliminated, and, not incidentally, the legal fees are minimized.

Settlement is achieved only if each side in a negotiation approaches the negotiation looking for not only what is in that process for them, but also keeping in mind what is in the process for their opponent. When you ignore this cooperative approach to the resolution of litigation, you may be risking an ultimate loss, even though the outcome might superficially appear to be a victory. This apparent victory is best illustrated by the union which demands a wage increase, and the company, after ultimately giving in, goes bankrupt a year later, because it can no longer be competitive with increased operating costs. This is probably one of the most simplistic examples of one-sided negotiations not keeping in mind the interests of the other side over the longer term. Within the context of civil litigation, the result usually is not a company which fails but rather a long memory of the opponent and the opponent's attorney when litigation may again arise over a different set of facts in the future with the same opponent or opposing lawyer.

The risk you run in an all-win or all-lose situation is poisoning future relationships and perspectives on the negotiating and resolution process. Such win-lose relationships, as opposed to win-win relationships, can have the effect of leaving one side or the other bitter at the outcome and believing that it has either been taken advantage of or unfairly and unjustly treated. Although there is oftentimes a temptation to approach the settlement process, particularly when liability has been admitted, as an all-or-nothing process, the tenure of such resolutions and their aftermath rarely make such an approach a good idea in the context of long-term future dealings. However, if you choose to negotiate on the basis of an all-or-nothing proposition, you should keep in mind that this is, more often than not, to be viewed as a single-time occurrence, because any long-term relationship with your opponent will likely be harmed by virtue of the memory of what happened in the past.

If you intend to use the "go for the throat" technique of negotiations, keep in mind that there will rarely be a second time. Because a large proportion of lawyers practice in a discrete area of substantive specialization, it is likely you will encounter the same opponents on future occasions. Similarly, you will oftentimes be either representing or opposing the same clients. If you put yourself in the position of having soured a relationship with an opponent by virtue of an all-or-nothing settlement in the past, you will not be doing yourself any favor with respect to the successful representation of your client in the future.

Another aspect of negotiation style involves becoming aware of your opponent's negotiation style and using that information to your advantage.

Experience has probably indicated to you that people of all types, including lawyers, generally act in a relatively predictable manner. The plaintiff's lawyer will typically make a large demand while the defense lawyer will typically make a small offer. Thus, you are generally able to make some sort of relatively accurate prediction in advance as to how your opponent will behave when you present your damages demand in the negotiating setting. Although you will encounter individuals who respond differently under different circumstances, you may generally assume that opposing counsel is wary of the uncertainties and unpredictability associated with the outcome of a trial. The best way to use this uncertainty is to be aware of it and take it into account in formulating your negotiating style.

Generally speaking, there are cues which are associated with your opponent's negotiating style which can tip you off to a great deal regarding the ability to prevail in the negotiation. Oftentimes, the unspoken needs and requirements of your opponent will come across either through his or her style or in some other fashion. It is incumbent upon you to pick up on these cues in order to be able to use them to your maximum advantage. See **§ 10.20**. If you are able to satisfy the needs and hopes of your opponent in the negotiating process, your opponent will typically be amenable to fulfilling your needs. By the same token, you should consider how guarded you want to be in disclosing your own needs. Remember, knowledge is power, and any knowledge your opponent has about the underlying weaknesses, needs, or requirements of your position can put your opponent in a superior bargaining position.

§ 10.3 The Negotiation Setting

Two general sources of information which you may utilize for the purpose of "reading" your opponent in the negotiation process are the setting of the negotiation and the statements of your opponent during the negotiation process.

Perhaps one of the best examples of the manner in which the setting or frame of reference for negotiations influences the outcome of those negotiations is a simple real estate sale. Assume that the owner of a home is attempting to sell that home through a real estate agent. The home is vacant, and all the furniture has been removed from the premises. Experience indicates that the owner probably attempted to sell the house while still occupying it. As a result of an inability to sell that house because the asking price was too high, the market was depressed, or any other number of reasons, the owner was in a position of having to move before selling the house. The house now sits vacant and unsold with the owner probably living in some other house making mortgage payments to two banks.

Any real estate agent who goes in to make an offer on that house for a prospective purchaser is immediately aware of the fact that the seller or opposing real estate agent representing the client is under some pressure to sell. In this negotiation setting, it would be imprudent to offer the asking price of the house, because the owner would probably be receptive to something less than the asking price. The fact that there is probably a second mortgage on a second piece of property, the owner is in a distant city and simply wishes to unload the property, or any number of other factors would, in all likelihood, influence the owner of the house to take something less than he or she might otherwise take under more ideal circumstances.

Obviously, a great deal of information can be gleaned from the setting of these negotiations. That information is readily translatable into a negotiating strategy. The negotiating strategy is to offer a price which is favorable to the purchaser but at the same time permits the seller to meet his or her needs.

Similar to the physical setting of the negotiation or the thing to be negotiated over are statements made by your opponent. More often than not, if you pay attention to what your opponent says in the context of the negotiating process, you will find that he or she discloses a great deal of information about not only his or her thought processes regarding resolution of the case but also those of his or her client. Properly recognized, these observations can be turned into a powerful negotiating tool. For example, assume that you are in the process of negotiating with an opposing attorney regarding a large wrongful death settlement. Your opponent comments that his client, a widow with two children, is anxious to get this case resolved either through trial or settlement, because there are a number of expenses coming up in the immediate future.

As a practical matter, the resolution of any litigation through trial is not an expedient process. The discovery process, the trial itself, and then post-trial proceedings including appeal all cause this process to be lengthy and drawn out.

The attorney who says, even in an offhand manner, that his or her client is looking forward to receiving the money to take care of some defined or even undefined expense is delivering a message either deliberately or inadvertently that the client might be ripe for settlement and that the setting for negotiations is positive from an opponent's point of view.

Cases settled under such circumstances can typically be negotiated and resolved in a rather amicable fashion with both sides believing that they got a settlement which favored their particular client. Ironically, it really doesn't matter whether the settlement does in fact favor one client or the other as long as there is a perception by each side that the settlement does favor that client.

§ 10.4 Negotiation Setting Logistics—In General

The practical aspects of the negotiation process include such things as the medium through which negotiations take place, be it by mail, by telephone, or face-to-face, as well as the physical location of the negotiations. Taking these factors into consideration is crucial to the success of negotiations. Not only is there a convenience factor associated with successfully structuring the logistical aspects of negotiating, but also there are a significant number of tactical and psychological considerations that can strengthen one party's hand while weakening that of another.

Generally, there are three means of communication during the negotiating process. There are communications by mail, by telephone, and face-to-face confrontations. In any negotiating process in a single case you may find yourself using one or all three of these means of communications. More often than not, the medium of communication which you choose is simply a function of either convenience or happenstance. However, there are a number of tactical considerations associated with each medium which you should keep in mind when deciding how you are going to approach the overall negotiating process. Each of these methods of communication has advantages and disadvantages associated within the context of settlement discussions. It is in these advantages and disadvantages that you can find yourself at a tactical advantage or, on some occasions, at a tactical disadvantage.

§ 10.5 —Negotiating by Mail

From a general perspective, using the mail as a negotiating medium has a number of advantages associated with it. The first of these is that you are able to establish a written record of communications. This record focuses not only on the timing of the negotiations but also on the substance of those negotiations. It allows you to substitute the written record for your own recollection and that of your opponent and will frequently avoid any disputes in the future as to what may have gone on in the past.

In using the mail as a negotiating medium, you will typically find yourself better prepared in terms of both responding to the negotiating posture of your opponent and setting forth your own negotiating position. This is not so much a function of the mail but rather of the written medium. You will typically spend a significantly greater amount of time and utilize more effort in preparing written settlement documents than you might otherwise commit when negotiating on the telephone or on a face-to-face basis. Because you are better prepared and, at least on paper, better represented, there is less chance for mistakes when using the mail as a negotiating tool. Typically, you will have reviewed the negotiation position in a letter on multiple occasions before it is sent off to your opponent. As a result, the inadvertent error or misstatement is less likely to occur in negotiating by mail.

Perhaps one of the greatest advantages to using the mail as a negotiating vehicle is that it is far easier to say no in a letter than it is to do so either on the telephone or especially in a face-to-face confrontation. Almost unconsciously, you probably already use the mail whenever you want to deliver bad news to an opponent or take a position that you might have felt uncomfortable taking if you had to do so in person either sitting across the table or in the same courtroom with your opponent.

Just as the mail as a negotiating vehicle has a number of advantages, it also suffers from a number of disadvantages of which you should be aware. The first of these is the reciprocal of one of the advantages; it is quite easy for your opponent to respond no through the mail. In addition, you are not able to get any visual feedback from your opponent in the negotiating process when negotiating by mail. In a face-to-face confrontation and, to a lesser extent, over the telephone, you are able to get either visual or aural feedback by which you can temper your comments or react accordingly. For example, your opponent may be saying no, but his visual expressions or other gestures may clearly indicate to you that he is in agreement with you. That is not possible through the mail, and thus you lose an important aspect of being able to shape and formulate your negotiating position on a dynamic basis.

Finally, perhaps one of the greatest disadvantages of negotiating through the mail is the fact that it is a lengthy and time consuming process. Oftentimes, settlements are struck on a very rapid basis when parties are in a position to move quickly. If the negotiating process is carried out exclusively through the mail, this rapid exchange often leading to settlement will not occur. Thus, while negotiating by mail results in far fewer errors, it is less likely to bring about immediate or short-term resolutions of problems.

§ 10.6 —Negotiating by Telephone

Negotiating by telephone has both advantages and disadvantages. On the advantage side of the ledger is the fact that, quite similar to using the mail, you are generally better prepared by the time you make the phone call. Because the phone call itself typically is an "event," it is likely that you have sketched out ideas and put them down in some sort of outline form. The lack of a face-to-face confrontation also makes it relatively easy to say no compared to in-person negotiations.

Perhaps the single greatest advantage of using the telephone for the purpose of settlement negotiations, at least over using the mail, is the speed with which the negotiations can occur. More often than not, however, what may be stated during a telephone conversation will be followed up with a letter to your opponent setting forth the nature of the telephone negotiations. This is done for the purpose of taking advantage of the great strength of negotiating by mail, namely creating a permanent record of the negotiations. One of the problems with this follow-up procedure, however, is that oftentimes you may find that an opponent abuses this follow-up as a means for putting down in writing his recollection of what occurred as distinguished from what actually occurred.

A potential disadvantage which you may encounter in using the telephone for negotiations is dealing with an opponent who is better prepared for the telephone conversation than you are. Another disadvantage, which also occurs when using the mail, is the fact that there is no visual feedback. However, you do have the advantage of at least getting aural feedback by virtue of listening carefully and being able to detect changes or uncertainty in your opponent's voice. Perhaps the single greatest disadvantage of the telephone as a settlement tool is the fact that it is quite easy to misunderstand an opponent. This is why it is advisable to follow up all settlement discussions which take place on the telephone with a letter setting forth precisely what transpired.

A good tactic to utilize when you are involved in negotiations over the telephone is always to attempt to initiate the telephone call. This way, you can plan the time of the call and maximize this timing factor to your advantage. If, however, you find yourself on the receiving end of a telephone call, you should advise your opponent that you will call back. Use the opportunity prior to calling back to prepare yourself for the negotiating process and maximize any tactical advantage of setting the time for the call yourself. Thus, orchestrate the telephone call as to timing to maximize your advantage and minimize it for your opponent. If this requires you in effect to make up an excuse regarding the inconvenience of the telephone call at that particular time, do so, because being caught unexpectedly will put you at a disadvantage in the negotiating process. If you negotiate during an unexpected call, you will not be well prepared nor will you have thought out the best tactical approach to take.

Once you are involved in a negotiating process on the telephone with your opponent, you should ensure that you will be free from distractions. Before taking the call or placing the call, advise your secretary that you are not to be interrupted by colleagues or associates. Such distractions can cause you to operate at a disadvantage since you will not be attuned totally to what is transpiring on the telephone.

In terms of taking notes during a telephone conversation, you should try to do so sparingly, because the notetaking process itself will be a distraction. However, immediately upon hanging up, you should either write detailed notes from skeleton notes as to what transpired or, alternatively and perhaps even better, dictate a detailed memorandum as to what went on. From this memorandum, you will then be able to draft a letter to your opponent confirming and fixing for the record what transpired.

§ 10.7 —Face-to-Face Negotiations

The final medium available to you for the purpose of negotiating settlements is face-to-face negotiations or confrontations. By and large, you should recognize at the outset that the negotiating process is confrontational, with each party to the negotiation looking to get what is best for him or his party. The plaintiff wants as much money as possible, while the defendant wants to spend as little as required to end the litigation. Recognition of this fact is essential to successful negotiating.

Face-to-face negotiations are typically the most productive and perhaps the best of the available negotiating tools. This is generally true since, unlike the use of either the mail or the telephone, you get immediate visual and other feedback from your opponent. Time delays and other disadvantages associated with other negotiating processes are not present in the face-to-face confrontation.

Separate from the very powerful advantage of having instantaneous feedback during the negotiating process, face-to-face negotiations allow you to rivet the attention of your opponent and maintain that attention. After all, there is less possibility of outside distractions and no delay built into the process. Presumably your opponent is in your office, or you are at some other location and are able to control the outside distractions. Coupled with this is an even more compelling advantage: if you are involved in a face-to-face confrontation for the purpose of settlement negotiations, there is a certain degree of commitment displayed by both sides, your opponent as well as yourself, to the negotiation process. After all, if you weren't going to negotiate, the meeting typically would not take place.

The commitment to negotiations in a face-to-face meeting may not be present with negotiations by mail or by telephone, because they are initiated by one party through the use of a letter or telephone call. However, the degree of effort associated with initiating and carrying out settlement negotiations in a face-to-face or personal meeting is considerably greater. As a result, it is typical that the commitment to reaching a satisfactory settlement on the part of all sides is manifested more strongly in the personal negotiating session.

§ 10.8 The Site of Negotiations

One aspect of the negotiating process to which enough attention is frequently not paid is the question of where the negotiations take place.

Generally speaking, you will have three choices available to you: at your opponent's office, at your office, or at some neutral site such as the courthouse. Each of these sites has advantages and disadvantages which you will want to keep in mind when determining the location for the negotiations.

The way in which you raise the question of where the negotiations will take place oftentimes dictates how that particular aspect of the negotiating process is resolved. If it is raised as a matter of fact, almost in an offhand manner, you stand a better chance of prevailing in carrying out your choice than if you make a major point of this aspect of the process.

The advantages of meeting in your office to negotiate with your opponent fall into three general categories. The first of these is that your opponent has already expended a certain degree of effort and commitment in reaching the bargaining table. By having your opponent come to you, there is an advantage to the overall bargaining process, no matter how small it may be perceived to be. In addition, by requiring your opponent to come to your office for the purpose of negotiations, there is not as great a likelihood that the negotiations will be terminated prematurely. You control the situation to a greater extent, short of your opponent's walking out. Finally, from a personal logistical perspective, the fact that your office, your secretary, and other resources are immediately available makes having negotiations sessions in your office advantageous. You are not put in the position of having to expend either time or money through travel or other arrangements for negotiating in some other city or across town.

Unfortunately, you may find that you cannot always control where the settlement negotiations take place. On occasion, perhaps more often than you might like, you will find that you will be negotiating at your opponent's office. Even in such circumstances, there are certain advantages to be enjoyed which should be kept in mind. These advantages are, in fact, disadvantages when viewed from the perspective of negotiating in your own office.

Essentially, the advantages of negotiating in your opponent's office fall into four categories. Being accessible in your own office is conducive to interruptions. This is true under even the best of circumstances. Accordingly, if you enter into settlement negotiations and conduct them at your opponent's office, you will not have the interruptions that you might otherwise be susceptible to when negotiating in your office. Coupled with this fact is the availability of your opponent's facilities and resources, including secretarial assistance, during the negotiating process without the need of having to tax your own office facilities or resources.

Separate and apart from these logistical advantages are two very real tactical advantages to negotiating out of your office. First, by being away from your office, your colleagues, and others, you are in a position to play for time by indicating to your opponent during the negotiating process that your files are not accessible or, alternatively, that approval for taking some position is needed from a superior. This allows you to use distance and location as a stalling tactic. The reciprocal of this fact is that, by being on your opponent's own turf, you are in a position to press your opponent harder for a decision, because presumably his or her colleagues or superiors are available.

§ 10.9 Dealing with Principals

One fact to keep in mind during the negotiating process, especially as it may relate to the damages aspect of negotiations, is that approval is needed from the client. This is a fact of life for any lawyer, whether representing the plaintiff or the defendant. You may find it desirable to let your opponent know at an early stage of the negotiations that your authority with respect to negotiations is limited to the ability to engage in the negotiation process and make a recommendation to either your superior or your client. However, you should point out that the ultimate decision whether to accept an offer will be made by someone not present, namely a colleague or the client, with whom you must consult before any agreement or settlement can be culminated. As a result, you are able to negotiate more freely.

What happens if, in fact, you as the attorney have the ultimate settlement authority? On occasion, you will have been given authority in advance to act on behalf of your colleague or client. The question which presents itself in this account in this context is whether you should exercise this authority.

Generally speaking, even if you do exercise this settlement authority without prior consultation with a client, you should not do so immediately at the time of the settlement offer. You can accomplish this by retiring to a conference room and either going through the motions of making a phone call to a colleague or simply sitting in the conference room and thinking about the settlement offer. The advantage of not acting immediately, even when armed with advance settlement authority, is that a certain "cooling off" may allow you to examine the settlement offer in an objective light to determine whether it is a good settlement offer. This is true whether the offer was put forward by you or your opponent. Accordingly, when you have settlement authority, you should still devise some sort of plan with a colleague by which you can engage in a discussion with respect to the settlement offer. By doing so, you are able to determine on a better basis whether the settlement offer should be accepted.

On the other hand, sometimes it may not be desirable to engage in such prior consultation before accepting a settlement offer. In those situations, in order to ensure that you do not act precipitously, you should go into the settlement negotiations, armed not only with the settlement authority given to you by the client, but also with a point-by-point, preferably written, plan for evaluating the settlement agreement. In this situation, the point-by-point plan should be focused on the goals and objectives of the settlement agreement that you are intending to bring about. As a result, you will more likely reach a settlement which achieves predetermined goals as opposed to fashioning a settlement agreement in which the goals *may* be found. The most typical situation in which you may find it less than desirable to have a cooling off is when you perceive the settlement offer to be highly favorable to your client and you want to move quickly to avoid your opponent's withdrawing. Under such circumstances, the best course of action is to agree to the settlement immediately and act accordingly.

Once you have reached a settlement that you believe to be highly favorable but indicate to an opponent that you wish to take some time to consider the settlement agreement before accepting it, your opponent may react that you have negotiated in less than good faith. The problem with this is not so much the accusation of negotiating in less than good faith but rather as long as the settlement offer remains outstanding, that your opponent is in a position to either modify or withdraw it. This obviously is not desirable, especially if you are armed with settlement authority and have already perceived the settlement agreement as highly favorable.

If you go into negotiations making it clear that, prior to approval of the settlement agreement, you will have to confer with either the client or superior, the fact that you indicate to your opponent that it is your intention to recommend a particular settlement agreement will convey a sense of confidence to your opponent that the agreement will be concluded. This is, in fact, a two-edged sword. First, if you then come back and suggest changes to your opponent based upon these consultations, your opponent may already have set it in his or her mind that the original settlement agreement was satisfactory. This may raise some difficulty for making the changes. However, a far more likely scenario is that if you come back and say that, unless certain changes or concessions are made, your superior or client will not approve the agreement, your opponent may see the entire settlement falling apart unless he or she concedes to the changes. This puts a tremendous amount of pressure on your opponent to go along with the changes and may put you in a superior bargaining position.

§ 10.10 Drafting the Settlement Agreement

As a general rule, you, and not your opponent, should always undertake the actual drafting of the settlement agreement. Although this certainly adds to your workload, it provides you with the ability to structure the agreement around your particular needs. Specifically, you are able to use your language and organization and, as a result, put more of your own thinking in the settlement agreement.

A very good tactic to pursue in settlement negotiations is to present your opponent at an early stage of the negotiations with a draft agreement that sets forth all the terms of the settlement proposal which you would either accept or be willing to recommend to your client. This allows you to use your settlement agreement as the starting point for negotiations, and you can begin discussions on those aspects of the agreement over which no real controversy exists. Then, the disputed provisions of the agreement will be provisions drafted by you, and, in all likelihood, the final version will retain some or all of the language of your original draft.

A good approach when a settlement agreement is not prepared in draft prior to the commencement of the discussions is to take careful notes during the settlement discussions and, during a recess in the settlement discussions, embody those notes into a draft agreement. You can then present that draft agreement to your opponent utilizing your language and organization and expressing what you understood to be the tenor of the discussion in your own words. This permits you to assume a greater degree of control over the direction of the settlement negotiations in a way that focuses your opponent on those areas which you believe to be important.

§ 10.11 Preparing to Negotiate

In negotiations, as in many other aspects of the trial process, information is power. Obviously, the negotiating process should not be entered into on a haphazard or ad hoc basis. Similar to the process of cross-examination, you will not be able to accomplish your goals in achieving a settlement favorable to your client unless you know exactly what those goals are and what you intend to accomplish.

There is nothing worse than watching an attorney cross-examine a witness when it is apparent that the attorney has not thought out the purpose for the cross-examination and thus finds himself or herself being taken advantage of by the witness. The very same result will ensue if you enter into settlement negotiations, particularly in the damages phase of litigation, without having carefully thought out what you wish to accomplish.

One of the very first things which you should do is to know your opponent. This requires you to obtain as much information as possible about not only the opposing client, in order to determine what type of settlement might be feasible, but also the attorney representing that client. One of the best ways to do this is to consult colleagues who have been involved in litigation both against as well as on the same side as that attorney. This will permit you to get a good bit of insight about your opponent and determine whether there are particular aspects of your opponent's personality that may be taken advantage of in the negotiating process. Inquiries regarding previous settlements that the opposing client has entered into may give you some additional information. You can use the same approach for additional information about the opposing attorney.

Be sure to keep in mind what your opponent may wish to take away from the settlement negotiation. Remember, a need-based analysis may reveal to you that what you perceived as being necessary in order to settle the case is not necessarily inconsistent with what your opponent may feel is necessary. For example, you may find that your opponent is representing the same client in several different lawsuits all of which are similar to yours. Going into your negotiations it is well to recognize that whatever amount your opponent agrees to pay in your case is going to be thrown back at your opponent in the other cases. Although this may not necessarily mean that you are willing to take less money, it does mean that you must be conscious of the broader implications of a particular settlement strategy.

Part of effectively preparing for a settlement negotiation is making a realistic assessment of your own case. By this I do not necessarily mean only the liability aspects of the case, but also the minimum amount of money which you are willing to accept for the case. Coupled with this should be a determination of whether you are going to be in a position of requiring an all-cash settlement or whether some alternative approach such as a structured settlement may be acceptable. Obviously, this is a position which must be developed in concert with the client. However, the client is not necessarily in the best position to know whether an all-cash versus some alternative approach to settlement is advisable. As a result, be prepared to bring in settlement professionals, economists, and other types of financial planners when formulating your settlement strategy. You will then be in a better position to advance a settlement proposition, and you will be able to rapidly evaluate settlement proposals.

One very important thing to keep in mind, particularly when there are multiple attorneys representing a side, is to be sure that your team of attorneys is of like mind with respect to settlement negotiations. It is imperative that any disagreements be settled before negotiations begin. One situation in which you might encounter this is personal injury or wrongful death litigation when there is a forwarding counsel or co-counsel relationship. Generally speaking, as long as one individual attorney has been designated as the lead attorney for the purpose of the negotiation process, there should be no problem with having more than one attorney present at the negotiations and still speaking with a single voice. Indeed, there may be circumstances in which it is desirable to obtain several views toward the particular aspect of the negotiations and to have another attorney available for moral and other support. Just as obvious is the fact that, if the attorneys representing a particular client openly disagree, there can be disastrous results, because opposing counsel is then in a position to make certain demands that would have the effect of driving a wedge even farther between the divided attorneys. In addition, opposing counsel is then in a position to act as a negotiator between disputing attorneys representing the same side.

Remember, there is virtually no advantage to having multiple attorneys speaking on behalf of a single client. By the same token, there are several advantages to be gained by having a lead attorney. First and foremost, a single attorney speaks with a stronger voice. Other advantages include the fact that the other members of the negotiating team or co-counsel are always available for information or to have ideas bounced off them. In addition, when there are multiple attorneys representing a single side, the weaker attorneys in terms of weaker personalities may better be kept in the background during the negotiating process. Finally, multiple attorneys are better able to focus on various aspects of the settlement proposal without the need to be actively involved in the settlement negotiations. This allows the other attorneys who are not acting as spokesperson to keep the lead attorney apprised of various aspects of the proposal that might otherwise have slipped by unnoticed.

§ 10.12 Negotiation Techniques

As with most other parts of litigation, there are a number of tactics and techniques associated with successful negotiations. The manner in which you use these, which of them you use, and your timing with respect to their use are all dictated by the particular situations which you may confront in any given case. Also to be considered in making these decisions is whether you are dealing from a position of strength or weakness. For example, if you have a good case on liability but a poor one on damages with liability no longer an issue, you may choose certain tactics which might not be appropriate were the situation reversed.

No matter which tactics you may utilize, a risk-benefit analysis should be made with respect to each tactic prior to its use. In effect, what you must do is focus on the worst possible consequences if the tactic which you choose backfires. Against this you must weigh the best possible result if the tactic succeeds. Based on this evaluation, you are in a much better position to determine whether a particular tactic is appropriate for given circumstances.

Keeping the foregoing in mind, let us turn to a number of tactics that may be appropriate under different circumstances depending upon the facts involved, the personalities of the parties, and the risk-benefit analysis process.

§ 10.13 —Good Guy versus Bad Guy

One of the classic negotiating processes which we oftentimes see portrayed on television is the good guy-bad guy approach, typically in the criminal context with two detectives interrogating a suspect. One of them takes the bad guy role, attempting to bully the suspect into a confession, indeed almost physically attacking him. The other detective acts as an intermediary and good guy, interrupting and restraining the other detective and preventing the suspect from being abused. At least this is what the suspect is led to believe through this good guy-bad guy charade.

Within the context of damage negotiations, this approach changes very little from the way we've seen it portrayed on television. Essentially what is required is representation by more than one attorney in order that one can play the good guy and one can play the bad guy. What this means within the context of civil litigation involving money damages is that one plays a hard-nosed role, while the other is more of a conciliator.

The whole idea underlying this approach to negotiations is to attempt to obtain a psychological edge over your opponent. This is especially effective when there are multiple attorneys representing one party and only a single attorney representing the other side. In such a circumstance, one lawyer can act in an unreasonable fashion, while the other can act in a reasonable fashion and attempt to control his or her colleague. This can best be accomplished by having the so-called reasonable attorney seemingly agree with the opponent while at the same time seeking minor concessions from the opponent in order to satisfy the unreasonable colleague. Obviously, these so-called concessions are carefully thought out in advance by the team of negotiators and truly represent what they wish to obtain, as distinguished from the public position being put forward by the unreasonable lawyer.

In order to utilize this negotiating style and tactic most effectively, the bad guy member of the negotiating team must at least appear as the lawyer with the final say. This is necessary in order to make it seem as if the reasonable negotiator has to have something to bring back to the unreasonable negotiator in the form of a concession in order to get an agreement. If it appears to the opposing side that the reasonable attorney is the one with the ultimate control over the disposition of the case, the obvious response will be to ignore the unreasonable lawyer.

§ 10.14 —"Take It or Leave It"

At one time or another in our careers, we have all been involved in settlement negotiations when we have said to our opponent, "this is the most we're willing to offer; take it or leave it." On occasion we mean it;

probably in an equal number of circumstances, we're simply using this as a negotiating tactic.

This approach can have certain advantages. However, it is one of the riskiest styles of negotiating. There is a substantial possibility that you can lose your credibility as a negotiator if, after putting out your final offer or demand in a take-it-or-leave-it format, you actually do make some additional movement. The problem with this is that your opponent will think that you have some additional flexibility over and above that which you've already displayed; perhaps even more importantly, in future negotiations with you, your opponent may never be persuaded by a take-it-or-leave-it type of proposition.

The question then presents itself whether there are any circumstances in which a take-it-or-leave-it approach is a sound one to take in settlement negotiations. Although the answer to this is yes, the circumstances are limited and must be carefully considered before utilizing this tactic. First, and perhaps more important, you must have other options and be in a position to take a chance on the take-it-or-leave-it approach. If your opponent actually does walk away from the settlement negotiations, you must be prepared to try the case or have some fallback position. Coupled with this is the practical requirement that, before taking this approach, you must either have completely discussed it with your client or satisfied that the approach is in the best interest of the client. Don't put yourself in the position of taking this sort of negotiating tack on the spur of the moment only to find yourself backed into a corner.

Perhaps most frequently encountered is the situation in which you have made your best and final offer. There is simply no more money or no more room for movement. In such a situation, you can be up front with your opponent about it; indicate that there is no further negotiating room for you because your client is not willing to make any more movement and that your final offer is a take-it-or-leave-it proposition. Obviously, in such a situation you must be prepared to go to trial in the event that your opponent does not go along with your position.

§ 10.15 —"Bit by Bit"

One very effective technique of negotiating style is to approach the negotiation on a "bit-by-bit" basis. For example, assume that your case is made up of several different major points. Three of them are not very strong in terms of elements of proof or evidentiary foundations, while the other two are quite strong and you will have several witnesses testify with respect to each of them. By providing your opponent in the negotiating process with a sample or bit of the evidence on the two stronger points and either providing no information on the weaker points or simply generalizing about them, you can oftentimes portray your case in its most effective fashion. Unless your opponent thinks about it, something which, quite surprisingly, many opponents will not do, he or she will tend to make the psychological transfer of the stronger parts of your case to your entire case.

The obvious tack to take when confronted with this approach by somebody against whom you are negotiating is to require that the opposing attorney present the entire case to you with respect to what evidence he or she intends to produce. Obviously, sometimes you may find this to be a less than practical approach in terms of the examination of documents. For example, assume that the medical records are voluminous. In this situation, there is absolutely no justification for simply accepting the medical records being presented by your opponent as an example of the kind of injuries being suffered. Rather, you have the option of either examining all the medical records or, alternatively, asking for all the records and then simply choosing those portions of the medical records which you conclude should be examined in detail.

§ 10.16 —The "Add-On" Technique

Another approach to the negotiating process is the "add-on" technique. This technique is used to win the battles as a means for winning the war. Essentially what it allows you to do is to, in effect, strike a bargain and then come back and attempt to improve your own bargaining position and result.

A simple example out of everyday life is illustrative. Assume that you are involved in the purchase of a house. You have gone back and forth negotiating with the seller of the home and have reached a price of $150,000. You noticed in the garage a lawn tractor and accessories and have also determined that it would be advisable for you to have an inspection of that home. After the bargain is struck at the $150,000 price, but before the contract is signed, you ask the seller what she would charge to throw in the tractor and its accessories as well as whether she will pay for the home inspection. The seller comes back and says that she'll charge you $1,000 for the tractor and its accessories but won't pay for the home inspection. At that point you indicate that you think $1,000 is too much and you believe it to be justified that she pay for the home inspection since she is making certain representations about the quality of the home. The seller indicates in response that she won't do so with respect to the home inspection and is firm on the price of the tractor. You respond that it's really too bad to have the sale of the home hung up over such inconsequential points, but they are important to you and you want to think overnight about whether to go forward with the deal.

Confronted with the possibility of losing the house sale over a relatively small amount, you come back and say that, in order to obviate any further delay, what you would suggest is that the seller charge $500 for the tractor and that you will split the cost of the home inspection with her. Not wanting to lose the sale and sensing that this may be important to you, or at least important enough not to go forward with the sale without thinking about it, the seller relents.

Obviously, the scenario just described presents the application of this technique in an ideal setting. It may not work this way all the time. However, there are certainly circumstances in which it can work in a very similar fashion. For example, in the area of worker's compensation insurance, assume that you are representing a plaintiff who has a workers' compensation lien of $5,000 against any recovery. After the settlement discussions have been resolved and a figure for the settlcment has been arrived at, you come back and request that the opponent take care of satisfying the settlement lien. If the opponent says no, you take the position that you will have to think about whether to go through with this settlement at all. You reason that now the settlement is, effectively, for less money, because you've got to satisfy the lien out of the settlement amount. You are now in a position to negotiate the disposition of the settlement lien as an additional factor and perhaps either have the defendant take care of it entirely, depending on how anxious the defendant is to settle the case, or at least reach a disposition of the workers' compensation lien which has each side contributing to its resolution, probably for a reduced amount.

The way to respond to this approach is by affirmatively taking the initiative and indicating to your opponent, who is now attempting to "nickel and dime" you, that you don't have authority to give the concessions which he seeks. You should suggest that the negotiations be terminated so that you can consider what further steps to take at that point. Oftentimes, this will be sufficient to cause an opponent who is attempting to use this sort of tactic to back off.

§ 10.17 —The Counteroffer

Another technique to negotiating involves the counteroffer. More often than not, the process of making counteroffers is routine in settlement negotiations. Used as a tactic, a counteroffer may take your opponent's offer and add to it your own terms and conditions. For example, assume that you are negotiating on behalf of the defendant in a personal injury case. The plaintiff has offered to settle the case for $1 million. Your counteroffer, using a structured settlement approach, would call for a pay-out over time of $1 million. Essentially you have embodied your opponent's terms but rearranged it in a more favorable fashion.

§ 10.18 —Other Negotiation Techniques

There are a number of other tactical aspects to successful negotiating which should be kept in mind in the settlement process. They fall into four broad categories:

1. Never accept negotiating deadlines or cutoffs from your opponent.
2. Seek outside support and authority for your position.
3. Recognize the frame of reference in which you are negotiating at any particular time and be able to adapt or playact.
4. Remember that your opponent is simply another lawyer.

A favorite negotiating technique of both plaintiffs and defendants is to indicate that a particular offer must be accepted by a particular time on a particular day or it is deemed withdrawn. The whole idea to this approach is to add artificial pressure to the negotiating process and cause an opponent to believe that unless a particular offer is accepted at a particular time, it will be withdrawn. Obviously, the side in the negotiations which has the greatest time flexibility will benefit from such artificially imposed deadlines. By the same token, the ability to demonstrate a high degree of restraint and calm in the face of negotiating deadlines will often pay large dividends.

An attorney who imposes a deadline also hopes to cause an opponent to feel pressured by the deadline and thus display greater flexibility with respect to its negotiating position than might otherwise be the case. A good technique for dealing with such artificially imposed deadlines is to advise your opponent that you will simply not be able to evaluate the settlement offer or demand properly within the time constraints being imposed and that you will respond as soon as possible. Another approach is to counter with another deadline that is more to your liking. Under no circumstances, however, should you structure your settlement negotiations or consideration of a settlement proposal around a deadline which has been imposed by your opponent.

Any position which you take oftentimes comes down to the amount of credibility which you have as a lawyer. The ability to enhance the likelihood of your position having an impact on your audience, be it your opponent or a jury, can be dramatically affected by the ability to introduce extraneous evidence that your position is well accepted. The ability, in the context of the negotiation process, to demonstrate that certain hypotheses, assumptions, or other bases for your negotiating position have been written about or otherwise discussed by people other than yourself can be an invaluable aid.

Audiences, be they opponents or juries, are more receptive to the written word than they may be to the spoken word. Along these lines, any time you set forth a negotiating position, you should consider as a predicate to presenting that negotiating position whether there are articles by experts in the field which give some support to your position. The United States Bureau of Labor Statistics is one source of excellent information that bears upon the damage negotiating process.

The typical context in which we see this done is when we engage an economist to do a damage calculation. Inevitably that economist will rely upon and incorporate any number of economic texts, articles, and other information to bolster his or her own opinion as to what a human life or injury is worth. There is no reason why this can't be done equally well without the physical presence of an economist. The same sources of information are available to us, and they have an equally strong capacity to legitimize our position, no matter how outrageous they may be under other circumstances.

A third technique of which you should be aware in the negotiating process is playacting. I am a strong believer in the fact that a trial is much like a theatrical production in terms of its preparation as well as its production in the courtroom. The lawyer is at the same time a writer, a director, a producer, and an actor. In the courtroom, however, we as lawyers on both sides of the controversy are restricted with respect to staying in the confines of the evidence and being bound by the rules of procedure and rules of evidence. No such restrictions exist, however, outside the courtroom within the context of the negotiating process. Indeed, when negotiating settlements, there is very little that is not fair game with respect to tactical approaches and considerations. Oftentimes, it pays not to be yourself and to truly playact. Outrageous positions can be taken, irrational conduct can be displayed, and approaches which might not otherwise be you can be tried to see what effect they have on your opponent and on the overall negotiating process.

How many times have you seen an opponent, either in a deposition or in a negotiating setting, who displays a great deal of confusion about what is going on? In effect, he is playing the "poor dumb country lawyer" role. You know as well as he does that such an approach is merely playacting and meant to throw off the other lawyers in the case, because that lawyer is just as shrewd, if not shrewder, than anybody else in the case. The negotiation process is ripe with the opportunity to use such techniques in order to determine what effect they have on an opponent. If you learn that they are not effective, you can drop them just as quickly as you assumed them and try some other tack.

A final consideration of which you should be aware when negotiating is to not be awed by your opponent. This can be brought about in one of two ways and can clearly work to your substantial disadvantage if you are not careful about the approach you take to negotiations. On occasion, you will be litigating against an opponent who you consider to be a nationally-known attorney operating with a big reputation and who, at least in your opinion, is truly one of the so-called lions of the bar. More frequently, you will find yourself negotiating against somebody whom you know quite well. However, he will have with him as his consultant during the negotiations an economist or some other expert in the field who speaks in phrases that only other experts understand.

These circumstances can be intimidating unless you are of equal stature with your high-powered opponent or you have your own economist with you. It is quite easy in such circumstances to be intimidated by the opponent because you tend not to hear what is being said but rather are overwhelmed by the person who is saying it. This may make you more pliable in accepting positions that you would not accept from some other lawyer.

This tactic should be guarded against at all costs, and you should recognize that in the negotiating process all lawyers are equal—it is only cases and facts which are different. Don't permit your opponent to inject his or her personality or that of others into the negotiating process as an actual element of the case. If you see an opponent attempting to do that, you should respond in a strong fashion and attempt to take control of the negotiations. One good tactic to utilize when you find your opponent attempting to overwhelm you either through the use of his own personality or that of someone else is to become an aggressive negotiator. You should try various personalities under these circumstances to see what response you get. In addition, you should consider having the negotiations on your home ground, so to speak, or in your office, in order that you are more comfortable with the surroundings and not a guest in the negotiations.

§ 10.19 Getting Information

In virtually every aspect of litigation, knowledge is power. This is no less true and, indeed, is probably more true in the negotiating process. The side which possesses the greatest amount of information has a negotiating edge. This includes information about both cases, your opponent's as well as yours, information about your opponent, and information about what the needs and requirements of both your opponent and your own client are in the settlement process.

The trial process itself through pretrial discovery will provide a substantial amount of information for you. The usual manner of gaining such information will be through the use of pretrial discovery techniques.

However, perhaps even more valuable information will be obtained through the informal process of exchanging information with your opponent. More often than not, this will be through simple questions.

In addition to using questions to obtain information, you can also use questions to give information as well. The way this is done in the trial setting in the courtroom is through leading questions. Thus, the question, "What time is it?" gives no information but seeks some. However, the question, "It's four o'clock, isn't it?" not only seeks information in the form of a confirmation but also gives information in the form of time.

Transposing this process into the settlement context, the manner in which a question can both seek and give information at the same time would be something along the lines of, "If I were able to offer you $500,000, would your client accept it?" This allows you to set forth a position without committing yourself with respect to the position itself.

Experience indicates that questions have multiple functions. They get information. They give information. They get someone's attention. They initiate the thought process and they hasten the resolution of problems. It's your task in the negotiating process to use questions to their fullest extent and to your advantage.

An effective tactic to use when commencing negotiations is to attempt to ascertain the needs of your client and your opponent before actually embarking on the process of negotiating. The failure to do this can result in the seeking of a commitment from an opponent, as well as a commitment from yourself, before either side has had an opportunity to ascertain what type of commitment is in his or her best interests. As a result, negotiating without a needs analysis is more likely to bring about unhappy negotiations, unsuccessful negotiations, and/or unsatisfying negotiations.

The use of questions to ascertain the needs of your opponent can help you get better insight into how to structure the negotiating process. A good example of this technique is commencing negotiations with the question, "I think we both agree that it's in our mutual interest to resolve this case without going to trial, don't you?" Through this question, you have conveyed the position that you desire to settle and are seeking confirmation from your opponent. The commitment that is being sought from your opponent is not a major one, but it is one which, if given, paves the road for further discussions.

This could be followed by the next question, "Could we talk about, for the moment, what your client needs to resolve this case?" Once again you're not seeking any commitment from your opponent but are shaping the direction which the negotiating process will take. This could be followed by the kind of question I referred to before, "Would your client be amenable to a structured settlement of this case?" Once again, you're not seeking commitments but rather shaping the direction of the discussions and at the same time conveying information.

The greatest advantage in the negotiating process goes to the side who controls the direction of the negotiations. Control of the negotiating process is a direct function of the amount of knowledge which one has about an opponent. The key to successfully negotiating settlements which are favorable to your client while at the same time maintaining an advantageous, long-term relationship with your opponent is to ascertain the needs of your opponent while satisfying the needs of your client.

§ 10.20 Negotiating Needs

In *The Art of Negotiating* (Simon & Schuster Cornerstone Library 1981), Gerard I. Nierenberg talks about the need theory and divides it into six categories.

1. The negotiator works for the opponent's needs.
2. The negotiator lets the opponent work for the negotiator's needs.
3. The negotiator works for the opponent's and his or her needs.
4. The negotiator works against his or her own needs.
5. The negotiator works against the opponent's needs.
6. The negotiator works against the opponent's and his or her own needs.

A recognition of not only your own needs but those of your opponent is necessary in order to negotiate successfully. The best perception which you can foster is one on the part of your opponent that you are working in favor of his or her needs while against your own best interests. Obviously, this is an impression which you desire to foster but one which you don't want to actually exist. This requires that you determine what your opponent's needs are. In order to do this, there are several sources of information.

1. Observation of your opponent's actions
2. Observation of your opponent's expressions
3. Analysis of your opponent's words
4. Observation of your opponent's body language
5. Information about your opponent from public records
6. Information from colleagues and other key people who have been involved in the negotiating process with your opponent.

In making the analysis of your opponent's needs, you should consider the various types of needs which people in general strive for. The following list is by no means inclusive of everything, nor is it meant to suggest that every individual has each of these needs or has them equally strongly. It is, however, meant as a guide in terms of analyzing your opponent and determining what his or her particular needs are.

1. Security
2. Self-image
3. Self-achievement
4. Acceptance
5. Excitement
6. Upward mobility
7. Recognition
8. Love
9. Wealth
10. Financial security
11. Job security
12. Knowledge
13. Resolution

§ 10.21 The Computer Analysis

The advent of the personal computer has introduced a new dimension to business as well as personal dealings. Computers have entered the courtroom not only in the accounting area of law office operations but in document management, graphics, computer reconstruction of accidents, and a whole host of other applications. At least insofar as the legal profession is concerned, the computer has only scratched the surface of possible uses.

In the area of negotiations, the computer has been used to construct financial simulations, do damage analyses, and project future losses.

A more unusual application of the computer can be useful in another area of the negotiating process. At least one developer of software for computer applications has come up with a series of computer programs that apply psychological principles to human analysis. Developed by the Human Edge Software Corporation of Palo Alto, California, Mind Prober is a software program which allows you to rely upon your impressions of a person with whom you are dealing and express agreement or disagreement with a list of adjectives that potentially describes a person whom you wish to understand. Remembering that one of the most important aspects of successful negotiations is understanding your opponent and his or her needs, the ability to analyze and assess the personality variables of your opponent is invaluable.

In utilizing the Mind Prober type of assessment, you express agreement or disagreement with 75 different adjectives which describe an individual's personality. In effect, these adjectives focus on the needs of an individual as described in **§ 10.20**. For example, you would evaluate your opponent's personality in terms of these adjectives and their definitions:

Adjective	*Definition*
achieving	accomplishing, persevering, striving
defensive	protective, shielded, careful
innovative	creative, new, original
open minded	aware, unbiased, receptive
rigid	stiff, unchanging, inflexible
socially striving	seeking respectability

Once you have completed what is in effect the needs analysis of the individual, the computer provides to you a personality assessment of the individual with whom you are working. Although certainly it doesn't pretend to be the total answer to successful negotiating strategy or understanding your opponent, such an assessment provides additional information for you in the negotiating process.

CHAPTER 11

VOIR DIRE AND JURY INSTRUCTIONS

§ 11.1 Voir Dire Regarding Insurance

Given the environment in today's society regarding insurance companies, all lawyers must be attuned to the biases and prejudices of jurors in the context of questioning during the selection process. Thus, although it may be inappropriate to mention an insurance company, insurance coverage, or related issues during the presentation of the evidence, there is little doubt that it is, in most cases, a proper area of inquiry during the jury selection or voir dire process. Accordingly, you must be aware of a few of the available techniques and allowable bounds in this area.

In *Kiernan v. Von Schaik,* 347 F.2d 775 (3d Cir. 1965), the plaintiff appealed from a defense verdict in a personal injury action. The plaintiff claimed that the trial judge had committed an error in refusing to put five questions to prospective jurors on the voir dire. Three questions involved the jurors' connections with the insurance business and two questions asked whether the jurors had read any literature indicating a relationship between the amounts of a personal injury verdict and the increase in insurance premiums.

The United States Court of Appeals for the Third Circuit stated that questions about the jurors' relationship to the insurance industry were relevant in ascertaining bias, and exclusion of these questions was an error by the trial judge. However, the court found that two questions regarding the so-called insurance crisis were properly excluded. A survey of other jurisdictions reveals varying results focusing on this and related questions.

§ 11.2 —Alabama

A defendant appealed the trial court's order denying a new trial in a fraud action, claiming that the trial court erred in overruling the objection to the plaintiffs' question on voir dire whether any potential jurors' family members worked for an insurance company or any company connected with an insurance company. The appellate court held that the trial court correctly overruled the objection to the plaintiffs' question. Information about jurors' family members' connections with the insurance business is clearly material to the parties' right to peremptory strikes. The dissent in this case stated that the majority opinion changes the long-established rule in Alabama that counsel are restricted to asking whether potential jurors (or family members) are officers, stockholders, employees, servants, or agents of a named insurance company and not just any insurance company. *Alabama Power Co. v. Bonner,* 459 So. 2d 827 (Ala. 1984).

§ 11.3 —Arkansas

In an action arising out of an automobile collision, the defendant alleged on appeal that the trial court erred in permitting plaintiff's counsel to ask potential jurors whether they had liability insurance and whether they believed the size of jury verdicts in personal injury cases affects auto liability insurance premiums. All but two jurors indicated that they had seen advertisements by insurance companies aimed at jurors to the effect that the jurors themselves were affected by the verdicts they rendered, in that such verdicts resulted in increased premiums. The appellate court upheld the verdict, stating that the voir dire of the jury was "obviously" in good faith and, as such, was proper. Nothing in the record supported the defendant's claim that the voir dire inevitably indicated to jurors that the plaintiff had insurance. *King v. Westlake,* 246 Ark. 555, 572 S.W.2d 841 (1978).

§ 11.4 —California

The defendant appealed from plaintiff's verdict in a personal injury action. The defendant claimed that plaintiff's counsel committed prejudicial misconduct when, on voir dire, he questioned potential jurors about the source of money for the judgment, including whether any juror had an interest in an insurance company. The trial court during voir dire admonished the jury that the defendant was not insured and that insurance coverage was not a relevant factor in the trial. The appellate division upheld the verdict, stating that the trial court's admonishment cured any potential prejudice which may have occurred by reason of the plaintiff's questions. *Bigboy v. County of San Diego,* 15 Cal. App. 3d 397, 201 Cal. Rptr. 226 (1984).

§ 11.5 —Connecticut

The plaintiff appealed from a defendant's verdict in an action for personal injury. The plaintiff claimed that the trial court committed error in refusing to permit on jury selection the question, "Would you feel that you have any financial interest in this lawsuit, or might you in any way be affected by awarding damages to the plaintiff?" A series of articles to the effect that high plaintiff's verdicts were the cause of a rise in insurance premiums had appeared in the local papers around the time of the trial, but the plaintiff made no attempt to ask potential jurors whether they had read any such articles. The appellate court upheld the defendant's verdict, stating that there was no error in the trial court's ruling, in light of the fact that the plaintiff's questions as framed was vague and ambiguous. *Lowell v. Daley,* 148 Conn. 226, 169 A.2d 888 (1961).

§ 11.6 —Florida

The plaintiff pedestrian sued the driver of a car that hit him while he was standing near a road. At trial, defendant's counsel, during voir dire, asked the potential jurors whether the fact that his client had insurance coverage would affect their decision as to his client's potential liability. During closing arguments, defendant's counsel stated that the defendant should not have to pay for the plaintiff's injuries, because the accident was unavoidable. Plaintiff's counsel, in summation, stated: "He keeps talking about [the defendant] having to pay. It is the insurance company that will have to pay." The jury returned a verdict for $200,000, and the defendant had a $10,000 policy. The appellate court stated that defendant's counsel's comments were proper and a retaliatory response would not be justified if no improper statements were made by the opposing counsel. The court found the argument of plaintiff's counsel that the insurance company would have to pay might have adversely affected the jury verdict with respect to liability and damages, given that the evidence on the issue of liability was so close, and therefore reversed and remanded for a new trial on all issues. *Sislak v. Wilson,* 472 So. 2d 776 (Fla. 1985).

§ 11.7 —Indiana

On an appeal from a defendant's verdict in a personal injury action, the plaintiff claimed that the trial court erred by granting the defendant's motion in limine prohibiting the plaintiff from inquiring into prospective jurors' interest in any insurance company. The appellate court upheld the verdict, stating that a mere showing that the court improperly limited the scope of voir dire examination does not require reversal without a further showing that the plaintiff entered a proper objection or made an offer of proof, because the court has no means to measure the harm potentially suffered by the plaintiff without such a showing. The dissenting judge stated that the plaintiff's written objection did not waive an error of the trial court when it sustained the defendant's motion in limine, and that the trial court's error was sufficient to substantiate a reversal. *Rohrkaste v. City of Terre Haute,* 470 N.E.2d 738 (Ind. Ct. App. 1984).

§ 11.8 —Kentucky

During voir dire in a personal injury action, a prospective juror informed the court that a close relative of hers may have been an insurance adjustor whose company may have been involved in one of the accidents at issue in the case. On appeal from the plaintiff's verdict, the defendant assigned as error the trial court's refusal to have the case continued on the basis of this juror's statement. The appellate court upheld the verdict, stating that the innocuous mention of insurance by a prospective juror did not in any way deprive the defendant of a fair trial, and if there was any error, it was harmless. *Vanhook v. Stanford-Lincoln County Rescue Squad, Inc.,* 678 S.W.2d 797 (Ky. 1984).

§ 11.9 —Missouri

The defendant appealed from a verdict in a personal injury action, alleging that the trial court's denial of a mistrial was in error. The defendant moved for the mistrial following voir dire statements about insurance offered by a potential juror and the plaintiff's questions inquiring whether any jurors or their family members were insured with or employed by a particular insurance company. The appellate court upheld the verdict, stating that the trial court did not abuse its discretion in denying the mistrial and that mentioning a specific insurance company may have signaled to the jury that there was liability insurance in the case, "but that would be inevitable in any trial." *Schell v. Kiersey,* 674 S.W.2d 268 (Mo. 1984).

In another Missouri case, the plaintiff moved for a mistrial when defense counsel asked the jury panel on voir dire: "Do you all understand that the defendant in this case is not an insurance company—the defendant is Hofer, Inc." The trial court denied a mistrial but sustained the plaintiff's objection and instructed the jury to disregard the statement. The appellate court found no error in denying the mistrial and said the trial judge was in the best position to determine whether the issue was injected into the case in good or bad faith. The judgment was affirmed. *Smith v. Hofer, Inc.,* 701 S.W.2d 451 (Mo. 1985).

In a final Missouri example, the plaintiff appealed from a defendant's verdict in a medical malpractice action, claiming that the trial court erred in barring plaintiff's counsel from asking prospective jurors on voir dire if they or members of their families had financial interest in or were employed by the defendant's insurance company. The trial court had determined that the plaintiff had failed to demonstrate good faith for asking the insurance question, because the defendant's insurer was an association of hospitals which were self-insured and had no office or employees in the area. In upholding the verdict, the appellate court stated that the trial court did not abuse its discretion and the plaintiff failed to allege or suggest that she was prejudiced in any way by the trial court's ruling. *Skinner v. Sister of St. Mary's,* 686 S.W.2d 858 (Mo. 1985).

§ 11.10 —New Hampshire

During a trial for driving while intoxicated and driving without proof of financial responsibility, the court applied a blanket prohibition to defense counsel's request that the court ask potential jurors if any of them had ever been a victim of an automobile accident in which the parties involved were not insured or in a position to pay for damages. The defendant was convicted, and he appealed. The appellate division found that the trial court's refusal to allow such questioning was an abuse of its discretion, because the ruling denied the defendant his right to expose possible biases of prospective jurors. *State v. Goding,* 124 N.H. 781, 474 A.2d 580 (1984).

§ 11.11 —New York

The plaintiff appealed from an order granting the defendant's motion for a mistrial based upon remarks made by plaintiff's counsel during voir dire. The appellate court stated that "speaking generally, we believe that without undue emphasis on the subject the matter of dissemination through various news media of the impact of monetary awards in the negligence cases upon automobile liability insurance rates may be a proper subject for exploration upon voir dire examination of a jury panel." *Graham v. Waite,* 23 A.D.2d 628, 257 N.Y.S.2d 629 (1965).

§ 11.12 —North Carolina

The defendant manufacturer appealed from judgment for the plaintiff in a property damage action, claiming that the trial court committed prejudicial error in prohibiting the defendant from mentioning during voir dire that the plaintiff's insurer was the party plaintiff. In upholding the verdict, the appellate court stated that there was no prejudicial error in the ruling, even though the plaintiff's insurer's identity was admissible once the insurer was joined as a party plaintiff. In any event, all of the details of the insurance settlement were brought out on cross-examination of the plaintiffs, and the plaintiffs could have prosecuted the action alone. *Howard v. Smoky Mountain Enterprises, Inc.,* 76 N.C. App. 123, 332 S.E.2d 200 (1985).

§ 11.13 —Ohio

On voir dire, plaintiff's counsel questioned a juror about her employment with an insurance agency, and asked her further whether her employer provided insurance for the defendant. The defendant appealed, claiming as error the trial court's refusal of a motion for mistrial. The appellate court, while recognizing that the plaintiff's question regarding a specific insurance company was erroneous, found that it did not call for a mistrial because it should not have given rise to bias or prejudice so as to prevent a fair verdict. *Blay v. Hart Stores, Inc.,* No. 83-J-34 (Ohio Ct. App. 1984).

In another Ohio case, a plaintiff's verdict in a medical malpractice case was appealed when the defendant argued that the trial court erred in failing to grant a motion for a mistrial, based upon improper reference to insurance during plaintiff's voir dire. During voir dire, counsel for plaintiff questioned one juror about her husband's job at an insurance company and any potential bias she might have because of her husband's position. The appellate court upheld the verdict, stating that, given the nature of the case and the fact that the insurance questions were immediately followed by a cautionary instruction by the court, this was a proper area to explore on voir dire. *Wolfe v. Hawkes Hospital,* No. 84AP-1007 (Ohio Ct. App., Sept. 24, 1985).

§ 11.14 —Oregon

In an Oregon case, the concurring judge stated that the relatively slight prejudice to the defendant which could arise by reason of questions about the insurance industry is far outweighed by the probability of bias against the plaintiffs created by advertising campaigns by insurance companies. The majority felt that although the question was improper, it was not so prejudicial as to require reversal. *Johnson v. Hansen,* 289 P.2d 380 (Or. 1964).

§ 11.15 —South Dakota

During voir dire in a personal injury action, plaintiff's counsel questioned a prospective juror regarding her relationship with an insurance company while commenting, "insurance companies are always the defendants in these kinds of cases." Defense counsel moved for a mistrial, which was granted, when the trial court ruled that the questions were not asked in good faith. After verdict for the defendant, the plaintiff appealed from a court order taxing jury costs and attorneys' fees to plaintiff and plaintiff's counsel for causing two mistrials. The appellate court upheld the verdict, stating that, although it was proper to inquire whether a prospective juror has any interest in or affiliation with an insurance company, it was totally improper to state that insurance companies are always the defendant. The majority overruled the trial court's award of jury costs and attorneys' fees on the basis that the trial court did not have authority to award such costs, but two of the justices would have allowed the award to stand. *Lowe v. Steel Construction Co.,* 368 N.W.2d 610 (S.D. 1985).

§ 11.16 —Texas

The defendant appealed from a plaintiff's verdict in a wrongful death action. The defendant claimed that plaintiff's counsel's questioning of potential jurors about work relating to "claims" and reference to one defendant's "personal counsel" improperly informed the jury that one of the defendants was covered by liability insurance. The appellate court upheld the verdict, stating that the questioning of prospective jurors about their work related to claims was in good faith and did not create a reasonable inference that the defendant was insured. *Cavnar v. Quality Control Parking, Inc.,* 678 S.W.2d 548 (Tex. Ct. App. 1984).

§ 11.17 Voir Dire Questioning

In most personal injury actions, the selection of a jury is the key factor in the outcome of the case. Most state courts permit counsel to conduct questioning of the jury. In federal courts, however, the trial judge conducts the voir dire, and counsel may submit questions to the judge.

The voir dire submission which follows in **§ 11.18** is suitable for either use by counsel or submission to the court.

§ 11.18 Sample Voir Dire Proposal

PROPOSED VOIR DIRE OF DEFENDANT

(Defendant) submits the annexed proposed voir dire for the jury in the above-referenced action.

Respectfully submitted,

____

(Attorney)

PROPOSED VOIR DIRE EXAMINATION

1. Please state your name.
   a. What is your marital status?
   b. Do you have any children?
      (1) How many?
      (2) What are their ages?
2. Are you currently employed?
   a. By whom?
   b. What position do you hold with your current employer?
   c. How long have you worked for your current employer?
3. Are you or has any member of your family ever been licensed as a pilot?
   a. How is the individual who is or was a pilot related to you?
   b. Is he or she currently licensed?
   c. What types of aircraft does he or she fly?

4. Have you or has any member of your family ever been involved in any serious accidents involving an aircraft? If so, please elaborate.

5. Have you or has any member of your immediate family ever suffered any serious personal injury as a result of any accident?
   a. How is the individual who was involved in the accident related to you?
   b. Please explain briefly what occurred.
   c. Who was injured as a result of the accident?
   d. What was the extent of the injuries?
   e. Were any lawsuits filed as a result of the accident?
      (1) Who filed suit?
      (2) Whom did they sue?
      (3) What was the result of the case?

6. Have you or has any member of your family sustained or incurred any serious physical injury or illness?

a. If the injured person is a family member, what relation is he or she to you?

b. What is the nature of the illness or injury?

c. What was the type of illness or cause of the injury?

d. Do you or does your family member still suffer from the injury or illness?

e. Were you or was your family member unable to work?

f. For how long were you or was your family member unable to work?

7. Have you ever been on disability? For how long?

8. Approximately how many days have you been sick from work over the past three years?

9. What is the longest period you have not worked because of illness or physical injury?

a. What was the nature of the illness or injury?

10. Have you or has any member of your immediate family ever sued or been sued?

a. If so, when was this lawsuit brought?

b. Were you or was your family member the plaintiff or the defendant?

c. Please briefly describe the basis of the suit.

d. What was the outcome of the suit?

11. Have you ever served on a jury before?

a. When?

b. Was the case a criminal or civil matter?

c. Please briefly describe what the case was about.

d. What was the outcome of the case?

12. Do you have—from a hobby, profession or prior training—any knowledge of aviation, airplanes, or piloting? Please explain your connection with the subject and your interest in it.

13. Have you ever heard of (defendant) before?

a. If so, what have you heard?

b. Do you have any opinions or feelings about (defendant) or any individual who might be associated with (defendant)?

c. What are those opinions or feelings?

d. Do you think you could fairly assess evidence and not be swayed by your preexisting knowledge and views about (defendant)?

14. Have you ever flown on a small aircraft?

a. What do you think of them generally?

b. Do you believe that they try to operate safely?

c. What was your experience like?

15. Will you follow the law as given to you by the Court in its instructions, regardless of any sympathies you may feel for any of the parties?

16. Do you understand the difference between evidence relating to whether the defendants may be liable to the plaintiff for her injuries and evidence relating to the severity of the plaintiff's injuries?

17. Do you believe that you can fairly evaluate the evidence regarding whether the defendants in this case are liable for the plaintiff's injuries regardless of the extent of the plaintiff's injuries? Even when the injuries are very severe burns as depicted in these photographs? (Show photographs.)

18. Do you understand that the fact that the defendants in this lawsuit are being sued does not indicate that they have done anything wrong or that they are in fact liable for the plaintiff's injuries?

§ 11.19 Jury Instruction Techniques

One area of trial practice which seems frequently to be shortchanged in most trial practice books and courses is jury instructions. Experienced trial lawyers, however, know that the tactics and techniques which surround the instructions given by the judge to the jury immediately before they decide the case can be the most crucial part of the entire trial process.

Opening statements, the cross-examinations of witnesses, expert testimony, and closing arguments are highly visible and important parts of the trial, but each of these segments of the trial is presented by an attorney or a witness—that is, by someone other than the judge. The jury instructions, however, are presented by the judge, who is the authority figure in the courtroom. When the judge instructs the jury about the law they are to apply in deciding the case, he or she is not playing the role of an advocate. To the contrary, the judge is perceived as the living symbol of justice. The lawyers are being paid to advocate a position, as are the experts. Many witnesses are perceived as having a vested interest in the outcome of the case or, perhaps, as advocates of the position on behalf of which they are testifying.

In light of these facts and perceptions, the jury typically listens more closely to and weighs more heavily almost everything said to them by the judge, including the jury instructions. What they usually do not know, however, is that the jury instructions given to them are frequently the suggestions by counsel, oral argument to the court, and, in some respects, negotiation among all parties. In effect, the jury instructions being given to them by the judge are oftentimes more the product of counsel than of the court. However, since the court is the vehicle for conveying them, the jurors inevitably attach more weight to them than if they came from the lawyers.

Because the jury instruction process is so important, it is incumbent upon all attorneys to treat the process as providing an additional opportunity to persuade the jury of the rightness of their position. To help accomplish this task, several techniques are available to make the jury instruction process an effective trial tactic.

§ 11.20 Form Jury Instructions

When embarking on the process of drafting proposed jury instructions, the first place most attorneys turn is to the pattern jury instruction book appropriate for the particular court in which the case is pending or perhaps the kind of case, e.g., criminal or civil. All too frequently this is a serious mistake, because counsel will quite literally lift the pattern instructions out of the form book, perhaps have them retyped, and submit them to the court with a cover page and caption. As with many other boilerplate types of information used by lawyers (e.g., interrogatories), form jury instructions are prepared for no case in particular and, for the most part, they show it. Even to many lawyers, the language they typically use is convoluted, difficult to understand, and, considering the role they play in litigation, just as likely to confuse the jury as not.

Although certainly form jury instructions have a role to play in the trial process, this role is more properly to serve as a pattern against which customized instructions for your case should be prepared. In doing so, there are a number of guidelines which, if observed, will make your jury instructions more effective advocates of your position.

1. Avoid negative sentences. This is particularly true with respect to those which contain double negatives. For example, "The fact that the defendant did not testify on his own behalf is not to be used against him." Inevitably double negatives cause trouble to many people trying to understand them.
2. If you find yourself having to use single or double negatives, follow them up with affirmative explanatory sentences. For example, if you must have the instruction just given, consider using an explanatory sentence along the following lines: "Even though the defendant chose not to testify, the United States Constitution provides that a person cannot be required to testify against himself."
3. Personalize the instructions. For example, the "plaintiff" should be "Mary Smith," and the "defendant" should be "XYZ Corporation." Not only does this make the instructions more personal, but it also makes it easier for the jury to follow them and keep the parties straight.

4. Ambiguous words or phrases should be avoided. Remember, although lawyers may not consider something ambiguous, the jurors may find it difficult to understand, especially if it is written in "legalese." As a result, look for double meanings. For example, don't use "court" for "judge," "bar" for "prohibit," "counsel" for "lawyers," or "disregard" for "ignore." Unlike pleadings prepared for a judge, jury instructions must be prepared for nonlawyers.
5. Draft your instructions in a narrative format that permits them to be presented to the jury in a conversational style. You will find this approach to be far more conducive to understanding the jury than the choppy approach which results when form-type instructions are just strung together.
6. Request the judge to preinstruct the jury. This technique requires jury instructions to be submitted and ruled upon *prior* to opening statement. The great advantage to this approach is that it permits you to structure your opening statement in such a manner as to present the standards of law the jury will later hear repeated at the end of the case. Preinstructions should also include a summary of the case and perhaps the basic positions of each side. The obvious strength of including such statements is that the jury will have a far better ability to put the evidence in perspective as it is presented.
7. Always press to get rulings on jury instructions, at a minimum, prior to your closing argument. Absent such rulings, you will be at a substantial disadvantage in presenting your closing argument to the jury, because you cannot structure your closing argument around the law which is controlling.
8. If the jury instructions have been ruled upon prior to closing argument, use phraseology like "as the judge will tell you . . ." during your closing argument. Later, when the judge instructs the jury along the lines you have pointed out to them, you may be given the benefit of being perceived by several jurors as insightful.
9. Written jury instructions. One technique which some judges use in more complex cases involving lengthy jury instructions is to provide the jury with written copies of the jury instructions, along with special interrogatories, after the jury has been instructed orally. This is particularly effective when the jury instructions have been prepared in a narrative form. Another advantage of this approach is that, when there are multiple parties with different standards of proof or law applicable to each, giving the jurors "packages" of instructions provides them with a structured format for considering the case during deliberation and in reaching their decision.

From an overall perspective, more consideration given to the process of drafting and using jury instructions will pay substantial dividends in successful trial results. The use of jury instructions as part of the preinstruction process, as a checklist against which to measure your proofs and as elements incorporated into your closing argument, can be one of the most effective trial tactics you have available.

The form jury instructions and special verdict form in the next sections are the type which defense counsel may find useful, because they are adversarily slanted.

§ 11.21 Sample Form Jury Instructions

PROPOSED JURY INSTRUCTIONS AND SPECIAL VERDICT FORM OF DEFENDANT

Defendant submits the attached proposed jury instructions and special verdict form. Defendant reserves the right to submit additional jury instructions or change existing instructions depending upon the nature of any new issues that plaintiff may raise prior to or during trial, and depending on the Court's rulings on jury instructions and other legal issues.

Respectfully submitted,

____

(Attorney)

Note: If the jury instructions which you submit are lengthy, *always* include a table of contents to make the job of the judge easier.

TABLE OF CONTENTS

Verdict Not to Be Based on Sympathy, Bias, Guesswork, or Speculation

C. Instructions on Issues and Burdens of Proof
Issues and Allocation of Burdens of Proof
Standard of Proof—Definition of Greater Weight of the Evidence
Burden of Proof—Negligence
Burden of Proof—Contributory Negligence
Burden of Proof—Assumption of Risk
Burden of Proof—Employer/Employee Relationship

D. Instructions on Negligence Claims
Definition of Negligence
Fact of Accident Is Not Proof of Negligence
Definition of Gross Negligence
Definition of Willful and Wanton Negligence
Definition of Proximate Cause
Definition of Intervening Cause
Definition of Contributory Negligence
Contributory Negligence: Parties' Negligence Not Compared
Definition of Assumption of the Risk

E. Instructions on Employer/Employee Claims
Definition of Employer and Employee
Employer's Liability for Employee's Negligence
Definition of Scope of Employment
Definition of Independent Contractor
Test for Independent Contractor or Employee
Principal Not Liable for Acts of the Independent Contractor
Acts Not Considered to Be Inherently or Intrinsically Dangerous Activity

F. Instructions on Landlord/Tenant Relationship
Landlord's Duty upon Surrendering Control
Liability of Landlord upon Surrender of Control

G. Finding Instructions
Finding Instruction on Negligence Claims
Finding Instruction on Vicarious Liability

H. Instructions on Damages
Reasonable Proof for Damages
Duty to Mitigate Damages
Aggravation of Preexisting Condition
Punitive Damages
Definition of Common Law Actual Malice

I. Concluding Instruction
Verdict—"Allen Charge"

§ 11.22 —Opening Instructions

REQUESTED INSTRUCTION NO. _____

PRELIMINARY INSTRUCTIONS TO JURY

Members of the jury, your function in the trial of this case is to reach a verdict that is based solely on the evidence and the instructions of law which I will give you after all the evidence has been presented.

You are the triers of fact. You are to decide, after considering all the evidence presented, what happened—what the facts are—and you are to apply the facts you find to the instructions of law. You should use your common sense in considering the evidence, and you may draw reasonable inferences from the evidence.

My function as Judge is to preside over the trial: to rule on points of law and to instruct you on the law. It is our responsibility to see that this case is decided in accord with the facts and the law.

To begin this case, the lawyers may make an opening statement. In their opening statements, the lawyers may tell you what they expect the evidence to be. This should help you to understand the evidence as it is presented through the witnesses later and make you aware of conflicts and differences that may arise in the testimony. What the lawyers say is not evidence; you must not consider it as evidence.

After opening statements, you will hear and see the evidence.

The only evidence you may consider in reaching your verdict is what comes from witnesses who testify before you (or by deposition), from any exhibits presented, or from stipulations of counsel. If there is a stipulation, it will be explained when it is presented.

Each witness will be examined by the lawyer who calls him or her and may then be cross-examined by the lawyer for the other side. During the questioning of a witness, one lawyer may object to a question asked by the other. You must not consider this as an effort to keep something from you. It is the duty of the lawyer to object to a question at times if the lawyer believes it violates the rules of evidence, and it is my duty to rule upon such objection. This case—like all cases—must be tried in accord with the rules of evidence which have been developed over many years. These rules of evidence control what can be presented to a jury; their purpose is to protect the fairness and accuracy of the factfinding process in which you are engaged. Therefore, do not concern yourself with any objection or hold it against the side making the objection.

You must not consider any evidence that is stricken or that you are told to disregard.

You are the persons who have to decide what the facts are. If, while a witness is on the witness stand, you are unsure or uncertain as to what he or she said, or if you have any questions relating to the case which you think the witness may be able to answer, you may ask a question. I suggest that you wait until the lawyers have completed their questioning of the witness before you ask your question, because they may ask the same question. If you do have a question, when the lawyers have concluded their examination of the witness, let me know by raising your hand or speaking up.

If a juror asks a question which may be objectionable, the Court may want to have the jury leave the courtroom before ascertaining if there is any objection.

Please listen closely to each witness. Ordinarily, a witness will not be recalled to the stand simply because you missed something the witness said or did not understand what he or she said.

After all the evidence has been presented, then the instructions on the law will be prepared. You will then return to the courtroom, and I will read the instructions to you.

After I read the instructions, the lawyers make their closing arguments. In their closing arguments, the lawyers will refer to the testimony you have heard—but, here again, what they say is not evidence. Their statements are only their recollection of the testimony.

There will be occasional recesses during the trial. During these recesses, you must not discuss the case with anyone, including your fellow jurors, or go to the scene, or make any independent investigation, or receive any information about the case from the radio, television, or the newspapers.

Please keep an open mind as the evidence is presented. Remember that your job is to reach your verdict only after you have heard and considered all the evidence, the instructions of law, and the final arguments of the lawyers.

When you do retire to your jury room after the case has been submitted to you, you should first select a foreman and then exchange your views on the case with the other jurors fully and openly. All jurors should have the benefit of hearing the views and observations of the other members of the jury.

Your verdict must be unanimous.

The faithful and proper performance by you of your duty is vital to the administration of justice. I ask your complete attention to the case as it is presented.

SOURCE:

GIVEN ______________

REFUSED ______________

MODIFIED ______________

Note: Check local rules or local model jury instructions for source citations.

§ 11.23 —General Instructions

REQUESTED INSTRUCTION NO. _____

INTRODUCTORY INSTRUCTION

Now that you have heard the evidence, it becomes my duty to give you the instructions of the Court as to the law applicable to this case.

It is your duty as jurors to follow the law as I shall state it to you, and to apply that law to the facts as you find them from the evidence in the case. You are not to single out one instruction alone as stating the law, but must consider the instructions as a whole. Neither are you to be concerned with the wisdom of any rule of law stated by me.

Counsel have quite properly referred to some of the governing rules of law in their arguments. If, however, any difference appears to you between the law as stated by counsel and that stated by the Court in these instructions, you are of course to be governed by the Court's instructions.

Nothing I say in these instructions is to be taken as an indication that I have any opinion about the facts of the case, or what that opinion is. It is not my function to determine the facts, but rather yours.

You must perform your duties as jurors without bias or prejudice as to any party. The law does not permit you to be governed by sympathy, prejudice, or public opinion. All parties expect that you will carefully and impartially consider all of the evidence, follow the law as it is now being given to you, and reach a just verdict, regardless of the consequences.

Unless otherwise stated, the jury should consider each instruction given to apply separately and individually to the plaintiff and to each defendant in the case.

SOURCE:

GIVEN ______________

REFUSED ______________

MODIFIED ______________

REQUESTED INSTRUCTION NO. _____

ALL PERSONS EQUAL BEFORE THE LAW—ORGANIZATIONS

This case should be considered and decided by you as an action between persons of equal standing in the community, of equal worth, and holding the same or similar stations of life. A corporation is entitled to the same fair trial at your hands as a private individual. All persons, including corporations, partnerships, unincorporated associations, and other organizations, stand equal before the law, and are to be dealt with as equals in a court of justice.

SOURCE:

GIVEN ______________

REFUSED ______________

MODIFIED ______________

Note: This is an important instruction if you represent a corporation.

REQUESTED INSTRUCTION NO. _____

MULTIPLE DEFENDANTS

Although there are three defendants in this action, it does not follow from that fact alone that if one is liable, all are liable. Each defendant is entitled to a fair consideration of his own defense, and is not to be prejudiced by the fact, if it should become a fact, that you find against the other. Unless otherwise stated, all instructions given you govern the case as to each defendant.

SOURCE:

GIVEN _______________

REFUSED _______________

MODIFIED _______________

REQUESTED INSTRUCTION NO. _____

CREDIBILITY OF WITNESSES

You are the judges of the facts, the credibility of the witnesses, and the weight of the evidence. You may consider the appearance and manner of the witnesses on the stand, their intelligence, their opportunity for knowing the truth and for having observed the things about which they testified, their interest in the outcome of the case, their bias, and, if any have been shown, their prior inconsistent statements, or whether they have knowingly testified untruthfully as to any material fact in the case.

You may not arbitrarily disregard believable testimony of a witness. However, after you have considered all the evidence in the case, then you may accept or discard all or part of the testimony of a witness as you think proper.

You are entitled to use your common sense in judging any testimony. From these things and all the other circumstances of the case, you may determine which witnesses are more believable and weigh their testimony accordingly.

SOURCE:

GIVEN _______________

REFUSED _______________

MODIFIED _______________

REQUESTED INSTRUCTION NO. _____

EXPERT WITNESSES

In considering the weight to be given to the testimony of an expert witness, you should consider the basis for his or her opinion and the manner by which the expert witness arrived at it and whether all of the material facts that he or she relied on have been proved.

SOURCE:

GIVEN _______________

REFUSED _______________

MODIFIED _______________

REQUESTED INSTRUCTION NO. _____

SCIENTIFIC AUTHORITY NOT EVIDENCE

An expert witness has been asked if he agreed or disagreed with the opinion of an authority whom the witness recognized as a standard authority in the field. The only purpose for which this evidence is permitted is as a test of the knowledge and accuracy of the expert witness. It is not proof that what was written in the authority is true.

SOURCE:

GIVEN _______________

REFUSED _______________

MODIFIED _______________

REQUESTED INSTRUCTION NO. _____

PARTY BOUND BY OWN TESTIMONY

When one of the parties testifies unequivocally to facts within his or her own knowledge, those statements of fact and the necessary inferences from them are binding upon the testifying party. He or she cannot rely on other evidence in conflict with his or her own testimony to strengthen his or her case.

However, you must consider the testifying party's testimony as a whole, and you must consider a statement made in one part of his or her testimony in the light of any explanation or clarification made elsewhere in that testimony.

SOURCE:

GIVEN ______________

REFUSED ______________

MODIFIED ______________

Note: Remember, you will not generally win a case on cross-examination and not direct examination. After all, your witnesses are supposed to do well on direct examination. That is what this instruction points out.

REQUESTED INSTRUCTION NO. _____

CIRCUMSTANTIAL EVIDENCE

Any fact that may be proved by direct evidence may be proved by circumstantial evidence; that is, you may draw all reasonable and legitimate inferences and deductions from the evidence.

SOURCE:

GIVEN ______________

REFUSED ______________

MODIFIED ______________

REQUESTED INSTRUCTION NO. _____

LIMITED ADMISSIBILITY—PRIOR INCONSISTENT STATEMENTS

During the trial, evidence was introduced that a witness had previously made a written statement or given testimony that was inconsistent with his or her testimony at this trial. The only purpose for which that evidence was admitted was its bearing on the witness's credibility. It is not proof that what the witness may have said earlier is true.

SOURCE:

GIVEN ______________

REFUSED ______________

MODIFIED ______________

Note: Always include a jury instruction which addresses the use of documentary evidence by the jury.

REQUESTED INSTRUCTION NO. _____

REJECTED AND STRICKEN EVIDENCE

You must not consider any matter that was rejected or stricken by the Court. It is not evidence and should be disregarded.

You must also not infer from any rulings on the admission of evidence or on motions made with respect to the applicable law, or from anything I have said during the course of the trial, that I hold any views for or against any of the parties to this lawsuit. Any views of mine, in any event, would be totally irrelevant, since it is your recollection of the evidence and your determination of the issues of fact which control.

SOURCE:

GIVEN _____________

REFUSED _____________

MODIFIED _____________

Note: An instruction such as this is of doubtful value, particularly when given at the close of the case. Always request a cautionary instruction at the time opposing counsel makes an objectionable statement.

REQUESTED INSTRUCTION NO. _____

REFERENCE TO AMOUNT SUED FOR IS NOT EVIDENCE

Any statement of counsel for the plaintiff referring to the amount sued for is not evidence in this case; you should not consider it in arriving at the amount of your verdict, if any.

SOURCE:

GIVEN _____________

REFUSED _____________

MODIFIED _____________

Note: If you are representing the defendant, always request this instruction so the jury does not place too much weight on the amount plaintiff's counsel's request for damages.

REQUESTED INSTRUCTION NO. ______

VERDICT NOT TO BE BASED ON SYMPATHY, BIAS, GUESSWORK, OR SPECULATION

You must not base your verdict in any way upon sympathy, bias, guesswork, or speculation. Your verdict must be based solely upon the evidence and instructions of the court.

SOURCE:

GIVEN ________________

REFUSED ________________

MODIFIED ________________

§ 11.24 —Instructions on Issues and Burdens of Proof

REQUESTED INSTRUCTION NO. ______

ISSUES AND ALLOCATION OF BURDENS OF PROOF

Your verdict must be based on the facts as you find them and on the law contained in all of these instructions.

The issues in this case are:

(1) Were the defendants negligent?

(2) If they were negligent, was their negligence a proximate cause of the airplane accident at issue in this lawsuit?

On these issues the plaintiff has the burden of proof.

(3) Was the plaintiff negligent?

(4) If she was negligent, was her negligence a proximate cause of the airplane accident at issue in this lawsuit?

(5) Did the plaintiff assume the consequences of a known risk?

On these issues the defendants have the burden of proof.

(6) In operating ________________ Airport, did ____________ Aviation act as an employee of ________________?

(7) In operating ________________ Airport, did ____________ Aviation act as an independent contractor of ________________, and, if so, did ____________ Aviation engage in an intrinsically or inherently

dangerous activity in operating the airport that proximately caused the airplane accident and resulting damages to plaintiff?

(8) If the plaintiff is entitled to recover, what is the amount of her damages?

On these issues the plaintiff has the burden of proof.

Your decision on these issues that I have briefly set out for you must be governed by these instructions.

SOURCE:

GIVEN ________________

REFUSED ________________

MODIFIED ________________

Note: An instruction regarding burden of proof is always crucial, particularly if you are a defendant. Although the jurors may not immediately understand the concept of burden of proof, they typically will understand the concept if it is applied for them vis-à-vis the facts. The instructions which follow focus on burden of proof issues.

REQUESTED INSTRUCTION NO. _____

STANDARD OF PROOF—DEFINITION OF GREATER WEIGHT OF THE EVIDENCE

When a party has the burden of proof on an issue, then he or she must prove that issue by the greater weight of all the evidence. This is sometimes called the preponderance of the evidence. It is that evidence which you find more convincing. The testimony of one witness whom you believe can be the greater weight of the evidence.

SOURCE:

GIVEN ________________

REFUSED ________________

MODIFIED ________________

REQUESTED INSTRUCTION NO. _____

BURDEN OF PROOF—NEGLIGENCE

The plaintiff has the burden of proving by the greater weight of the evidence that the defendants were negligent and that the defendants' negligence proximately caused the accident and any of the injuries to the plaintiff. Plaintiff also has the burden of proving by the greater weight of the evidence that the defendants were grossly negligent or willfully or wantonly negligent to obtain any punitive damages in this case. As you were instructed earlier, negligence may be shown by any of the defendants' evidence or by the plaintiff's evidence.

SOURCE:

GIVEN _______________

REFUSED _______________

MODIFIED _______________

REQUESTED INSTRUCTION NO. _____

BURDEN OF PROOF—CONTRIBUTORY NEGLIGENCE

When the defendants claim contributory negligence as a defense, they have the burden of proving by the greater weight of the evidence that the plaintiff was negligent and that her negligence was a proximate cause of the plaintiff's injuries. Contributory negligence may be shown by the defendants' evidence or by the plaintiff's evidence.

SOURCE:

GIVEN _______________

REFUSED _______________

MODIFIED _______________

REQUESTED INSTRUCTION NO. _____

BURDEN OF PROOF—ASSUMPTION OF RISK

Where the defendants claim assumption of the risk as a defense, they have the burden of proving by the greater weight of the evidence that the plaintiff fully appreciated the nature and the extent of a known danger; that the plaintiff voluntarily exposed herself to it; and that the plaintiff was injured as a result of the danger assumed. Assumption of the risk may be shown by any of the defendants' evidence or by the plaintiff's evidence.

SOURCE:

GIVEN _______________

REFUSED _______________

MODIFIED _______________

REQUESTED INSTRUCTION NO. _____

BURDEN OF PROOF—EMPLOYER/EMPLOYEE RELATIONSHIP

The plaintiff has the burden of proving by the greater weight of the evidence that ____________ Aviation was an employee of ______________, that __________ Aviation was negligent while acting within the scope of its employment, and that this negligence proximately caused damage to the plaintiff.

SOURCE:

GIVEN ____________

REFUSED ____________

MODIFIED ____________

§ 11.25 —Instructions on Negligence Claims

REQUESTED INSTRUCTION NO. _____

DEFINITION OF NEGLIGENCE

Negligence is the failure to use ordinary care. Ordinary care is the care a reasonable person would have used under the circumstances of this case.

SOURCE:

GIVEN ____________

REFUSED ____________

MODIFIED ____________

REQUESTED INSTRUCTION NO. _____

FACT OF ACCIDENT IS NOT PROOF OF NEGLIGENCE

The fact that there was an accident and that the plaintiff was injured does not, of itself, entitle the plaintiff to recover.

The plaintiff has the burden of proving by the greater weight of the evidence that the defendants were negligent and that their negligence caused the plaintiff's injuries.

SOURCE:

GIVEN _______________

REFUSED _______________

MODIFIED _______________

Note: This is an important instruction which all defense counsel should ensure is given, because it will tend to disabuse some of the jurors of a mistaken notion about liability. The same is true of the several instructions which follow.

REQUESTED INSTRUCTION NO. _____

DEFINITION OF GROSS NEGLIGENCE

"Gross negligence" is that degree of negligence which shows such indifference to others as constitutes an utter disregard of caution amounting to a complete neglect of the safety of another person. It is such negligence as would shock fair-minded people, although it is something less than willful recklessness.

SOURCE:

GIVEN _______________

REFUSED _______________

MODIFIED _______________

REQUESTED INSTRUCTION NO. _____

DEFINITION OF WILLFUL AND WANTON NEGLIGENCE

"Willful and wanton negligence" is acting intentionally in disregard of another person's rights or acting with a reckless indifference to the consequences to another person when the defendant is aware of his conduct and is also aware, from his knowledge of existing circumstances and conditions, that his conduct would probably result in injury to another.

SOURCE:

GIVEN _______________

REFUSED _______________

MODIFIED _______________

REQUESTED INSTRUCTION NO. _____

DEFINITION OF PROXIMATE CAUSE

A proximate cause of an accident, injury, or damage is a cause which in natural and continuous sequence, unbroken by an efficient intervening cause, produces the accident, injury, or damage. It is a cause without which the accident, injury, or damage would not have occurred. There may be more than one proximate cause of an injury.

SOURCE:

GIVEN ______________

REFUSED ______________

MODIFIED ______________

REQUESTED INSTRUCTION NO. _____

DEFINITION OF INTERVENING CAUSE

An intervening cause is an independent event, not reasonably foreseeable, that completely breaks the connection between the defendant's negligent act and the plaintiff's injury. An intervening cause breaks the chain of events so that the defendant's original negligent act is not a proximate cause of the plaintiff's injury in the slightest degree.

If you believe from the greater weight of the evidence that the defendants were negligent and that such negligence created a situation of potential danger, but that a person not a party to this lawsuit—a third party, for example—became aware, or by the exercise of ordinary care should have been aware, of the existence of such situation of potential danger, and that thereafter the third party, by an independent intervening act of negligence, brought about the accident, and that the defendants in the exercise of ordinary care could not reasonably have foreseen such intervening negligent act of the third party, then the situation of danger created by the defendants' negligence became merely a circumstance of the accident but not a proximate cause thereof, and you shall return your verdict in favor of the defendants.

SOURCE:

GIVEN ______________

REFUSED ______________

MODIFIED ______________

Note: This is another crucial instruction which defense counsel should insure is given.

REQUESTED INSTRUCTION NO. _____

DEFINITION OF CONTRIBUTORY NEGLIGENCE

Contributory negligence is the failure to act as a reasonable person would have acted for her own safety under the circumstances of this case.

SOURCE:

GIVEN _____________

REFUSED _____________

MODIFIED _____________

Note: Affirmative defenses should always be addressed, whether you are representing plaintiff or defendant. The burden of proof relative to them must be addressed as well.

REQUESTED INSTRUCTION NO. _____

CONTRIBUTORY NEGLIGENCE: PARTIES' NEGLIGENCE NOT COMPARED

If you find from the greater weight of the evidence that the plaintiff and any of the defendants were negligent and that their negligence proximately contributed to the accident, you may not compare the negligence of the parties. Any negligence of the plaintiff which was a proximate cause of the accident will bar the plaintiff from recovering in this case.

SOURCE:

GIVEN _____________

REFUSED _____________

MODIFIED _____________

REQUESTED INSTRUCTION NO. _____

DEFINITION OF ASSUMPTION OF THE RISK

If you find by the greater weight of the evidence that the plaintiff fully understood the nature and extent of a known danger, and if she voluntarily exposed herself to it, she assumed the risk of injuring herself from that danger. The plaintiff cannot recover for injuries that proximately resulted from assuming the risk of a known danger.

SOURCE:

GIVEN ______________

REFUSED ______________

MODIFIED ______________

§ 11.26 —Instructions on Employer/Employee Claims

REQUESTED INSTRUCTION NO. _____

DEFINITION OF EMPLOYER AND EMPLOYEE

An employer is a person who has the right to control the way his employee does his work.

An employee is the person whom the employer has a right to control in the way he does his work.

SOURCE:

GIVEN ______________

REFUSED ______________

MODIFIED ______________

Note: Whenever you have an employer-employee relationship, jury instructions must clarify that relationship and the ways in which it can give rise to liability. This instruction and the ones which follow address this issue.

REQUESTED INSTRUCTION NO. _____

EMPLOYER'S LIABILITY FOR EMPLOYEE'S NEGLIGENCE

An employer is liable for all damages caused by the negligence of his employee while acting within the scope of his employment.

If you believe from the evidence that defendant __________ Aviation was an employee of defendant ________________, and that at the time of the accident __________ Aviation was then going about its business and acting within the scope of its employment, then any negligence is chargeable to ________________.

If you further believe from the evidence and the other instructions of the Court that __________ Aviation was negligent and that any such negligence was a proximate cause of the collision, then (unless the plaintiff was guilty of negligence proximately contributing to cause the collision) you shall find your verdict in favor of the plaintiff.

SOURCE:

GIVEN ___________

REFUSED ___________

MODIFIED ___________

REQUESTED INSTRUCTION NO. _____

DEFINITION OF SCOPE OF EMPLOYMENT

An act is within the scope of employment if it is incidental to the employer's business and is done to further the employer's interest. If an employee departs so far from his or her duties that the employee's acts are no longer for his or her employer's benefit, then the acts are not within the scope of employment.

SOURCE:

GIVEN _______________

REFUSED _______________

MODIFIED _______________

REQUESTED INSTRUCTION NO. _____

DEFINITION OF INDEPENDENT CONTRACTOR

An independent contractor is a person who is employed to produce a specific result but who is not subject to the control of the employer as to the way he brings about that result.

SOURCE:

GIVEN _______________

REFUSED _______________

MODIFIED _______________

Note: Always clarify the status of an independent contractor versus an employee. The risk in failing to do so is that the jury may improperly impose liability.

REQUESTED INSTRUCTION NO. _____

TEST FOR INDEPENDENT CONTRACTOR OR EMPLOYEE

If you believe from the evidence under the lease between the defendants that _______________ had the right to prescribe not only what the results of the work should be, but also to direct the means and methods by which ___________ Aviation should do the work, then ___________ Aviation was an employee of _______________, and in such event the liability of _______________, if any, is governed by the other instructions of the Court.

SOURCE:

GIVEN ______________

REFUSED ______________

MODIFIED ______________

REQUESTED INSTRUCTION NO. _____

PRINCIPAL NOT LIABLE FOR ACTS OF THE INDEPENDENT CONTRACTOR

A person who hires an independent contractor is not liable for his actions. However, if the work given the independent contractor was unlawful, a nuisance, or inherently dangerous, the employer is liable for injuries arising out of that work.

If you believe from the evidence under the lease between defendants _______________ and ___________ Aviation that _______________ had the right to specify the results of the work only, and that ___________ Aviation could adopt such means and methods as it chose to accomplish those results, then _______________ Aviation was an independent contractor and ____________________ would not be responsible for any negligence of ___________ Aviation, in which event you should return your verdict in favor of _______________.

SOURCE:

GIVEN ______________

REFUSED ______________

MODIFIED ______________

REQUESTED INSTRUCTION NO. _____

ACTS NOT CONSIDERED TO BE INHERENTLY OR INTRINSICALLY DANGEROUS ACTIVITY

An activity is not ultrahazardous or inherently or intrinsically dangerous if it is of such a character that, if properly done, no injurious consequences arise.

SOURCE:

GIVEN _______________

REFUSED _______________

MODIFIED _______________

Note: This instruction is crucial whenever an activity of this type is involved. Jurors must be made to understand the nature of such activities and the way in which the law treats them.

§ 11.27 —Instructions on Landlord/Tenant Relationship

REQUESTED INSTRUCTION NO. _____

LANDLORD'S DUTY UPON SURRENDERING CONTROL

A landlord who knows that a dangerous condition exists has a duty to warn the tenant about it before the tenant enters into possession. The landlord does not have this duty when the condition is open and obvious or if the tenant knows of the condition or should have discovered it by making a reasonable inspection.

If a landlord fails to perform this duty, then he is negligent.

SOURCE:

GIVEN _______________

REFUSED _______________

MODIFIED _______________

Note: Always clarify the landlord/tenant relationship. This is an area which jurors can relate to and which must be addressed.

REQUESTED INSTRUCTION NO. _____

LIABILITY OF LANDLORD UPON SURRENDER OF CONTROL

Where the landlord surrenders control of the premises to his tenant, he is not liable to the tenant or to the tenant's invitees for defects known to the tenant, or which the tenant could have discovered by reasonable inspection, unless the landlord made a warranty of the condition of the premises or fraudulently concealed known defects.

SOURCE:

GIVEN _____________

REFUSED _____________

MODIFIED _____________

§ 11.28 —Finding Instructions

REQUESTED INSTRUCTION NO. _____

FINDING INSTRUCTION ON NEGLIGENCE CLAIMS

You shall find your verdict for the plaintiff and against Defendant A if the plaintiff has proved by the greater weight of the evidence that:

(1) Defendant A was negligent; and that

(2) Defendant A's negligence was the sole proximate cause of the plaintiff's accident and damages.

You shall find your verdict for the plaintiff and against Defendant B if the plaintiff has proved by the greater weight of the evidence that:

(1) Defendant B was negligent; and that

(2) Defendant B's negligence was the sole proximate cause of the plaintiff's accident and damages.

You shall find your verdict for the plaintiff and against Defendant C if the plaintiff has proved by the greater weight of the evidence that:

(1) Defendant C was negligent; and that

(2) Defendant C's negligence was the sole proximate cause of the plaintiff's accident and damages.

You shall find your verdict for the plaintiff and against two or more defendants if the plaintiff has proved by the greater weight of the evidence that:

(1) two or more defendants were negligent; and that

(2) the negligence of two or more defendants was the sole proximate cause of the plaintiff's accident and damages.

You shall find your verdict for any or all defendants if:

(1) as to that defendant, the plaintiff has failed to prove either negligence or proximate cause; or

(2) you find by the greater weight of the evidence that the plaintiff was contributorily negligent and that her contributory negligence was a proximate cause of the accident; or

(3) you find by the greater weight of the evidence that the plaintiff assumed the consequences of a known risk.

SOURCE:

GIVEN ______________

REFUSED ______________

MODIFIED ______________

Note: Special interrogatories should almost always be used, because they force the jurors to focus upon the issues at hand. In addition, they assist counsel in better structuring an appeal. Always request that the judge give the jury instructions in written form.

REQUESTED INSTRUCTION NO. _____

FINDING INSTRUCTION ON VICARIOUS LIABILITY

You shall find your verdict for the plaintiff if she has proved by the greater weight of the evidence that:

(1) __________ Aviation was negligent; and that

(2) __________ Aviation was an employee or agent of ______________; or that

(3) ____________________ Aviation was an independent contractor of ________________ and engaged in an intrinsically or inherently dangerous activity in operating the airport; and that

(4) __________ Aviation's negligence was the sole proximate cause of plaintiff's accident and resultant damages.

You shall find your verdict for ________________ if:

(1) the plaintiff failed to prove by the greater weight of the evidence the elements above with __________ Aviation being proved to be either an employee or agent of ______________, or an independent contractor that engaged in an intrinsically or inherently dangerous activity; or if

(2) the defendants have proved by the greater weight of the evidence that the plaintiff was contributorily negligent and that her contributory negligence was a proximate cause of the accident; or if

(3) the defendants have proved by the greater weight of the evidence that the plaintiff assumed the consequences of a known risk.

SOURCE:

GIVEN ____________

REFUSED ____________

MODIFIED ____________

Note: This type of instruction helps direct the jury in the decision making process and focuses them on the issues. It should always be prepared as one of the last instructions to be given. Generally, the more damage instructions given to the jurors, the more their attention will be focused on damages and the greater the likelihood of a damages award.

§ 11.29 —Instructions on Damages

REQUESTED INSTRUCTION NO. _____

REASONABLE PROOF FOR DAMAGES

The burden is on the plaintiff to prove by the greater weight of the evidence each item of damages he claims and to prove that each item was caused by the defendants' negligence. She is not required to prove the exact amount of her damages, but she must show sufficient facts and circumstances to permit you to make a reasonable estimate of each item. If the plaintiff fails to do so, then she cannot recover for that item.

SOURCE:

GIVEN ____________

REFUSED ____________

MODIFIED ____________

Note: Damages are an important part of all jury instructions. Instruction on damages should be prepared so as to represent the view of the law most favorable to your client.

REQUESTED INSTRUCTION NO. _____

DUTY TO MITIGATE DAMAGES

The plaintiff has a duty to minimize her damages. If you find that the plaintiff did not act reasonably to minimize her damages and that, as a result, they increased, then she cannot recover the amount by which they increased.

SOURCE:

GIVEN ______________

REFUSED ______________

MODIFIED ______________

REQUESTED INSTRUCTION NO. _____

AGGRAVATION OF PREEXISTING CONDITION

If you find that the plaintiff had a condition before the accident that was aggravated as a result of the accident or that the preexisting condition made the injury she received in the accident more severe or more difficult to treat, then if you find your verdict for the plaintiff, she may recover for the aggravation and for the increased severity or difficulty of treatment, but she is not entitled to recover for the preexisting condition.

SOURCE:

GIVEN ______________

REFUSED ______________

MODIFIED ______________

REQUESTED INSTRUCTION NO. _____

PUNITIVE DAMAGES

If you find that the plaintiff is entitled to be compensated for her damages, and if you further believe by the greater weight of the evidence that the defendants acted with actual malice toward the plaintiff or acted under circumstances amounting to a willful and wanton disregard of the plaintiff's rights, then you may also award punitive damages to the plaintiff to punish the defendants for their actions and to serve as an example to prevent others from acting in a similar way.

If you choose to award punitive damages, you must state separately in your verdict the amount you allow as compensatory damages and the amount you allow as punitive damages.

SOURCE:

GIVEN _______________

REFUSED _______________

MODIFIED _______________

Note: Punitive damage standards vary greatly from state to state. Check your state and local law carefully. From a defense perspective, avoid instructions such as this, if possible, because they suggest a punitive award. Always move for a severance as a defendant.

REQUESTED INSTRUCTION NO. _____

DEFINITION OF COMMON LAW ACTUAL MALICE

"Actual malice" is a sinister or corrupt motive such as hatred, personal spite, ill will, or a desire to injure the plaintiff.

SOURCE:

GIVEN _______________

REFUSED _______________

MODIFIED _______________

§ 11.30 —Concluding Instruction

REQUESTED INSTRUCTION NO. _____

VERDICT—"ALLEN CHARGE"

As you have been told, your verdict must be unanimous. If you can possibly reach a verdict, it is your duty to do so. You should listen to the views and opinions of your fellow jurors with fairness and candor, and you should give consideration to what they say. However, you must decide the case for yourself, and you should reach an agreement only if it can be done without sacrificing your individual judgment. During the course of your deliberations, each of you, whether in the majority or the minority, should not hesitate to reexamine your own views and change your opinion if you are convinced it was wrong. No juror, however, should give up his or her honest opinion as to the evidence solely because of the opinion of fellow jurors or for the mere purpose of returning a verdict.

If you can reach a decision without surrendering your conscientious opinion, it is your duty to do so.

Please return to the jury room and give the matter your further consideration.

Thank you.

SOURCE:

GIVEN ______________

REFUSED ______________

MODIFIED ______________

CHAPTER 12

OPENING STATEMENTS

§ 12.1 Introduction

In court, your first experience with what can be considered unfair tactics is usually during an opening statement. The opening statement is one of the two parts of a trial during which you or your opponent are the only individuals in the spotlight. There are no witnesses or pieces of evidence before the jury or the judge with whom or which you must compete for attention, and so anything you do during an opening statement receives that much more attention because the attention is focused.

Before turning to particular types of unfair techniques and how to combat them, it is important that you realize the nature of an opening statement: what it is and, perhaps more important, what it is not.

In general, an opening statement should accomplish several things. It must inform the judge and jury of what your evidence will prove and what your case will establish. It should set a theme. The opening statement should explain and preview the evidence so the jury understands what is about to occur. In addition, the opening statement should define terms and concepts which the jury will encounter and, when appropriate, admit facts which are essential to the case or, when the facts are adverse, which require admission in order to minimize the damage they do to your side.

More important is what an opening statement is not and what it should not do. An opening statement is not an argument, and so it should not argue the facts or the law. It is in this area that you will find the most abuse by opposing counsel during opening statements.

§ 12.2 Statements versus Arguments

An opening statement in its purest form is just that—a statement, distinguished from an argument directed at advocating or persuading a particular point of view. The opening statement is supposed to inform and explain things but not argue them. Unfortunately, the line between stating and arguing is so thin and so blurred that it is easy to step over it inadvertently. More important, a well-crafted opening statement can step over the line and become an argument without ever alerting you to the fact that your opponent has stopped stating facts and is now arguing them.

As a rule of thumb, the difference between a statement and an argument for purposes of openings and closings has virtually nothing to do with the substance of what is said but rather is a function of how it is said. In general, three things distinguish statements from arguments. First is the distinction between what the evidence "will prove" and what the evidence "has proved." If your opponent starts to take the approach during an opening statement of presenting facts without qualifying them with an assertion that this is what the evidence will prove, you should note an objection, because this is a misleading tactic to take before a jury. One favored technique is to make a blanket statement at the outset of one side's reaction of facts that the evidence "will prove the following things" and thereafter never repeat that statement. This is clearly capable of being misleading, and is a tactic to which you should consider objecting.

A second distinction between the opening statement and the closing argument has to do with tone of voice and is, in large measure, the factor which most distinguishes statements from arguments. You should listen carefully to the words being spoken by your opponent and isolate the tone of voice. Statements which are clearly argumentative, presented in a very low-keyed, nonaggressive, and nonargumentative tone of voice, will often fail to evoke an objection from you, because your aural senses are not offended. This is not to say that the statements are any less argumentative or any less objectionable. Your opponent has simply eliminated some of the clues which would have alerted you to the fact that an argument is being made as distinguished from a statement. The best way to guard against becoming a victim of this tactic is to be wary of soft-spoken advocates.

Finally, try to be aware of the inevitable "red flag," alerting you to something which is about to occur or which is actually occurring that is probably improper under the circumstances. Tone of voice can be such a red flag. When your opponent's voice starts to take on an argumentative or louder tone, this should alert you to the fact that an impropriety is probably occurring to which you will want to object.

On occasion, you may find that your opponent has a personal characteristic which acts as a red flag. For example, you may find that prior to doing something which is probably improper your opponent has a habit of looking at you or using a certain word or phrase. Such things are done almost unconsciously. By paying careful attention to the personal characteristics and mannerisms of your opponent, you will learn to recognize these red flags and protect yourself from the tactics which they mark. You might be well advised for general background purposes to read any one of the many available books on body language. By recognizing the way a human being speaks without words, you will find yourself anticipating the words about to be spoken and be better prepared to turn unfair tactics upon their user.

§ 12.3 Reserving Opening Statements

A perfectly legitimate defense tactic is to reserve an opening statement. In the normal course of things, an opening statement is made by both sides at the beginning of the case. The defendant generally has an option to reserve its opening statement until the conclusion of the presentation of the plaintiff's evidence and prior to commencement of its own presentation.

Two points should be noted in connection with reserving opening statements. First, when representing a plaintiff and confronted with a defendant who has reserved an opening statement, you may find yourself susceptible to being severely prejudiced by a deftly prepared and presented opening statement made at the conclusion of your evidence. Keep in mind that defense counsel has had the benefit of hearing and cross-examining your case. Properly prepared, an opening statement delivered under such circumstances can be argumentative and more in the nature of a closing argument. You may find your opponent responding to your evidentiary presentation rather than stating what his or her evidentiary presentation will be during the defense portion of the case. If this is done in a nonargumentative fashion, it will not sound like an argument but will seem like a simple statement of the case.

When your opponent uses this tactic, you should consider making an objection based, not on the fact that the opening statement is argumentative, but on the fact that it is not stating the evidence to be presented by the defendant but is instead a statement in response to the plaintiff's evidence. Thus, the "opening statement" is improperly and unfairly in the nature of a closing argument or rebuttal.

Second, the point to be considered by defense counsel who has reserved an opening statement is to avoid an ambush by the plaintiff's attorney during the presentation of your evidence. You are particularly susceptible to such an ambush as defense counsel when you have reserved an opening statement and the jury has had nothing to measure the plaintiff's evidence against, because you have not presented your theory of the case or the evidence that you expect to present. In order to avoid being prejudiced in these circumstances, you should request an instruction from the court regarding your having reserved the opening statement. One such instruction might be as follows:

> Ladies and gentlemen of the jury, you are about to hear the opening statement made by plaintiff's counsel. The purpose of this opening statement is so that the lawyers can present to you what they expect the evidence will prove and, in effect, preview the case. Each counsel has the right to make an opening statement. However, defense counsel has the right to reserve an opening statement. By this I mean that defense counsel has the right to make an opening statement after the plaintiff has presented its evidence and prior to the defense putting on its case. Defense counsel in this case has exercised that right and reserved his opening statement. As a result, once the plaintiff has completed its opening statement the plaintiff will call its first witness and you will not at that time hear the defense opening statement. Rather you will hear it after the plaintiff has presented all of its evidence. You should keep an open mind and remember that there are two sides to this lawsuit.

You should also consider requesting a similar, shorter instruction at the conclusion of the plaintiff's opening statement and prior to the calling of the plaintiff's first witness. Such an instruction might go as follows:

> Remember, ladies and gentlemen of the jury, the defense has reserved its opening statement and you will hear that presentation at the conclusion of the plaintiff's case. You should give no greater or less weight to the plaintiff's evidence in light of the fact that the defense has reserved its opening statement.

Remember, as a defense attorney you may have sound reasons for reserving your opening statement. However, do not subject yourself to any speculation in the minds of the jurors regarding why you have not presented an opening statement and thereby lend additional weight to your opponent's case. One way to avoid this is to insure that the jurors clearly understand what it means to reserve an opening statement and that they will in fact hear your opening statement at a later point.

§ 12.4 Broken Promises

Many of the tactics used during opening statements are verbal in nature. By this I mean that your opponent will use language so as to unfairly prejudice your case, unfairly advantage his or her case, or put you on the defensive. The comments made during an opening statement may not be substantive in the context of the case but merely verbal devices with a purpose of challenging you before the jury; in the event you accept the challenge but cannot deliver, you will lose standing and credibility before the jury.

One essential premise of such verbal techniques is that they are not and should not be confined in their effect to the context in which you are using them. An opening statement does not end when you sit down. Rather, the opening statement really ends during the closing argument when you tie that argument into the overall case and refer back to the opening statement. This is best illustrated by the widely recognized fact that your cross-examination of any witness is completed not during the questioning of the witness but rather during your closing argument.

If you approach the opening statement as a roadmap or summary of the case to follow, you will soon realize that what you are doing is making promises to the jury. As noted in **§ 12.2**, you are indicating to the jury that the evidence "will prove" something. It then becomes your obligation to prove whatever you said you would prove, through the introduction of evidence. If you fail to do so, you will have disappointed the jury and failed to meet what is, in effect, a promise to the jury.

In an opening statement, such a technique can be used in any number of ways. One of the most effective is as follows:

> Ladies and gentlemen of the jury, an opening statement is a promise—a promise of what the evidence will prove. When the attorneys state to you that they expect to show something or they expect to prove something or the evidence will demonstrate something, they are making a promise to you, and it is a promise which should not be lightly taken or lightly made. Rather, you should remember that promise and carefully scrutinize the evidence which is introduced to see if, in fact, that attorney has kept his promise to you.

During the closing argument, an attorney who has referred to a promise during the opening statement may return to it in the following manner:

> During the opening statement I told you that there were promises being made. Those promises, both made by my opponent and made by myself, related to what the evidence would prove. Quite frankly, ladies and gentlemen, my opponent has broken his promises. He has failed to live up to your expectations and he has failed to prove that which he indicated he would during the opening statement. Broken promises!

This technique has, from its users' point of view, a tremendously beneficial effect of not so subtly attacking the personal credibility of the opposing attorney. Remember, no one, including a juror, likes to have the promises which have been made to him or her broken. A statement made about promises having been broken relates to the individual attorney who made the promises. The lack of credibility which is implicit in the charge of breaking of promises puts a negative light on the case of the person charged with that offense.

If an opponent refers to promises during an opening statement, you should anticipate that there will be a reference to broken promises during the closing argument. An effective countermeasure to this technique is, in the first instance, to be sure that you do not break any promises. At the same time, you should turn the tactic around on your opponent during the opening statement in the following fashion, assuming that your opponent has gone first and referred to promises and that either you are immediately following with your opening statement or you have reserved your opening statement and are delivering it at the close of the plaintiff's case:

> You have heard my opponent refer to the fact that an opening statement is a promise. Indeed it is, ladies and gentlemen, and it is a promise which should not be lightly made. I invite you to listen to the evidence carefully and to compare that evidence against the promises which my opponent has made. I further invite you to compare that evidence against the promises I am about to make, and would suggest to you that on weighing that evidence at the conclusion of this case, there will only be one outcome which you could reach in terms of who has made the promises and who has kept the promises.
>
> Now there will come a time during the closing argument at the conclusion of the evidence when both my opponent and I will have the opportunity to argue this case to you. At that time you and I together will examine the promises which each side has made and examine the evidence which each side has introduced in support of the keeping of those promises. I would suggest to you now that the outcome will clearly demonstrate and prove to you that there is only one result to be reached in this case—for Mary Jones.

The great strength to responding to the broken promises technique during opening statement by alerting the jury to the fact that it will be brought up again during closing argument is that you in effect steal the thunder from your opponent and adopt this verbal technique as your own. This counter-offensive technique is most effective when you are representing the defendant and have already been confronted with the broken promises presentation during the opening statement of the plaintiff.

§ 12.5 Instructing in the Law

As a general rule, a judge will caution counsel during either an opening statement or closing argument not to instruct the jury in the law since that is reserved for the court. When the jury has been preinstructed in the law, e.g., prior to opening statement during an introductory statement by the court, or when the jury instructions have been agreed on prior to the closing arguments, counsel may frequently state the law to the jury or, in the latter instance, argue the law to the jury.

During an opening statement, you should be wary of an attorney who either states the law to the jury when there has been a preinstruction, or, if there has not been a preinstruction, proceeds to state to the jury the law which will be applied. This tactic aims at placing counsel in a position in the eyes of the jury as the more knowledgeable party in directing the legal focus of the case. Thus, when the jury has not been preinstructed but your opponent is making statements bearing on matters such as burden of proof and burden of going forward, or similar remarks, you should be prepared to act appropriately and quickly.

Typically the intentions of your opponent may be ascertained by directing a question to your opponent through the court as to whether your opponent expects to or intends to state, during the opening statement, any standards of law either in the general sense or as they may specifically apply to the instant case. Alternatively, you may inquire of the court as to its position on whether counsel may make such statements to the jury during the opening statement without regard to whether there has been preinstruction of the jury. By doing so you are able to deliver a message to your opponent without need for a direct focus or suggestion.

If you have had no reason to believe that your opponent was going to state the law to the jury during an opening statement but learned this for the first time during the opening statement, you have a number of possibilities. Obviously, the first and most reactive response is to object. One of the problems with making objections during an opening statement is that you frequently draw greater attention to the statement to which you have made an objection than would have been paid if there had been no objection at all. In addition, juries frequently will resent an individual who interrupts another, even with an objection, especially during opening statements and closing arguments. If you make an objection and then request a side bar conference, the jury may resent you for holding up the trial and making their jury service that much longer. Finally, the ultimate downside risk of making an objection of this type is to have it overruled and suffer a defeat in the eyes of the jury.

Notwithstanding all the risks to making an objection to the statement, there will be times when you will be compelled to make such an objection.

Under such circumstances, it is best to indicate, in order to protect yourself against an unfavorable ruling, something along the following lines:

> Objection, your Honor. With all due respect to my opponent, I feel compelled to register an objection for the record at this point. Counsel is stating the law to the jury at what I believe to be an inappropriate time and, in addition, is taking over the function of this Honorable Court in doing so. I respectfully make this objection in order to protect my client's rights and would request that counsel confine his opening statement to what the evidence will prove and not what the law is to be applied to that evidence.

Assuming that your decision, where confronted with a statement of law, is not to object, your option is to simply "white knuckle" the statement, and you can probably safely assume that it will not significantly register in the minds of the jury. If you do so, you can always come back on your opening statement and, in effect, counterstate the law. An objection by your opponent at that point may prove ineffective, because it will be quite apparent to the court that your opponent has done the very thing to which he or she is now objecting. Note that if you do object and the objection is overruled, you should definitely consider making a counterstatement of the law yourself since you now have a preview of how the judge will rule in such a situation.

When jury instructions have been agreed upon prior to trial, there is a technique which will place you in a superior position in the eyes of the jury. In this comparatively unusual situation, you should say something to the jury along the following lines:

> Ladies and gentlemen of the jury, this is the opening statement in which I have the opportunity to state the facts and the evidence which will be introduced and presented to you. In addition, I believe that Judge ________________ will at the appropriate time state to you what the law is to be applied to those facts. I believe that Judge ________________ will at that time indicate to you the following.

Having made a statement as to what the judge will say at a later time without arguing that law, you will, after the judge actually so instructs the jury, appear that much more in command of the case. Unless your opponent points out that the jury instructions have been agreed on, there is virtually no chance that the jury will be aware of the fact unless there has been preinstruction.

§ 12.6 Creating Exhibits

There is little doubt that an opening statement is not evidence. However, it is equally true that you should not usually tell the jury that an opening statement is not evidence. By doing so you are immediately raising the unspoken question in their minds, "Then why am I listening to this?" Similarly, unless exhibits have been stipulated into evidence prior to commencement of opening statements, nothing may be used during an opening statement for evidentiary purposes. This fact is simply demonstrated by your statements that the evidence "will prove"; since no evidence has been received as yet, you are simply making a statement of expectations. If you fail to deliver, you must suffer the consequences in the minds of the jury and at the hands of your opponent.

Although as a general rule you may not use any exhibits during an opening statement which are not part of the evidence stipulated or agreed to prior to trial, there is a technique sometimes used which in effect creates evidence during the opening statement to help the jury better remember the opening statement they are hearing. In addition, the samc "evidence" may be used later in thc trial and thus gain an imprimatur of validity and credibility which, in part, carries over to the comments of counsel.

In its simplest form, this technique calls for the preparation of a chart listing witnesses or facts which will be proven. This chart is prepared during the opening statement as counsel speaks and is simply a concise shorthand list of the evidence, made up of numbered statements. Because the chart is nothing more than a written version of the listing in the opening statement itself, the basic document to be examined to determine whether there is a viable objection is the statement.

An example of how this technique might be used is as follows:

> Ladies and gentlemen of the jury, during the presentation of the case for plaintiff Mary Jones you will hear from six live witnesses. They are Dr. Tim Johnson, [etc.].

At this point you would write the number *1* on a large 30″ × 40″ artist pad and next to it write *Dr. Tim Johnson.* As you named additional witnesses you would also write their names and, depending on the manner in which you wish to use this technique, you might write a few buzz words regarding their testimony as you state it.

The advantage of this technique of creating an exhibit is that not only do you assault the juror's aural senses with the opening statement, but you also assault their visual senses. As a result, the likelihood of your being able to imprint your message on their minds is that much greater. The long-term advantage of this technique is that during your closing argument you can come back to this chart and use it to outline the evidence from the various witnesses and couple it to the promises you made during your opening statement, thereby providing continuity between the opening statement, the case, and the closing argument.

When confronted with this tactic there are a range of options available to you, from doing nothing, to objecting, to using the approach yourself.

All the advantages and disadvantages of making objections during an opening statement discussed in § **12.5** are equally applicable here. Thus, you have a risk-benefit analysis in determining whether to make an objection to the creation of an exhibit. The risk of doing nothing must be measured by the individual exhibit you are confronting. Perhaps the best response is to turn the tactic around on your opponent. This can be done most effectively by taking your opponent's exhibit and, to the extent possible, using it to demonstrate what your evidence will prove.

In most cases, you will be cross-examining your opponent's witnesses for the purpose of not only getting concessions from them but also disproving their positions. By taking your opponent's list of witnesses or evidence and turning it around to the perspective of your case and stating what that witness or evidence will prove in the context of your case, you will be gaining a tremendous tactical advantage. You will probably want to add additional witnesses and exhibits to your opponent's list, thereby adopting the exhibit and turning it into your exhibit. You will then have an even more powerful, persuasive tool, and the list will probably be rendered useless for your opponent's future purposes.

§ 12.7 Making Objections

As a general matter, the making of objections during any portion of a trial, be it to an opening statement made by your opponent or to the examination of a witness conducted by an opponent, amounts to a risk-benefit proposition. The analysis you must go through in making an objection is whether the benefits associated with an objection, whether you win or lose, outweigh the risks inherent in proceeding.

Very briefly, on the benefit side of the ledger in connection with making objections is the fact that you will prevent your adversary from making objectionable and possibly prejudicial remarks. In addition, you may have the opportunity to make a statement in the presence of the jury which will throw doubt on the credibility not only of your opponent's case but of your opponent as well. Finally, and perhaps most importantly, a properly timed objection can have the benefit of throwing your opponent off and interrupting his or her train of thought at a crucial time. This may affect the balance of your opponent's presentation or break up his or her communication with the jury. This latter area is the one in which objections are most frequently used during opening statements.

There are a number of techniques which can protect you against inappropriate and unfair interruptions during your opening statement. You should make a judgment as to whether your opponent is likely to interrupt you for reasons other than those that might validly relate to inappropriate comments by you. If you determine that unfair interruptions are not unlikely, the approach you take will fall into one of several categories:

1. Prior to commencement of your opening statement and out of the presence of the jury, you should request that all objections to the opening statement be reserved until the opening statement is concluded. You should suggest that any objections be resolved thereafter at side bar, or out of the presence of the jury, with appropriate instructions from the court directed at the jury for purposes of curing any problems. The difficulty with this suggestion, which you may find made by an opponent or perhaps the court itself, is that curative instructions, whatever their effect or lack thereof, will certainly be much less effective if they are given at the conclusion of the entire opening statement and not immediately following what may have been an improper comment by counsel.
2. As soon as your opponent makes an objection, you should immediately request a side bar conferencc. In order to respond to an interruption of this type as effectively as possible, you should be aware that your opponent is about to make an objection. As you see your opponent start to rise, you should immediately stop talking, even if this requires you to stop in midsentence. You should then turn to your opponent and permit him or her to go no further than stating the word *objection* before you request a side bar conference.
3. You can then have the objection resolved at side bar. You will find yourself in one of two situations: either you have prevailed on the objection or you have lost.
4. If you have prevailed on the objection, you should walk back to the podium and request that the court reporter read back the last statement to which there was an objection. Once it has been read back, you should *repeat* that statement and continue with your opening statement. This makes it apparent to the jury that you have won whatever took place out of their hearing. In addition, you have the benefit of having delivered to the jury the statement to which there was an objection, and presumably which has some importance in the case, no fewer than three times, first, during the original statement, second, when it was read back to the jury, and third, when you repeated it at the point of picking up your train of thought.
5. A more difficult proposition presents itself when you go to side bar during the objection to the opening statement and lose the objection. The task which you face is to make it appear to the jury as if you have prevailed while at the same time obscuring any perception that your opponent has beaten you. While there is no surefire approach to such a situation, one effective tactic is to return to the podium after the objection has been sustained, say "As I was saying prior to counsel objecting . . . ," and continue your opening statement leaving out the objectionable area completely. Verbally, you are communicating to the jury that you are repeating what you said previously,

making it appear as if you have prevailed. Substantively, you will be moving on to a different subject and leaving the objectionable area. The lapse of time between the objectionable statement, the objection, and resumption of the opening statement usually means the jurors will not really be able to connect what transpired before with what happens later.

6. A far more difficult problem arises when in addition to sustaining the objection, the court instructs the jury as to the impropriety of your prior comment or strikes the prior comment. Quite obviously, it is impossible to unring a bell. The jury has heard your statement and will not be able to forget it or factor it completely out of their decision making process. Under such circumstances, the approach which you should take is not dissimilar to the one you would have taken in the absence of any such instructions from the court. Specifically, you should continue your opening statement with a transitional comment along the lines of, "Prior to the objection being made, ladies and gentlemen of the jury, I was commenting upon . . . ." This permits you to close up the gap verbally between your comments prior to the objection and your resumption of the opening statement. Although you certainly are not able to dispel the comments of the judge completely, you can hope to minimize their impact on the jury and take advantage of the fact that unringing bells is not a physical possibility.

7. Another good verbal technique to combat the sustaining of an objection is, upon your return to the podium, to turn to the judge and, in a rather casual and low-key fashion, say, "Thank you, your Honor." If anything, you are simply expressing common courtesy toward the court, as you will no doubt be doing on numerous occasions throughout the trial. However, the beneficial fall-out effect is to throw the jurors into a frame of mind, especially if the judge has given them a cautionary instruction or instruction to disregard certain comments, that you are an ally of the judge on this point and that the instructions of the court should not reflect negatively on you or your case. Another comment of this type which might be directed to the court following an instruction to the jury is, "Thank you, your Honor, for clarifying that point." The risk that you must guard against is that of making it appear in your tone of voice that such comments are either flip or cynical. You run the added risk under that circumstance of being rebuked by the judge in front of the jury and losing standing or credibility in the eyes of the jury.

8. One of the most effective tactics against the opponent who repeatedly interrupts you during an opening statement can be a direct confrontation. A good way of doing this is to accept the first two or three objections and handle them at side bar as discussed. After a few such objections, you might consider responding in the presence of the jury by saying, "Your Honor, with all due respect to my opponent, I have been quite patient during repeated objections made during my opening statement. I would respectfully request that your Honor instruct counsel to stop interrupting my opening statement. If he is doing so for the purpose of interrupting my train of thought and my ability to present my case during this opening statement to the jury in a logical and uninterrupted fashion, I would suggest that this is improper. I would further suggest that he will have an opportunity to make an opening statement and present to the jury what he believes the evidence will show. However, I would also suggest that such repeated objections and interruptions are not justified."

9. If the above statement is made in a respectful tone of voice directed to the court, and the appropriate groundwork has been laid through the prior objections of your opponent, you have a pretty good shot at having the judge rebuke your opponent in the presence of the jury. The benefits are tremendous, because the psychological impact of having the judge, who is the authority figure in the courtroom, direct what are tantamount to disciplinary words at an attorney in the presence and hearing of the jury reflects adversely upon that attorney.

§ 12.8 Side Bar Conferences

Most judges trying cases before juries are especially conscious of the added time which the presence of a jury means for the overall trial process. The mere fact of bringing the jury in and out of the courtroom and the fact that shorter trial hours must frequently be maintained are always in the mind of the judge. When objections or other matters which must be resolved out of the hearing of the jury arise in court, there is frequent resort to side bar conferences. The problem with a side bar conference is that it is often time consuming and may sometimes result, even after the side bar conference, in the jury's being taken out of the courtroom while counsel argue a point to the judge.

The risk of side bar conferences is that the jury is left sitting in the courtroom, now knowing what is going on, sometimes for long periods of time. This often results in some degree of resentment and impatience among the jurors. If the judge is the one who requested the side bar conference, this will not typically reflect adversely in the eyes of the jurors on either attorney. However, if the side bar conference or a number of such conferences is requested by one or the other of the attorneys, there is a very real risk that the jurors will perceive that particular attorney, and through the attorney the client, as delaying and perhaps not as well-organized in the conduct of the case.

Although certainly there are situations when a side bar conference is absolutely required and must be requested by you, as in dealing with objections, you must recognize that a side bar conference or, more particularly, repeated side bar conferences are a risk-benefit proposition. This is most true when you make your request for a side bar conference in the hearing of the jury and the judge denies your request, again in the hearing of the jury. This result can often be perceived as reflecting on either your skills or your credibility vis-à-vis the judge. This should be avoided if at all possible.

You may run into an opponent who either deliberately or for other reasons requires you to ask for repeated side bar conferences to resolve either matters of counsel behavior or objections to your presentation of the case. An effective approach in this situation is to raise the point with the judge at one of the side bar conferences indicating something along the following lines:

> Your Honor, with all due respect, I do not wish to keep requesting side bar conferences in order to resolve these matters. They interrupt the proceedings and slow the case down. Counsel, however, has repeatedly required me to request them as a result of his constant interruptions. I would request an instruction from your Honor that he cease making frivolous objections (or as appropriate).

This statement is delivered in a low-keyed, nonoffensive tone and can often spur the judge to caution your opponent. Remember, judges are interested in expediting the trial pending before them. They are looking for ways to shortcut procedures and move the case along. The point of the side bar conference is to save time and not have the jury removed from the courtroom. If counsel is, through behavior, precipitating a number of side bar conferences and requiring others to request them, it is not at all inappropriate for the court to discipline counsel who is requiring an inordinate number of interruptions.

§ 12.9 Sample Opening Statement

Good morning, ladies and gentlemen. Let me do something a little bit unusual at the outset of my opening statement. I'd like to tell you what this case is not about before I tell you what this case is about.

It's not about what caused that tragic accident which claimed the lives of 248 passengers and eight employees of Z Air.

It's not about compensating the families of the people whose lives were taken or the families of those men and women in the crew.

Well then, you might ask, what is this case about? Well, plain and simple, it's a commercial dispute between an organization which chartered an aircraft and the airline from which that aircraft was chartered.

On the one hand we have the organization which chartered a DC-8 aircraft from Z Air. On the other, we have G.Z., who founded Z Air; J.Z., his son, who at the time was president of Z Air; Harry Weisberg, who is the Vice-President and General Counsel of Z Air; B Air, an FAA-certified maintenance facility which maintained the aircraft; and Multinational Air Leasing, which leased the aircraft to Z.

What this case is about—what this commercial dispute is about—is whether the plaintiff organization ought to be required to live up to their obligations under the contract of charter with Z Air. Now the organization doesn't want to do that. They don't want to live up to their obligations and they would like you to find, and will present evidence which they say justifies your relieving them of those obligations. What they're going to attempt to do in that regard is persuade you that the charter contract which the organization had with Z Air is void because they say Z Air fraudulently induced them into entering into it.

Now before I turn to what the evidence will prove regarding the dealings between Z Air and the organization, let me tell you a little bit about the parties to this case and what the evidence will demonstrate in that regard.

The organization was formed for the purpose of administering certain international agreements. But perhaps more importantly, the evidence will demonstrate that it is a sophisticated business organization. It is that role which is in question in this lawsuit and not any other role.

Specifically, the evidence in this case will demonstrate that much like any business entity, the organization has an administrative operation and that part of that administrative operation deals with the contracting process. Now the contracting process the organization engages in is not unlike any other contracting process for any other company. Indeed, the evidence will clearly demonstrate that in many respects the organization's contracting process is far more sophisticated than that of many businesses.

In this regard, the organization relied upon three separate elements for the purpose of entering into contracts, and specifically in this case, entering into the charter contract with Z Air. Now, you should also know that this wasn't the first charter contract which the organization had entered into with Z. Rather, it was the last of a series of contracts which spanned some three years. The evidence in this regard will prove that, throughout the entire course of this relationship, the organization was, in their own words, more than satisfied with the service of Z Air.

Now in entering into these charter contracts the organization relied upon technical advice from their own aviation technical personnel, legal advice from their own lawyers, and contracting advice from their own contracting officers. The evidence in this regard will demonstrate that the technical advice they received in the area of aviation was from an employee of the organization, J.W., who had spent virtually his entire career on the technical side of the aviation business. Not only was he a career military pilot and officer, but he had also inspected and supervised the inspection of large aviation organizations. In addition, Mr. W. held a bachelor's degree in aviation management as well as a master's degree in aviation management.

For the purpose of obtaining legal advice regarding the contracting process, the organization relied upon their in-house lawyers. In this case, you will hear testimony from J.F., a former organization lawyer who, like J.W., spent most of his career on the legal side of the aviation business dealing with maintenance organizations, aircraft, air charter arrangements, and the very types of things which the organization had contracted for with Z Air.

Finally, in order to bring all of this together and enter into contracts, the organization had contracting officers, whose job it was to insure that the contractors with whom the organization contracted were not only capable of performing the services but of performing them safely. Furthermore, these contracting officers carefully monitored performance of the contractors, including Z Air, throughout the performance of the contract.

You will hear evidence from the organization's own contracting officers that Z Air was fully capable of performing the services for which it had contracted with the organization. Specifically, the organization's own contracting officers in this case will testify to the fact that Z Air had a good reputation in the industry, an excellent safety record, good management, good pilots, and good maintenance. They will tell you that the organization's contracting officers had reviewed the past performance for the organization and had found it to be very satisfactory.

In addition to all of the foregoing evidence, you will also hear that not a single organization employee, be it a technical person, a lawyer, or contracting officer, ever heard or had reason to believe that Z Air was ever unsafe. In fact, what you will hear is that it was only after talking to the organization lawyers in this case that they heard for the first time any such statements.

Now before talking about Z Air and what the evidence will demonstrate in that regard, let me mention one other thing. The fact that the aircraft crashed and tragically took the lives of so many people doesn't mean that Z Air and G.Z. and H.W. and J.Z. and the others didn't intend to comply with the regulations, didn't intend to have safe operations, and didn't intend to have the very best operation which they could.

What the evidence will demonstrate in this regard is that perhaps, just perhaps, on a given day at a given time somebody, the crew, or something, the airplane, made a mistake. This accident no more means that the airline was unsafe or that the individuals involved deliberately intended to run an unsafe operation or deliberately intended not to comply with the regulations than in any other situation when an accident occurs.

Indeed, ladies and gentlemen, the conclusion that any particular airline, train company, or other organization or business is unsafe just because they have an accident is no more true than your being uncoordinated if you stumble, or your being an unsafe driver if you have a car accident.

Now it's been said that a lawyer should never use humor in the courtroom. I believe in that because experience has taught me that even with my wife or my daughter that what I believe may be funny as a lawyer may not necessarily be funny to anyone else. Well, for the sake of making a point, I'm going to break that rule and relate something to you which I heard as early as law school.

Back then one of my professors said that if you are in court, if you're in trial, and the facts are against you—you have bad facts—you should pound the law.

By pounding the law, you can hope to distract the jury from the facts. And obviously, as you might expect, a hand went up and the question was asked, "What if the law is against you?" Equally obviously, the response from the professor, having heard the same question from countless young law students before, gave the obvious answer, namely, that if the law is against you, you pound the facts, and this distracts the jury from the law.

Well, again a hand shot up and the final and perhaps most obvious question was asked, and that is, "Professor, what happens when both the facts and the law are against you?" The professor, having taught the course for a number of years, not only anticipated the question, but relished its being asked. His answer was really quite simple, namely, when the facts and the law are against you, you pound the table.

Now, I tell you that story for a very important reason. Because I submit to you, ladies and gentlemen, that during the days to come, we will hear a great deal of table pounding from counsel for the organization. Do not permit it to distract you from the facts.

Having said that, let me turn to what the evidence will demonstrate regarding G.Z., J.Z., H.W., Z Air, and the other defendants.

G.Z. started Z Air back in 1981 for the purpose of providing scheduled passenger service, military service, cargo service, and chartered air transportation services. At the time G.Z. already was involved in a number of aviation activities including B Air, an FAA-certificated repair station, which would ultimately perform maintenance services for Z Air, as well as for numerous other scheduled air carriers. G.Z. was also the founder of Multinational Air Leasing, whose business it was to lease, buy and sell airplanes. And so G.Z. had, in effect, a family of aviation businesses, and he started Z Air for the purpose of completing that family.

In forming Z Air, G.Z. had the benefit of utilizing the services of these other companies and so he had a leg up. He was able to draw upon the experience, the resources and the credit of those organizations. The evidence will demonstrate that this was a benefit, since it allowed Z Air to have access to aircraft without making major capital expense duties to purchase those aircraft, as well as first class maintenance services at costs equal to or below usual market rates. The evidence will also show that contracting out maintenance services in the aviation industry is common. It will also show that Z Air's operation of leased aircraft was also common in the aviation industry.

Now the plaintiffs will argue that Z Air was never started for the purpose of making a profit since, among other reasons, it was started with \$1,000 cash. The evidence will indicate that nothing could be further from the truth. While it was started with \$1,000 cash, it also was started with millions of dollars of lines of credit. Not only did Z Air seek to make money—at the time of this tragic accident, it was starting to make money.

Now Z Air was successful in obtaining a number of contracts. These contracts were to provide air transportation services between various points in the United States and overseas. Now in order to operate an airline, I should tell you, approval and certification is needed from the United States government.

The evidence in this regard will demonstrate that at all times—in fact even as we sit here today—Z Air has had that certification and been considered to be a safe operator by the Federal Aviation Administration. By virtue of the fact that Z Air held a certificate under Part 121 of the Federal Aviation Regulations, they were subjected to numerous surveillances. In 1985 alone there were over 220 inspections of Z Air done by just the FAA. The FAA inspectors will tell you that Z Air was absolutely clean in this regard. The crews were well trained, operated the flights safely, and the airplanes were well maintained.

Now you will hear a great deal of evidence regarding the FAA inspections and surveillance of Z Air by FAA inspectors.

You'll hear an FAA inspector testify that most of the discrepancies found during a special inspection were recordkeeping problems and that even though the paperwork may not have been done, there was little doubt in the FAA team's mind that the lack of record keeping did not reflect the state of the airline. The crews were well trained, the aircraft were well maintained, the airline was well operated and the new management team was both responsive and dedicated to doing the best they could.

Now in 1982, Z Air, responding to a request for proposals put out by the plaintiff organization, offered to provide certain air transportation services to the plaintiff. Z Air in fact provided those services in 1982 and did so again in 1983 and 1984. The evidence will demonstrate that in choosing to use Z Air, the organization reviewed Z Air's qualifications as an air carrier and all of the information which you would expect any commercial organization entering into a business deal with any other commercial organization to review. Z Air hid nothing, responding to all questions fully and forthrightly.

The evidence will show that in late 1984 negotiations started for the 1985 contract. The organization claims that Z Air misrepresented to it certain facts of how much weight the aircraft to be used could carry. Now before I tell you what the evidence will prove, let me tell you something about which you'll hear a great deal—zero fuel weight. The plaintiffs will argue that the zero fuel weight limitation of the accident aircraft was exceeded. In fact, however, the evidence will indicate that no one knows whether or not it was exceeded, and that even if it was exceeded, it didn't in any way affect the safety of the aircraft, the performance of the aircraft, or the happening of this accident. Furthermore, even assuming the zero fuel weight of the accident aircraft was exceeded, that's a far cry from fraud. You'll hear evidence that Z Air's management and supervisors, on a prior occasion, told Z Air's pilots that if there was any question—any question at all—regarding weight problems, that they shouldn't operate a flight. Shut it down! You'll also hear an engineer from McDonnel Douglas testify that even if the zero fuel weight of this aircraft was exceeded that, first, it had nothing to do with the aerodynamic performance of the aircraft and, second, was irrelevant to the takeoff of the aircraft. He will also testify that at the time the aircraft took off, it was airworthy. He will tell you, as will others, that the aircraft was operated within center of gravity limits and within gross takeoff weight limits. Based on these facts, he will tell you that the zero fuel weight was, as I said, irrelevant and that the aircraft was not overweight.

I submit to you that at the time you hear all the evidence from the plaintiff and weigh it against that to be presented by Z Air and G.Z., you will conclude that this is nothing more than a smokescreen. Even assuming that zero fuel weight was exceeded, at most the evidence will indicate that perhaps a pilot or pilots made a mistake, but that neither Z Air nor any of the other defendants are guilty of fraud.

You will also hear a great deal of additional nitpicking about discrepancies and recordkeeping errors and ratcheting sounds and the like. Once again I submit that, upon listening to the evidence carefully, both that to be presented by the plaintiff as well as that presented by Z Air, G.Z., and the others, you will conclude that we are dealing with smokescreens. Under no circumstances will there be any evidence that Z Air was unsafe or that Z Air didn't intend to comply with Federal Aviation Regulations or that Z Air or anyone else committed fraud.

You'll also hear testimony from a former administrator of the FAA. He will tell you that certainly Z Air had blemishes but that every airline, and indeed, everything in life, has blemishes. However, he'll also tell you that Z Air was neither unsafe nor incapable of complying with the Federal Aviation regulations. To the contrary, he'll tell you that Z Air was a safe airline and that they not only met and continue to meet the standards of the Federal regulations, which is all that they're required to do, but they exceed those minimum standards. He'll tell you that the fact that a crew may make a mistake on a given day, assuming that's what happened here, doesn't make the airline unsafe in any way.

Now I've already told you that you're going to hear a great deal about whether this aircraft which crashed was capable of carrying what the plaintiff says Z Air had agreed to carry. The one thing that you should pay careful attention to in this regard is the fact that Z Air, specifically the Vice President of Planning and his assistant, both of whom are highly experienced and knowledgeable in the charter industry and both of whom have dealt with the organization over many, many years, specifically told the organization that the aircraft in question were not capable of carrying the amount of weight which the organization wanted. The evidence will show that when negotiations for the contract were going on, the organization came to Z Air and indicated that the contract should allow each of the 250 passengers to bring 70 kilos of baggage. Z Air, in response, told the organization that this wasn't possible and that if each passenger showed up with 70 kilos of bags, that it wouldn't fit on the aircraft. In response, the organization indicated that they understood, and further understood that the 70 kilos in the contract was a maximum and not an average, but that they wanted the 70 kilos in the contract. With a full understanding of the limitations of the aircraft which were going to be used, the organization agreed to go forward. They were, in every respect, fully informed and fully advised by Z Air. Despite having been told of the limitations of the DC-8 aircraft, the evidence will clearly demonstrate that the organization wanted that weight provision in the contract but just as clearly understood what the limitations of the aircraft would be.

Now the organization comes before you and says, "we didn't understand, we didn't know, Z Air is guilty of fraud." Ladies and gentlemen, I submit to you that by the time you hear the evidence on this issue, you too will conclude that the only fraud present in this case is the one which is going to be perpetrated in this courtroom if the organization is permitted to get away with its position.

What occurred on the date of the accident was a tragedy then and continues to be a tragedy today. No one feels worse about this accident than G.Z., J.Z., and H.W. and the others. Their company, Z Air, was involved. No one feels more sympathy and more concern for the families who are involved. However, the fact that this accident occurred doesn't indicate that Z Air is uncaring or guilty of some fraud.

The only thing which the evidence will prove and which the happening of this accident demonstrates, is that perhaps, and I say perhaps, on a given day at a given time, a group of pilots made a mistake. In fact, the McDonnell-Douglas engineer will testify that in his opinion the aircraft crashed due to ice on its wings and fuselage and assuming this is what happened, the crew made a mistake in not having the aircraft de-iced. He will also tell you that in his opinion if the crew had de-iced the aircraft, it would have taken off and flown safely. And so, ladies and gentlemen, at worst we have a mistake by the aircraft crew. A mistake in judgment, which the evidence will prove is a world away from fraud. Assuming that the engineer is correct, that mistake by the crew is no more evidence of fraud or willful intent to mislead and misrepresent on the part of G.Z., J.Z., H.W., Z Air, and the others than your being involved in an auto accident is any evidence of your recklessness as a driver.

At the conclusion of the evidence in this case, I will once again have the opportunity to stand before you and make a closing argument. I know that you will listen to the evidence between now and then conscientiously keeping in mind always your obligations as jurors. Keep in mind also what I have said during this opening statement for, in many respects, it is like a road map of what is to come. In some respects I have attempted to point out some of the landmarks which you might encounter along the way.

There is little doubt that you will conclude at the end of this journey, and based on all of the evidence to be presented before you, that Z Air was an airline which cared, which wanted to and intended to do a good job and which, despite this tragic accident, was in fact doing a good job. The organization will say so and the FAA inspectors who inspected Z Air on a day-to-day basis will say so.

Remember, this litigation is not about what caused this accident and it's not about compensating the families of those whose lives were so tragically snatched from them. What it is about is whether or not Z Air and these gentlemen and others are guilty of deliberate and intentional misrepresentations.

They are not.

§ 12.10 Trial Briefs

A cardinal rule of trial practice is *always* to file a trial brief *prior* to trial, notwithstanding whether local rules or the court require such a brief. As a practical matter, even if local rules make no provision for filing a trial brief, it is doubtful that such a brief would be rejected. Properly prepared, a trial brief will be a tremendously effective tool of advocacy for you. Another point which should be considered is that a trial brief is like an opening statement without any restrictions whatever on what can be stated or indeed argued. If properly prepared and timely filed, a trial brief can give you a decided advantage over your opponent.

A trial brief should be adversarial in the sense that it should lay out the facts as you view them while at the same time not putting any unfair reading or interpretation on those facts. In addition, a trial brief should set forth your position in your best adversarial and argumentative fashion, citing cases when appropriate, and have attached to it copies of anything which you wish the judge to look at and have at hand. This will include copies of key exhibits, even though they may not yet have been received into evidence, as well as copies of slip opinions or reported cases which are central to your position.

You should file a trial brief without regard to whether the case is a jury trial. It may occur to you that in a jury trial, a trial brief is comparatively useless, because the jury makes the decision and not the judge. However, remember that the judge is the one who establishes the pretrial parameters of the case, makes all of the rulings on evidentiary and other types of objections during trial, and undertakes an examination of witnesses despite having indicated to the jury that "the fact that the court has asked questions should not lead you to give any greater weight to those questions or answers than you would give to the questions asked by counsel and the answers of the witnesses to those questions." As we all know, such cautionary instructions are frequently of little value, because jurors value the perception of the judge and often lean in the direction in which they perceive the judge to be leaning. As a result, it is incumbent on a litigant to do everything possible to cause the judge to lean in his or her direction. A trial brief does this regardless of whether there is a jury in a particular case.

In a nonjury case, a trial brief is even more imperative, because you may not even have an opening statement. An opening statement is not evidence in the case and, as a result, judges who are trying the facts frequently do not permit them or, if they do, allow them only in an abbreviated form. In these circumstances, the trial brief takes the place of any opening statement and assures you of being able to get your position before the judge in your best adversarial fashion.

§ 12.11 —Timing of Filing

One of the tactics most frequently associated with filing of trial briefs is the last-minute filing. In what can be considered the most abused form of this tactic, a trial brief is filed with the clerk on Thursday for a trial beginning on Monday. A copy is sent by regular mail to opposing counsel on Thursday so it can be assured that delivery will be delayed until Saturday or Monday, while at the same time—and unfairly—a courtesy copy is hand delivered to the judge's chambers at the time the filing occurs or, even worse, the judge's courtesy copy is mailed or delivered to the judge's chambers by some expedited mail system such as Federal Express or Express Mail.

If you find yourself on the receiving end of such an unfair tactic, which has a net result of placing your opponent's position in the trial before the judge while—in the event you are not going to file a trial brief—your position goes unrepresented, you have several options, none of which is as satisfactory as having filed your own brief.

Assuming that you intend to file a trial brief, it may be a good idea either to agree on a time for simultaneous filings or to request that the judge set such a time. This will obviate the problem in the first instance and will also avoid any ambush that you might encounter by filing early only to have your opponent file later with an opportunity to respond to your points.

If, for whatever reason, you find yourself not having filed a trial brief but subject to an ambush in the sense that your opponent's trial brief was filed at a time which gave you either no opportunity to respond or no opportunity even to read the brief, you should determine when your opponent's trial brief was in fact filed and, if possible, when it was delivered to the judge. One possible recourse is a motion to strike the brief as untimely and unfairly filed in that it deprived you of an opportunity to respond meaningfully or indeed even to review the brief prior to commencement of trial.

In such a circumstance, as a fallback position, you should be prepared to file your brief. Indeed, after reviewing your opponent's brief, no matter how untimely filed, you may find that your interests are better served by filing your own brief and not moving to strike your opponent's brief. You may want to note on the record that your opponent's brief was filed in what might be considered a "fast and loose" fashion but that, for the sake of permitting each attorney to fully and completely advocate the position of his or her client, you will not raise an objection but simply request leave to file your own brief, a copy of which is attached.

By taking this approach you not only point out to the judge the tactic that has been pursued by your opponent, but you also get your position before the court. Notwithstanding the ability to effectively counter this sort of tactic by your opponent, there is still no substitute for filing your own trial brief.

Always provide the judge with a courtesy copy, unless the judge indicates that documents must be delivered to the clerk for filing. A trial brief is one pleading which you will want to have delivered to the judge's chambers in order to ensure that the judge has it and treats it somewhat differently from the other pleadings in the case.

When you do file a trial brief directly with the judge as a courtesy, you should consider giving it a distinctive cover or binding. For example, you might want to put the trial brief in a three-holed looseleaf notebook of brightly colored vinyl. It should be heavily indexed, with index tabs for quick and ready reference on the bench. The distinctive cover is to permit you to determine at the outset of the trial or at any point thereafter whether the judge is using your trial brief on the bench as a trial guide.

Remember, a trial brief is very similar to the opening statement in that it gives you an opportunity to lay out your roadmap of the case. The great advantage of the trial brief, however, is that it may be adversarial and argumentative. As a result, it is helpful for you to know whether the judge actually has the trial brief on the bench and is referring to it. If so, you have somewhat of a leg up over your opponent in that the judge presumably has in mind your scenario of what occurred and you can direct the judge's attention to particular portions of your trial brief or to materials included in the appendix to the brief.

§ 12.12 Jury Books

As litigation becomes more and more complex, a technique seeing increased use in the courtroom involves what has been referred to as a *jury book.* The jury book is nothing more than a compilation of, among other things, key exhibits which are duplicated and placed in three-ring binders, with a copy prepared for each juror. Other possible items for inclusion in a jury book, especially in technical cases, might be a glossary of terms and perhaps a "cast of characters" of the witnesses and individuals who will be referred to during the trial. In addition to the names of the witnesses and other individuals, there might be a one-sentence explanation of who the people are. The reason for using the three-ring notebook or pressboard binder is that you may want to include additional exhibits as they are received into evidence during the trial itself.

From an overall perspective, the jury book technique is finding much greater use and widespread acceptance among trial judges. However, it is also true that the use of such a technique lies within the discretion of the trial judge and is not likely to be addressed under local rules. Notwithstanding the widespread acceptance of this technique, the manner of its use in a particular piece of litigation often gives one party an unfair advantage in the eyes of the judge.

Yours should be the side which suggests that the jury book be used, and you should provide the court with a draft copy of a jury book along with inclusions prepared by you. You should indicate to the judge at that time that you are prepared, after your opponent has had an opportunity to review your jury book, to sit down with your opponent and go over any objections or suggested additions to it.

Once that process has been completed, you will be in a position to submit the final version of the jury book to the judge along with a suggested instruction to be given to the jury before they see the jury book.

The following is a pattern instruction which you might consider:

> Ladies and gentlemen of the jury, as part of counsel's preparation for this case they, working with the court, have prepared what we call a "jury book." It is nothing more than a three-ring binder containing copies of certain key exhibits which it has been agreed are admissible in evidence, along with a glossary of technical terms as well as a "cast of characters" consisting of names of individuals who will testify here either by deposition or live. We will give you this jury book each morning when you arrive for the trial and pick it up each evening as you depart. The purpose of this jury book is to permit you to better follow the introduction of the evidence into the record as it progresses and relate what is then being discussed with what has been discussed at some prior time. It is not in any way meant to distract you or substitute for the live evidence then being presented by counsel.

Of course, the ultimate decision whether to give such a jury book to the jury rests with the court. However, if you make such a suggestion and take the offensive by giving the book to the judge in draft form along with a proposed instruction and an offer to sit down with opposing counsel, you will certainly appear to the court to be the individual who is taking the initiative and thereby will gain an advantage over your opponent. Even though the jury may never know that you were the party who suggested using the technique, the judge will know and cannot help but keep it in mind during the progress of the trial.

When should the jury book first be introduced into the proceedings? The very nature of the book largely answers that question. The jury book should be given to the jurors at the beginning of the case, preferably following the opening statement or possibly prior to the opening statement, with instructions not to look at it until the opening statements are completed. Thus the contents of the jury book and the use of the technique must be approved and completed prior to opening statements.

Typically, if you are going to suggest use of the procedure, you should do so no later than the final pretrial conference. However, if the final pretrial conference is, as is sometimes the case, only a few days prior to the commencement of the trial, you may want to initiate the procedure through a pleading at a much earlier date. In this situation, you would file a motion suggesting implementation of the jury book technique and attach to that motion a copy of the proposed jury book. At the same time, you would certainly want to call your opponent and suggest a meeting to go over the jury book in order to seek an agreement as to its use. If your opponent declines, you would then be in a position to attest that you attempted to resolve the matter with your opponent but were unable to do so as a result of your opponent's desire not to participate. This gives you an advantage in the eyes of the court by making you the litigant who wants to move the case along more expeditiously and effectively, while casting your opponent in the opposite role.

When your adversary proposes use of a jury book, you may find yourself in a quandary. You do not want to be perceived as obstreperous, but at the same time, you do not want your opponent to gain the full benefit of having suggested the technique. One approach to this is to file your own version of the jury book, incorporating items suggested by your opponent to the extent that they are not objectionable to you, and supplementing them with your own proposals. Do this before any filing of pleadings or suggestion of disagreement.

Typically, the best you can do when your opponent has gotten the jump on you by proposing a jury book is to pick up on the suggestion immediately and in effect run with it, thereby dispelling any notion that this is a technique belonging to your opponent and for which he or she should receive credit.

§ 12.13 Judge Books

A *judge book* combines a trial brief with a jury book and constitutes either an agreed-on document to be provided to the judge, incorporating items which might be included in the jury book as well as adversarial matters, or, if the contents are agreed on, a document which incorporates those items in the jury book along with one-sided adversarial matters. It differs from most pretrial statements or orders in the sense that, if it is filed by one party, the judge book is truly adversarial in nature and allows you, as the trial brief does, to prebrief the judge regarding your case.

You may often find that a good trial brief takes on the characteristics of a judge book in that it contains a section on witnesses who will be called and a summary of their testimony, an outline of the facts, a list of exhibits to be introduced by you, a legal section discussing the law as it relates to your case, a legal section that relates to the law as it touches on your opponent's case, and an appendix which might include a glossary of technical terms, a cast of characters, copies of key exhibits or documents, whether or not they have been received into evidence or stipulated to, and copies of key cases which you feel are especially important for the judge to keep in mind.

In other respects, the judge book should be treated like the trial brief in terms of time of filing and use as well as preparation. It should be filed in a distinctive binder, heavily indexed, and provided to the judge early enough to permit meaningful review prior to trial while at the same time not giving your opponent a chance to timely counterfile if he or she failed to do so in the first instance.

CHAPTER 13

EXAMINATION OF WITNESSES

§ 13.1 Introduction

The direct and cross-examination of witnesses provide innumerable opportunities for the use of tactics which may be considered unfair by counsel against whom they are directed. However, remember that the mere fact that you or your opponent may consider a tactic unfair does not mean that it is improper within the context of litigation.

You are an advocate, and you naturally consider unfair anything that injures your case or is unfavorable to your position. It is only when you or your opponent oversteps an invisible line that something considered unfair by one side or the other becomes improper and inadmissible.

In the examination of witnesses, a new element is introduced into the trial situation—a third person, the witness. Some unpredictability is present when dealing with your own witnesses as well as when cross-examining those of your opponent. The unpredictability associated with direct examination of your own witnesses is that even the best-prepared witness can take you by surprise. With respect to cross-examination of your opponent's witnesses, a good attorney has laid traps for an opponent, and the problem is to avoid these traps.

Overlying the entire situation is a series of techniques and tactics which can be used by an opponent to prejudice your case and put you at a disadvantage. Unless these are recognized either before they are used against you or in time to prevent damage being done to you, you may find yourself in the situation of having to make repairs. Unfortunately, your repair efforts usually become apparent to all in the courtroom. The trick in this situation is to turn an unfavorable circumstance around and use the tactic against your opponent.

This chapter explores a number of techniques which you should be aware of and which have the potential for favoring one side or the other, depending on how they are used. In addition, it suggests responses to these techniques when you are on the receiving end that can often turn an unfavorable situation into one which gives you the upper hand.

The chapter is divided into two parts. The first part examines a variety of tactics and techniques which pertain to the examination of all types of witnesses. The second part considers the special case of expert witnesses.

EXAMINATION OF WITNESSES IN GENERAL

§ 13.2 Burdens, Presumptions, and Inferences: A Tactical Perspective

Burdens and presumptions are rules of law that are given little thought by most lawyers until they find themselves on the wrong end of one. In its simplest form, a *burden* determines the minimum amount of evidence that a party must produce to sustain a genuine factual dispute. Along the same lines, a *presumption* is a conclusion that a factfinder must draw when confronted with certain evidence. If it is a *rebuttable presumption,* the party against whom the presumption operates must persuade the factfinder not to accept or be guided by the presumption.

Burdens and presumptions affect the entire case, from the drafting of the pleadings to motions for summary judgment to motions for a new trial. **Sections 13.3–13.6** focus on that part of the trial at which burdens and presumptions take on their greatest importance, demanding immediate action and response by counsel for both sides—the process of preparing, submitting, and objecting to jury instructions. This process, however, in order to be effective, begins long before the trial with a recognition of the role which burdens and presumptions play in pretrial motion practice, during discovery, and in developing an effective strategy for presenting evidence at trial.

§ 13.3 —Burdens in General

In general, the obligations of the parties to litigation with respect to establishing the elements of a claim or defense are allocated in accordance with precedent or statute. The party upon whom some duty lies to satisfy a given element of a course of action is said to have the *burden* as to that element. In this regard, there are two types of burdens: (1) the *burden of proof* and (2) the *burden of going forward.*

As a general rule, the party with responsibility for initially *pleading* something has the burden of proof. Thus, the plaintiff carries the overall burden of proof for the elements (for example, duty, breach, causal relationship, damages) of its cause of action, for example, negligence, throughout the trial. The defendant, however, may also bear a burden of proof for such elements in any affirmative defenses, such as contributory negligence, that it may assert. Each party must then persuade the jury that it has met its burden of proof by a preponderance of the evidence.

The plaintiff, with the burden of proving to the jury the existence of the elements in its cause of action, must also produce evidence in support of each element of that cause of action. When the evidence offered is so inadequate that no reasonable factfinder could be persuaded that a given element exists, the judge may decide, as a matter of law, that the plaintiff has failed to meet its burden. Thus, in ordinary circumstances, the plaintiff faces the threshold requirement of *going forward* and introducing enough evidence to create a genuine issue before it even gets the opportunity to try to meet its burden of proof.

The burden of going forward is satisfied when the plaintiff introduces evidence which, when viewed most favorably, is sufficient to enable the jury reasonably to find each element of the cause of action more probably true than not true. When a plaintiff has introduced such evidence regarding each element of the cause of action pleaded by it, a *prima facie* case has been presented.

As a procedural matter, the trial judge decides whether a plaintiff has met its burden of going forward and presented a prima facie case. This decision is typically made in the form of a ruling on a motion for a directed verdict by the defendant at the close of the plaintiff's case. If the judge grants the motion, the jury is never given a chance to weigh the evidence but is directed by the judge to render a verdict for the defendant. Because the plaintiff has not presented a prima facie case, the defendant is not even put to the task of refuting it. The burden of proof, then, consists of the plaintiff's responsibility of coming forward with sufficient evidence to forestall an adverse ruling by the judge on the defendant's motion for a directed verdict.

Assuming the plaintiff meets its burden of going forward, the burden of going forward then shifts to the defendant. In other words, the defendant must rebut the plaintiff's case by raising one or more questions of fact. Once this is accomplished, the defendant has met its burden. The defendant does *not,* however, assume the burden of actually *persuading* the factfinder that its version is more likely true than not. The burden of proof, unlike the burden of going forward, does not shift during the trial but always remains upon the plaintiff. If the defendant fails to meet its burden of going forward, the plaintiff is entitled to a directed verdict in its favor.

If both sides meet their burdens on all elements, then the case goes to the jury. At this point, the plaintiff will prevail if the jury decides that a preponderance of the evidence supports its position.

§ 13.4 —Presumptions and Inferences in General

Presumptions repeatedly cause practical difficulties for even the most experienced lawyer. Much of the confusion stems from an imprecise and inconsistent vocabulary. Case law and statutes speak of "inferences," "conclusive presumptions," "permissive presumptions," "presumptions of 'fact' and of 'law'," and "rebuttable presumptions." Usage may vary not only from state to state and from civil to criminal cases, but from judge to judge within the same or different jurisdictions. The underlying logic and legal effect of presumptions are, in the final analysis, really quite straightforward.

An *inference* may be broadly defined as a conclusion about the existence of a particular fact reached by considering other facts in the usual course of human reasoning. Throughout a trial, juries repeatedly arrive at conclusions based on inferences, as opposed to direct evidence. They work from a basic fact, the existence of which is supported by the evidence, to an inferred fact, the likely existence of which is supported by common sense. The decision as to whether to make a given inference is completely discretionary with the individual juror. Based on his or her own experience, a juror is free to infer or not to infer the existence of B from A.

A presumption differs from an inference primarily in that a presumption is not discretionary. In some ways, a presumption is an inference that has been given special status in the interests of procedural convenience or public policy. A *presumption* may be defined as a rule of law that *requires* that the existence of a fact be taken as established when one or more other facts are established. However, a presumption must embody an underlying logical inference. Indeed, one major rationale for raising certain inferences to the status of presumptions is that the inferences are so universally supported by common sense and experience that, in the interest of judicial economy, the court may dispense with the need for a party to present unnecessary evidence.

Generally speaking, presumptions are *rebuttable.* That is, presumptions are mandatory only in a conditional way. The jury must find in favor of the presumed fact when the party with the burden of proof has established the basic facts—*unless* the opposing party then comes forward with evidence sufficient to overcome the presumption. The legal effect of presumption is to shift at least the burden of going forward—and in some instances the burden of proof—for a given factual question onto the opposing party. In essence, presumptions are burden shifters. However, under the Federal Rules of Evidence and the majority of state rules, a presumption shifts only the burden of going forward and not the burden of proof.

§ 13.5 —Trial Considerations

Presumptions, functioning as automatic burden shifters, can be powerful weapons in a trial lawyer's arsenal. At a minimum, they can save time at trial as well as time and expense in discovery. However, there may also be occasions when a presumption can make the difference between winning or losing a case.

Once a trial has begun, presumptions take on special procedural significance at two points, at least: (1) in moving for or resisting a motion for a directed verdict and (2) in formulating, submitting, and objecting to jury instructions.

Motions for directed verdicts are usually made (1) after the opening statement of opposing counsel, (2) at the close of opposing counsel's evidence, or (3) at the close of all evidence. The precise standard used by the judge when dealing with such motions may vary slightly from state to state and between state and federal courts. However, in essence, the moving party is asking the court to rule that the opposing party has not met its burden of going forward—that is, the party has not presented evidence sufficient to raise a question of fact on one or more elements of the cause of action based upon which the jury could reasonably find in that party's favor.

It should be immediately obvious that presumptions, as burden shifters, may have a pivotal role to play in making or overcoming motions for a directed verdict. In a jurisdiction that recognizes, for example, that death may be presumed from a person's unexplained absence for seven years, a plaintiff in a wrongful death action may defeat a motion for a directed verdict even though the plaintiff has offered evidence only of seven years of absence, not the victim's actual death.

Practice varies among jurisdictions and even among courtrooms in the same jurisdiction whether motions for directed verdicts must be in writing, what degree of specificity is required, and whether oral argument or briefs are to be employed. As a practical matter, however, once the trial has begun, there is usually little time to prepare either the moving or the opposing papers. As a result, it is typically a good idea to prepare at least a draft or "skeleton" motion in advance of trial and to fill in necessary details as the opposing party puts on its case.

Judges often recognize and apply presumptions as a matter of course, both in making threshold determinations whether a party has met its burden of going forward and later as triers of fact in bench trials. Remember, however, that even in the case of a bench trial, it is incumbent upon you to bring presumptions to the attention of the judge and argue either for their application or for their being overcome.

§ 13.6 —Jury Instructions

Juries must be instructed as to both the relevant presumptions in the case and the operation of those presumptions on specific factual questions. A crucial distinction between inferences and presumptions is that the former are discretionary with the jury, and the latter are mandatory.

In addition to relevant presumptions, the jury will be instructed on such other matters as burdens and standards of proof, the factual issues to be decided, and the law to be applied. Although the judge approves and presents the instructions to the jury, the parties themselves fashion them initially and argue to have their versions adopted. About half the states and the federal courts have developed "pattern jury instructions" to cover most commonly encountered legal areas. In some jurisdictions, the use of pattern instructions is optional; in many, their use may be required when they accurately state the law. When the pattern instructions do not contain an instruction on a subject on which a party believes an instruction is warranted, that party is free to draft its own instruction.

Practically speaking, you should prepare jury instructions as far in advance of trial as possible. This can help crystallize your theory of the case, cut down on the proofs, and save time at trial. From a tactical standpoint, your proposed instructions should reflect the theory of the case as you see it and cover every material issue of fact to be decided. When you draft your own instructions, rather than using pattern instructions, they should be in simple language, brief, nonargumentative, and impartial. This is not to say, however, that instructions favorable to your case are improper.

Suggesting a large number of instructions is to be avoided, and repetitive instructions are improper. An instruction based on a statute should reflect any judicial construction or modification of that statute, although it is not recommended that you try to convert the language of judicial decisions into instructions.

Instructions should be prepared and submitted on separate, numbered pages, in the sequence in which you want the court to read them. The citation, pattern instruction number, case, or statute for the legal authority supporting each instruction should appear on its page. The page should also identify the submitting party.

The judge has broad discretion in giving the instructions that the parties have tendered. He or she may refuse or modify an instruction or propose his or her own sua sponte. In most states, the parties must request that instructions be given, and, if not timely made, the request may be waived. Some courts request that the parties submit their instructions at the outset of the trial; others, after all the evidence is in. Generally, approval of jury instructions occurs before closing arguments, so that the parties know better how to structure their last appeals to the jurors.

In most states, certain instructions must be given, even though neither party requests them. These generally include instructions as to which party bears the burden of proof on each factual issue, as well as the proper standard of proof to be applied by the jury. For example, in a criminal trial, the judge may be required to instruct the jury on the presumption of the defendant's innocence and on the specific elements of the offense. The judge may also give *cautionary* instructions on the jury's duty to follow the law, determine the facts from the evidence, ignore personal prejudices or sympathies, and others.

Generally, proposed instructions are submitted to the court and simultaneously served on all other parties. The judge may schedule a conference to hear argument on the instructions. At this conference, each party can raise and meet objections to the instructions proffered by others or by the judge and suggest alternatives or compromises. Some judges may require the parties to submit written objections in advance. In any event, each party must be prepared to support its position with legal authority. The grounds of an objection must be specific, and, if a modified version of an instruction would cure a defect, you should be ready to submit it.

The judge will ultimately rule on every instruction tendered, usually noting in its margin whether it was "given," "modified," or "refused." In order to preserve objections for appeal, an objecting party typically must reiterate any objections *after* the judge has ruled, or the objections may be deemed to have been waived. A party may also be required, depending on the applicable rules, to take exception to the court's giving of or refusal to give a specific instruction after all instructions have been given and before jury deliberations begin. In any event, the burden is on the objecting party to preserve the record of the conference and the objection.

Appellate courts grant trial courts broad discretion on approving, modifying, or refusing jury instructions. As a general rule, the fact that a single instruction is improper does not constitute reversible error if it is cured by the effect of the instructions taken as a whole. There is extensive case law in every jurisdiction regarding the propriety of particular instructions and whether they merit reversal. Of the plethora of reasons for objecting to a specific jury instruction, a listing of those most frequently raised can be instructive.

1. Repetitious, duplicative, or redundant
2. Comments on the evidence
3. Argumentative
4. Gives undue prominence to a single theory, issue, or defense
5. Minimizes the importance of a theory, issue, or defense
6. Misstates the law or facts
7. Unsupported by the evidence
8. Goes beyond the pleadings or issues of the case
9. Misleads or confuses the jury
10. Injects a party's faulty contentions
11. States abstract principles of law
12. States inferences to be drawn from facts
13. Unqualifiedly assumes the truth of a disputed or controverted material fact
14. Expresses an opinion on the facts, merits, or evidence
15. Determines a witness's credibility or the weight of testimony
16. Determines the weight given to elements of evidence
17. Inconsistent with other jury instructions
18. Fails to state the entire law as modified or qualified; is too general, too broad, or too narrow
19. Vague, ambiguous, indefinite, or obscure
20. Uses double negatives or Latin words
21. Incorrectly indicates the character of the evidence necessary to establish facts and the degree of evidence required
22. Invades the province of the jury
23. Excludes issues from the jury
24. Directly or impliedly determines a fact at issue
25. Directly or impliedly determines matters relating to the amount of damages
26. Belittles evidence
27. Is incorrect or exhibits bias.

Clearly, only a few of these objections relate substantively to burdens or presumptions, although almost any one could be applicable in general terms to an instruction containing a presumption.

A list of objections specifically relating to presumptions in jury instructions might include the following:

1. The instruction incorrectly shifts the burden of proof.
2. The instruction is worded permissively instead of in mandatory terms.
3. The presumption finds no legal support in case law or statute.
4. The presumption, though supported by legal authority, has no rational basis in fact.
5. The instruction uses the word "presumption," thereby creating an unnecessary conclusion for jurors.
6. An instruction as to a presumption has been improperly omitted.

An understanding of the role of burdens, inferences, and presumptions in the overall trial process is crucial to the successful presentation of a case. Coupled with an understanding of their relationship to motions for a directed verdict and any jury instructions, a trial lawyer has a valuable weapon for both successfully presenting his or her case and defeating that of his or her opponent.

§ 13.7 Cautionary Instructions—"The Back Door"

One of the tritest phrases used in the legal profession in relation to improper statements in court and their effect on a jury is that you can't unring a bell. Human experience indicates that this is true, because once an individual—particularly a juror whose primary role is to listen and assimilate facts—hears something, it is virtually impossible to wipe that statement or other piece of information completely out of his or her mind. Instructing an individual to forget something or, in the case of a juror, to disregard an improper statement and not to permit it in any way to affect the decisionmaking process is of questionable value.

The typical circumstance in which you will encounter the back-door or cautionary instruction approach involves either an honest error by an opponent or, as may unfortunately sometimes occur, a deliberate act of putting something before a jury with the knowledge that it is improper. The latter usually takes the form of an inadvertent act, despite its deliberateness. Your opponent's immediate follow-up to such an act is, "Your Honor, I apologize."

You then face a difficult predicament, not unlike the one which may confront you with regard to making objections. If you seek an instruction from the judge that the jury should disregard a particular statement of an attorney made during the questioning of a witness, you run the very real risk of drawing the jury's attention to the statement and emphasizing its importance. On the other hand, if you do nothing, you run the equally great risk of having the jury assimilate what is often a damaging exchange or comment into the decisionmaking process.

Your overall approach to such back-door attempts is not unlike the risk-benefit analysis that you must go through in other aspects of litigation, particularly motions practice. In many respects, when you attempt to unring the bell, you are in a *no win* position, and you must pay more attention to minimizing and containing the damage than you do to curing the problem. Cautionary instructions are of little help, because they can do nothing more than attempt to aid the jury in considering the improprieties to which they have been exposed; they cannot wipe the slate clean. Unfortunately, short of a successful motion for mistrial, which is unlikely except in the case of the grossest abuse, the cautionary instruction is about all that can be hoped for in this regard.

In dealing with opponents who you either suspect or know will take a back-door approach and then seek to use the cautionary instruction as a means of curing the problem they have created, there are several tactical points which you should keep in mind and techniques which may be helpful.

1. If you anticipate that your opponent is going to make a statement or pursue a line of questioning with a witness that will result in presenting something improper before the jury, you should take prior steps to prevent it. One approach is a motion in limine filed before trial or an oral motion made either prior to or during examination of the witness. Obviously, if you are making the motion during examination of the witness, you should make it at side bar.
2. One way to approach this task (when you are uncertain as to whether your opponent is going to pursue such a tactic) without looking bad yourself is to direct a question through the court suggesting your desire to obviate objections which would otherwise slow the trial down. For example, you might say, "Your Honor, if counsel at this point is going to pursue [describe the area of your concern], I would respectfully object and request that counsel be instructed not to pursue that line of questioning as, despite any instructions which your Honor may give to the jury with respect to disregarding the questions and answers, the questions and answers will still have been put before the jury and it will be difficult if not impossible for them to wipe them from their minds completely."
3. One highly aggressive approach to this problem which focuses the spotlight on your opponent is to object in open court and point up the tactic for what it is. For example, you might say, "I object to this

line of questioning [or statement by counsel, as appropriate] and would suggest to your Honor that the only reason counsel has pursued this area is to present in front of the jury that which counsel knows is improper for the purpose of prejudicing the jury. I would further suggest that counsel knows that despite a cautionary instruction by your Honor that the jury should disregard what has just occurred, the jury has heard the statement nonetheless. I would further request that your Honor admonish counsel not to pursue such tactics."

4. The obvious advantage of taking an offensive approach is that you are, in effect, "attacking" your opponent for unethical behavior. If the court does in fact admonish your opponent, you have gained a considerable tactical advantage. However, remember that the jury will still have heard the objectionable statement, question, or answer.

§ 13.8 Motion to Strike

A motion to strike is nothing more than a formal pleading, in written or oral form, directed at having something stricken from the record. Obviously, when made during the examination of a witness, a motion to strike a statement which was made in the presence of the jury results only in a cautionary instruction to the jury to disregard something. The value of such relief is questionable. However, such motions and resulting instructions are obviously necessary to protect the record.

When you move to strike a comment which is particularly prejudicial or improper, you should consider requesting that the court direct the comment to be physically stricken in order to prevent it from becoming part of the record in the event the case is appealed. If the material to which the motion is directed is not of an evidentiary nature but rather is something else which is clearly improper or which involves the behavior of counsel, motions and orders granting motions can frequently be obtained which direct that certain material be physically stricken from the record.

One tactic of which you should be aware is the improper use against you of a motion to strike. Such a motion, especially in the presence of a jury which does not really understand the ramifications of a motion to strike, casts a cloud of suspicion on the part of your examination which is the subject of the motion. Thus, an opponent who makes a motion to strike without good basis is in effect saying to the jury that you did something wrong. If the motion is denied, you have been, in large measure, vindicated.

Even when you are vindicated, however, the question has still been raised, and you should be sure to obtain some sort of remedial instruction from the judge clarifying what has transpired in connection with a motion to strike. Such motions should certainly be made out of the hearing of the jury, and this would, assuming you are the target of a motion to strike, necessitate a bench conference.

In the event that a motion to strike is granted, it will typically be followed by an instruction to the jury to "disregard" certain information, statements, questions, or answers. When you find yourself having to move to strike, you should also consider suggesting cautionary instruction language. Often, you can gain an advantage in such an instruction, because it casts a negative light on your opponent and amounts to an admonition against your opponent's conduct. An example of such an instruction might be as follows:

> Ladies and gentlemen of the jury, you are to disregard the last question and answer wherein counsel sought to elicit material which is clearly irrelevant to this case and your consideration of a verdict. Furthermore, counsel is admonished not to raise this area again.

The obvious advantage of having your opponent admonished in the presence of the jury is that the jurors put great weight on the perceptions of the judge and will see the conduct of counsel as they think the judge sees it. If you believe that the jurors try lawyers any less than they try cases, your belief is simply a product of inexperience and will change over time.

§ 13.9 "I'll Link It Up Later"

During examination of a witness, you will often hear an opponent formulating a question make what purports to be factual statements as part of the basic premise of the question. If the questions as phrased are answered, those premises become factual parts of the record. This may occur with either fact witnesses or expert witnesses, in the latter category with respect to hypotheticals, for example, "Doctor, assume (a), (b), and (c). Do you have an opinion as to whether or not the defendant was negligent?"

Whether you are dealing with a fact witness or an expert witness, your typical response when your opponent has integrated certain facts or assumptions into the questions and there is no evidence in the record to support those statements is to object. Absent some further statement from your opponent, such objections frequently will be sustained.

A tactic often used and frequently abused is for an opponent to respond to your objection along the following lines: "Your Honor, I would request the court's indulgence at this point, because the facts or information to which counsel refers will be introduced through the next (or later) witness." Alternatively, when your objection may go to the relevance of a certain line of questioning, the response may be: "Your Honor, I would suggest to the court that the relevance of this line of questioning will become apparent in a very short time."

When confronted with such explanations, judges frequently overrule an objection subject to reconsideration at a later point in the event that counsel either does not introduce the required facts or evidence or fails to make the vital link of relevance. The problem with this type of ruling is that frequently your opponent does fail to introduce or connect the necessary evidence as earlier represented to the court. When this happens, even assuming a successful motion to strike at a later point, the offending evidence has been presented to the jury, and they are now being told to unring a bell.

To maximize the protection to your case against such a tactic or against such a response by your opponent to a valid objection, recognizing that many judges permit evidence to be presented before the jury on assurances of counsel that certain other evidence will be introduced or that a relevance link will be made, there are two points which you should consider.

First, when confronted with the response of counsel as indicated, you should request an offer of proof out of hearing of the jury as to what the later evidence or link of relevance will be that justifies the court's permitting the evidence then being elicited into the record. If your opponent is simply running a bluff or attempting to abuse the rules of evidence, it will become apparent. Alternatively, if your opponent makes such an offer of proof and then fails to live up to it by introducing the evidence later, you stand a very good chance of not only having all the evidence stricken but having your opponent disciplined or admonished in the presence of the jury. Although you cannot unring the bell, you can at least maximize the situation to the extent of making it uncomfortable for your opponent.

Second, one of your greatest problems when an opponent indicates that certain later evidence will be adduced is that you may fail to follow up and make sure that the evidence is in fact adduced, and thus you forget to bring a motion to strike and seek whatever additional relief may be justified. In such circumstances, you should take steps to remind yourself about the "promises" of your opponent and ensure that he or she lives up to them. It is helpful to note any promises in a specific section of your trial notebook, particularly the section dealing with the witnesses referred to during the offer of proof. In the event that the evidence is stricken on your motion at a later point, you will be unable to refer to the occurrence itself in your closing argument. However, you can most certainly refer to the concept of promises as referred to in **Chapter 12** on opening statements and as discussed in **Chapter 16** on closing arguments.

§ 13.10 Lawyer-Judge Confrontations

At some time in their careers, all lawyers have had the misfortune to find themselves appearing before a judge whom they believe is being hostile or unreasonable. Sometimes the judge is being equally unfair to both sides. In most instances, however, when for whatever reason a judge has embarked on a course of judicially irrational behavior, it benefits one side to a significant extent while operating to the prejudice of the other.

In such circumstances, the task facing a lawyer is twofold: how to keep confrontational situations from occurring and, assuming they do occur, how to deal with them so as to neutralize the potential for damage to the case or to the continued long-term relationship between the lawyer and the judge. In terms of the first consideration, preventing a situation from developing that puts you on the receiving end of a "judge gone wild," certain basic truths must be recognized.

First and foremost is that everybody has bad days and that judges are no exception. On occasion, the pressures and difficulties of our personal lives have a disproportionate impact on our professional relationships. In the context of the judge-lawyer relationship, this can mean extreme difficulties when one considers the decisionmaking power the judge has over the lawyer. Unfortunately, there is no way to really recognize that the judge is having a bad day until it manifests itself in the courtroom. One way to get a head start is to observe the judge in action before your case is called. This approach only works, of course, if your case is not the first one on the calendar, but when you do have a chance to observe, you frequently will be able to get some insight into what to expect by watching the judge with other lawyers.

The second basic truth to be recognized is that trial-level judges—particularly federal district court judges—are among the most powerful human beings in the United States. Consider that within the context of the judiciary, of all the thousands and thousands of decisions and orders made daily by federal district court judges, only a handful ever enter the appellate process. A district court judge's power of civil and criminal contempt is awesome. Indeed, although the power of an individual member of Congress or the power of the president is certainly substantial, for all intents and purposes either of these is subject to a far greater system of checks and balances than the power of a federal district court judge. For any number of reasons, lawyers frequently do not take appeals, and this makes many decisions invincible. In addition, the review standard of *clearly erroneous* and the wide latitude afforded trial judges in matters of discretion and judgment make it a formidable and expensive task to take on a decision in the appellate courts.

The third basic truth to be recognized in dealing with a difficult judge is that sometimes there is simply nothing you can do but roll with the punches and avoid making the situation any worse. This requires an accurate and often instantaneous appraisal of what has occurred, immediate formulation of a plan of action, and an accurate assessment of damage.

After accepting these basic truths, whether you are happy with them or not, the question becomes how to deal with a situation in which the judge goes on the rampage. While by no means surefire in their results, there are a number of things that a litigator can or should do in such situations.

Honest Assessment

In the heat of battle or in the adversarial atmosphere of litigation, it is often difficult to step back from a situation and honestly assess where you are and how you got there. It is even more difficult when you are standing before a judge who has launched a shouting, bench-pounding tirade against you for what you perceive as no valid reason. In dealing with such a situation, the very first thing to do—unless speech is absolutely necessary—is to keep your mouth shut and use the time to make an honest assessment of what you did and whether it justified the judge's reaction.

Remember, all litigators are combatants, paid to have and preserve a biased view of the circumstances that gave rise to a particular piece of litigation. All too frequently, their views miss the big picture and the fact that no matter how valid one side of an issue may be, there are inevitably valid points to be made on the other side as well. The judge stands between both sides and presumably takes a more balanced view of the case. On occasion, this balanced view may be the initial cause of a judicial rampage that may not be totally unwarranted. By stepping back from the battle and trying to look at the situation as the judge sees it, you can often come to understand what provoked the judge.

The next step is to decide what to do in order to defuse the situation. In some circumstances, it may mean doing nothing; in others, it may mean apologizing to the court in the hope of ending the confrontation. In all circumstances, however, there should be an attempt to obtain a dispassionate understanding of what occurred and why.

Baiting the Judge

Just as it is mandatory to make an honest assessment of the confrontation situation, one thing no lawyer should do or appear to do is to bait the judge. One of the usual ways of doing so—although it is frequently unappreciated—is to mention the appellate process. No one likes to have decisions second-guessed. Although judges frequently make casual statements from the bench along the lines of, "If you don't like it, you know the road to the circuit," human nature being what it is, judges do not want to be reversed.

In the emotionally charged atmosphere of a courtroom confrontation with the judge, the raising of the appellate process by an attorney who is the object of a tirade is virtually guaranteed to aggravate the situation further. Statements like "Your Honor, my clients will be taking this matter to the appellate court" are tantamount to throwing gasoline on a fire. It is one thing for a judge to make such comments; it is quite another for an attorney to make them.

The principle to follow in a courtroom confrontation with a judge is not to speak out of reflex. Remember, words that may not be inflammatory in a more routine courtroom situation have the potential to take on vastly different meanings in a confrontation with a judge who is unreasonably upset.

Protecting the Record

Although waving the appellate flag in the courtroom is ill-advised, the record must be protected. Absent total inability to control the situation, a litigator should never permit confrontation with a judge to occur off the record. Without a doubt, judges feel less restricted in their comments when they are off the record. When they are on the record, and subject to appellate and public scrutiny, many judges will moderate their attitudes, statements, tempers, and actions.

In the context of a confrontation, the record should be protected in two ways—by a stenographic record and by a posthearing pleading. A lawyer placed in an off-the-record confrontation situation with a judge should respectfully request that the proceedings be placed on the record. Such a suggestion, even if made in the most low-key and neutral fashion, has definite potential for further aggravating the situation. If the request is denied, there is very little that can be done about it. However, the denial most assuredly should be addressed in a posthearing motion or pleading focused on getting your entire presentation on the record in written form.

Motions for Reconsideration

When rulings that you believe to be unsound or unfair have been made against you by an enraged judge, a promptly filed motion for reconsideration sometimes will result in modifications. In addition, the filing of such a motion has the benefit of building the appellate record in the event that the matter is to be pursued further. If necessary, affidavits or copies of pertinent transcript excerpts from the hearing should be appended. If the judge refuses your request for a court reporter, this should be noted as well.

The downside risk of filing such a motion is that it keeps the confrontation alive and may poison the judge against your entire case. However, as with many other areas of litigation, this is a risk-benefit analysis question that must be answered separately for each case and for which there is no single solution.

The entire area of judge-lawyer interpersonal dealings is one to which a great deal of attention should be given by all litigators. Recognition of the danger signs and the ability to deal with such difficulties effectively frequently can mean the difference between winning and losing a motion—and, on occasion, a case. Although not all confrontations can be resolved favorably, careful handling and an awareness of what is occurring will always help contain the damage and minimize its effects.

§ 13.11 Out-of-Order Witnesses

Virtually every jurisdiction today, federal or state, requires the filing of some sort of pretrial statement or witness list which delineates with a high degree of specificity the evidence and witnesses to be called during the trial. Sometimes this must be done as a joint filing, and sometimes it is done through separate filings. In addition to advising the court of the overall parameters of the proofs at trial, this also alerts opposing counsel to the nature of the proofs to which they will have to respond.

In addition to allowing an opponent to prepare cross-examinations and rebuttal examinations, the filing of such information also represents, in part, a recognition that the plaintiff has a burden of going forward as well as a burden of proof. In short, the burden of going forward relates to the fact that a plaintiff must get past a motion for a directed verdict by introducing enough evidence for a trier of fact or jury to find for the plaintiff. Once that has been done and a motion for a directed verdict has been denied or a ruling thereon held in abeyance, the plaintiff still has the burden of proof. In effect, the burden of proof never shifts, for it always rests on the plaintiff and, theoretically, once the plaintiff has completed the presentation of its evidence, the defendant then has the burden of proving everything which it affirmatively advances, including things like affirmative defenses.

In the normal order of things, the plaintiff will call all of his or her witnesses, the defendant will call witnesses to respond, and, on occasion, both sides will call rebuttal witnesses to address things not otherwise covered in the case-in-chief. One tactic sometimes used is the out-of-order witness, particularly as it relates to the defense's putting a witness on during the plaintiff's case or vice versa. Properly done, this can be a devastating tactic.

Putting a witness on out of order during your opponent's case has obvious advantages in that it provides the jury with a preview of the evidence to come in a case which has not yet been started. Furthermore, it presents the preview when the case being presented has not yet been completed and thus gives the jury a benchmark or measure against which to compare the evidence then being presented.

An example of how this can be done effectively is when an expert, because of time availability problems, is put on by the defense during the plaintiff's case. The expert gives opinions and offers testimony that is obviously directly contrary to the plaintiff's case and is presented at a time when the plaintiff's case is not yet complete. This gives the jury a measure against which to hold the plaintiff's case as the balance of it is presented. If the expert or witness who has been put on out of order is strong in terms of both substance and presentation of the testimony, the advantages are tremendous.

The burden which a plaintiff must overcome is not only the traditional one of going forward/burden of proof; it now includes the burden of overcoming strong and effectively presented adverse testimony right in the middle of its case. In addition, this preeducation of the judge and jury can have the effect of shaping rulings on objections and, in its most effective form, can require the plaintiff or the party finding itself on the receiving end of this approach to change its entire tactical approach to the remainder of the case. By the time this has occurred, it is often too late in the case to undertake a major tactical change that would affect the balance of the presentation.

The most effective means of keeping from having an opponent's witness presented in the middle of your case is not to provide an opportunity for it. Typically, this situation might arise either as a result of your not having a witness available because, for example, testimony has finished early on a given day and your next witness is not physically available until the following morning or, alternatively, when your opponent requests permission from the judge to put a witness on out of order because of schedule conflicts. One of these situations you can do something about; the other presents more problems.

Running out of witnesses often occurs during trial, because testimony may take less time than anticipated or a judge may work longer hours than expected. Its very unexpectedness might indicate that it cannot be planned for and protected against. However, careful logistical and schedule planning of your witnesses should keep you operating one witness ahead. Just as the expert pool or chess player is several moves ahead of the move being made at any given time, you should always have a minimum of one witness physically available and ready to testify while another of your witnesses is on the witness stand actually testifying.

A more effective and easier approach to this "one ahead" technique may be to have a deposition testimony in the wings and ready to go, either through use of deposition summaries, as discussed in **Chapter 1**, or through actual verbatim deposition materials. The whole idea is not to be caught with a void which your opponent may fill in order to use jury time productively.

You face a somewhat more difficult problem, although not of your own making, when your opponent requests permission to put a witness on out of order during your case because the witness will be unavailable at a later time. You can easily appear unreasonable if you refuse to allow this or if you strenuously object to the court. When confronted with this situation, there are several points which you should keep in mind.

If this request is made to the court, be sure that proper inquiry has been made either by you or by the judge into the reason for the unavailability of the witness and the amount of notice which has been given the witness. If the unavailability of the witness turns out to be contrived because of improper or lack of adequate notice by counsel, this should become clear upon such inquiry, especially when the inquiry is made by the judge. In the event that the unavailability seems to be contrived, you can be assured that the judge will not permit the out-of-order presentation.

In the event that the unavailability is genuine, your problem is to walk the fine line between objecting to an out-of-order witness who breaks up your case and has the potential to give your opponent the advantage and being cooperative in a way that minimizes any damage to your case. You should note an objection to the out-of-order presentation, pointing out that each of your witnesses builds on the other witnesses and on the evidence which precedes that witness's testimony.

By allowing your opponent to put on a witness out of order during your case, you are being prejudiced by interruption of your chain of evidence and of your whole story during its unfolding and presentation to the jury. Just as a novel would lose all sense and reason if a chapter from the end of the book were placed at the beginning, your case will lose its persuasive value and your client will be done a grave injustice if, through faulty planning by your adversary and through no fault of your own, your opponent is given an unfair advantage.

In the event that your objections are overruled and your opponent is permitted to put on a witness out of order during your case, your backup positions could include the following.

1. Request that the witness's testimony be videotaped and presented in its normal position during the trial. You should indicate that you are available for such a videotape deposition at the conclusion of the trial day and that this would be far preferable to prejudicing your client by having your case interrupted.
2. Suggest that a written deposition be used in lieu of the live testimony.
3. In the event that all other suggested alternatives fail, including the use of either a videotape or oral deposition, determine the point in your case where the insertion of an adverse witness will have the least effect. This approach is obviously one of "minimizing damage" and should be avoided. However, in the event that this alternative

becomes your only one, you should ascertain where the testimony of an adverse witness could be inserted without breaking the flow of evidence and where its effect will be minimized. One approach is immediately to follow the testimony of such a witness with your strongest expert in direct rebuttal. By having your opponent's witness go first and then having your expert present your case-in-chief, you not only have the opportunity to present your evidence in the first instance but also have your expert incorporate rebuttal-type testimony into your direct case. If there is any attempt by your opponent to call a rebuttal witness thereafter, you can legitimately object on the basis that such rebuttal evidence is improper, because the situation was of your opponent's own making.

§ 13.12 Examining Adverse Witnesses

No doubt there will come occasions in your life as a trial lawyer when it will be necessary for you to call an adverse party to the witness stand as part of your direct case. In these instances, you have no doubt already taken a deposition from the party and are prepared to impeach that individual should his or her testimony change. However, assuming that the party is available, he or she will be called live at trial. The approach typically best taken when examining this sort of witness is something equivalent to the friendly cross-examination of a witness.

Rule 43B of the Federal Rules of Civil Procedure and state counterparts permit you to call an adverse party to the stand to testify as part of your direct case. Rule 611(c) of the Federal Rules of Evidence and its state counterparts permit you to use leading questions when you call a hostile witness, an adverse party, or a witness identified with an adverse party as part of your direct case. In effect, the examination becomes a cross-examination. Practically speaking, however, if it is to become a hostile-type examination, this is an approach which you should allow the witness to initiate, as opposed to introducing that tone on your own.

Be aware of the following points when you call an adverse party to testify as part of your direct case:

1. Determine in advance of calling the adverse party why you are calling him or her. Typically, the soundest reason for doing so is to secure facts or admissions favorable to your case. It is typically not the best idea to call an adverse party as part of your direct case for the purpose of impeaching his or her credibility. This is better left to your cross-examination of that party during your opponent's case.
2. You should listen carefully to the answers and ensure that the witness is limiting his or her answer to your question. As a result, you should

always use leading questions in order to limit the range of freedom which the witness has in answering the question.

3. If the witness is not being responsive, you should insist upon responsive answers through a motion to strike directed at the nonresponsive answer.
4. Remember that, because the adverse party is not having his or her credibility vouched for by you, you are granted a great deal more latitude in the conduct of your examination, even though it is a direct examination.
5. When the witness answers a question other than the one you are asking, a good tactic to point this out to the jury is to say, "Sir, now would you answer my question" and then repeat the question.
6. Frequently, when calling an adverse party as a witness during your direct case, you will confront a witness who has lost all memory of the areas being inquired into. In such a situation, you should not insist upon an answer, because what has occurred will become evident to the jury. A better approach is to emphasize the witness's lack of memory and, within the context of the questions being asked, make it appear improbable that such a lack of recollection would exist.
7. A good time to follow this up is your cross-examination of the adverse party during your opponent's case. Obviously, if the witness has a sudden recollection during questioning by his or her counsel but evidenced a complete lack of such recollection during your questioning, this will not escape the jury.

In almost every case, there will be witnesses you must call as part of your direct case who are in a position to testify about a major flaw or problem with your case. Obviously, if this problem is significant enough, perhaps you would have been better advised either not to call the witness at all or simply to settle the case. However, the larger number of such problems are neither major nor fatal to the successful prosecution or defense of the lawsuit. The problem is how to present those in their best light to the jury.

The immutable rule in this area is to leave no weaknesses in your case for your opponent to bring out on cross-examination of your witnesses. When weaknesses are brought out on cross-examination, they inevitably become major weaknesses and major flaws, and your credibility suffers in the eyes of the jury for not bringing them out on direct examination.

Tactically, you would be well advised to bring the weaknesses out early in the witness's testimony, get them explained, and move on to the stronger aspects of the testimony. This allows you to open big with the witness, get the weakness out of the way, get to the substance of the testimony, and close strong. By stealing your opponent's thunder, you can take away the shock value the testimony may have had and the impression that you were concealing something. Although you can be assured that your opponent will attempt to make the most of the weakness, there is little you will be able to do about that and probably nothing which you will need to do if you have done an adequate job in dealing with it during the direct case.

Rule 43B of the Federal Rules of Civil Procedure, in addition to permitting you to call an adverse party during your case, also allows you to interrogate any unwilling or hostile witness through the use of leading questions. In addition, the same provision is contained in Federal Rule of Evidence 611(c). We have already discussed the examination of an adverse party who is presumed to be hostile. What about the situation in which a witness thought originally to be favorable and friendly to your case turns hostile on the stand and starts to give testimony adverse to your case?

Generally speaking, what is required is for you, in good faith, to claim surprise. Once the court has determined that the witness is indeed hostile or unwilling, you will be permitted to examine that witness as if you were on cross-examination. Thus, leading questions will be allowed, and you will probably be permitted to impeach the witness in the event that there have been earlier inconsistent statements. For example, if you have taken the deposition of the witness or have a written statement from him or her, you will be able to use that deposition or written statement to impeach him or her as if the witness had been turned over to you on cross-examination.

It is well known that when you call a witness to the stand, you are vouching for that witness's credibility. What this means in practical terms is that, absent some surprise by that witness, you are not going to be able to ask leading questions of the witness, because it is presumed that the witness is going to give testimony friendly to your side. As a result of this, you will rarely find yourself in the situation of impeaching your own witness, although you may have in your possession inconsistent evidence previously testified to or written by the witness that you intend to use to impeach the witness's testimony at trial.

Rule 607 of the Federal Rules of Evidence provides that the credibility of a witness may be attacked by any party, including the party who called him or her. This represents a departure from the traditional rule that a party calling a witness may not impeach him or her and a recognition of the fact that parties do not choose witnesses but rather have them chosen for them by the facts and circumstances of the case. The question, then, of impeaching your own witness is one of tactics and timing.

You will want to call a witness whom you intend to impeach only if you know you will be able to impeach that witness. This requires you to have clearly impeaching evidence, such as a prior inconsistent statement given either in writing or at a deposition. Then you must consider timing.

Do you want to impeach the witness as part of your direct case, or do you want to have that witness testify as part of your direct case and impeach the witness later by introducing testimony or evidence through another witness? In some measure, this decision is dictated by the means which you intend to use to impeach the witness.

If you have a prior inconsistent statement given in deposition from that witness, the most effective time to impeach the witness is while you are examining him or her. This is the traditional type of impeachment, using prior inconsistent testimony, and is not hearsay under Federal Rule of Evidence 801(d)(1). The alternative approach is a written statement contained in a letter or some other document that directly impeaches the witness. Here you have a greater latitude, because you may be able to introduce that letter through some other witness at a later point.

The risk you run in deferring impeachment is that the jury may integrate the witness's testimony and evidence into their overall consideration of the case. By later impeaching, you may find that the impact of the impeachment is lost or at least substantially lessened. Thus, the primary factor to be considered is the impact value. Generally speaking, the strongest impact is gained by impeaching the witness immediately and then later calling other witnesses or introducing other evidence which furthers the impeachment.

An ability to respond quickly to these types of situations in the courtroom can frequently spell the difference between success and disaster. Although each case must be dealt with based upon its own unique set of facts and personalities, an ability to have a predetermined strategy allows a measured response that has been well thought out and planned in an environment separate and distinct from the adversary atmosphere of the courtroom.

§ 13.13 Pocket Briefs

Litigation is marked by written filings. Most of these take place either prior or subsequent to the trial itself. Very few take place during the trial as the oral testimony unfolds. However, use of *pocket* or short briefs on specific evidentiary points is an extremely effective way of placing an opponent on the defensive and at a substantial disadvantage during the trial itself.

In every case you litigate, there are a number of evidentiary points which you can be sure will arise and resolution of which depends on the exercise of discretion by the trial judge. Frequently these may involve hearsay and its admissibility under either one of the specific exceptions or a general exception, privilege, or narrower questions that relate to the particular character of evidence involved in the case you are litigating.

Sometimes these evidentiary questions have been briefed in advance. Frequently they have not.

Perhaps the single most effective way to handle such evidentiary questions when you can anticipate them and they have not been prebriefed prior to trial is by use of a pocket brief at trial. For example, assume that a question involving what is asserted to be hearsay arises during your direct examination of a particular witness. Your opponent objects that the area of inquiry involves hearsay and that the evidence is inadmissible under the applicable rules. Your response is that, first of all, it is not hearsay and, even assuming it to be hearsay, it should be admissible under the catchall exception as meeting the requirements of reliability and trustworthiness. Your opponent makes an argument, you respond, and the judge is left with a question whether the proposed evidence is hearsay and, even assuming it to be hearsay, whether it should be allowed into evidence under the catchall exception by an exercise of judicial discretion.

In deciding the question, the judge certainly has some awareness of the appellate review process and wishes to make the right decision. It is not unheard of for a judge to reach for an evidence book right on the bench, or, if convenient, to take a recess for some quick research in chambers. Assume further that, as the judge is pondering after each side has had its say, you say:

> Your Honor, I have anticipated this particular problem and would like to hand up to the court a three-page brief setting forth the applicable rules and legal precedent in support of my position. I also have a copy for counsel and one for the clerk to include in the record.

You have now given the judge specific, on-point support for your position. You have further given the judge a push toward ruling in your direction. In addition, you have demonstrated to the judge that you are prepared, organized, and in control of the proceedings. By making the brief short and concise, you have assured that not much time need be devoted to either its reading or its understanding. Your opponent is placed on the defensive and at a considerable disadvantage. The odds are that, if your position appears on its face to be sustainable and, coupled with the legal authorities presented to the court, one with which the court feels comfortable legally and otherwise, you will prevail.

Use of pocket briefs in this way gives you a tremendous tactical advantage, because your opponent does not really know how many more such briefs you have in your briefcase. In addition, the court will give greater weight to your position on objections and evidentiary questions knowing that you have undertaken research to prepare such briefs.

The key is to keep them, in fact, *brief.* Only with short, concise arguments that can be digested and understood in a few minutes can you be assured that they will have the desired impact of motivating the judge toward a favorable ruling during the trial itself. Otherwise, your opponent will ask for time to respond, and, if the brief is of the type which must be read by the judge in chambers, the judge will typically agree to this request and ask you to move on to another area of questioning until the evidentiary objection is resolved. This delay can be avoided by conciseness in your brief.

Another advantage of the pocket brief technique is that you can prepare boilerplate or "canned" pocket briefs which may be useful during trial of all kinds of cases as they relate to questions of hearsay, privilege, and other evidentiary matters with broad, general applicability. Pocket briefs focusing on the court's discretion or on the law in general as distinguished from the particular facts or elements of the case then pending before the judge can be prepared over time on a broad range of evidentiary points. All you will need to do in the circumstances as they relate to any particular case is to have a caption prepared for the particular case with appropriate signature and service pages.

Over a period of time, you will build up a library of pocket briefs which can be drawn on for virtually any case in any of a multitude of situations. Indeed, by having four copies of each brief in your briefcase and keeping a supply of cover and signature sheets, you can virtually prepare and assemble the briefs in court as the evidence unfolds. This can be a tremendously effective technique which can steamroll your opponent on evidentiary questions and objections.

§ 13.14 Offers of Proof

Certain trial techniques available to litigators unfortunately are either not fully understood or frequently overlooked. One of these is an offer of proof. A typical situation calling for an offer of proof in the context of a trial might be when you are examining a witness and draw an objection from your opponent. The objection may or may not be valid. In any event, if it is sustained, you have to ask a different question or perhaps move on to a different area of questioning. In this situation, the offer of proof is a valuable technique.

When an objection is sustained, you should request to "make an offer of proof for the record." The effect is twofold. First, your offer of proof educates the judge about the line of questioning to which an objection has been made and presumably sustained. On occasion, this process itself can result in a reversal of the judge's decision. The more likely use of the offer of proof is to permit the appellate court to, in effect, peek behind the record and see what the evidence would have been had the objection not been sustained and had counsel been permitted to pursue a particular line of questioning or question. The advantage is obvious in the sense that neither the trial judge nor the appellate court confronts a blank wall, so to speak, regarding the objection, without any hint as to what might have happened or what the evidence might have been had the objection been overruled.

Abuse of the offer of proof by an opponent can occur when it is made in inappropriate circumstances. Typically, the offer of proof is most appropriate in relation to an area of questioning as opposed to a single question. If your opponent attempts to make multiple offers of proof for the obvious purpose of educating the judge, you should be sure to point out that the offer of proof device is being used inappropriately. By the same token, you should not be so intimidated that you become reluctant to make an offer of proof under appropriate circumstances.

You should not assume that the judge will permit an offer of proof, but you should insure that if you do object to the making of an offer of proof by your opponent that the record is protected and that any denial by the judge of an offer of proof request is sustainable on appeal. This can be accomplished at side bar without the necessity of an offer of proof, by pointing out to the court during your objection what the offer of proof in effect would be. This permits you to characterize the evidence as opposed to your opponent, who will most certainly characterize it in a way advantageous to his or her case.

§ 13.15 Bench Conferences

During the conduct of any trial before a jury there will arise any number of occasions in which counsel will request a bench conference or will be asked to approach the bench. The obvious purpose of this is to conduct some sort of discussion with the judge out of the hearing of the jury. Often these discussions focus on evidentiary matters and rulings thereon. From an individual attorney's point of view, the liability of a bench conference is that by requesting such a private discussion you are lengthening the term of the jury service and slowing down the trial.

The obvious risk in doing this, especially repeatedly, is that you may alienate the jury by what they may perceive as an obstreperous approach to the case. However, you may have to request repeated bench conferences when your opponent is either making objections or causing you to make objections that require disposition out of the hearing of the jury and when removal of the jury from the courtroom is too time-consuming. Thus, as with many other elements of trial practice, you will be in a weighing and balancing situation; i.e., you will be weighing the benefits of a bench conference against the liabilities associated with the perceptions which may form in the jurors' minds.

You will have very little control over the conduct of bench conferences and situations when you find you must request them. You should be aware, however, that many judges do not as a matter of course permit a bench conference or may respond to your request with a denial. This puts you in a difficult position if the denial occurs in front of the jury, as it usually does. Thus, you must be particularly careful not to permit your opponent to put you into a corner where you must request repeated bench conferences, so that you run the risk of being perceived by the jurors as obstreperous or of having the judge lose patience or otherwise deny your request for a bench conference, even though you may be correct in your underlying reasoning.

One point which you should consider is to affirmatively raise with the judge, at an opportune moment during a bench conference or perhaps in front of the jury, an objection to either your opponent's repeated requests for bench conferences or the conduct of counsel which requires you to ask repeatedly for bench conferences. By pointing out to the judge, perhaps in front of the jury, your concern that conduct of counsel is causing the trial to slow down and not to proceed as efficiently and expeditiously as it otherwise could, you may score points with the jurors as well as the judge. Similarly, this will often give your opponent more than second thoughts regarding conduct which may precipitate another confrontation.

§ 13.16 Objections—In General

From an overall perspective, the making of objections during trial, particularly during the examination of witnesses, is a tremendously effective device for shaping and molding the other side's evidentiary presentation. Not only does an objection have the effect of focusing or commenting on the substantive nature of the areas being inquired into, but it has the additional and sometimes more powerful effect of breaking up the presentation and adversely affecting the demeanor of the attorney making the presentation. The devastating nature of a well-timed objection can be appreciated by any attorney who has carefully prepared a direct or cross-examination of an important witness, only to have these plans destroyed by an objection from an opponent.

When you make trial objections, a number of techniques should be taken into account to be sure your opponent does not take unfair advantage of you. Recognition that objections really are two-edged is crucial to being able to make or meet objections effectively during examination of witnesses. A determination of why a particular objection has been made, whether an objection should be made, how to respond appropriately to an objection, or how to press an objection forward is essential in tactical litigation. For purposes of the next section, a general understanding of objections in terms of both what they are and how to make them is assumed. For a general discussion of objections, *see* M. Dombroff, *Key Trial Control Tactics: A Guide to Winning the Ultimate Verdict* (1983).

§ 13.17 —Making and Responding

There is nothing magical about making or responding to objections. However, there are some techniques which can make your objections more effective, while at the same time forestalling undue prejudice either to your case or to you through objections made by your opponent.

1. Objections should be made loudly, in a manner calculated to terminate or interrupt the question or answer then in progress without provoking the comment, "Wait until counsel has finished the question!" Once the answer is given, you will find yourself attempting to unring the bell. If the witness then being examined by your opponent is the type who quickly latches onto the end of the question and gives the answer, you should request that the judge instruct the witness to give you an opportunity to object prior to commencement of the answer.
2. When you make objections, they should be complete, unless you are otherwise instructed by the court. They should include the basis of your objection and be calculated to persuade the judge. Be particularly wary, however, of opponents who make adversarial-type arguments during their objections which are tantamount to instructions to witnesses or arguments to the jury. If this happens, you should bring it to the attention of the judge and note your objection to counsel's arguing to the jury or instructing the witness under the guise of an objection.
3. When you are examining a witness and an objection is made to your examination, one of the first things you should consider is going to side bar. As soon as you notice counsel starting to rise for an objection, you should stop talking and allow your opponent to start the objection. As soon as the word *objection* is spoken, you should ask to go to side bar to forestall any attempt by other counsel to present argument in the hearing of the jury.
4. You may run into an opponent who uses objections to attempt to shake you instead of to define the contours of the evidence. Typically, such an opponent will make frequent objections and attempt to break your train of thought or concentration during your examination of a witness. If you run into this tactic, a good approach is to allow your opponent to make three or four objections. At that point you should consider making a statement to the judge, in the hearing

of the jury if possible, along the following lines: "Your Honor, with all due respect to counsel, I object to his attempts to interrupt my questioning of this witness or interrupt my train of thought. Counsel will have an opportunity to cross-examine this witness, and I would suggest that his continuous objections to this point are not sound and are solely calculated and made for improper reasons." If you prevail and obtain an affirmative ruling from the judge, you will have done incalculable damage to the credibility of your opponent.

5. Deliberately or inadvertently, many counsel will use the phrase, "Isn't it a fact, . . ." and then go on to ask a question of a witness, either on cross-examination or, more typically, on direct examination. On direct examination, such a question may be leading in nature in that it suggests an answer. This preface to a question amounts to testimony by your opponent and is an attempt to lend greater significance and credibility to information contained in a question that may or may not be a fact. A well-timed objection after two or three repeats of this phrase will often draw an admonition from the judge not to continue with such questions.

§ 13.18 Attacking Credibility

Surprisingly, in this age of what is supposed to be sophisticated litigation, trick questions are still asked. The most typical of these is "Have you talked to anyone about this case?" This question implies that there is something wrong with talking to somebody, particularly the attorneys, about the case. Not having otherwise been instructed, and being somewhat concerned about whether it was all right to talk about the case, witnesses on cross-examination by an opponent may in fact lie and indicate that they did not talk to anyone about the case.

As I have pointed out in my trial tactics book, *Key Trial Control Tactics: A Guide to Winning the Ultimate Verdict* (1983), your ability to increase the improbability of a witness's version of the facts can frequently yield substantial benefit when credibility is important. This is particularly true when things like eyewitness testimony are involved. A technique which you may run into is directed at increasing the improbability that the witness is correct and reflects negatively on the credibility of the witness. It essentially involves use of three questions:

1. "Have you talked with anyone about this case?" All witnesses should be advised to admit readily that they spoke to the lawyers regarding a case. If the witness denies that he or she spoke to anyone prior to testifying, a point can be made during closing argument regarding the improbability of the witness's version of the facts if the witness

has not spoken to anyone, whether another witness to the event or counsel.

2. "When did you talk with him?" If the witness indicates in response to the first question that he or she spoke to the attorney, it is important to establish a time frame for that discussion. The improbability of the witness's story theoretically increases with the recentness of the talk. Thus, if the witness indicates that he or she spoke with the lawyer just days or moments before testifying and the incident which is the subject of the litigation took place some years prior to trial, an argument regarding improbability is further strengthened.
3. "Where did this conversation take place?" and "Who was present?" These additional questions provide more basis for argument as to the improbability of the witness's version of the facts. If the meetings or conversations included other witnesses, an argument may be made regarding the consistency of various witnesses' testimony and the fact that the testimony may be contrived.

When you confront an attorney who uses this tactic to increase the improbability that your witnesses are telling the truth, two basic approaches can be taken. The first is to object that the inquiries of counsel are not directed to the substantive nature of the testimony or indeed toward the credibility of the witness, but rather are solely directed at implying that the witness is fabricating. Most judges and juries will resent an attempt by counsel at underhanded behavior in dealing with a witness and will feel a natural protectiveness toward the witness, especially if that witness is not a professional in the sense of being an expert witness. An attempt to impugn the credibility of a witness by an "underhanded" technique of implying that the testimony is contrived or otherwise fabricated can often boomerang on the counsel making this attempt.

An alternative approach is to note your objections for the record and then, on redirect examination of the witness, take the witness back through the same questions and in effect fill out the rest of the picture by removing the inferences and answering the unasked questions. For example, simply by asking whether anyone coached the witness relative to testimony or whether the witness contrived the testimony in connection with other witnesses, you can often elicit an angry denial from the witness with which many jurors can sympathize. Such emotional responses are usually completely spontaneous, and can do much to damage the standing of opposing counsel who has attempted to impugn the integrity of a person by implication.

Another effective way to increase the improbability of the witness's testimony relates to eyewitness testimony and is based on Federal Rule of Evidence 702, which allows the testimony of an expert witness if that witness's knowledge will help the trier of fact to understand evidence or make a determination regarding a factual issue.

Oftentimes, in litigation involving any number of things, both on the civil and criminal side of the dockets, your opponent will attempt to prove facts through the use of eyewitness testimony. Perhaps one of the simplest examples of this is a motor vehicle accident case in which an eyewitness testifies as to who did what at any particular time.

Such testimony is usually accepted once certain basic foundational considerations can be established. These may include the fact that the witness was in a position to see what transpired and indeed is competent to testify. The question of credibility then becomes paramount. Cross-examination of the witness is the typical means used to attempt to affect the weight which the jury will attach to this testimony.

An extremely effective tactic which should be considered in attempting to challenge eyewitness testimony is the presentation of an expert in the field of human perception and memory regarding the reliability of eyewitness testimony. A case addressing this question in the criminal context is *United States v. Downing,* 753 F.2d 1224 (3d Cir. 1985). In *Downing,* the defendant was convicted on charges of mail fraud, wire fraud, and interstate transportation of stolen property. On appeal, the Third Circuit held that Federal Rule of Evidence 702 pertaining to expert testimony would permit the defendant to adduce from an expert in the field of human perception and memory testimony concerning the reliability of eyewitness identifications. In addition, the Third Circuit held that it was an error on the part of the district court to refuse to admit such testimony of the defense psychologist. The trial judge had precluded that evidence on the basis that he believed such testimony could never meet the helpfulness standard of Rule 702. In light of the fact, as pointed out by the Third Circuit, that the defendant was convicted solely on the basis of eyewitness testimony, such evidence should have been admissible.

The *Downing* case is in the criminal context, with its far stricter standard and constitutional concerns regarding the rights of the defendant. The transfer of the *Downing* reasoning applying Rules 702 and 704 to the civil context can be accomplished with a minimal amount of trouble.

In *Downing,* the defendant made a proffer as to what the evidence of the expert would be. Specifically, the proffer indicated that the expert would testify concerning:

1. The *forgetting curve,* i.e., the fact that memory does not diminish at a uniform rate
2. The fact that, contrary to common understanding, stress causes inaccuracy of perception and distorts one's subsequent recall
3. The *assimilation factor,* which indicates that witnesses frequently incorporate into their identifications inaccurate information gathered after the event and confused with the event

4. The *feedback factor,* which indicates that, when identification witnesses discuss the case with each other, they can unconsciously reinforce their individual identifications; and
5. The fact that studies demonstrate the absence of a relationship between the confidence a witness has in his or her identification and the actual accuracy of the identification.

The applicability of these factors in any sort of eyewitness testimony situation is obvious, and they should be utilized whenever you find yourself confronted with a case being put on by an opponent which in large measure relies upon eyewitness testimony. Whether you are successful in precluding the evidence entirely is, in some respects, academic. The ability to put such expert testimony on relative to the question of the weight which the jury should assign to the eyewitness testimony is itself of significant value.

§ 13.19 Witness Mind Games

One of the most difficult aspects of presenting evidence at trial is working with witnesses. I have heard it said that, were it not for witnesses, cases would take significantly less time and be much easier to present. There is a great deal of truth to this because, in effect, witnesses are oftentimes the only unknown about the trial process.

By the time of trial, the documentary evidence has all been discovered and prepared. The opening statement and closing argument have been drafted out and rehearsed. Virtually every other aspect of the trial itself has been orchestrated and pored over by counsel and the court alike. Witnesses, however, add an element of spontaneity and drama to the proceedings. All too frequently, they are a disappointment to the counsel presenting them. This is true whether we are talking about direct or cross-examination.

The mind games a witness must work through as part of presenting his or her testimony at trial are significant. Not only must the witness know the facts of the case and his or her area of testimony, but also the witness must adjust to the courtroom setting and the interrogation mode. There are a number of factors you must be aware of in order to ensure that your opponent has not conducted a successful examination of your witness even before the trial starts. This is particularly important when the witness has been exposed to your opponent prior to trial. For example, assume that the witness has been deposed. During that deposition your opponent, who conducted the examination, was abrasive, unrelenting, and, from an overall perspective, quite intimidating. The fact of having to meet this particular attorney again in the highly unfamiliar atmosphere of the courtroom, where every word counts, is not a particularly bright prospect for most people. As a result, your opponent in these circumstances has planted elements of worry, doubt, anxiety, and concern in the mind of a witness even before the trial starts. In order to understand and be able to deal effectively with these concerns of your witness and overcome any advantage which your opponent may have going in, it is important to understand what you need from that particular witness.

§ 13.20 —Lawyer Requirements from Witnesses

Quite apart from the need to get certain factual information from a witness while that witness is testifying, be it on direct or cross-examination, is the fact that the witness must fulfill several requirements to make that testimony persuasive and convincing to the jury. A recognition of these needs allows you to appreciate the concerns which the witness has as a person when he or she prepares to take the witness stand.

First and foremost, virtually all lawyers are concerned with the fact of how the witness will be as a witness. In essence what this amounts to is apprehension over the fact that the witness will be operating in an unfamiliar environment and, despite all of the best preparation, may not be able to withstand questioning from your opponent.

You are also going to be concerned with your ability to direct and control not only the examination by your opponent through judiciously placed objections, but also the direction of the testimony during your own examination of the witness. Remember, just because you are asking the questions and this is your witness, there is no assurance that the witness will perform as you wish.

Lawyers are always concerned about whether the jury will understand the testimony. Remember, you as a lawyer will have lived with the case for years, and the witness will have been rehearsed to the point of near perfection. However, the jury will quite likely never have been exposed to any of the information in the case and will, by virtue of the system in which we operate, be presented with a highly compressed version of a large body of facts and unfamiliar law. They will then be expected to make a decision in the face of two competing interests. As a result, it is mandatory when preparing your witnesses that you not only give a great deal of thought to the witness himself or herself but also to the impact of the witness's story on the jury.

The final consideration which you must keep in mind when approaching your witnesses for the purpose of preparing them to testify is whether they will be credible when they present their testimony. In the final analysis, credibility is probably everything. It really doesn't matter whether the witness is telling the truth unless the jury perceives the witness to be telling the truth. Equally important is the fact that the witness must be able to stand up to cross-examination not only in terms of sticking by his or her story but also conveying the message to the jury that he or she is a truthful witness who has simply come to set out the facts before them for their decision.

Once you have analyzed the important considerations which you as a lawyer must confront with respect to preparing witnesses to testify at trial, you are then in a position to understand and appreciate the concerns which the witness has over and above those dealing with the factual substance of the testimony.

§ 13.21 —Witness Concerns

Quite apart from whether the witness remembers particular facts, it is important that you understand the concerns of an individual who is going to testify as a witness. More often than not, these concerns will manifest themselves in the courtroom and make a witness vulnerable to your opponent's attacks. By taking them into consideration in preparing your witness, you will be in a better position to anticipate the problems which may occur and enable the witness to deal with these concerns both before he or she enters the courtroom as well as while testifying.

Among the most important concerns of any witness are those relating to the unfamiliarity of the courtroom. The witness will ask himself or herself the following questions about entering this unfamiliar territory.

1. Will I remember what I am supposed to say?
2. Do I really know what I am going to say?
3. Will I be embarrassed?
4. Will I make a mistake?
5. Will people like me?
6. What is cross-examination going to be like?

These concerns do not relate so much to the substance of a particular witness's testimony; rather, they focus more upon the human relationships which will exist between yourself and the witness, your opponent and the witness, the jury and the witness, and, finally, the judge and the witness. If your witness already has had an encounter with your opponent through, for example, a deposition, the apprehensions which may exist in your witness's mind can be substantial, because sparks may already be flying, and the level of the relationship which exists between your opponent and the witness may already be less than favorable. The question then is how to psychologically condition your witness to maximize the likelihood that such factors will not adversely affect his or her testimony while at the same time arming the witness for the kinds of tactics or mind games which your opponent might be inclined to play during cross-examination.

§ 13.22 —Special Preparation Techniques: Checklist

Central to the ability to assure that a witness does not lose the case in a manner which does not relate to the substance of that witness's testimony is understanding the witness's concerns about testifying. The ability of your opponent to take your witness and turn him or her into the opponent's witness oftentimes turns on these concerns rather than on the substance of the testimony. Recognizing this fact and dealing with it in the witness briefing stage is the key to avoiding such an occurrence.

Traditional types of witness-briefing checklists are available in any number of places. Some very extensive witness preparation materials may be found in M. Dombroff, *Dombroff on Direct and Cross-Examination* (John Wiley & Sons 1985).

The checklist items in this section are distinct from the simple, ordinary briefing considerations which you should take into account when preparing any witness to testify. Rather, these items cater to and recognize the validity and importance of the special apprehensions a witness may have and which can effectively be played upon by a shrewd opponent. It is especially important for you to keep them in mind when you are preparing a "first-time" witness.

Checklist

____ **1.** Find out exactly how the witness feels about testifying. Rarely do attorneys question a witness in this area. You must find out if the witness is scared.

- ____ Ask the witness what most concerns him or her, apart from the facts of the case or a general apprehension of the unknown.
- ____ Discuss these concerns, because they can overwhelm the ability of the witness to make a convincing presentation. (Remember, presumably opposing counsel is comfortable in the courtroom environment or, at the very least, more comfortable than the witness.)
- ____ Be sure to confront these apprehensions of the witness precisely and not in a peripheral or condescending manner.

____ **2.** Be sure that you tell the witness what your role will be during direct and cross-examination.

____ Explain how you will assist the witness during the direct examination to get over rough spots, remember areas that may be omitted, and generally shape the testimony as the witness delivers it.

____ Explain the objection process and how you will use it to control the flow of evidence during cross-examination.

____ **3.** Explain not only your themes but the themes of your opponent.

____ Tell the witness how his or her testimony fits into the overall case so that the witness cannot be blindsided or compartmentalized by your opponent on cross-examination. Good preparation in this area also will prevent the witness from delivering an answer or presenting a position, in the expectation that he or she will be helping you, which is inconsistent with your overall theme.

____ **4.** Take the witness to the courtroom.

____ Allow the witness to sit in the witness chair, the jury seats, counsel table, and, if possible, the judge's chair. This will allow the witness to see himself or herself as others will and will give him or her a better sense of perspective on the presentation.

____ **5.** When you rehearse the witness, use a videotape, if available.

____ This also permits the witness to see himself or herself as others do. It will inevitably be a humbling experience which will point up weaknesses in the witness's presentation that the witness never believed existed or was aware of in his or her personality.

____ **6.** Moot court the witness in the most aggressive, hostile fashion you can.

____ Don't tell the witness that you are doing this; rather, gauge the reaction and allow it to develop spontaneously.

____ Coupled with this examination should be a physical placement of the witness, preferably either standing away from any table or chairs or sitting away from a table or chairs. This physical isolation will require the witness to, in effect, stand alone and will make him or her feel more vulnerable.

____ **7.** Be very careful about giving general advice to a witness.

____ A good example of this is telling the witness, "Answer only the question that is asked." As a practical matter, this is good advice. But remember that the witness has no frame of reference in which to place your advice.

____ Therefore, give examples of what you mean. For instance, say, "Answer only the question that is asked. What this means is that if you are asked your name, give the attorney your name but not your age or address."

____ **8.** Teach the witness to be an aggressive listener.

____ It is natural for a witness while being examined to want to have the examination over with. As a result, the witness generally will think ahead of the question being asked or answered, and will not be listening to the question because he or she is thinking about the answer or, perhaps, the next question.

____ Aggressive listening permits the witness to actively listen to and hear the question. Frequently, this will mean the difference between a correct answer and an incorrect or misleading answer.

§ 13.23 Hearsay

One of the most significant "non-rules" of evidence deals with hearsay. Under the Federal Rules of Evidence or state counterparts, the hearsay rule, insofar as it attempts to keep evidence out of the record which is not susceptible of in-court cross-examination unless it falls within one of the specified exceptions, is in large measure a fiction. Unfortunately, far too many attorneys are unfamiliar with the key which unlocks the catchall exception to the hearsay rule, and thus they fail to take full advantage of the fact that the hearsay rule is basically a series of exceptions without a rule.

Hearsay is generally defined as a statement, other than one made by the declarant while testifying at a trial or a hearing, offered into evidence to prove the truth of the matter asserted in that statement. Fed. R. Evid. 801(c).

The essential reason why hearsay is not admissible into evidence is an opponent's inability to cross-examine the evidence, because the statement in question was made out of court. There are a number of exceptions to the hearsay rule. Fed. R. Evid. 803. Unless a particular statement is found either not to be hearsay or to fall within one of the hearsay exceptions, the statement is not admissible into evidence.

All too frequently, this is the point at which many attorneys' analyses of a particular piece of evidence cease. In this regard, however, you must be especially aware of the *catchall* or *back-door exception* to the hearsay rule. As set forth in the Federal Rules of Evidence, statements not specifically covered by any of the exceptions to the hearsay rule but which have equivalent circumstantial guarantees of trustworthiness are admissible if the judge determines:

(A) The statement is offered as evidence of a material fact;

(B) The statement is more probative on the point for which it is offered than any other evidence which the proponent can procure through reasonable efforts; and

(C) The general purposes of the rules and the interests of justice will best be served by admission of the statement into evidence.

Fed. R. Evid. 803(24), 804(5).

The first level of analysis you must make regarding an attempt to get evidence into the record is whether it is hearsay. If you determine that the statement is hearsay, the next level of analysis is whether it falls into one of the specific hearsay exceptions set forth in either the Federal Rules of Evidence or your state's equivalents. If you determine that it does not fall within one of the specified exceptions, you should then look at the catchall exception to the hearsay rule with which you are working. In using the catchall exception, you must be prepared to argue three points to the judge:

1. The evidence being offered, whether an oral statement or a physical act, is offered to prove a fact material to the case.
2. There is no other evidence which you can secure through reasonable efforts which is more probative on the point for which you are offering the particular evidence.
3. The "interests of justice" will be served by admission of the oral statement or act into evidence.

In effect, the admission into evidence of a statement under the catchall exception to the Federal Rules of Evidence and state equivalents amounts to an appeal to the judge's discretion. What you are saying is, "Your Honor, this is hearsay evidence, but I need it, and it's the best I can do under the circumstances." If the judge is persuaded that the evidence is material and relevant to the issue under contention and that there is no other evidence reasonably available of equal weight, it will be received.

Notwithstanding that the catchall exception to the hearsay rule allows the judge wide latitude as to what to admit into evidence, there is still a way to stop this evidence from coming into the record when the judge turns to you and says, "Counsel, I am inclined to admit this evidence into the record as being more probative than anything else on this point that can be reasonably obtained, it being otherwise material. Do you have any comments or response to its offer?" The Federal Rules of Evidence and virtually all state rules which parallel the Federal Rules of Evidence also provide some caveats against the admission of evidence using the back-door approach. According to Federal Rules of Evidence 803(24) and 804(5), evidence which is otherwise admissible under the catchall exception is still not admissible:

> unless the proponent of it makes known to the adverse party sufficiently in advance of the trial or hearing to provide the adverse party with a fair opportunity to prepare to meet it, his intention to offer the statement and the particulars of it, including the name and address of the declarant.

What this caveat means is that the catchall exception to the hearsay rule typically may not be invoked during trial, because this does not provide an adequate opportunity for you to "prepare to meet" the offer of evidence. As a result, when confronted with this type of offer during trial, you should object that you have not had a fair opportunity to cross-examine or otherwise take discovery steps regarding this offer. Further, you should inquire through the judge as to when your opponent actually formed the intention to offer the evidence, as well as when your opponent knew the substance of the evidence itself, including the declarant's identity.

If you can establish that your opponent knew about this evidence some time prior to trial but failed to disclose this fact to you, you are in a far better position to prevent it from being received into evidence. Even if you received notice prior to trial, the argument still exists that there was not sufficient time to give you an opportunity to meet the offer. Accordingly, the same factor which permits the introduction of hearsay under the catchall exception, i.e., discretion, also allows that evidence to be kept out because it unduly prejudices you, not because of its substance, but because of the circumstances under which it is being offered.

Another exception to the hearsay rule, dealing with public records and reports, is found in Federal Rule of Evidence 803(8)(c). Specifically, it provides for the receipt into evidence of:

> Records, reports, statements, or data compilations, in any form, of public offices or agencies, setting forth . . . (C) in civil actions and proceedings and against the government in criminal cases, factual findings resulting from an investigation pursuant to authority granted by law, unless the sources of information or other circumstances indicate lack of trustworthiness.

Essentially, this exception to the hearsay rule permits the receipt into evidence, despite the fact that they may be hearsay, of certain government reports. This is true in all civil actions by virtue of the words of the rule itself.

The question is what happens when you are confronted with an opponent who seeks to introduce a report prepared by the state or federal authorities that presumably bears upon causation or some other element in issue in your case. Assuming that the government entity preparing the report is not a party to the litigation, the typical objection would relate to the hearsay rules. However, under the 803(8)(c) exception, the report would arguably be admissible insofar as it contained factual findings resulting from an investigation made pursuant to authority granted by law.

Oftentimes, such reports are the result of the work product of numerous people carried out over a long period of time. The backup documentation for the reports is voluminous, and the opportunity to delve into that information for the purpose of impeaching it is limited. Frequently, the governmental authority involved will not make the people available, will advise you that the people are either retired or no longer with the government, or simply will not cooperate in any way at all. Geographic distance is also a factor frequently confronted, and the overall ability to respond to the particular report and its conclusions, factual in nature though they may be, is in far too many instances limited, if it exists at all.

Ellis v. International Playtex, Inc., 745 F.2d 292 (4th Cir. 1984), addressed this question in the products liability context. *Ellis* was a wrongful death action brought by the representatives of a woman who died as a result of toxic shock syndrome (TSS). Suit was instituted on a products liability theory against the manufacturer of the tampon she was using.

At trial, the plaintiff offered into evidence certain studies which had been prepared by the United States Center for Disease Control in Atlanta, Georgia, and certain state health authorities. Those studies indicated a factual correlation between toxic shock syndrome and the tampon that had been used by the plaintiff's decedent that was manufactured by the defendant. The trial judge determined, in excluding the studies, that an insufficient foundation had been laid by the plaintiff with respect to the methodology of the studies in question.

On appeal, the Fourth Circuit reversed a judgment for the defendant and found that under Rule 803(8)(c), public records of the type in question were presumed admissible because of the high degree of reliability and neutrality associated with investigations of a public agency such as the Center for Disease Control. Under such circumstances, the Fourth Circuit found that the burden falls on the party opposing the evidence being received into the record and that the burden includes demonstrating the untrustworthiness of the evidence. Insofar as arguments may relate to the question of the age and currency of the data in question, problems with the methodology involved in the study, or bias built into the study, the Fourth Circuit found that those elements affected the weight to be afforded the evidence and not its admissibility.

Finally, the Fourth Circuit also would not accept the argument put forward by International Playtex, Inc. that the general acceptance test established in *Frye v. United States,* 293 F.2d 1013 (D.C. Cir. 1923), precluded receipt of the evidence. In this regard, the Fourth Circuit determined that investigations carried out by the public agencies that fall within Rule 803(8)(c) of the hearsay exceptions are presumed to reflect generally accepted methodologies.

The burden which the Fourth Circuit placed upon the defendant in the *Ellis* case, and the problem you will confront whenever *Ellis*-type reasoning is used to underlie the offer into evidence of investigations carried out by governmental authorities, is the ability to respond to those investigations. It is all well and good for the court to say that things such as methodology, bias, and age go to weight and not admissibility, but the practical effect of arguing this distinction to the jury is minimal.

Perhaps the most effective argument you can make when confronted with the offer of evidence under Rule 803(8)(c) relates to Rules 401 and 403 of the Federal Rules of Evidence. Rule 401 sets forth the relevance standards for admissibility and defines *relevant evidence* as "evidence having any tendency to make the existence of any fact that is of consequence to the determination of the action more probable or less probable than it would be without the evidence."

Rule 403 deals with the question of excluding relevant evidence. "Although relevant, evidence may be excluded if its probative value is substantially outweighed by the danger of unfair prejudice, confusion of the issues, or misleading the jury, or by considerations of undue delay, waste of time, or needless presentation of cumulative evidence."

The approach to take then when confronted with an evidentiary offer of the type discussed in *Ellis* might be to acknowledge that the evidence may be relevant; however, then point out that all relevant evidence is not admissible. Then, turning to Rule 403, you can point out to the court that the use of such evidence in the case, assuming that you are still in the pretrial stages, would require extensive discovery by you of governmental authorities and that to do so would unduly delay the trial. Along the same lines, you should also argue that the use of such evidence will unduly prejudice you, because there will be an imprimatur attached to such government-generated evidence that it will be virtually impossible for you to overcome.

If you are in the midst of trial and such evidence is offered, you should immediately object and indicate to the court that, if the evidence is admitted, over your Rule 403 objection, you will be required to request a continuance in order to permit you to take certain discovery. This will certainly result in a delay of the case and, just as likely, will result in unfair prejudice and a confusion of the issues of the case.

§ 13.24 Graphic Testimony

You should always be looking for ways to make the most of the testimony of your witnesses. The primary means of communication in the courtroom is the spoken word. However, this is not always the most effective way of imparting information you want to have retained and understood by the audience to whom you are directing your message. *See* M. Dombroff, *Dombroff on Demonstrative Evidence* § 1.2 (1983). Your task as a litigator is to make sure that your witness's message is communicated in a fashion which maximizes its effectiveness and increases the ability of the jury to understand and retain it. The use of graphic or demonstrative devices to accomplish this is particularly effective. If you are able to reduce the spoken word to a hard copy exhibit, you not only stand a better chance of having it retained in the memories of the jurors, but you may also be able to actually send it into the jury room and incorporate it physically into the record beyond the transcript of speech.

There are two primary means of achieving increased understanding and retention of spoken testimony, both of which use graphic exhibits. The first approach is a *shopping list summary* of testimony; the second is a *chart summary.*

The shopping list approach to summarizing testimony is simply a numbered list which, in the case of an expert, for example, depicts the expert's opinions in a summarized and numerical form. The more reasons there are for the expert's holding the opinion to which he or she has testified, the longer the list will be, and the more visual impact it will have on the jury. On being offered into evidence, the list provides a permanent and graphic record of the testimony, which may be referred to to sum up the testimony with which it is associated. It is easily included in post-trial briefs or motions as well as appellate briefs.

A chart summary follows the same general idea but enhances the concept by relying on a more concise and visual format. In its simplest form, a chart summary of testimony incorporates the testimony of the witness in a chart or graph.

Assume that the plaintiff in a personal injury action has alleged that your client should have taken certain precautionary measures to avoid the accident which resulted in the plaintiff's injuries. In response, your expert witness is prepared to testify that the safety measures taken by your client were proper and adequate and that the precautionary measures advocated by your opponent would not have provided any further safety margin. This example is drawn from *id.,* ch. 4, dealing with the use of summaries in evidence. A full discussion of this and other techniques for dramatically presenting evidence in a demonstrative form can be found in that book.

In a graph form, this testimony can be effectively summarized as the witness testifies. The existing safety measures are listed first on the lefthand side (e.g., reflective tape, signs, handrails, etc.), with the last safety measure listed being the one advocated by your opponent (e.g., flashing lights). Listed along the top of the chart are the various safety parameters which are effected by the safety measures listed on the lefthand side (e.g., depth perception, height judgment, distance judgment, etc.). Both the lefthand and the top lists would be filled in as your expert testifies. **Illustration 13-1** is an example of this type of chart.

Illustration 13-1

CHART SUMMARY OF TESTIMONY

	Depth Perception	Height Perception	Distance Perception
Reflective Tape	No	No	Yes
Signs	No	No	Yes
Handrails	Somewhat	Yes	Somewhat
Flashing Lights	No	No	No

Once you have finished laying out the parameters of the summary chart, the witness may give an opinion as to whether any given safety measure provides assistance relative to a particular safety aspect simply by answering "yes," "no," or "somewhat." You insert the answers in the appropriate position on the chart as the testimony is given.

In the ideal circumstance, the row of answers reading from left to right opposite the existing safety measures will be a combination of "yes," "no," and "somewhat," with a solid row of "no" answers for the safety measures advocated by your opponent. Depending on the type of case, the elements or format of the summary chart may change. In more complex cases involving a large number of chart elements to be drawn from the witness's testimony, the chart or diagram may be prepared out of court and still be admissible, even though it is prepared by a person who is not produced as a witness. *See, e.g., Cohen v. Kindlon,* 366 F.2d 762 (2d Cir. 1966); *Grayson v. Williams,* 256 F.2d 61 (10th Cir. 1958); *Union Transportation Co. v. Sacramento County,* 255 P.2d 831, *aff'd on this issue,* 42 Cal. 2d 235, 267 P.2d 10 (1954); *Tennessee Gas Transmission Co. v. Moorhead,* 305 S.W.2d 81 (Tex. Civ. App. 1966).

The graphic summary chart focuses the jury's attention on the essence of the testimony and provides an extremely effective device for concisely summing up the testimony during closing argument. Additionally, it eliminates the need for reliance on notes. In fact, depending on the scope of the summary chart or charts prepared during the presentation of evidence, you may find that you do not need any other notes.

§ 13.25 —Dealing with Graphic Testimony

As a general matter, the admissibility of charts, graphs, and diagrams into evidence is well established. *See* M. Dombroff, *Dombroff on Demonstrative Evidence* §§ 2.27, 4.17 (1983). However, the fact that evidence in a graphic format may be generally admissible does not mean that a *particular* application of the evidentiary technique of graphic testimony will always be proper. When you deal with this particular brand of evidence, because it is so effective when properly prepared, there are a number of techniques of which you should be aware.

1. The evidence being offered in the courtroom is coming from the witness in the form of oral testimony or documentary material which arises out of the transaction in issue. The graphic testimony used to enhance the presentation of the other types of evidence can be asserted to be merely cumulative and repetitive of the direct testimony and to be offered for no other purpose than recording the direct testimony in a particular format, as distinguished from aiding the jurors in judging the weight or credibility to be afforded the witness or the testimony. Pursuant to Federal Rule of Evidence 403 and equivalent state rules of evidence, relevant evidence may be excluded from the record if its probative value "is substantially outweighed by the danger of unfair prejudice, confusion of the issues, or misleading the jury, or by consideration of undue delay, waste of time, or needless presentation of cumulative evidence."
2. The objection to be made in connection with use of the graphic testimony technique involves an appeal to the court's discretion to exclude the evidence based on the fact that it is nothing more than a "needless presentation of cumulative evidence."
3. In the event that you do not prevail on an objection premised either on substantive grounds directed at the evidence itself or on the argument that the format of presentation is cumulative, you should consider attacking the creation of the exhibit itself. Your inquiry should be into whether the exhibit has been contrived. This may be brought out by questions directed at such matters as whether the witness or the attorney came up with the idea of formatting the evidence in the fashion being used, when the format was determined, whether the attorney and the witness practiced or rehearsed the so-called graphic depiction of the testimony, whether the witness ever used such a depiction in the past, whether the depiction itself adds anything of a substantive nature to the testimony or whether it is simply another way of presenting the same information contained in the oral testimony. This last area of inquiry is directed at the type of objection available under federal and state rules regarding cumulative evidence.
4. Another approach to graphic testimony when it is used against you in connection with your opponent's examination of a witness is to use the technique yourself. It is typically not a good idea, however, to use the same graphic presentation prepared by your opponent; you should immediately remove it from the view of the jury when it is

your turn to examine. You should then proceed to prepare your own graphic presentation in view of the jury or during a recess for use during your examination. This may call for some quick planning on your part, but typically, once having seen your opponent's type of presentation, you can do this sort of planning fast.

5. If a graphic depiction of testimony is used, you should object to its receipt into evidence notwithstanding that the witness may have used it during his or her testimony. Even if your objection to the actual preparation of the exhibit during the testimony does not work, you may find the judge receptive to your objection directed at keeping it out of the record.
6. A further objection should be raised against allowing the graphic exhibit into the jury room during deliberations.

§ 13.26 —Chalk Boards

If there is a single fixture present in almost every federal, state, and local courtroom in this country, it is the chalk board or blackboard. Even though readily available and easy to use, a chalk board presents a number of problems as a courtroom visual aid, especially if there is any desire to retain the information set forth on the chalk board, because there is no means of having the information marked and received into evidence.

A chalk board can be an effective demonstrative aid during an opening statement or a closing argument when what you may present is not evidence and cannot be received into evidence. It may, however, also be used effectively during the presentation of evidence when your opponent's desire is to deprive you of the full ability to cross-examine.

Assume that an opponent is presenting an expert whose testimony and opinions are filled with statistical information. A good example would be an economist. The bottom line of the economist's opinion will be a number. However, reaching this number requires a series of calculations and assumptions. As the economist testifies to these assumptions and calculations, they are put up on the blackboard by either your opponent or the witness.

Once the blackboard is completely filled with the assumptions and calculations, a final number is determined. Your opponent then proceeds to erase the blackboard and make one or two additional, rather innocuous entries before completing direct examination and turning the witness over to you for cross-examination. Later in the trial, unknown to you, your opponent intends to offer into evidence large charts of the expert's calculations and assumptions. However, unless you have taken notes on what the expert assumed or calculated, you are left without the immediate ability to cross-examine effectively.

In dealing with such a situation, there are a couple of matters which you should consider. First, when you confront an opponent who intends to use a blackboard for the purpose of presenting an extensive amount of information to the jury, request at the outset that the information not be erased until you have had an opportunity to copy all of it for purposes of effectively and expeditiously cross-examining the witness. Also, you should consider having a Polaroid camera available and requesting the judge's permission to photograph the blackboard and its contents prior to its being erased.

§ 13.27 Phantom Evidence

A questioning technique which some lawyers engage in is leading the court, counsel, and the witness to believe that evidence exists when no such evidence is present at all. Lawyers, while cross-examining a witness, may cause the witness and the jury to believe that a statement, tape recording, or other type of document exists which contradicts the testimony then being presented. Even if the testimony of the witness is truthful, the seed of doubt, an element of mistrust, is planted with the jury and is sometimes difficult to overcome. A recent case by the United States Tax Court in which a government attorney attempted just such a tactic highlights the consequences of taking this sort of approach to trial tactics and demonstrates what the result can be.

In *Kalish v. Commissioner,* No. 5663-85 (U.S. Tax Ct. Oct. 14, 1986), an attorney for the Internal Revenue Service was suspended from practice for 60 days before the Tax Court for using the precise questioning tactic just described. In so doing, the court found the attorney's conduct to be "unprofessional and unacceptable."

The problem arose in the context of the IRS counsel's questioning of a witness whom he believed was testifying falsely. During the questioning, the attorney apparently attempted to create the impression that the attorney had a tape recording between the witness and another individual and, in fact, confronted the witness with a tape implying that it was a recording of the prior conversation.

In arguing against the imposition of sanctions upon this attorney, the position was taken that "he did not intend to mislead the court and had no intention of offering into the evidence the tape which he apparently had at counsel's table." It was pointed out by the Tax Court in imposing the sanction that the IRS attorney's lawyer stated that by attempting to "mislead the witness into believing that his telephone conversation had been recorded is not a trial tactic which the Office of Chief Counsel [IRS] condones, [and] counsel seeks to excuse it . . . on the basis of inexperience and exuberance of a young trial counsel."

Unfortunately the very tactic which counsel in the *Kalish* case attempted to use with obvious disaster is one which we frequently see portrayed on television when the cross-examining attorney stands before the witness holding a sheet of paper, implying that there is something on that sheet of paper contrary to what the witness said. As we see it played out in such dramas, the witness recants a statement just made or otherwise admits he is a liar, although in truth the piece of paper is blank or entirely unrelated to what is going on in the courtroom. The *Kalish* case demonstrates that this tactic has no place in court.

Whenever you confront a situation in which you believe that such impeaching evidence may be present and it has not otherwise been produced, you should immediately object to the line of questioning and seek to approach side bar. At side bar, you should ask for an offer of proof as to exactly what evidence exists and a determination by the trial court whether it is properly usable.

You should also consider whether the impeaching document, tape recording, or other item should have been produced in response to pretrial discovery request. If your definition sections in pretrial discovery requests were broad enough you may find that the tactic your opponent attempts to use on you can be turned around on him, because the document should have been produced during discovery, but production was not made.

§ 13.28 Rebuttal Witnesses

On occasion, following presentation of the case in chief, your opponent will turn to a rebuttal case. Obviously, this is the more usual circumstance when you are on the defense and the plaintiff is putting in a rebuttal following the conclusion of your case. It is unlikely that such a situation will occur when representing the defense, because it is unlikely that you will be permitted to call any witness in response to your opponent's rebuttal case.

The rebuttal phase of evidence is one aspect of a case which is subject to abuse, because, in large measure, it returns an element of trial by ambush to the case. Thus, one matter which you should consider carefully and be attuned to during the trial is whether the rebuttal case being presented by the plaintiff is, indeed, true rebuttal or whether it should have been anticipated during the case in chief and presented at that time.

You may encounter a situation in which the witness who is testifying as to the matters on rebuttal is indeed testifying as to proper rebuttal matters. However, there may come a time during that direct testimony when the witness is relying on certain exhibits or other documents that could not have conceivably been prepared or utilized without prior planning well in advance. Under such circumstances, you should raise an immediate objection that such evidence properly belongs in the case in chief and that to permit it to be presented through the device of rebuttal is simply too prejudicial and improper.

Emerick v. United States Suzuki Motor Corp., 750 F.2d 19 (3d Cir. 1984) was a products liability action which arose from a motorcycle accident and presented just such a situation. A judgment was entered on a verdict in favor of the defendants, and a motion for a new trial was denied. The plaintiffs appealed, asserting that the district court judge abused his discretion in refusing to admit certain expert and videotape testimony of accident-site tests offered during the plaintiff's case in chief as well as during rebuttal.

In rejecting this connection, the Third Circuit found that there was no abuse of discretion when the plaintiffs had clearly violated local rules in that no testing had been reported during the discovery or the pretrial conference. Furthermore, the videotape evidence was not listed as a possible exhibit in the case, and the testing was in fact done three days after the trial had commenced, despite the contention by the plaintiff that the testing could not have been done until after the plaintiffs first had the opportunity to view the defendant's videotape on the day after the pretrial conference. Finding that the evidence belonged in the case in chief rather than on rebuttal, when the true purpose of the testimony in evidence was to demonstrate the defective nature of the product, the court of appeals affirmed the lower court's decision to reject the evidence, because it would unduly prejudice the defendant and violate the rules.

When your opponent attempts to introduce evidence during the rebuttal phase of the case and you find yourself on the receiving end of what is, in fact, a trial by ambush, immediately examine that evidence for the purpose of determining whether it actually belongs to the case in chief. The *Emerick* case provides excellent authority for rejecting such evidence when there will be less than an orderly presentation of proof were it to be received during rebuttal. On this point, *see also Skogen v. Dow Chemical Co.*, 375 F.2d 692 (8th Cir. 1967); *Olsen v. United States*, 521 F. Supp. 59 (E.D. Pa. 1981), *aff'd sub nom. Olsen v. Ford Motor Co.*, 688 F.2d 823 (3d Cir. 1982).

EXAMINATION OF EXPERT WITNESSES

§ 13.29 Introduction

There is little doubt that litigation of all types depends in large part on expert witnesses. Broadly speaking, an expert in litigation is a person who, by virtue of special training or special knowledge in some technical or substantive area, is in a position to aid the trier of fact—the judge or jury—in reaching a decision.

As a practical matter, unless called by the court as an impartial expert, a person who has been retained by one or the other side to testify as an expert is identified with that side, and the testimony takes on certain adversarial overtones. Your problem when using experts is to present them in as authoritative and convincing a fashion as possible, while at the same time not permitting them to be perceived as advocates of your cause with a stake in the outcome, even if that stake involves only their credibility.

It is also highly desirable to portray your opponent's expert as an individual who is unqualified or biased. Similarly, anything which you can do to minimize the impact of the testimony presented by your opponent's expert, especially if that expert is both well-qualified and convincing, will aid your client.

Although the use of expert witnesses, including their proper preparation and integration into the overall litigation, is a subject more attuned to a general book on trial advocacy, there are a number of techniques and tactics that can dramatically alter the effectiveness of an expert witness. An understanding of these tactics, for the purpose of using them effectively as well as for blunting their impact, is essential.

§ 13.30 Timely Notice

A case well worth reading, dealing with timely notice of expert witnesses to your opponent, is *Sturgeon v. Airborne Freight Corp.,* 778 F.2d 1154 (5th Cir. 1985). In *Sturgeon,* the court's refusal to allow testimony of an expert was found not to be an abuse of discretion, in that the plaintiff never informed the district court that he was having difficulty in obtaining an expert witness before discovery cutoff dates. Furthermore, the plaintiff should have been aware from the beginning of the action of the need for expert testimony. The court also found that, since the witness had been designated as an expert after the expiration a local rule deadline, the plaintiff had to be prepared to try the case without the witness even if the witness was thereafter available for trial.

All too frequently it seems that judges "waive" the rules in favor of a plaintiff. The *Sturgeon* case illustrates one of those situations where this did not occur and, at least in terms of providing some sort of example which can be put before the judge for the purpose of showing that other judges have done as defense counsel would wish them to do in a particular case, the *Sturgeon* case provides good precedent.

§ 13.31 Qualifications

As a general proposition, the examination of an expert may be broken down into two broad areas. The first of these areas has to do with the qualifications or background of the expert; the second part is the substantive testimony, including materials relied upon. The line between these areas within the normal direct examination of an expert is typically quite perceptible in the questioning. For example, the question, "Did you review certain materials?" would mark the transition between qualifications and substantive testimony. Similarly, the question, "Did you form an opinion?" would mark the transition from the general foundation area to the giving of opinions.

The role of the qualifications or voir dire area of expert testimony is integral to overall success in presenting an expert. As a general rule, qualifications, background, training, and related matters are areas with which most experts feel entirely comfortable, even if they are uncomfortable in the surroundings of the courtroom. Even in unfamiliar surroundings, most people testifying as expert witnesses feel quite at ease testifying about their personal background and history. During this phase of the testimony, the jurors will form their initial impressions regarding an expert's demeanor and credibility, and those impressions will determine their overall empathy and identification with the expert then testifying. Thus, it is important that the qualifications of an expert be presented orally and in open court before the jury, when jurors will be able to make their own observations regarding credibility and demeanor.

Recognizing that the voir dire aspect of expert testimony is so crucial to the overall question of believability, there are a number of techniques available to affect this aspect of expert witness presentation.

On occasion you may find an opponent who, in the name of judicial economy and efficient use of jury time, suggests that the qualifications of experts be submitted by written statement or affidavit, with only voir dire or cross-examinations permitted. This suggestion would be implemented by having either the witness or counsel read the statement or affidavit and thereafter be asked essentially one question: "Is what I just read an accurate and complete statement of your background qualifications?" Thereafter, opposing counsel would have the opportunity to cross-examine on qualifications for purposes of challenging the ability of the witness to testify as an expert.

Suggestions which have the effect of shortcutting the presentation of an expert witness should be resisted when your expert has especially impressive credentials that you know can be presented to the jury in a convincing and appealing way. By pointing out to the court that the ability of the expert to present qualifications orally is integral to the overall ability of the jury to judge credibility, you will be likely to prevail on this question. You should ensure, however, that your direct examination, insofar as it relates to qualifications and background, is not too long or drawn-out, so as not to give any sort of ammunition to your opponent.

The question is more difficult when the suggestion is made that qualification be by affidavit in a nonjury case. In this situation, there may be greater justification for using this technique, because the judge is the sole arbiter of the credibility of witnesses and will have the opportunity to listen to the witness testify on both direct and cross-examination. Even here, however, an appropriate response to the suggestion that qualification be through affidavit is that the qualifications of the witness and the ability to testify about them are important in enabling the court to judge credibility of the witness, because this is the area the witness should know the best.

Another motivation for suggesting the affidavit technique of qualifying a witness and its use for direct testimony as well may be that the expert is weak as a witness. This does not reflect on the substantive qualifications or nature of the expert's testimony, but rather on the ability of the witness to present that testimony in a convincing fashion. Remember, a courtroom is an intimidating setting, and a trial is not the ideal frame of reference for clear, calm, and level-headed thinking, especially when the individual being examined is inexperienced in that setting. Many individuals under such circumstances, including lawyers, become uncomfortable and do not equip themselves very well.

Thus, you may find that your opponent suggests the use of qualifications through affidavit in order to cut down the amount of live testimony which his or her expert must present in an already uncomfortable setting. You should be suspicious of such a suggestion, because the motive may be not only to minimize the quality of your expert but also to minimize the weakness of your opponent's expert. Frequently, you will be able to ascertain the precise motivation of an opponent in making such a suggestion if you have deposed the experts in the case and already have a sense of how they will perform under pressure. However, even then, performance in the courtroom is not necessarily equatable to performance in either the deposition room or the classroom.

The initial judgment which you must make in cross-examining the qualifications of your opponent's expert either on voir dire or as part of your substantive cross-examination is, in fact, whether to cross-examine or not. If you conduct a cross-examination on voir dire you will, in effect, be challenging the competence of the witness to testify at all. If you are successful in challenging those qualifications, the witness may be prohibited from testifying totally or at least in part. Alternatively, if you challenge the qualifications of the witness as part of your substantive examination, such an examination is targeted more to the weight to be afforded specific testimony based upon the qualifications of the witness than to the ability of the witness to testify.

The most important consideration to keep in mind when challenging the qualifications of a witness is the question of why you are challenging those qualifications. Be objective in determining whether the witness is qualified to testify. Even if there are a number of areas in which you can make a valid inquiry regarding qualifications, it will take a convincing showing of lack of competence on the part of the witness for the judge to disqualify him. You may be better off in such situations if you reserve such cross-examination for the substance of the testimony rather than directing it at the qualifications and ability of the witness to testify. If you are unsuccessful in challenging the qualifications of the witness during a voir dire, especially in the presence of the jury, you will quite likely be unable to raise those same points for the purpose of lessening the credibility of the witness's testimony. Even if the judge rules that the witness may testify and that the qualifications go to weight, the fact that the judge is, in effect, putting his stamp of approval on the witness by permitting him to testify will reduce the effect of any argument regarding the weight to be afforded the witness's testimony by virtue of what has transpired.

The single most important consideration in preparing to examine the qualifications, and for that matter the substance, of an expert witness is to go in fully prepared in all areas. The first step involves a determination why you are examining the witness on his qualifications—admissibility or credibility. Once you have made this determination, you must gather as much information as you possibly can regarding this witness. There are a number of sources of information and factors to be considered:

1. Your own previous experience with the witness
2. The experience of colleagues both in your firm and with other firms with the witness
3. Your own experts. Because they presumably operate in the same profession as your opponent's experts, your experts are a valuable source of information and should be able to learn a great deal about opposing experts
4. Encyclopedias of specialties in specific technical areas
5. Anything which the expert has written
6. Transcripts of prior testimony given by the witness
7. Newspaper files that may contain articles or information about the witness
8. Catalogs and other types of school literature at any university or other institution where the witness is on the faculty or otherwise associated
9. Any professional or advertising literature that is published by the expert or any organization with which he is associated, such as consulting organizations
10. The expert's curriculum vitae
11. The depositions that were taken of the expert in not only your case but any other case you are able to learn about in which he testified.

The most effective way to prepare for the cross-examination of your opponent's expert is through pretrial discovery. Such discovery should take several forms, including interrogatories, requests for production of documents, requests for admissions, and, if possible, depositions. Each of these has a definite role in the process of preparing to cross-examine an expert, and each provides certain benefits.

The prime objective of interrogatories directed to your opponent's expert is to obtain as much factual and opinion information as possible. This will certainly enable you to be better prepared for the actual examination of the expert and, in view of the cost considerations associated with taking a deposition, may save you a considerable amount of money.

When structuring interrogatories directed at your opposing expert, you should take the position that the identity of the expert must include more than his name and address and should contain the full qualifications of the expert. Along these same lines, you should broaden the interrogatories to include all of the facts upon which he will be testifying.

An excellent approach to using interrogatories for expert discovery is to propound contention interrogatories to your opponent and ask if the opposing experts will testify as to any of the contentions contained in the interrogatories. If you get an affirmative answer, you should elicit the full range of information relative to the expert's position on each contention.

Your questions should be as detailed as possible and, as is consistent with the effective use of interrogatories in general, you should never ask more than one question in a given subsection. One question which should always be included in a general interrogatory is who prepared the answers to the interrogatories and who assisted or provided information for that process. In particular, you should ask if an expert assisted in the preparation of the responses or provided any information for them, and if so, what assistance or information he provided.

Another good approach in using interrogatories to take expert discovery and prepare for cross-examination is to ask if the expert will use the validation technique of Federal Rule of Evidence 703 as part of his or her grounds for testifying. If you get an affirmative answer, you should elicit information as to what facts or data will be coming in through use of this technique and obtain full information as to the circumstances surrounding the particular facts or data and their use.

A good technique is to combine interrogatories with requests for admissions and indicate that if a request to admit has been denied, the expert should set forth all information upon which the denial is based. This has the added effect of discouraging your opponent from denying requests for admissions since, under these circumstances, it may be more work than it is worth to deny the request rather than simply to admit it.

Be sure to ask whether the opposing expert has done any testing or has requested tests. If so, you should obtain full information relative to the results of the testing and determine whether the expert will be relying upon the results. In this regard, you should also ascertain whether the opposing expert has prepared a report, and, if so, at a minimum, you should get its title, date, and subject matter. This should be followed up with either a separately filed request for production or, even better, a request for production combined with the interrogatories.

You should also determine whether the opposing expert will be using any books or articles as part of his testimony. If so, you should determine what items he will use and what part of his testimony will rely upon them for support.

You should determine whether the opposing expert will rely on any facts or data to be established by any exceptions to the hearsay rule as part of his testimony or the grounds therefor. If so, you should ascertain which exceptions are involved and obtain as much information as possible relative to the facts or data involved in those exceptions.

You must guard against an attempt by your opponent to place an expert's opinion report within the context of the work product doctrine set forth in Federal Rule of Civil Procedure 26(b)(3) and its state counterparts. As a practical matter your opponent will, under most circumstances, probably direct that a report not be prepared. In any event, the specific rule relative to the giving of information by experts should be argued to supersede the more general rule against the production of materials under the so-called work product doctrine.

Your interrogatories should also focus on whether there were any communications to or from the expert and any representative of your opponent relative to acquiring the services of the expert, the expert's opinion, and similar matters. If so, you should ascertain the date of the communications, to whom they were sent, their subject, and the full circumstances surrounding their preparation and transmittal. You should also combine a request for production of documents with your interrogatories, seeking copies of any such materials.

With the outcome of more and more litigation turning on the ability to persuade the jury through the use of expert witnesses, it is crucial that trial counsel be able to deal effectively with the task of preparing for and cross-examining an expert's qualifications. This ability is frequently the difference between a credible expert and one who the jury listens to but doesn't hear.

§ 13.32 —Examination Checklist

Once you have all of the information you are able to accumulate on the expert, you are then in a position to conduct a voir dire. The following checklist is a good approach to ensure that all areas of inquiry regarding the qualifications of the expert are covered during your examination.

Checklist

____ **1.** Examine deficiencies in the education and/or training of the witness.

____ **2.** Examine deficiencies in the specific areas of expertise needed to testify in the case.

____ **3.** Determine whether the witness was the primary author of articles which bear his or her name as well as that of other authors. It is not unusual that, even though the witness is listed as an author, he did none of the work and was merely listed as an author because of peripheral involvement or supervision of the actual authors.

____ **4.** Are the qualifications and credentials of the expert what he or she states them to be? For example, oftentime experts will be members of advisory boards for organizations or publications. However, upon minimal inquiry, you may find out that an expert's being an advisory board member really means virtually nothing, with no responsibilities or activities associated with membership.

____ **5.** Even though the witness may be broadly qualified to testify as an expert, is he or she out of her field of specialization? Perhaps the most simplistic example of this is the physician who is essentially an ear, nose, and throat specialist who may be testifying in an area which, though involving medicine, is more particularly suited to an internist.

____ **6.** Is the witness practicing in the area of expertise that is required for the testimony at the current time? This is important not only for its own value as a means of attacking the expert, but it also raises the question of whether he or she is aware of the latest developments in the area of expertise involved. You would be surprised how many so-called experts in the particular area have moved on to other fields and like to have their names associated with the field in which they are no longer practicing.

____ **7.** Has the expert practiced in the relevant area involved in the litigation, and does he or she know the applicable standard of care in the jurisdiction?

____ **8.** Why did the expert leave certain positions which he held, and, assuming there are circumstances other than those considered to be favorable, is there room for bias or prejudice to be explored?

____ **9.** Has the expert overstated his credentials by, for example, indicating that he or she is a professor but actually is only an associate professor? In addition, does the expert have tenure at the institution, or was he or she ever denied tenure?

____ **10.** Has the expert ever been qualified as an expert in litigation on previous occasions? Associated with this area of inquiry is whether the expert has ever been denied qualification as an expert and, if so, why.

____ **11.** If certification is available in the field of expertise in which the expert is testifying, does he or she have such certification? If not, you should certainly inquire into the reasons for this failure. Good examples are board-certified physicians or certified public accountants. Did the expert fail the certification examination?

____ **12.** One good tactic is to ask whether the expert was ever an officer of any professional organization in which membership was indicated on direct examination. In addition, ask if he or she belongs to any international organizations or other similar organizations in which membership is elective rather than simply based on paying dues.

By taking this approach, you will be able to make as many points as possible against the expert before direct testimony begins. Moreover, if your voir dire is sufficiently effective, the judge may not let the witness testify at all. In the event this occurs, your opponent may be left without an expert. However, be advised that experience shows this is not likely.

If you wait for cross-examination to challenge the qualifications of the expert, the jury may consider the points you make as going just to the weight to be accorded the testimony of the expert rather than excluding the expert's testimony. Unless you are reasonably certain that you will successfully challenge the qualifications and competence of the expert to testify on direct examination, there is a substantial argument to be made for reserving the qualifications area of examination for the cross-examination.

§ 13.33 —Sample Qualification by Affidavit

IN THE UNITED STATES DISTRICT COURT
FOR THE ____________ DISTRICT OF ____________

	}		
In re Air Crash Disaster	}		
at Pago Pago, American	}	SS.:	M.D.L. Docket No. 176
Samoa on January 30, 1974	}		All Cases Liability
____________	}		

Affidavit of Captain ______________

I am 61 years old and married with three sons, each of my three sons being an engineer and a pilot. I presently reside in Ridgefield, Connecticut and am a retired airline captain having retired from ______________ [Airline] at the mandatory retirement age of 60 years old.

I. *Educational and Employment Background*

I graduated from high school in 1934 and from Purdue University in 1938. I graduated from Purdue with a Bachelor of Science Degree in Mechanical Engineering with a specialty in Aeronautical Engineering. I participated in ROTC and was commissioned a second lieutenant in the field artillery in 1938. I then entered the Air Corps Flight School at Randolph Field, Texas, and graduated as a second lieutenant in the U.S. Air Corps in 1939. I was then assigned as an advanced school flight instructor at the U.S. Air Corps Flight Training Center, Kelly Field, Texas. During my Air Corps flight training I completed courses in, among other things, communications, engineering, meteorology, safety and navigation. During my employment with ______________ [Airline], I also took further courses in communications, meteorology, navigation, sea law, international law, engineering, maintenance, and safety. In 1942, I obtained a degree as a Master pilot of Ocean Flying.

My initial employment would be considered as of 1938 when I joined the U.S. Army Air Corps as a flying cadet. I was located at Randolph Field, Texas. During that time, I trained and flew primary training airplanes such as the PT-11, PT-13 and BT-9's. I advanced to Kelly Field, Texas, advanced flight school and graduated in 1939. I was trained at Kelly Field and flew advanced training airplanes such as the P-12, BC-8, BT-2, AT-6 and BC-13. In 1939 I was assigned to the Advanced U.S. Air Corps Flight School as a flight instructor and instructed cadets and flew airplanes such as the AT-6, BC-8, A-11, A-11A, O-38, O-43, P-12, P-35, B-10 and the B-18.

On August 15, 1940, I joined ______________ [Airline] at Brownsville, Texas as a co-pilot on DC-2, DC-3 and Stinson Reliants. I then transferred to New York with ______________ [Airline] to qualify on flying boats, navigation and instrument flying. I qualified on flying boats in the Boeing 314 and Grumman G-44 and transferred back to Brownsville, Texas to qualify in command on DC-3A's in 1942. Following my qualification as a command pilot, I transferred back to New York to qualify in command on four engine flying boats in 1944 and operated four engine flying boats under contract for the U.S. Navy (NATS) until 1945.

In 1945 I transferred to Miami, Florida to operate Air Force C-54 aircraft to Africa and Europe, and subsequently returned to New York to operate Air Force C-54 aircraft, following which I returned to civil operations with ______________ [Airline] and continued to operate as a pilot in command and an instructor pilot from New York until my retirement in 1975.

The aircraft which I have operated as pilot in command from the end of the war until my retirement are the DC-4, Constellation Lockheed L-049, Constellation

Lockheed L-749, DC-6, DC-7, Boeing 377, Boeing 707, Boeing 747. I have a total aircraft time to date of approximately 31,450 hours.

II. *General Knowledge of Pan American Operations, Training, Etc.*

In 1940, when I started my career with ________________ [Airline] at Brownsville, Texas, I was a co-pilot flying to Mexico and Central and South America. In 1941, I transferred to New York to qualify as an Ocean Navigator and pilot of four engine flying boats. In 1942, I returned to Brownsville, Texas to command DC-3 type aircraft flying to Mexico, Central and South America. During this period I was appointed check pilot with ________________ [Airline] and had the responsibility for training and qualifying other pilots within the Western Division. Also, during this time, I co-authored the first pilot training manual for ________________ [Airline] flight crew personnel. In 1944, I returned to New York to command four engine flying boats, operating to Bermuda, South America, Africa and Europe under a U.S. Navy contract (NATS). In 1944, I transferred to Miami, Florida to operate four engine land airplanes (C-54) for the U.S. Air Force (ATC) to Africa, Europe and the Azore Islands. In 1945, I transferred back to New York to continue operating the same equipment to Europe, Africa, and the Azore Islands for the Air Force. From 1945, until my retirement in 1975, I continued to operate from ________________ [Airline's] New York base as the pilot-in-command of various aircraft as listed above. During this time, I was appointed a check pilot, as well, on various types of commercial aircraft from DC-4's to Boeing 707's. I estimate that I spent more than 20 years as a check pilot during my 35 years with ________________ [Airline] training and qualifying other pilots on various airplanes and over various routes of the ________________ [Airline] System.

During this entire time of my tenure with ________________ [Airline], I was a member of the Air Line Pilots Association and was active in the fields of air safety and engineering. I was Chairman of the Air Line Pilots Association's SST Concorde Committee from 1962 until my retirement. I chaired the International Federation of Airline Pilots (a world wide organization) Supersonic Transport Study Group until my recent retirement. I was a member of the International Civil Aviation Organization SST Panel at Montreal, Canada until the SST Panel concluded its duties last year. I have also served on pilot committees to evaluate new commercial aircraft including the Boeing 747.

I have flown research vehicles produced by U.S. manufacturers, the National Aeronautics and Space Administration, the United States Air Force and various European manufacturers. These included piston powered jet rockets, supersonic military and supersonic transport simulators and the Concorde simulator and Grumman's Apollo Lunar Module simulator. At present, I own and operate my own single engine amphibian airplane.

Following my retirement, I was selected by the Administrator of the Federal Aviation Administration to be one of six recently retired airline pilots to conduct an aviation safety study. This group is known as the Special Air Safety Advisor Group and conducted a six month study rendering its report which was released in January, 1976. During this study, I observed over 100 airline crews on more than 20 different U.S. airlines as part of my duties. Many safety recommendations made by this group are either now being implemented or under study.

III. *Materials Reviewed*

I have, to this date, reviewed the investigatory report of the National Transportation Safety Board, certain exhibits marked for use in this litigation including the ________________ [Airline] Simulator/Flight Recurrent Training and Proficiency Records, the National Transportation Safety Board Final Report, the ________________ [Airline] 1975 Final Report and the ________________ [Airline] Follow-Up Special Inspection 1975, as well as each attachment to the NTSB investigative report. I have not, as of this date, undertaken an in-depth review of the depositions or an overall review of ________________ [Airline] documents produced in this litigation except to the extent that many of those documents may be duplicated in my own library or may contain information and knowledge already possessed by myself as a result of my experience. I do intend to review the pertinent depositions prior to testifying in this case and supplement my opinions and basis thereof accordingly.

IV. [*Preliminary Areas of Proposed Testimony and Outline of Opinions*]

____

Sworn to before me this

____________ day of ____________, 1976.

____

NOTARY PUBLIC

My Commission Expires: ____________

§ 13.34 Testimony by Affidavit

An extension of the technique of presenting the qualifications of an expert through an affidavit or in writing is to present the direct testimony of the expert by affidavit. This is used in court similarly to an affidavit in the qualification area. The only question which may be asked of the expert in court is, "Is your statement of direct testimony as contained in Exhibit ______ accurate?" Once this has been done, absent any supplemental but nonrepetitive questions, the witness is turned over for cross-examination. In the jury setting, the statement is read to the jury by either the attorney or the expert, while in the nonjury situation, the statement is received into evidence in lieu of the oral testimony of the expert, and the judge simply reads it either on the bench or prior to trial if it is submitted in advance.

Cross-examination of the expert based on the written testimony, complete with impeachment, then takes place just as if the testimony had been presented orally in court. The manner in which the trier of fact may judge the credibility of the witness in these circumstances is clearly through cross-examination and a physical observation of the witness, as opposed to an opportunity to judge the credibility of the witness during direct testimony.

This technique tends to be suggested when one of two situations exists. If your opponent is presenting an expert who is particularly weak in terms of ability to present testimony but is capable of defending his or her opinions, you may find your opponent suggesting that the testimony of all experts be presented by written affidavit. The rationale supporting this suggestion typically is that the jury can still judge the credibility of the witness by how he or she does under cross-examination and that this technique will move the case along more rapidly. In the nonjury situation, this whole rationale makes more sense. The second situation is when your expert is particularly strong and your opponent wishes to minimize the impact of that expert's testimony. In such a situation, the less exposure the jury has to your expert, the better your opponent will fare. Whatever the motivation for the suggestion, your response, when you want to present your expert live for direct testimony, will be the same.

The direct testimony of an expert or of any witness is rarely where one wins a case. Remember, direct testimony is in large part staged, and all listeners expect that if you present a witness, that witness, whether an expert or fact witness, will say something favorable to your case. As a practical matter, the only thing direct testimony can do for you is lose the case. Thus, you may well find yourself suggesting the use of testimony through affidavit when your own experts are weak and you are fearful that you will lose the case on their direct testimony. Unfortunately, you may also find yourself the recipient of the appropriate responses to this technique.

Also, as discussed in **§ 13.31** with regard to affidavits for the presentation of qualifications, the ability of the jurors to perceive with their own eyes and ears the expert witness presenting the direct testimony, separate and apart from the substance of the testimony itself, is crucial to a determination of credibility. This is even more the case when there are experts on each side with diametrically opposed opinions regarding causation. Under these circumstances, the trier of fact should have the opportunity to make its own credibility judgments. If you are limited to the presentation of experts through written affidavit on qualifications or direct testimony, you might just as well have mailed the testimony in and permitted the jurors to read it themselves at home. You must be wary, however, about a direct examination that is too long and self-defeating. This quires careful preparation of the expert and careful staging of the testimony itself. When you have a strong expert or when you suspect your opponent has a weak expert, however, your response to any suggestion that a shortcut be used in the presentation of the testimony should be to resist the suggestion. This approach should be taken notwithstanding that these suggestions are often clothed in the rationale of judicial expedition and economy, because that is only used as a justification when the true justification cannot be openly stated.

§ 13.35 —Sample Testimony by Affidavit

IN THE UNITED STATES DISTRICT COURT
FOR THE ______________ DISTRICT OF ______________

	}		
In re Air Crash Disaster	}		
at Pago Pago, American	}	SS.:	M.D.L. Docket No. 176
Samoa on January 30, 1974	}		All Cases Liability
______________________	}		

Affidavit of ______________________

______________, being duly sworn, deposes and says:

I. [*Background and Qualifications*]

II. [*Documents and Materials Reviewed*]

III. *Preliminary Opinions and General Testimony Relative to [Airline] Flight 806*

Having been an operations representative for ______________ [Airline] throughout the world for a number of years, as well as having held a certificate from the Federal Aviation Administration as an airline dispatcher, I am intimately familiar with both the meteorological and dispatch factors surrounding ______________ [Airline] flights as well as aircraft operations in general. Additionally, due to my present consultation activities and activity in the meteorological area, including long-range forecasting, I am also familiar to a very high degree with tropical weather conditions and the weather conditions existing in the South Pacific.

My preliminary review has indicated that for nearly a week prior to the night of the accident, the weather at Pago Pago had been affected in varying degrees by a low of tropical origin. Interestingly enough, the crew of Flight 806 went through Pago Pago on its outbound flight on January 23, 1974, so they should have been intimately familiar with the weather conditions then existing and developing. Beginning within a week earlier, there was a very small low approximately 600 miles southeast of Pago Pago. It moved slowly westward passing several hundred miles south of Pago Pago on January 26, 1974, then took a northwesterly course reaching a point approximately 600 miles west northwest of Pago Pago. The center of circulation can be quite accurately fixed by the surface observations and satellite pictures.

During the time of travel, this system had intensified and greatly expanded its area of influence so that Pago Pago, although 600 miles from the center at the time of the accident, was still well within the area of circulation about the low. Since wind flows clockwise about a low in the southern hemisphere, the wind direction in the vicinity of the Samoan Islands was predominantly from the north. This was true of Pago Pago although the direction did oscillate from 320 degrees true to 40 degrees true during the 24 hours prior to and 24 hours following the accident. The wind velocity during this period was averaging 15 to 20 knots with frequent gusts to 25 to 30 knots and a peak gust of 44 knots. The peak gust near the time of the accident was 35 knots. Such is in no way unusual of a tropical weather situation and is certainly typical of South Pacific weather during the tropical weather months in the winter such as is described by the ________________ [Airline] Route and Weather Manual for the South Pacific.

In addition to influencing the wind, there was associated with the low an extensive area of clouds, and beneath this cloud cover were smaller but active areas of showers, some very heavy. These were visible on satellite pictures as brighter spots or brighter bands within the cloud cover.

On infrared pictures, the degree of brightness is an approximate indication of the height of the clouds so that the brighter the cloud, the higher the top. Therefore, a bright spot would likely be the top of a well-developed cumulus or cumulonimbus cloud or cluster of such clouds. A narrow bright band could indicate a line of such clouds. Soundings taken at Pago Pago were conditionally unstable from the surface to higher levels and would support vertically developed clouds to 30 or 35 thousand feet or higher. However, vertically developed clouds to that height would most likely have associated thunderstorms but none had been reported at Pago Pago, and in my opinion, the towering cumulus had not developed into cumulonimbus in the vicinity of Pago Pago and the accident.

Under the influence of these conditions, Pago Pago had experienced cloudy weather for several days prior to and for 24 hours following the accident. Also during that time, there were periods of showers, some briefly very heavy. However, based upon my review of the facts of this accident, it is my opinion that during the approach of the aircraft and up until the time of impact, Flight 806 was not operating in an area of heavy showers. Neither the dynamics of the weather nor the eyewitness statements allow me to conclude that the aircraft was in heavy showers or heavy rain during its operation. Rather, however, the aircraft was operating in some rain but the rain did not become heavy until after the impact.

I have reviewed the possibilities that either wind shear, gust front conditions, or severe downdrafts affected the operations of the aircraft during its approach. My review of the weather dynamics and factual information herein leads me to conclude that the existence of any wind shear in this instance, if in fact it did exist, can only be classified as slight. I base this upon the surface weather observations and the winds aloft indicating to me that any existing wind shear was not of any significant magnitude.

With respect to the question of a gust front, I have also reviewed the possibility that a gust front in some way came into play in this situation and have concluded that such is not probable. Considering the location of the National Weather Service facility, the location of the accident site, the approach path, the times of the surface weather observations and the dynamics of the moving weather, it is my conclusion that the gust front associated with the moving weather did not yet reach the approach path of the aircraft or the aircraft itself prior to the accident. Assuming, however, that some portion of the gust front was in the vicinity of the aircraft, I do not believe that the weather or winds contained therein were of sufficient magnitude to have any effect upon the operation of the aircraft. Similarly, insofar as the question of possible downdrafts is concerned, I again feel that the existence of any downdrafts is not probable in sufficient magnitude to have had an effect upon the operation of the aircraft. This again is based upon an analysis of the weather data both before and after the accident as well as witness statements and the accident report.

Based upon my overall review, it is my opinion that the weather conditions existing at Pago Pago throughout the time period of the accident as well as prior thereto were typical of the tropical weather conditions encountered during the winter weather months in the South Pacific. My review of the documents in this litigation has indicated to me that the crew of the aircraft should have been aware of such weather conditions and been prepared for them. Additionally, I would have fully expected the crew of the aircraft to utilize all available sources of information in determining the weather conditions existing during their approach including, if appropriate, their airborne weather radar. This is especially true in view of the fact that Pago Pago does not have any ground based radar of any type. It is my opinion that the crew of Flight 806 was in a position to be infinitely more familiar with the weather conditions affecting their approach as well as the weather conditions that they might expect to encounter than either the FAA personnel or Weather Service personnel. This is based upon my knowledge of ________________ [Airline] procedures, my review of the documents herein as well as the fact that the crew went through Pago Pago on its outbound leg.

I have also reviewed the procedures utilized by the weather observers at Pago Pago both in observing the weather and in transmitting the weather, and find that their actions are consistent with all that would have been expected of them. Indeed, I find that Mr. ________________ was competent and conscientious in the execution of his duties. Having been told that there was a bad rain shower at the airport, it is my opinion that the crew of the aircraft was in a far better position to determine whether or not to continue this approach than anybody on the ground.

With respect to the dispatch function of ________________ [Airline], I have reviewed those materials relevant to the dispatch of Flight 806 as well as those materials relevant to the overall dispatch responsibilities and functions of ________________ [Airline], especially for the South Pacific. It is my opinion that the dispatch function of the South Pacific, especially considering the testimony of Mr. ________________ as well as his letters to the company, left much to be desired. It is my opinion, based upon my review of the documents herein as well as my own experience, that the dispatch function was not one that was taken seriously by ________________ [Airline] and not one for which it properly trained or upgraded its dispatchers. While the dispatchers may have met the minimum requirements of the Federal Air Regulations for certification, they did not, in my opinion, possess sufficient knowledge of weather, route or airport characteristics to properly assist a pilot in making decisions.

____

Sworn to before me this

__________ day of __________, 1976.

____

NOTARY PUBLIC

My Commission Expires: __________

The following excerpt from an actual trial transcript demonstrates how this technique is used in court. Following the presentation of qualifications is supplemental questioning by counsel.

Kenneth Reginald Hardy, called as a witness on behalf of Pan American, having first been duly sworn, was examined and testified as follows:

THE CLERK: Will you please be seated and state your full name and spell the last name, please.

THE WITNESS: Kenneth Reginald Hardy, H-a-r-d-y.

THE COURT: Was Mr. Hardy's deposition taken?

MR. TUCKER: Yes, your Honor.

THE COURT: Is it filed?

MR. TUCKER: Your Honor, I don't know what your Honor's pleasure is. Pursuant to your suggestion we have prepared a narrative statement. I don't know if your Honor wants to circulate it or distribute it or read it—

THE COURT: May I see it, please?

MR. TUCKER: Certainly. May I hand it up, your Honor?

THE COURT: Yes. Thank you.

(Brief pause.)

THE COURT: Mr. Hardy, have you read this statement of your qualifications?

THE WITNESS: Yes, your Honor.

THE COURT: Mr. Tucker, either you may read it or I will have the witness read it. I think that is easier than circulating it.

MR. TUCKER: Fine, your Honor.

THE COURT: All right.

DIRECT EXAMINATION

BY MR. TUCKER:

Q. Will you read your statement of qualifications, please.

THE COURT: Ladies and gentlemen, it is written as if he is not speaking it. When he says "he is," he is talking about himself. There is also a list of publications. The list of publications, we will handle in a moment.

BY THE WITNESS:

A. (Reading)

"Dr. Kenneth R. Hardy is a member of the American Meteorological Society and his expert testimony will be offered in the area of meteorology.

"Dr. Hardy commenced his studies at the University of Saskatchewan where in 1952 he received an A.B. degree with honors in the field of physics. While an undergraduate at the University of Saskatchewan, Dr. Hardy's study included classes in optics, nuclear physics, mechanics, electomagnetism, chemistry and calculus.

"From the University of Saskatchewan, Dr. Hardy went on to obtain his Master's degree in meteorology from the University of Toronto in 1953. While studying for his Master's in meteorology, Dr. Hardy's course of study included thermodynamics, synoptic meteorology, dynamic meteorology, fluid dynamics and climatology.

"While at the University of Toronto, Dr. Hardy also began employment with the Canadian Meteorological Service. Upon graduation from the University of Toronto, Dr. Hardy's studies with the Canadian Meteorological Service first covered forecasting in Moncton, New Brunswick, where he was responsible for preparing forecasts for the public and for the aviation industry.

"While with the Canadian Meteorological Service, Dr. Hardy's duties took him to an arctic weather observing station in Resolute in the Northwest Territories where he was in charge of a weather station and providing weather briefings for all flights into the station.

"While still with the Canadian Meteorological Service, Dr. Hardy then moved to the Central Analysis Office in Montreal where his duties included the preparation of weather maps which were then distributed to forecast offices throughout Canada.

"Prior to returning to school to receive his Doctorate, Dr. Hardy was also employed by a private weather consulting firm in Canada where he was responsible for preparing weather forecasts for public and for various industrial concerns.

"In 1958 Dr. Hardy enrolled at the University of Michigan in the doctorate program. While studying for his doctorate, he was employed by the University of Michigan Research Institute as a research associate in the field of meteorology. Dr. Hardy's thesis dealt with the observations taken of raindrop size distributions and their variation with heights. Dr. Hardy received his Doctorate in Meteorology in 1963 from the University of Michigan.

"After receiving his Doctorate, Dr. Hardy was employed by the Air Force Cambridge Research Laboratories, which is an independent research laboratory of the United States Air Force where he was employed for approximately 11 years. His work with the Cambridge Research Laboratories was on a project basis primarily involved with the analysis of ground based weather radar information. In 1966 he became Chief of the Weather Radar Branch. While at the Cambridge Research Laboratories, Dr. Hardy was involved in the investigation of severe storms and in the use of sophisticated ground based weather radar systems to study clear air turbulence and wind shear.

"In 1974, Dr. Hardy left the Cambridge Research Laboratories and joined Environmental Research and Technology, Inc., as Manager of the Earth Resources and Atmospheric Physics Division. In this position he is responsible for studies involving the remote sensing of the earth's surface and atmosphere by satellite and for basic research in cloud physics, radar meteorology and atmospheric dynamics.

"Dr. Hardy is currently a member of the American Meteorological Society and from 1968 to 1970 was Chairman of the American Meteorological Society's Committee on Severe Local Storms. Dr. Hardy has completed the necessary examination requirements for nomination as a certified consulting meteorologist and currently only awaits formal approval by the American Meteorological Society. Dr. Hardy is also a member of the Royal Meteorological Society, the Scientific Research Society of America, and the International Union of Radio Science."

THE COURT: Dr. Hardy, there is a list of publications that has been presented to me, three and a half pages. Are these the books that you have published or articles that you have published?

THE WITNESS: Yes, Your Honor. They aren't scientific papers.

THE COURT: Are there any of those that particularly relate to the area of your testimony today?

THE WITNESS: Yes, there are several.

THE COURT: If you can just briefly state the subject matter of those articles.

THE WITNESS: One has to do with the raindrop size distribution within showers and their variability with height.

Others generally have to do with the observations of severe storms using radar and other types of meteorological measurements.

A good number of them have dealt with the nature of wind shear in the atmosphere and the detection of clear air turbulence using extremely sensitive and powerful radar systems which are based on the ground.

MR. TUCKER: Thank you, your Honor.

BY MR. TUCKER:

Q. Dr. Hardy, you used a term. Let's get right to that term, sir. What is wind shear?

A. Wind shear is the change of the wind speed or direction over some distance.

Q. Is that just a change in direction or just a change in velocity or just a change in speed, or a combination of the two?
A. It can be one or the other or both.
Q. All right, sir. Is this wind shear as you have defined it, sir, a new phenomenon to meteorologists?
A. No. We have known about wind shear for decades, since some of the early observations of wind fields within the atmosphere.
Q. How long have you been associated, sir, in part of your work with the aviation community or the aviation industry?
A. I was involved in the aviation industry starting in 1953.
Q. And have you been continuously involved in one phase or another with the aviation community?
A. Not continuously but on an on-and-off basis I have been involved.
Q. All right, sir. With respect to the knowledge of the aviation community, particularly as wind shear affects the operation of aircraft, can you tell us when that phenomenon first became known?
A. It became known to—

MR. DOMBROFF: Objection, your Honor. I think the question is too broad and vague.

THE COURT: Sustained.

BY MR. TUCKER:

Q. With respect to the knowledge of those other than meteorologists and with respect to the knowledge of the effect of wind shear on aircraft operations, can you tell us when materials first became available?

MR. DOMBROFF: Objection, your Honor. The question is still vague and ambiguous. It is compound.

THE COURT: Just use the latter part of the question.

MR. TUCKER: All right, sir.

BY MR. TUCKER:

Q. When, sir, outside the field of meteorologists did the phenomenon of wind shear and its effects upon aircraft operations first become known?

MR. DOMBROFF: Objection, your Honor. Known to whom? We are concerned with Pan American here.

THE COURT: Sustained as to form, but it seems like a battle over nothing.

Did you first read any publications about wind shear that had been written by other than those in your specialty?

THE WITNESS: Yes.

THE COURT: When did you first read it?

THE WITNESS: Approximately the mid-sixties.

THE COURT: What was it that you read, what type of publication?

THE WITNESS: They were still in the meteorological field published in meteorological journals, and the description of wind shear within the scientific papers had obvious applications to aircraft flight.

THE COURT: Have there been any writings on the effects of wind shear on aircraft flight?

THE WITNESS: Yes, sir—yes, your Honor.

THE COURT: When did those writings first appear?

THE WITNESS: In the late sixties, approximately.

THE COURT: What type of publication?

THE WITNESS: They would often be in aviation-type journals.

BY MR. TUCKER:

Q. Such as what type of journals, sir?

A. Some in Aviation Week and Space Technology.

Q. Now, let me ask you this. With respect to the actual effect upon the operation of aircraft, how wind shear is to be overcome, can you tell us when you first saw any articles along those lines outside of the scientific field?

MR. DOMBROFF: I am going to object, your Honor. It is not relevant when this man first saw them. There is no showing that he is a pilot or subscribes to any of the manuals or publications of the aviation flying field or that he has the knowledge or ability to know what Pan American knew in the mid-sixties.

THE COURT: Overruled.

THE WITNESS: May I have the question read back?

THE COURT: Yes. Read it back.

(The record was read as follows:

Q. Now, let me ask you this. With respect to the actual effect upon the operation of aircraft, how wind shear is to be overcome, can you tell us when you first saw any articles along those lines outside of the scientific field?")

BY THE WITNESS:

A. It would be in the early seventies.

BY MR. TUCKER:

Q. Have you prepared some charts here which graphically portray various aspects of wind shear?

A. Yes, sir, I have.

Q. What do you mean, first, by wind speed, sir?

A. It is the change of the speed or the motion of the air across a point.

Q. Is that sometimes used synonymously with "wind velocity?"

A. Yes, sir, it is. In the scientific field, "velocity" is meant to include both wind speed, how fast the air is moving, and the wind direction. It is often used in a rather sloppy sense, where wind velocity is just wind speed, but in the scientific literature, "velocity" includes both wind speed and wind direction.

§ 13.36 Scope and Admissibility of Expert Testimony

The following survey of several federal courts demonstrates the scope of expert testimony which is generally permitted by the courts.

First Circuit. In *Computer Systems Engineering, Inc. v. Quantel Corp.,* 740 F.2d 59 (1st Cir. 1984), the trial court allowed the plaintiff's accountant to testify as to profits lost as a result of a claimed failure to provide usable software pursuant to a contract. The defendant objected and appealed from plaintiff's favorable trial verdict. The appellate court upheld the trial court's decision to admit the accountant's opinion as to lost profits, because his specialized knowledge might have been of assistance to the jury. The trial court did not abuse its discretion in admitting the testimony.

In *McDonald v. Federal Laboratories, Inc.,* 724 F.2d 243 (1st Cir. 1984), a police officer who was injured when a mace canister he was carrying accidentally discharged brought an action against the manufacturer alleging breach of warranty and negligent design. The defendant manufacturer offered testimony by an expert witness as to the claimed design defects. The court refused to permit the expert to testify as to the design of the canister but allowed the expert to testify as to the chemical aspects of mace. After a favorable plaintiff's judgment, the defendant manufacturer appealed. The appellate court upheld the trial court's decision, because the witness had demonstrated no education or familiarity with the engineering principles involved in the design of a canister.

In *Coleman v. DeMinico,* 730 F.2d 42 (1st Cir. 1984), the plaintiff sued two police officers alleging violations of his civil rights through the use of excessive force. Over the plaintiff's objection, the trial court allowed the defense expert's doctor to testify that the plaintiff's injuries did not seem severe enough to have been caused by being hit with a nightstick. The expert also admitted that his opinion was speculative. The defendant police officers were successful at trial, and the plaintiff appealed. The appellate court stated that the defense expert's doctor's opinion was admissible, because he was not testifying from pure conjecture and his testimony was supported by other testimony in the case.

Second Circuit. In *Shatkin v. McDonnell Douglas Corp.,* 727 F.2d 202 (2d Cir. 1984), the mother of an airline passenger killed in a plane crash brought a wrongful death action against the airline and the manufacturer of the plane. The plaintiff offered expert testimony as to the value of future gifts which would be expected by the mother from her son, based upon projections of the son's future income, tax rates, economic trends, and possible disposable income. The trial court refused to admit the expert testimony. The defendants appealed an award for pain and suffering, and the plaintiff mother cross-appealed, alleging that the expert testimony should have been admitted. The appellate court stated that the testimony proffered by the plaintiff contained assumptions and assertions that were so unrealistic as to suggest bad faith and that were likely to confuse and mislead the jury. The trial court's decision to deny admission of the testimony was upheld. The court noted that the expert was working from assumptions which did not seem to have a basis in fact.

Third Circuit. In *United States v. Downing,* 753 F.2d 1224 (3d Cir. 1985), the defendant was convicted on charges of mail fraud, wire fraud, and interstate transportation of stolen property, solely on the testimony of an eyewitness. The district court refused to admit the testimony of a psychologist offered by the defendant to testify as to the reliability of eyewitness identifications. The psychologist was an expert in the field of human perception and memory. The trial court stated that the psychologist's testimony could never meet the "helpfulness" standard of Federal Rule of Evidence 702. See **§ 13.39**. The appellate court reversed, stating that the trial court should have conducted a hearing on the admissibility of the expert's testimony. If the hearing concluded that the testimony should not have been admitted, no new trial was required. The "helpfulness" standard centered on two factors: (1) the reliability of the scientific principles upon which the expert testimony rests and the potential of the testimony to aid the jury in reaching an accurate decision and (2) the likelihood that the testimony would mislead or confuse the jury. The court also suggested that there must be a specific showing that the particular features or facts surrounding the eyewitness identifications involved in the subject case may have impaired the accuracy of the specific identification.

Fifth Circuit. In *Holmes v. J. Ray McDermott & Co.,* 734 F.2d 1110 (5th Cir. 1984), the plaintiff sued his employer under the Jones Act and general maritime law and won a substantial verdict. The defendant claimed that a safety expert called by the plaintiff should not have been allowed to testify beyond his area of expertise and that the admission of his testimony was reversible error. The appellate court affirmed the trial court's decision to admit the expert testimony, stating that the court properly allowed the testimony and instructed the jury that any lack of expertise or basis for the expert's testimony applied to the weight of the testimony rather than its admissibility.

In *Dixon v. International Harvester Co.,* 754 F.2d 573 (5th Cir. 1985), the plaintiff was injured when a pine sapling entered the cab of a tractor he was operating while plowing fire lanes following a hurricane. The plaintiff won a substantial verdict, and the defendant moved for judgment notwithstanding the verdict and a new trial. The court granted the motion notwithstanding the verdict and dismissed the case. In granting the dismissal, the trial court excluded testimony of the plaintiff's expert witness, a design engineer and consultant, because the design engineer had never participated in checking the design of a "crawler tractor" and because he failed to demonstrate how the tractor could have been made safer. Both parties appealed. The appellate court reversed the trial court's judgment n.o.v. and reinstated the jury verdict, stating that it was within the jury's province to determine the weight to give the expert's testimony based upon his experience and credentials.

Sixth Circuit. In *United States v. Smith,* 736 F.2d 1103 (6th Cir. 1984), a defendant offered expert testimony regarding the reliability of eyewitness testimony. The trial court refused to allow the testimony, and the defendant was convicted. On appeal, the court stated that, although the testimony of an expert regarding the reliability of eyewitness identification is proper and should, in all likelihood, have been admitted, in this particular case it constituted "harmless" error.

In *Davis v. Combustion Engineering, Inc.,* 742 F.2d 916 (6th Cir. 1984), the plaintiff brought an age discrimination action against his employer, and the trial court allowed the plaintiff's expert to testify on the issue of age discrimination. The expert had two degrees in business administration, had worked in finance and personnel, and had written personnel policies. The expert, however, had not previously been involved in the area of age discrimination and was unfamiliar with the specifics of the Age Discrimination in Employment Act of 1967. The plaintiff was successful, and the defendant appealed. The appellate court, affirming the trial court judgment, stated that, although the expert was unfamiliar with the pertinent statutory definitions and standards, this lent to his credibility rather than his qualifications to testify. It noted that the court's instructions as to the witness's credibility were carefully explained to the jury and that the defendant employer was given—and took full advantage of—the opportunity to challenge the expert's credibility. There was no error, even when the testimony constitutes an opinion on the ultimate fact.

Seventh Circuit. In *Kalsay v. Consolidated Rail Corp.,* 749 F.2d 437 (7th Cir. 1984), the plaintiff appealed from a defendant's verdict on the basis that the trial court erred in qualifying a police officer as an expert in a train-automobile accident. The appellate court upheld the defendant's verdict, stating that the officer's skill and experience were sufficient to qualify him as an expert. The court stated that, when an expert witness had a reasonable factual basis for his conclusions and was available for cross-examination, his testimony is sufficient even though he did not make exact measurements of the accident site.

Eighth Circuit. In *Federal Crop Insurance Corp. v. Hester,* 763 F.2d 723 (8th Cir. 1985), the Federal Crop Insurance Corp. brought an action against a farmer for underestimating his crop yields. The trial court allowed the farmer's neighbors who grew the same type of crops for a number of years to testify as experts. The district court, in a jury trial, ruled in favor of the FCIC on three of its four claims. The farmer appealed. The appellate court upheld the decision to admit the expert testimony, stating that a witness's practical experience can qualify the person as an expert and that the relative skill of the farmers went to their credibility and not the admissibility of the testimony.

In *Clayton Center Associates v. Schidler Haughton Elevator Corp.,* 731 F.2d 536 (8th Cir. 1984), the owner of a building sued an elevator company for breach of contract to maintain elevators in the building. The trial court refused to allow plaintiff's expert to testify concerning repair estimates of the elevators and that none of the problems were due to excessive heat or dust in the building. The trial court awarded a directed verdict in favor of the defendant. The appellate court reversed, stating that the decision to exclude the expert testimony was reversible error. The building owner had established the witness's experience in the elevator maintenance field and his particular familiarity with the elevator system in the case.

Ninth Circuit. In *United States v. Marabelles,* 724 F.2d 1374 (9th Cir. 1984), the trial court's decision to prohibit a loan officer from testifying as an expert in a criminal tax evasion case was upheld on the basis that the loan officer was not an expert on taxation and was not fully familiar with the defendant's business expenses.

In *United States v. Binder,* 769 F.2d 595 (9th Cir. 1985), a child molestation and sexual conduct criminal action, the trial court allowed two psychologists and a psychiatrist to testify concerning the children's ability to distinguish truth from falsehood and reality from fantasy. The defendant was convicted and appealed, stating that the expert testimony improperly buttressed the credibility of the complaining witnesses who were, by the way, five and seven years old. The appellate court reversed, stating that it was error to admit expert testimony that the children could be believed, because the testimony was to bolster the children's testimony and to usurp the factfinding function of the jury. The court went on to state that the error might not have been grounds for reversal had the testimony been admitted solely to aid the jury in understanding credibility evaluations or if it had been limited to references to psychological literature or to a discussion of a general class of victims.

Computer Systems Engineering, Inc. v. Quantel Corp., 740 F.2d 59 (1st Cir. 1984), demonstrates the kind of expert testimony that is admissible. In *Computer Systems,* the trial court allowed the plaintiff's accountant to testify as to the profits lost as a result of a claimed fee to provide usable software pursuant to a contract. The defendant objected and appealed from the plaintiff's favorable trial verdict.

On appeal, the First Circuit upheld the trial court's decision to admit the accountant's opinion as to lost profits, because his specialized knowledge might have been of assistance to the jury. In admitting that testimony, the appellate court found that the trial court had not abused its discretion.

A contrary result was reached in *McDonald v. Federal Laboratories, Inc.,* 724 F.2d 243 (1st Cir. 1984). In *McDonald,* a police officer was injured when a mace canister he was carrying accidentally discharged. An action was brought against the manufacturer of the mace canister alleging breach of warranty and negligent design. The defendant manufacturer offered testimony by an expert witness to rebut the claimed design defects. The court refused to permit the expert to testify as to the design of the canister but allowed him to testify as to the chemical aspects of the mace.

After a favorable plaintiff's judgment, the defendant manufacturer appealed. The appellate court upheld the trial court's decision, because the witness had demonstrated no education or familiarity with the engineering principles involved in the design of the canister.

The *Computer Systems* and *McDonald* cases demonstrate the nature of the qualifications which an expert must have for the purpose of being able to testify at trial pursuant to Rule 702 of the Federal Rules of Evidence.

Another case demonstrating the use of expert witnesses is *United States v. Downing,* 753 F.2d 1224 (3d Cir. 1985). *Downing* involved a defendant who was convicted on charges of mail fraud, wire fraud, and interstate transportation of stolen property. He was convicted solely on the testimony of an eyewitness. The district court refused to admit the testimony of a psychologist offered by the defendant to testify as to the reliability of eyewitness identifications. The psychologist who was proffered by the defendant was an expert in the field of human perception and memory. In rejecting that testimony, the trial court stated that the psychologist's testimony could not meet the "helpfulness" standard of Federal Rule of Evidence 702.

On appeal, United States Court of Appeals for the Third Circuit reversed the district court's finding and stated that the trial court should have conducted a hearing on the admissibility of the expert's testimony. If the hearing concluded that the testimony should not have been admitted, no new trial was required. The Third Circuit also found that the "helpfulness" standard of the rule centered on two factors: (1) the reliability of the scientific principles upon which the expert testimony rests and the potential that the testimony will aid the jury in reaching an accurate decision and (2) the likelihood that the testimony would mislead or confuse the jury. In addition, the Third Circuit also suggested that there must be a specific finding that the particular features or facts surrounding the eyewitness identifications involved in the case under consideration may have impaired the accuracy of the specific identification. The *Downing* case is discussed in a different context in § **13.18**.

It is clear that when offering or utilizing expert testimony in the context of your case, you must keep in mind not only the qualification standards that attach to the expert witness under consideration in the case, but also the "helpfulness" standard of the rules insofar as it relates to the jury. The failure to do this may find you with an expert but no place to testify.

§ 13.37 —"Do You Have an Opinion?"

The Federal Rules of Evidence and a number of state rules have been amended to permit experts to testify regarding their opinions and to give the reasons for those opinions without giving the underlying facts or data on which they base those opinions, unless the court otherwise directs. In any event, the expert may be required to disclose the underlying facts or data upon which he or she bases an opinion on cross-examination.

Fed. R. Evid. 705 provides:

> The expert may testify in terms of opinion or inference and give his reasons therefor without prior disclosure of the underlying facts or data, unless the court requires otherwise. The expert may in any event be required to disclose the underlying facts or data on cross examination.

In this regard, *see also, e.g., Wilson v. Clark,* 417 N.E.2d 1322 (Ill. Sup. Ct. 1981), a medical malpractice case in which the court prospectively adopted Rule 705; *Roberts v. Tardif,* 417 A.2d 444 (Me. 1980), in which a medical expert was permitted to testify based on data which had been neither authenticated nor admitted into evidence.

In obviating the need for laying a foundation in terms of facts or data upon which an expert bases an opinion, Rule 705 is aimed primarily at doing away with lengthy and adversarial types of hypothetical questions which gave an attorney the opportunity to argue a case during its presentation as distinguished from arguing it during closing argument. However, in actual use, this rule can work a tremendous hardship on you when dealing with your opponent's experts.

Suppose an expert is called during your opponent's case who testifies as to his qualifications and then is simply asked whether he has an opinion regarding the conduct of your client. He indicates that he does, and he is asked for that opinion, which he then gives along with the reasons why he holds that opinion. Your opponent then turns that witness over to you for cross-examination. The predicament which you face is deciding whether to walk into what could be an ambush.

As you confront an expert presented by an opponent who has given an opinion without the underlying data on which he or she bases that opinion, the most significant factor which you should consider is the believability or credibility of that expert. You must consider the overall nature of the testimony and the objective impression which the expert has made in the courtroom. This requires you to look not only at the nature of the opinion but also at the demeanor of the expert and prior testimony as it may have related to qualifications and other matters. If you conclude either that the expert is not credible or that your own expert is strong enough to rebut your opponent's expert totally, you may well be advised not to cross-examine and inquire into areas where you might meet with the response, "I am glad you asked that question," which is a sure sign of trouble.

On the other hand, your usual response to an opponent's expert who gives what amounts to conclusionary testimony without providing underlying support must be to cross-examine in order to attack not only the credibility of the witness individually but also the substance underlying the opinion. Your first assault on this testimony should be through the judge. Most of the rules of evidence which permit experts to testify in this manner also require those experts to give the underlying justification for their opinions when this is ordered by the court. In any sort of technical case, whether commercial, tort, or otherwise, an appeal should be made to the judge that, because of the technical nature of the case, the jury is being done a disservice in being deprived of the full breadth of the expert's testimony and the bases for it, which they need to make an informed judgment as to the credibility of that expert and his or her opinions.

An alternative approach is to request that the judge order your opponent to provide you, prior to the commencement of your cross-examination, with the bases of the opinions of the expert, whether or not the expert is going to testify as to those bases. You will thus be able to prepare for and properly cross-examine the expert and, most importantly, know what areas not to get involved with on cross-examination.

§ 13.38 —Hypotheticals

The reason behind state and federal rule amendments making it unnecessary for experts to testify as to the bases of their opinions relates to problems with the use of hypothetical questions. Generally, hypothetical questions are used to elicit opinions from experts. Typically, a hypothetical presented to an expert starts with the words, "Assume for me the following facts . . ." and then goes on until a hypothetical is constructed premised on the facts of the case then in question. The line of questioning then continues with the questions, "Based on the facts that I have just given to you, do you have an opinion as to whether or not . . . ?" and "What is that opinion?"

With the changes in rules of evidence, detailed hypotheticals setting forth the basis of an expert's opinion as a means of eliciting those opinions are no longer typically required. However, it is not at all unusual, and indeed it is quite common, to find such hypotheticals being used. The problem with the hypotheticals is that they give rise to a number of ills. For one thing, they frequently contain assumptions of facts which are not in evidence or embody arguments or adversarial statements of counsel which are more properly contained within a closing argument. On occasion, these improprieties are inadvertent. Unfortunately, on occasion they can be deliberate.

When your opponent uses complicated hypotheticals, you should be especially watchful about the facts built into the hypothetical. You should request, at a minimum, that the hypothetical be read back after completion of the question, if it is of any length, so you can break down the facts individually and determine whether they are in fact in the record. Another approach is to request prior to trial that, if hypotheticals are to be used, they be written out and provided in advance. If you follow this approach, however, you will also be imposing a burden on yourself, because you will undoubtedly have to provide written hypotheticals for your own experts as well.

When you encounter a hypothetical with facts that are not in the record and you note an objection, a frequent response from your opponent is that evidence of the facts will be introduced at a later point and that everything will be "linked up." Unfortunately, experience indicates that often this is not done, and because of the failure of counsel to raise the point again, the hypothetical and the answer will stand.

Your first response to a comment by counsel that the facts will be introduced later is to object. Sometimes the judge will sustain the objection. Often the judge will overrule the objection based on an understanding that the evidence validating the hypothetical will be introduced later. If this happens, you must be careful to raise the objection later if counsel has not fulfilled the promise to the court. You must also be prepared to move to strike the hypothetical. The problem with this is that, once the jury has heard the hypothetical and the answer, you are again in the position of trying to unring the bell and having them instructed to disregard something. The difficulties are obvious, especially when there has been a substantial amount of testimony since the offending exchanges and the jury has integrated the hypotheticals and answers into its impression of the case.

Although you will be unable to completely wipe from the recollection of the jury the statements which may later turn out to have been improper because of failure of counsel to introduce the appropriate evidence, one approach might be to seek to characterize your opponent as having breached the trust of the court and the jury. The very best way to do this is to have the judge admonish your opponent in front of the jury for failing to introduce the required evidence despite earlier assurances to the contrary. You would want the judge to say something like the following:

> Ladies and gentlemen of the jury, during the testimony of Mr. Smith's witness John Adams, the expert who testified in the area of accident reconstruction, the court permitted, over the objection of counsel for the defendant, certain hypothetical questions to be addressed to the witness. The objection of counsel at that time was that the hypothetical facts which the witness was asked to assume as being true for the purpose of answering the questions were not yet present in the record. The response of counsel asking the question was that the facts would later be introduced into the record. Based upon those assurances made to me by counsel that the facts would later be introduced

> into the record, I permitted the hypotheticals to be asked and answered over the objection of counsel. The plaintiff's case has now been completed, and the facts which counsel assured me would be introduced into the record [have not been introduced] [were offered into evidence but were ruled inadmissible]. As a result, the hypothetical questions and the answers based upon those questions which were permitted over objections were improper, and the objections which were earlier overruled on the bases of assurances of counsel are now sustained. As a result, I am granting the defendant's motion to strike the questions and answers, and you are instructed to totally disregard and give absolutely no weight whatsoever to the questions and answers posed by counsel and given by the witness on the subject matter of . . . .

Even with an instruction as extensive as this one, you still face the problem of how to direct the jury's attention to the questions and answers so they can isolate what they are supposed to ignore. Obviously, the mere attempt to isolate what they are supposed to ignore highlights that information and perhaps reinforces it in their minds. If you request that the judge have the reporter read back the question for the purpose of refreshing their recollection as to what they are instructed to strike from their memories, you also risk reinforcing that recollection. This latter approach may be acceptable if only the question is read back, together with the objections being sustained. However, the question itself probably will stimulate a recollection of the answer, and you will probably be refreshing what had already become a stale recollection.

The great advantage that you gain in this situation is not so much the jury's disregarding of the evidence, because in some indefinable way it will probably enter into the overall decision-making process anyway, but rather the fact that the personal integrity and credibility of your opponent have now been impugned by the court. The jury inevitably will place a great deal of weight on the judge's perceptions and impressions, despite instructions to the contrary, and anything you can do to boost your own standing in the eyes of the judge as perceived by the jury and lessen that of your opponent will benefit your case.

§ 13.39 —The Learned Treatise Exception to the Hearsay Rule

Federal Rules of Evidence 702 and 703 delineate to what an expert may testify and the bases upon which the testimony must be founded.

> Rule 702. *Testimony by Experts*
>
> If scientific, technical, or other specialized knowledge will assist the trier of fact to understand the evidence or to determine a fact in issue, a witness qualified as an expert by knowledge, skill, experience, training, or education, may testify thereto in the form of an opinion or otherwise.

> Rule 703. *Bases of Opinion Testimony by Experts*
> The facts or data in the particular case upon which an expert bases an opinion or inference may be those perceived by or made known to him at or before the hearing. If a type reasonably relied upon by experts in the particular field in forming opinions or inferences upon the subject, the facts or data need not be admissible in evidence.

An expert who is properly prepared and fully conversant with the facts and issues of the case becomes a surrogate advocate. As long as the fine line between lawyer and expert is not perceived as being overstepped, the successful resolution of a case frequently turns more on the credibility assigned to the expert's opinions than the opinions themselves.

As effective as experts can be, there are a number of liabilities which can be associated with their use. One of the more significant can be cost. With expert fees rising from a few hundred dollars per day to several thousand dollars per day, the financial aspect of using an expert can, on occasion, be prohibitive. Expert expense, however, is a relative matter dependent upon what is at stake in the case.

Perhaps an even more significant problem associated with experts is the risk of the experts cancelling one another out. Consider a jury confronted with two well-qualified experts, one for the plaintiff and one for the defendant. Each expert testifies in a manner diametrically opposed to the other. Both come across convincingly. Both are well-dressed, and both know how to sell themselves. The jury has no really effective way to choose between the two, except perhaps by reference to other witnesses. Oftentimes, the jury will simply cancel out the two experts in its consideration of the case and decide it by reference to the balance of the evidence.

As discouraging as a prospect like this may be, experts are nonetheless necessary. The task facing a litigator in light of these risks is how to enhance and buttress expert testimony to make it more believable, more credible, and more likely to be accepted over that offered by an opponent.

One technique which is available but which has been virtually overlooked by most litigators is the use of a learned treatise as affirmative proof to buttress live expert testimony and make it more credible. Federal Rule of Evidence 803(18) is the exception to the rule against hearsay which addresses this area.

> *Learned treatises.* To the extent called to the attention of an expert witness upon cross-examination or relied upon by him in direct examination, statements contained in published treatises, periodicals, or pamphlets on a subject of history, medicine, or other science or art, established as a reliable authority by the testimony or admission of the witness or by other expert testimony or by judicial notice. If admitted, the statements may be read into evidence but may not be received as exhibits.

Apart from adding additional weight to the testimony of the expert who testifies live at trial, the use of a learned treatise is a cost-effective means of presenting additional expert testimony. Two recent cases address this technique and make it clear that it is worth considering when structuring proofs.

The first case, *Burgess v. Premier Corp.,* 727 F.2d 826 (9th Cir. 1984), involved litigation arising out of allegations of misrepresentation by the defendant about the quality of a cattle herd. The district court found for the plaintiff, and the Ninth Circuit affirmed. In doing so, the court found that the admission into evidence based on Rule 803(18) by the trial judge of books on cattle investing was proper when the plaintiff's expert testified that the author was a recognized expert on the subject.

The Fifth Circuit also addressed this subject in *Alexander v. Conveyors & Dumpers, Inc.,* 731 F.2d 1221 (5th Cir. 1984), a products liability action involving a skip hoist device which malfunctioned and caused the death of plaintiff's decedent. The district judge permitted the plaintiff's expert to read from the 1957 American Standard Safety Code for Conveyors but refused to admit the document into evidence. On appeal, the Fifth Circuit affirmed a directed verdict for the defendant and found no prejudice to the plaintiff in the judge's refusal to permit the document into evidence. However, the court of appeals also made several other observations, including the fact that although the learned treatise exception to the hearsay rule in Rule 803(18) may preclude receipt of the document into evidence, the catchall exception in Rule 803(24) could be used as a means to admit it. *See also Tart v. McGann,* 697 F.2d 75 (2d Cir. 1982) (disputed medical literature, if shown to be reliable and authoritative, may be read into the record as substantive evidence, regardless of whether it was relied upon by an expert during direct examination or called to his attention during cross-examination); *Dawson v. Chrysler Corp.,* 630 F.2d 950 (3d Cir. 1980) (excerpts from the two reports on automobile crashworthiness prepared by the U.S. Department of Transportation, the authoritativeness of which was inferentially conceded by another expert, were properly read into the record after being called to the attention of an expert during cross-examination).

Although statements in learned treatises may be used as substantive evidence once the appropriate foundation has been laid, they are most frequently used to impeach an expert's credibility. Ideally, the best approach is to have the expert acknowledge that the treatise is recognized as an authoritative source in the field and then go on to contradict the expert's testimony using excerpts from the treatise.

A point to be aware of is the fact that the experts cannot prevent the effective use of a learned treatise by denying that the treatise is reliable and authoritative. Such foundation can come from either the testimony of another expert or judicial notice.

A criticism often leveled at the use of the learned treatise exception as a device of substantive evidence is that a battle of the books results. Such a criticism is of little significance when one considers the battle of the experts which frequently occurs in litigation. The use of learned treatises as substantive expert testimony presents a generally unexploited area of trial proof which is a cost-effective supplement to live testimony.

Although the cases just discussed present the use of the learned treatise as a means for presenting substantive expert testimony, *Ellis v. International Playtex, Inc.,* 745 F.2d 292 (4th Cir. 1984), takes the tack of, in effect, shifting the burden completely. *Ellis* arose out of the wrongful death of the plaintiff's decedent as a result of toxic shock syndrome (TSS) allegedly caused by her use of tampons manufactured by the defendant.

At trial the plaintiff in *Ellis* offered into evidence certain epidemiological studies that had been prepared by the United States Center for Disease Control and various state health agencies. These studies indicated the existence of a correlation between toxic shock syndrome and the type of tampons which the plaintiff's decedent had used. The trial judge sustained an objection to the studies, finding that there was not a sufficient foundation laid by the plaintiff as it related to the methodology utilized.

The Fourth Circuit reversed a judgment for the defendant. In doing so, the court of appeals found that Federal Rule of Evidence 803(8)(c) made public records admissible because of what is usually a high degree of reliability and neutrality by public agency investigations. The court then found that this fact placed a burden on the party opposing admission into evidence of such records or investigations to establish their untrustworthy nature. Finding that matters such as defects in the method of the studies, bias, and age of the data went to the weight of the evidence and not to its admissibility, the Fourth Circuit found that the district court had been in error in refusing to receive the studies into evidence. In addition, the court of appeals found that, because investigations of the type in question were presumed to reflect generally accepted methodologies, the general acceptance test which applies to scientific evidence and which was enunciated in *Frye v. United States,* 293 F.2d 1013 (D.C. Cir. 1923), did not preclude admission.

Both learned treatises and public records represent potential means of presenting substantive expert testimony in a manner which is low cost and, at minimum, difficult to cross-examine.

§ 13.40 —Misuse of the Learned Treatise Exception

The learned treatise exception to the rule against hearsay permits statements from a reliable, published treatise on some science or art to be read into evidence, to the extent that such statements are called to the attention of an expert witness upon cross-examination or relied upon by him in direct examination. *See* Fed. R. Evid. 803(18); Unif. R. Evid. 803(18).

In *Haney v. DeSandre,* 692 S.W.2d 214 (Ark. 1985), a jury verdict in favor of the defendant in a medical malpractice action was reversed, in part for improper use of a learned treatise to bolster the testimony of the defendant's expert witness. The complaint in this case alleged that the defendant physician had negligently failed to test the plaintiff-patient for pregnancy before performing a hysterectomy. The defendant produced evidence tending to show that the physicians do not routinely order pregnancy tests before performing a hysterectomy. In order to further bolster this evidence, defendant's expert witness produced an authoritative treatise on gynecology and testified that "nowhere in the book 'does it state that you should order routinely a pregnancy test prior to a hysterectomy.'" *Id.* at 215. The Arkansas Supreme Court held that the admission of that testimony supported reversal because the treatise referred to contained no statement one way or the other as to whether physicians routinely order pregnancy tests before performing a hysterectomy. It appears that the learned treatises exception did not apply in this case because the treatise contained no statement that logically could have been relied upon by the defense expert.

The case serves to remind us to caution expert witnesses not to bolster their testimony through references to a learned treatise unless that treatise contains statements that logically support the witness's testimony, although the treatise in *Haney v. DeSandre* merely failed to express a contrary position.

§ 13.41 Preparing Medical Experts: Checklist

Medical witnesses often pose problems which tend to be more difficult than the other kinds of expert witnesses. The fact of medical training and the sensitivity of doctors to malpractice litigation requires special steps to be taken in the preparation and presentation of medical witnesses. The checklist which follows and the hints for physicians as witnesses in the next section will help you avoid having your own medical witnesses take unfair advantage of you.

Checklist

Preliminaries:

____ **1.** Name

____ **2.** Professional address

____ **3.** Occupation
____ **4.** Educational background
  ____ **a.** Schools attended (undergraduate; graduate; postgraduate)
  ____ **b.** Specialty status (board qualified; certified; diplomate)—explain
  ____ **c.** Offices held—local; state; national
  ____ **d.** Appointed positions
  ____ **e.** Member of any boards
  ____ **f.** Any published writings
  ____ **g.** Any teaching duties
  ____ **h.** Any lecturing before societies
  ____ **i.** Special awards
  ____ **j.** States licensed to practice in
  ____ **k.** Licensed to practice in this state?

Examination:

____ **1.** Doctor, have you on occasion had the opportunity to see, take history from, examine, and treat [patient's name]?
____ **2.** On what date? Where?
____ **3.** Was a history taken at that time? If so, relate.
____ **4.** Was history obtained from other sources (previous reports)?
____ **5.** What were the patient's primary complaints at the time of the history?
____ **6.** Did the injuries appear to be compatible with the complaints and history taken, including history of trauma as described to you?
____ **7.** Did you take a past history? If so, explain (previous accidents; diseases; surgical; impairments).
____ **8.** Was an examination made at that time?
____ **9.** Where was the examination held?
____ **10.** Was the patient cooperative?
____ **11.** What observations were made at that time?
____ **12.** What examination procedures were used?
____ **13.** Did the patient appear to be in pain?
____ **14.** Was the patient taking anything for relief of pain?
____ **15.** If so, what was it (who prescribed it)?
____ **16.** Did the patient appear to be hurt?
____ **17.** Was the patient bleeding when first observed?
____ **18.** Describe lacerations (black and blue; etc.).
____ **19.** Was the patient in shock?

____ **20.** Did the patient complain of pain during the examination?
____ **21.** Were x-rays taken?
____ **22.** If so, were they taken under your supervision and control?
____ **23.** Did you interpret them?
____ **24.** What did the x-rays show (fractures; dislocations; malformations; subluxations; etc.)?
____ **25.** Point out areas indicating existence of abnormality.
____ **26.** How did the patient describe the area and location of pain?
____ **27.** Do you have an opinion that you can state within a reasonable degree of medical certainty as to whether the pain was real or simulated?
____ **28.** If so, state.
____ **29.** Doctor, describe the difference between objective and subjective findings?
____ **30.** Explain the meaning of objective symptoms.
____ **31.** Explain the meaning of subjective symptoms.
____ **32.** Was there anything in the examination to cause you to disbelieve complaints of the patient (malingering tests—explain)?

Diagnosis:

____ **1.** Did you arrive at a diagnosis?
____ **2.** State the diagnosis based on findings as a result of the examination.
____ **3.** Were the complaints of the patient in proportion to your findings?
____ **4.** Was your diagnosis based on your findings of the examination and history?
____ **5.** Was your diagnosis yours alone or in consultation with other doctors?

Treatment:

____ **1.** Did you undertake treatment?
____ **2.** If so, describe (be prepared to have daily records reviewed on a day-by-day basis).
____ **3.** Was the plaintiff hospitalized (prior to or after your treatment)?
____ **4.** How long was the patient hospitalized?
____ **5.** Do you anticipate further hospitalization?
____ **6.** Did the patient respond to the treatment?
____ **7.** Did the patient cooperate with treatment?
____ **8.** What future treatments do you anticipate?

____ **9.** Is the patient still under your care?

____ **10.** How long and with what frequency will such treatments continue?

____ **11.** Do you expect to treat the patient in the future? If so, how long?

____ **12.** What is your estimated cost of such treatment?

____ **13.** Did you prescribe vitamins, belts, etc.?

____ **14.** Is the patient still taking this supplementation?

____ **15.** Did the patient undergo therapy?

____ **16.** If so, what type?

____ **17.** For how long was therapy rendered?

____ **18.** By whom?

____ **19.** Do you expect that it will be required in the future?

____ **20.** If so, what is the estimated cost?

____ **21.** Did treatment to the patient require any braces, casts, splints, collars, traction, or other devices?

____ **22.** If so, describe.

____ **23.** For how long a period?

____ **24.** Will it be required in the future?

____ **25.** If so, for how long?

____ **26.** Will there be any additional costs?

____ **27.** Was the patient in pain during the treatments?

____ **28.** Was the pain recurrent or constant?

____ **29.** Was the patient disabled during the treatment?

____ **30.** If so, to what extent?

____ **31.** When did you last examine the patient?

____ **32.** Describe his or her condition at that time.

____ **33.** Was the patient in pain at that time?

____ **34.** What were the character and severity of pain at the time?

____ **35.** Was the patient disabled at that time?

____ **36.** To what extent?

Future:

____ **1.** Doctor, in your expert opinion, can you state within a reasonable degree of medical probability whether the patient has reached maximum medical improvements?

____ **2.** Can you state within a reasonable degree of medical certainty whether the patient will suffer any permanent impairment in the future?

____ **3.** Can you state within a reasonable degree of medical probability the length of time treatment will have to continue in the future and the approximate necessary expenses of said treatment?

____ **4.** Do you have an opinion that you can express within a reasonable degree of medical certainty whether the patient will have to suffer pain in the future as a result of this injury?

____ **5.** Upon what factors do you base your opinion?

____ **6.** Doctor, what recommendations or limitations have you placed on this patient?

____ **7.** Have you done all you can for the patient?

____ **8.** In your opinion, within a reasonable degree of medical probability, can you state whether you feel that the injury sustained by the patient was a direct result of the accident of ________ date?

____ **9.** Did you render a statement to the patient for your services?

____ **10.** In what amount?

____ **11.** Is this reasonable for like services in the community?

§ 13.42 —Tips for Medical Experts

To many people, appearing in court to give expert testimony may prove to be an unpleasant experience. The following suggestions should help to minimize the possible unpleasantness of this experience.

1. Be objective. Even though the patient's welfare may be at stake, your particular role as an expert witness in the courtroom must be a totally impartial one, trying to help the court and the jury arrive at the truth. It is not your function to see that one side or the other "wins." When you allow yourself to become partisan, you become emotional, defensive, unnecessarily and improperly involved.
2. Keep within your field of expertise. Know the extent of your knowledge; admit your limitations. Never permit an attorney to lead you out of your field into another area where you may be unsure of yourself or have to guess—and where your guess could be wrong. Simply respond that you lack the qualifications to render an opinion because you lack either the knowledge or the expertise in the field.
3. Remain on firm ground. Do not be persuaded by an attorney to testify to opinions that go beyond what you honestly and sincerely believe.
4. Adequately prepare. Make sure you have done all your homework: review all available information about the area in which you are

being called on to testify. If you make reference to professional literature, make sure it is authoritative.

5. Do not confuse the legal distinction between "possibility" and "probability." Anything is hypothetically possible, but in the law, nothing is possible unless it is more likely than not to occur; that is, 51 percent or greater.
6. Do not answer questions you do not fully understand. Never attempt any response unless you fully realize what is being asked. It is far better to say you don't understand and to ask counsel to repeat the question than to give an answer which may not be responsive to the question or which may destroy your ultimate credibility. If the question is unclear, ask for clarification.
7. Do not guess at answers. If you don't know the answer, your best answer is: "I don't know." If asked why, you can respond by saying either that you are out of your field of expertise or, quite simply, that you don't know.
8. Do not volunteer information. Listen attentively to the question and answer it simply and concisely. It is the obligation of the attorney to obtain the information from you and not your duty to provide unsolicited information.
9. Do not lose your temper. As long as you keep your composure, your answers and your credibility with the jury remain. If you lose your temper or in any way display agitation, you place yourself at a disadvantage, particularly when an experienced cross-examiner sees that you can be easily provoked. If you lose your temper, you lose your credibility and, worse, may say things you may regret.
10. Distinguish between testimony as an expert witness and a fact witness. A *fact witness* testifies about personal knowledge of an incident. An *expert witness* offers opinions, interpretations, and conclusions based on facts presented to the expert. For example, a treating physician can testify about the treatment provided (fact witness) or testify about the appropriate standard of care to the particular patient (expert witness).
11. When using medical terminology, define in lay terms what you mean.

§ 13.43 Court-Appointed Experts

As litigation becomes more complex, trials are frequently becoming "battles of the experts." Whether any trier of fact, be it a judge or a jury, confronted with two experts whose opinions are diametrically opposed, is in a position to rationally make an informed choice is all too frequently less than certain. This does not mean, though, that such choices are not made. The fact that cases in which experts play a pivotal role are decided every day makes it clear that such choices are made and, probably more frequently than not, made correctly.

There exists in the Federal Rules of Evidence a device designed to aid the trier of fact in making informed decisions in such complex cases. It is infrequently resorted to, however, and is typically overlooked by litigators more for tactical reasons than anything else. Federal Rule of Evidence 706 provides a procedure by which the court, either on its own motion or that of any party, may appoint a "court expert."

> (a) Appointment. The court may on its own motion or on the motion of any party enter an order to show cause why expert witnesses should not be appointed, and may request the parties to submit nominations. The court may appoint any expert witnesses agreed upon by the parties, and may appoint expert witnesses of its own selection. An expert witness shall not be appointed by the court unless he consents to act. A witness so appointed shall be informed of his duties by the court in writing, a copy of which shall be filed with the clerk, or at a conference in which the parties shall have opportunity to participate. A witness so appointed shall advise the parties of his findings, if any: his deposition may be taken by any party; and he may be called to testify by the court or any party. He shall be subject to cross-examination by each party, including a party calling him as a witness.

An excellent example of the use of this procedure is *Leesona Corp. v. Varta Batteries, Inc.,* 522 F. Supp. 1304 (S.D.N.Y. 1981), a patent infringement action tried to the court sitting without a jury. The issues presented to Judge Robert J. Ward were highly technical, involving "electrode chemical cells using specific electrode structures." The court was also confronted with multiple, highly qualified experts testifying on behalf of each side.

Rather than make his decision solely on the basis of what experts oftentimes indicate is experience testifying as advocates, Judge Ward utilized Rule 706 to appoint an expert. He asked each side to submit a list of nominations. One name appeared on both lists, and, after the judge conferred with the expert and gave him an opportunity to review summaries of each side's position as well as other documents, the expert agreed to serve. *Id.* at 1311.

In appointing the court expert, Judge Ward entered a consent order setting forth the parameters of the expert's compensation and responsibilities:

> (b) In advance of trial Dr. Cairns is to prepare himself to become adequately knowledgeable to serve as a consultant to the Court with respect to the technical or scientific aspects of this litigation. Said preparation shall include, but not be limited to a review of the following:
>
> (1) The disclosure and teaching of U.S. Patent Nos. 3,419,900 (Elmore '900) and (Moos '909).

> (2) The prior art cited by the United States Patent Office in the proceedings of the Elmore '900 patent.
>
> (3) The prior art cited by the United States patent office in the proceedings of the Moos '909 patent.
>
> (4) Other patents, patent applications, and publications relied upon by the parties (see updated exhibit list).
>
> II. To attend the trial during the testimony of witnesses relating to the technical or scientific aspects of the case so as to permit fulfillment of the duties of I above.
>
> III. To offer testimony at trial subsequent to the completion of the parties' cases as a Court expert on any technical or scientific subject requested by the Court on direct examination by the Court, subject to cross-examination counsel for the parties.

Id. at 1311 n. 17

Following this expert's appointment, each side was permitted to submit written questions to the expert who, in turn, prepared a written report. Thereafter, a structured deposition of the expert was permitted, followed by his testimony at trial after he listened to the experts called by each party. *Id.* at 1312.

In commenting upon the use of a court-appointed expert, the judge first made a number of observations.

> The Court found Dr. Cairns' testimony to be of enormous assistance. Not only was the court expert's evaluation and testimony thorough and careful, but he also explained his views with a patience and clarity that any court trying a scientifically difficult patent case would find invaluable. The parties' expert witnesses, as a reading of this opinion should reveal, also were quite helpful. Indeed, without their testimony the value of Dr. Cairns' services, as well as the Court's understanding of the technical issues, would have been severely disminished. But, in an action such as this, a court expert serves not only as a witness on whose opinion the Court can rely for assistance, but also as both a teacher who, unaffected by his having been called as a witness by one side or the other, can explain the technical significance of the evidence presented.

Id. at 1312.

From a tactical viewpoint, there may be an enormous risk associated with the use of a court-appointed expert. Unfortunately, in many instances this risk may not become known until after the expert is appointed and it is too late.

Perhaps the single most determinative factor in the courtroom is the judge. Even in a jury situation, it is the judge who rules on jury instructions, questions witnesses, handles objections, rules on evidence, and, in all too many instances, clearly manifests an attitude toward the case which is crystal clear to the jury. Despite instructions to the contrary, experience indicates that the jury gives a great deal of weight to the attitudes manifested by the judge.

Consider the jury confronted with a court-appointed expert who quite clearly testifies in a manner favorable to one party. In some respects this would be equivalent to the judge expressing his or her opinion to the jury on the merits of the case.

Assuming the expert is testifying in a manner favorable to you, the benefits are significant. Equally significant is the damage to your case when the expert testifies, in effect, against you.

The problem with this situation is that, at least using the *Leesona* procedure, the parties might not know the leanings of the court-appointed expert until his or her first report was issued. Thereafter, all the efforts of the party which will be helped by the testimony would be directed at bolstering and supporting the expert's credibility, while all the efforts of the other side will be directed at impeaching the expert.

Although there may be no way to control the appointment of a court expert, there are a number of factors to keep in mind. First, the risks are substantially greater in the jury situation than in the nonjury one. By the same token, the benefits are also potentially greater. Be sure to point out to the judge the risks of prejudice in the eyes of the jury.

Consider suggesting that the appointment not include the expression of any opinions on the merits of the case, but rather be limited to testimony only on an informational or explanatory basis. Although this restricts the role of the expert, it also eliminates the possibility of prejudice. Another approach is not to have the court-appointed expert testify at trial at all, but simply act in the role of a consultant to the court. This completely avoids the problem of the expert's being perceived as favoring one side or the other.

The major benefit from the use of court-appointed experts is the better working of the system. From an adversarial point of view, use of a court-appointed expert is, in many respects, not a good technique. Notwithstanding this latter fact, however, Rule 706 commits total discretion over making the decision whether to appoint a court expert to the trial judge. Given the stronger management role being played by judges and the more complex litigation being dealt with by the court, it is not unlikely that the use of court-appointed experts will increase.

§ 13.44 Expert Interrogatories

The following form interrogatories are suitable for use in inquiring about your opponent's experts. Remember, the *only* discovery you are entitled to as a matter of right involving experts is interrogatories. Take advantage of that discovery.

1. State the names and addresses of all witnesses, including fact (nonexpert) and expert witnesses that you expect to or may call to testify at trial.
2. For each witness (fact and expert) identified in response to Interrogatory 1, state the subject matter of his or her likely testimony in this regard and whether each such witness will be proffered as an expert qualified to render expert opinion.
3. For each witness that you intend to proffer as an expert qualified to render opinion testimony, please provide his or her full name, academic degrees, professional and employment affiliations and qualifications. (A resumé attached to your answer will be sufficient response.)
4. For each witness that you intend to proffer as an expert qualified to render opinion testimony, state the substance of the facts on which he or she is expected to testify.
5. For each witness that you intend to proffer as an expert qualified to render opinion testimony, state the opinions that he or she is expected to express.
6. For each witness that you intend to proffer as an expert qualified to render opinion testimony, give a summary of the grounds for each opinion that he or she is expected to express.
7. For each witness that you intend to proffer as an expert qualified to render expert testimony, state all materials reviewed by such person in preparation for their testimony.
8. For each witness that you intend to proffer as an expert qualified to render expert opinions, state any investigation, tests, or analysis that were made by or on behalf of such witness in preparation for their testimony.
9. Describe the nature, source, and content of all documents that you expect to or may seek to offer at the hearing as exhibits.
10. Describe any visual or auditory aids that you expect to attempt to use at the hearing, including but not limited to a videotape, film, slides, charts, or figures set forth on a blackboard, tape recording, blowups of documents or charts, or photographs.

§ 13.45 Limiting Discovery Regarding Experts

On occasion, you may encounter an opponent who seeks to limit the discovery you can take from his expert. This may arise because the expert has a number of opinions which are unfavorable to the party who is offering him or her and, notwithstanding this fact, the attorney is still using the expert. In order to prevent these unfavorable opinions from coming out, counsel argues that the expert has a dual role. On the one hand, the witness is a testifying expert, while on the other, he or she is a consultant. In the former capacity, the witness is not going to testify to opinions which may have been formulated in the latter capacity. Although this is an imaginative approach to trying to prevent an expert witness from offering unfavorable opinions, this approach likely will fail. The brief in **§ 13.46** lays out the reasoning why it most likely will not succeed. Although Virginia law is discussed in this brief, the Virginia rules are virtually identical to the Federal Rules.

§ 13.46 —Sample Brief in Support of Motion to Compel Discovery

MEMORANDUM OF LAW IN SUPPORT OF RESORT'S MOTION TO COMPEL DISCOVERY

B Resort, Inc. ("Resort") submits this memorandum of law in support of its motion to compel plaintiff to produce its expert witnesses for deposition and to permit them to answer all questions relating to facts known and opinions held by them regarding the circumstances surrounding the airplane crash that is the subject of this lawsuit. This motion is necessary because, at the deposition of the first of plaintiff's three expert witnesses, plaintiff's counsel directed the witness not to answer questions that sought such facts and opinions.

STATEMENT OF FACTS

The relevant facts are set forth in detail in the accompanying declaration of Mark A. Dombroff, executed on September 10, 1987. Those facts are only summarized here.

BACKGROUND

This litigation arises out a crash on December 11, 1984, of a small private airplane shortly after takeoff from Open Airport near Roanoke, Virginia. Plaintiff was one of the plane's four occupants, all of whom survived.

Before bringing this lawsuit, plaintiff received several million dollars in settlement of her claims arising from the crash from parties other than the defendants in this litigation. She then brought this action, shortly before the statute of limitations elapsed, against the owner and the operator of the airport. Although the National Transportation Safety Board investigation found that the crash was principally caused by the failure of the pilot to adequately inspect the aircraft and to remove ice that had formed on the aircraft's wings prior to takeoff, plaintiff has alleged in this lawsuit that her injuries were caused by negligent activities of the defendants relating to the design, maintenance and operation of the airport.

The defendants have denied plaintiff's allegations that they were negligent and have asserted, *inter alia,* the affirmative defense that plaintiff's injuries were caused by negligent acts or omissions of persons and parties other than the defendants. *See* Answer of Defendant B Resort, Inc., p. 10, third affirmative defense; grounds for defense of defendants.

PLAINTIFF'S COUNSEL'S IMPROPER DIRECTION TO THE WITNESS NOT TO ANSWER

Plaintiff has designated three experts to testify regarding the safety of the airport for use by the public and the operation of the aircraft on the day of the crash. Dombroff Dec., ¶¶ 7–8. Plaintiff agreed to the depositions of those experts and produced the first expert witness, Mr. M., for deposition on September 9, 1987. *Id.*, ¶¶ 9–10.

During the questioning of Mr. M., however, plaintiff's counsel objected to, and directed Mr. M. not to answer, questions that sought facts known or opinions held by Mr. M. that relate to the acts or omissions of parties other than defendants who may have contributed to the cause of the crash. In particular, even though Mr. M. had reviewed the performance of the pilot and the aircraft involved in the crash and was qualified to form opinions regarding such performance, plaintiff's counsel directed Mr. M. not to answer any questions relating to those subjects. Dombroff Dec. ¶¶ 12–15.

Plaintiff has taken the position that even though plaintiff's experts have studied all the circumstances surrounding the crash and are qualified to form opinions regarding the causes of the crash, they should only have to answer questions that relate to the actions of the defendants in this lawsuit. *Id.* In essence, plaintiff argues that her experts should only be permitted to testify to some of their opinions regarding the crash—namely their opinions that may be favorable to plaintiff's case.

The only justification offered by plaintiff's counsel for this extraordinary position is on the ground of relevancy, (e.g., Tr., p. 11), and on the ground that plaintiff did not intend for her experts to testify regarding the potential negligence of third persons, (e.g., Tr., p. 10). As demonstrated below, those are clearly inadequate grounds for objecting—let alone directing a witness not to answer—under the Virginia rules.

ARGUMENT

THE INFORMATION SOUGHT BY RESORT IS DISCOVERABLE.

1. Rule 4:1(b)(1) of the Rules of the Virginia Supreme Court, which sets forth the scope of discovery, provides in relevant part:

> Parties may obtain discovery regarding any matter, not privileged, which is relevant to the subject matter involved in the pending action, whether it relates to the claim or defense of the party seeking discovery or to the claim or defense of any other party. . . . *It is not ground for objection that the information sought will be inadmissible at the trial if the information sought appears reasonably calculated to lead to the discovery of admissible evidence.*

(Emphasis added). It is precisely because of the broad scope of discovery permitted under Rule 4:1 that Rule 4:5, which sets forth the specific procedural rules for depositions, provides in relevant part:

> Evidence objected to [at depositions] *shall be taken* subject to the objections.

Rule 4:5(c) (emphasis added).

In interpreting these liberal discovery rules, the Virginia Supreme Court has held that it is improper to direct a deposition witness not to answer questions simply because the answer may be inadmissible, because the Virginia discovery rules authorize "*extensive* discovery of inadmissible evidence 'if the information sought appears reasonably calculated to lead to the discovery of admissible evidence.'" *Turner v. Manning Maxwell & Moore, Inc.*, 216 Va. 245, 217 S.E.2d 863, 870 (1975) (emphasis added).

Indeed, federal courts, in interpreting the virtually identical language of the federal discovery rules, *see* F.R.C.P. [Fed. R. Civ. P.] 26 and 30, have repeatedly held that absent a claim of privilege, questions asked at discovery depositions should be answered even if the answers would not be admissible at trial. For example, the United States District Court for the District of Massachusetts has interpreted F.R.C.P. 30(c) [which is identical to Rule 4:5(c)] to mean:

> *as a general rule, instructions not to answer are improper.* The only exceptions are those [that] deal with questions which seek information in the form of trade secrets and privileged information. Even in the case of questions of this type, it is the duty of the attorney instructing the witness not to answer to immediately seek a protective order.

American Hangar v. Basic Line, Inc., 105 F.R.D. 173, 175 (D. Mass. 1985) (emphasis added) (citations omitted). *Accord Ralston Purina Co. v. McFarland*, 550 F.2d 967, 973 (4th Cir. 1977) ("'Counsel for party had no right to impose silence or instruct witnesses not to answer and' . . . if plaintiff's counsel had any objection to the questions, under Rule 30(c) he should have placed it on the record and the evidence would have been taken subject to such objection.") (citations omitted); *International Union of Elec., Radio and Mach. Workers, AFL-CIO v. Westinghouse Elec. Corp.*, 91 F.R.D. 277 (D.D.C. 1981) (objection based on relevance does not justify a direction not to answer even when answer would not be discoverable under other discovery rules).

Here, there can be no question that counsel's relevancy objection and direction not to answer was highly improper. First, under the federal interpretation of F.R.C.P. 30(c), which contains identical language as Rule 4:5(c), it is *always* improper to direct a witness not to answer on relevancy grounds. *See, e.g., International Union of Elec., Radio and Mach. Workers, AFL-CIO v. Westinghouse Elec. Corp., supra,* 91 F.R.D. 277 (D.D.C. 1981).

Second, the questions objected to by plaintiff's counsel are certainly "reasonably calculated to lead to the discovery of admissible evidence," even if the answers themselves are ultimately determined not to be admissible for some reason. Thus, under Rule 4:1(b)(1), the answers are clearly discoverable. *See Turner v. Manning Maxwell & Moore, Inc., supra,* 216 Va. 245, 217 S.E.2d 863, 870 (1975).

Finally, there can be no serious doubt that the questions to which plaintiff has objected in this case seek relevant and admissible information. Plaintiff's cause of action focuses on the cause of the tragic airplane crash in which she was injured. Certainly all of the witness' knowledge and opinions regarding the circumstances of that crash are relevant to the "claims or defenses" of the parties in this litigation—especially in light of the defendant's affirmative defense that the crash was caused by the negligence of others.

2. [Fed. R. Civ. P.] Rule 4(1)(b)(4)(A)(ii) provides that facts known and opinions held by experts are discoverable through depositions upon motion by the party seeking discovery. In this case, because plaintiff agreed to the depositions of her experts, there was no need for B Resort to seek leave to depose them. Even if plaintiff had not agreed to the depositions, however, B Resort would have been entitled to take them upon motion to this Court. Indeed, federal courts interpreting F.R.C.P. 26(6)(4), which is identical to the language of Rule 4:1(b)(4), liberally permit depositions of experts that are expected to testify at trial once, as has been done here, interrogatories directed to the experts' testimony are served and answered. *See, e.g., Herbst v. ITT,* 65 F.R.D. 528 (D. Conn. 1975); *see generally,* 4 *Moore's Federal Practice,* ¶ 26.66[3] (1986).

Moreover, the fact that the deponents are experts does not effect the scope of permissible discovery. While there does not appear to be any relevant Virginia cases interpreting Rule 4:1(b)(4), federal courts that have interpreted the virtually identical language of F.R.C.P. 26(b)(4), have held that the rule "provides for quite liberal discovery of the opinions of experts." *United States v. Piquette,* 52 F.R.D. 370 (E.D. Mich. 1971). *Accord Dennis v. BASF Wyandotte Corp.,* 101 F.R.D. 301 (E.D. Pa. 1983); *Herbst v. ITT,* 65 F.R.D. 528 (D. Conn. 1975); *see generally* 4 Moore's Federal Practice, para. 26.66[3] (1986).

Indeed, both Rule 4:1(b)(4) and F.R.C.P. 26(b)(4) provide for discovery of "facts known and opinions held by experts, otherwise discoverable under the provisions of subdivision (b)(1) of this Rule . . . ." The rules do not place any other restrictions or limitations on the substantive facts or opinions discoverable. As demonstrated *supra,* the questions objected to by plaintiff's counsel call for answers that are fully discoverable under Rule 4:1(b)(1).

While subdivision (A)(ii) of Rule 4:1(b)(4) provides that the Court, in its discretion, may impose restrictions on the scope of expert depositions, the circumstances in this case do not justify any such restrictions. On the contrary, ________________ Resort merely seeks to discover (i) the opinions of plaintiff's experts as to what they believe caused the crash in which plaintiff suffered her injuries; and (ii) the factual basis for those opinions. Plaintiff takes the position that her experts should be required to testify only as to their opinion regarding some of the factors that they believe contributed to the crash—apparently plaintiff wants to limit their testimony to the factors that plaintiff believes will support her case against defendants. ________________ Resort seeks discovery of all the relevant opinions of plaintiff's experts and the facts on which those opinions are based.

While plaintiff's position, on its face, is unfair to defendants and wholly unsupported by the Virginia discovery rules, it is particularly inappropriate in a case such as this that involves an airplane crash. In such cases, there are always numerous factors that potentially contribute to the crash, such as the condition of the airplane, environmental and weather conditions, the performance of the pilot, including his or her mental and physical condition, and the role of third persons that may have interacted with the pilot or the plane (such as air traffic controllers). The identification of any one factor or group of factors as the cause of the crash necessarily depends upon a complete analysis of all potential factors and their interrelationship. In other words, even in the unlikely case where the cause of the crash can be traced to a single factor, it is impossible to give a fair analysis of why the airplane crashed without providing an analysis of other potential factors.

Plaintiff apparently expects her experts to do just that—to identify and analyze only those factors that support plaintiff's case against defendants. Such a procedure would be grossly prejudicial, as well as contrary to the Virginia rules of discovery and evidence.

3. Finally, Rule 4:12(4) provides, in relevant part:

> If the motion [to compel discovery] is granted, the court shall, after opportunity for hearing, require the party or deponent whose conduct necessitated the motion or the party or attorney advising such conduct or both of them to pay to the moving party the reasonable expenses incurred in obtaining the order, including attorney's fees . . . .

B Resort is accordingly entitled to the reasonable expenses that it incurred in connection with its motion, especially in light of the highly improper nature of plaintiff's counsel's direction to the witness not to provide clearly discoverable answers.

§ 13.47 Turncoat Employees as Expert Witnesses

A significant problem for many lawyers is the former employee who, without warning, shows up as an expert witness for the other side. In such circumstances, there are two means of attack available to counsel. The first of these involves the contractual obligations or relationships which run between the employer and the former employee. However, these contractual undertakings are sometimes less than effective as a means of precluding a former employee from testifying. Their language may be general, and they may fail to focus on the specific problem at hand. The common law obligations which exist between employers and employees or former employees are frequently a better weapon for obtaining injunctive relief than any other available means.

To establish that it is entitled to injunctive relief, a plaintiff must show that the balance of equities favors the granting of preliminary injunctive relief.

> Four factors are particularly important in determining whether a preliminary injunction is proper: (1) the likelihood of plaintiff's success on the merits; (2) whether the injunction will save the plaintiff from irreparable injury; (3) whether the injunction would harm others; and (4) whether the public interest would be served by the injunction.

In re DeLorean Motor Co., 755 F.2d 1223, 1228 (6th Cir. 1985). *Accord USACO Coal Co. v. Carbomin Energy, Inc.,* 689 F.2d 94, 98 (6th Cir. 1982) (affirming district court's entry of preliminary injunction freezing defendants' assets to protect rights of plaintiffs who had asserted constructive trust-restitution claims).

An employee's "confidential relationship implicit in his employment" affirmatively obligates him "'to exercise the utmost good faith, loyalty and honesty toward . . . [his] principal or employer.'" *Triangle Sheet Metal Works, Inc. v. Silver,* 154 Conn. 116, 125, 222 A.2d 220, 224 (1966) (*quoting Town & Country House & Homes Service, Inc. v. Evans,* 150 Conn. 314, 317, 189 A.2d 390, 392 (1963)).

> The law is well settled that knowledge acquired by an employee during his employment cannot be used for his own advantage to the injury of the employer during the employment; and after the employment has ceased the employee remains subject to a duty not to use trade secrets, or other confidential information which he has acquired in the course of his employment, for his own benefit or that of a competitor to the detriment of his former employer.

Allen Manufacturing Co. v. Loika, 145 Conn. 509, 514, 144 A.2d 306, 309 (1958).

Thus, "regardless of the existence of any express agreement touching the subject . . . [an employee may] not use a trade secret acquired in the course of [his] employment for [his] own benefit to the detriment of plaintiff." *Triangle Sheet Metal Works,* 154 Conn. at 123–124, 222 A.2d at 224. *Accord, Town & Country House & Homes Service,* 150 Conn. at 319, 189 A.2d at 393; *Restatement (Second) of Agency* § 396(b) and comments b, d (1958).

These express and implied promises not to possess or disclose trade secrets and confidential information without authorization are enforceable both by the award of damages and by the imposition of equitable relief, including an injunction and an accounting. *Town & Country House & Homes Service,* 150 Conn. at 318, 189 A.2d at 394. *See also Triangle Sheet Metal Works,* 154 Conn. 116 (affirming trial court's order enjoining former employees from using former employer's trade secrets in competing business).

The unauthorized disclosure of confidential information traditionally has been recognized as irreparable injury warranting preliminary injunctive relief. In *E.I. DuPont de Nemours Powder Co. v. Masland,* 244 U.S. 100 (1917), for example, the Supreme Court upheld the validity of a preliminary injunction restraining the petitioners' former employee from disclosing trade secrets. Writing for the Court, Justice Holmes explained:

> The starting point . . . is that the defendant stood in confidential relations with the plaintiffs, or one of them. These have given way to hostility,

> and *the first thing to be made sure of is that the defendant shall not fraudulently abuse the trust reposed in him. It is the usual incident of confidential relations.*

Id. at 102 (emphasis added). *See also Restatement (Second) of Agency* § 399(f) and comment f ("An injunction is of special importance where an agent . . . is threatening to disclose confidential information.").

Nothing in such injunctions will typically cause former employees any cognizable harm. The injunction would not prevent them from legitimately carrying on any new business, and they would remain free to use "acquired skill and knowledge." *Allen Manufacturing Co. v. Loika,* 145 Conn. at 517, 144 A.2d at 310.

The only "injury" they would experience as a result of such injunctions is that they could not violate at will contractual and fiduciary duties to former employers by selling confidential proprietary and privileged information. That "injury"—the deprivation of unlawful gains—is entitled to no weight in the equitable balance. As Justice Holmes recognized, "[i]f there is any disadvantage in the fact that he knew the plaintiffs' secrets, he must take the burden with the good." *Dupont,* 244 U.S. at 102.

On another level, the requested injunction will promote the public interest in the "encouragement of technological advancement." *Sperry Rand Corp. v. Rothlein,* 241 F. Supp. 549, 564 (D. Conn. 1965). "If protection of trade secrets is withheld, research and development will be impaired, for no employer would be willing to spend large sums on research and development of new ideas, methods and processes, if they can be freely taken and used." *Id.*

Particularly with respect to product manufacturers, granting an injunction will vindicate the public interest in encouraging manufacturers to develop sophisticated accident assessment procedures and to scrutinize continually and to refine their product designs, operating instructions, and recommended maintenance procedures. Conversely, denying the injunction could cool manufacturers' product-safety research efforts based on their fear that they might thereby be increasing their potential exposure to product-liability claims. Even minimal deterrence of such ameliorative efforts would be against the public interest.

CHAPTER 14

DEMONSTRATIVE EVIDENCE

§ 14.1 Introduction

As a general proposition, *demonstrative evidence* as used in this chapter refers to evidence that has been created for purposes of the trial as distinguished from evidence which exists incident to the transaction in litigation. One example which illustrates this definition is a bank check. *See* M. Dombroff, *Dombroff on Demonstrative Evidence* § 1.1 (John Wiley & Sons 1983) [hereinafter *Dombroff on Demonstrative Evidence*]. The check itself is *direct* evidence of the financial transaction which it is meant to represent. However, if you in any way process that check, by blowing it up into a 40″ by 60″ enlargement, blowing up the signature block to an enlargement, or preparing a flow chart to represent the underlying financial transaction, you have created *demonstrative* evidence.

The significant difference in the courtroom between the check as direct evidence and any of its processed formats is that relatively traditional foundation requirements must be met to get the check into evidence, while you are dependent almost entirely on the discretion of the court to get the demonstrative evidence resulting from the processing of the check into evidence. However, the effectiveness of the demonstrative approach to introducing evidence as a means of increasing jury comprehension and understanding and increasing the persuasiveness of a particular point of view typically justifies the risk associated with dependence on the court's exercise of discretion in these areas. As long as a proper foundation is provided, the risks should be minimized in most respects.

Because demonstrative evidence is so powerful at trial, it is susceptible of considerable misuse. It is important that you understand and appreciate the manner in which you can be victimized by an opponent who uses demonstrative evidence in a way that is either unfair or calculated to prejudice your case beyond the bounds of retrievability. Such dirty tactics can be recognized and countered effectively. This chapter should help you understand demonstrative evidence techniques in general and how they may benefit your case in particular.

§ 14.2 Prejudicial Evidence and Cautionary Instructions

Demonstrative evidence, a powerful persuasive tool, has the capability of being highly prejudicial. The word *prejudicial,* however, is not synonymous with *inadmissible.* As used in this context, *prejudicial* means that the evidence is meant to persuade the trier of fact in favor of the side making the offer. Accordingly, the fact that the word *prejudicial* is associated with a particular piece of evidence is in itself of no significance.

In response to an objection that a particular piece of evidence is prejudicial and thus inadmissible, a fallback position is to suggest a *cautionary instruction.* The idea behind the cautionary instruction is that the judge will instruct the jury that the particular evidence at issue is being offered and received for limited purposes and that the jury should not use it for other purposes or infer any other facts from the particular piece of evidence. Consider the case of a model of an airport offered by a defendant. Both the vertical and horizontal scales were correct relative to one another and the degree of detail was extensive, yet it did not reach the point of being so prejudicial as to be incapable of foundation. Despite this fact, and even though it was possible to document the foundation every step of the way, an objection to the admissibility of the exhibit was raised and briefed by opposing counsel. **Section 14.3** contains a copy of the brief filed by the party against whom the model was being offered, and an affidavit submitted by the producer of the model.

(Cautionary instructions and the "back-door" approach to getting evidence into the record, particularly in regard to the hearsay rule, are discussed in another context in **Chapter 13.**)

§ 14.3 —Sample Brief on Motion to Exclude Evidence

Attorneys for Defendant, Third-Party
Plaintiff, and Third Party
Defendant ________________ [Airline]

UNITED STATES DISTRICT COURT
________________ DISTRICT OF ________________

In re

Pago Pago Aircrash	}		
of January 30, 1974	}	SS.:	MDL No. 176 WMB
________________	}		All Cases—Liability

Brief re Motion of ________________ [Airline]
to Exclude the Model of a Portion
of American Samoa (Exhibit 1600)
Constructed by the Government

Defendant, Third-Party Plaintiff and Third-Party Defendant, ________________ [Airline], submits this Brief in support of their Motion to Exclude the Model of a Portion of American Samoa (Exhibit 1600) Constructed by the Government.

[*Index*]

[*Table of Cases and Other Authorities*]

1. Introduction

The newly enacted Federal Rules of Evidence do not deal directly with demonstrative evidence other than writings, recordings, and photographs. *Fed. Rules of Evidence,* Rule 1001. Thus, the propriety of other types of demonstrative evidence is determined by the general sections of the Federal Rules of Evidence and in particular Rule 403.

> Although relevant, evidence may be excluded if its probative value is substantially outweighed by the danger of unfair prejudice, confusion of the issues, *or misleading the jury,* or by considerations of undue delay, waste of time, or needless presentation of cumulative evidence. *Fed. Rules of Evidence,* Rule 403. (Emphasis added.)

This brief will discuss the misleading aspects of the Government's topographical model of a portion of American Samoa (Exhibit 1600). There can be no doubt that the model would leave a false impression in the mind of a juror with respect to the pertinent issues in this case.

In addition to misleading the trier of fact, this exhibit also has foundational and hearsay problems. These issues will also be discussed.

2. The Model of a Portion of American Samoa Constructed by the Government Is Misleading and Should Not Be Permitted to Be Seen by the Jury.

The expression, "a picture is worth a thousand words," although trite, is nevertheless true. Demonstrative evidence has a power of persuasion over the trier of fact often lacking with verbal testimony.

> Since "seeing is believing," and demonstrative evidence appeals directly to the senses of the trier of fact, it is today universally felt that this kind of evidence possesses an immediacy and reality which endow it with particularly persuasive effect. *McCormick on Evidence,* 2d ed., Hornbook Series, Section 212, p. 524, 525 (1972).

McCormick went on to say:

> Again, even if no essentially emotional response is likely to result, demonstrative evidence may convey an impression of objective reality to the trier. Thus, the courts are frequently sensitive to the objection that the evidence is "misleading," and zealous to insure that there is no misleading differential between objective things offered at trial and the same or different objective things as they existed at the time of the events or occurrences in litigation. *Id.,* at 525.

The underlying reason for this zealous guard by the courts is poignantly set forth in an often-quoted section of *Wigmore on Evidence:*

> It is, briefly, that a material object, particularly a writing, when presented as purporting to be of a certain origin, always tends to impress the mind unconsciously, upon the bare sight of it, with the verity of its purport. Does it purport to be a contract signed by A and B? We immediately assume it to be such; though it may be the merest forgery. Does it purport to be a picture of the place of murder? We look at it with an interest based on the unconscious assumption that it *is* that house. In short, we unwittingly give the document the credit of speaking for itself, though no human being has yet spoken for it. Now this tendency has to be rigorously repressed, and as it is in the present relation that this tendency finds one of its most frequent manifestations, so it is here that the tendency has so frequently to be struck at by judicial rulings. *Wigmore on Evidence, Chadbourn Revision* (1970), Section 790, p. 218.

And so the jurors, upon seeing the model of a small portion of American Samoa, will probably keep that picture in their minds long after the verbal testimony has grown hazy. For that reason, the model must be entirely accurate, not only in what is seen on the model, but also from the viewpoint of what has been omitted.

Anyone looking at the model without happening to see the brass legend might believe that this model represents the final approach to an airport in the flatlands of Indiana. The jury will not be able to see the cliff-like one- to two-thousand foot ridge located just off the area represented by the ridge which will figure so prominently in the discussions concerning wind shear. The jury will be misled into believing that there [were] no obstructions in the airspace over Logotala Hill which were in violation of FAA requirements and regulations. The terrain there is immensely rough, and the trees which protruded into the airspace of the approach on the day of the crash created to a large degree, the "black hole" effect during the approach. The model can only be viewed as if one were looking out of an airline window, not 100 to 500 feet above ground level (AGL), but from the lofty perch of 12,000 to 20,000 feet. Such a view gives the jury no inkling of the terrain factors which contributed to the cause of the crash. The glide slope line appears to be a gentle slope from the vantage point of 20,000 feet, but in reality it is one of the steepest glide slopes in the world. In short, the model predisposes one to think in terms of pilot error because of the seemingly easy approach. Such prejudice greatly outweighs the probative value, if any, of this exhibit.

A case closely related in fact to the above issue warns of the misleading effects which models can have on the minds of the jurors when there is a great disparity of size. In *County of San Mateo v. Christen* (1937) 22 Cal. App. 2d 375, the trial court excluded a small model of a tract of land in an eminent domain proceeding. The holding of the court is worth noting.

> Conceding that a foundation was laid for the introduction of the model, the use of models must lie largely within the discretion of the trial court. While models may frequently be of great assistance to a court and jury, it is common knowledge that, even when constructed to scale, *they may frequently, because of the great disparity in size between the model and the original, also be very misleading,* and trial courts must be allowed wide discretion in ruling upon whether to admit them into evidence or not. Upon the general subject of the admission of material objects into evidence section 1954, Code of Civil Procedure, provides: "The admission of such evidence must be regulated by the sound discretion of the court." *County of San Mateo, supra,* at 378. (Emphasis added.)

The rule is no different in the federal courts. Admissibility of demonstrative evidence is largely within the discretion of the trial judge. *Sedlack v. General Motors Corp.,* 253 F.2d 116 (7th Cir. 1958). A model should be excluded if the jury is apt to be misled by its use. 29 Am. Jur. 2d, *Evidence,* section 804, p. 893.

Not only do the omissions and misleading vantage point of the model distort reality, but also the model has not been constructed to scale. See attached Affidavit of professional model maker ________________. For example, the relatively short distance between the center point of the runway and the VASI lights was distorted by 90 feet in real life. The glide slope center line was off by 220 feet in real life. Every measurement taken by Mr. ________________ found that the details measured were not placed according to scale. On a model constructed to scale, and of a size comparable to that of the Government's model, the maximum error allowable in the location of details is plus or minus 10 feet in order for the model to be called a "scale model." It is manifestly apparent from the findings in Mr. ________________'s Affidavit that this model is not to scale.

A model not to scale was rejected in the case of *Burriss v. Texaco,* 361 F.2d 169 (4th Cir. 1966), because of its potentially misleading effect on the jury.

> Rejection of the model was particularly justified here, as the tubing used to represent the drainage pipes was admittedly not to scale, rendering the conditions of the proposed experiment substantially different from those existing at the fire. *Id.,* at 175.

In summation, the Government's model prepared to give the viewer a three-dimensional view of a section of American Samoa could have been a very valuable aid in giving the jury a "feel" for the testimony of the witnesses. The Government's obvious attempt to mislead by omissions of pertinent features, carelessness in construction, and its high altitude point of view has rendered it not only useless, but also highly prejudicial.

It would be manifestly unfair to allow the jury to view this erroneous model for weeks on end and come to conclusions about the ease of the approach that are not warranted by the actual facts of the site.

3. The Model of a Portion of the Island of American Samoa Must Be Accompanied by a Percipient Witness Who Is Familiar with the Area Being Described by the Model.

While it is true that the federal courts permit the introduction of demonstrative evidence such as models, maps, sketches or diagrams, *Brinegar v. San Ore Construction Co.,* 302 F.Supp 630 (E.D. Ark. 1969), it is imperative that this evidence be illustrative of verbal testimony which has been given to describe whatever is at issue.

> Models, maps, sketches, and diagrams (as distinguished from duplicates) are by their nature generally not confusable with real evidence, and are admissible simply on the basis of testimony that they are substantially accurate representations of what the witness is endeavoring to describe. *McCormick on Evidence,* Hornbook Series, Section 213, p. 530 (1972).

Wigmore on Evidence, Chadbourn Revision (1970), Section 793, p. 239, describes the requirement in more absolute terms:

> It follows, then, that the map or diagram must first, to be admissible, be *made a part of some qualified person's testimony.* Someone must stand forth as its testimonial sponsor; in other words (as commonly said), it *must be verified.* (Emphasis by the author).

Furthermore:

> A witness must have had observation of the data in question (Sec. 650 supra), must recollect his observations (Sec. 725 supra), and must correctly express his observation and recollection (Sec. 766 supra). *Id.,* at 239.

The model of a portion of American Samoa is at issue because it does not accurately reflect the topography and location of certain monuments. This is all the more reason why a person describing this topography and monument placement, must have some personal knowledge as to their location. For example, the model attempts to depict the location of impact. The model maker has demonstrated no personal knowledge of the location of point of impact on the model. He was obviously told by others where to place the marker, a classic hearsay situation.

In a case, factually on point with this previous example, *Fleming v. Commonwealth,* 284 Ky. 209, 144 S.W.2d 220 (1940), the Kentucky Supreme Court reversed an involuntary manslaughter conviction because of the hearsay involved. The city engineer provided a blueprint showing the point of an accident impact by means of some white stars on the blueprint. The blueprint absent the white stars was acceptable, however. The engineer had placed the white stars where another person had indicated the accident to be.

In addition, the creator of this model has not demonstrated any personal knowledge whatsoever of any features of American Samoa, as represented in the model. While the topographical map itself from which the model was constructed, if properly authenticated, would meet the hearsay exception, *Wigmore, supra,* Section 794, and would be admissible to illustrate testimony, the model which purports to represent American Samoa and not the map, would be improper unless authenticated by someone with personal knowledge of the physical characteristics of American Samoa.

> The witness thus standing sponsor must be *qualified by observation* (Secs. 650, 657 *supra*) to speak of the matters represented in the picture [model]. (Emphasis by the author.) Wigmore, *supra,* at Section 794, p. 240.

The only exception to this rule, which is not applicable here is in the case of photographs. Such evidence once properly authenticated speaks for itself in some jurisdictions; but only for the reason that a photograph "is without question more accurate and reliable than that of a human witness." *People v. Bowley* (1963) 59 Cal.2d 855, 861.

Thus, the model presented by the UNITED STATES Government does not speak for itself, but is only useful when it does not mislead and when testified to by a witness who has competent knowledge of the scene depicted. That model must be affirmed by that witness to represent the scene. *Wigmore, supra,* at Section 794, p. 239.

4. Conclusion

7 Am. Jur. *Proof of Facts,* p. 604, lists seven criteria which should be satisfied before this model can be introduced into evidence as illustrative of verbal testimony:

- Exhibit prepared according *to scale*
- Exhibit verified by witness as reliable and correct representation of area or *subject matter in issue*
- Exhibit of such a nature as to be *explanatory* of verbal testimony
- Exhibit of such a nature as not *to mislead jury* or cause confusion or undue influence
- Prepared model *identical* with original except as to size
- Witness *qualified* to testify as to accuracy of proposed exhibit
- Nature of testimony such that reference to prepared model is necessary to understanding of testimony by jury. (Emphasis added.)

With the possible exception of the last criterion, none of the prerequisites for the use of this model by the Government have been met.

Because this model is inherently defective and incapable of meeting the evidentiary requirements set forth by the law, the Court is requested to forbid the trier of fact from viewing this model.

Affidavit of ________________ re the Model of
a Portion of American Samoa Constructed
by the United States Government

STATE OF CALIFORNIA }
COUNTY OF LOS ANGELES } SS.:
____________________ }

I, ________________, being duly sworn, depose and say:

I am a citizen of Brazil and have lived in the State of California for 11 years. I am over 18 years of age.

I am currently President of ________________ located in ____________ and I have been actively engaged in the model industry for over 20 years. My present clientele includes Hughes Aircraft, I.B.M., TRW Systems, Litton Industries, and many others. During my career in the model industry I have had occasion to construct topographical models to scale.

On January 11, 1978, I inspected a model located in the United States District Courthouse, at 312 North Spring Street, Los Angeles, California, constructed by the UNITED STATES GOVERNMENT. This model attempted a representation to scale of a portion of the Island of American Samoa, namely a portion of the approach to Pago Pago International Airport.

Using the brass plate scale attached to the model itself, I calibrated a measuring device with which to measure distances on the model. I constructed my own measuring device because the unattached measuring device which was used by the Government when constructing the model, was unavailable. The device which I calibrated to measure the distances was the straight edge of a manila folder. This folder was used because the rulers which I have are not flexible enough for the type of measurement that had to be done and I did not wish to damage the Government's exhibit. I can state that I carefully calibrated the straight edge and that my measurements were accurate to plus or minus 10 feet (distances as they would appear at American Samoa in life size). The calibrations on my straight edge were done so as to give me distances on the model as they would appear life size. As I measured each distance from various checkpoints on the model, I would compare these distances with the measurements which were given on the drawing blueprint number PCD2267-2 (Exhibit 220).

I verbally gave the results of the measurements and the comparisons to an employee of the law firm of ________________, who recorded these measurements on a yellow pad. The recordations were repeated back to me so that I could confirm them.

I found that overall the model was not constructed to scale. None of the distances which I measured, accurately corresponded with the distances given on drawing blueprint number PCD2267-2 (Exhibit 220).

My findings were as follows:

> (All distances given correspond to life-size distances)
> Distance of the localizer antenna from the Northern threshold of the runway:
> Blueprint—975 feet; model—1150 feet
> Distance from the Northern runway threshold to waterline:
> Blueprint—200 feet; model—300 feet
> Distance from the runway centerline to the localizer antenna:
> Blueprint—303 feet; model—375 feet
> Distance from the runway centerline to the center point of the token representing the VASI Lights:
> Blueprint—150 feet; model—240 feet
> Distance (horizontal) from the lower ILS glide slope line represented on the model by the lower yellow string to the beacons:
> Blueprint—280 feet; model—500 feet
> The distance represented by the line which was the shortest distance from the curve in Larson Bay to the ILS glide slope represented by the lower yellow line:
> Blueprint—550 feet; model—200 feet
> The distance from the runway centerline to the glide slope antenna:
> Blueprint—350 feet; model—425 feet

In constructing models to scale it is customary to have the center point of the representative token represent the actual center point of the item in real life as measured on the blueprint.

I was not permitted to check vertical elevations. Such a measurement entails the inserting of pins in the model.

Based on my years of experience in the scale model industry, I would conclude that the builder of this model only wanted to approximate the placement of the details on the model with respect to their location in the real world. On models built to scale, details as represented on the model should not differ in distance more than 10 feet (life size) from their actual locations in real life.

§ 14.4 —Sample Cautionary Instruction

The fallback position of the offering party was to suggest a cautionary instruction to the judge, meant to limit the purposes for which the model was being used. That cautionary instruction was as follows:

Exhibit 1600 is a model of Pago Pago International Airport and certain portions of the terrain underlying the approach path. The portions of the terrain shown do not include obstructions, trees, lava bank or other objects that may extend above the surface. The model is not to scale nor does it represent the topography of the island in scale. Not all of the terrain surrounding the airport is shown, nor is all of the land between the coast and the airport.

For further discussion of this instruction, *see Dombroff on Demonstrative Evidence* § 5.2.

Notwithstanding the cautionary instruction, the model was in scale in every respect. However, to overcome objections which may or may not have been well founded, the cautionary instruction approach was taken and accepted by the judge. The model was accepted into evidence at the beginning of the case and became the focal point of much testimony, being used as a prop not only by the attorneys but by the witnesses as well.

This is simply the old problem of unringing the bell. Even though the jury may be cautioned as to something they should or should not do in connection with their own mental processes and assimilation of certain evidence into their decisionmaking, it is virtually impossible to limit the use they will make of a particular piece of demonstrative evidence. The fact of the matter is that the cautionary instruction provides a pretense for getting evidence into the record. Accordingly, when you are in such a situation, the position you should take is that the cautionary instruction does not cure the problem.

Acknowledging that the evidence itself is powerful, you should point out that the cautionary instruction is merely the proverbial finger in the dike, and that there is no way to stem the inferences or actual use which the jury may make of a particular exhibit notwithstanding a cautionary instruction. When you call the court's attention to the fact that opposing counsel's use of a cautionary instruction is nothing more than a pretense for getting an otherwise prejudicial and inadmissible exhibit into evidence, you can often place the burden on the other side to show how a cautionary instruction has more than a superficial effect in a particular situation.

§ 14.5 Captions

Many pieces of demonstrative evidence, particularly those in chart, graph, or diagram form, have captions associated with the graphic portrayal. In its simplest form, a caption affixed to a list of opinions prepared by an expert in graphic form might be "Plaintiff's Negligence" or "Defendant's Negligence." Captions, however, are often far more deviously used to convey messages to the viewer that would be inadmissible if presented in some other format.

Assume an exhibit prepared by an opponent is meant to represent a transfer of funds. The exhibit is in the form of a flow chart and is an accurate graphic portrayal of how the funds moved between your client, the defendant, and the corporation which the plaintiff alleges was a "front" for the diversion of funds away from their intended recipient to your client's own interest. The factual information contained within the graphic portrayal is an accurate reflection of the underlying facts and the movement of the money.

Opposing counsel intends to use the exhibit with a fact witness, as distinguished from an expert, for the purpose of describing the movement of funds. The exhibit has a caption, "Fraudulent Diversion of Grant Money," which is not in any way integral to the exhibit but is meant to describe what is portrayed in it. The problem with the description is that it is actually a point of view or adversarial position that the otherwise accurate chart reflects the wrongful diversion of money. Accordingly, an objection should be raised, not necessarily to the underlying exhibit, but rather to the caption on it.

Such an objection should be directed to the overall exhibit unless it is in your interest to allow the exhibit to be used. If it is in your interest to permit the exhibit to be used or if your overall objection is overruled, you should seek to have the caption blocked out or physically removed. Physical removal of a caption or other offending information is generally preferable to blocking it out with opaque tape or paper, because the jurors may spend more time wondering what they are not seeing than thinking about what they are seeing in terms of factual information.

All exhibits, no matter how innocuous they may appear to you, should be carefully examined for information which is essentially extraneous to the underlying exhibit but which is descriptive of the exhibit in a manner which is, in effect, argumentative. Argumentative captions should be objected to, and exhibits which contain them should not be permitted in front of the jury.

§ 14.6 Colors and Highlighting

From childhood we are exposed to the merchandising of products and ideas. Recognizing that the courtroom is in some ways a marketplace and that a particular point of view or position is being sold to the jury as the ultimate consumer, it is clear that many of the concepts and techniques used in the advertising industry have equal applicability in the courtroom and in litigation in general. One means of delivering an unconscious message is by use of color.

As a general rule, demonstrative evidence can be tremendously powerful. Since the ability to use demonstrative evidence requires a favorable exercise of the trial judge's discretion, anything which compromises the exercise of that discretion so as to give rise to a claim that a proposed exhibit is indeed prejudicial within the rules of evidence is something to be avoided. As a result, unless color is essential to a particular depiction, as in a model or chart, color used for artistic purposes is generally to be avoided.

The purpose of a chart, graph, diagram, or model is to convey factual information or to simplify information presented in another format. The purpose of demonstrative evidence techniques is not to deliver an independent message. However, it is easy to convey such a message, and, unless you are on your guard, colors and highlighting techniques incorporated into an exhibit can deliver a silent message to the jury unknown to you.

Assume that your opponent in a personal injury case is presenting an economist to testify regarding the damages occasioned by the alleged negligence of your client. The economist has prepared a chart which, in effect, summarizes his opinions of the various damage components. That chart, prior to his giving an ultimate opinion and adding up all of the figures, appears as follows.

Loss of income	$850,000
Loss of care, comfort, and support	$100,000
Loss of affection	$100,000
Medicals	$ 52,000

Upon being asked the ultimate question, "What is the total amount of damages occasioned to Barbara Jones as a result of this accident in your opinion?", the witness either flips down an overlay with a total located in the proper position relative to the other numbers, or, alternatively, although he has been using a black felt tip marker to write the numbers, he now uses a red felt tip marker. In either event, the finished exhibit appears as indicated below.

Loss of income	$ 850,000
Loss of care, comfort, and support	$ 100,000
Loss of affection	$ 100,000
Medicals	$ 52,000
	$1,102,000

Color is clearly used in a chart or diagram—or, in this case, calculations—to highlight and draw attention to a particular aspect of the exhibit. If the color is red, it is possible that the unconscious message *blood money* is conveyed. Accordingly, when an exhibit is presented to you prior to its offer into evidence, as typically happens under most rules of civil procedure today, you should be particularly careful about and on guard against colors which unnecessarily draw attention to particular aspects of charts or diagrams and convey messages by themselves.

For example, from birth we are taught to associate the color red with *danger* or *stop.* The color yellow is associated with *caution.* Softer pastels tend not to excite people, while grays and browns are neutral and can often avoid an objection that a piece of evidence is prejudicial when the exhibit itself conveys an extremely powerful message without the addition of unnecessarily prejudicial elements such as color.

This is not to say that, if color is integral to a particular exhibit, it should not be used. For example, in a case which involves an electrical junction box with a red danger sign, you would be perfectly justified in having that sign portrayed in its accurate colors. Indeed, failure to do so would probably be a serious error. The color itself is *meant* to convey a message, and there should be no unfairness or prejudicial argument associated with such an accurate portrayal.

§ 14.7 Statistical Presentations

Persons in the world of corporate finance are intimately familiar with the presentation of statistics in forms designed to convey information and, on occasion, to disguise information. In the courtroom as well, attorneys often confront the task of conveying statistical information for purposes of establishing liability (in many commercial cases) or proving damages. Use of statistics to prove damages is required in all shapes and kinds of litigation, from the small fender-bender case to large antitrust/commercial litigation.

Statistics presented in court in an original format, as simply taken from business records, are not usually very effective. This is because the business format is not conducive to a public presentation of records, nor is it aimed at general understanding as distinguished from the more particularized understanding of corporate personnel or accountants. The task confronting an attorney presenting this information in court is to translate its format and vehicle of presentation, i.e., accounting records, ledger sheets, and profit and loss statements, into something which is understandable and effective.

The general subject of presenting statistical information, in terms of both technique and format, is discussed in *Dombroff on Demonstrative Evidence* §§ 2.2–2.7.

Statistics can be used in court to convey misleading information to the jury and, more important, to convey incorrect conclusions based on that information. Sometimes the presentation of this information in a misleading or unfair format is inadvertent. However, there are techniques available which can disguise the true import of statistical information and live up to the adage that statistics can be used to prove anything. These techniques and tactics must be guarded against, no matter what the motivation for their use. You must carefully scrutinize any presentation of statistical information to ensure that it demonstrates what its proponent urges. All too often, the conclusion which is urged based on statistics is not supported by the numbers. The next five sections demonstrate techniques for presenting statistical information in a misleading fashion.

§ 14.8 —Scales

Generally, the vertical and horizontal scale of any particular chart should be in proportion. Thus, a scale chart which provides statistical information in a graphic form that has a proportionate relationship both vertically and horizontally might appear as in **Illustration 14-1**.

However, if the scales are changed, as in the examples in **Illustration 14-2**, the physical appearance of that chart changes rather dramatically as well. Although the information is the same, the visual perception is clearly distorted and delivers a different message.

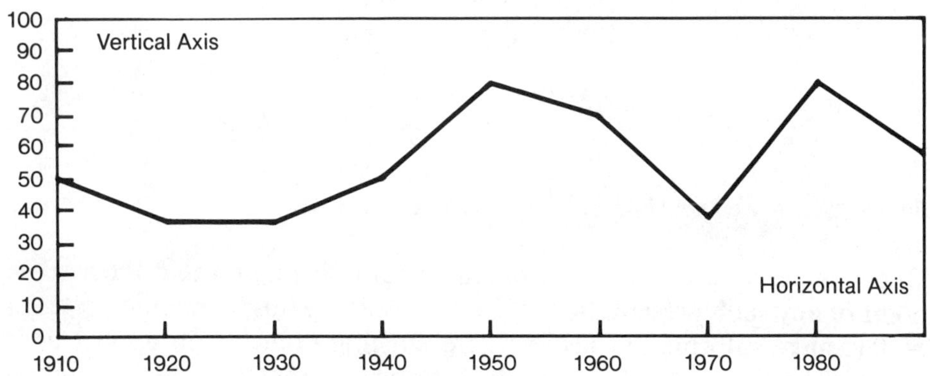

Illustration 14-1

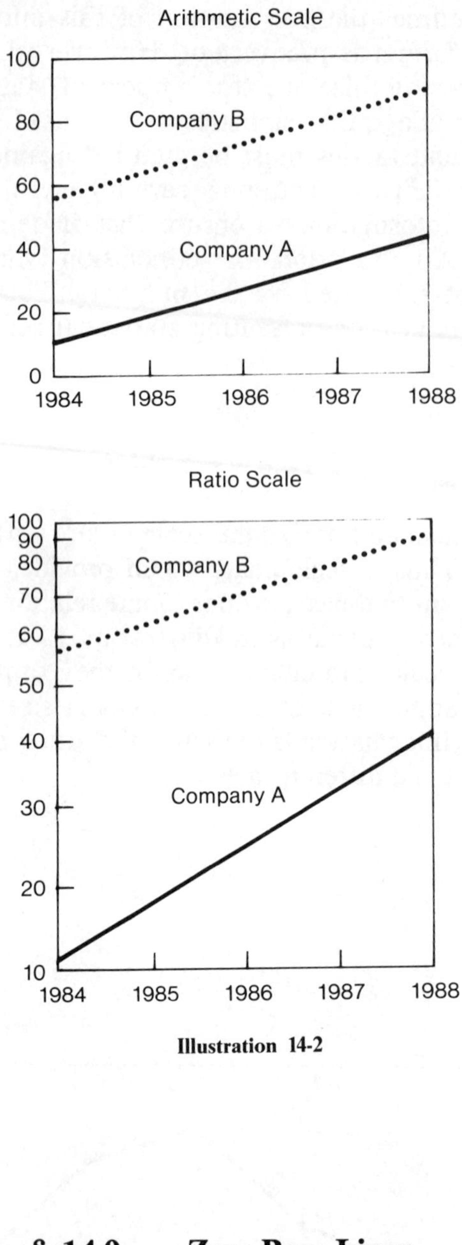

Illustration 14-2

§ 14.9 —Zero Base Lines

One assumes in a presentation of statistical information that the starting point of any such presentation is the zero point. Thus, a graphic portrayal of statistical information using a zero starting point might appear as in **Illustration 14-3**. However, to distort that presentation yet retain the same substantive information, the zero line can be moved as in **Illustration 14-4** thus making lesser amounts appear greater and greater amounts appear lesser. This technique takes advantage of the fact that people believe what they think they see. The visual and mental impressions which such a graphic technique accomplishes often outlast the substantive message of the information itself.

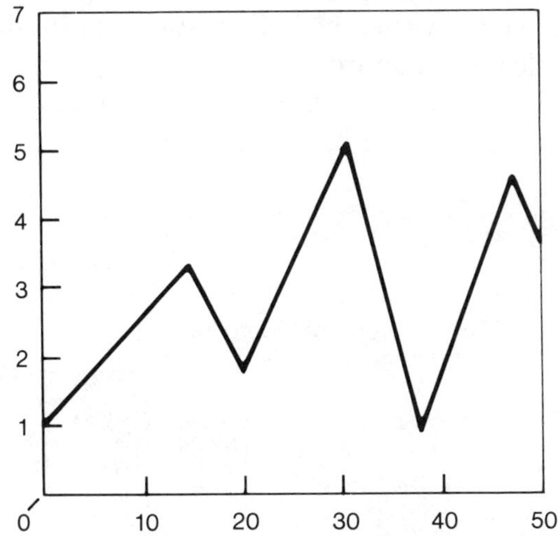

Illustration 14-3

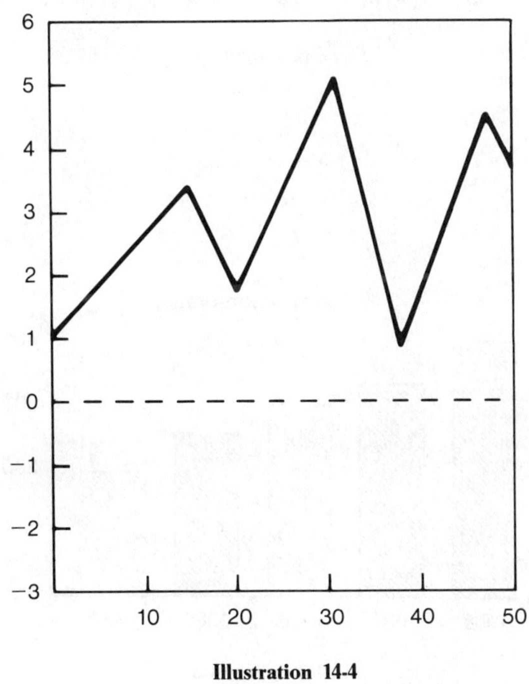

Illustration 14-4

§ 14.10 —Left to Right and Right to Left

Americans in general are used to reading from left to right on a page. There are psychological expectations that information given to them will read from left to right. Thus, a bar chart presenting certain statistical information as one might expect to see it would appear as in **Illustration 14-5**. However, if you reverse the information, as in **Illustration 14-6**, you present a misleading picture. The same thing happens when, as in **Illustration 14-7**, information is presented through a graphic portrayal.

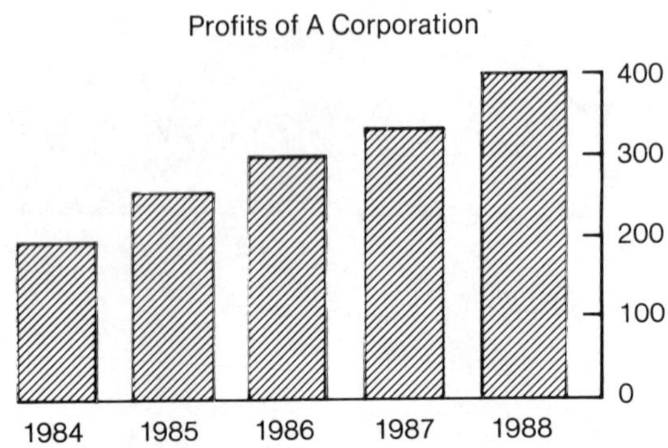

Illustration 14-5

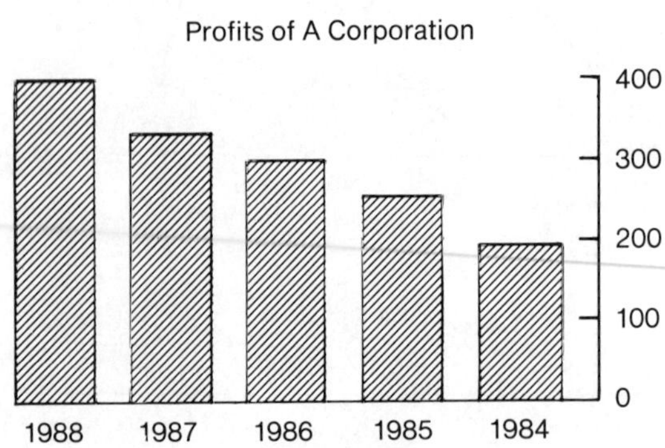

Illustration 14-6

Profits of A Corporation

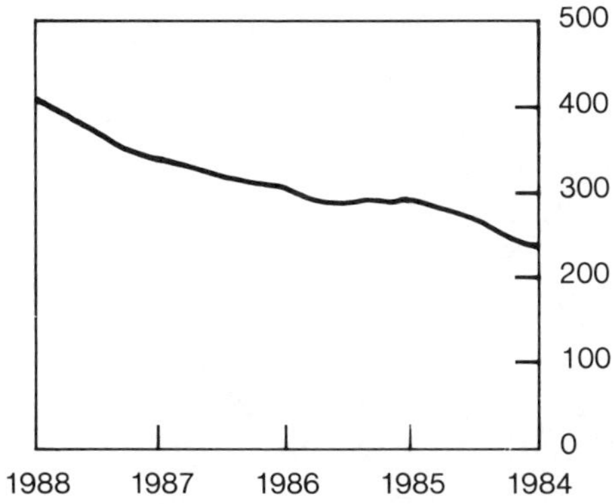

Illustration 14-7

§ 14.11 —Edited Charts

Just as litigants often try to take substantive information out of context and present it as persuasive of their position, charts and other graphic information can also be presented out of context. An example of this approach is the presentation of statistical information in a graphic format which is meant to illustrate either increasing numbers or decreasing numbers. An appropriate format for showing sales increases appears in **Illustration 14-8**. The problem with this approach is that, unless you have

Sales are Increasing

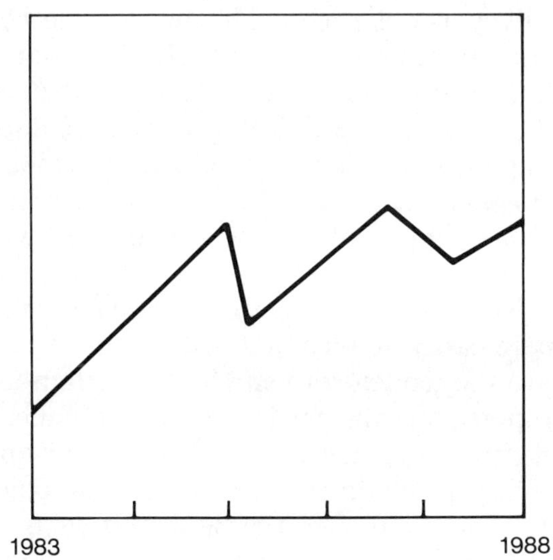

Illustration 14-8

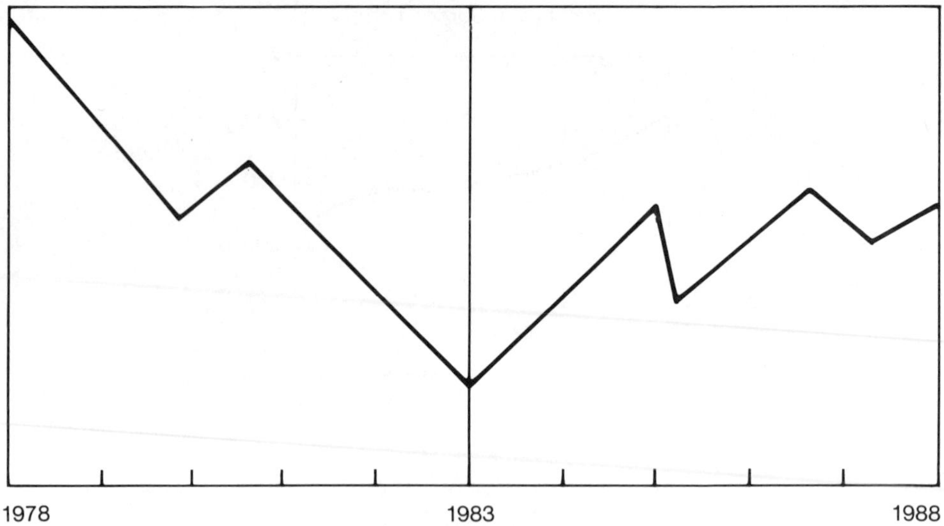

Illustration 14-9

made discovery inquiries regarding this information, you will not know that the actual chart itself if fairly presented would appear as indicated in **Illustration 14-9**.

§ 14.12 Size of Exhibits

A rule of thumb whenever you deal with demonstrative evidence is that you should make the particular piece of evidence, whether a chart, graph, diagram, model, or any other technique available to you, as large as possible. Indeed, the limiting factor should not be what you think is too large, but rather how large an exhibit the courthouse doors and elevators permit you to bring into the courtroom. Obviously, there are some practical limitations to this, and you should exercise common sense. However, there is a very definite unfair aspect associated with the view that "bigger is better."

Although there is no doubt that bigger exhibits are better exhibits because they can more easily be seen and demand more of the jury's attention, they also have the tendency to emphasize certain aspects of a case, perhaps out of proportion to the particular point in issue. Thus, when you face large demonstrative aids being presented by your opponent who has had them blown up, you should consider whether an objection should be founded on the fact that, although the blowup itself is an accurate portrayal of substantive information, the act of increasing the size of the information tends to give it undue importance and to emphasize it out of proportion in the case.

When your opponent has blown up 8″ by 11″ copies to produce a large exhibit, the position you should take is that the large blowup is prejudicial not by virtue of the information, but rather by virtue of the portrayal. The basis of your objection is that your opponent has smaller copies, accurate in terms of both size and scale.

The reality, however, the court may not sustain your objection because larger exhibits can more easily be seen and used by experts. All the same, you should be on the lookout for situations in which large blowup delivers a message separate and apart from the words or information on it.

One example of such a situation is a selective enlargement. Assume that you are involved in a case in which one piece of evidence is a map. In evidence is the actual map used by a witness or a party to the case. Your opponent, ostensibly for the purpose of clarity, has had a segment of that map blown up to a large scale, perhaps 30″ by 40″. Thus, the information contained on the enlarged portion is taken out of context. If the issue in the case is how someone read the map, such a selective out-of-context enlargement will have the effect of simplifying the task of reading the map for the jury and, by extension, making it look as if it should have been easy for the person charged with having misread the map.

Another good example relates to photographs. Blowups of photographs are frequently used in litigation. Indeed, it is not at all uncommon for both sides to use large blowups of photographs for the purpose of "taking" the jurors to the particular scenes which they might not otherwise be able to conveniently visit. The question is not whether the information contained within the photograph is accurate, but rather whether the portrayal itself distorts the message being delivered.

For example, assume that a photograph is meant to represent an accident scene from the perspective of an eyewitness. If that photograph is blown up, ostensibly to make it easier for the jury to follow testimony, the enlargement of details in that scene will make it that much easier for the jury to see them. If this photograph is being presented against your case and the question of what a particular eyewitness could or could not see is important, the very fact of the blowup distorts the information and the ability of the trier of fact to perceive it. Thus, the vehicle for presenting what is otherwise accurate substantive information is prejudicial, and you should object to it.

The judge may overrule your objection and indicate that it should be directed to the weight to be afforded the exhibit by the jury as distinguished from its admissibility. Thus, you must be prepared to examine such exhibits through the witnesses and point out their defects during examination.

§ 14.13 Models

A model, because it is a three-dimensional, physical portrayal, can be one of the most effective types of demonstrative evidence available to a trial lawyer. *See Dombroff on Demonstrative Evidence* ch. 5. It can also be one of the most unfairly presented. You must be especially aware of the context of the case vis-à-vis the model being presented.

Assume that you are representing the defendant in a relatively simple slip-and-fall case. Your opponent has had prepared a detailed model of the entire scene or premises which includes a large area totally irrelevant to the issues under consideration. In fact, most of the model has no connection with the physical premises actually involved in the transaction. For example, assume the slip and fall took place at a supermarket, and, instead of portraying just the aisle where the accident occurred, the model portrays the entire supermarket.

Such models can be quite impressive and can distract the jury from the true issues in the case. The possible overkill associated with a model should be kept in mind and an objection directed at any such attempt.

§ 14.14 —Cautionary Instructions

Whenever a model is used in litigation, by you or against you, you must first determine the purpose for which the model is being used. Although some models are used for scale purposes, most should be used for illustrative purposes. The distinction is that a model presented for illustrative purposes cannot have measurements taken from it nor can it be used to compare relative locations, because the scales may not be properly prepared, either within the vertical plane alone or within the vertical as against the horizontal plane.

A technique used to overcome an objection that a model is not prepared to scale and that it thus distorts the information it is meant to present is the cautionary instruction. What this means, in effect, is that, even if you intend to present a model for illustrative as distinguished from scale purposes, it should still be prepared to scale.

When your opponent attempts to introduce a model into evidence for "illustrative" purposes with a cautionary instruction, you should be especially wary, because cautionary instructions are likely to be ignored. See §§ **14.2** and **14.4**. The distinction between something being introduced for scale versus illustrative purposes is frequently not clear in the minds of jurors. Thus, when you use models of geography and the like, you should have them prepared to scale but be ready to present them for other than scale purposes. You should be aware of an opponent who has a cautionary instruction already prepared for the judge to deliver to the jury. I have done this myself, but I have also seen opponents do so to disguise flaws in their exhibits, for example, vertical and horizontal scales that are so out of proportion to one another that they distort what the jury actually sees.

You must acknowledge to the judge when arguing such an objection that you are capable of pointing out such distortions to the jury through cross-examination, but you should then note that you are not capable of changing their perception of the exhibit. Often this distorted perception will outweigh, both in terms of understanding and retention, their exposure to a cross-examination focused on credibility.

§ 14.15 —Photographs of Models

Notwithstanding the issue of scale, any model used in a courtroom requires a close physical and visual inspection for the jury to appreciate any detail and perhaps to be able to connect it to the issues in the case.

No matter where a model is placed in the courtroom, someone always has difficulty seeing it—the judge, the jury, or witnesses who have to use the model. Furthermore, the model is not always relevant to what is going on in the courtroom at any given time, and sometimes it is inconvenient to move the model in and out of a location where it can be seen by the jury.

One technique which can be used in connection with actual use of a model is photographs of the model. Although they lack the three-dimensional perspective immediately associated with models, coupled with the use of the model, photographs allow the jury to have close-up views while at the same time they have the convenience that may not attach to the use of an actual model. The problem with such photographs, especially if they are enlarged, is the problem associated with photographs in general, as noted in §§ **14.12** and **14.16**. Not only does an enlargement distort the perspective, but it also permits jurors to see aspects of a particular scene which may or may not be accurate within the context of the litigation.

A good example of this is photographs taken from the interior of models using a close-up lens or other technique. Thus, observers can be made to feel as if they are inside a particular scene looking out, which they would not be able to do unless they were actually present for a view.

As long as the perspectives are precisely the same and the model is in scale, there would seem to be nothing wrong with this. However, when the jury makes such a viewing in absentia, there is a tremendous amount of distortion inherently present. The mere fact of not being on the scene removes all the true-to-life details and makes the photographic view still and unrealistic.

Your best defense is to be aware of this technique and not to accede readily to the use of any such photographs. Along these lines, you should not only be prepared to note an objection, but you might have photographs of the actual scene present or suggest that in lieu of photographs of a model, photographs of the actual scene be used. Remember, it is an excellent argument that, by going from scene, to models, to photographs of the models, an attorney has gone a full circle, and that one can actually skip the model and photograph-of-model steps, going simply to photographs of the actual scene. In many respects, the *best evidence* argument is valid in this instance, because the photographs of the scene are the best evidence of what appears on the scene as distinguished from photographs of a model.

§ 14.16 Photographs in General

Photographs are one of the most commonly used of all demonstrative aids in the courtroom, particularly in personal injury, wrongful death, or property damage cases. In *Dombroff on Demonstrative Evidence,* I discussed in some detail techniques for using and abusing photographic evidence, both slides and prints, and the proper means of cross-examining photographs offered against your case. *See* ch. 3.

When examining photographic evidence offered by your opponent, your primary objection to it typically relates to relevance.

Other common objections that you may have to deal with include the possible prejudicial or inflammatory nature of what the photograph portrays; the fact that the photograph is cumulative or unnecessary within the context of the issues before the jury; that the photograph is misleading in being black and white while it portrays a scene in which color is important; or, generally, that your opponent has failed to present an adequate foundation for the admission of the photograph.

Quite separate and distinct from these well-known objections are others which you should keep in mind; these are unique to photograph evidence and may be sufficient either to disqualify the evidence from coming into the record at all or to lessen substantially any weight or credibility to be attached to the photograph. Sometimes these relate to matters which have simply been overlooked by your opponent, but, on occasion, they will relate to deliberate techniques.

Exaggeration. It is possible to photograph a scene so that distances between objects appear far greater than they are in fact or so that objects appear to be much larger than they really are.

Minimization. A still photograph may minimize distance, heights, lengths, and other conditions.

Elaboration. A photograph or series of photographs may show far more of a scene or object than is necessary to a proper understanding of the relevant facts. Close-ups usually show enough of the subject to avoid deception by omission and may be supplemented by more distant views.

Omission. A partial photographic view of a scene or object, standing by itself and unsupported by more general pictures, may constitute a dangerous deception. This fault may be fatal when only one picture is taken, because there may be no way to supply the essential missing details which were beyond the viewfinder.

Reversal of left and right. In prints, reversal occurs whenever the negative is turned with the wrong side toward the paper when the print is made. In color slide viewing, it occurs when the slide is put in the projector backwards.

Optical illusions. In general, a light-colored object appears larger than a dark object of the same dimensions; vertical lines appear longer than horizontal lines of the same length; and the length of an empty space appears less than the length of a similar space containing details.

Single viewpoint and compression of time. A single photograph is a selected framed picture taken from a given point of view, depicting an instant of time. It may reflect a mere fragment of a complex legal situation; this fragment is imprinted on the minds of the jurors and cannot be modified effectively by explanation.

Color of photograph. Color photographs frequently reproduce certain colors in unrealistic hues which tend to exaggerate the conditions being illustrated to a prejudicial extent. Use of improper film for the lighting conditions present may give a photograph an unrealistic overall color cast or tint.

Correct viewing distance. For every photograph there is one and only one viewing distance which guarantees that the angular size of the objects in the picture is the same as the angular size of the objects in the original scene. Remember that the proper viewing distance is equal to the product of the focal length of the lens and the magnification of the enlargement.

One matter which oftentimes receives little attention is whether opposing counsel took the photographs. If so, a question arises as to the propriety of opposing counsel testifying as to the photographs, foundation considerations, substantial similarity questions, and the whole host of other matters based upon which photographs can be attacked while, at the same time, remaining as attorney of record in the case.

A difficult situation can present itself when there are real or contrived questions regarding the admissibility of photographs and those questions go to foundation considerations. In such circumstances, if the photographs have been taken by counsel, there is a substantial argument to be made that counsel must seriously consider withdrawing. Obviously, when a case is well along in the discovery process or, indeed, in some instances in trial, this can pose a difficult problem.

§ 14.17 Summaries

In **Chapter 1**, I discussed the use of summaries in some detail. However, the demonstrative evidence aspect of summaries should be mentioned here, because a summary has a value over and above the fact that it compresses information and expedites trial.

As demonstrative evidence, summaries raise a number of issues, the first of which relates to accuracy. It is often difficult to oppose the offer into evidence of a summary, because you may be perceived by the judge as attempting to make the case resolution process longer and more expensive. Thus, your most appropriate approach when an opponent offers a summary is to ensure that the summary is accurate.

The concept of accuracy is somewhat elusive in this context, because the very act of compressing evidence that may otherwise be contained in voluminous documents has the effect of making it more effective. One of the first things you should consider when reviewing a summary proposed by an opponent, whether it is of documentary evidence or a deposition, is whether the summary contains a balanced account of the facts present in the underlying document. Although at least one court has held that a prosecution summary chart need not contain a defendant's version of the facts, *United States v. Ambrosiani,* 610 F.2d 65 (1st Cir. 1979), an objection directed at the fact that a summary is a distortion should be vigorously argued. Thus, an attempt to create a one sided summary and have it received into the record should be resisted.

Pursuant to Rule 1006 of the Federal Rules of Evidence, a summary is itself evidence as distinguished from the underlying records. An attack on the accuracy of a summary is perhaps the best way of short-circuiting an opponent who attempts to take unfair advantage of you. Along these same lines is the question of titles or captions of summaries used as documentary or graphic evidence. For example, if an opponent attempts to present a misleading caption that includes buzz words such as *illegal* or *negligence* or other words which connote some aspect of liability, you should resist this even though the information contained within the summary itself may be accurate. You should also examine your opponent's summaries to be sure that the captions or titles do not characterize what your opponent is intending to prove through the use of the summary. Thus, if, for example, bank records are used to show that funds were diverted for improper uses, you should not permit an opponent to have a caption which incorporates that conclusion instead of one which simply indicates that the information in the summary is from bank records. Further discussion of captions appears in **§ 14.5**.

One important point in your favor regarding the use of summaries as demonstrative evidence, in the sense that the information contained in the summary is processed from underlying records, is that full disclosure is now required in civil cases. Generally, demonstrative evidence of any type, especially summaries which take some time to examine for accuracy before you can properly claim an objection, typically is not admitted into evidence if the first time it is disclosed to you by your opponent is at trial itself.

Federal Rule of Evidence 1006 and most of its state counterparts require the advance disclosure of documents underlying any summary to allow the opponent to prepare a cross-examination or an opposing summary. This should be done sufficiently in advance of trial to satisfy either local rules or common sense regarding the time needed by your opponent to review the summaries and underlying documents. You should also, if you are offering the summary, be prepared to have available for deposition or testimony the person who prepared the summary, in the event that foundation testimony is required.

The purpose of disclosing the existence of a summary and the foundation for it prior to trial is either to make it possible to obtain stipulations regarding accuracy and admissibility or to allow for a pretrial examination and ruling by the court. The likelihood of getting into the trial record demonstrative evidence which has not been disclosed prior to trial is, given today's full pretrial disclosure rules in both the state and federal systems, substantially impaired. Accordingly, it is in your best interest to do everything you can to obviate any objections to your exhibits prior to trial. An especially effective technique in using demonstrative evidence, including summaries, is the request for admission. See **Chapter 1**.

United States v. Marchini, 797 F.2d 759 (9th Cir. 1986) dealt with the admissibility of summary charts. The chart in question was prepared by the government's expert witness for the purpose of assisting the jury in understanding a tax case. The court held the chart to be admissible in a prosecution for underreporting of wages subject to withholding when the calculations represented in the chart were based upon evidence adduced to trial. Furthermore, the expert, an Internal Revenue agent, was available for cross-examination by the defendant as to the basis of his testimony and the chart itself.

Gomez v. Great Lakes Deal Division, National Steel Corp., 803 F.2d 250 (6th Cir. 1986), held that the decision to admit summaries of voluminous writings, recordings, or photographs which cannot be examined conveniently in court is within the sound discretion of the trial court. If the summary fairly represents and is taken from the underlying documentary proof in a manner that is accurate and nonprejudicial, the summary should be admissible.

Crowder v. Aurora Co-op Elevator Co., 393 N.W.2d 250 (Neb. 1986) provides that summaries which are illustrative of evidence in the record for the purpose of making evidence clear to the jury are admissible within the discretion of the court.

§ 14.18 Television and Videotape

There is little doubt that one of the most profound influences on the American public today is television. A significant proportion of all Americans use television as their primary means of communication and information gathering, not only for entertainment but for news as well.

Translating this phenomenon into the legal process has primarily involved depositions. However, motion pictures and, particularly, videotape are seeing wider and wider use and acceptance in the demonstrative evidence field. For further discussion, *see Dombroff on Demonstrative Evidence* ch. 6; see also **Chapter 9** on videotaped day-in-the-life presentations.

The major advantage of videotape and television lies in the psychological effect of the presentation. Videotape played through a television is something with which virtually all jurors are familiar. They are exposed to it every day, and so they essentially trust the message which it delivers. Thus, when your opponent is going to use videotape to present demonstrative evidence, whether it is a videotape deposition, a dynamic reconstruction of an event through animation process, or a day-in-the-life presentation, the potential for adversarial prejudice is so great that you must be careful in your approach to this technique. Keep in mind the following points:

1. You should recognize that most judges are receptive to any technique which holds the interest of the jury and is structured to simplify the issues in the case. Usually the use of videotape as the medium for presenting information fulfills these goals. However, you must be careful, when you review the evidence to be presented in whatever format it existed in before, that the presentation is merited by the issues in the case. Thus, looking at a slip-and-fall case, a videotape presentation by a plaintiff which involves an animation of how the human body, presumably the plaintiff, suffered the fall and was injured can be objected to on the basis that its prejudicial effect outweighs any probative or educational value it may have. In effect, you are arguing overkill.

2. When dealing with videotape, be especially wary of any sound tracks on the tape. Thus, for example, in case of a day-in-the-life presentation or videotape animation, you should object to inclusion of any prerecorded sound tracks. Although a sound track makes for a far slicker presentation from your opponent's perspective, it puts you in a tremendously prejudiced and unfair position because you are incapable of cross-examining it.
3. In addition to being aware of any extraneous material in the presentation, you should keep in mind that a presentation on videotape can be out of context—that is, edited. You should carefully scrutinize what is being offered to be sure that it has not been edited, and, if it has, you should seek discovery of anything edited out. If that material is unavailable, you should have a well-founded objection which can preclude the evidence from coming into the record.

When you are preparing to cross-examine a videotape exhibit, you should keep in mind a number of areas which can provide fertile grounds for objection:

1. Whether a witness who was present at the time the film or videotape was shot will be required to testify that it accurately depicts events as the witness saw them when they occurred
2. Whether the witness will be required to testify regarding the competence of the camera operator
3. Information regarding the type of camera used and its mechanics
4. Information regarding the type, sensitivity, speed, and other characteristics of the film
5. Information regarding the type of lens and lens adjustment used, including any distortion factor which may be associated with the lens
6. Lighting arrangements during the filming
7. Weather conditions existing at the time of filming
8. The speed at which the film was taken, in order to obviate any objections regarding the fact that the film has been speeded up or slowed down
9. The sound process, if any, used in connection with the filming
10. The manner and circumstances surrounding the development of the film, including such things as brightness, clarity, color accuracy and rendition, and printing process
11. Any editing, with outtakes saved for screening prior to trial if necessary
12. The competence of the projectionist or technician to operate the equipment in the proper fashion

13. The speed at which the motion picture or videotape is shown relative to the speed at which it was shot

14. The distance of the projector from the screen and whether an element of distortion is associated with that distance

15. The brightness of the motion picture or videotape during presentation in relation to the brightness level actually present at the scene (primarily, this relates to the light level of the courtroom as it may exist during presentation)

16. The lens on the projector and whether it is introducing an element of distortion

17. Whether the soundtrack is distorted or altered through the projection process.

See also Dombroff on Demonstrative Evidence § 6.16.

If the above information is not available, you may be able to keep the exhibit out of evidence, or you may have fertile ground for cross-examination that goes to both weight and credibility.

Typically the most effective way of presenting a demonstration in court is through the use of videotape. *Rocky Mountain Helicopters v. Bell Helicopters Textron,* 805 F.2d 907 (10th Cir. 1986) is a decision dealing with the question of admissibility of the results of experiments. In *Rocky Mountain Helicopters,* the district court was found by the United States Court of Appeals for the Tenth Circuit properly to have admitted evidence from a photo-elastic study of stress in helicopter parts that was conducted by the seller after a helicopter accident. The court found there was no showing that the admission of the evidence was erroneous and of a subsequent remedial measure. The court felt that evidence of the test was admissible as a post-accident test or report and that Federal Rule of Evidence 407 does not exclude evidence of post-event investigative tests and reports.

In addition, focusing on Federal Rule of Evidence 702 dealing with expert witnesses, the Tenth Circuit found that the trial court had not abused its discretion in admitting testimony of a witness who had a doctorate degree in metallurgical engineering and experience in investigating several hundred helicopter accidents when the witness stated that only a faulty design could have caused the accident.

The utilization of post-accident tests or experiments is always a difficult subject. All trial counsel would be well advised not to conduct those tests or experiments in the courtroom, because they can be turned around and used against you. The alternative approach, and the one to be desired, is to conduct them outside the courtroom and introduce evidence of the post-accident testing through the use of videotape. This maximizes the opportunities for an effective presentation while minimizing any possibility that your opponent may be able to utilize that same evidence.

§ 14.19 Home Movies

In **Chapter 9**, I dealt at some length with day-in-the-life presentations. *See also Dombroff on Demonstrative Evidence* § 6.13. One aspect of these presentations has the potential for tremendous prejudice when used against your client.

As a general matter, a day-in-the-life presentation is nothing more than a videotape, prepared outside the courtroom, which is intended to depict what life is now like for the plaintiff living with the injuries inflicted by the alleged negligence of the defendant. The purpose of the presentation is to depict the quality of life and, in effect, prejudice the jury so far against the defendant that sympathy and emotion will take over and a verdict will be returned in favor of the plaintiff.

In themselves, day-in-the-life presentations are extremely prejudicial and are right on the line between admissibility and inadmissibility. This is true in virtually every instance. However, a properly prepared day-in-the-life presentation inevitably is admissible.

One technique which can be used in a day-in-the-life presentation is to splice into the day-in-the-life presentation scenes from family home movies. By incorporating and editing scenes from home movies into a day-in-the-life presentation, a seeming before-and-after injury comparison can be presented. Editing simply involves combining comparable before-and-after scenes when the technical specialists prepare the presentation.

The argument which you should raise when confronted with such a tactic is that a day-in-the-life presentation prepared in such a manner goes beyond what is proper and does nothing but play to the sympathy and emotions of the jury by wrenching jurors back and forth between what was and what is. Although it can certainly be helpful in showing what the loss was as part of proving damages, doing so through this editing process amounts to a Hollywood technique of highlighting and magnifying the injuries. At least one court, in not permitting pained facial expressions, grimaces, or audible expressions of pain to be played to a jury, has concluded that these expressions would destroy the jury's objectivity because they would enflame the average person. *Thomas v. C.G. Tate Construction Co.,* 465 F. Supp. 566 (D.S.C. 1979). The same is true of the technique of joining a day-in-the-life presentation with home movie shots from the plaintiff's life before the injury. Although the plaintiff will argue that this is a valid comparison, it is the format of the comparison which is objectionable and not the fact of the comparison. This comparison can far more easily and less prejudicially be presented through testimony and, indeed, can be quantified by an economist.

§ 14.20 Videotape and Home Movie Evidence

The author thanks David L. Abney and the *Federal Bar News & Journal* for the use of materials in **§§ 14.20** through **14.36**, which are adapted from Mr. Abney's article, *The Plaintiff Goes to Hollywood,* 34 Fed. Bar J. 217–23 (No. 5, June 1987).

The claimant in a personal injury or worker's compensation action is often the ending actor in a video production made by one side or the other. Plaintiff films are proffered to graphically depict the impact of an injury upon the victim. Defense motion pictures are produced to refute and impeach the disability claims made by the plaintiff. Although both types of presentations have appeared in American courtrooms since the 1920s, great confusion persists about the propriety of this type of evidence. Although there are some technical differences between videotape and motion picture film, for simplicity of discussion they will be treated as similar types of motion picture visual presentation. *See Dombroff on Demonstrative Evidence* §§ 6.2–6.8.

§ 14.21 Presentations Made by the Plaintiff

The first reported plaintiff motion picture presentation came in the 1923 New York decision of *Gibson v. Gunn, 206 A.D. 464,* 202 N.Y.S. 19 (1923), *aff'd,* 208 A.D. 745, 202 N.Y.S. 927 (1924). In that case, an automobile accident victim proffered a motion picture depicting his precrash agility as a vaudeville performer. Voicing concerns that would echo over the years, the appellate court overturned a jury verdict for the plaintiff:

> Aside from the fact that moving pictures present a fertile field for exaggeration of any emotion or action, and the absence of evidence as to how this particular motion picture film was prepared, we think the picture admitted in evidence brought before the jury irrelevant matter, hearsay and incompetent evidence, and tended to make a farce of the trial.

202 N.Y.S. at 20.

Plaintiffs in later cases have been allowed to show films of their condition before and even during the injury. For instance, in *Tanuvasa v. City and County of Honolulu,* 2 Haw. App. 102, 626 P.2d 1175 (1981), a promising young football player alleged that a severe police beating had caused head trauma which had destroyed his promising athletic career. The court permitted the introduction of high school football films to support the claims that his activities were now limited. 626 P.2d at 1181. In an action for the death of a young boy, a Florida court even allowed the father to show motion pictures of the parents at the drowning scene. *Larnel Builders, Inc. v. Martin,* 105 So. 2d 580 (Fla. Dist. Ct. App. 1958).

Overwhelmingly, however, plaintiff films focus on the condition of the victim following the injury which generated the lawsuit. Some of the presentations center on a specific trait or quality. For example, in *Rogers v. City of Detroit,* 289 Mich. 86, 286 N.W. 167 (1939), the trial court allowed the introduction of a motion picture showing the abnormally rapid pulsation of the victim's throat. *See also Sheahan v. Dexter,* 91 Ill. Dec. 120, 136 Ill. App. 3d 241, 483 N.E.2d 402 (1985) (trial court refused to allow audiovisual recording demonstrating damage to victim's voice); *Foster v. Crawford Shipping Co.,* 496 F.2d 788 (3d Cir. 1974) (admission of short film showing impaired mental state of victim was error under circumstances); *Carvell v. Winn,* 154 So. 2d 788 (La. Ct. App.) (trial judge properly refused to allow demonstrative X-ray motion picture of skeletal structure of human body in motion), *cert. denied,* 245 La. 71, 156 So. 2d 603 (1963). Other motion pictures feature the dramatic and often revolting therapy and treatment programs required by certain injuries. *See, e.g., Douglas v. G.H.R. Energy Corp.,* 463 So. 2d 5 (La. Ct. App. 1984) (graphic videotapes of painful burn therapy held inadmissible); *Jesco, Inc. v. Shannon,* 451 So. 2d 694 (Miss. 1984) (admission of film depicting burn treatment procedures). The bulk of the plaintiff motion pictures purport to depict a portion or all of a typical day in the life of the plaintiff after the date of the allegedly wrongful injury. *See, e.g., Lee v. Volkswagen of America, Inc.,* 688 P.2d 1283, 1290 (Okla. 1984) (introduction of day-in-the-life film was permissible). The use of these displays has increased in recent years. *See, e.g., Stanton by Brooks v. Astra Pharmaceutical Products,* 718 F.2d 553, 558 n.7 (3d Cir. 1983) (objection against use of day-in-the-life film not pursued on appeal); *Seese v. Volkswagenwerk A.G.,* 648 F.2d 833, 847 n.20 (3d Cir. 1981) (no error in admission of day-in-the-life film); *Powers v. United States,* 589 F. Supp. 1104, 1106 (D. Conn. 1984) (perusal of day-in-the-life film helped convince trial judge of reality of plaintiff's injury).

These types of movies are generally styled as *day-in-the-life* films. *See generally* Nielson, *Admissibility of Day in the Life Films in Personal Injury Litigation,* 32 Fed'n Ins. Couns. Q. 235 (Spring 1982). They have generated a great deal of comment, most of it approving, which is not surprising, since most of the legal articles have been written by members of the plaintiffs' bar. *See, e.g.,* Joseph, *Demonstrative Videotape Evidence,* 22 Trial 60 (June 1986); Passanante, *The Use of Clinical and "Day-in-the-Life" Presentations In Personal Injury Litigation: A Rising Star in the American Courtroom,* 20 Wake Forest L. Rev. 121 (Spring 1984); Funk &

Hicks, *Admissibility of "Day in the Life" Films in Virginia,* 18 U. Rich. L. Rev. 751 (Summer 1984); Pikula, *The Evidentiary Aspects of "Day in the Life" Films,* 69 Mass. L. Rev. 59 (Summer 1984); Comment, *Plaintiffs' Use of "Day in the Life" Films: A New Look at the Celluloid Witness,* 49 U.M.K.C. L. Rev. 179 (Winter 1981); Preiser & Hoffman, *'Day-in-the-Life' Films—Coming of Age in the Courtroom,* 17 Trial 26 (Aug. 1981) (Part One), 17 Trial 41 (Sept. 1981) (Part Two). For an interesting article on Canadian law in this area, *see* Goldstein, *Using Videotape to Present Evidence in Civil Proceedings,* 6 Advoc. Q. 89 (June 1985). The day-in-the life motion pictures normally last no more than a half-hour and show a carefully selected series of supposedly representative daily activities. *See, e.g., Lawton v. Jewish Hospital,* 679 S.W.2d 370, 372 (Mo. Ct. App. 1984) (videotape of victim's daily routine); *Pisel v. Stamford Hospital,* 180 Conn. 314, 430 A.2d 1 (1980) (plaintiff's activities while a hospital patient).

§ 14.22 —Laying the Foundation

The first hurdle in obtaining admission for any of the plaintiff's productions is to show that they are relevant. Rule 401 of the Federal Rules of Evidence states that evidence is relevant if it has "any tendency to make the existence of any fact that is of consequence to the determination of the action more probable or less probable than it would be without the evidence." Since they present a national standard, the Federal Rules of Evidence will be the system utilized in these sections. Because the condition of the victim is a central issue in almost all personal injury cases, movies depicting the injuries, activities, and abilities of the plaintiff generally will be highly relevant. *See, e.g., Grimes v. Employers Mutual Liability Insurance Co.,* 73 F.R.D. 607, 609 (D. Alaska 1977) ("Both the film of the plaintiff engaging in daily activities and the film of the plaintiff performing clinical tests are relevant to the issue of the nature and extent of damages. The defendant's relevancy objection is frivolous"). Authentication of the motion pictures is more problematic.

Trial courts will admit only motion pictures which have been authenticated properly. The Federal Rules of Evidence are liberal in this area: "The requirement of authentication or identification as a condition precedent to admissibility is satisfied by evidence sufficient to support a finding that the matter in question is what its proponent claims." Fed. R. Evid. 901(2). A proper foundation must be given that the motion pictures are a true, correct, and accurate portrayal of what they purport to represent. *See, e.g.,* 32 C.J.S. *Evidence* § 715 (1964 & Supp. 1986). The authentication testimony is customarily given by the person who operated the filming equipment, although the testimony of another person present at the time the motion picture was made will suffice if he or she is able to state that the final product is an accurate depiction of what actually occurred. *See, e.g.,* 29 Am. Jur. 2d *Evidence* § 801 (1967 & Supp. 1985). Technicalities concerning the camera, photographic medium, editing, and lighting speed the authentication process, but they are window dressing to the main concern of accuracy. *See, e.g.,* Pikula, *The Evidentiary Aspects of "Day in the Life" Films,* 69 Mass. L. Rev. 59, 66–67 (Summer 1984).

Once relevancy and authenticity are established, any plaintiff motion picture is still subject to a wide range of objections centering on unfair prejudice and hearsay.

§ 14.23 Objections by the Defense

The majority of defense objections swirl around the concerns raised by Federal Rule of Evidence 403:

> Rule 403. *Exclusion of Relevant Evidence on Grounds of Prejudice, Confusion, or Waste of Time.* Although relevant, evidence may be excluded if its probative value is substantially outweighed by the danger of unfair prejudice, confusion of the issues, or misleading the jury, or by considerations of undue delay, waste of time, or needless presentation of cumulative evidence.

Defense concern over these types of motion pictures is well-founded. See **Chapter 9**. *See also* German, Merin & Rolfe, *Videotape Evidence at Trial,* 6 Am. Jur. Trial Advocacy 209, 224 (Fall 1982) ("The film's purpose is essentially inflammatory") (discussion of day-in-the-life presentations).

§ 14.24 —Unfair Prejudice

Many plaintiff motion pictures would by their very nature arouse extreme sympathy in an average jury. For instance, in *Butler v. Chrestman,* 264 So. 2d 812 (Miss. 1972), the plaintiff proffered a movie film depicting an agonizing period in the victim's recovery. The camera zoomed in periodically to show the plaintiff's pain grimaces and ended "with a parting shot of her seemingly crying from excruciating pain." *Id.* at 816. In reversing the admission of this film, the Mississippi Supreme Court held that the movie was "more likely to inflame and prejudice the jury rather than serve any evidentiary purpose." *Id. See also Transit Homes, Inc. v. Bellamy,* 282 Ark. 453, 671 S.W.2d 153, 158–59 (1984) (day-in-the-life movie featuring victim who already was a quadriplegic before the accident was too prejudicial to admit).

This vivid plaintiff's presentation was repeated in *Thomas v. D.G. Tate Construction Co.,* 465 F. Supp 566 (D.S.C. 1979). The victim in that case had been badly burned in an automobile accident. The film depicted a physical therapy session which had a profound impact on the patient.

> During the entire process plaintiff was grunting, groaning and crying out and his face forming various contortions and grimaces evidencing much pain.
>
> It is impossible in the foregoing brief summary to completely depict what is revealed by the audio and visual presentation of this tape. The tape positively shows plaintiff is experiencing extreme pain and mental anguish. During the viewing of this tape, one has a tendency to try to disregard it and to direct his attention to something more pleasant, and if one has the slightest tendency to be squeamish, a feeling of nausea arises.
>
> The tape definitely incites extreme sympathy for the plaintiff and would inflame the average person.

Id. at 569. The trial judge held that any probative value in the production was overwhelmed by the danger of unfair prejudice and excluded the film. *Id.* at 571. *See also Douglas v. G.H.R. Energy Corp.,* 463 So. 2d 5, 6–7 (La. Ct. App. 1984) (similar tape of burn debridement procedures held inadmissible).

Any motion picture showing a suffering injured human being necessarily will be distasteful for the jury and prejudicial to the defense. Motion pictures can be a vivid aid to the jury in understanding the victim's condition. *See, e.g., Apache Ready Mix Co. v. Creed,* 653 S.W.2d 79, 83–84 (Tex. Ct. App. 1983) (20-minute videotape of a day in the victim's life admitted to assist jury in comprehending case). *See also Barenbrugge v. Rich,* 490 N.E.2d 1368, 1374–75 (Ill. Ct. App. 1986) (admission of videotape showing day in the life of victim was not unduly prejudicial). Even if the film is as accurate as possible, if the depiction engenders impassioned prejudgment, it will be inadmissible in court. Mere unpleasantness, of course, is not enough to bar such films. *See, e.g., Grimes v. Employers Mutual Liability Insurance Co.,* 73 F.R.D. 607, 609–10 (D. Alaska 1977) (probative value of day-in-the-life film outweighed the prejudicial impact). Drawing upon his own experience, feelings, and training, the trial judge must ascertain in each case the fine distinction between unreasoning sympathy and informed impartiality. Even if the plaintiff production is not found to be unfairly prejudicial, there is always the danger that such a film might lead to confusion as to the real issues in the case, turning the trial from a search for truth to a quest to succor a person in distress. *See, e.g.,* German, Merin & Rolfe, *Videotape Evidence at Trial,* 6 Am. Jur. Trial Advocacy 209, 224–26 (Fall 1982).

§ 14.25 —Cumulativeness

In addition to concerns over unfair prejudice and confusion of the issues, objections commonly are made that plaintiff motion pictures are merely cumulative to testimony about the plaintiff's condition already given by the victim, his friends and family, and by appropriate health-care professionals. Some courts have accepted the cumulative evidence objection, especially when the film is offered after the bulk of the plaintiff's case has been presented. *See, e.g., Ashley v. Nissan Motor Corp.,* 321 So. 2d 868, 872–73 (La. Ct. App.) (day-in-the-life film held cumulative), *cert. denied,* 323 So. 2d 478 (La. 1975). Other courts give short shrift to the cumulative evidence concerns:

> Moreover, the mere fact that there is ample uncontradicted medical testimony concerning the nature and extent of plaintiff's injuries should not, in and of itself, prevent a plaintiff from showing to the jury a motion picture illustrating in an informative and non-inflamatory manner the impact that the accident has had on his or her life.

Caprara v. Chrysler Corp., 71 A.D. 2d 515, 423 N.Y.S.2d 694, 699 (1979) (cumulative film admitted that showed injuries of victim), *aff'd,* 52 N.Y.2d 114, 436 N.Y.S.2d 545 (1981). *See also Trapp v. Cayson,* 471 So. 2d 375 (Miss. 1985) (plaintiff allowed to present full day-in-the-life movie with narration even though the presentation came at the end of his case).

In any event, the plaintiff should be able to avoid this objection by presenting the film at the start of his case. The most important and legitimate danger in the plaintiff movies is that they will mislead the jury.

§ 14.26 —Misleading Film or Videotape

Although the plaintiff's film is an accurate representation of what was seen by the camera, it still may be that what was presented to the camera was in no sense an accurate reflection of the plaintiff's true condition. For instance, a short day-in-the-life movie will depict only those matters deemed interesting by the plaintiff and his helpers. The victim's side will also edit away all material that fails to forcefully and effectively convey the desired message. The combined filming and editing procedure makes the film selective, noncontinuous and self-serving. This is compounded by the fact that even a brief motion picture is a series of many thousands of persuasive and memorable images; the film is a stage set and managed by the plaintiff. *See, e.g., Haley v. Byers Transportation Co.,* 414 S.W.2d 777, 780–81 (Mo. 1967) (motion pictures of victim's daily activities properly not admitted by trial court). It is only to be expected that the plaintiff will always portray the actors, backgrounds, and activities which will have the maximum permissible wallop on the jury. *See, e.g., Protective Casualty Insurance Co. v. Killane,* 447 So. 2d 316, 317 (Fla. Dist. Ct. App. 1984) (day-in-the-life video admissible despite objectionable background of Christmas and household decorations); *Grimes v. Employers Mutual Liability Insurance Co.,* 73 F.R.D. 607, 610 (D. Alaska 1977) (scenes of emotional interplay between family members should be eliminated from the day-in-the-life film).

§ 14.27 Hearsay

The final serious objection to a plaintiff's motion picture is that it constitutes hearsay. It may be surprising at first glance to conclude that a movie is hearsay. In dealing with this theory, it is helpful to start with the definition of hearsay: "'Hearsay' is a statement other than one made by the declarant while testifying at the trial or hearing, offered in evidence to prove the truth of the matter asserted." Fed. R. Evid. 801(c). A film made with a narration or a verbal communicative soundtrack is more obviously an out-of-court statement presented for the truth of the material contained with it. *See, e.g., Sprynczynatyk v. General Motors Corp.,* 771 F.2d 1112, 1117 (8th Cir. 1985) (admission of videotapes of driver's hypnosis session absent proper cautionary instruction constituted prejudicial error, especially since the videotapes were hearsay); *United States v. Dorell,* 758 F.2d 425, 434 (9th Cir. 1985) (videotape expressing defendant's political and religious reasons for damaging government military property was hearsay). Even a totally silent film, however, easily can fit the definition of hearsay. This is true because a hearsay statement need not be oral or written. Completely nonverbal conduct will constitute a hearsay statement if the person performing the actions intends to make an assertion through his conduct. Fed. R. Evid. 801(a).

If the plaintiff knows that he is the star attraction in a film designed to show the nature and extent of his disability, his actions and expressions will form a statement about his plight. *See, e.g., Haley v. Byers Transportation Co.,* 414 S.W.2d 777, 780 (Mo. 1967). The finished movie will, after all, be a central part of his damage suit. A believable performance will mandate more money to the victim and his family. If the resulting film shows assertive conduct, as is likely, then it will be hearsay. The significance of a finding that the plaintiff movie is hearsay is that hearsay is inadmissible unless it falls within an accepted exemption or exception. Fed. R. Evid. 801(d), 802. *See, e.g., Grimes v. Employers Mutual Liability Insurance Co.,* 73 F.R.D. 607, 611 (D. Alaska 1977), in which the trial court held the day-in-the-life film to be hearsay but allowed it admission under the residual hearsay exception of Fed. R. Evid. 803(24) because the movie was trustworthy and "more probative on the material issues of pain and suffering and loss of enjoyment of life than any other evidence which the plaintiff could procure through reasonable efforts." 73 F.R.D. at 611. It is hard to see how conventional testimony from lay and expert witnesses, coupled with still photographs, would not have been more trustworthy, equally probative, and less blatantly hearsay.

§ 14.28 Discretion and Function of the Judge

Traditionally, trial judges have enjoyed broad leeway in determining the admissibility of plaintiff motion pictures. *See, e.g., Lehmuth v. Long Beach Unified School District,* 53 Cal. 2d 544, 348 P.2d 887, 2 Cal. Rptr. 279 (1960) (trial judge has discretion to admit film showing medical condition and unconscious reactions of victim); *Luther v. Maple,* 250 F.2d 916, 921 (8th Cir. 1958) (admission or exclusion of movie depicting medical treatment of plaintiff was left to discretion of judge). Decisions concerning admissibility will be reversed only if there has been an abuse of discretion, *see, e.g., Reggio v. Louisiana Gas Service Co.,* 333 So. 2d 395, 402 (La. Ct. App.) (admission of videotape of physical therapy sessions not abuse of discretion), *writ denied,* 336 So. 2d 187 (La. 1967), or if the trial judge rules on admission without even examining the film presentation, *Reimer v. Delisio,* 296 Pa. Super. 205, 442 A.2d 731 (1982) (plaintiff films are not inadmissible per se), *aff'd,* 501 Pa. 662, 462 A.2d 1308 (1983). The trial court is free to order that the motion picture be edited to remove objectionable material and played without sound if those measures will lessen the unfair prejudice and hearsay problems. *See, e.g., Lawton v. Jewish Hospital,* 679 S.W.2d 370 (Mo. Ct. App. 1984) (trial court allowed to edit film of victim's daily routine). In appropriate cases, the judge may order that the trial be bifurcated, reserving any disclosure or showing of the victim's movie until after liability has been established. *See, e.g., Grimes v. Employers Mutual Liability Insurance Co.,* 73 F.R.D. 607, 610 (D. Alaska 1977). While these ameliorative capabilities assist in the search for justice, the broad range of discretion has lead to divergent admission decisions on films that seem identical. *See, e.g.,* Annotation, *Admissibility of Visual Recoding of Event or Matter Other than that Giving rise to Litigation or Prosecution,* 41 A.L.R. 4th 877, 893–903 (1985). What is needed is a common approach which will fairly deal with the plaintiff motion pictures and give some consistency of outcome.

Formulating a workable general rule about the admissibility of plaintiff injury movies would bring some coherence to the law of evidence in this area. Almost any victim film creates genuine and multiple concerns over unfair prejudice, misleading the jury, cumulative evidence, and hearsay. A possible solution to this dilemma is presented in the recent opinion of

Federal District Judge Carter in *Bolstridge v. Central Maine Power Co.*, 621 F. Supp. 1202 (D. Me. 1985).

The plaintiffs in that case sought admission of a day-in-the-life videotape allegedly showing the typical activities of accident victim Samantha Bolstridge. The defense made all of the objections mentioned earlier in this article. After examining the movies and the applicable case law, Judge Carter declined to admit the production. His rationale deserves quotation at length:

> The question of permitting the showing of a motion picture film or videotape at trial is one for the sound discretion of the Court. The propriety of allowing videotapes of this type into evidence is questionable for several reasons. Almost always an edited tape necessarily raises issues as to every sequence portrayed of whether the event shown is fairly representational of fact, after the editing process, and whether it is unduly prejudicial because of the manner of presentation. Further the fact that a plaintiff is aware of being videotaped for such purpose is likely to cause self-serving behavior, consciously or otherwise. Next, use of videotape for such purposes is troublesome because it dominates evidence more conventionally adduced simply because of the nature of its presentation. Finally, such a videotape may serve to distract the jury from the other cogent issues which properly must be considered to produce a fair verdict conscientiously derived from an impartial consideration of the evidence with strict attention to the applicable principles of law.

Id. at 1203–04 (citations and footnotes omitted). The footnotes discussed the possible atypicality and hearsay issues.

Judge Carter concluded that the answer to these thorny problems would be a limited exclusionary rule:

> For all of the above reasons admitted, the Court concludes that videotapes should be admitted as demonstrative evidence only when the tapes convey the observations of the witness to the jury more fully or accurately than for some specific, articulable reason the witness can convey them through the medium of conventional, in-court examination. Samantha Bolstridge appears to be able to testify on her own behalf. She can demonstrate to the jury in open court activities similar to those depicted in the videotape. Further, relatives and physicians of the Plaintiff Samantha Bolstridge may offer similar testimony. Thus, the videotape, in any event, will be merely cumulative of testimonial evidence which is available to the Plaintiff. Also, admission of the tape into evidence will create the risk of distracting the jury and unfairly prejudicing the Defendant, principally, though not exclusively, because the benefit of effective cross-examination is lost. Therefore, it should be excluded under Fed. R. Evid. 403.

Id. at 1204 (citations omitted).

The *Bolstridge* rule seems to provide the most flexible and rational approach in this area. There may indeed be occasions where a unique combination of factors require the use of plaintiff personal injury movies. For example, if the victim is in a coma or otherwise unable to communicate or come to court, and other witnesses cannot convey adequately the victim's condition, a motion picture might be the only recourse. In general, however, the pitfalls of plaintiff films would seem to militate against their routine use in court. For several reasons, the same is not true of motion pictures of the plaintiff prepared by the defense, as will be discussed in the next section.

§ 14.29 Presentations Made for the Defendant

The defendant is also often interested in introducing motion pictures depicting the plaintiff's physical condition and activities. Many of the foundational requirements and evidentiary objections are similar to those involving the plaintiff productions. The final goal, however, is quite different. The defense hopes to procure and present motion pictures which will demonstrate that the plaintiff is a healthy, mendacious malingerer. Since by their very nature defense films are candid, unrehearsed and made without the plaintiff's consent or knowledge, the judicial response to them is generally more tolerant. Indeed, they have been a common sight in American courtrooms since the 1920s. *See, e.g., Massachusetts Bonding & Insurance Co. v. Worthy,* 9 S.W.2d 388, 393 (Tex. Ct. Civ. App. 1928) (surveillance movie properly excluded because of insufficient foundation); *Snyder v. American Car & Foundry Co.,* 322 Mo. 147, 14 S.W.2d 603, 606–67 (Ct. App. 1929) (motion picture admitted to show rapid gait of plaintiff). *See generally* P. Kelly, *Blashfield Automobile Law & Practice* § 435.5 *Motion Pictures* (Rev. 3d ed. 1977 & Supp. 1985).

§ 14.30 —Surveillance Movies

Surveillance movies are a standard defense production. *See, e.g.,* Annotation, *Use of Motion Pictures as Evidence,* 62 A.L.R.2d 686 § 6 (1958 & Supp. 1984). They are made by defense or investigators who surreptitiously monitor the plaintiff and secretly make motion pictures of relevant activities indicating a physical condition at odds with the asserted disability. *See, e.g., Crawford v. Maryland Casualty Co.,* 39 So. 2d 102, 104 (La. Ct. App. 1949) (surveillance movie of unimpeded physical activities of allegedly injured plaintiff). *See also Pacific Mutual Life Insurance Co. v. Marks,* 230 Ala. 417, 161 So. 543 (1935), an interesting case in which the defendant sought unsuccessfully to display in court post-injury vacation movies made by the plaintiff that showed normal physical ability). In many personal injury and workers' compensation cases, these defense movies will be a crucial factor in establishing the defendant's contention that the plaintiff is uninjured or is not as disabled as he alleges. *See, e.g., Alford v. Bailey,* 202 Pa. Super. 324, 196 A.2d 393, 396 (1963) (in personal injury action defendant introduced films showing victim carrying and lifting heavy bags). A vital secondary purpose is to impeach and damage the credibility of the claimant who is testifying that his injuries are much worse than they patently and visibly are. *See, e.g., Harmon v. Board of Retirement,* 62 Cal. App. 3d 689, 133 Cal. Rptr. 154 (1976) (pictures of disability claimant playing golf); *Gagliano v. Boh Brothers Construction,* 44 So. 2d 732 (La. Ct. App. 1950) (in workers' compensation permanent-total-disability case defense provides films showing the claimant stooping, bending, and doing laborious work); *Harley v. Hockey,* 199 Misc. 512, 103 N.Y.S.2d 717, 719 (N.Y. Sup. Ct. Jefferson County 1950) (film of victim on a ladder offered to impeach plaintiff's credibility). The defense motion pictures, standing alone, might not be enough to conclusively establish the defendant's theory and defeat the plaintiff's claim. *See, e.g., Glover v. Southern Pipe & Supply Co.,* 408 So. 2d 352, 353, 355–56 (La. Ct. App. 1981) (workers' compensation case reversed when trial court gave too much weight to short defense surveillance film). Combining the surveillance move with corroborating expert medical testimony will often be an overwhelming combination. *See, e.g., Mertz v. Mellon National Bank & Trust Co.,* 11 Pa. Commw. 541, 314 A.2d 570, 571–72 (1974) (films offered corroboration of defense expert testimony concerning propriety of terminating workers' compensation total-disability benefits.

§ 14.31 —Laying the Foundation

The basic foundational predicates for the admission of defense films are similar to those for plaintiff-sponsored motion pictures. The defendant must establish by competent testimony that the films are a true, accurate, and correct representation of the scene. *See, e.g., Hayward v. Ginn,* 306 P.2d 320, 324 (Okla. 1957) (professional photography of plaintiff walking). *See, e.g., Jordan v. New Amsterdam Casualty Co.,* 353 S.W.2d 256, 259 (Tex. Ct. Civ. App. 1961) (pictures of plaintiff showing normal work performance), *rev'd on other grounds sub nom. New Amsterdam Casualty Co. v. Jordan,* 359 S.W. 2d 864 (Tex. 1962). This testimony may be provided by the photographer, *see, e.g., Thomas v. Fleming,* 241 Miss. 26, 128 So. 2d 854 (1961) (movies of supposedly immobile plaintiff performing heavy work in garage), or by any person present when the films were made who can positively state that they are a true and correct likeness of the things he saw at the time, *see, e.g., Kortz v. Guardian Life Insurance Co.,* 144 F.2d

676, 679 (10th Cir.) (background information given by non-photographer witness), *cert. denied,* 323 U.S. 728 (1944). Because surveillance movies are often filmed long-distance or under marginal conditions, courts seem to be more demanding in establishing that the actor is indeed the plaintiff, *see, e.g., Barnham v. Nowell,* 243 Miss. 441, 138 So. 493 (1962) (film adequately clear to allow identification of plaintiff); *General Accident Fire & Life Assurance Corp. v. Camp,* 348 S.W. 2d 782 (Tex. Ct. Civ. App. 1961) (exclusion of surveillance movie due to lack of adequate identification of actor), and in ensuring that the final product is clearly presented to the jury's view, *see, e.g., Wren v. St. Louis Public Service Co.,* 333 S.W.2d 92 (Mo. 1960) (case remanded for proper projection of surveillance movie); *Will v. Merrill,* 210 F.2d 132, 133 (4th Cir. 1954) (proper repair of torn film allowed display of defense film to jury). Even after the authentication and identification requirements are fulfilled, these movies still face numerous objections by the plaintiff.

§ 14.32 Objections to Defense Motion Pictures

The main objections to defense motion pictures have centered on the unfair prejudice concepts embodies in Federal Rule of Evidence 403. See **§ 14.23**. Even if the defense film has a soundtrack with speech of the plaintiff-actor, a hearsay objection would fail before the exemption allowing admissions by a party-opponent. Fed. R. Evid. 801(d)(2)(A). Plaintiffs have argued, with mixed success, that the defense films are inflammatory, cumulative, an unfair surprise, and misleading. As with the plaintiff films, the cumulative evidence objection largely depends on the order of presentation. *See, e.g., North Miami Beach v. Horan,* 181 So. 2d 366 (Fla. Dist. Ct. App. 1966) (defense films cumulative of earlier material); *Finn v. Wood,* 178 F.2d 583, 584 (2d Cir. 1950) (surveillance movie merely cumulative of earlier testimony). The defense films certainly have sensational overtones, since they are often a dramatic and direct refutation of both the plaintiff's case and his credibility. *See, e.g., Metropolitan Life Insurance Co. v. Wright,* 199 So. 289 (Miss. 1940) (surveillance movies improperly excluded by trial court). *Boyarsky v. G.A. Zimmerman Corp.,* 240 A.D. 361, 270 N.Y.S. 134 (1934) (refusal to admit probative defense movies at trial results in reversal). However, so long as the motion pictures constitute "relevant, material and instructive evidence" about the plaintiff's true condition, they will not be excluded because they are inherently sensational. *See, e.g., Steele v. Gossen,* 329 S.W.2d 703, 712 (Mo. 1959) (surveillance movies of allegedly disabled plaintiff doing strenuous farm labor). A more legitimate concern is that the defense will unexpectedly spring the movies on an unsuspecting plaintiff, leaving little opportunity to properly explain the seemingly damning presentation.

§ 14.33 —Unfair Surprise

The defendant would undoubtedly prefer to bushwhack the plaintiff with an apparently devastating surveillance movie. There may indeed be no right to be apprised in advance that films will be made of the plaintiff's activities, *but see Gulf Life Ins. Co. v. Stossel,* 131 Fla. 268, 175 So. 804 (1937) (an unusual case in which the court actually suggested that a court commissioner be appointed to assist both sides in making a surveillance movie; Stossel apparently stands alone), or to be provided with a copy of the movie once it has been made. *See, e.g., Peak v. Industrial Accident Commission,* 82 Cal. App. 2d 926, 187 P.2d 905 (1947) (petitioner in workers' compensation action not entitled to copies of movie made by insurance carrier. However, a preview in advance of trial would certainly obviate the ambush objection, *see, e.g., Jones v. Texas Employers Insurance Association,* 352 S.W.2d 318, 320 (Tex. Ct. Civ. App. 1961) (advisable to allow preview of surveillance film in workers' compensation cases), and would properly give the plaintiff a reasonable chance to exercise his rights of rebuttal and explanation, *see, e.g., Glover v. Southern Pipe & Supply Co.,* 408 So. 2d 352, 255 n.1 (La. Ct. App. 1981) (plaintiff was improperly denied awareness of defense film and right to explain its contents). This is especially true when the plaintiff has employed discovery devices such as interrogatories in an effort to uncover any surveillance films and prepare to cope with them at trial. *See, e.g., Hoey v. Hawkins,* 332 A.2d 403 (Del. 1965) (intentional secretion of defense movie after request for production results in reversal on damages issue). *See also Lawler v. Industrial Commission,* 24 Ariz. App. 282, 537 P.2d 1340 (1975) (state law requiring pre-hearing notice of intent to offer films in workers' compensation actions specifically excluded surveillance films from the notice provisions).

The arguments over unfair surprise are cogently addressed in the Delaware decision of *Olszewski v. Howell,* 253 A.2d 77 (Del. Super. Ct. 1969). The plaintiffs in that case requested the production of defense surveillance movies "in order to prevent surprise and to develop, if necessary, counter evidence." *Id.* at 77. The defendant resisted the production motion, alleging that there was no good cause to disclose matters of which the plaintiff had equal awareness. Judge Quillen saw worth in each approach:

> Both positions strike the Court as having merit insofar as general litigation policy is concerned. On the one hand, a plaintiff shows need for protection against the rather distasteful business of having an opposing litigant possibly use, and even misuse, motion pictures of the plaintiff, taken secretly without the plaintiff's knowledge and consent, in a manner deliberately designed to impeach the plaintiff's credibility and to degrade the plaintiff generally. On the other hand a defendant demonstrates a need to protect himself against a

> possible exaggerated claim, and even false claim, of personal injury and shows that a premature disclosure of the impeachment evidence could result in a conscious or subconscious tailoring of plaintiff's case in chief to meet the challenge.
>
> On balance, the Court decides for several reasons that "good cause" has been shown for disclosure. First, even assuming the plaintiffs can recall the event of the two days in question, the precise evidence which the defendant has, the film, is now unique and cannot now be reproduced. Second, moving picture evidence is subject to misuse by splicing, angle of shooting, misleading condensation, selective lighting, either natural or artificial, and many other variables. It may take an expert to discover and analyze the product and techniques. Third, there is now, at least in civil cases, a well established policy of pretrial disclosure which is based on a rationale that a trial decision should result from a disinterested search for truth from all the available evidence rather than tactical maneuvers based on the calculated manipulation of evidence and its production. Fourth, disclosure should expedite the disposition of the case by encouraging settlement, by bringing to head any objections to evidence, and by giving the plaintiffs an advance opportunity to develop counter-evidence. These policy reasons support disclosure.

Id. at 77–78 (citation omitted).

Judge Quillen granted the plaintiffs' motion to produce the surveillance films. *Id.* at 78.

§ 14.34 —Misleading Film or Videotape

Once apprised of the defense film, plaintiffs will typically object that it is inherently misleading, especially if the production is selectively noncontinuous and apparently projected at an incorrect speed. As a theoretical matter, it is true that motion pictures are subject to deceptive techniques. For example:

> Telescopic lenses, ingenuous settings of the stage, the elimination of unfavorable portions of a film, an angle from which a picture is taken, the ability to speed up the reproduction of the picture and the genius of a director may tend to create misleading impressions. *Harmon v. San Joaquin Light & Power Co.,* 37 Cal. App. 2d 169, 98 P.2d 1064, 1067 (1940) (surveillance movie in personal injury suit not entitled to conclusive effect). The fact that numerous "pranks and tricks" may be played on movies does not mean that they are per se suspect, especially when testimony is introduced to the effect that the moving pictures are indeed a true representation of the scene and events witnessed at the time of the filming. [*Heiman v. Market Street Ry. Co.,* 21 Cal. App. 2d 311, 69 P.2d 178, 180 (1937) (films showing visibly impaired plaintiff admissible in personal injury action).] In order to make a successful objection on the misleading theory, the plaintiff must focus on the particular deceptive ploy allegedly used.

As a general rule, if the plaintiff can demonstrate that the motion picture film has been speeded up so that the resulting projected image does not match the actual speed of the actor, the trial court will exclude the film. *See, e.g., Powell v. Industrial Commission,* 4 Ariz. App. 172, 418 P.2d 602, 610 (1966) (films offered which showed workers' compensation claimant working at plainly unnatural speed), *vacated on other grounds,* 102 Ariz. 11, 423 P.2d 348 (1967). As a less-preferred alternative to exclusion, the judge may instruct the jury to disregard the shifted speed. *See, e.g., Utley v. Heckinger,* 362 S.W.2d 13, 17 (Ark. 1962) (surveillance movies showing alleged accident victim walking with[out] crutches). At the very least, the plaintiff is entitled to testify that the defense movie does not accurately portray his normal gait and movements. *See, e.g., Williamson v. St. Louis Public Service Co.,* 363 Mo. 508, 252 S.W.2d 295, 300 (1952) (surveillance movies of plaintiff walking).

The most effective objection to the defense films has stressed their lack of continuity. Since the star of these productions is not aware of the filming operation, the defense agents must take their pictures as opportunities arise over a period of hours or of days. *See, e.g., McGoorty v. Benhert,* 305 Ill. App. 458, 27 N.E.2d 289, 294 (1940) (discontinuity of filming a necessary part of surveillance). Courts are mindful of the fact that evidence in the form of moving pictures must be used with great caution, because such pictures show only very brief intervals of the activities if the subject is suffering pain, and they do not show the after effects of his activities. *Lambert v. Wolf's Inc.,* 132 So. 2d 522, 527 (La. Ct. App. 1961) (pictures of plaintiff doing strenuous work at a garage completely refuted disability claim). Occasionally, when the length of the inconsistent plaintiff activity has been very short in comparison with the total observation time, the surveillance movie has not been given conclusive effect. *See, e.g., Oregon v. Tri-State Road Boring, Inc.,* 434 So. 2d 65 (La. 1983) (tapes showing 3½ hours of total activity over a 3-day period); *John B. Kelly Co., Inc. v. Workmens' Compensation Appeals Bd.,* 8 Pa. Commw. 589, 303 A.2d 255 (1973) (surveillance from 1966 to 1969 results in "miniscule" final film); *DeBattiste v. Anthony Laudadio & Sons,* 167 Pa. Super. 38, 74 A.2d 784, 787 (1950) (pictures only showed claimant's activities for "very limited periods of time"); *Equitable Life Assurance Soc. v. McDonald,* 280 Ky. 825, 134 S.W.2d 953, 954 (Ct. App. 1939) (film of only 71 minutes from entire afternoon of surveillance). The defense movie will be weakened further if the filmed activities are both brief and entirely consistent with the admitted limited capabilities of the claimant. *See, e.g., Klein v. Himbert,* 474 So. 2d 513, 516 (La. Ct. App. 1985) (inconclusive film of plaintiff's activities); *Niles Police Department v. Industrial Commission,* 83 Ill. 2d 528, 48 Ill. Dec. 212, 416 N.E.2d 243, 246 (1981) (brief filmed exposure of photosensitive claimant to light did not disprove disability); *Costanzo v. Southern Farm Bureau Casualty Insurance Co.,* 124 So. 2d

621, 625 (La. Ct. App. 1960) (limited film of farm work was consistent with the claimed disability). Naturally, if the film is too short or completely consistent with the plaintiff's position, the film may be irrelevant to the trial and hence inadmissible. *See, e.g., Cutting v. John V. Cowper Co.,* 7 A.D. 2d 348, 183 N.Y.S.2d 171 (1959) (film did not contradict asserted partial disability). The quest to obtain a useable motion picture of adequate length and content may lead the defendant to some rather unorthodox methods.

§ 14.35 —"Unclean Hands"

Plaintiffs have argued in several cases that the defendant has underhandedly set up a situation in which the victim will be forced or tricked into exerting himself and revealing his true physical abilities for the benefit of hidden cameras. *See, e.g., Bernardy v. O.K. Furniture & Rug Co.,* 385 P.2d 909, 910 (Okla. 1963) (defense investigator allegedly set up flat tire on plaintiff's car in order to take film of him changing the tire). These defense ploys normally seem to include the services of a young woman who induces the male plaintiff to perform feats of athletic prowess. *See, e.g., Snowhill v. Lieurance,* 72 Wash. 2d 718, 435 P.2d 624, 625 (1967) (tossing large plastic ball at a picnic); *McGoorty v. Benhart,* 305 Ill. App. 458, 27 N.E.2d 289 (1940) (female investigator persuades allegedly disabled plaintiff to swim, row, golf, throw baseballs, and play football). While these techniques may be unsavory, judges will admit the resulting movies if they are relevant to the issues of the case. *See, e.g., Maryland Casualty Co. v. Coker,* 118 F.2d 43, 44 (5th Cir. 1941) (defendant obtained pictures of plaintiff rowing a boat by using "female companions and the usual liquid refreshment").

§ 14.36 Discretion of the Judge

As with the plaintiff presentation, appellate courts will reserve only the admission decision of a trial judge concerning a defense film when there has been an abuse of discretion. *See, e.g., Harris v. St. Louis Public Service Co.,* 270 S.W.2d 850, 853 (Mo. 1954) (admission of defense film governed by abuse of discretion standard); *Denison v. Omaha & C.B. St. Ry. Co.,* 135 Neb. 307, 280 N.W. 905 (1938) (admission of films showing plaintiff working in the stockyard was within the discretion of the trial judge). As with the plaintiff movies, the judge will rule on admission and the jury will consider the weight to accord the film, *see, e.g., DeTunno v. Shull,* 75 Ohio L. Abs. 602, 144 N.E.2d 669, 672 (Ohio Ct. App. 1956) (movies showing plaintiff changing a wheel several years after the accident); *Wagner v.*

McDaniels, 9 Ohio St. 3d 184, 9 Ohio B.R. 469, 459 N.E.2d 561 (1984), unless the judge is hearing the matter alone, in which case he will perform both functions, *see, e.g., Jones v. Employers Mutual Liability Insurance Co.,* 114 So. 2d 602, 606 (La. Ct. App. 1959) (films of allegedly disabled plaintiff performing ordinary manual labor). The scope of judicial discretion, however, is significantly smaller for defense motion pictures. Unlike the plaintiff films which are an embellishment of the victim's case, defense movies are a direct refutation of the plaintiff's credibility. *See, e.g., Mathias v. Baltimore & Ohio Railroad,* 93 Ill. App. 2d 258, 236 N.E.2d 331 (1968) (trial court erred in not allowing showing of defense films contradicting the plaintiff's case). Since the defense films are a pivotal point in the defendant's case, they cannot be brushed aside or ignored without substantial justification. *See, e.g., Georgia-Pacific Corp. v. McLaurin,* 370 So. 2d 1359 (Miss. 1979) (failure to admit film results in reversal); *McClung v. Delta Shipbuilding Co.,* 33 So. 2d 438 (La. Ct. App. 1948).

§ 14.37 Computer Evidence

The use of a computer, which is simply a high speed calculator, has given experts providing services to lawyers far wider latitude in formulating and supporting their opinions, whether the expert is an economist or an individual engaged in accident reconstruction. Whenever there are statistics or a wide range of possible variables in a set of assumptions, computers have made it possible for experts formulating opinions for litigation to do so with extraordinary freedom and assurance.

The fact of the matter is that the assumptions themselves are no more valid than they were before the use of the computer, since the computer does nothing more than speed up the process. However, the very fact of a computer does seem to add weight and credibility to the evidence with which it is associated. I have discussed computer-generated demonstrative evidence in detail in *Dombroff on Demonstrative Evidence* ch. 9, pointing out that computers and the mystique associated with them can be used in any number of ways, including the processing of damage statistics or of a time sequence of events. In addition, the computer is capable of doing simulations that were impossible prior to computers because of the wide range of variables that may be involved.

The problem with computer-generated evidence is the fact that the computer itself is involved and generates a *hard copy* product. It goes through the minds of members of the jury that, "it says it on that paper, therefore it must be true." For example, assume that you are defending a wrongful death claim against a client. The economist testifying regarding the economic loss suffered by the plaintiff has made certain assumptions and calculations. Your opponent has just elicited the following questions and answers:

Q. Doctor, based on the assumptions and information which we have just discussed, did you perform certain calculations?
A. Yes.
Q. What was the purpose of those calculations?
A. I ran these calculations in order to project over the expected life expectancy of Mr. Burns what the lost income was by virtue of his death.
Q. How did you perform these calculations?
A. I used a computer program which incorporates all of the assumptions and factual information and, in a high-speed manner, does the calculations and produces the results on a printout which is projected from the date of death through the date of trial, to the date of Mr. Burns's projected death had he lived his full life expectancy.
Q. Do you have the results of that computer computation with you?
A. Yes, sir, I do.
Q. Your Honor, I would request that computer printout be marked as exhibit 5.
THE COURT: It will be so marked.
Q. Doctor, would you explain to the jury what this computer printout sets forth in detail?

The expert goes on to testify in detail as to what the computer printouts mean and hands out copies of the summary sheets of the printouts while he testifies from a large blowup of the printout in full view of the jury. At the conclusion of this line of questioning, the expert gives his opinions regarding the economic loss, and your opponent moves the exhibit into evidence. The credibility associated with this technique is substantial because the computer is involved.

Your task in view is to remove any mystique associated with this tactic and expose it for what it is. A line of questioning which you might pursue is as follows:

Q. Doctor, you have indicated that you used a computer for the purpose of doing certain calculations, is that correct?
A. Yes, I did.
Q. The computer itself did not make any assumptions, is that right?
A. That's correct.
Q. So what you did, if I understand you correctly, is to take certain factual information which came out of the discovery in this case or from the attorney for the plaintiff and feed it into the computer?
A. That's correct.
Q. And you also fed certain assumptions into the computer regarding rates of inflation, reduction to present value and other matters?
A. That is correct.

Q. And then the computer did calculations, isn't that right?
A. That is correct.
Q. And it did those calculations at a rather high rate of speed?
A. Yes, sir, a very high rate of speed.
Q. In fact, Doctor, it did those calculations faster than you could do them using even a calculator, isn't that correct?
A. Yes, sir, quite a bit faster.
Q. And it doesn't make any mathematical errors, does it, sir?
A. No, sir, it shouldn't.
Q. But its mathematical calculations are only as good as the underlying information, both facts and assumptions, which you feed into the computer, isn't that right?
A. That is correct.
Q. And those mathematical calculations, again assuming no error, are just as good, and in fact no better, than calculations which you might do using either a pencil or a calculator, again assuming no error, isn't that right?
A. Yes, sir, that is right.
Q. So the real question is whether the facts which went into those calculations and the assumptions on which those calculations are based are valid, isn't that right?
A. That's correct, sir.
Q. Doctor, have you ever heard the phrase, "garbage in-garbage out?"
A. Yes I have.
Q. What does it mean, sir, to you?
A. Well, sir, computer specialists or programmers use it and it essentially means that the result which you get out of a computer is only as good as the information which you put into the computer.
Q. [picking up the plaintiff's computer printout] Then what you are saying to me, sir, is that if you put garbage information into the computer you will get garbage results out of the computer?
A. That is right.
Q. So the computer doesn't make the information any better or more valid or more valuable, does it, sir?
A. No, sir, it doesn't.
Q. All it does is it gives you some mathematical calculations much faster and without any mathematical errors?
A. Essentially, sir, that is correct.

As you can see, this simple line of questioning on cross-examination of an expert who has used statistical data that have been processed by a computer, whether in the form of reconstructions, simulations, or statistical printouts, is extremely effective in pointing up the computer for what it is: a high-speed, error-free pencil. This is an effective way of meeting what can otherwise be an unfair tactic.

In addition to taking this line of approach in cross-examining the evidence, there are a number of other techniques with which you should be familiar when you deal with computer-generated demonstrative evidence offered by an opponent (this list first appeared at *id.* § 9.14):

1. Do not waste your effort attacking the accuracy of the computer's arithmetic.
2. Establish and pursue lines of questioning and testimony which make it clear that the computer is only doing what it is instructed and that the results are only as valid as the instructions. Remember, "garbage in-garbage out."
3. Test the reasonableness of the results with simple hand calculations. Bad programming or bad assumptions can cause computer results to be way off base. Although it is not possible to check all of the results, it is frequently and typically possible to make a spot check or two. Nothing makes a set of complex computations look worse or more foolish than a simple convincing calculation which shows the computer answer is clearly wrong. If you are presenting computer-generated demonstrative evidence, insure that both you and your expert make spot checks of the calculations prior to trial to satisfy yourselves as to the general validity of the results and to immunize yourself against embarrassing cross-examination.
4. All computations intended to depict physical events are accomplished using some type of mathematical model which describes the physics of the situation. You should carefully examine this model and its programming. Obviously, your expert will play an invaluable role in this area.
5. Because mathematical models are approximations of the real world, find out what approximations were made by your opponent or your opponent's expert. Make a list of the items which would affect the results, and find out if each of these has been included in the model and, if so, what assumptions are involved in each physical process.
6. After formulating a mathematical model, it is necessary to make numerical assumptions about each of the variables in order to permit the computer to make computations. For example, vehicle speed must be assumed. Make a list of these variables, and find out what assumptions were made with respect to each one. Determine which assumptions may be incorrect or which ones could change the results drastically if only slightly inaccurate.
7. If there are variables which can only be limited to a range of possible values, it may be desirable to repeat the computations for the two extremes. If both computations lead to the same conclusions, then the results are solid. If they do not, then either the computation must be abandoned or means found to justify further reduction of the

range of the variables. These areas should be inquired into on cross-examination in order to determine whether your opponent's expert discarded one of the extremes in order to permit the results to more closely parallel the desired results.

8. Certain simple modeling is well established. For example, the distance that an automobile can travel in a given period of time at a given speed is generally well known. However, if the physics involved are reasonably complex, you should inquire as to the extent to which this specific mathematical modeling has been previously used, subjected to tests, and verified. Has it ever been published in any text or journal? If you are able to reduce the mathematical model in the computer-generated evidence and the subsequent results to an experiment, you may be able to take advantage of the fact that experiments do not always work.

In *West v. Martin,* No. 57,191 (Kan. Ct. App. Jan. 30, 1986), the Kansas Court of Appeals concluded that a computer printout analyzing the result of a psychological test did not fit the business records exception to the hearsay rule. Because the printout was not simply a compilation of data but rather an analysis or interpretative summary, it would not fall within the requirements set forth in Federal Rule of Evidence 803(b). Furthermore, a physician was not a proper foundation witness, because his function was limited to transferring or providing the data to be analyzed and he was totally unqualified to provide the necessary foundation showing the computer printout's accuracy and trustworthiness.

§ 14.38 Views—In General

The use of a view presents the questions to counsel whether it is permissible and, in the ultimate sense, whether it is tactically desirable. On many occasions, the court will not permit a view, because it is time-consuming and expensive, depending upon where the jury must be taken to conduct the view.

A survey of jurisdictions, both state and federal, focusing on this question demonstrates the kinds of circumstances and situations when a view has been permitted in civil and criminal cases and when it has not.

§ 14.39 —View Denied

First Circuit. When a jury view would have been time-consuming and cumulative, if not repetitive, photographic exhibits were used to illustrate the relevant features of the scene, and defense counsel had repeatedly expressed concern about the possibility of the jury talking to one another or to counsel, the denial of the defendant's motion for a view of the scene was proper and within the court's discretion. *United States v. Drougas,* 748 F.2d 8 (1st Cir. 1984).

Eleventh Circuit. In a case in which the defendant was convicted of conspiring to possess and possessing with intent to distribute narcotics, a quantity of cocaine had been secreted in a packing crate.

The district court appropriately exercised its discretion in denying a jury view of the warehouse and the packing crate, which was removed by the United States Customs Service from the warehouse. The appellate court stated that the jury view would have likely confused the jury and misled it into thinking that knowledge that the crate was in customs custody was an element of the crime, when the offense of removing goods from customs custody does not require such knowledge. *United States v. Sarmiento,* 744 F.2d 755 (11th Cir. 1984).

The district court's decision declining a request for a jury view of a boat which was used to import cocaine was well within its discretion. *United States v. Martinez,* 763 F.2d 1297 (11th Cir. 1985).

Connecticut. The diagram to which the defendant had access in conjunction with the testimony was sufficient to provide the jurors with a clear picture of the premises; therefore, the court did not abuse its discretion in denying the defendant's motion to allow a view of the premises. *State v. Taxiltaridis,* 2 Conn. App. 617, 481 A.2d 98 (1984).

Georgia. Denial of the defendant's motion to view the scene in an aggravated assault and attempted armed robbery action was within the court's discretion. *Jackson v. State,* 172 Ga. App. 359, 323 S.E.2d 198 (1984).

Indiana. A jury's view of the place relevant to the crime charged is not essential to a fair trial and is wholly within the discretion of the court. There was no showing that a view of the vehicle used in the crime would have materially assisted the jury; therefore, there was no error in the denial of the motion to view the vehicle. *Johnson v. State,* 472 N.E.2d 892 (Ind. 1985).

Michigan. Because the conditions had changed considerably between the time of the automobile accident and the motion to view the scene of the accident, a view of the scene would not have been proper and the judge's denial of the request was well within his discretion. The accident occurred in the winter, and the trial took place in the summer. *West v. Livingston County Road Commission,* 131 Mich. App. 63, 345 N.W.2d 608 (1983).

Minnesota. The court did not abuse its discretion in refusing to let the jury view the crime scene, because a viewing would not have been helpful to the jury in this burglary case. *State v. Stewart,* 360 N.W.2d 430 (Minn. 1985).

New York. In a case in which the defendant was charged with criminal possession of a weapon in the third degree, the court did not abuse its discretion when it denied the defense motion for a jury view of the scene. The court held that the cumulative impact of a number of changes affecting the visibility of that area at night was sufficiently substantial so as to preclude such a viewing. The changes occurred between the time of defendant's arrest in late November of 1981 and the time of the trial in late June of 1982 and included alterations in the natural light and the artificial illumination from street lamps and store fronts, as well as the appearance of foliage on the trees. *People v. Rao,* 107 A.D.2d 720, 484 N.Y.S.2d 76 (1985).

Ohio. A police officer brought an action against a driver, alleging that the driver negligently operated his motor vehicle which ran over the officer's foot and negligently and intentionally failed to remove the vehicle. After a judgment in favor of the officer, the driver appealed, claiming that the court's refusal to demonstrate the impossibility of the accident using his 1976 Volkswagen van was reversible error. The court held that it was within the discretion of the trial court to deny the request because there were some differences between the 1976 Volkswagen van with which the demonstration would have been performed and the 1971 Volkswagen van that was involved in the accident. *Carter v. Simpson,* 16 Ohio App. 3d 420, 476 N.E.2d 705 (1984).

§ 14.40 —View Permitted

Georgia. After being convicted of murder and sentenced to life imprisonment, the defendant appealed. The court held that the absence of the defendant at the jury viewing of the crime scene, when made for the purpose of better understanding the evidence and not introducing new evidence, was not a denial of due process. *Forney v. State,* 255 Ga. 316, 338 S.E.2d 252 (1986).

Massachusetts. Defendant was convicted of assault and battery with a dangerous weapon, and he appealed. Both the decision to permit a view of the crime scene and the limits of the view are within the discretion of the trial judge. In this case, although the view was allowed, the judge denied the defendant's request that each juror be seated in the automobile in order to better appreciate its interior layout and dimensions. *Commonwealth v. Gabbidon,* 17 Mass. App. 525, 459 N.E.2d 1263 (1984).

New York. The defendant, a city police officer, was convicted in county court of manslaughter in the first degree, and he appealed. The court did not abuse its discretion in authorizing a jury view of the murder scene, nor had the scene so materially changed as to render the view improper. Additionally, when the court granted the view in order to temper any prejudice emanating from the possibility that two jurors may have viewed the area despite the court's admonition to avoid that area and to familiarize all jurors with the area, the area was sufficiently uncommon so that a view would be helpful to the jurors. *People v. Purcell,* 103 A.D.2d 938, 479 N.Y.S.2d 268 (1984).

South Carolina. The defendants in *State v. Plath* were convicted of murder and sentenced to death. The court allowed a jury view of the scene outside the presence of the defendant's counsel. The appellate court held that the viewing in the absence of appellants' counsel did not deny the defendants their constitutional rights to counsel and confrontation.

Because a jury view of the scene is not a taking of testimony, constitutional protections are not implicated or denied when, as here, the trial judge in fact accompanied the jury in the absence of the defendants and their counsel, who neither objected to the arrangement nor requested to be taken along. *State v. Plath,* 281 S.C. 1, 313 S.E.2d 619 (1984).

Virginia. The defendant was convicted in circuit court of possession of heroin with intent to distribute, and he appealed. The trial judge viewed the scene of the crime during a bench trial. The appellate court held that the presence of the defendant at a jury view of a crime scene is not an absolute jurisdictional prerequisite, overruling *Noell v. Commonwealth,* 135 Va. 600, 115 S.E. 679 (1923).

Because the defendant had waived his right to be present at the view and the event was conducted in a manner free from prejudice, there was no irregularity tending to influence the trier of fact. Although this case deals with a trial judge's view of the scene, the court's ruling encompasses a jury view. *Jones v. Commonwealth,* 227 Va. 425, 317 S.E.2d 482 (1984).

Washington. The defendant was convicted of first degree murder. On appeal, the court stated that the prejudicial effect of a jury view did not outweigh the probative value, because the view was permissible to aid the jury in understanding the logistics of the crime scene, and the court properly instructed the jury that the view did not constitute evidence. *State v. Bernson,* 40 Wash. App. 729, 700 P.2d 758 (1985).

Wisconsin. The insurer brought an action in subrogation seeking recovery from the driver involved in a rear-end collision with its insured. The judge viewed the scene. On appeal, the appellate court stated that the review of the scene rests within the judge's sound discretion and may be initiated through the judge's own motion or by motion of either party. Because of the similarity in purpose, the procedures applicable to a jury view should be applied to the judge's view of the scene. *American Family Mutual Insurance Co. v. Shannon,* 120 Wis. 2d 560, 356 N.W.2d 175 (1984).

§ 14.41 —Sample Motion for a View

The following motion can be used as a basis for seeking a view in almost any type of case. Although this motion deals with the view of a helicopter, the subject matter of the view is irrelevant.

UNITED STATES DISTRICT COURT
FOR THE NORTHERN DISTRICT OF NEW YORK

AUDREY L. BRYANT, as Administratrix of the Estate of CHARLES EDWARD BRYANT, deceased, Plaintiff, —against— SIKORSKY AIRCRAFT, a Division of United Technologies Corporation, (Delaware); SIKORSKY AIRCRAFT, a Division of United Technologies Corporation (Alabama); TEXTRON, INC., a foreign corporation. Defendants.	Case No. 83-CV-992 Judge Neal P. McCurn

MEMORANDUM IN SUPPORT OF DEFENDANT'S
MOTION *IN LIMINE* FOR A VIEW OF A
BLACK HAWK HELICOPTER

Introduction

This memorandum is submitted in support of the motion of defendant Sikorsky Aircraft Division of United Technologies Corporation (Delaware)

("Sikorsky") for an *in limine* ruling pursuant to Federal Rule of Evidence 402, permitting a view of a Black Hawk helicopter at trial.

Sikorsky, subject to being able to make the appropriate arrangements, is prepared to fly a Black Hawk helicopter to the place of trial in order that the jury may view the various systems of the Black Hawk in operation. Sikorsky will have the Black Hawk placed in a heated hanger for the view. In addition, Sikorsky will also make arrangements to have the view videotaped so that it may be a part of the full record on appeal. However, before undertaking the steps necessary, including the permission of the U.S. Army, Sikorsky would like to ascertain through this motion whether or not the Court is inclined to permit this view if Sikorsky is able to arrange it.

Discussion

This court may, in its discretion, permit such a view. The three factors to be taken into consideration in deciding whether to grant a view are the importance of the view to the litigation, the availability of the information by other means and whether the object has changed in appearance since the dispute began. J. Weinstein & M. Berger, *Weinstein's Evidence* ¶ 403[05] (1986). *See La France v. New York, New Haven & Hartford R.R.*, 191 F. Supp. 164 (D. Conn. 1961); *see also Northwestern Casualty Co. v. Global Moving & Storage, Inc.*, 533 F.2d 320 (6th Cir. 1976).

First, a view of an actual Black Hawk helicopter is of great importance to this litigation. The Black Hawk itself is the real defendant here, and its safety and performance are at issue. The jury will be presented with a great deal of highly technical evidence and asked to evaluate it. It will be impossible to understand the evidence in this case without a good general understanding of how the Black Hawk works. A helicopter is a highly sophisticated and complex piece of machinery and one with which very few people have any acquaintance. A view demonstrating how this machine works will aid the jury in understanding how this machine works.

Second, an understanding of how this machine works can best be conveyed to a jury of laypersons by having them actually see a Black Hawk. Although a trained mechanic might be able to understand how a Black Hawk works from charts and diagrams, it is unlikely that the jury will be composed either in whole or in part of mechanically adept persons. The operation of the Black Hawk as a unified system simply cannot be demonstrated by diagram or film or in any other way than by seeing it.

Third, although Sikorsky cannot, of course, produce the Black Hawk involved in the crash, the Black Hawk it is offering is substantially similar to the Black Hawk involved in the crash.

For the above reasons Sikorsky's motion *in limine* should be granted and a view of a Black Hawk permitted at trial.

Dated: October ______, 1986

HUGHES HUBBARD & REED

By: ______________________________
Mark A. Dombroff, Esquire
1201 Pennsylvania Avenue, N.W.
Suite 300
Washington, D.C. 20004

and

DEGRAFF, FOY, CONWAY, HOLT-HARRIS & MEALY
Christopher Massaroni, Esquire
90 State Street
Albany, New York 12207-1780

ATTORNEYS FOR DEFENDANT
SIKORSKY AIRCRAFT

Of counsel:

Ruth L. Piekarska, Esquire
Hughes Hubbard & Reed
One Wall Street
New York, New York 10005

CHAPTER 15

DAMAGES

§ 15.1 Introduction

While most proceedings in litigation, whether in the settlement, pretrial, or trial process, are oriented toward the facts, whenever the question of damages arises, there is a tremendous injection of emotion and passion. The potential for use of unfair tactics against your client in the context of either proving damages or defending damages increases dramatically. Because an appeal to the emotions and prejudices of the jury on the question of damages can have either a conscious or an unconscious effect on their liability decision, the ramifications of tactics or techniques which can prejudice your case on the damages issues must be recognized and protected against.

In the trial setting, the very fact of proving damages raises emotion. Similarly, evidence, especially such effective evidence as day-in-the-life presentations, may be prejudicial albeit, if properly prepared with appropriate foundation, admissible. It is not these techniques against which one must guard, but rather those which overstep the bounds of propriety and are clearly inadmissible. Even many admissible techniques are unfair in the adversarial sense. As an advocate, you must be capable of blunting their effectiveness and protecting your client.

§ 15.2 Computer Printouts

In **Chapter 14**, I discussed the use of computer-generated demonstrative evidence to take unfair advantage of the mystique surrounding computer-processed materials. Computer printouts have become more and more pervasive in the damages proof area. The same computations which economists used to do using a pencil or a calculator for determining loss due to personal injury/wrongful death/commercial damage are now being done by a computer.

There are both valid and invalid reasons for using a computer. The valid purpose is the higher degree of speed and mathematical accuracy which can be achieved by using the computer to process the numbers. However, remember that the computer does not make any subjective judgments or evaluations, and it processes only the facts and assumptions which are programmed into it. It is nothing more than a high-speed, error-free pencil which is able to do what is, for practical purposes, an unlimited number of calculations using any number of assumptions or facts. However, the result invariably is viewed as having greater validity by virtue of having been processed through a computer.

You may confront an opponent who brings in an economist for the purpose of proving damages or, for that matter, any other witness testifying on damages who has prepared the damages calculations and information using a computer. The dimension which this technique adds to the substance of the information is the format in which it is presented. Thus, you should be prepared to point out that the calculations or numbers are no more or less valid by virtue of having been done by a computer but that it is merely a matter of mathematical convenience. The line of cross-examination discussed in **Chapter 6** is appropriate to follow in this area.

Particularly in personal injury and wrongful death cases, when using an economist of your own, you should consider whether you should provide the court and jury with what is in effect a counter printout for the purpose of supporting your assumptions and conclusions. The obvious disadvantage of this technique is not directly associated with the use of a computer printout but is more directly related to the fact that, as a defendant, if you use an economist of your own, this places a "floor" on the damages. Thus, if your opponent's expert has testified and has computer printouts supporting damages in the amount of $1 million, but your expert testifies and has printouts supporting damages in the amount of $500,000, you have put the jury in the position of being able to split the difference. While the numbers are no more or less valid, the advantages obtained by your opponent from a computer printout will also be obtained by you. However, you will also have provided the jury with a floor and thus made it easier for them to award damages of some significant amount.

When representing a plaintiff, use of a computer printout in a personal injury or wrongful death case has a very distinct benefit quite separate and apart from its tendency to validate the statistics which it presents. Often it is difficult for jurors who themselves earn relatively modest incomes to think in terms of the large verdicts being sought in personal injury or wrongful death cases. As a result, it is imperative that a plaintiff's attorney condition the jury to awarding large damages. This conditioning typically starts during the opening statement, when plaintiff's counsel advises the jurors that they will be asked to award a large amount of money, perhaps several million dollars. Indeed, there may well be questioning during jury selection which focuses on this point as well.

During the actual presentation of the evidence, plaintiff's counsel must present economic experts, whether actuaries, accountants, or economists, for the purpose of supporting a million-dollar request. Even with such testimony, it is sometimes difficult for the jury to overcome the hurdle to make the seven-figure award. Use of the computer printout makes it easier, because the jury does not have to rely on the spoken word provided by some expert who is being paid to testify but may now rely instead on the printed number which an "objective" computer has produced. As used by some plaintiffs' counsel, the computer printout becomes a prop, taking on a life of its own quite separate and distinct from any testimony which may have been offered in connection with it.

The approach in responding to this tactic is not unlike the approach when cross-examining the expert who produced the printout. It must be pointed out to the trier of fact that the computer printout itself is irrelevant, that the numbers which it contains are essentially meaningless. Those numbers are only as good as the assumptions which went into making them up and the facts which were manipulated by those assumptions.

By using such words and phrases as "manipulated" when referring to what the computer did to the numbers, "processed," "garbage in-garbage out," "high-speed pencil" or "high-speed calculator" when referring to the computer printout, you will be able to instill in the minds of the jury that you are really talking about a way to veil the true import of the information. This has the further effect of belittling the computer and continually reminding the jury that they are being subjected to what is essentially a tactic of persuasion.

§ 15.3 Verdicts and Judgments in Similar Cases

As a defense attorney, you are likely to encounter unfair tactics used by plaintiffs' attorneys more often in personal injury and wrongful death cases than in property damage cases, because the latter area typically involves liquidated damages and documentary proof thereon. When economists are used to prove damages, including lost profits, you can run into certain problems.

An economist typically relies on statistical information from governmental agencies such as the Bureau of Labor Statistics and the Labor Department. There may be occasions, however, when an economist who is testifying for a plaintiff in a personal injury or wrongful death action uses information which is not permissible. It is generally held to be improper for an award to be premised on or take into account what may have been awarded by a jury in another case. On the subject generally, particularly within the context of closing arguments, *see* 15 A.L.R.2d 1144, 1146 (1951); *see also Salgo v. Leland Stanford Jr., University Board of Trustees,* 154 Cal. App. 2d 560, 317 P.2d 170 (1957).

This might arise either through the economist testifying as to the foundation information used or relied on in reaching a result or during the cross-examination of the economist. In this latter context, it may come about by the economist's revealing that he or she either worked on other cases in which a certain result was reached and took into account what a jury did in that particular situation or was aware of results reached in a similar case. You should move to strike any testimony premised on these bases, inasmuch as either a failure to object or a failure to move to strike typically will be viewed as a waiver. If the calculations and opinions of the economist are too intertwined with this sort of objectionable and improper foundation information, you should be prepared to argue the motion to strike and seek to have all the testimony excluded. Similarly, when you use an economist for your own case, you should ensure that he or she does not rely on information which is itself objectionable.

§ 15.4 Collateral Source Information

One area of damages proof that is often hotly contested involves payments from what is characterized as a *collateral source*. Briefly stated, the whole controversy focuses on attempts of defense counsel to introduce into evidence through a witness or, on occasion, during closing argument discussion regarding payments the plaintiff has received or may receive in the future from other sources. For example, defense counsel may want to introduce evidence that the plaintiff has received payments as a result of insurance, workers' compensation, or medical benefits. In addition, the defense may want to introduce evidence of the remarriage of the plaintiff in order to instill in the minds of the jury a cutoff date for the award of damages.

You will have to determine the precise law in your jurisdiction, but generally, any attempt to introduce this evidence is unfair and improper because it is considered to be prejudicial to the plaintiff's case, *see* 47 A.L.R.3d 234 (1973); *Deighan v. E. Turgeon Construction Co.,* 95 R.I. 130, 182 A.2d 438 (1962); *Werner v. Lane,* 393 A.2d 1329 (Me. 1978); *Goldstein v. Gontarz,* 64 Mass. 800, 309 N.E.2d 196 (1974); in that payments or benefits received from other sources do not relate to the issue of the defendant's liability or any money or damages to be paid as a consequence of that liability.

Notwithstanding the law, a defendant may attempt to introduce such evidence by the back door. For example, on the question of remarriage, in referring to the plaintiff's widow, the defendant may refer to her by her new married name, thus conveying the message to the jury that Mrs. Jones is no longer Mrs. Jones but is now Mrs. Smith. Nothing more need be said, because jurors now have it firmly in their minds that there has been a remarriage and the message of the cutoff date for damages will have been conveyed.

How, then, can a plaintiff prevent such an unfair tactic? The key to this problem is to file a motion in limine prior to trial to define clearly the limits of permissible activity by defense counsel in this area. If the court has issued an order on your motion precluding mention of collateral source payments or benefits, including remarriage, and defense counsel makes any such mention, you are in a position to seek sanctions, an instruction, and, in some cases, a mistrial.

Following discussions of liability insurance (**§ 15.5**) and remarriage (**§ 15.6**), **§ 15.7** contains a sample motion re collateral sources and supporting memorandum and a sample response motion opposing the exclusion of collateral source evidence.

§ 15.5 —Liability Insurance

Most courts will deem any mention in the record of a defendant's liability insurance to be highly prejudicial and improper. *Freidl v. Hennard,* 66 A.D.2d 1024, 411 N.Y.S.2d 731 (1978); *Kresel v. Geise,* 231 N.W.2d 780 (N.D. 1975); *Hertz v. Hudson Motor Car Co.,* 8 F.R.D. 431 (D.D.C. 1939). Thus, when representing a defendant, you should guard against any unfair mention or attempt to introduce into evidence the fact either that your client is an insurance company or that your client is insured. Of course, when the insurance company is the named defendant, this particular problem does not present itself.

Notwithstanding the general rule that a mention of the presence of liability insurance is improper and unfair, there are exceptions to this rule. For example, evidence of insurance introduced to show an agency relationship or to show ownership or control quite distinct from any other purpose may be proper. *See, e.g., Leavitt v. Glick Realty Corp.,* 362 Mass. 370, 285 N.E.2d 786 (1972).

However, this technique is clearly susceptible to abuse by plaintiff's counsel, and thus, when representing the defense, you should carefully examine any attempt by the plaintiff's attorney to introduce evidence of insurance supposedly for an appropriate purpose. This is not unlike a situation involving the hearsay rule when a party attempts to introduce evidence which is clearly hearsay but professes that its introduction is for a purpose other than to prove its truth and claims it is not within the ambit of the rule against hearsay.

When counsel representing the plaintiff attempts to introduce evidence of insurance for purposes of showing something else, such as ownership or control, you should carefully point out to the judge that the jurors' ability to distinguish the various purposes of such evidence and to limit its use to proper purposes is a virtual impossibility. As a result, you are being unfairly prejudiced with regard to your ability to properly respond.

The reciprocal of this first rule is the rule that counsel representing a defendant is not able and should not be able to mention that there is no insurance available. *Kresel v. Geise,* 231 N.W.2d 780 (N.D. 1975); *Waid v. Bergschneider,* 94 Ariz. 21, 381 P.2d 568 (1963). From a plaintiff's perspective, this is an unfair tactic, because a jury may be persuaded not to enter a verdict for the plaintiff or to enter a smaller verdict for the plaintiff if they believe that the defendant has little or no means to pay. Once again, this is subject to the general exception that if such evidence is introduced to prove an absence of ownership or absence of control or some other collateral matter, it may be admissible. However, when this happens, the plaintiff should take the same position that defense counsel may take when evidence of existence of insurance is offered—namely, that it is unfair and prejudicial, putting the plaintiff in a position of being unable to respond fairly.

What happens when there has been a mention of insurance, either of its presence by the plaintiff or its absence by the defendant? The key issue is whether such a mention constitutes prejudicial error to the point of requiring a reversal or a mistrial. The cases that have been decided on this point, either within the context of closing argument or otherwise, are very factually oriented. In particular, such remarks were found not to be prejudicial when the jury was instructed to disregard the remark, *Clarke v. Hudson,* 265 Ala. 630, 93 So. 2d 138 (1956), when no objection was made and was thus waived, *Deschaine v. Deschaine,* 148 A.2d 746 (Me. 1958), or when the remark regarding insurance was in response to opposing counsel's improper remark during closing argument, *VanDerlinde v. Wehle,* 274 Minn. 477, 144 N.W.2d 547 (1966). The question then depends on the initial circumstances. However, in order to keep your client from being unfairly prejudiced and to maximize any advantage of such a situation, there are a number of considerations which you should keep in mind at all times:

1. A motion in limine should be filed seeking an order specifically describing the limits of what is proper in terms of both evidence and argument. If your opponent violates this order and introduces evidence of a collateral source nature, you are in an excellent position to seek sanctions and, under appropriate circumstances, a mistrial or reversal.
2. If your opponent introduces improper evidence, the value of a successful objection, even if followed by a cautionary instruction or admonition, is questionable. However, you should most certainly seek such relief, especially the latter. This type of relief reflects on the personal credibility of your opponent and makes further statements suspect.
3. Another avenue of relief to be considered when you have been subject to unfair comments or evidence is to respond in kind. Essentially, this will amount to your being given the opportunity to introduce evidence which would otherwise be unfair and perhaps improper as a curative measure. However, you should not undertake to do this without the assent of the court, or you may find yourself compounding a situation which is already a problem and creating reversible error.

§ 15.6 —Remarriage

Remarriage as a collateral source should be considered within the context of representing the defense in a jurisdiction where awards of punitive damages are not permitted. The position to be taken by the defense is that evidence of actual remarriage is offered only to establish a cutoff date beyond which plaintiffs should not receive damages for loss of society, comfort, and security, all of which are presumably provided by a new spouse. In such a situation, so the argument goes, the two essential objections to admitting evidence of remarriage should not apply.

The first objection, that damages are fixed at the time of death, is really no reason at all, and, in those jurisdictions where awards of punitive damages are prohibited, this approach is in fact punitive. Many things are considered in determining damages. For example, a court usually considers and allows for increases in the deceased's wages over his or her work life expectancy, a concept which is inconsistent with fixing damages at the time of death. If indeed damages were fixed at the time of death, future expectations of the deceased in regard to employment and future wage increases should be ignored. Furthermore, the court also considers such factors as the date of a minor child's majority, always a future event if the child is a minor when the parent dies, in determining when the loss of support should cease. As a practical matter, courts really do not follow the principle that damages are completely fixed at the time of death. In admitting evidence of an actual remarriage only for the purpose of establishing a cutoff date for loss of comfort, society, and companionship, a court does not in any way violate or do injustice to the general rule. A widow's damages are fixed at the time of the husband's death, and the remarriage establishes only a cutoff date.

The second objection associated with the general preclusion of evidence of remarriage is that too much speculation is involved in comparing the future earning abilities of the two husbands. In addition to being unrealistic, this rule is not violated if evidence of actual remarriage is used only to establish a cutoff date for damages for loss of society, comfort, and security. There is no speculation or comparison involved. In fact, such matters as life expectancy, future earnings, habits, and character of the deceased, all of which are in fact considered by the court, are usually much more speculative in nature. It is indeed inconsistent, the argument by the defendant should proceed, that a plaintiff may recover as compensable damages numerous intangible items clearly incapable of being calculated, but the court must close its eyes to a concrete fact which unquestionably affects the damages suffered.

The argument outlined should be presented by a defendant with an eye toward limiting any unfairness visited on his or her client by virtue of the fact that the general rule in a jurisdiction or the prevailing practice may be not to admit any evidence on the subject of remarriage. When representing the plaintiff in the same situation, the position you should take is more in line with the traditional concept that the defendant should not profit from its own negligence and so should not be entitled to limit the damages of plaintiff by introducing evidence of such a collateral source as remarriage.

§ 15.7 —Sample Motions re Collateral Sources

PLAINTIFF'S MOTION TO EXCLUDE EVIDENCE OF PAYMENT FROM COLLATERAL SOURCES

COMES NOW the plaintiff, by undersigned counsel, and moves this Honorable Court for an order excluding any inquiries or the introduction of any evidence relating to payments the plaintiff has received from collateral sources for her personal injuries. The grounds for this motion are set forth more fully in the accompanying memorandum of law.

Pursuant to this Court's Pretrial Conference Order, this motion will be heard on ____________, 19__, at 9:00 A.M.

PLAINTIFF'S MEMORANDUM OF LAW IN SUPPORT OF MOTION TO EXCLUDE EVIDENCE OF PAYMENT FROM COLLATERAL SOURCES

I. Introduction

Plaintiff Lisa Moore submits this memorandum of law in support of her motion for an order excluding any inquiries or the introduction of any evidence relating to payments the plaintiff has received from collateral sources for her personal injuries. Plaintiff moves for an order at this stage because of inquiries made by the defendants during discovery. The defendants' inquiries suggest that they will attempt to prejudice the plaintiff's case by showing the jury that she has already received payments from other sources.

The Court should prevent the defendants from sneaking in through the back door evidence which is clearly inadmissible through the front door. The collateral source rule in Virginia prohibits not only the admission of collateral payments, but mere inquiry which tends to suggest that the plaintiff has received such payments. For this reason, the Court should make it clear before the trial even begins that it will not permit any inquiries which evidence payments from collateral sources.

II. The Collateral Source Rule

It is firmly established in Virginia that damages recoverable for personal injuries caused by the negligence of another are not to be reduced because of compensation received from a collateral source wholly independent of the defendant. *Johnson v. Kellam,* 162 Va. 757, 175 S.E. 634 (1934); *Burks v. Webb,* 199 Va. 296, 99 S.E.2d 629 (1957); 5C Michie's Jurisprudence *Damages* § 49 (1983). More importantly, "[t]he collateral source rule also ordinarily *prohibits inquiry* as to whether the plaintiff has received payments from collateral sources." *Id.* at 111–12 (emphasis supplied). The rule is necessary because "the jury may well reduce the damages based on the amounts that the plaintiff has been shown to have received from collateral sources." *Id.* at 112. Indeed, the danger of prejudice is such that evidence "tending to prove" that the plaintiff has received proceeds from a collateral source "is not admissible." *Burks v. Webb,* 99 S.E.2d at 636.

III. Argument

A. Direct Evidence and Inquiries Relating to Prior Claims and Settlement Agreements Should Be Excluded.

At plaintiff's deposition, the defendants asked her a series of questions regarding amounts she was paid pursuant to demands made against Aviation Aircraft, Inc., W.G. Smith ["the pilot"], and P.B. Open. *See* Deposition of Lisa Moore 6–14, 139, 146–52. Specifically, plaintiff was asked the following questions:

> Q. Now, am I correct in understanding that you received $1,500,000 in settlement from Aviation Aircraft Corporation?

Id. at 146.

> Q. Were you ever told that during the course of the next twenty-five years, you would be paid nine-and-a-half million dollars, in excess of

nine-and-a-half million dollars tax-free [from the pilot's insurance company]?

Id. at 147.

Plaintiff's counsel stated a continuing objection to this line of questioning based on the collateral source rule but provided the defendants with copies of the settlement agreements which showed the amounts paid or to be paid. *Id.* at 9–10, 12, 137–39. Such direct ("front door") questions about collateral payments, while permissible during discovery, should be absolutely prohibited at trial. The Court should enter an order which ensures that no attempts are made to prejudice the plaintiff's case with improper questions about collateral sources.

B. The Court Should Exclude Indirect Evidence and Inquiries Which Tend to Prove That Plaintiff Has Received Payments from Collateral Sources.

During discovery, the defendants also made indirect inquiries which would suggest to a jury that the plaintiff has already received large amounts of money from other sources. For example, the defendants asked the following questions at plaintiff's deposition:

Q. Do you have a pool at your ranch, swimming pool?
Q. How big is the ranch, by the way?

Deposition at 20.

Q. [Do you have] horses on the property?
Q. Are you getting horses?
Q. Does [your husband] have, or do you have any ranch hands or hired help on the property?

Id. at 38.

Q. Incidentally, does [your husband] own the ranch?

Id. at 50.

Q. Did you buy [the ranch] together?

Id. at 51.

Q. Well, did you use half your money and half his money [to buy the ranch]?

Id. at 53.

These types of questions, while not asking directly about collateral payments, "tend to prove" that the plaintiff has received money from collateral sources. *Burks v. Webb,* 99 S.E.2d at 636. These questions are nothing more than an attempt to sneak in through the back door evidence which is inadmissible through the front door. The Court should not permit the defendants improperly to influence the jury through the use of these "back door" questions. The collateral source rule closes both doors and compels an order excluding indirect evidence and inquiries which tend to prove collateral source payments. *Id.*

IV. Conclusion

For the foregoing reasons, plaintiff prays that the Court enter an order excluding any inquiries or the introduction of any evidence relating to payments plaintiff has received from collateral sources for her personal injuries.

ORDER

Upon consideration of the plaintiff's Motion to Exclude Evidence of Payment from Collateral Sources, the Memorandum of Law in support thereof, any opposition thereto, and the arguments of counsel, it is this ______ day of __________, 19__ hereby ORDERED:

(1) Plaintiff's motion is granted;

(2) At trial, defendants shall not directly inquire about matters relating to payments the plaintiff has received from collateral sources for her personal injuries; and

(3) At trial, defendants shall not directly or indirectly inquire about matters which tend to prove that the plaintiff has received payments from collateral sources.

____

Judge

OPPOSITION TO PLAINTIFF'S MOTION TO EXCLUDE EVIDENCE OF PAYMENT FROM COLLATERAL SOURCES

B Resort, Inc. ("B Resort") submits this memorandum in opposition to plaintiff's motion for an order "excluding any inquiries or the introduction of any evidence relating to payments the plaintiff has received from collateral sources for her personal inquiries." Plaintiff's Supporting Memorandum ("Pl. Mem.") 1.

Plaintiff claims that "inquiries made by the defendants during discovery" prompted her motion because those "inquiries suggest that [defendants] will attempt to prejudice the plaintiff's case by showing the jury that she has already received payments from other sources." As an example of these "inquiries," plaintiff cites questions asked at her deposition that relate to the multimillion dollar prior settlement agreements into which she has entered. *Id.* at 3. Plaintiff's motion should be denied because the collateral source rule does not apply to settlement proceeds and the order sought is far too broad since it would preclude the defendants from eliciting testimony that is both probative and admissible.

ARGUMENT

A. Settlement Proceeds Are Not Subject To The Collateral Source Rule.

As plaintiff points out, the collateral source rule applies only to sources of compensation that do not reduce plaintiff's recoverable damages. Pl. mem. at 2 (citing *inter alia Burks v. Webb,* 199 Va. 296, 99 S.E.2d 629 (1957)). The collateral source rule therefore does not apply to the proceeds of a settlement with a joint tortfeasor since a Virginia statute specifically provides that recovery against non-settling tortfeasors *shall be reduced* by such proceeds. *See* Va. Code Ann. § 8.01–35.1(A)(1) ("the Virginia Settlement Statute"). *See also Kossman v. American University,* 546 F.2d 1029 (D.C. Cir. 1976) (collateral source rule does not apply to proceeds of settlement). Plaintiff points to no authority to the contrary.

The admissibility of evidence relating to plaintiff's prior settlements is accordingly governed not by the collateral source rule but by the Virginia settlement statute. That statute simply provides, without elaboration, that "[a] release or covenant not to sue given pursuant to this section shall not be admitted into evidence in the trial of the matter." Va. Code § 8.01–35.1(A)(1). Thus, statutory authority provides only for the exclusion of direct evidence of the prior settlements. There is neither authority nor reason to exclude, as plaintiff argues, indirect evidence of those prior settlements.

It is not surprising that the scope of the exclusionary rule for prior settlements should be narrower than the scope of the collateral source rule for collateral payments. For collateral payments, the substantive law specifically provides a right of double recovery. For settlements, the Virginia settlement statute specifically prohibits double recovery.

B. Even If the Collateral Source Rule Applies, Evidence of Collateral Payments Is Admissible If It Is of Sufficient Probative Value.

As plaintiff explains, the collateral source rule is designed to avoid the prejudice that might result if the jury knew that plaintiff had already been compensated for some of his or her injuries. Pl. mem. at 2. As such, it is a specific instance of the more general rule that "[a]lthough relevant, evidence may be excluded if its probative value is substantially outweighed by the danger of unfair prejudice, confusion of the issues, or misleading the jury." *See* Fed. R. Evid. 403.

By her motion, plaintiff apparently is attempting to preclude defendants from inquiring into highly relevant areas of her personal life that directly relate to her recovery from the accident. Plaintiff has asked the Court to order defendants' counsel not to make inquiry into areas that "would suggest to a jury that the plaintiff has already received large amounts of money from other sources." Pl. mem. at 4. Such an order would be inappropriate in that it would preclude defendants' counsel from eliciting probative, relevant evidence. For example, plaintiff's enjoyment of life is certainly relevant to the plaintiff's claim for $10 million in compensatory damages and may be demonstrated by questions that incidentally indicate material wealth. Even if the collateral source rule applied, plaintiff's remedy in such a situation would not be to exclude the evidence entirely but for a limiting instruction to be issued to the jury. *See, e.g.,* Fed. R. Evid. 105.

CONCLUSION

For the foregoing reasons, B Resort requests that the Court deny plaintiff's Motion to Exclude Evidence of Payment From Collateral Sources.

§ 15.8 Pain and Suffering

One of the most difficult concepts for a plaintiff to prove is pain and suffering. If damages for pain and suffering are recoverable in a wrongful death case (under the controlling law) or in a personal injury case, a plaintiff has the difficult task of getting a concept across to a jury and then attaching a dollar value to that concept. One common approach is the *per diem* approach. Essentially, the per diem approach to proving pain and suffering consists of dividing a period of time into smaller units, for example, dividing years into days, and then assigning a dollar value to each of these units. Because pain and suffering is an intangible item, when you attempt to quantify the period of time into more familiar units, it is sometimes easier to assign a dollar value to smaller units and then simply multiply the smaller unit amount by the applicable period of time. Plaintiffs' attorneys find this method of presenting evidence on pain and suffering particularly helpful.

The per diem approach to proving pain and suffering is somewhat misleading, because it diverts the jury's attention from affixing a dollar value to an element of damages, assuming pain and suffering is an appropriate element for consideration, and focuses attention on a time frame which can be easily quantified. By then assigning a smaller dollar value to that small time frame, and performing a simple multiplication, plaintiff's counsel is able to come up with what is typically a relatively large number.

For example, assume that the life expectancy of the plaintiff in a particular case is 25 years and the plaintiff asserts that pain and suffering as a result of injury will have been incurred each and every day of the plaintiff's life. The argument would simply take 25 years and multiply it out, 365 days for each year, coming up with 9,125 days. Plaintiff's counsel may then argue to the jury: "Ladies and gentlemen of the jury, would you pay $50 per day to be relieved of this pain and suffering? $100 a day?" It is easy to see, then, that the suggestion is being planted in the minds of the jury through the prior evidence that all they need to do is multiply out the number of days by some amount suggested by the attorney or selected by them.

As a general matter, courts do not agree on the propriety of this approach in measuring pain and suffering. *See, e.g., Weeks v. Holsclaw,* 55 N.C. App. 335, 285 S.E.2d 321, *aff'd,* 306 N.C. 655, 295 S.E.2d 596, *reh'g denied,* 307 N.C. 273, 302 S.E.2d 884 (1982); *Felder v. Johnson,* 273 S.C. 479, 257 S.E.2d 714 (1979); *Yates v. Werk,* 363 Mich. 311, 109 N.W.2d 828 (1961). *See also Decicco v. Methodist Hospital,* 74 A.D.2d 593, 424 N.Y.S.2d 524 (1980); *Tjas v. Proctor,* 591 P.2d 438 (Utah 1979); *Calley v. Manicke,* 24 Ill. 2d 390, 182 N.E.2d 206 (1962); *Cox v. Valley Fair Corp.,* 83 N.J. 381, 416 A.2d 809 (1980).

Even when you as defense counsel face such an argument, you should seek an instruction from the court or be permitted to argue yourself that the value determination remains discretionary with the jury and that the suggested value is not evidence itself. This practice has generally been upheld even by those federal and state courts which permit the per diem approach to proving pain and suffering. *Baron Tube Co. v. Transport Insurance Co.,* 365 F.2d 858 (5th Cir. 1966); *Mileski v. Long Island Railroad,* 499 F.2d 1169 (2d Cir. 1974); *Vanschike v. ACF Industries,* 665 F.2d 188 (8th Cir. 1981); *see also Worsley v. Corcelli,* 119 R.I. 260, 377 A.2d 215 (1977); *Thompson v. Kyles,* 48 N.C. App. 422, 269 S.E.2d 231 (1981).

As a general matter, whether you represent the plaintiff or the defendant, use of the per diem approach to proving pain and suffering bears little relevance to whether a jury will enter a large or a small verdict. One possible approach from a defense point of view when such argument is permitted is to point out that the per diem approach to calculating this intangible aspect of damages is overly simplistic and inaccurate. Defense counsel should urge that jurors not be "suckered" into using a shorthand formula for calculating an element of damages but rather should rely on their own good sense in this regard. Although it will be difficult to disabuse them of the notion, even unconsciously, that pain and suffering can be calculated through the per diem technique, by raising the question of a more reasoned approach you should at least be able to get the jury thinking along these lines.

§ 15.9 The "Golden Rule" Approach

One tactic used by some counsel during either the presentation of evidence or closing argument is to have the jurors place themselves in the position of the plaintiff and ask either through an expert witness or during closing argument what members of the jury would like to be awarded if the same tragedy or injury which the plaintiff suffered were to strike them. This is generally known as "the golden rule" approach or argument, and can be summed up in the phrase "do unto others as you would have them do unto you." It is also generally held to be an improper approach to proving or arguing damages. *Chicago, R.I. & Pac. Railroad v. American Airlines, Inc.,* 408 P.2d 789 (Okla. 1965); *Stanley v. Ellegood,* 382 S.W.2d 572 (Ky. 1964); *Estis Trucking Co. v. Hammond,* 387 So. 2d 768 (Ala. 1980).

When representing the defense, you should vehemently object to any attempt to introduce evidence along the lines of the golden rule approach or to make such an argument during the closing argument. Typically, the use of this tactic is considered to be prejudicial and may result in reversible error or mistrial. *Brokopp v. Ford Motor Co.,* 71 Cal. App. 2d 841, 139 Cal. Rptr. 888 (1977); *Insurance Co. of the West v. Dills,* 145 Ga. App. 183, 243 S.E.2d 549 (1978). The failure to object may well result in a waiver. *LeRitilley v. Harris,* 354 So. 2d 1213 (Fla. Dist. Ct. App. 1978); *Brisbee v. Ruppert,* 306 Minn. 39, 235 N.W.2d 364 (1975). Furthermore, you may find that after you have made an objection and had it sustained, the trial judge will issue a cautionary instruction to the jury that they are to disregard the evidence. This may result in denial of any motion for a mistrial or in the cure of any reversible error. *Crump v. Geer Brothers,* 336 So. 2d 1091 (Ala. 1976); *Beaumaster v. Crandall,* 576 P.2d 988 (Alaska 1978).

Finally, in some situations, notwithstanding that improper evidence was received and counsel objected, the verdict itself is found to be reasonable. In one such situation, the improper evidence did not affect the verdict and, as a result, no reversible error occurred. *Phoenix v. Boggs,* 1 Ariz. App. 370, 403 P.2d 305 (1965).

§ 15.10 Housewives

Often the decedent or injured person in a personal injury or wrongful death litigation is or was a housewife. From a plaintiff's perspective, this is certainly not as strong a case from a dollars and cents point of view as a case involving a full-time member of the labor force who is earning a regular weekly income. Calculation of damages in the latter category is rather easy.

From a defendant's perspective, until a few years ago, the economic value of a housewife was at best minimal; in some instances, her value was even considered to fall under the category of "nuisance" value. There are defense counsel who still attempt to take the position that a death or personal injury suffered by a woman who is not a member of the labor force but who is a housewife is of minimal value in terms of damages.

There are two risks associated with defense counsel's taking what is today an unrealistic position. The first is that thinking has changed quite a bit, and most people assume, without having any real dollars-and-cents bases for their assumption, that the work performed by a housewife has monetary value. An attorney who takes the position that a housewife has minimal value runs a risk of alienating the jury.

Perhaps more important is the fact that there are what can be characterized as relatively objective standards for assigning a dollars-and-cents value to the work of a housewife. Such standards are supported by government research, which has concluded that a market cost approach can be applied to this area. The market cost approach assumes that the wage rate for tasks performed in the marketplace can be applied to the same work performed outside the marketplace. Thus, very simply, dollar values can be attached to various tasks performed in the home. Once these dollar values have been attached, it is a simple matter to determine the economic value after certain survey information is compiled. The application of a market cost approach in 1975 by the United States Department of Health, Education and Welfare revealed that the average 1972 value of a housewife was $4,705. Research and Statistics Note No. 9, Economic Value of a Housewife, August 28, 1975, Office of Research and Statistics, Social Security Administration, United States Department of Health, Education and Welfare. The information in this note is still current. Economists using this note utilize current values in order to update the statistics.

There is little doubt that activity in the home performed by housewives accounts for a very large amount of unpaid work. Any attempt by defense counsel to characterize it otherwise is unfair and, quite simply, wrong. Such tactics on the part of defense counsel can quickly be turned around into a powerful weapon against the substantive position being taken by the defense as well as the personal credibility factor associated with counsel.

§ 15.11 Minors and Infants

Issues similar to those discussed in the preceding section arise in cases involving the economic value of a minor or infant. Many personal injury and wrongful death cases involve minors. They have no demonstrated earning capacity, and, thus, the single greatest and perhaps most reliable measure of economic loss suffered is not present. Defense counsel, careful not to incur the wrath of the jury, attempts to minimize the actual economic loss and restrict the jury's consideration to intangible factors such as care, comfort, and affection. This is clearly unfair and deprives the plaintiff of a substantial element and argument on the damages aspect of the case.

It is important that plaintiff's counsel in a personal injury or wrongful death case involving a minor not permit defense counsel to limit in any way the proof regarding damages to intangible factors. Although damages in all instances are controlled by the applicable statutes, the following elements of proof are usually material and should be considered in relation to both the intangibles and any pecuniary loss to be proved:

1. The child's age, sex, intelligence, health, disposition, character, and mental and physical characteristics, as well as any subjective or objective evidence that may relate to the child as a total human being

2. The age, health, and occupations of the parents
3. The age and health of any brothers or sisters
4. The educational background of the parents and any brothers or sisters
5. The nature of the relationship from a qualitative point of view between the minor and the parents or the minor and any brothers or sisters
6. Life expectancy of the minor as well as that of parents, brothers, and sisters
7. Any past contribution of money or services at home by the minor to the parents, brothers, or sisters
8. The probability that any future money or services will be provided to the parents, brothers, or sisters
9. The probability of any future inheritance by the parents, brothers, and sisters
10. Statutory obligations which may exist running toward parents or others
11. Any evidence on the probable career path which the minor might have pursued in life, based on the parents' occupations and education, as well as those of brothers or sisters
12. Any projection of probable earnings of the minor and, on reaching majority, during a projected work expectancy.

The great risk with presenting an argument or evidence for lost earnings on behalf of a minor is that you can do this in such great detail that defense counsel can characterize it as pure speculation. For example, how can the plaintiff assert that a six-year-old child will earn in excess of $2 million over his or her lifetime?

There is a certain amount of validity to this argument, at least so far as appearances are concerned, and, as a result, you must be particularly careful when assigning such values that you do not overstep the bounds of what the jury is willing or able to accept, because you will start out with the jurors on your side, and you do not want to lose them. For an excellent and extensive discussion, *see* Decof, *Damages in Actions for Wrongful Death of Children,* 47 Notre Dame Law. 197 (1971).

From a defense point of view, the best tactic is to acknowledge that there is some value to be assigned in a particular case involving a minor but to contest any speculative assertion that a situation is comparable to that of the member of the labor force on whom there is a proven earnings record or about whom one can make some reasonably probable assumptions.

§ 15.12 Reducing Damages for the Defense

Perhaps the greatest single unfairness visited on defense counsel (at least in their own eyes) in a personal injury or wrongful death case when there is doubtful liability is the fact that damages evidence affects the liability outcome of the case. Many defense counsel, when liability is doubtful, may therefore seek to separate the liability and damages portions of the case by having separate trials. Although on occasion a court may be agreeable and certainly has the power to do so under both federal and state rules of procedure, many judges are not so disposed. Certainly plaintiffs will oppose such requests, especially when evidence of liability is weak and evidence of damages is strong. In these instances, the plaintiff will emphasize damages with the hope of being able to overcome any problems in the liability area.

In this situation, it goes without saying that defense counsel must address the damages issue and cannot simply ignore it. Failure to address it amounts to conceding the issue to the plaintiff and raises more questions in the minds of the jurors than it answers. Indeed, failure to deal with the damages issue either through the presentation of evidence or on closing argument can give away the case.

The sounder tactic is to make some effort to reduce the amount demanded by plaintiff's counsel. This may be done through cross-examination of the plaintiff's witness, offering defense witnesses on the damages issue, or vigorous argument during the summations. Even when you engage in this sort of proof, there is always the unspoken thought that there must be some validity to the damages being sought by the plaintiff, or the defendant would not be so vigorous in arguing against them. How, then, does defense counsel overcome the inherent unfairness with which the system favors the plaintiff in such situations?

The most effective approach is for defense counsel during the closing argument to point out to the jury that a lesser amount of damages should be given only in the event that a verdict is entered in the plaintiff's favor. Thus, there is a conditional statement associated with this line of argument, in that only if damages are to be awarded at all, that is, only if liability is established against the defendant, should a lesser amount than what is being sought be awarded.

The following line of argument can be used in such a situation:

> The fact that I am discussing the plaintiff's damages claim and the amount being sought by the plaintiff is not to be considered any sort of admission of liability on our part. Nor is it meant to be construed by you or presented by me as an acknowledgment that liability has been established or that the plaintiff is entitled to anything. On the contrary, we take the position and have proved through the evidence that the plaintiff is not entitled to

> anything and that there is no liability on the part of my client. However, under our system, the plaintiff is entitled in this trial to introduce evidence on the damage issues. This does not mean that the plaintiff is entitled to anything, just as my presentation of damages evidence and cross-examination of that evidence as presented by the plaintiff is not an acknowledgment of the plaintiff's entitlement. Rather, the purpose of my introducing evidence on the damages issues and discussing the plaintiff's damage claim in my closing argument is its effect on the issue of liability. Indeed, even assuming that the plaintiff is entitled to something, even assuming that the plaintiff has established liability, the amount requested by the plaintiff far exceeds any real injury that he may have suffered.

Following this discussion, you are then in a position as defense counsel to delve into the specifics of the damages element of the case both as presented by the plaintiff and as presented by you. Also, to dispel further the unfairness inherent in the system, an effective responsive tactic by defense counsel is to discuss the damages issues early in the closing argument and close the summation by hitting hard on the absence of liability.

An effective transition between the damages and liability portions of the argument is illustrated by the following:

> I have just discussed in some detail the damages issue as it relates to this case. Not only have I discussed the evidence introduced by the plaintiff, but I have also discussed the evidence which we have introduced both by way of questioning the plaintiff's witnesses as well as through our own witnesses. Remember, I did this not for the purpose of in any way admitting or implying that the plaintiff is entitled to any damages, but rather to show you that the amount sought by the plaintiff under any set of circumstances is unreasonable.
>
> Now let me turn to the question of liability, and let me show you that even if the amount being sought by the plaintiff were reasonable under the evidence introduced in the record, my client here owes the plaintiff nothing. The issue in this case concerns whether the defendant is guilty of negligence and whether, if so, that negligence caused any injury whatsoever to the plaintiff. The evidence presented here has proved that my client is not guilty of any negligence, and, as a result, the plaintiff is entitled to nothing under any construction of the facts.

Although you are not able as defense counsel to completely take the issue of damages out of the case unless the judge goes along with you and orders a separate trial on the issue of damages and liability, you can minimize the inherent unfairness involved in damages being a part of the case. This must be done from the outset of the case and continued through the closing argument to ensure that the jury does not get swept up in the damages aspect of the trial and get carried along through liability.

Another approach to reducing damages is to seek an order lowering the amount of the damage award by the amount of any prior settlement payments. A sample motion regarding such a setoff is contained in § **15.13**.

§ 15.13 —Sample Motion re Setoff

MOTION FOR A DECLARATION THAT ANY DAMAGE AWARD TO PLAINTIFF BE REDUCED BY THE AMOUNT OF PLAINTIFF'S PRIOR SETTLEMENTS

Please take notice that on ____________, 19__, at 9:00 A.M., or as soon thereafter as counsel may be heard, defendant B Resort, Inc., by counsel, will move this court for an order declaring that any damage award to plaintiff resulting from this action should be reduced by the amount of plaintiff's prior settlements of claims arising from the accident that is the subject of this lawsuit.

B Resort makes this motion on the ground that defendants are entitled to such a setoff pursuant to Va. Code Ann. § 8.01–35.1(1). A proposed order and a memorandum of law are submitted herewith in support of this motion.

[PROPOSED] ORDER

Upon consideration of B Resort's motion for a declaration that any damage award to plaintiff in this action will be reduced by the amount of plaintiff's prior settlements, and the oral argument of counsel for all parties:

IT IS ORDERED that B Resort, Inc.'s motion is hereby GRANTED, and that any award of damages to plaintiff resulting from this lawsuit will be reduced by the amount of plaintiff's prior settlements of claims arising from the accident that is the subject of this lawsuit.

Dated: ____________, 19__

____
Judge

MEMORANDUM OF LAW IN SUPPORT OF B RESORT'S MOTION FOR A DECLARATION THAT ANY DAMAGE AWARD TO PLAINTIFF BE REDUCED BY THE AMOUNT OF PLAINTIFF'S PRIOR SETTLEMENTS

B Resort, Inc. ("B Resort") submits this memorandum in support of its motion for a declaration that any damage award to plaintiff resulting from this lawsuit be reduced by the amount of plaintiff's prior settlements of claims arising from the accident that is the subject of this lawsuit.

Evidence in support of this motion is contained in the accompanying Document Supplement to B Resort's Pre-Trial Conference Motions. Citation to that evidence is by tab number in the Document Supplement, cited herein as "Doc. Supp."

1. Prior to bringing this litigation, plaintiff asserted claims against the pilot of the aircraft in which she was injured and the manufacturer of that aircraft. *See* Doc. Supp. Tab 9, at 9–10. (plaintiff's Dep.). Those claims resulted in multimillion dollar settlements that provide for the payment of more than $10 million to plaintiff over her life. Those settlement agreements, as produced by plaintiff, are contained in Tabs 2 through 6 of the Document Supplement. Plaintiff also entered into a settlement agreement with two of the original defendants in this lawsuit that provided for a one time payment of $25,000. *See* Doc. Supp. Tab 1.

2. Va. Code § 8.01–35.1 (the "Virginia Settlement Statute") provides, in relevant part:

> When a release or a covenant not to sue is given in good faith to one of two or more persons liable in tort for the same injury . . .
>
> any amount recovered against the [non-settling] tort-feasors or any one of them *shall be reduced by any amount stipulated by the covenant or the release, or in the amount of the consideration paid for it, whichever is the greater.*

Va. Code § 8.01–35.1(A)(1) (1950, Supp. 1987) (emphasis added).

3. There is no question that plaintiff's prior settlements come within the scope of the Virginia settlement statute. The two releases produced by plaintiff specifically refer to the statute. Doc. Supp. Tab 1 (Release of P.B. Open and B Resort, Inc.) ("The release . . . is made pursuant to the Virginia Code § 8.02–35.1 [sic] . . .") and Doc. Supp. Tab 2 (Release of Aviation Aircraft Co.) ("This Release is made pursuant to Virginia Code § 8.01–35.1 . . ."). Moreover, plaintiff's claims against all of the settling parties were based on the injuries she received from the airplane crash that is the subject of this lawsuit. *See* Doc. Supp. Tab 9, pp. 139–43 (plaintiff's Dep.).

4. Defendants are accordingly entitled to a declaration that any damage award to plaintiff resulting from this lawsuit be reduced by the total amount stipulated in the plaintiff's prior settlement agreements, or the amount of consideration paid for those settlements, whichever is greater.

CHAPTER 16

CLOSING ARGUMENTS AND JURY INSTRUCTIONS

§ 16.1 Introduction

There are two occasions during a trial when you as the lawyer have the spotlight and do not have to share it with anyone. The first is the opening statement, and the second is the closing argument. The obvious difference between the two is that an opening statement is not supposed to contain any argument. However, as any good advocate knows, there is a fine line between stating things and arguing them. Within the context of litigation, this difference often boils down to use of the phrase *the evidence will prove* as distinguished from *the evidence has proved.* In addition, tone of voice frequently makes the difference between an opening statement and a closing argument in that an argumentative tone of voice will raise red flags in the mind of an opponent, while a calm and relatively even tone of voice can often succeed in stating the same words in a nonobjectionable fashion.

There is little question, however, that the closing argument, in that it follows the presentation of the evidence and is supposed to be an argument, provides an opportunity to a litigator to "pound the table" and present the facts and law in an adversarial fashion. Emotion can run high, and, on occasion, lawyers can either lose control of themselves or get carried away with the feelings of the moment. Frequently the tactics used during a closing argument are far more effective as persuasive tools than any others used during trial, because it is during the closing argument that an attorney has the greatest freedom to address the jury in a direct, person-to-person fashion on an emotional ground. Recognizing this fact, it is incumbent on you as an advocate to recognize such tactics, be aware of their potential effect, and be knowledgeable on how to deal with them, because the likelihood of their negatively affecting your case when left unchecked is substantial.

One caveat should be noted, however. Jury studies have shown that jurors, for the most part, make up their minds who will win the case during the opening statements. This is a rather frightening notion, assuming that there is any degree of truth in it, because it means that jurors decide cases at that point in a trial when they know the least about it. In light of this fact, one may ask why a closing argument is important if the jury has for the most part already made up its mind. The answer is probably that, if we all knew what the individual decisions of the jurors were at the point of the opening statement, we probably would not need the closing argument except to keep them in line or change their minds. However, it is this very fact which makes the closing argument so important. The closing argument is your last opportunity to speak to the jurors, and by this point in the trial process you have classified the jurors into those who are decided for you, those who are decided against you, and those who are on the middle line.

Experienced trial lawyers are probably correct in their judgments about jurors a good percentage of the time, and thus their task during closing argument is to reinforce the beliefs and decisions of those who have decided for their case and push those who are undecided over to their side, while at the same time dissuading and converting those who have decided against their case. Thus, no matter when individual jurors make up their minds, it is not until the jurors set foot in the jury room that the lawyers lose all capability of affecting the decisionmaking process. Accordingly, the closing argument is of crucial importance, and any tactic which increases the effectiveness of the closing argument for your opponent has a negative effect on your case.

§ 16.2 Broken Promises

Any experienced litigator knows that an effective closing argument actually commences during the opening statement. In effect, an opening statement amounts to a preview of the evidence or, in many respects, a promise of what the evidence to be introduced by each side will be. During the closing argument, each side has the opportunity to sum up and argue that evidence has been introduced to keep promises made during the opening statement, as discussed in **Chapter 12**.

An extremely effective technique in terms of focusing the jury's attention on the credibility of an attorney is to refer to broken promises along the following lines:

> Ladies and gentlemen of the jury, I told you during the opening statement that what I was making to you was a series of promises. These were promises as to what the evidence to be introduced by my client would prove. I submit, based on the discussion which we have just had about the evidence, that those promises have been kept. I also submit to you that my opponent, who made essentially the same types of promises regarding what his evidence would prove, has, in fact, broken his promises to you. He has not proved what he said he would prove. He has not introduced evidence to support the conclusions for which he argues. He has broken his promises.

Although it may seem to be nothing more than a rhetorical technique, the true effectiveness of this approach is that no one, a member of the jury or anyone else, likes to feel that promises have been made and then broken. There will be a certain amount of resentment about the breaking of promises. Thus, when the argument is presented that you have broken your promises to the jury, the focus is not so much on the merits of the case, but rather on your credibility. Only a naive lawyer believes that juries do not try lawyers as well as cases.

The best tactic in responding to this approach is, in the first instance, to preempt your opponent. Thus, you should be the attorney who argues about broken promises. This will have the effect of putting your opponent rather than you on the defensive. This may not always be possible, especially when you are representing a defendant and the plaintiff has the opportunity to both open first and close first, as well as the opportunity to present a rebuttal. In those instances when, because of the party you are representing, you are unable to preempt your opponent with the broken promise argument, an effective technique for blunting this approach is demonstrated by the following argument:

> Ladies and gentlemen of the jury, my opponent speaks to you about broken promises. He speaks to you about what the evidence will prove. He tells you that he has kept his promise and yet my client has broken his. I know that you are not in any way taken in by these essentially rhetorical techniques, these word games. I know for a fact that you will judge the evidence on its merits and not based upon any attempt by either my opponent or myself to shift your attention through such word games involving questions of broken promises.

In truth, the ploy of broken promises *is* a word game, and, by pointing this out to the jury, you will have the benefit of exposing the tactic for what it is.

Although it is far better to be on the giving end of this particular tactic, you do not always have the luxury of this position, and you must be prepared to deal with it. By refocusing the jury's attention on the facts and away from the rhetoric of your opponent's closing argument, you will typically be able to blunt the impact of such techniques.

§ 16.3 Challenging Your Opponent

Along the same lines as the broken promises argument is the challenge thrown on the table during closing argument. During an opponent's closing argument, you may hear some point made with the follow-up statement, "How does the plaintiff or defendant answer that?" or "Ladies and gentlemen of the jury, I invite you to listen very carefully to my opponents' argument to see what they have to say about that point."

The problem which you run into with this tactic is that if you fail to respond to this spoken challenge, you may well find yourself leaving an unanswered question in the jury's mind not only with respect to the substance of the challenge, but, more importantly, with respect to why you said nothing in response. The jury is then free to reach the conclusion that whatever point is being discussed, your opponent is correct.

By the same token, if you avail yourself of this challenge you are, in effect, meeting on your opponent's battleground and playing by your opponent's rules. The question then becomes one of responding to this particular verbal technique during a closing argument in a way that shifts the focus of attention and turns the tactic around on your opponent. As a practical matter, the only way to respond is, notwithstanding whatever downside risks accompany it, to accept the challenge and respond. Although you may be playing by your opponent's rules in this limited regard, the downside risk of not responding and leaving an unanswered question in the minds of the jurors is far in excess of that associated with responding.

A suggested framework for a response might be:

> During his argument, ladies and gentlemen, my opponent challenged me to answer a question. He asked you to listen very carefully to my answer. Now this is not a game of verbal challenges. This is something far more serious. I know that you will not be distracted by such techniques of lawyers. Such lawyers' tactics. I know, rather, and I am fully confident that you will deal with the facts. However, my opponent raises a good question and indeed, a fair question. He further raises a question to which you

> should have an answer. Unfortunately, my opponent will not like this answer, for the evidence does not support his position.

You will then go on and discuss the evidence. Once again, by taking this approach you will be exposing the verbal tactic for what it is and turning it around on your opponent by making it appear as if your opponent's approach to the case is petty.

The major downside risk of using this tactic, i.e., making the challenge, is that it will be accepted and you will find yourself beaten on your own battlefield. The whole idea is to use the tactic only if you know that you cannot be beaten or to respond to it in a fashion calculated to completely turn it around on your opponent.

§ 16.4 Arguing the Law

As a general matter, it is proper for you or an opponent to comment on the law. *Hardy v. Schirmar,* 163 Cal. 272, 124 P. 993 (1912). What this means is that it is proper to comment on how the law should be applied to the facts and argument of the case. However, it does not mean that you should not object to comments on the law when the judge has not resolved the question of jury instructions. In some cases, prior to commencement of the closing argument, the court will have resolved what jury instructions will be presented, typically in order, to permit the attorneys to comment on the law to be applied. However, even in this situation, when it is proper to comment on the law, there is a tactic which can unfairly prejudice your case.

Assume that your opponent is about to embark on the portion of his or her argument which relates to the law to be applied by the jury when they retire. An argument along these lines might run as follows:

> Ladies and gentlemen of the jury, his Honor will shortly instruct you as to the law to be applied by you to the facts in this case when you reach your decision. I believe his Honor will instruct you along the following lines.

If the jury is not aware that the issue of the law they will be instructed in by the judge has already been resolved by the judge and the parties, it can seem as if the attorney making this kind of argument, i.e., "his Honor will instruct you," is omniscient. Although this has very little substantive effect on the case itself, it has a far greater effect on the credibility of the attorney making the argument. Unless it is pointed out to the jury that the question of the law has already been resolved by the judge and the attorneys together, it can appear as if one of the attorneys has an "inside track" as to what the judge will instruct.

In this situation, you must make sure the jury is aware of the other side of the question. This can be done simply by pointing out to the jury during your argument that there is no magic associated with your commenting on the law. For example:

> Ladies and gentlemen of the jury, counsel and the court have already resolved the question of what jury instructions will be provided to you. These jury instructions are the law which you are to apply in this case to the facts when you deliberate.

An alternative approach is to do exactly the same thing your opponent does, by saying to the jury, "I believe his Honor will instruct . . . ." Either of these approaches can blunt any intimation by your opponent that he or she has some sort of special knowledge as to what the judge will do.

It is not improper for your opponent to comment on the law, but there is more uncertainty on the question of reading the law to the jury during summation, in the same fashion as the attorney might read particular evidence from the record, or perhaps a deposition transcript, to the jury. Although certainly all attorneys desire to clarify and discuss the law and its application to the facts, the holdings of courts generally are that it is improper to read from a case decision or legal treatise to support an interpretation of or to comment on the law. *State v. Maye,* 286 N.W.2d 387 (Iowa 1979); *contra Horne v. State,* 155 Ga. App. 851, 273 S.E.2d 193 (1980).

If your opponent attempts to enhance the credibility of an argument through a verbatim reading of the law, you should object. This goes beyond a comment on the law and attempts to lend some greater air of authority beyond permissible bounds.

§ 16.5 Objections

Just as you have the right to interrupt your opponent's argument to make an objection, your opponent has the right to interrupt you during your closing argument. Both of you have the right to obtain rulings from the court on objections in order to guide your argument. There is probably no area as capable of being abused by attorneys than the making of objections, during closing argument or in some other part of the trial.

Considering that closing argument is counsel's final opportunity to address members of the jury, it remains one of the most effective parts of the trial to capture, shape, and focus the attention of the jurors. Because you are the only performer on stage during your closing argument, it is important to be aware of the problems associated with objections.

When an objection is made, argument in progress is interrupted. More important, the train of thought and concentration of the jury is interrupted, as is any rapport which you may have established with the jury. You should keep in mind several techniques for effectively dealing with objections made by your opponent or to use when you are considering making an objection.

Many objections are made simply to interrupt the flow of an argument or break the rapport established between the jury and you. If you suspect this is the case, there are several possible ways of handling such a tactic. The first is not to do anything while your opponent objects, but let one or two objections go by. The third time, you should make a comment to the court along the following lines:

> Your Honor, I certainly don't begrudge counsel the opportunity to object when there is an improper comment being made. However, you have overruled two of his objections and yet he continues to raise objections. I would submit that he is doing so for the purpose of interrupting my train of thought and any rapport that I may be able to establish with the jury and would further submit that this is an improper purpose for objecting. Counsel will have his opportunity to argue his case and I would respectfully request that he save his objections for proper purposes and not the improper ones for which they have been raised to this point.

The risk which you run is that the judge may view you with some disfavor for having said such a thing in open court. Accordingly, you must carefully establish the ground rules which the judge wishes to follow during closing argument and, in order to keep this very thing from happening to you, i.e., the making of statements by your opponent which may result in your being admonished during your closing argument, the first thing you should be prepared to do when you see your opponent about to make an objection during your closing argument is to go to side bar and seek to have the objection resolved. Thus, you should cut off your opponent's objection after the word *objection* with a request that counsel approach side bar.

This procedure should be determined prior to commencement of the closing argument so that it is understood by both parties.

There is always a downside risk of seeking side bar conferences in that you can be perceived as delaying the proceeding. The same risk is associated with the making of objections in general, although not perhaps to the same extent. The way to handle this particular problem is to make extremely careful judgments about interrupting with an objection of your own, realizing that when you make an objection you highlight what is being said.

Where you feel compelled to request a side bar conference because of an objection made during your closing argument, there is an extremely effective tactic for turning the objection around on your opponent. If you prevail at the side bar conference and have the objection overruled, what you should do when you return to the podium is make a request of the judge to have the court reporter read back your last few remarks so that you can gather up your train of thought. This will usually be permitted. The next thing you should do is repeat exactly what the court reporter just said as a means of getting started again. The effect of this is to make the same statement to the jury three times, first when you originally made it and drew the objection, second when it is read back by the court reporter, and third when you repeat it again. Not only does the jury get to hear the same statement three times, but the jury also gets the clear message that you won on the issue of the objection.

A trickier problem is presented when you lose the objection at side bar. Regardless of the original motivation for having made the objection, whether to break your train of thought or anything else, your opponent runs the risk of incurring the disfavor of the jury when he or she objects. However, having weighed those risks, your opponent may still feel that the possible benefit from breaking your train of thought justifies taking them. If your opponent prevails at side bar and an objection is sustained, you are placed in a somewhat more difficult predicament.

The first thing you should do is fight off any attempt to have a cautionary instruction made to the jury that they should "disregard" a particular statement of yours. As a practical matter it is impossible to unring a bell; however, any such instructions do tend to reflect on your credibility. What you should try to do at side bar is simply to indicate to the judge that you will move along to another topic and not pursue the objectionable line of argument. Whether or not you are able to prevail on this particular point, the thing to do when you return to the podium after a period of delay resulting from the side bar conference is to address the jury with the following words: "Ladies and gentlemen of the jury, as I was saying before the objection . . . ." and then move on to a nonobjectionable area. As a practical matter, because of the delay between the statement which drew the objection and your resumption of your argument, the jury will probably not be able to connect the substance of your argument when it is resumed with the substance of the argument when it was interrupted. You will make it seem as if you are simply picking up the train of your argument and will convey a message to the jury that you won on the issue of the objection. Because appearances are extremely important in this matter, you may actually win in the minds of the jurors.

A technique to consider during closing argument designed to make the presentation of your argument not only smoother but also less likely to be interrupted by your opponent is to suggest to the judge that all objections during closing argument be reserved until the closing argument is complete. As a practical matter, the decision whether or not to object during an opponent's closing argument is one which can be made only with a great deal of difficulty, because an interruption by you during an opponent's closing argument can oftentimes by viewed by the jury in a very unfavorable light. After all, you are lengthening the trial and, as a practical matter, perhaps being viewed as rude. In addition, the fact that you object also can work to your substantive disadvantage; it highlights whatever your opponent is saying and, in the event you lose the objection, the jury is advised of the fact that you have suffered a setback just by virtue of the objection's not being sustained.

The response of some opponents to this particular situation is not only to ask that the court reporter read back the statement to which the objection was made, but then to go ahead and repeat that statement, thereby reiterating to the jury that in fact you lost the objection. This permits your opponent to have the statement which he made to which an objection was lost repeated to the jury three times.

The technique which you should consider using during closing argument is to request of the judge that all objections be reserved, save grievous objections to which the court may sua sponte raise an objection. In this regard and dealing with this procedure, see *Hammill v. United States,* 498 A.2d 551, 555 (D.C. 1985), which upheld the trial judge's imposing a noncontemporaneous objection rule whereby he advised counsel prior to argument that unless "it shocks the court's conscience," there would be no objection on the part of any counsel until after argument. Such a ruling does not, however, lessen or diminish the obligation of the trial judge to assure that counsel's arguments remain within proper balance. *See United States v. Young,* 105 S. Ct. 1038, 1044 (1985).

§ 16.6 Emotional Pleas

There is little doubt that the closing argument is the most emotional part of the trial. Of course, there are emotional moments at various points in personal injury or wrongful death cases, but it is during closing argument when an attorney can pull everything together and literally bring tears to the eyes of the jurors with an argument that is entirely proper. It is during the closing argument that attorneys who are actors at heart can display their talents and do everything they can to persuade jurors who are not inclined to decide for them to change their minds. This is particularly true when you are representing a plaintiff, because the sympathy factor in those situations is enormous. However, as an attorney representing a defendant, you must be aware of the unfair tactics to which your client can be subjected which can have a prejudicial value far beyond the mere words in the statement.

The real problem with emotional arguments is that the curative step is normally a cautionary instruction to the jury to disregard something, even though it is unrealistic to believe that the jurors will ever completely forget what they heard, and no one can determine the extent to which it is a factor in the decisionmaking process. You must be prepared to object in the event that your opponent attempts to address the jury's religious or racial prejudices. Clearly these are improper and unfair tactics which should draw an instruction from the judge as well as an admonition to your opponent. *Fintak v. Catholic Bishop,* 51 Ill. App. 2d 191, 366 N.E.2d 480 (1977); *George v. Travelers' Indemnity Co.,* 81 Mich. App. 106, 265 N.W.2d 59 (1978).

You should also not permit your opponent to indulge in any sort of appeal to social, economic, or political associations of the jurors. In addition, personal attacks on you or on other individuals are not permitted, except as they may relate to credibility; such attacks are also not permitted on corporations. *Cook v. Cox,* 478 S.W.2d 678 (Mo. 1978).

When you are listening to an opponent's argument and making the decision whether to object on the basis that the argument is unfair and improper, there are a number of points or guidelines which you will do well to consider:

1. For what purposes is your opponent making the remark?
2. Does the remark have, objectively speaking, a substantially prejudicial effect on your client?
3. Is the remark made by your opponent supported by the facts, notwithstanding any prejudicial effect it might have?
4. Is the remark relevant and material to the issues in the case?
5. Will you, by objecting, direct more attention to the remark than you would by simply letting it pass?
6. What are the probabilities of an objection being sustained, and if it is sustained, will you be able to get opposing counsel admonished in the hearing of the jury?

As with any aspect of the trial, a risk-benefit analysis is crucial when dealing with emotional pleas made by opposing counsel. It is particularly important in this area because of the potential for adverse effects on your case when undue emotion is injected into a closing argument. Because this is the last opportunity for either counsel to address the jury, emotional and possibly prejudicial remarks must not go without response.

The great risk of a closing argument is that it presents an opportunity in a highly supercharged and emotional atmosphere for an attorney to bring about a mistrial. A recent case demonstrating precisely this problem is *Cole v. Bertsch Vending Co.,* 766 F.2d 327 (7th Cir. 1985). Defense counsel during his closing argument openly asked the jury to feel sympathetic toward his client. There is little question but that such overt pleas playing upon the sympathy of the jury are not permissible, and, despite the fact that they may be waived as grounds for objection if not raised at the time, they are indeed grounds for objection and may well be grounds for a mistrial depending upon the nature of the plea.

The statements in *Cole* were found to be particularly inappropriate, because the defendant had earlier in the trial suffered a heart attack on the witness stand, and the jury could easily have interpreted the remarks of defense counsel as a plea for pity in determining the extent of liability. Fortunately, experience indicates that such emotional pleas are rarely made in circumstances of this type. It would seem as if the comments by defense counsel were, at a minimum, ill advised in light of a situation in which the jury was probably quite susceptible to an emotional plea.

The Seventh Circuit also found that the District Court's order prohibiting any reference to the defendant's consumption of alcoholic beverages immediately prior to the accident was overly broad and restrictive. Although it had been admitted that the defendant was negligent, the evidence of alcohol consumption was still relevant to the defendant's credibility, and such references should have been permitted.

The closing argument is one time when the discretion of the trial judge manifests itself in the broadest possible fashion. *Cole* is an extreme example of a situation in which counsel unwisely made an improper argument in an already emotional surrounding.

When preparing for your closing argument, you would be well advised to "moot court" it before an audience which is able to judge the merits of that argument vis-à-vis its containing objectionable material. Oftentimes you as a trial lawyer are so close to the case that you are unable to make an objective judgment as to whether the argument itself is proper.

In addition to "rehearsing" the argument for maximum spontaneity, you should also subject it to a content review for just this sort of problem. Don't let the emotion of the moment get the better of you and work its way into an otherwise proper closing argument.

§ 16.7 Dos and Don'ts: Comments to the Jury

The closing argument may be the area of trial in which an attorney is given the greatest latitude with respect not only to what is said but also to the manner in which it is said. Nevertheless, there are obvious limitations. It is crucial that you be aware of these so that your opponent does not take unfair advantage of the wider latitude allowed during closing argument.

1. Counsel may comment on the conduct of the parties as long as the comment is factually accurate and relevant to the issues being tried. *Burgdorff v. International Business Machines Corp.*, 74 Ill. App. 3d 158, 392 N.E.2d 183 (1979).

2. Verbal abuse of opposing counsel is not permitted.

   Cross v. Houston B. & T. Railroad, 351 S.W.2d 84 (Tex. Civ. App. 1961); *Community Public Service Co. v. Andrews,* 590 S.W.2d 563 (Tex. Civ. App. 1979) (counsel cannot state that opposing counsel "would do anything to win the case"); *People v. Weller,* 123 Ill. App. 2d 421, 258 N.E.2d 806 (1970) (it is improper to state that opposing counsel could qualify "as an SS trooper").

3. Your opponent may not verbally abuse your client or witness.

   People v. Smith, 52 Ill. App. 2d 583, 367 N.E.2d 756 (1977) (cannot state the witness was lying); *People v. Thomas,* 37 Ill. App. 2d 320, 346 N.E.2d 190 (1976) (cannot call expert witness a "nut").

4. Sarcastic humiliation of counsel's abilities as a trial attorney must be avoided. This is true even if the match-up in talents makes it obvious that one of the attorneys lacks trial abilities. One of the great risks with commenting in this area is that you may find yourself having the jury sympathize and side with the less talented lawyer.

5. The use of swear words or epithets should be avoided.

   Queen City Land Co. v. State, 601 S.W.2d 527 (Tex. Civ. App. 1980).

6. Any suggestion by your opponent that you attempted to suppress the facts is improper.

   Missouri-Kansas-Texas Railroad v. Ridgway, 191 F.2d 363 (8th Cir. 1951).

7. Any comment by your opponent that you failed to call a witness is improper if that witness was unavailable for you to call for testimony.

It may be even more important for you to be aware of what remarks *can* appropriately be made during a closing argument. As a general matter, you should rid yourself of any preconceived notions regarding what may or may not be said during closing argument. As any experienced trial lawyer knows, most courts will deem it improper to say to the jury, "Put yourself in the plaintiff's [or defendant's] shoes." Indeed, any demand or request by counsel that the jury think in a subjective or personal manner, rather than the desired objective and detached manner, is considered to be improper.

However, instead of asking jurors what each would personally feel, think, or believe, it is better to ask a rhetorical question, using an adversarially fair technique couched in terms of a "reasonable person's" beliefs.

A troublesome area during both the opening statement and the closing argument for defendants is how to appeal to the jury to keep an open mind and consider both sides of the question. It is improper to ask the jurors to put themselves in the position of having two conflicting versions of an event put to them by, for example, their children. Obviously, the argument would go, the juror or parent would listen to both sides and not simply accept the version of the facts presented by one of the children.

Since this puts the jurors into the position of having to decide the facts on a personal basis, it will arguably be improper and unfair. The most effective approach is to ask jurors how a reasonable parent would respond when confronted by two differing versions of a set of facts. Would the parent simply accept one version without listening to the other? Surely not. The reasonable parent or reasonable person would listen to both children's versions of the facts and then make a decision based on what each had to say regarding what occurred. The argument continues, a reasonable juror or trier of fact should do no less and should listen and consider both sides of the argument and the facts before making a decision.

In addition to the listed comments which are improper and unfair, it is also improper for your opponent to refer to the jurors by name. Furthermore, it is improper to speak about the wealth or poverty of the parties.

The question of how to respond to these unfair tactics is perhaps more important than the tactics themselves. No discussion of dos and don'ts can be complete without addressing this area. Do you have an opportunity to retaliate by making similarly improper comments? As a general matter you should not try to retaliate with highly improper remarks, whatever the conduct of your opponent. You may find yourself running into the same trouble which your opponent had with the judge. However, where your comments are on point and relevant, most courts will permit you to make unfair retaliatory comments. Typically, such comments would be in the nature of an explanation and can be viewed as a balancing of the scales. For example, if your opponent explains why a witness or party failed to take the stand, then you should be given an opportunity to give your version of the reason even if, under other circumstances, your remarks would have been characterized as unfair and prejudicial, had the initial argument not been made.

You must consider whether responsive comments made by you tend to highlight the unfair comments made by your opponent to your detriment. The countervailing consideration is whether to simply let the comments go unresponded to and, with luck, deemphasized. The risk with this course of action is that you do not know what use the jurors will make of the unfair comments in their overall deliberative process.

The scope of permissible conduct and comment during closing argument is shown by the following cases which focus upon the kinds of comment by counsel which may be appropriate or inappropriate depending upon the given circumstances.

First Circuit. After conviction, the appellate court stated that the prosecutor's closing argument was improper when, upon the defendant's failure to testify, the prosecutor stated the burden of proof shifted to the defendant and implied that the governmental evidence was uncontradicted. This error, however, was a harmless error. *United States v. Skandier,* 758 F.2d 43 (1st Cir. 1985).

Fourth Circuit. It was not reversible error for the prosecutor to argue that F.B.I. agents were "agents of the people" and that if the jury did not believe in the agents, the jury should "cut the defendant loose." The prosecutor was not improperly vouching for the credibility of his witnesses, and, in any event, the comments would have been permissible rebuttal to a defense argument that the government had presented a "half-baked case" and that the testimony of the F.B.I. agents was "inaccurate and not complete." *United States v. Silva,* 745 F.2d 840 (4th Cir. 1984), *cert. denied,* 470 U.S. 1031 (1985).

In closing argument in *United States v. Samad,* 754 F.2d 1091 (4th Cir. 1984), defense counsel argued that an F.B.I. agent's affidavit was inconsistent with the trial testimony and therefore urged the jury not to believe the F.B.I. agent's testimony. In rebuttal, the prosecutor, after referring to the defense counsel's comments regarding the F.B.I. agent's affidavit, stated, "Well, I'll tell you something, I'm the one that wrote that affidavit." The appellate court upheld the conviction but stated that, although the prosecutor's overzealous attempt in closing argument to bolster his own witness was clearly improper and should have been subject to a curative instruction by the trial court, the remarks did not constitute reversible error, because they tended only to support evidence which favored the defendant.

Fifth Circuit. The court in *United States v. Saenz,* 747 F.2d 930, *reh'g denied,* 752 F.2d 646 (5th Cir. 1985), upheld a conviction, notwithstanding a barrage of comments exchanged by defense and prosecution counsel. The court stated that the alleged improper prosecutorial comments had to be considered in context when determining their propriety and that a prosecutor may respond to improper arguments by defense counsel. The prosecutor's statement that the defense lawyers were better attorneys and that, if it were a contest between lawyers, the prosecutor would lose, was proper response to defense counsel's statement that the prosecutor was a good lawyer who was going to tell the jury many things about defendants and defense counsel. The prosecutor's statement that defendants had 10 attorneys in the courtroom, though improper, did not mandate reversal, because the jury was aware that there were a number of defense lawyers in the courtroom and the statement was a fair response to defense counsel's argument that the prosecutor had all the resources of the F.B.I. and the Texas Rangers at his disposal.

The prosecutor's statements vouching for his witnesses and asserting their bravery was fair response to defense counsel's argument that the government's witnesses were coached, programmed, and intimidated. The prosecutor's statement suggesting that defense counsel was attempting to confuse the jurors and keep the truth from them by objecting to evidence did not amount to reversible error, because defense counsel had accused the prosecutor of hiding evidence. The prosecutor's statement suggesting that he only prosecuted the guilty did not amount to reversible error, because the defense had directly attacked the prosecutor's integrity in maintaining the prosecution and accused the prosecutor of abusing the system.

On an appeal from a conviction in *United States v. Eiland,* 741 F.2d 738 (5th Cir. 1984), the court stated that, although it is reversible error for a prosecutor to comment on a defendant's silence, the particular statement made by the prosecutor could not naturally or necessarily be construed as a statement on the defendant's silence. However, the court's failure to charge the jury against drawing adverse inferences from the defendant's failure to testify after a proper objection could not be dismissed as a technical error; therefore, the conviction was overturned.

A state prisoner in *Richardson v. Lucas,* 741 F.2d 753 (5th Cir. 1984), was convicted of burglary after he refused the assistance of public defenders and made "a voluntary waiver of right to counsel." The appellate court stated that a refusal to give a requested "failure to testify" instruction can be harmless error, and, in the instant action, it was harmless beyond a reasonable doubt.

In *Matteson v. King,* 751 F.2d 1432 (5th Cir. 1985), a prosecutor's reference to the victim's head having been blown off and in the ceiling did not render a trial unfair, according to the appellate court. Although the prosecutor acted improperly in suggesting to the jury that it should find the petitioner guilty of first degree murder so that the death penalty could be imposed, the court found that any prejudice which resulted, when viewed in context of the entire trial, was not so egregious as to violate the Constitution and require reversal of the conviction.

Defendant police officers were convicted of denying civil rights of persons arrested and confined in county jail in *United States v. Garza,* 754 F.2d 1202 (5th Cir. 1985). The convictions were affirmed despite prosecutor's remark regarding a defendant's prior conviction, which was never proved.

The defendant in *United States v. Perez-Leon,* 757 F.2d 866 (7th Cir. 1985), was convicted of conspiracy to possess with intent to distribute cocaine. The defendant had used an entrapment defense. In summation, the defense counsel stated that the prosecution could give evidence of prior drug dealing after the prosecutor's objection misstated the law. The court held that, in view of the prohibition placed on the prosecution not to question the defendant about his prior arrests, the objection was proper and that defense counsel properly stated the law only after the prosecutorial objection.

Illinois. The defendant in *People v. Eckhardt,* 465 N.E.2d 107 (Ill. App. Ct. 1984), was convicted of murder, despite her claim of innocence by reason of insanity. The prosecutor in his rebuttal closing argument stated that the insanity defense requires proof of uncontrollable behavior as a continuing condition. The state law defines insanity merely as a person who lacks substantial capacity to appreciate the criminality of his conduct or to conform his conduct to the requirements of law. The appellate court found that the misstatement of law was grounds for reversal because in effect it distorted the burden of proof by suggesting incorrectly what the jury must find in order to determine that the defendant was insane.

In *People v. Estes,* 469 N.E.2d 275 (Ill. 1984), the defendant was convicted of voluntary manslaughter. On appeal, the conviction was reversed. The prosecutor's statement to the jury during closing argument that the defendant's prior experiences with the victim, including her broken tailbone and being threatened with a gun, did not "count," because evidence of both the violent disposition of the victim and threats directed at the defendant by the victim had probative value in establishing that the defendant reasonably believed that the use of force likely to cause death or great bodily harm was necessary to prevent the killing or inflicting of great harm upon the defendant. The prosecutor's suggestion to the jury during closing arguments that to find defendant had acted legally in self-defense would be equivalent to morally condoning her shooting of her husband was clearly prejudicial and outside the bounds of fair comment.

After a conviction of murder, the appellate court found that the defendant in *People v. Reese,* 105 Ill. 2d 275, 460 N.E.2d 446 (1984), was not substantially prejudiced by the prosecutor's reference in closing argument to evidence not admitted at trial, to the murder victim's two children, and to the nature of reasonable doubt standard when evidence establishing the defendant's guilt was overwhelming. The trial court properly charged jury and sustained defendant's counsel's objections to improper closing argument.

The defendant in *People v. Holman,* 103 Ill. 2d 133, 469 N.E.2d 119 (1984), was convicted of armed murder, aggravated kidnapping, burglary, and other offenses and was sentenced to death. The appellate court found that numerous comments by the prosecutor in closing and rebuttal arguments in the sentencing phase of the capital case were improper. The court found that the prosecutor's statement during closing argument highlighting the possibility that the defendant would kill again if he were not executed, even if supported by the evidence, was speculative and so prejudicial as to outweigh its probative value and had no function other than to appeal to the passions and fears of the jury. The prosecutor also commented on legal concepts, such as self-defense and voluntary manslaughter, which were not involved in the case, so as to give the jury the idea that the death penalty was proper in all cases except those which constituted voluntary manslaughter, and suggested that the jury had the same right to use deadly force against the defendant that an individual has against a person who threatens imminent bodily harm to him or to another. The prosecutor also made references to various studies and public opinion polls concerning the death penalty, all of which the court found to be improper.

The court found that the numerous comments by the prosecutor which suggested that the prosecutor had reliable information outside the record which proved his assertions were clearly likely to elicit an emotional response and went far beyond what the defense invited and further distracted the jury from giving the case the individualized consideration essential in all death cases. Even though the defendant had not objected to the comments at trial, the closing argument by the prosecutor mandated a remand for sentencing.

The following comments were not found to be so prejudicial as to warrant reversal: the mentioning of a murder victim's family, *People v. Cunningham,* 473 N.E.2d 506 (Ill. 1984); that the victim of a prior murder perpetrated by the defendant was survived by spouse and child and the defendant served only eight years for the previous murder conviction, *People v. DelVecchio,* 105 Ill. 2d 414, 475 N.E.2d 840 (1985); that the previous conviction of the defendant was substantial proof that defendant was familiar with the legal system, *People v. Simpson,* 473 N.E.2d 350 (Ill. 1984); calling the defendant a liar, *People v. Wilson,* 463 N.E.2d 890 (Ill. 1984); characterizing the defendant as "an animal," *People v. Kashney,* 472 N.E.2d 164 (Ill. App. Ct. 1984); attacks on defense counsel accusing counsel of distorting evidence, referring to counsel as a "high-priced lawyer" hired to get the defendant off, and that statements in counsel's arguments were something he presented "in every murder that he defends in this building," *People v. Howard,* 460 N.E.2d 432 (Ill. 1984); referring to the defense as a "smoke screen," "veil of smoke," and "smoke bomb" together with reference to the defendant as a "leech on the street," *People v. Williams,* 468 N.E.2d 807 (Ill. App. Ct. 1984).

However, it seems that when *all* of these things are put into one case, reversal might be warranted. A conviction of murder was overturned in *People v. Ray,* 467 N.E.2d 1078 (Ill. 1984), despite an eyewitness's testimony which established the defendant's guilt, because of prosecutorial misconduct. The prosecutor repeatedly attacked the professional integrity of the defense counsel, charged defense counsel with lying and misstating applicable law, and commented on the defendant's failure to testify. The prosecutor also intimated existence of favorable state's evidence inadmissible at trial because of the defendant's objections, suggested witnesses were afraid to testify because the defendant had threatened or intimidated them, improperly intimated that the defendant had prior criminal history, and suggested that the defendant was manipulating his constitutional rights to escape conviction.

New York. It was error to permit plaintiff's counsel to argue to the jury that he took the case only because he believed the plaintiff was an honest woman. *Kritz v. Manufacturers Hanover Trust Co.,* 33 A.D.2d 753, 305 N.Y.S.2d 887 (1969).

The prosecutor's misconduct during summation was deemed error and convictions were reversed in *People v. Grice,* 100 A.D.2d 914 (N.Y. 1974). During summation the prosecutor argued the facts not in evidence, expressed personal belief in defendant's guilt, mischaracterized and denigrated the defense counsel, appealed to jurors' emotions, and vouched for the credibility of state witnesses. *See also People v. Simmons,* 100 A.D.2d 497 (N.Y. 1984).

Portraying the defendant as a middle-level drug dealer was highly prejudicial to the defendant's case and deprived him of a fair trial by shifting the jury's focus away from the primary issue of the case, i.e., whether or not the defendant sold $100.00 worth of cocaine to an undercover officer, in *People v. Ortiz,* 99 A.D.2d 497, 470 N.Y.S.2d 445 (1984).

In an action for false imprisonment and malicious prosecution, *Pascavige v. City of Cohoes,* 95 A.D.2d 969, 414 N.Y.S.2d 306 (1983), a defendant's verdict resulted. The appellate court upheld the verdict, stating that the defendant's summation was so prejudicial as to require reversal. The defense counsel had stated that "as to damages, that money will come from taxpayers' money, and it is not a proper use of taxpayers' money."

§ 16.8 Rebuttal and Waiver

In a civil case in which the plaintiff has the burden of proof, the plaintiff is said to have the right to open and close during the closing argument phase of litigation. Essentially this just means that the plaintiff has the right to make closing argument first, followed by the defense closing argument, followed by the plaintiff's rebuttal. When representing the defense, you must be aware of weaknesses in your case so you can anticipate and deal with them during your argument-in-chief; you will not have any further opportunity to address the jury, even though the plaintiff has the right to make a rebuttal. Thus, in some ways, the plaintiff has an unfair advantage built into the system.

You should remember a number of points, including the fact that a rebuttal argument is not necessarily a matter of right. *Varella v. State,* 561 S.W.2d 186 (Tex. Crim. App. 1978). Because the rebuttal argument is to be directed at the comments of defense counsel and may not be used to restate the plaintiff's case or to state things which were not presented in the plaintiff's argument-in-chief, plaintiff's counsel has no right to use rebuttal argument as the primary vehicle for presenting a summation to the jury. Thus, when you confront a rebuttal argument which has become a primary vehicle, as opposed to simply a responsive vehicle, you should object that plaintiff's counsel has attempted to take unfair advantage of what is already an unfair situation.

An interesting situation arises when you as a defense lawyer waive a closing argument. Although I do not recommend this as a general practice, there are certainly times when you may consider waiving your closing argument. In that event, is your opponent entitled to any rebuttal at all? This can be crucial when the plaintiff has obviously reserved a large segment of the argument-in-chief for rebuttal, certain that it will be responsive to your closing argument. If you waive a closing argument, the position to be taken by you as defense counsel is that no rebuttal argument is proper, because rebuttal is only for purposes of response to your argument-in-chief, and if there is no such argument, there can be no response.

You should also note that a waiver should not reflect on the merits of the case and should not be treated as any concession to the plaintiff. Indeed, you might consider requesting that the judge instruct the jury along these lines.

Another tactic which you may on occasion run into is a request by the plaintiff to split closing argument between liability and damages. This may be done for several reasons, including the fact that the plaintiff may want more time and may, along with the request to split the argument, also request that equal amounts of time be allotted to arguments on liability and damages. From a defense perspective, this request is to be opposed, because it gives the plaintiff an unfair advantage which is not present in the normal closing argument situation. A plaintiff must argue both liability and damages and thus has a much heavier burden in terms of allocating time among the various aspects of the case which must be presented to the jury. A plaintiff will often lean more heavily toward arguing damages, because it is in the damages area that emotional and sympathy factors can be used to shore up what might otherwise be a weaker argument on liability. However, if the plaintiff is given separate chances to argue liability and damages and an equal amount of time to argue each, the tactical judgments which must be made by the plaintiff regarding allocation of time are no longer necessary, and the plaintiff has an unfair advantage. Such requests should be opposed by you as defense counsel on the grounds that any such allocation is unwarranted.

§ 16.9 Time Allowed and Number of Attorneys

As a general matter, the time to be allotted to closing argument falls within the discretion of the court. Among the specific factors which a judge will consider may be the length of the trial, the complexity of the issues, the amount of evidence which has been presented, and the number of witnesses who testified.

As a general rule, a decision to limit closing argument or, for that matter, to allow a longer period of time for closing argument will rarely, if ever, be reversed. To obtain a reversal, you must be able to demonstrate that the limitation or grant of time had such a prejudicial effect on your case that the case would have had a different result had the court not acted as it did.

As discussed in **§ 16.8**, your best strategy as a defense lawyer is to urge the court to limit the length of closing arguments. The reason for this is that your opponent representing the plaintiff must argue both liability and damages and thus has a far harder time dealing with a limited amount of time in which to present a summation. When plaintiff's counsel argues for additional time or to split the argument allocating an equal amount of time to each portion, you should, as defense counsel, argue against such a proposition. Similarly, when representing a plaintiff, you should argue against any attempt by defense counsel to unfairly prejudice your case by limiting the time available.

Plaintiff's counsel may encounter the tactic of being forced to oppose, in the presence of the jury, an attempt to limit time for closing argument or to seek extra time for closing argument based on the need to argue both liability and damages. Any such argument in the presence of the jury can lead jurors to believe that plaintiff's counsel needs additional time to compensate for a weak case. Such arguments should be made outside the presence of the jury, and any attempt by defense counsel to do otherwise is improper.

Another tactic sometimes used to increase the amount of time which a particular side has for purposes of presenting a closing argument is to have multiple attorneys argue the case, even though, as a general matter, the amount of time available for closing argument has no relationship to the number of counsel which the court may permit to engage in closing argument. One must always seek permission from the court to have more than one attorney argue on behalf of a particular side. Limitation of the number of attorneys who can argue for either side is typically committed to the court's discretion. *Mikchel v. State,* 164 Tex. Civ. App. 303, 298 S.W.2d 829 (1957); *Moldovan v. Allis-Chalmers Manufacturing Co.,* 83 Mich. App. 373, 268 N.W.2d 656 (1978).

On occasion, you may find an opponent who requests permission to have more than one attorney argue a particular case during summation. The proposed breakdown of this argument typically is along fact issue lines with respect to liability or, more likely, liability and damages.

Although there is nothing inherently wrong with such a division of labor from an advocate's point of view, it is not usually a very good idea to have any splitting of argument, because you end up interrupting the flow of your case as it is being presented and probably breaking the jury's concentration. Therefore, if your opponent seeks to split his or her argument, it is usually a sound idea to permit such a splitting.

When your opponent attempts to split an argument among multiple counsel, there is one potentially unfair tactic which you must guard against. Although theoretically a division of argument among multiple counsel should not result in any greater time for the total presentation of the argument, your opponents may either use more time or actually request more time on the grounds that there is more than one attorney involved. Any request for additional time should be vigorously opposed, because the decision to split an argument was made by counsel and there is no reason for the court to grant additional time. Furthermore, you should, prior to commencement of your opponent's closing argument, make it clear through the court that no greater amount of time is to be permitted and impose that requirement by objection during the argument if in fact counsel exceeds the allowed time. An objection on this point is problematical; all the risks associated with making an objection during a closing argument, including possible alienation of the jury, are present in this situation. However, you should at least be able to count on the fact that the judge will give you an equal amount of time when your opponent has exceeded the permissible time.

Another problem associated with multiple attorneys arguing for one side is repetition. Although counsel may indicate that they will not be repetitive, they may in fact go ahead and be repetitive. Alternatively, they may indicate that for the sake of "foundation and continuity" they will be repetitive, but only very briefly.

Any attempt by your opponent to repeat the closing argument under any guise, as foundation or otherwise, should be resisted. Remember, all your opponent is doing when he or she repeats an argument is hammering a point home to the jury and having an opportunity through a second attorney to make the same point. Although certainly counsel may be redundant during a closing argument, that same redundancy is not proper when an argument has been split, because the very idea of splitting an argument is that the break point is natural, either issue-oriented or liability-versus-damages-oriented.

§ 16.10 Getting into the Jury Room

The closing argument or summation is your last opportunity to address the jury—your last chance to win over those who are intending to decide the case against your client. However, there is a way to enter the jury room during the deliberations by proxy and ensure that your position is clearly and persuasively before the jury while they deliberate, while at the same time minimizing the chance that they may misconstrue or misinterpret some piece of evidence. This is through the use of demonstrative evidence as discussed in **Chapter 14**, namely, processed evidence.

A good example of processed evidence would be to take a bank check which may be direct evidence in the case and blow it up to 30 inches by 40 inches. You might take that bank check and the financial transaction which it represents and use a flow chart to present the same information. In either event, what you have done is to *process* the direct evidence of the bank check which may be received into evidence with minimal foundation. As far as admissibility is concerned, you are resting almost entirely on the discretion of the court.

As with any other kind of evidence, demonstrative evidence of this type may be used during closing argument if and only if it refers to or is made up of things which have already been accepted into evidence during the course of the trial. This is a matter of common sense; obviously, evidence of any sort used during closing argument for the very first time is not susceptible to cross-examination and is being used during a portion of the case which itself is not evidence.

Although there is nothing wrong with using demonstrative evidence during the closing argument, there are techniques and tactics for its use which have the potential for unfairly prejudicing your case when used by your opponent.

Demonstrative evidence properly used during closing argument can give you or your opponent a tactical advantage in that each juror enters the jury room with a mental and visual impression of the key points of the argument presented. However, careful consideration must be given to the use of demonstrative evidence, inasmuch as its improper use not only can have negative effects on your case but, perhaps more important, can also have positive effects on your opponent's case.

When an individual reads something at the same time when the very same message is delivered orally, it is retained for a much longer period of time and comprehended to a much fuller extent than when that individual is either told something or shown something. For example, television is a most effective means of communicating information which you wish people to act upon, because the viewer both sees and hears the message. In the litigation situation, demonstrating as well as stating the evidence has special applicability in the area of closing argument, because immediately following the closing argument, the jury will retire to the jury room. Thus, the jury upon retiring will have just been exposed to the most effective means of communicating persuasive information to them, and they will undertake the deliberation process when that information and message is freshest in their minds.

§ 16.11 —Creating Demonstrative Evidence

All the techniques of demonstrative evidence are potentially available to you and your opponent during a closing argument. However, there is one technique in particular with the potential for being abused and used in an unfair fashion—the creation of demonstrative evidence during the closing argument that has not, prior to that time, been used in the trial. Assume you are dealing with a case involving allegations of negligence against your client arising from a slip and fall on your client's premises. The plaintiff has previously testified as to what occurred. In addition, there was testimony from the plaintiff's mother as to what occurred and from a witness who arrived on the scene just a few seconds after the alleged slip and fall took place.

Your client is the owner of the supermarket involved. In addition to the testimony being offered by your client, there are two additional witnesses who testified as part of your case. The first of these witnesses stated that she cleaned the floor in the area of the alleged fall within 30 minutes prior to the incident, and the second testified that he saw the plaintiff fall outside the store on city property within a few minutes after the alleged fall was supposed to have occurred.

The testimony of all of these witnesses during trial was offered orally. While some of them used a floor plan of the store, none of them prepared any charts, graphs, or diagrams, nor did any of them use written statements.

In lieu of using notes during his closing argument, your opponent presents two large sheets of paper which appear as indicated in **Illustration 16-1**.

Illustration 16-1

PLAINTIFF'S EVIDENCE

1. Plaintiff
2. Plaintiff's mother
3. Witness who arrived after incident

DEFENDANT'S EVIDENCE

1. Defendant
2. Witness who cleaned floor before incident
3. Witness who saw plaintiff fall outside store

The manner in which your opponent incorporates these demonstrative aids into his closing argument is as follows:

> Let me turn to an examination of the evidence at this point, ladies and gentlemen of the jury. In order to better assist you in being able to not only review and deliberate regarding the evidence but to organize it as well, I have taken the liberty of listing the witnesses on these large sheets of paper. The first sheet which you are looking at right now contains a list of the witnesses who appeared on behalf of the defendant. Let's talk about each one of these witnesses and the merits of the testimony presented by them. [At this point counsel would discuss each of the defendant's witnesses in a fashion which minimizes their testimony, rebuts their testimony, etc.] Now let's turn to the witnesses who appeared here on behalf of Mary. [The sheet is taken down, changed, and the list of plaintiff's witnesses is shown.] Let's talk about the testimony of each of these witnesses and let's see what really happened, what the defendant would have you believe occurred.
>
> [At this point counsel would discuss the plaintiff's evidence.]

This is an extremely effective technique for several reasons. First, the jurors are given an outline of how to organize the evidence. What they do not realize is that the attorney has, not so subtly, organized the evidence in a manner which is more advantageous for his case. Second, there has been a selective presentation of the evidence, once again along the lines the attorney wishes. Third, counsel is taking advantage of the fact that the jurors will remember things they see and read for themselves better than things which are simply told to them. Since an oral argument is being presented to them at the same time they are reading these things, their level of comprehension and retention immediately before they retire to the jury room to deliberate will be at its peak. Finally, counsel is relieved of the need to use notes, because the notes are contained on the chart in full view of the jury.

The impact of this technique is considerable. It is unfair in capitalizing on a number of different advantages, as discussed, and it does so at a time when it is most important to be able to get yourself into the minds of the jurors.

§ 16.12 —Defensive Tactics

There are limited ways to combat the technique described in **§ 16.11** and either blunt its effectiveness or turn it into a weapon for your case. The most obvious way is to do it yourself and preempt your opponent's ability to do it. This is not always possible, because, if your opponent is representing the plaintiff, you may find yourself second in time in terms of presenting the argument and thus not capable of using this technique to your advantage.

The next possibility is an objection to the use of "evidence" which has not been presented at any earlier time during the trial. Although this should certainly be attempted, you should be prepared for it to be overruled, because charts of this type can probably be characterized as nothing more than a written version of the oral argument and a compilation of evidence which is in the record as distinguished from the creation of new evidence or introduction of evidence not received into the record earlier.

Finally, the third line of defense is to turn this technique to your own advantage by considering the advisability of using your opponent's chart to prove your point. Remember, as a general rule, cases are not won on the direct examination or presentation of witnesses on your behalf. Juries expect witnesses for a particular side to favor that side. Practically speaking, cases can only be lost on direct examination by one of your witnesses not coming across well. On the other hand, cases are often won on cross-examination of the other side's witnesses.

The same concept is true in closing argument. If you are able to take your opponent's argument or, in this case, your opponent's exhibits, and successfully turn them against your opponent, you will have a far more powerful weapon than the one used by your opponent in the first instance.

As a practical matter, within the context of outline charts, one approach which might be used is illustrated by the following argument:

> Ladies and gentlemen of the jury, during his closing argument my opponent used two charts in order to outline the evidence which he indicated supported his case and his argument that you should decide the case in favor of his client. Let's examine those charts and see what they really say as distinguished from what the plaintiff would like them to say. [At this point the charts should be taken out or replaced in view of the jury and used as a prop to support your own argument.]
>
> Now, it's been said that statistics lie or numbers can be made to say anything which the person using those numbers would like them to say. I guess what this really means is that somebody who is creative with numbers can make them say or support virtually anything. I think that we have just seen how the facts of this case as illustrated by these charts actually support your deciding for John Smith in this case and not for the plaintiff as my opponent would have you do and would argue in favor of.
>
> I suppose that you can take any set of facts and argue that they support a particular conclusion regardless of whether they may actually support that conclusion. The fact that you may put those arguments or facts up on a blackboard or on a chart as was done here lends no greater validity to those conclusions and lends no greater support to those facts. Rather, it's merely a tactic or technique that is used to shift the attention of the audience from

> the true import of what is being said and what is meant by the facts being presented.
>
> I submit to you that there is little doubt based upon the plaintiff's own exhibits that there is one decision to be reached in this case and that is in favor of the defendant.

The exact nature of the argument to be presented is virtually totally dependent on the facts and circumstances of the individual case. However, any creative advocate can fashion an argument which turns on the points raised by an opponent with the props used to support the advocate's own argument as distinguished from that of the opponent. The example just given is but one avenue of approach; it walks a fine line between attacking the approach taken by counsel personally and focusing on the merits of the case.

§ 16.13 "Your Recollection Controls"

In most cases, the judge will instruct the jurors that it is *their* recollection of the evidence, and not the recollection of counsel or the court, that controls. Your task as an advocate is to ensure that the jury's recollection of the evidence is consistent with your recollection, and that your recollection supports your conclusions.

In many cases, it is advantageous to use certain testimony during your closing argument which is favorable to your case. When you make the decision to incorporate a specific part of a witness's testimony into your closing argument for purposes of greater credibility, you should immediately make arrangements with the court reporter to have that particular testimony transcribed.

Once you have the testimony in hand you may then present an argument along the following lines:

> Ladies and gentlemen of the jury, his Honor will shortly instruct you that in your consideration of the evidence, it is your recollection of that evidence which controls. It is not my recollection or the way I relate the evidence to you. It is not even his Honor's recollection. Rather it is your recollection. Now this has been a rather long trial and we have both presented as attorneys, and you have heard as jurors, a number of witnesses on a number of different subjects. In addition, you have also had presented to you and seen a number of documentary exhibits. On balance, the amount of information which has been presented to you has been substantial.
>
> Now you may recall that we heard from [insert name of witness] during the trial and that he testified on the general subject of [insert general subject]. Now, as the trial progressed and as various testimony and evidence were presented, I attempted to make careful notes in order that I would be in

> a position to better aid you during this closing argument with understanding not only the evidence but the conclusions which the evidence should lead you to reach. These notes have included careful notes of what [insert name of witness] said because of the importance of his testimony on the issues which you must decide.
>
> However, my memory and my ability to take notes is sometimes just not able to keep pace with the speed with which events unfold in the courtroom. This does not mean by any stretch of the imagination that what I am saying to you is any way inaccurate, but rather I don't have the ability, just as a matter of mechanical speed, to take down in shorthand precisely what everyone says while at the same time participating in what is going on in the courtroom. As a result of this fact, I asked that the testimony of [insert name of witness] be transcribed and prepared in this little booklet by the court reporter. Now this is a verbatim transcript of what he said on these important issues and I would like to read to you, if I may, exactly what he said on certain matters so that neither you, nor I, nor his Honor have to rely upon our memories.

The clear advantage of this technique is that it is no longer the recollection of the jurors which controls, but rather your selective presentation of verbatim testimony. A modified approach occurs when daily copy is used and the entire trial transcript is available for the closing argument. In that case, although you may not want to read repeatedly, you may want to cite page numbers to the jury to lend further support and credibility to your recollection of the evidence, thereby encouraging them to substitute your judgment for theirs.

The problem which any of these techniques presents is that it can be used with equal effectiveness against you. You should be aware that when verbatim testimony is read to the jury, it is typically read out of context, and unless you are able to place it into context, your opponent will have the advantage, because it will be your opponent's verbatim reading against your recollection. Accordingly, you must be careful to guard against any such readings out of context and be sure to point them out to the jury. The effect of exposing a reading as made out of context is most assuredly to turn the jury against your opponent and discredit the other side's case as well as your opponent personally.

Somewhat more troublesome are those situations in which your opponent presents his or her recollection of the evidence and the jury has not taken any notes. Possible distortions may be rampant under the guise of "recollection," and these can unfairly prejudice you if you take a stricter approach to presenting evidence during your own argument. All you can do is listen closely and be prepared to object. One type of objection during closing argument that can provide benefit with a minimal amount of downside risk is an objection that your opponent is mischaracterizing the evidence. If you can object that your opponent is mischaracterizing the evidence, whether purposefully or inadvertently, you stand an excellent chance of having the jury instructed that it is their recollection and not counsel's recollection that controls. This immediately puts your opponent on the defensive, because he or she is virtually in the position of having to apologize to the jury, and this can only benefit your case. Even if your objection is overruled, you have still raised a spectre of doubt in the jurors' minds as to whether they can trust what they are hearing.

§ 16.14 Jury Instruction Techniques

One area of trial practice which seems frequently to be shortchanged in most trial practice books and courses is jury instructions. Experienced trial lawyers, however, know that the tactics and techniques which surround the instructions given by the judge to the jury immediately before they decide the case can be the most crucial part of the entire trial process.

Opening statements, the cross-examinations of witnesses, expert testimony, and closing arguments are certainly highly visible and important parts of the trial. They all have something in common: each of these segments of the trial is presented by an attorney or a witness. Maybe a better way of saying the same thing is that they are all presented by someone other than the judge. The jury instructions, however, are presented by the judge who is, as is well known, the authority figure in the courtroom. When the judge instructs the jurors about the law they are to apply in deciding the case, he or she is not playing the role of an advocate. To the contrary, the judge is perceived as the living symbol of justice. The lawyers are being paid to advocate a position, as are the experts. Many witnesses are perceived as having a vested interest in the outcome of the case or, perhaps, as advocates of the position on behalf of which they are testifying.

In light of these facts and perceptions, the jurors typically listen more closely and weigh more heavily almost everything said to them by the judge, including the jury instructions. What they usually do not know, however, is that the jury instructions given to them are frequently the results of suggestions by counsel, oral argument to the court, and, in some respects, negotiation among all parties. In effect, the jury instructions being given to them by the judge are oftentimes more the product of counsel than of the court. However, because the court is the vehicle for conveying them, the jurors inevitably attach more weight to them than if they came from the lawyers.

Because the jury instruction process is so important, it is incumbent upon all attorneys to treat the process as providing an additional opportunity to persuade the jury of the rightness of their position. To help accomplish this task, a number of techniques are available to make the jury instruction process an effective trial tactic.

When embarking on the process of drafting proposed jury instructions, the first place most attorneys usually turn is to the pattern jury instruction book appropriate for the particular court in which the case is pending or perhaps the kind of case, e.g., criminal or civil. All too frequently this is a serious mistake, if counsel literally lifts the pattern instructions out of the form book, perhaps having them retyped, and submits them to the court with a cover page and caption. As with many other boilerplate types of information used by lawyers (for example, interrogatories), form jury instructions are prepared for no case in particular, and, for the most part, they show it. Even to many lawyers, the language they typically use is convoluted, difficult to understand, and, considering the role they play in litigation, just as likely to confuse the jury as not.

Although certainly form jury instructions have a role to play in the trial process, this role is more properly that of serving as a pattern against which customized instructions for your case should be prepared. In doing so, there are a number of guidelines which, if observed, will make your jury instructions more effective advocates of your position.

1. Avoid negative sentences. This is particularly true with respect to instructions which contain double negatives. For example, "The fact that the defendant did not testify on his own behalf is not to be used against him." Inevitably, double negatives cause trouble to many people trying to understand them.
2. If you find yourself having to use single or double negatives, follow them up with affirmative explanatory sentences. For example, if you must have the instruction given in **No. 1** above, consider using an explanatory sentence along the following lines: "Even though the defendant chose not to testify, the United States Constitution provides that a person cannot be required to testify against himself."
3. Personalize the instructions. For example, the "plaintiff" should be "Mary Smith," and the "defendant" should be "XYZ Corporation." Not only will this make the instructions more personal, but it will make it easier for the jury to follow them and keep the parties straight.
4. Avoid ambiguous words or phrases. Remember, although lawyers may not consider something ambiguous, the jurors may. As a result, look for double meanings. For example, don't use "court" for "judge," "bar" for "prohibit," "counsel" for "lawyers," or "disregard" for "ignore." Unlike pleadings prepared for a judge, jury instructions must be prepared keeping in mind that nonlawyers will be using them.
5. Draft your instructions in a narrative format that permits them to be presented to the jury in a conversational style. You will find this

approach far more conducive to understanding by the jury than the choppy approach which results when form-type instructions are just strung together.

6. Request that the judge preinstruct the jury. This technique requires jury instructions to be submitted and ruled upon *prior* to opening statement. The great advantage to this approach is that it permits you to structure your opening statement in such a manner as to present the standards of law the jury will later hear repeated at the end of the case. Preinstructions should also include a summary of the case and perhaps the basic positions of each side. The obvious strength of including such statements is that the jury will have a far better ability to put the evidence in perspective as it is presented.
7. Always press to get rulings on jury instructions, at a minimum, prior to your closing argument. Absent such rulings, you will be at a substantial disadvantage in presenting your closing argument to the jury, because you cannot structure your closing argument around the law which is controlling.
8. When the jury instructions have been ruled upon prior to closing argument, use phraseology like, "As the judge will tell you . . ." during your closing argument. Later on, when the judge instructs the jury along the lines you have pointed out to them, you may well be given the benefit of being perceived by several jurors as insightful.
9. Ask for written jury instructions. One technique which some judges use in complex cases involving lengthy jury instructions is to provide the jury with written copies of the jury instructions, along with special interrogatories, after the jury has been instructed orally. This is particularly effective when the jury instructions have been prepared in a narrative form. Another advantage of this approach is that when there are multiple parties with different standards of proof or law applicable to each, by giving the jurors "packages" of the instructions, they are provided with a structured format for considering the case during deliberation and in reaching their decision.

From an overall perspective, substantial consideration given to the process of drafting and using jury instructions will pay substantial dividends in successful trial results. The use of jury instructions as part of a preinstruction process, as a checklist against which to measure your proofs and, finally, as elements incorporated into your closing argument, can be one of the most effective trial tactics you have available.

CHAPTER 17

POST-TRIAL TACTICS

§ 17.1 Introduction

All too often, the rendering of a verdict in a case does not mark the end of litigation but instead begins a new phase. The post-trial maneuvers that take place even prior to the taking of an appeal are frequently lengthy and seek to retry many, if not all, of the issues that were tried to the jury. Otherwise legitimate tactics are frequently pursued in a manner which renders the motivation of counsel suspect. However, it is a fact of life that litigators never give up but continue to pursue the cause of their client until they reach a point of diminishing returns or an instruction to stop.

Among the various post-trial options available to litigants prior to appeal are extensive post-trial motions practice as well as the possibility of pursuing costs and possible settlement. Depending on whether you represent a prevailing party at trial, you may wish to seek certain post-trial relief, or you may desire to settle the case rather than continue along the litigative route.

The motions most typically made at the conclusion of the trial or after the verdict is rendered by the jury include a motion for a directed verdict, a motion for a new trial, or a motion for judgment notwithstanding the verdict (judgment n.o.v.). These motions are interrelated, but each also has specific characteristics depending on the basis for the motion. The factual basis for a post-trial motion frequently will be the same regardless of which motion is brought. Indeed, you may often find yourself bringing several motions seeking different kinds of relief from the court, all premised on the same factual framework.

Of all the substantive bases for bringing a post-trial motion, the one related to juror conduct, separate and apart from rendering of the verdict, is the most frequently encountered. Such a motion may relate to juror misconduct or withholding of information and is typically advanced by an unsuccessful litigant as bearing on the denial of a right to a fair trial.

§ 17.2 Juror Misconduct

It is not at all unusual following a trial for both lawyers and representatives of the lawyers, whether they are on the winning or the losing side, to interview the jurors. This may be done for any number of reasons, including determination of the basis on which the jury decided, the perceptions which the jurors had of the evidence, the impressions the jurors had of the lawyers or witnesses, and the operation of the jury system in general in that case.

Many uses of juror interview information may be legitimate in revealing matters of concern to lawyers. There is one use made of juror interview information, however, which attempts to undermine and impeach the jury verdict in a manner inconsistent with existing law and practice. This tactic must be guarded against when possible and, when filed, exposed for what it is—an improper and collateral attack on the jury verdict.

The motion in **§ 17.3** is an example of the substance of a motion for mistrial based on a juror interview and an allegation premised on that interview that the juror in question, who subsequently became the foreman of the jury during deliberations, was guilty of intentionally withholding material information regarding his experience with aircraft navigational equipment. The moving party alleged that this had the effect of denying a defendant, who had been found guilty of willful misconduct, the opportunity to challenge him for cause and nullifying the right of peremptory challenge.

Counsel are confronted occasionally with the question of impeaching a jury verdict. Obviously this is quite difficult to do, because the sanctity of the jury verdict typically cannot be disturbed. The following is a summary of the standards established regarding such issues as focused on by a number of federal circuits, including the Second, Third, Sixth, Seventh, and Ninth.

Second Circuit. Affidavits and statements by jurors may not ordinarily be used to impeach a verdict once the jury has been discharged, unless extraneous influence invaded the jury room. *Jacobson v. Henderson,* 763 F.2d 12 (2d Cir. 1985).

Third Circuit. A juror's hearing impairment which allegedly rendered him incompetent to serve at the defendant's trial was not an extraneous influence which could be the subject of any post-verdict inquiry. A strong showing of juror incompetence is required, and a hearing problem does not come under either of the two exceptions to Federal Rule of Evidence 606(b), because a hearing problem is not "extraneous prejudicial information . . . improperly brought to the jury's attention," and it is not an "outside influence . . . improperly brought to bear upon any juror." The court reasoned that it was obvious the drafters of the rule were primarily concerned with jury tampering and improper communication to the jury and not any physical disability of a juror. *Government of Virgin Islands v. Nicholas,* 759 F.2d 1073 (3d Cir. 1985).

The fact that the district court spoke in camera to two jurors during damages deliberations and did not allow counsel to review a transcript of the in camera discussion until after a verdict had been returned would not support error sufficient for reversal. *VanBuskirk v. Carey Canadian Mines, Ltd.,* 760 F.2d 481 (3d Cir. 1985).

Sixth Circuit. Because a juror's affidavit admitted that she told the judge that she knew and had formed an opinion about the case, her contention that she was prejudiced thereby may be regarded as incompetent testimony regarding the "effect of anything upon his or any other juror's mind or emotions" rather than evidence that she committed perjury during voir dire. The predominant interpretation of the language contained in Federal Rule of Evidence 606(b) is that even when the jury has testified about extraneous information or an outside influence, he or she may not be interrogated about its impact. *Brofford v. Morris,* 751 F.2d 845 (6th Cir.), *cert. denied,* 106 S. Ct. 194 (1985).

Seventh Circuit. After a jury brought in a guilty verdict, the defense learned that a juror who had received a threatening telephone call during the trial had, contrary to court instructions, informed other members of the jury about the telephone call.

The appellate court stated that, rather than question jurors directly in determining whether extrajudicial contact with a juror was prejudicial to the defendant, the district court must make findings of fact at two separate levels: (1) the district court must find the basic, or subsidiary, facts, e.g., the nature, content, and extent of the extrajudicial contact; and (2) based on this, the court must then make the ultimate factual determination whether the contact likely affected the jury's impartiality. In this instant case, the appellate court felt that petitioner was denied his constitutional rights to an impartial jury by reason of the threat of one of the jurors and the communication by that juror to other members of the jury. *Owen v. Duckworth,* 727 F.2d 643 (7th Cir. 1984).

After a defense verdict, the plaintiff wished to question the jury, but the district court judge denied this request in light of a local district rule which gives the judge discretion as to when to allow such action. The appellate court affirmed the denial of the plaintiff's request even though the plaintiff had shown that the wife of a juror apparently had casual conversation with the wife of an investigator for the defendant and with counsel for both sides. There was no showing of direct contact with a juror. *Delvaux v. Ford Motor Co.,* 764 F.2d 469 (7th Cir. 1985).

Ninth Circuit. A juror told the plaintiff after the trial that part of the jury charge asked the jury to reach a decision quickly, if possible, because the judge had another trial some 200 miles away. After the plaintiff asked the juror if that affected the decisionmaking process, the jurors said, "Some jurors grudgingly went for the guilty verdict." The appellate court stated that jurors may not be questioned about the deliberative process or subjective effects of extraneous information, nor can such information be considered by the trial or appellate courts. Reviewing courts will not disturb jury verdicts on appeal when extraneous information relates only to issues not material to the guilt or innocence of the defendant. Intrinsic jury processes will not be examined on appeal and cannot support reversal. *Albantino v. United States,* 750 F.2d 1442 (9th Cir. 1985).

Texas. As a general rule, jurors may not impeach their verdict by testifying to events that occurred during their deliberations. However, they may testify to show that, through inadvertence or mistake, the verdict actually entered differed from what the jury intended. This required all the jurors to agree that such inadvertence or mistake had occurred. In this case, only one or two of the jurors were confused, and, therefore, there was not a sufficient showing of mistake. *Smith v. City of Seven Points, Texas,* 608 F. Supp. 458 (E.D. Tex. 1985).

Wisconsin. A juror's racially prejudicial remark during jury deliberations was protected by Federal Rule of Evidence 606(b) and, therefore, the petitioner's request for habeas corpus relief was denied. *Shillcutt v. Gagnon,* 602 F. Supp. 1280 (E.D. Wis. 1980).

§ 17.3 —Memorandum of Points and Authorities

1. INTRODUCTION

________________ [Airline] has been denied its right to a fair trial. The foreman of the jury, ________________, has stated under oath that during voir dire he intentionally withheld material information about his experience with aircraft navigational equipment. He denied ________________ [Airline] the opportunity to challenge him for cause and nullified the right of peremptory challenge.

Had ________________ answered the questions put to him by the court, he would have been challenged either for cause, as was ________________, a radar technician, or peremptorily removed from the jury. His failure to do so requires the declaration of a mistrial.

2. ____________ INTENTIONALLY CONCEALED MATERIAL INFORMATION DURING VOIR DIRE

The court instructed the jury panel that every question asked of them should be understood by them to be addressed to each member of the panel individually. Tr. 4440. The jurors were told that they would be required to decide the case based only on the evidence, not on their experience. Tr. 4539. As ________________ said with reference to another juror during the voir dire, "In the land of the blind the one-eyed man is king. You are going to have a one man jury in this case." Tr. 4547. The court, too, was concerned that the special knowledge or experience of one juror might pervert the integrity of the jury process:

> In other words, ladies and gentleman—and I don't address this just to you ________________, but to everybody, counsel and myself and the parties want a six person jury to resolve this case. We don't want a one person jury or a two person jury and we expect that when the jurors hear the case and deliberate on the case, that all of the collective judgments and observations of all six of you come into play, and we would not want—nor would it be proper for one juror to take the position that "I have had more experience in some area than you other jurors, so, therefore, this is the way things are."
>
> All right, again, in other words, just hypothetically, it would be very improper for some juror . . . to go into the jury room and say—let's say evidence has been presented a certain way, and for the juror to say, "When I was sitting in the cockpit of X plane, Charlie Jones was the pilot and told me that this is the way the instruments work," because that is not evidence in the case, and it is the evidence that is presented—and you will have lots and lots of evidence over a six month period, and you won't need any outside material to help you resolve this case. Tr. 4737–38.

The concern led the court to ask ________________, who was later excused for cause, several questions about his experience with and knowledge of aircraft navigational instruments. Tr. 3732 *et seq.* Similar questions were put to ________________. Tr. 4705.

________________'s sworn statement makes it clear that he appreciated the importance of the inquiry about aircraft navigational instruments and that he intentionally withheld material information about his experience. During voir dire the court asked ________________ "Did you have any instruction at all on the navigational apparatus on the aircraft?" ________________'s answer was "No sir." Tr. 4787.

________________'s sworn statement makes the concealment clear:

Question: I want to bring up a point. I understand that you have had eight years experience in the Navy and you can give me some idea of what—

Answer: I had—they asked at the beginning of the trial what experience we have had, or you know, our jobs and everything so that they could get someone that was not bias [sic] you know. I had flown planes for twenty years. I am sure that they wouldn't have taken me as a juror, but I told them I was a fire control technician in the Navy four years and they never asked me another question.

Now, either they knew what fire control technician was or they chose not to ask me, but it's a radar technician, aviation radar technician. I work [sic] on fighter aircraft, I rode in the backseat once in a C-47 a couple of times. Every day that I was working on the flight line, I was working in aircraft.

And they chose not to ask me any more questions. So I don't know whether it was important to them or not, but these other guys, they were asking questions too—they specifically had jobs working on radar. Let's say, you know, that they stated this, you know, that they worked on radar, you know.

They asked me a lot of questions. They didn't ask me because—because the name I gave to the job I had fire control technician is what they call it.

Question: You thought they might have been confused?

Answer: I felt guilty about it at first when they chose me as a juror, but I told them I was in the Navy for four years and stuff, so I don't know whether that should have been something that I should have talked more about, but they had—what, about 300 people in the courtroom when they were choosing the jury. And four days sitting there, asking everybody questions, and they would say, "Okay, everybody that has a nurse in the family raise your hand." I mean, the questions just—days got long.

So I figured I wasn't going to volunteer any information unless I hit a nerve with them. I would explain anything they wanted. So they asked about—I can't remember the question, but it was something similar, "Does anyone have any experience with aircraft" or something like this.

I said, "I was a fire control technician." And that was it.

But, like I say, it's all the navaids, it's the radar, it's radio altimeters. It was everything they are talking about.

Question: Then you had considerable experience with the whole bit?

Answer: Right.

3. ___________'S CONCEALMENT VITIATED THE PROTECTION AFFORDED BY VOIR DIRE AND DENIED ___________ [AIRLINE] ITS RIGHT TO A FAIR TRIAL

The purpose of voir dire is to allow the court and the attorneys to determine bias and to exercise judgment concerning the selection of jurors. Obviously, the purposes cannot be realized unless the jurors truthfully and fully respond to the questions put to them by the court.

The very purpose of voir dire examination is to develop the whole truth concerning the prospective jurors' state of mind, not only to enable the trial judge to determine actual bias, but to enable counsel to exercise his intuitive judgment concerning the prospective jurors' suspected bias or prejudice. "[T]he right of challenge includes the incidental right that the information elicited out of voir dire examination shall

> be true." As so well stated by Judge ______________, while a trial judge, "The answers to questions put by the court necessarily form the basis for the court's excusing a juror on its own motion or challenges for cause . . . and the exercise of peremptory challenges by each side. Necessarily, it is expected and required that jurors in their answers shall be completely truthful and that they shall disclose, upon a general question, any matters which might tend to disqualify them from sitting on the case for any reason. It therefore becomes imperative that the answers be truthful and complete. False or misleading answers may result in the seating of juror[s] who might have been discharged by the court, challenged for cause by counsel or stricken through the exercise of peremptory challenge. The seating of such a juror could and probably would result in a miscarriage of justice and therefore courts and attorneys, who are officials of the court, are ever mindful of the importance of jurors' answers to questions regarding their qualifications." *Photostat Corporation v. Ball,* 388 F.2d 783, 786 (10th Cir. 1964); *accord, United States v. Freedland,* 111 F. Supp. 852, 853 (D.N.D. 1953).

Because of the critical importance of voir dire to our jury system, it is the duty of every juror to answer fully and truthfully all questions put to him:

> It is the duty of a juror to make full and truthful answers to all questions propounded to him touching his qualifications to serve as a juror in any case, since full knowledge of all material relevant matters is essential to the fair and just exercise of the right to challenge, either peremptorily or otherwise. A juror who falsely conceals a material fact relevant to his qualifications is guilty of such misconduct as is prejudicial and obstructive to the fair administration of justice in our courts. *United States v. Lampkin,* 66 F. Supp. 821, 824 (S.D. Fla. 1946).

The meaningful exercise of the right to peremptorily challenge jurors is fundamental to the right to trial by jury.

> The right is a traditional, arbitrary and capricious one and "it must be exercised with full freedom, or it fails of its full purpose." *Lewis v. United States,* 146 U.S. 370, 378 . . . thus, under statutory law, the court is the judge of actual bias, but counsel is the sole and exclusive judge of whom he shall challenge for suspected bias or prejudice against his client's cause. No one will gainsay that the denial or substantial impairment of the statutory right of peremptory challenge is prejudicial to the constitutional right to a fair and impartial jury. *Photostat Corporation v. Ball, supra,* 338 F.2d at 786; *accord, Consolidated Gas and Equipment Co. of America v. Carver,* 257 F.2d 111 (10th Cir. 1958).

The Ninth Circuit has recognized the important connection between the right to jury trial and the right to receive truthful responses from prospective jurors to the questions put to them by the court during voir dire.

> A defendant is entitled to be tried by an unprejudiced and legally qualified jury. *United States v. Napoleone,* 3 Cir., 349 F.2d 350, 353. A defendant is entitled to exercise challenges for cause and, under Rule 24(b) Federal Rules of Criminal Procedure, he may exercise a specified number of peremptory challenges, excusing prospective jurors for any reason the defendant deems sufficient. In aid of these rights, Rule 24(a) provides for voir dire examination of prospective jurors. It is self-evident that for such voir dire examination to serve these purposes, the answers

> given by prospective jurors must be truthful and complete. *Jackson v. United States,* 408 F.2d 306, 308–09 (9th Cir. 1969).

The United States Supreme Court has stated that to allow an individual who has knowingly made untrue statements during voir dire to sit on a jury makes a sham of the right to a jury trial:

> A talesman when accepted as a juror becomes a part or member of the court. The judge who examines on the voir dire is engaged in the process of organizing the court. If the answers to the questions are wilfully evasive or knowingly untrue, the talesman, when accepted, is a juror in name only. His relation to the court and to the parties is tainted in its origin; it is a mere pretense and sham. What was sought to be attained was the choice of an impartial arbiter. What happened was an intrusion of a partisan defender. If a kinsman of one of the litigants had gone into the jury room disguised as the complaisant juror, the effect would have been no different. The doom of mere sterility was on the trial from the beginning. *Clark v. United States,* 209 U.S. 1, 11 (1932) (Cardozo J.).

________________'s knowing and intentional concealment of information which he knew to be material both to the court and to counsel, prevented ________________ [Airline] from seeking his removal from the jury for cause and made it impossible for ________________ [Airline] to meaningfully exercise its right to peremptorily challenge him.

4. ________________'S INTENTIONAL CONCEALMENT OF MATERIAL FACTS MANDATES THE DECLARATION OF A MISTRIAL

The controlling decision of the Ninth Circuit requires that a mistrial be granted:

> We agree with the court in *State v. Simmons,* 59 Wash. 2d 381, 368 P.2d 378, 384 (1962) that "[w]here a person serves on a jury who, if not excused for cause, would certainly have been peremptorily challenged if certain questions on voir dire had been answered truthfully, it has been held to be an abuse of discretion not to grant a new trial." *Marshall v. United States,* 355 F.2d 999, 1009–10 (9th Cir. 1966).

Had ________________ answered the questions put to him on voir dire truthfully, it is probable that he, like ________________, who was a radar technician employed by RCA, would have been excused for cause. At the very least, ________________ would have been subject to peremptory challenge, and he would have been removed. It is clear that what ________________ [Airline] and the court got was indeed a one man jury.

5. CONCLUSION

________________ intentionally and knowingly concealed material information about his background during the court's voir dire. In doing so, he prevented ________________ [Airline] from intelligently exercising its rights to seek his removal for cause and to peremptorily challenge him. ________________ [Airline] was denied its right to a fair and impartial jury, and this motion should be granted.

DATED: October 2, 1978

By ________________________
Attorney for Defendant

Declaration of ____________________

State of ________________ }
} SS.:
County of ________________ }

1. My name is ______________________, and I am an attorney admitted to practice before this court. I am one of the attorneys representing ____________ [Airline] in this litigation. I have personal knowledge of the facts herein set forth, and, if called upon to do so, I could and would competently testify thereto under oath.

2. In late August, 1978, ________________ [Airline] retained a private investigator to interview the jurors in this case. Mr. ________________ was interviewed on August 27, 1978. The interview was recorded by a certified court reporter, and Mr. ________________ swore that the statements that he made during the interview were true and correct.

3. Attached hereto as Exhibit "A" are five pages of the transcript of that interview. They are a true and correct copy of the original transcript which has been filed *in camera* with this court.

I declare under penalty of perjury that the foregoing is true and correct.

Executed on October ____________, 1978.

____

EXHIBIT A
[Photocopies of transcript pages quoted in Memorandum]

§ 17.4 —Dealing with Jury-Related Motions

On its face, the tactic illustrated by the motion in the preceding section could appear meritorious. Certainly the argument is cogent. However, your response to any such attempt to impeach a jury verdict premised on jury interviews, short of patent jury misconduct such as bringing a law book into the jury room, should be the same regardless of the allegations made.

As a general matter, a juror may not testify about statements made during the jury's deliberations. In addition, a juror may not "testify about the effect of anything upon his or any other juror's mind or emotions as influencing him to assent to the verdict or about his mental processes in connection with the verdict." *See* 11 C. Wright & A. Miller, *Federal Practice and Procedure* § 2810 (1973).

A litigant may not rely on juror opinion as to what the evidence proved. *See Koenig v. Frank's Plastering Co.,* 227 F. Supp. 849 (D. Neb. 1964), *aff'd,* 341 F.2d 257 (8th Cir. 1965) (jurors could not testify whether they found a party contributorily negligent); *Northern Pac. Railway v. Mely,* 219 F.2d 199 (9th Cir. 1954) (jurors could not testify that they would have decided otherwise if not for discussion of one particular railroad policy); *Holden v. Porter,* 405 F.2d 878 (10th Cir. 1969) (jurors could not testify as to effect of speculation that defendant was insured).

In addition, a litigant unhappy with a jury verdict may not rely on juror opinions premised on juror interviews as to what the juror personally or the jury as a whole believed or based its verdict on. *See, e.g., York Chrysler-Plymouth, Inc. v. Chrysler Credit Corp.,* 447 F.2d 786 (5th Cir. 1971) (single juror may not attempt to impeach the verdict of the whole jury by purporting to state the intention of the jury); *Smith-Blair, Inc. v. R.H. Baker & Co.,* 232 F. Supp. 484 (C.D. Cal. 1962), *aff'd,* 331 F.2d 506 (9th Cir. 1964) (affidavits of jurors offered to show what they meant by their answer to a special verdict properly stricken). When an opponent attempts to impeach a jury verdict, especially when there have been no special findings of fact but only a general verdict, declarations prepared out of court through a jury interview and made after trial in the presence only of procuring counsel should not be allowed into the record.

The judge deciding the case in which the defendant moved for a mistrial (see § **17.3**) found that the responses of the juror did not contain any false statements or conceal any information. Furthermore, the court found that the juror had not intentionally misled or deceived the court. This was upheld on appeal. *In re Pago Pago Aircrash of Jan. 30, 1974,* 525 F. Supp. 1007 (C.D. Cal. 1981), *aff'd,* 692 F.2d 704 (9th Cir. 1982).

Even if a post-trial interview with a juror reveals juror misconduct, not all juror misconduct requires post-trial relief in the form of judgment notwithstanding the verdict or a new trial. In *United States v. Klee,* 494 F.2d 394 (9th Cir. 1974), the court stated:

> Assuming that there was jury misconduct, it is still true that not every incident of jury misconduct requires a new trial. [Citations omitted.] The test is whether or not the misconduct prejudices the defendant to the extent that he has not received a fair trial. *Cavness v. United States, supra,* 187 F.2d at 723.

494 F.2d at 396; *see also United States v. Hendrix,* 549 F.2d 1225, 1229 (9th Cir. 1977), *cert. denied,* 434 U.S. 818 (1977).

§ 17.5 —Tactical Considerations

In responding to a post-trial motion premised on an allegation of juror misconduct and supported by a post-trial interview with a juror, there are a number of points which you should take into account:

1. Any response should strongly assert that post-trial interviews with jurors are in no way a proper inquiry into the foundation of a jury verdict and that such actions are improper and a faulty premise for post-trial relief.
2. The circumstances of the interview should be determined as further ammunition for attacking an opponent. For example, it may be that, although a court reporter was present at the interview or, alternatively, a tape recorder was used, the juror was not asked to swear to the truth of the statement until after the interview was concluded. This "after the fact" type of interview is unfair and improper.
3. If a motion for post-trial relief is premised on a juror interview and portions of the interview are included, you should immediately demand the entire interview. It is not at all unlikely that there will be substantial portions of the interview which undermine the movant's own position and which have not been put forward for that reason.
4. Any response to the tactic of a post-trial juror interview should also point out that, even if there was juror misconduct, it was neither harmful nor prejudicial. It should also point out that the means used to obtain this information, i.e., post-trial interview, are more harmful than the conduct complained of in the case.

§ 17.6 Appeal versus Settlement

After a trial, whether you are on the winning or the losing side, a number of avenues of relief are still open to you. If you are on the winning side, you hope that the defendants will not take an appeal and will simply pay you whatever the jury said you are entitled to in the case. You will also want your costs and whatever else the judge may have awarded you.

Perhaps it is a weakness of the system, but the loser in litigation actually has a great many more options. In addition to the wide-ranging post-trial motions practice discussed in §§ **17.2** through **17.5** and appeal itself, there may be settlement prospects.

Although the greatest impetus to settlement may be the setting of a trial date and many cases may be settled on the courthouse steps, another significant motivator to settlement is a verdict, regardless of which side it favors. The winner does not want further delay in receiving the fruits of victory caused by an appeal process and is frequently willing to settle for less than the verdict value of the case, while the loser has substantial leverage through the appeal process and the ensuing delay.

The losing side, whether the plaintiff or the defendant, is typically willing to settle for an amount significantly greater or significantly less, as the case may be, than it was willing to settle for prior to commencement of the trial. The irony of this situation is that, even though somebody has won the case, the parties are in many ways closer to settlement than they were before the trial began, because at least one trier of fact has expressed its opinion as to who was right and who was wrong. While there are valid settlement prospects to be explored following a verdict, the very existence of a verdict makes it possible for one side or the other unfairly to take advantage of the situation.

There is nothing wrong with using a verdict as a lever to end the litigation. The continuation of litigation through the appellate process is an expensive proposition, and anything which can be done to short circuit entry into the appellate system is desirable. However, there are limits to how far one should and can go, and the following considerations must be kept in mind:

1. When evaluating the prospects of settlement, especially when you are on the losing side, you must weigh the costs associated with pursuing the appeal against your likelihood of prevailing. Remember, you already have a decision against you, and no matter how unfair the demands for settlement may be, the other side is in the catbird's seat. Accordingly, you must often swallow your pride and be willing to pay out more money than you otherwise would have under a more favorable set of circumstances.
2. When you are on the winning side, you must walk a fine line between encouraging losers to pay more than they would have been willing to pay in a pretrial settlement and not further aggravating or wounding the self-esteem of counsel to the point that they recommend against any sort of settlement and urge their clients to pursue the appellate route.
3. Costs at trial can sometimes be used to bring about a settlement. In exchange for waiving costs and agreeing not to appeal, settlements can sometimes be initiated by the winner or the loser.
4. Settlement prospects should not be reserved after trial to either the winning side or the losing side. It may be in the best interests of all parties to pursue settlement prospects after trial.
5. An occasionally successful tactic is for a party desiring a settlement following a jury verdict to request that the trial judge become

involved in the process. This is not very different from the role which a trial judge may play prior to commencement of the trial, but the parties have been somewhat softened up as a result of the jury verdict.

6. The winning party must be careful not to gloat too much, inasmuch as that will tend to prejudice the winners' own position, of counsel and client, and infuriate the opponents. This could be destructive to any possibility of favorable settlement, while at the same time increasing litigation costs for all because of the appellate process.

Unawareness of the vitality of settlement prospects after a jury verdict is returned can only result in an opponent's taking advantage of you, using the jury verdict and the appellate process as leverage. The best defense is knowledge of how you can be manipulated and taking the steps which have been outlined to prevent it. By seizing the initiative in this area, you can make the situation work for you and often get a result which is more advantageous to your client than might otherwise have been the case.

TABLE OF CASES

Case	*Book §*
Anderson v. City of Bessemer City, 470 U.S. 564 (1985)	§ 8.5
Apache Ready Mix Co. v. Creed, 653 S.W.2d 79 (Tex. Ct. App. 1983)	§ 14.24
Armstrong Cork Co. v. Niagara Mohawk Power Corp., 16 F.R.D. 389 (S.D.N.Y. 1954)	§ 1.49
Aruba Bonaire Curacao Trust Co. v. Commissioner of Internal Revenue, 777 F.2d 38 (D.C. Cir. 1985), *cert. denied,* ___ U.S. ___, 106 S. Ct. 1469 (1986)	§§ 4.5, 6.4
Ash v. Cvetkow, 739 F.2d 493 (9th Cir. 1984), *cert. denied,* 470 U.S. 1007 (1985)	§ 5.2
Ashley v. Nissan Motor Corp., 321 So. 2d 868 (La. Ct. App.), *cert. denied,* 323 So. 2d 478 (La. 1975)	§ 14.25
Atlanta Coca-Cola Bottling Co. v. Transamerica Ins. Co., 61 F.R.D. 115 (N.D. Ga. 1972)	§ 1.7
Au Bon Pain Corp. v. Artect, Inc., 653 F.2d 61 (2d Cir. 1981)	§ 6.9
August v. Delta Airlines, Inc., 450 U.S. 346 (1980)	§ 9.14
August v. Delta Airlines, Inc., 600 F.2d 699 (7th Cir. 1979)	§ 9.14
Augustine v. United States, 810 F.2d 991 (10th Cir. 1987)	§ 6.4
Aurora Bancshares Corp. v. Weston, 777 F.2d 385 (7th Cir. 1985)	§ 3.10
Badgely v. Santa Croce, 800 F.2d 33 (3d Cir. 1986)	§ 8.4
Baker, *In re,* 744 F.2d 1438 (10th Cir. 1984), *cert. denied,* 471 U.S. 1014 (1985)	§ 5.10
Baker Indus., Inc. v. Cerberus Ltd., 764 F.2d 204 (3d Cir. 1985)	§§ 3.6, 7.2, 7.3
Bancohio Corp. v. Fox, 516 F.2d 29 (6th Cir. 1975)	§ 2.15
Bankers Life & Casualty Co. v. Holland, 346 U.S. 379 (1953)	§ 2.15
Barenbrugge v. Rich, 490 N.E.2d 1368 (Ill. Ct. App. 1986)	§ 14.24
Barham v. IDM Corp., 78 F.R.D. 340 (N.D. Ohio 1978)	§ 1.33
Barnd v. City of Tacoma, 664 F.2d 1339 (9th Cir. 1982)	§ 7.5
Barnham v. Nowell, 243 Miss. 441, 138 So. 2d 493 (1962)	§ 14.31
Baron Tube Co. v. Transport Ins. Co., 365 F.2d 858 (5th Cir. 1966)	§ 15.8
Barrett v. Singer Co., 60 Ohio St. 2d 7, 396 N.E.2d 218 (1979)	§ 2.11
Barta v. Long, 670 F.2d 907 (10th Cir. 1982)	§ 6.10
Bartsch v. Clarke, 293 F.2d 283 (4th Cir. 1961)	§ 2.15
Batson v. Neal Spelce Assocs., Inc., 805 F.2d 546 (5th Cir. 1986)	§ 7.2
Batson v. Neal Spelce Assocs., Inc., 765 F.2d 511 (5th Cir. 1985)	§§ 5.3, 6.5, 6.8, 7.7

Case	*Book §*
Brokopp v. Ford Motor Co., 71 Cal. App. 2d 841, 139 Cal. Rptr. 888 (1977)	§ 15.9
Brook Village N. Assocs. v. General Elec. Co., 687 F.2d 66 (1st Cir. 1982)	§ 1.13
Browning Debenture Holders' Comm. v. DASA Corp., 560 F.2d 1078 (2d Cir. 1977)	§ 7.3
Bulthuis v. Rexall Corp., 789 F.2d 1315 (1986)	§ 2.4
Burgdorff v. International Business Machs. Corp., 74 Ill. App. 3d 158, 392 N.E.2d 183 (1979)	§ 16.7
Burgess v. Premier Corp., 727 F.2d 826 (9th Cir. 1984)	§ 13.39
Burks v. Webb, 199 Va. 296, 99 S.E.2d 629 (1957)	§ 15.7
Burlington Coat Factory Warehouse v. Belk Bros. Co., 621 F. Supp. 224 (S.D.N.Y. 1985)	§ 4.2
Burriss v. Texaco, 361 F.2d 169 (4th Cir. 1966)	§ 14.3
Butler v. Chrestman, 264 So. 2d 812 (Miss. 1972)	§ 14.24
Calley v. Manicke, 24 Ill. 2d 390, 182 N.E.2d 206 (1962)	§ 15.8
Campbell, *In re,* 628 F.2d 1260 (9th Cir. 1980)	§ 8.5
Campbell v. General Motors Corp., 13 F.R.D. 331 (S.D.N.Y. 1952)	§ 1.49
Capitol Vending Co. v. Baker, 36 F.R.D. 45 (D.D.C. 1964)	§§ 1.49, 1.50
Caprara v. Chrysler Corp., 71 A.D.2d 515, 423 N.Y.S.2d 694 (1979), *aff'd,* 52 N.Y.2d 114, 436 N.Y.S.2d 545 (1981)	§ 14.25
Carter v. Albert Einstein Medical Center, 804 F.2d 805 (3d Cir. 1986)	§ 5.5
Carter v. City of Memphis, 636 F.2d 159 (6th Cir. 1980)	§ 5.5
Carter v. Seamans, 411 F.2d 767 (5th Cir. 1969)	§ 2.15
Carter v. Simpson, 16 Ohio App. 3d 420, 476 N.E.2d 705 (1984)	§ 14.39
Carter by Carter v. United States, 780 F.2d 925 (11th Cir. 1986)	§ 5.8
Carvell v. Winn, 154 So. 2d 788 (La. Ct. App.), *cert. denied,* 245 La. 71, 156 So. 2d 603 (1963)	§ 14.21
Casey v. Williams, 87 Nev. 137, 482 P.2d 824 (1971)	§ 2.11
Cavnar v. Quality Control Parking, Inc., 678 S.W.2d 548 (Tex. Ct. App. 1984)	§ 11.16
Cavness v. United States, 187 F.2d 719 (9th Cir. 1951)	§ 17.4
Celotex Corp. v. Catrett, 477 U.S. ______, 91 L.Ed. 2d 265 (1986)	§ 2.4
Central S.C. Chapter, Soc'y of Professional Journalists, Sigma Delta Chi v. United States Dist. Court, 551 F.2d 559 (4th Cir. 1977)	§ 2.15
Chandler Leasing Corp. v. Lopez, 669 F.2d 919 (4th Cir. 1982)	§ 6.5
Chapman v. Pacific Tel. & Tel. Co., 613 F.2d 193 (9th Cir. 1979)	§ 8.6

Case	*Book §*
Cook v. Cox, 478 S.W.2d 678 (Mo. 1978)	§ 16.6
Cooling Sys. & Flexibles, Inc. v. Stuart Radiator, Inc., 777 F.2d 485 (9th Cir. 1985)	§ 7.7
Cope v. McPherson, 781 F.2d 207 (D.C. Cir. 1985)	§ 6.7
Copeland v. Marshall, 641 F.2d 880 (D.C. Cir. 1980)	§ 7.4
Corchado v. Puerto Rico Marine Management, Inc., 665 F.2d 410 (1st Cir. 1981), *cert. denied,* 459 U.S. 826 (1982)	§§ 5.2, 5.5
Cordova Gonzalez, *In re,* 726 F.2d 16 (1st Cir.), *cert. denied,* 466 U.S. 951 (1984)	§ 8.5
Cornejo v. Landon, 524 F. Supp. 118 (N.D. Ill. 1981)	§ 1.49
Costanzo v. Southern Farm Bureau Casualty Ins. Co., 124 So. 2d 621 (La. Ct. App. 1960)	§ 14.34
Cotner v. Hopkins, 795 F.2d 900 (10th Cir. 1986)	§ 8.9
Cox v. Valley Fair Corp., 83 N.J. 381, 416 A.2d 809 (1980)	§ 15.8
Crawford v. Maryland Casualty Co., 39 So. 2d 102 (La. Ct. App. 1949)	§ 14.30
Cross v. Houston B. & T. R.R., 351 S.W.2d 84 (Tex. Civ. App. 1961)	§ 16.7
Crowder v. Aurora Co-op Elevator Co., 393 N.W.2d 250 (Neb. 1986)	§ 14.17
Crown Cork & Seal Co. v. Chemed Corp., 101 F.R.D. 105 (E.D. Pa. 1984)	§ 6.2
Crump v. Geer Bros., 336 So. 2d 1091 (Ala. 1976)	§ 15.9
Cutting John v. Cowper Co., 7 A.D.2d 348, 183 N.Y.S.2d 171 (1959)	§ 14.34
Damiana v. Rhode Island Hosp., 704 F.2d 12 (1st Cir. 1983)	§§ 6.5, 6.6
Davidson v. Beco Corp., 1986 Opinion No. CA-139 (Idaho Ct. App. Dec. 12, 1986)	§ 9.1
Davis v. Cluet, Peabody & Co., 667 F.2d 1371 (11th Cir. 1982)	§ 6.7
Davis v. Combustion Eng'g, Inc., 742 F.2d 916 (6th Cir. 1984)	§ 13.36
Davis v. Williams, 588 F.2d 309 (2d Cir. 1986)	§ 5.2
Dawson v. Chrysler Corp., 630 F.2d 950 (3d Cir. 1980)	§ 13.39
Day v. Allstate Ins. Co., 788 F.2d 1110 (5th Cir. 1986)	§ 6.8
DeBattiste v. Anthony Laudadio & Sons, 167 Pa. Super. 38, 74 A.2d 784 (1950)	§ 14.34
Decicco v. Methodist Hosp., 74 A.D.2d 593, 424 N.Y.S.2d 524 (1980)	§ 15.8
Deighan v. E. Turgeon Constr. Co., 95 R.I. 130, 182 A.2d 438 (1962)	§ 15.4
Delcastor, Inc. v. Vail Assocs., Inc., 108 F.R.D. 405 (D. Colo. 1985)	§ 1.21
Dellums v. Powell, 566 F.2d 231 (D.C. Cir. 1977)	§ 6.4
DeLorean Motor Co., *In re,* 755 F.2d 1223 (6th Cir. 1985)	§ 13.47

Case	*Book §*
Equal Employment Opportunity Comm'n v. New Enters. Stone & Lime Co., 74 F.R.D. 628 (E.D. Pa. 1977)	§ 1.8
Equitable Life Assurance Soc'y v. McDonald, 280 Ky. 825, 134 S.W.2d 953 (Ct. App. 1939)	§ 14.34
Estis Trucking Co. v. Hammond, 387 So. 2d 768 (Ala. 1980)	§ 15.9
Exxon v. FTC, 476 F. Supp. 713 (D.D.C. 1979)	§ 1.62
Fahey, *Ex parte,* 332 U.S. 258 (1947)	§ 2.15
Falstaff Brewing Corp. v. Miller Brewing Co., 702 F.2d 770 (9th Cir. 1983)	§§ 8.1, 8.5, 8.7
Farmers Plant Food, Inc. v. Fisher, 746 F.2d 451 (8th Cir. 1984)	§ 8.10
F.D. Rich Co. v. United States, 417 U.S. 116 (1974)	§ 7.1
Federal Crop Ins. Corp. v. Hester, 763 F.2d 723 (8th Cir. 1985)	§ 13.36
Felder v. Johnson, 273 S.C. 479, 257 S.E.2d 714 (1979)	§ 15.8
Finn v. Wood, 178 F.2d 583 (2d Cir. 1950)	§ 14.32
Fintak v. Catholic Bishop, 51 Ill. App. 2d 191, 366 N.E.2d 480 (1977)	§ 16.6
Fjelstad v. American Honda Motor Co., 762 F.2d 1334 (9th Cir. 1985)	§§ 5.9, 6.2, 6.3, 6.7
Fleming v. Commonwealth, 284 Ky. 209, 144 S.W.2d 220 (1940)	§ 14.3
Fletcher v. Southern Farm Bureau Life Ins. Co., 757 F.2d 953 (8th Cir. 1985)	§ 5.2
Folding Carton Antitrust Litig., *In re,* 83 F.R.D. 260 (N.D. Ill. 1979)	§ 1.8
Folding Carton Antitrust Litig., *In re,* 76 F.R.D. 420 (D.C. Ill. 1977)	§ 1.6
Fonseca v. Regan, 734 F.2d 944 (2d Cir.), *cert. denied,* 469 U.S. 882 (1984)	§ 6.4
Ford v. Alfara, 785 F.2d 835 (9th Cir. 1986)	§ 5.10
Ford v. Fogarty Van Lines, Inc., 780 F.2d 1582 (11th Cir. 1986)	§ 5.10
Ford v. Temple Hosp., 790 F.2d 342 (3d Cir. 1986)	§§ 7.2, 7.3
Forney v. State, 255 Ga. 316, 338 S.E.2d 252 (1986)	§ 14.40
Forro Precision Inc. v. IBM Corp., 673 F.2d 1045 (9th Cir. 1982)	§ 6.4
Foster v. Crawford Shipping Co., 496 F.2d 788 (3d Cir. 1974)	§ 14.21
Founding Church of Scientology v. Webster, 802 F.2d 1448 (D.C. Cir. 1986)	§ 6.1
Fox v. Capital Co., 299 U.S. 105 (1936)	§ 8.5
Freidl v. Hennard, 66 A.D.2d 1024, 411 N.Y.S.2d 731 (1978)	§ 15.5
Freschi v. Grand Coal Venture, 564 F. Supp. 414 (S.D.N.Y. 1983)	§ 2.10
Frye v. United States, 293 F.2d 1013 (D.C. Cir. 1923)	§§ 13.23, 13.39

Case	*Book §*
Grayson v. Williams, 256 F.2d 61 (10th Cir. 1958)	§ 13.24
Green v. Occidental Petroleum Corp., 541 F.2d 1335 (9th Cir. 1976)	§ 2.15
Greenbaum-Mountain Mortgage Co. v. Pioneer Nat'l Title Ins. Co., 421 F. Supp. 1348 (D. Colo. 1976)	§ 2.10
Griffin v. Swim-Tech Corp., 722 F.2d 677 (11th Cir. 1984)	§ 6.9
Grimes v. Employer's Mut. Liab. Ins. Co., 73 F.R.D. 607 (D. Alaska 1977)	§§ 9.8, 14.22, 14.24, 14.26, 14.27, 14.28
Grindell v. American Motors Corp., 108 F.R.D. 94 (D.N.Y. 1985)	§ 1.45
Groppi v. Leslie, 404 U.S. 496 (1972)	§ 8.3
Guerra v. Board of Trustees of Cal. State Univs., 572 F.2d 700 (9th Cir. 1978)	§ 2.15
Gulf Life Ins. Co. v. Stossel, 131 Fla. 268, 175 So. 804 (1937)	§ 14.33
Halderman v. Pennhurst State School & Hosp., 673 F.2d 628 (3d Cir. 1982) (en banc), *cert. denied,* 465 U.S. 1038 (1984)	§ 8.8
Haley v. Byers Transp. Co., 414 S.W.2d 777 (Mo. 1967)	§§ 14.26, 14.27
Haley v. Kansas City Star, 761 F.2d 489 (8th Cir. 1985)	§ 5.5
Hall v. Cole, 412 U.S. 1 (1973)	§ 5.9
Hall v. Commissioner, 805 F.2d 1511 (11th Cir. 1986)	§ 8.10
Hamilton v. Neptune Orient Lines, Ltd., 811 F.2d 498 (9th Cir. 1987)	§ 5.2
Hammill v. United States, 498 A.2d 551 (D.C. 1985)	§ 16.5
Hammond Packing Co. v. Arkansas, 212 U.S. 322 (1909)	§ 6.3
Haney v. DeSandre, 692 S.W.2d 214 (Ark. 1985)	§ 13.40
Harding v. Federal Reserve Bank of N.Y., 707 F.2d 46 (2d Cir. 1983)	§§ 5.2, 5.3
Hardy v. New York News, Inc., No. Civ. 1147 (MGC) (S.D.N.Y., Jan. 28, 1987)	§ 1.23
Hardy v. Schirmar, 163 Cal. 272, 124 P. 993 (1912)	§ 16.4
Harley v. Hockey, 199 Misc. 512, 103 N.Y.S.2d 717 (N.Y. Sup. Ct. Jefferson County 1950)	§ 14.30
Harmon v. Board of Retirement, 62 Cal. App. 3d 689, 133 Cal. Rptr. 154 (1976)	§ 14.30
Harmon v. San Joaquin Light & Power Co., 37 Cal. App. 2d 169, 98 P.2d 1067 (1940)	§ 14.34
Harris v. St. Louis Pub. Serv. Co., 270 S.W.2d 850 (Mo. 1954)	§ 14.36
Harris v. United States, 382 U.S. 162 (1965)	§ 8.7
Hastings v. North E. Indep. School Dist., 615 F.2d 628 (5th Cir. 1980)	§ 6.4
Hayden v. Oak Terrace Apartments, 808 F.2d 1269 (7th Cir. 1987)	§ 8.3
Hayden Stone, Inc. v. Brode, 508 F.2d 895 (7th Cir. 1974)	§ 6.9

Case	*Book §*
Jackson v. Schoemehl, 788 F.2d 1296 (8th Cir. 1986)	§§ 5.2, 5.8
Jackson v. State, 172 Ga. App. 359, 323 S.E.2d 198 (1984)	§ 14.39
Jackson v. United States, 408 F.2d 306 (9th Cir. 1969)	§ 17.3
Jacobson v. Henderson, 763 F.2d 12 (2d Cir. 1985)	§ 17.2
Jacques, *In re,* 761 F.2d 302 (6th Cir. 1985)	§ 8.1
Jaffe v. Grant, 793 F.2d 1182 (11th Cir. 1986)	§ 4.5
Jaffe v. Sundowner Properties, Inc., 808 F.2d 1425 (11th Cir. 1987)	§ 3.10
Jafree, *In re,* 741 F.2d 133 (7th Cir. 1984)	§ 8.7
James Julian Inc. v. Raytheon Co., 93 F.R.D. 138 (D. Del. 1982)	§ 1.62
Jee, *In re,* 799 F.2d 532 (9th Cir. 1986)	§ 5.8
Jesco, Inc. v. Shannon, 451 So. 2d 694 (Miss. 1984)	§ 14.21
J.M. Cleminshaw Co. v. City of Norwich, 93 F.R.D. 338 (D. Conn. 1981)	§ 8.9
John v. Louisiana, 757 F.2d 698 (5th Cir. 1985)	§ 8.10
John B. Kelly Co., Inc. v. Workmens' Compensation App. Bd., 8 Pa. Commw. 589, 303 A.2d 255 (1973)	§ 14.34
Johnny Pflocks, Inc. v. Firestone Tire & Rubber Co., 634 F.2d 1215 (9th Cir. 1980)	§ 3.10
Johnson v. Georgia Highway Express, Inc., 488 F.2d 714 (5th Cir. 1974)	§ 6.8
Johnson v. Hansen, 289 P.2d 380 (Or. 1964)	§ 11.14
Johnson v. Hubbard, 698 F.2d 286 (6th Cir.), *cert. denied,* 464 U.S. 917 (1983)	§ 5.6
Johnson v. Kellam, 162 Va. 757, 175 S.E. 634 (1934)	§ 15.7
Johnson v. State, 472 N.E.2d 892 (Ind. 1985)	§ 14.39
Jones v. Commonwealth, 227 Va. 425, 317 S.E.2d 482 (1984)	§ 14.40
Jones v. Continental Corp., 789 F.2d 1225 (6th Cir. 1986)	§ 7.2
Jones v. Employers Mut. Liab. Ins. Co., 114 So. 2d 602 (La. Ct. App. 1959)	§ 14.36
Jones v. Graham, 709 F.2d 1457 (11th Cir. 1983)	§ 5.3
Jones v. Texas Employers Ins. Ass'n, 352 S.W.2d 318 (Tex. Ct. Civ. App. 1961)	§ 14.33
Jordan v. New Amsterdam Casualty Co., 353 S.W.2d 256 (Tex. Ct. Civ. App. 1961), *rev'd on other grounds sub nom.* New Amsterdam Casualty Co. v. Jordan, 359 S.W.2d 864 (Tex. 1962)	§ 14.31
Kagan v. Caterpillar Tractor Co., 795 F.2d 601 (7th Cir. 1986)	§§ 5.5, 5.8
Kalish v. Commissioner, No. 5663-85 (U.S. Tax Ct. Oct. 14, 1986)	§ 13.27
Kalsay v. Consolidated Rail Corp., 749 F.2d 437 (7th Cir. 1984)	§ 13.36
Kamen v. AT&T Co., 791 F.2d 1006 (2d Cir. 1986)	§§ 3.6, 7.2
Kaps Transp., Inc. v. Henry, 572 P.2d 72 (Alaska 1977)	§ 2.11

Case	*Book §*
Lawton v. Jewish Hosp., 679 S.W.2d 370 (Mo. Ct. App. 1984)	§§ 14.21, 14.28
Leavitt v. Glick Realty Corp. 362 Mass. 370, 285 N.E.2d 786 (1972)	§ 15.5
Lee v. Volkswagen of Am., Inc., 688 P.2d 1283 (Okla. 1984)	§ 14.21
Leesona Corp. v. Varta Batteries, Inc., 522 F. Supp. 1304 (S.D.N.Y. 1981)	§ 13.43
Lehmuth v. Long Beach Unified School Dist., 53 Cal. 2d 544, 348 P.2d 887, 2 Cal. Rptr. 279 (1960)	§ 14.28
Lepkowski v. United States Dep't of Treasury, 804 F.2d 1310 (D.C. Cir. 1986)	§ 8.10
LeRitilley v. Harris, 354 So. 2d 1213 (Fla. Dist. Ct. App. 1978)	§ 15.9
Letelier v. Republic of Chile, 748 F.2d 790 (2d Cir. 1984), *cert. denied,* 471 U.S. 1125 (1985)	§ 6.7
Lewis v. United States, 146 U.S. 370 (1892)	§ 17.3
Light v. Semonoff, *In re,* 796 F.2d 569 (1st Cir. 1986)	§ 3.10
Link v. Wabash R.R., 370 U.S. 626 (1962)	§§ 3.7, 5.2, 5.3, 5.5, 5.8, 6.6
Lipsig v. National Student Marketing Corp., 663 F.2d 178 (D.C. Cir. 1980)	§§ 5.9, 7.2, 7.3
Little, *In re,* 404 U.S. 553 (1972)	§ 8.7
Litton Sys., Inc. v. AT&T Co., 700 F.2d 785 (2d Cir. 1983), *cert. denied,* 464 U.S. 1073 (1984)	§§ 6.7, 7.2
Loctite Corp. v. Fel-Pro, Inc., 667 F.2d 577 (7th Cir. 1981)	§§ 6.1, 7.7
Lomita Land & Water Co. v. Robinson, 154 Cal. 36, 97 P. 10 (1908)	§ 2.11
Lowe v. Steel Constr. Co., 368 N.W.2d 610 (S.D. 1985)	§ 11.15
Lowell v. Daley, 148 Conn. 226, 169 A.2d 888 (1961)	§ 11.5
Lucas v. Curran, 62 F.R.D. 336 (E.D. Pa. 1974)	§ 1.33
Luther v. Maple, 250 F.2d 916 (8th Cir. 1958)	§ 14.28
Lyell Theatre Corp. v. Loew's Corp., 682 F.2d 37 (2d Cir. 1982)	§§ 5.2, 5.3, 5.8
MacMeekin, *In re,* 722 F.2d 32 (3d Cir. 1983)	§ 6.6
Madesky v. Campbell, 705 F.2d 703 (3d Cir. 1983)	§ 5.2
Maggio v. Zeitz, 333 U.S. 56 (1948)	§ 8.4
Maness v. Meyers, 419 U.S. 449 (1975)	§ 8.8
M.A. Porazzi Co. v. Mormaclark, 16 F.R.D. 383 (S.D.N.Y. 1951)	§ 1.49
Marc Rich & Co., *In re,* 736 F.2d 864 (2d Cir. 1984)	§ 8.4
Marlboro Prods. Corp. v. North Am. Philips Corp., 55 F.R.D. 487 (S.D.N.Y. 1972)	§ 1.34
Marrese v. American Academy of Orthopaedic Surgeons, 726 F.2d 1150 (7th Cir. 1984) (en banc), *rev'd on other grounds,* 470 U.S. 373 (1985)	§ 8.8
Marshall v. Segona, 621 F.2d 763 (5th Cir. 1980)	§ 6.5
Marshall v. United States, 355 F.2d 999 (9th Cir. 1966)	§ 17.3

Case	*Book §*
Miller Elec. Constr., Inc. v. Devine Lighting Co., 421 F. Supp. 1023 (W.D. Pa. 1976)	§ 2.10
Miner v. Atlass, 363 U.S. 641 (1960)	§ 8.10
Mir v. Fosburg, 706 F.2d 916 (9th Cir. 1983)	§§ 5.2, 5.3, 5.4
Miranda v. Southern Pac. Transp. Co., 710 F.2d 516 (9th Cir. 1983)	§ 8.9
Missouri-Kan.-Tex. R.R. v. Ridgway, 191 F.2d 363 (8th Cir. 1951)	§ 16.7
Mitchell v. American Tobacco Co., 33 F.R.D. 262 (M.D. Pa. 1963)	§§ 1.49, 1.50, 1.51
Moldovan v. Allis Chalmers Mfg. Co., 83 Mich. App. 373, 268 N.W.2d 656 (1978)	§ 16.9
Monier v. Chamberlain, 35 Ill. 2d 351, 221 N.E.2d 410 (1966)	§ 1.6
Morris v. Ocean Sys., Inc., 730 F.2d 248 (5th Cir. 1984)	§ 5.2
Morris v. Redak, 124 Colo. 27, 234 P.2d 908 (1951)	§ 2.11
Morrison-Maierle, Inc. v. Selsco, 186 Mont. 606 P.2d 1085, 180 (1980)	§ 2.11
Motorola, Inc. v. Computer Displays Int'l, Inc., 739 F.2d 1149 (7th Cir. 1984)	§ 8.5
Mr. Hanger, Inc. v. Cut Weight Plastic Hangers, Inc., 63 F.R.D. 607 (E.D.N.Y. 1974)	§ 9.12
Mulay Plastics, Inc. v. Grand Trunk W.R.R., 742 F.2d 369 (7th Cir. 1984), *cert. denied,* 470 U.S. 1037 (1985)	§ 3.10
Murphy v. Magnolia Elec. Power Ass'n, 639 F.2d 232 (5th Cir. 1981)	§ 5.10
National Acceptance Co. of Am. v. Bathalter, 705 F.2d 924 (7th Cir. 1983)	§ 8.3
National Ass'n of Concerned Veterans v. Secretary of Defense, 675 F.2d 1319 (D.C. Cir. 1982)	§ 6.8
National Farmers' Org., Inc. v. Oliver, 530 F.2d 815 (8th Cir. 1976)	§ 2.15
National Hockey League v. Metropolitan Hockey Club, 427 U.S. 639 (1976)	§§ 6.3, 6.4
Nealey v. Transportacion Maritima Mexicana, S.A., 662 F.2d 1275 (9th Cir. 1980)	§ 5.3
Neely v. City of Grenada, 799 F.2d 203 (5th Cir. 1976)	§ 8.3
Nevijel v. North Coast Life Ins. Co., 651 F.2d 1380 (9th Cir. 1986)	§ 5.7
Newman, *Ex parte,* 81 U.S. 152 (1872)	§ 2.15
New York State Urban Dev. Corp. v. VSL Corp., 738 F.2d 61 (2d Cir. 1984)	§ 8.5
New York Times Co. v. Jascalevich, 439 U.S. 1317 (1978)	§ 8.5
Niblack, *In re,* 476 F.2d 930 (D.C. Cir.), *cert. denied,* 414 U.S. 909 (1973)	§ 8.7
Niles Police Dep't v. Industrial Comm'n, 83 Ill. 2d 528, 48 Ill. Dec. 212, 416 N.E.2d 243 (1981)	§ 14.34

Case	*Book §*
People v. Bowley, 59 Cal. 2d 855 (1963)	§ 14.3
People v. Cunningham, 473 N.E.2d 506 (Ill. 1984)	§ 16.7
People v. DelVecchio, 105 Ill. 2d 414, 475 N.E.2d 840 (1985)	§ 16.7
People v. Eckhardt, 465 N.E.2d 107 (Ill. App. Ct. 1984)	§ 16.7
People v. Estes, 469 N.E.2d 275 (Ill. 1984)	§ 16.7
People v. Grice, 100 A.D.2d 914 (N.Y. 1974)	§ 16.7
People v. Holman, 103 Ill. 2d 133, 469 N.E.2d 119 (1984)	§ 16.7
People v. Howard, 460 N.E.2d 432 (Ill. 1984)	§ 16.7
People v. Kashney, 472 N.E.2d 164 (Ill. App. Ct. 1984)	§ 16.7
People v. Ortiz, 99 A.D.2d 497, 470 N.Y.S.2d 445 (1984)	§ 16.7
People v. Purcell, 103 A.D.2d 938, 479 N.Y.S.2d 268 (1984)	§ 14.40
People v. Rao, 107 A.D.2d 720, 484 N.Y.S.2d 76 (1985)	§ 14.39
People v. Ray, 467 N.E.2d 1078 (Ill. 1984)	§ 16.7
People v. Reese, 105 Ill. 2d 275, 460 N.E.2d 446 (1984)	§ 16.7
People v. Simmons, 100 A.D.2d 497 (N.Y. 1984)	§ 16.7
People v. Simpson, 473 N.E.2d 350 (Ill. 1984)	§ 16.7
People v. Smith, 52 Ill. App. 2d 583, 367 N.E.2d 756 (1977)	§ 16.7
People v. Thomas, 37 Ill. App. 2d 320, 346 N.E.2d 190 (1976)	§ 16.7
People v. Weller, 123 Ill. App. 2d 421, 258 N.E.2d 806 (1970)	§ 16.7
People v. Williams, 468 N.E.2d 807 (Ill. App. Ct. 1984)	§ 16.7
People v. Wilson, 463 N.E.2d 890 (Ill. 1984)	§ 16.7
Perfect Fit Indus., Inc. v. Acme Quilting Co., 646 F.2d 800 (2d Cir. 1981), *cert. denied,* 459 U.S. 832 (1982)	§ 8.5
Perlman v. United States, 247 U.S. 7 (1918)	§ 8.8
Perry v. Winspur, 782 F.2d 893 (10th Cir. 1986)	§ 5.10
Pesaplastic, C.A. v. Cincinnati Milacron Co., 799 F.2d 1510 (11th Cir. 1986)	§ 8.6
Phelps v. Washburn Univ., 807 F.2d 152 (10th Cir. 1986)	§ 3.10
Phoceene Sous-Marine, S.A. v. U.S. Phosmarine, Inc., 682 F.2d 802 (9th Cir. 1982)	§ 5.9
Phoenix v. Boggs, 1 Ariz. App. 370, 403 P.2d 305 (1965)	§ 15.9
Photostat Corp. v. Ball, 388 F.2d 783 (10th Cir. 1964)	§ 17.3
Pisel v. Stamford Hosp., 180 Conn. 314, 430 A.2d 1 (1980)	§ 14.21
Platts v. Arney, 46 Wash. 122, 278 P.2d 657 (1955)	§ 2.11
Potlatch Corp. v. United States, 679 F.2d 153 (9th Cir. 1982)	§ 6.1
Poulis v. State Farm Fire & Casualty Co., 747 F.2d 863 (3d Cir. 1984)	§ 6.5

Case	*Book §*
Richardson v. Lucas, 741 F.2d 753 (5th Cir. 1984)	§ 16.7
Richardson v. United States, 465 F.2d 844 (3d Cir. 1972), *cert. denied,* 410 U.S. 955 (1973)	§ 2.15
Roadway Express, Inc. v. Piper, 447 U.S. 752 (1980)	§§ 3.9, 5.9, 6.9, 7.2, 7.3, 7.4
Roberson v. Ryder Truck Lines, Inc., 41 F.R.D. 166 (N.D. Miss. 1966)	§ 1.7
Roberts v. Tardif, 417 A.2d 444 (Me. 1980)	§ 13.37
Robinson v. Tanner, 798 F.2d 1378 (11th Cir. 1986)	§ 3.10
Roche v. Evaporated Milk Ass'n, 319 U.S. 21 (1943)	§ 2.15
Rocky Mountain Helicopters, Inc. v. Bell Helicopters Textron, 805 F.2d 907 (10th Cir. 1986)	§§ 2.2, 14.18
Rodgers v. Bowen, 790 F.2d 1550 (11th Cir. 1986)	§ 5.6
Roe, *Ex parte,* 23 U.S. 70 (1914)	§ 2.15
Rogers v. City of Detroit, 289 Mich. 86, 286 N.W. 167 (1939)	§ 14.21
Rogers v. Webster, 776 F.2d 607 (6th Cir. 1985)	§ 8.3
Rohrkaste v. City of Terre Haute, 470 N.E.2d 738 (Ind. Ct. App. 1984)	§ 11.7
Romandette v. Weetabix Co., 807 F.2d 309 (2d Cir. 1986)	§ 5.6
Rosahn, *In re,* 671 F.2d 690 (2d Cir. 1982)	§ 8.3
Ross v. Great Atl. & Pac. Tea Co., 447 F. Supp. 406 (S.D.N.Y. 1978)	§ 2.10
Rubin, *In re,* 769 F.2d 611 (9th Cir. 1985)	§ 6.5
Ruiz v. Hamburg-Am. Line, 478 F.2d 29 (9th Cir. 1973)	§ 1.8
Salahuddin v. Harris, 782 F.2d 1127 (2d Cir. 1986)	§ 5.10
Salgo v. Leland Stanford Jr. Univ. Bd. of Trustees, 154 Cal. App. 2d 560, 317 P.2d 170 (1957)	§ 15.3
Salter v. Upjohn Co., 593 F.2d 649 (5th Cir. 1979)	§ 1.50
San Mateo, County of v. Christen, 22 Cal. App. 2d 375 (1937)	§ 14.3
Savola v. Webster, 644 F.2d 743 (8th Cir. 1981)	§ 6.4
Scarboro v. Travelers Ins. Co., 91 F.R.D. 21 (E.D. Tenn. 1980)	§ 2.2
Scarborough v. Eubanks, 747 F.2d 871 (3d Cir. 1984)	§ 5.2
Schaible v. Michigan Mut. Ins. Co., 321 N.W.2d 860 (Mich. 1982)	§ 2.10
Schell v. Kiersey, 674 S.W.2d 268 (Mo. 1984)	§ 11.9
Schendel v. McGee, 300 F. 273 (8th Cir. 1924)	§ 2.15
Schilling v. Walworth County Parks & Planning Comm'n, 805 F.2d 272 (7th Cir. 1986)	§ 5.6
Schlagenhauf v. Holder, 379 U.S. 104 (1964)	§ 1.54
Schooley v. Kennedy, 712 F.2d 372 (11th Cir. 1983)	§ 5.6
Sealy, Inc. v. Easy Living, Inc., 743 F.2d 1378 (9th Cir. 1984)	§ 5.10
Searock v. Stripling, 736 F.2d 650 (11th Cir. 1984)	§ 6.5
SEC v. Ormont Drug & Chem. Co., 739 F.2d 654 (D.C. Cir. 1981)	§§ 8.3, 8.4

Case	*Book §*
Societe Internationale v. Rogers, 357 U.S. 197 (1958)	§§ 5.2, 6.3, 6.7
Southern Ry. Co. v. Lanham, 403 F.2d 119 (5th Cir. 1968)	§ 1.6
Sperry Rand Corp. v. Rothlein, 241 F. Supp. 549 (D. Conn. 1965)	§ 13.47
Sprynczynatyk v. General Motors Corp., 771 F.2d 1112 (8th Cir. 1985)	§ 14.27
Stanley v. Ellegood, 382 S.W.2d 572 (Ky. 1964)	§ 15.9
Stanton by Brooks v. Astra Pharmaceutical Prods., 718 F.2d 553 (3d Cir. 1983)	§ 14.21
State v. Bernson, 40 Wash. App. 729, 700 P.2d 758 (1985)	§ 14.40
State v. Goding, 124 N.H. 781, 474 A.2d 580 (1984)	§ 11.10
State v. Maye, 286 N.W.2d 387 (Iowa 1979)	§ 16.4
State v. Plath, 281 S.C. 1, 313 S.E.2d 619 (1984)	§ 14.40
State v. Simmons, 59 Wash. 2d 381, 368 P.2d 378 (1962)	§ 17.3
State v. Stewart, 360 N.W.2d 430 (Minn. 1985)	§ 14.39
State v. Taxiltaridis, 2 Conn. App. 617, 481 A.2d 98 (1984)	§ 14.39
Steele v. Gossen, 329 S.W.2d 703 (Mo. 1959)	§ 14.32
Sterling Energy, Ltd. v. Friendly Nat'l Bank, 744 F.2d 1433 (10th Cir. 1984)	§§ 7.2, 7.3
Stevens v. Greyhound Lines, Inc., 710 F.2d 1224 (7th Cir. 1983)	§§ 5.3, 5.6
Stocker v. Wells, 155 Neb. 472, 52 N.W.2d 284 (1952)	§ 2.11
Stock Pot Restaurant, Inc. v. Stockpot, Inc., 737 F.2d 1576 (Fed. Cir. 1984)	§ 5.2
Sturgeon v. Airborne Freight Corp., 778 F.2d 1154 (5th Cir. 1985)	§§ 5.2, 5.3, 8.10, 13.30
Sutter, *In re,* 543 F.2d 1030 (2d Cir. 1916)	§ 8.9
Tamari v. Bache & Co. (Lebanon) S.A.L., 729 F.2d 469 (7th Cir. 1984)	§§ 6.2, 6.5, 6.7, 6.8
Tamini v. M/V Jewon, 808 F.2d 978 (2d Cir. 1987)	§ 5.3
Tanuvasa v. City & County of Honolulu, 2 Haw. App. 102, 626 P.2d 1175 (1981)	§ 14.21
Tart v. McGann, 697 F.2d 75 (2d Cir. 1982)	§ 13.39
Taylor v. Combustion Eng'g, Inc., 782 F.2d 525 (5th Cir. 1986)	§ 5.5
Taylor v. Hayes, 418 U.S. 488 (1974)	§ 8.7
Tennessee Gas Transmission Co. v. Moorhead, 305 S.W.2d 81 (Tex. Civ. App. 1966)	§ 13.24
Textor v. Board of Regents of N. Ill. Univ., 711 F.2d 1387 (7th Cir. 1983)	§§ 7.3, 7.5
Thomas v. C.G. Tate Constr. Co., 465 F. Supp. 566 (D.S.C. 1979)	§§ 9.8, 14.19, 14.24
Thomas v. Fleming, 241 Miss. 26, 128 So. 2d 854 (1961)	§ 14.31
Thomas v. Gerber Prods., 703 F.2d 353 (9th Cir. 1983)	§ 6.3

Case	*Book §*
United States v. Cook, 608 F.2d 1175 (1979)	§ 2.2
United States v. DeFrantz, 708 F.2d 310 (7th Cir. 1983)	§ 6.9
United States v. Dorell, 758 F.2d 425 (9th Cir. 1985)	§ 14.27
United States v. Downing, 753 F.2d 1224 (3d Cir. 1985)	§§ 13.18, 13.36
United States v. Drougas, 748 F.2d 8 (1st Cir. 1984)	§ 14.39
United States v. Eiland, 741 F.2d 738 (5th Cir. 1984)	§ 16.7
United States v. Freedland, 111 F. Supp. 852 (D.N.D. 1953)	§ 17.3
United States v. Garza, 754 F.2d 1202 (5th Cir. 1985)	§ 16.7
United States v. Hendrix, 549 F.2d 1225 (9th Cir. 1977), *cert. denied,* 434 U.S. 818 (1977)	§ 17.4
United States v. Johnson, 736 F.2d 358 (6th Cir. 1984)	§ 8.5
United States v. Klee, 494 F.2d 394 (9th Cir. 1974)	§ 17.4
United States v. Koziy, 728 F.2d 1314 (11th Cir.), *cert. denied,* 469 U.S. 835 (1984)	§ 5.10
United States v. Lampkin, 66 F. Supp. 821 (S.D. Fla. 1946)	§ 17.3
United States v. Lee, 720 F.2d 1049 (9th Cir. 1983)	§ 8.7
United States v. Lipshy, 492 F. Supp. 35 (N.D. Tex. 1979)	§ 1.62
United States v. Lowery, 733 F.2d 441 (7th Cir.), *cert. denied,* 469 U.S. 932 (1984)	§ 8.7
United States v. Mack, 604 F.2d 336 (5th Cir. 1979)	§ 2.2
United States v. Marabelles, 724 F.2d 1374 (9th Cir. 1984)	§ 13.36
United States v. Marchini, 797 F.2d 759 (9th Cir. 1986)	§ 14.17
United States v. Martinez, 763 F.2d 1297 (11th Cir. 1985)	§ 14.39
United States v. McCargo, 783 F.2d 507 (5th Cir. 1986)	§§ 8.7, 8.8
United States v. Monteleone, 804 F.2d 1004 (7th Cir. 1986)	§ 8.1
United States v. Mucci, 630 F.2d 737 (10th Cir. 1980)	§ 2.2
United States v. Napoleone, 3 Cir., 349 F.2d 350	§ 17.3
United States v. National Medical Enters., Inc., 792 F.2d 906 (9th Cir. 1986)	§§ 3.5, 5.9, 6.4, 6.5, 6.7
United States v. Neal, 692 F.2d 1296 (10th Cir. 1982)	§ 2.2
United States v. Nesglo, Inc., 744 F.2d 887 (1st Cir. 1984)	§§ 7.3, 7.4
United States v. Nunez, 801 F.2d 1250 (11th Cir. 1985)	§ 8.7
United States v. Onu, 730 F.2d 253 (5th Cir.), *cert. denied,* 469 U.S. 856 (1984)	§ 8.7
United States v. Pearce, 792 F.2d 397 (3d Cir. 1986)	§ 8.8
United States v. Perez-Leon, 757 F.2d 866 (7th Cir. 1985)	§ 16.7
United States v. Piquette, 52 F.R.D. 370 (E.D. Mich. 1971)	§ 13.46
United States v. Richardson, 204 F.2d 552 (5th Cir. 1953)	§ 2.15

Case	*Book §*
Vergott v. Deseret Pharmaceutical Co., 463 F.2d 12 (5th Cir. 1972)	§ 2.2
Virginia Elec. & Power Co., *In re,* 539 F.2d 357 (4th Cir. 1974)	§ 2.15
Vuitton et Fils, S.A. v. Carousel Handbags, 592 F.2d 125 (2d Cir. 1979)	§ 8.3
Wagner v. McDaniels, 9 Ohio St. 3d 184, 9 Ohio B.R. 469, 459 N.E.2d 561 (1984)	§ 14.36
Waid v. Bergschneider, 94 Ariz. 21, 381 P.2d 568 (1963)	§ 15.5
Walker v. City of Birmingham, 388 U.S. 307 (1967)	§ 8.8
Washington v. Walker, 734 F.2d 1237 (7th Cir. 1984)	§ 5.3
Watson v. Miears, 772 F.2d 433 (8th Cir. 1985)	§ 6.7
Weaver v. Gross, 605 F. Supp. 210 (D.D.C. 1985)	§ 1.47
Webber v. Eye Corp., 721 F.2d 1067 (7th Cir. 1983)	§§ 5.2, 5.3, 5.5
Weeks v. Holsclaw, 55 N.C. App. 335, 285 S.E.2d 321 *aff'd,* 306 N.C. 655, 295 S.E.2d 596, *reh'g denied,* 307 N.C. 273, 302 S.E.2d 884 (1982)	§ 15.8
Weisberg v. Webster, 749 F.2d 864 (D.C. Cir. 1984)	§§ 6.3, 6.7, 6.8
Werner v. Lane, 393 A.2d 1329 (Me. 1978)	§ 15.4
West v. Livingston County Rd. Comm'n, 131 Mich. App. 63, 345 N.W.2d 608 (1983)	§ 14.39
West v. Martin, No. 57,191 (Kan. Ct. App. Jan. 30, 1986)	§ 14.37
Westhemeco Ltd. v. New Hampshire Ins. Co., 82 F.R.D. 702 (S.D.N.Y. 1979)	§ 1.7
Westmoreland v. CBS, Inc., 770 F.2d 1168 (D.C. Cir. 1985)	§ 6.1
White v. Raymark Indus., Inc., 783 F.2d 1175 (4th Cir. 1986)	§§ 8.9, 8.10
Whitlock, *Estate of* v. Commissioner of Internal Revenue, 547 F.2d 506 (10th Cir. 1976)	§ 2.15
Whittier v. Emmett, 281 F.2d 24 (D.C. Cir. 1960)	§ 2.15
Wilbur v. United States, 281 U.S. 206 (1930)	§ 2.15
Will v. Merrill, 210 F.2d 132 (4th Cir. 1954)	§ 14.31
Williamson v. St. Louis Pub. Serv. Co., 363 Mo. 508, 252 S.W.2d 295 (1952)	§ 14.34
Williamson v. United States, 207 U.S. 425 (1908)	§ 8.7
Wilson v. Clark, 417 N.E.2d 1322 (Ill. Sup. Ct. 1981)	§ 13.37
Winner Corp., *In re,* 511 F.2d 1010 (6th Cir. 1975)	§ 8.3
Wirtz v. Local 30, Int'l Union of Operating Eng'rs, 34 F.R.D. 13 (S.D.N.Y. 1963)	§ 1.49
Witt v. United States, 681 F.2d 1144 (11th Cir. 1986)	§ 8.10
Wold v. Minerals Eng'g Corp., 575 F. Supp. 166 (D. Colo. 1983)	§ 4.4
Wolfe v. Hawkes Hosp., No. 84AP-1007 (Ohio Ct. App., Sept. 24, 1985)	§ 11.13
Wood v. Gautier, 201 Kan. 74, 439 P.2d 73 (1968)	§ 2.11

TABLE OF FEDERAL RULES

Fed. R. Evid.	*Book §*
105	§ 15.7
401	§§ 13.23, 14.22
402	§ 14.41
403	§§ 2.2, 9.8, 13.23, 13.25, 14.3, 14.23, 14.28, 14.32, 15.6
407	§§ 2.2, 14.18
408	§ 9.1
606(b)	§ 17.2
607	§ 13.12
611(c)	§ 13.12
612	§ 1.62
702	§§ 13.18, 13.36, 13.39, 14.18
703	§§ 13.31, 13.39
704	§ 13.18
705	§§ 2.4, 13.37
706	§ 13.43
801(a)	§ 14.27
801(c)	§§ 13.23, 14.27
801(d)	§ 14.27
801(d)(1)	§ 13.12
801(d)(2)(A)	§ 14.32
802	§ 14.27
803	§ 13.23
803(b)	§ 14.37
803(5)	§ 1.5
803(8)(c)	§§ 13.23, 13.39
803(18)	§§ 13.39, 13.40
803(24)	§§ 9.8, 13.23, 13.39, 14.27
804	§ 1.5
804(5)	§ 13.23
901(2)	§ 14.22
1001	§ 14.3
1006	§§ 1.56, 14.17

INDEX